my Perspectives®

ENGLISH LANGUAGE ARTS

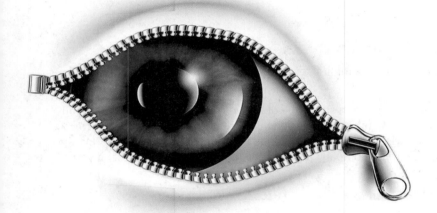

SAVVAS

LEARNING COMPANY

ISBN-13: 978-1-418-38614-6
ISBN-10:   1-418-38614-6

5   22

Welcome!

myPerspectives™ *English Language Arts* is a student-centered learning environment where you will analyze text, cite evidence, and respond critically about your learning. You will take ownership of your learning through goal-setting, reflection, independent text selection, and activities that allow you to collaborate with your peers.

Each unit of study includes selections of different genres—including multimedia—all related to a relevant and meaningful Essential Question. As you read, you will engage in activities that inspire thoughtful discussion and debate with your peers allowing you to formulate, and defend, your own perspectives.

myPerspectives ELA offers a variety of ways to interact directly with the text. You can annotate by writing in your print consumable, or you can annotate in your digital Student Edition. In addition, exciting technology allows you to access multimedia directly from your mobile device and communicate using an online discussion board!

We hope you enjoy using *myPerspectives ELA* as you develop the skills required to be successful throughout college and career.

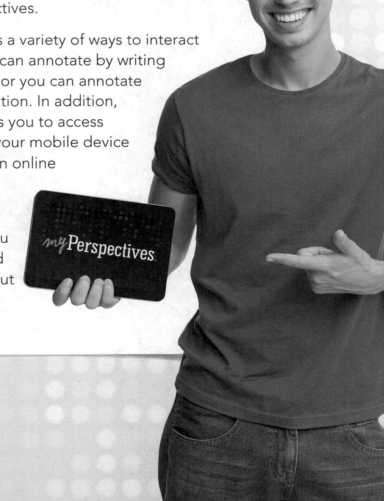

Authors' Perspectives

myPerspectives is informed by a team of respected experts whose experiences working with students and study of instructional best practices have positively impacted education. From the evolving role of the teacher to how students learn in a digital age, our authors bring new ideas, innovations, and strategies that transform teaching and learning in today's competitive and interconnected world.

> " The teaching of English needs to focus on engaging a new generation of learners. How do we get them excited about reading and writing? How do we help them to envision themselves as readers and writers? And, how can we make the teaching of English more culturally, socially, and technologically relevant? Throughout the curriculum, we've created spaces that enhance youth voice and participation and that connect the teaching of literature and writing to technological transformations of the digital age."

Ernest Morrell, Ph.D.

is the Macy professor of English Education at Teachers College, Columbia University, a class of 2014 Fellow of the American Educational Research Association, and the Past-President of the National Council of Teachers of English (NCTE). He is also the Director of Teachers College's Institute for Urban and Minority Education (IUME). He is an award-winning author and in his spare time he coaches youth sports and writes poems and plays. Dr. Morrell has influenced the development of *my*Perspectives in Assessment, Writing & Research, Student Engagement, and Collaborative Learning.

Elfrieda Hiebert, Ph.D.

is President and CEO of TextProject, a nonprofit that provides resources to support higher reading levels. She is also a research associate at the University of California, Santa Cruz. Dr. Hiebert has worked in the field of early reading acquisition for 45 years, first as a teacher's aide and teacher of primary-level students in California and, subsequently, as a teacher and researcher. Her research addresses how fluency, vocabulary, and knowledge can be fostered through appropriate texts. Dr. Hiebert has influenced the development of *my*Perspectives in Vocabulary, Text Complexity, and Assessment.

"The signature of complex text is challenging vocabulary. In the systems of vocabulary, it's important to provide ways to show how concepts can be made more transparent to students. We provide lessons and activities that develop a strong vocabulary and concept foundation—a foundation that permits students to comprehend increasingly more complex text."

Kelly Gallagher, M.Ed.

teaches at Magnolia High School in Anaheim, California, where he is in his thirty-first year. He is the former co-director of the South Basin Writing Project at California State University, Long Beach. Mr. Gallagher has influenced the development of *my*Perspectives in Writing, Close Reading, and the Role of Teachers.

"The *my*Perspectives classroom is dynamic. The teacher inspires, models, instructs, facilitates, and advises students as they evolve and grow. When teachers guide students through meaningful learning tasks and then pass them ownership of their own learning, students become engaged and work harder. This is how we make a difference in student achievement—by putting students at the center of their learning and giving them the opportunities to choose, explore, collaborate, and work independently."

"It's critical to give students the opportunity to read a wide range of highly engaging texts and to immerse themselves in exploring powerful ideas and how these ideas are expressed. In *my*Perspectives, we focus on building up students' awareness of how academic language works, which is especially important for English language learners."

Jim Cummins, Ph.D.

is a Professor Emeritus in the Department of Curriculum, Teaching and Learning of the University of Toronto. His research focuses on literacy development in multilingual school contexts as well as on the potential roles of technology in promoting language and literacy development. In recent years, he has been working actively with teachers to identify ways of increasing the literacy engagement of learners in multilingual school contexts. Dr. Cummins has influenced the development of *my*Perspectives in English Language Learner and English Language Development support.

UNIT 1 Inside the Nightmare

INDEPENDENT LEARNING

These selections can be accessed via the Interactive Student Edition.

 PERFORMANCE-BASED ASSESSMENT PREP

 PERFORMANCE-BASED ASSESSMENT

UNIT REFLECTION

DIGITAL PERSPECTIVES

- Unit Introduction Videos
- Media Selections
- Modeling Videos
- Selection Audio Recordings

Additional digital resources can be found in:
- Interactive Student Edition
- *my*Perspectives+

UNIT 2 Outsiders and Outcasts

DIGITAL  PERSPECTIVES

- Unit Introduction Videos
- Media Selections
- Modeling Videos
- Selection Audio Recordings

Additional digital resources can be found in:

- Interactive Student Edition
- *my*Perspectives+

UNIT 3 Extending Freedom's Reach

 INDEPENDENT LEARNING

MEDIA: INFORMATIONAL TEXT

**Law and the Rule of Law:
The Role of Federal Courts**

Judicial Learning Center

ESSAY

Misrule of Law

Aung San Suu Kyi

SHORT STORY

Harrison Bergeron

Kurt Vonnegut, Jr.

PERSONAL ESSAY

Credo: What I Believe

Neil Gaiman

These selections can be accessed via the
Interactive Student Edition.

PERFORMANCE-BASED
ASSESSMENT PREP

 PERFORMANCE-BASED
ASSESSMENT

UNIT REFLECTION

DIGITAL
PERSPECTIVES

- Unit Introduction Videos
- Media Selections
- Modeling Videos
- Selection Audio Recordings

Additional digital resources can be found in:

- Interactive Student Edition
- *my*Perspectives+

UNIT All That Glitters

INDEPENDENT LEARNING

These selections can be accessed via the Interactive Student Edition.

 PERFORMANCE-BASED ASSESSMENT PREP

 PERFORMANCE-BASED ASSESSMENT

UNIT REFLECTION

DIGITAL 🖱
PERSPECTIVES

- Unit Introduction Videos
- Media Selections
- Modeling Videos
- Selection Audio Recordings

Additional digital resources can be found in:

- Interactive Student Edition
- *my*Perspectives+

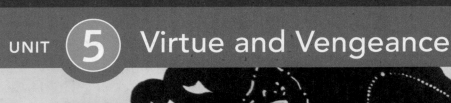

UNIT 5 Virtue and Vengeance

COMPARE

INDEPENDENT LEARNING

These selections can be accessed via the Interactive Student Edition.

 **PERFORMANCE-BASED
ASSESSMENT PREP**

 **PERFORMANCE-BASED
ASSESSMENT**

UNIT REFLECTION

**DIGITAL
PERSPECTIVES**

- Unit Introduction Videos
- Media Selections
- Modeling Videos
- Selection Audio Recordings

Additional digital resources can be found in:

- Interactive Student Edition
- *my*Perspectives+

UNIT 6 Blindness and Sight

INDEPENDENT LEARNING

These selections can be accessed via the Interactive Student Edition.

 PERFORMANCE-BASED ASSESSMENT PREP

 PERFORMANCE-BASED ASSESSMENT

UNIT REFLECTION

DIGITAL PERSPECTIVES

- Unit Introduction Videos
- Media Selections
- Modeling Videos
- Selection Audio Recordings

Additional digital resources can be found in:

- Interactive Student Edition
- *my*Perspectives+

All That Glitters

For many people, the longing for material goods extends well beyond the needs of survival. What drives our passion for things?

14-Year-Old Teaches Family the "Power of Half"

💬 **Discuss It** Why do people acquire more than they need?

Write your response before sharing your ideas.

UNIT 4

ESSENTIAL QUESTION: What do our possessions reveal about us?

LAUNCH TEXT
INFORMATIVE MODEL
I Came, I Saw, I Shopped

WHOLE-CLASS LEARNING

ANCHOR TEXT: SHORT STORY

The Necklace
Guy de Maupassant, translated by Andrew MacAndrew

ANCHOR TEXT: SHORT STORY

Civil Peace
Chinua Achebe

MEDIA: PHOTO ESSAY

Fit for a King: Treasures of Tutankhamun

PERFORMANCE TASK

WRITING FOCUS:
Write an Informative Essay

SMALL-GROUP LEARNING

JOURNALISM

In La Rinconada, Peru, Searching for Beauty in Ugliness
Marie Arana

POETRY COLLECTION

Avarice
Yusef Komunyakaa

The Good Life
Tracy K. Smith

Money
Reginald Gibbons

COMPARE

SHORT STORY

The Golden Touch
Nathaniel Hawthorne

POETRY

from King Midas
Howard Moss

MAGAZINE ARTICLE

The Thrill of the Chase
Margie Goldsmith

PERFORMANCE TASK

SPEAKING AND LISTENING FOCUS:
Deliver a Multimedia Presentation

INDEPENDENT LEARNING

MEDIA: INFORMATIONAL GRAPHIC

The Gold Series: A History of Gold
Visual Capitalist

NEWS ARTICLE

Ads May Spur Unhappy Kids to Embrace Materialism
Amy Norton

SHORT STORY

A Dose of What the Doctor Never Orders
Ihara Saikaku, translated by G. W. Sargent

MAGAZINE ARTICLE

My Possessions, Myself
Russell W. Belk

NEWS ARTICLE

Heirlooms' Value Shifts From Sentiment to Cash
Rosa Salter Rodriguez

PERFORMANCE-BASED ASSESSMENT PREP

Review Evidence for an Informative Essay

PERFORMANCE-BASED ASSESSMENT

Informative Text: Essay and Oral Presentation

PROMPT:

How do we decide what we want versus what we need?
What can result from an imbalance between want and need?

Unit Goals

Throughout the unit, you will deepen your understanding of materialism by reading, writing, speaking, listening, and presenting. These goals will help you succeed on the Unit Performance-Based Assessment.

Rate how well you meet these goals right now. You will revisit your ratings later when you reflect on your growth during this unit.

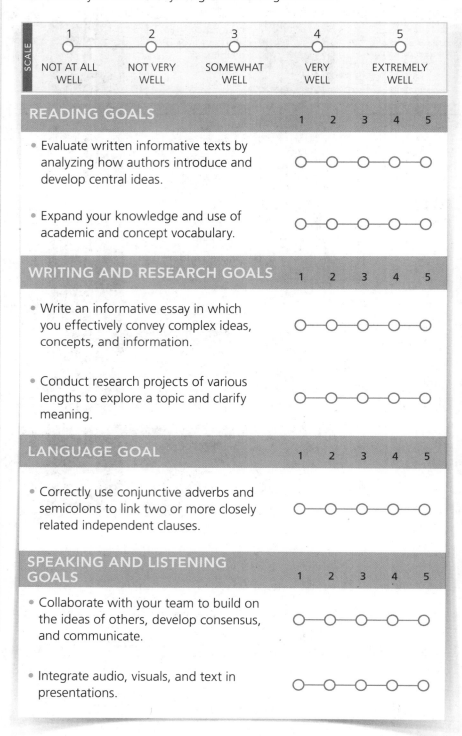

SCALE	1	2	3	4	5
	NOT AT ALL WELL	NOT VERY WELL	SOMEWHAT WELL	VERY WELL	EXTREMELY WELL

READING GOALS   1   2   3   4   5

- Evaluate written informative texts by analyzing how authors introduce and develop central ideas.

- Expand your knowledge and use of academic and concept vocabulary.

WRITING AND RESEARCH GOALS   1   2   3   4   5

- Write an informative essay in which you effectively convey complex ideas, concepts, and information.

- Conduct research projects of various lengths to explore a topic and clarify meaning.

LANGUAGE GOAL   1   2   3   4   5

- Correctly use conjunctive adverbs and semicolons to link two or more closely related independent clauses.

SPEAKING AND LISTENING GOALS   1   2   3   4   5

- Collaborate with your team to build on the ideas of others, develop consensus, and communicate.

- Integrate audio, visuals, and text in presentations.

Academic Vocabulary: Informative Text

Academic terms appear in all subjects and can help you read, write, and discuss with more precision. Here are five academic words that will be useful to you in this unit as you analyze and write informative texts.

Complete the chart.

1. Review each word, its root, and the mentor sentences.

2. Use the information and your own knowledge to predict the meaning of each word.

3. For each word, list at least two related words.

4. Refer to a dictionary or other resources if needed.

TIP

FOLLOW THROUGH
Study the words in this chart, and mark them or their forms wherever they appear in the unit.

WORD	MENTOR SENTENCES	PREDICT MEANING	RELATED WORDS
paradox ROOT: *-dox-* "belief"	1. Stuck in the middle of the ocean, I thought of the *paradox* "Water, water everywhere and not a drop to drink." 2. The teacher could not understand the *paradox*; the students were happy when they were given more homework.		paradoxical; paradoxically
chronicle ROOT: *-chron-* "time"	1. The film works both as an interesting story of one woman's life and as a *chronicle* of an era. 2. She is a good storyteller, able to *chronicle* events involving vast stretches of time and hundreds of characters.		
allocate ROOT: *-loc-* "place"	1. Rather than *allocate* blame, let's find a solution to the problem. 2. How should we *allocate* funds—to the playground project or to art supplies?		
deduce ROOT: *-duc-* "lead"	1. The detective is famous for her ability to *deduce* the truth from seemingly trivial details. 2. An animal's ability to *deduce* threatening changes in its environment can be key to its survival.		
primary ROOT: *-prim-* "first"	1. Ever since the big win, Shereen's *primary* feeling was one of elation. 2. You should support your ideas with evidence from both *primary* and secondary sources.		

LAUNCH TEXT | INFORMATIVE MODEL

This selection is an example of an **informative text**, a type of writing in which the author examines concepts through the careful selection, organization, and analysis of information. This is the type of writing you will develop in the Performance-Based Assessment at the end of the unit.

As you read, think about how the writer presents information in the form of examples, statistics, and expert opinion. How does the writer help the reader understand the importance of this information?

I Came, I Saw, I Shopped

NOTES

1   Perhaps you know what became of the robotic dog, ripped jeans, or gadget you couldn't live without a few years ago. Maybe you remember where you put that video game you used to love. It was a "must-have" item just last year. It's possible, though, that you've lost track of these things; consequently, they are forgotten, but not gone, collecting dust in a closet somewhere. In the meantime, you may have developed a taste for newer, fresher goods, such as a waterproof smartphone, designer shoes, or limited-edition sneakers.

2   When you want something with a passion, it can be difficult to picture a moment when that item might not mean much to you. A 2011 study showed that Americans upgrade their mobile phones every 21.7 months. This is the fastest turnover rate in the world. As the pace of technological change increases, replacement periods get even shorter. Are we just fickle and easily distracted, or are other forces at play?

3   All of the data suggest that America is a nation of shoppers. Instead of saving our money, we spend it. Recent research shows that only one in four Americans saves more than 10 percent of his or her income (Soergel 2015). In contrast, Europeans show personal savings rates of more than 10 percent over a 30-year period dating back to the early 1980s.

Are We Hardwired to Buy?

4   What drives our need to own the latest games, shoes, or phones? There are many notions. Some experts point to mirror neurons. These are cells in our brains that allow us to mirror, or reflect, the feelings

NOTES

and behavior of other people. Scientists believe that mirror neurons may tell us that we want what other people have, especially when we admire those people in other ways.

5   Social relationships may also affect our buying decisions. A study of Americans born between the early 1980s and the early 2000s finds that peer recommendations influenced many of the participants to make certain purchases. People from this "millennial" generation are also attracted to brands connected to social causes; they wish to buy products made by companies that donate profits to charity.

Emotional Spending

6   We can explain the desire for new shoes or a new phone at least in part as a practical concern. After all, we probably plan to wear the shoes and use the phone. However, some of our buying choices seem to be based almost purely on emotions.

7   As an example of emotional purchasing, consider the multi-billion-dollar market for collectible items from the past. In most cases, collectors don't plan to use these items. It is the rare driver who uses an antique car for her daily commute; likewise, the collectible doll from 1959 that sold at auction in May 2006 for $27,450 did not become a child's favorite toy. Advertising does not drive demand for collectibles; TV commercials for lunch boxes from the 1960s simply don't exist. Some purchases of collectibles may be investments in items that will grow in value; however, others are driven largely by emotions, such as longing for a time past.

8   All of the information we have about shopping and spending suggests that the desire for a particular item is not so simple. Our brains, our social connections, and even our feelings about the past may all contribute to a seemingly endless appetite to fill our homes and our lives with things.

WORD NETWORK FOR ALL THAT GLITTERS

Vocabulary A Word Network is a collection of words related to a topic. As you read the selections in this unit, identify interesting words related to the idea of materialism, and add them to your Word Network. For example, you might begin by adding words from the Launch Text, such as *gadget, upgrade,* and *collectibles*. Continue to add words as you complete the unit.

gadget

upgrade

collectibles

MATERIALISM

🔧 **Tool Kit**
Word Network Model

Summary

Write a summary of "I Came, I Saw, I Shopped." A **summary** is a concise, complete, and accurate overview of a text. It should not include a statement of your opinion or an analysis.

Launch Activity

Conduct a Discussion Consider this statement: **If they can afford it, people should buy whatever they want.** Decide how strongly you agree or disagree with the statement, and check the appropriate box. Briefly explain your reasons.

☐ Strongly Agree   ☐ Agree   ☐ Disagree   ☐ Strongly Disagree

_____

_____

Discuss your ideas with your classmates, and listen to their perspectives.

- Illustrate your ideas with examples from your own experiences or stories you have read or heard.
- As a group, consider the types of reasons classmates provide, and place them in broad categories. For example, are people's reasons practical, ethical, or emotional?
- Decide whether your initial position has changed. If so, write a brief statement explaining why.

QuickWrite

Consider class discussions, the video, and the Launch Text as you think about the prompt. Record your first thoughts here.

PROMPT: **How do we decide what we want versus what we need? What can result from an imbalance between want and need?**

✏ EVIDENCE LOG FOR ALL THAT GLITTERS

Review your QuickWrite, and summarize your initial thoughts in one sentence to record in your Evidence Log. Then, record evidence from "I Came, I Saw, I Shopped" that supports your initial position.

Prepare for the Performance-Based Assessment at the end of the unit by completing the Evidence Log after each selection.

 **Tool Kit**
Evidence Log Model

Title of Text: _____   Date: _____

CONNECTION TO PROMPT	TEXT EVIDENCE/DETAILS	ADDITIONAL NOTES/IDEAS

How does this text change or add to my thinking?   Date: _____

ESSENTIAL QUESTION:

What do our possessions reveal about us?

The objects we truly cherish often remind us of great experiences or people we love. What explains, then, our desire for the newest and latest gadgets, which do not evoke such personal connections? You will work with your whole class to explore the concept of materialism. The selections you are going to read present insights into people's wants and needs.

Whole-Class Learning Strategies

Throughout your life, in school, in your community, and in your career, you will continue to learn and work in large-group environments.

Review these strategies and the actions you can take to practice them as you work with your whole class. Add ideas of your own for each step. Get ready to use these strategies during Whole-Class Learning.

STRATEGY	ACTION PLAN
Listen actively	• Eliminate distractions. For example, put your cellphone away. • Keep your eyes on the speaker. •
Clarify by asking questions	• If you're confused, other people probably are, too. Ask a question to help your whole class. • If you see that you are guessing, ask a question instead. •
Monitor understanding	• Notice what information you already know and be ready to build on it. • Ask for help if you are struggling. •
Interact and share ideas	• Share your ideas and answer questions, even if you are unsure. • Build on the ideas of others by adding details or making a connection. •

CONTENTS

About the Author

A master of the short story, **Guy de Maupassant** (1850–1893) wrote tales that are both realistic and pessimistic and that frequently offer unforeseen endings. Following military service, Maupassant settled in Paris and joined a circle of writers led by novelist Emile Zola. With Zola's encouragement, Maupassant published his first short story, "Ball of Fat," which earned him immediate fame and freed him to write full time. "The Necklace" is his most widely read work.

🔧 **Tool Kit**
First-Read Guide and Model Annotation

The Necklace

Concept Vocabulary

You will encounter the following words as you read "The Necklace." Before reading, note how familiar you are with each word. Then, rank the words in order from most familiar (1) to least familiar (6).

WORD	YOUR RANKING
refinement	
suppleness	
exquisite	
gallantries	
resplendent	
homage	

After completing the first read, come back to the concept vocabulary and review your rankings. Mark changes to your original rankings as needed.

First Read FICTION

Apply these strategies as you conduct your first read. You will have an opportunity to complete the close-read notes after your first read.

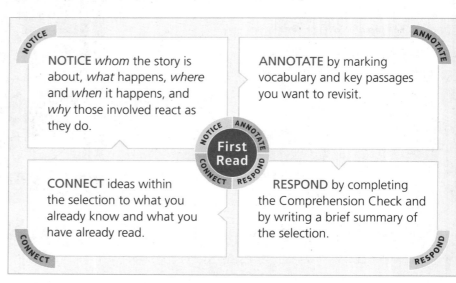

NOTICE whom the story is about, what happens, where and when it happens, and why those involved react as they do.

ANNOTATE by marking vocabulary and key passages you want to revisit.

CONNECT ideas within the selection to what you already know and what you have already read.

RESPOND by completing the Comprehension Check and by writing a brief summary of the selection.

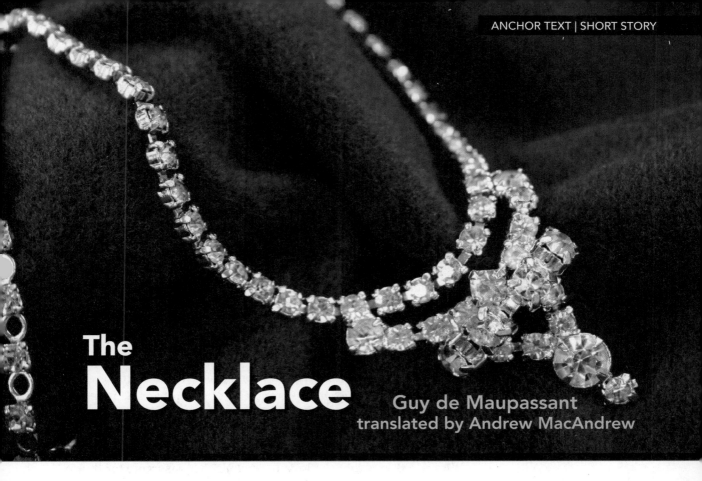

The Necklace

Guy de Maupassant
translated by Andrew MacAndrew

BACKGROUND

In the late nineteenth century, a type of literature known as Realism emerged as a reaction to the idealism and optimism of Romantic literature. Realism sought to describe life as it is, without ornament or glorification. "The Necklace," an example of Realist fiction, tells the story of an average woman who pays a significant price to experience a glamorous evening. As in all Realist fiction, there is no fairy-tale ending.

1 She was one of those pretty, charming young women who are born, as if by an error of Fate, into a petty official's family. She had no dowry,[1] no hopes, not the slightest chance of being appreciated, understood, loved, and married by a rich and distinguished man; so she slipped into marriage with a minor civil servant at the Ministry of Education.

2 Unable to afford jewelry, she dressed simply: but she was as wretched as a déclassée, for women have neither caste nor breeding—in them beauty, grace, and charm replace pride of birth. Innate **refinement**, instinctive elegance, and **suppleness** of wit give them their place on the only scale that counts, and these qualities make humble girls the peers of the grandest ladies.

3 She suffered constantly, feeling that all the attributes of a gracious life, every luxury, should rightly have been hers. The poverty of her rooms—the shabby walls, the worn furniture, the ugly

NOTES

refinement (rih FYN muhnt) *n.* politeness; good manners

suppleness (SUHP uhl nihs) *n.* smoothness; fluidity; ability to adapt easily to different situations

---

1. **dowry** (DOW ree) *n.* wealth or property given by a woman's family to her husband upon their marriage.

CLOSE READ

ANNOTATE: In paragraph 3, mark details related to size, luxury, and antiquity.

QUESTION: Why does the author use these particular details?

CONCLUDE: What image do these details paint of the life Madame Loisel desires?

exquisite (EHKS kwih ziht) *adj.* very beautiful or lovely

gallantries (GAL uhn treez) *n.* acts of polite attention to the needs of women

upholstery—caused her pain. All these things that another woman of her class would not even have noticed, tormented her and made her angry. The very sight of the little Breton girl who cleaned for her awoke rueful thoughts and the wildest dreams in her mind. She dreamed of thick-carpeted reception rooms with Oriental hangings, lighted by tall, bronze torches, and with two huge footmen in knee breeches, made drowsy by the heat from the stove, asleep in the wide armchairs. She dreamed of great drawing rooms upholstered in old silks, with fragile little tables holding priceless knick-knacks, and of enchanting little sitting rooms redolent of perfume, designed for teatime chats with intimate friends—famous, sought-after men whose attentions all women longed for.

4   When she sat down to dinner at her round table with its three-day old cloth, and watched her husband opposite her lift the lid of the soup tureen and exclaim, delighted: "Ah, a good homemade beef stew! There's nothing better . . ." she would visualize elegant dinners with gleaming silver amid tapestried walls peopled by knights and ladies and exotic birds in a fairy forest; she would think of **exquisite** dishes served on gorgeous china, and of **gallantries** whispered and received with sphinx-like smiles while eating the pink flesh of trout or wings of grouse.

5   She had no proper wardrobe, no jewels, nothing. And those were the only things that she loved—she felt she was made for them. She would have so loved to charm, to be envied, to be admired and sought after.

6   She had a rich friend, a schoolmate from the convent she had attended, but she didn't like to visit her because it always made her so miserable when she got home again. She would weep for whole days at a time from sorrow, regret, despair, and distress.

7   Then one evening her husband arrived home looking triumphant and waving a large envelope.

8   "There," he said, "there's something for you."

9   She tore it open eagerly and took out a printed card which said:

10   "The Minister of Education and Madame Georges Ramponneau[2] request the pleasure of the company of M. and Mme. Loisel[3] at an evening reception at the Ministry on Monday, January 18th."

11   Instead of being delighted, as her husband had hoped, she tossed the invitation on the table and muttered, annoyed:

12   "What do you expect me to do with that?"

13   "Why, I thought you'd be pleased, dear. You never go out and this would be an occasion for you, a great one! I had a lot of trouble getting it. Everyone wants an invitation: they're in great demand and there are only a few reserved for the employees. All the officials will be there."

14   She looked at him, irritated, and said impatiently:

---

2. **Georges** (zhawrzh) **Ramponneau** (ram puh NOH)
3. **Loisel** (lwah ZEHL)

15   "I haven't a thing to wear. How could I go?"

16   It had never even occurred to him. He stammered:

17   "But what about the dress you wear to the theater? I think it's lovely. . . ."

18   He fell silent, amazed and bewildered to see that his wife was crying. Two big tears escaped from the corners of her eyes and rolled slowly toward the corners of her mouth. He mumbled:

19   "What is it? What is it?"

20   But, with great effort, she had overcome her misery; and now she answered him calmly, wiping her tear-damp cheeks:

21   "It's nothing. It's just that I have no evening dress and so I can't go to the party. Give the invitation to one of your colleagues whose wife will be better dressed than I would be."

22   He was overcome. He said:

23   "Listen, Mathilde, how much would an evening dress cost—a suitable one that you could wear again on other occasions, something very simple?"

24   She thought for several seconds, making her calculations and at the same time estimating how much she could ask for without eliciting an immediate refusal and an exclamation of horror from this economical government clerk.

25   At last, not too sure of herself, she said:

26   "It's hard to say exactly but I think I could manage with four hundred francs."

27   He went a little pale, for that was exactly the amount he had put aside to buy a rifle so that he could go hunting the following summer near Nanterre, with a few friends who went shooting larks around there on Sundays.

28   However, he said:

29   "Well, all right, then. I'll give you four hundred francs. But try to get something really nice."

30   As the day of the ball drew closer, Madame Loisel seemed depressed, disturbed, worried—despite the fact that her dress was ready. One evening her husband said:

31   "What's the matter? You've really been very strange these last few days."

32   And she answered:

33   "I hate not having a single jewel, not one stone, to wear. I shall look so dowdy.⁴ I'd almost rather not go to the party."

34   He suggested:

35   "You can wear some fresh flowers. It's considered very chic⁵ at this time of year. For ten francs you can get two or three beautiful roses."

36   That didn't satisfy her at all.

37   "No . . . there's nothing more humiliating than to look poverty-stricken among a lot of rich women."

38   Then her husband exclaimed:

---

4. **dowdy** *adj.* shabby.
5. **chic** (sheek) *adj.* fashionable.

resplendent (rih SPLEHN duhnt) *adj.* dazzling; gorgeous

homage (OM ihj) *n.* something done to honor someone

39   "Wait—you silly thing! Why don't you go and see Madame Forestier[6] and ask her to lend you some jewelry. You certainly know her well enough for that, don't you think?"

40   She let out a joyful cry.

41   "You're right. It never occurred to me."

42   The next day she went to see her friend and related her tale of woe.

43   Madame Forestier went to her mirrored wardrobe, took out a big jewel case, brought it to Madame Loisel opened it, and said:

44   "Take your pick, my dear."

45   Her eyes wandered from some bracelets to a pearl necklace, then to a gold Venetian cross set with stones, of very fine workmanship. She tried on the jewelry before the mirror, hesitating, unable to bring herself to take them off, to give them back. And she kept asking:

46   "Do you have anything else, by chance?"

47   "Why yes. Here, look for yourself. I don't know which ones you'll like."

48   All at once, in a box lined with black satin, she came upon a superb diamond necklace, and her heart started beating with overwhelming desire. Her hands trembled as she picked it up. She fastened it around her neck over her high-necked dress and stood there gazing at herself ecstatically.

49   Hesitantly, filled with terrible anguish, she asked:

50   "Could you lend me this one—just this and nothing else?"

51   "Yes, of course."

52   She threw her arms around her friend's neck, kissed her ardently, and fled with her treasure.

53   The day of the party arrived. Madame Loisel was a great success. She was the prettiest woman there—**resplendent**, graceful, beaming, and deliriously happy. All the men looked at her, asked who she was, tried to get themselves introduced to her. All the minister's aides wanted to waltz with her. The minister himself noticed her.

54   She danced enraptured—carried away, intoxicated with pleasure, forgetting everything in this triumph of her beauty and the glory of her success, floating in a cloud of happiness formed by all this **homage**, all this admiration, all the desires she had stirred up—by this victory so complete and so sweet to the heart of a woman.

55   When she left the party, it was almost four in the morning. Her husband had been sleeping since midnight in a small, deserted sitting room, with three other gentlemen whose wives were having a wonderful time.

56   He brought her wraps so that they could leave and put them around her shoulders—the plain wraps from her everyday life whose shabbiness jarred with the elegance of her evening dress. She felt this and wanted to escape quickly so that the other women, who were enveloping themselves in their rich furs, wouldn't see her.

---

6. **Forestier** (fawr ehs TYAY)

57   Loisel held her back.

58   "Wait a minute. You'll catch cold out there. I'm going to call a cab."

59   But she wouldn't listen to him and went hastily downstairs. Outside in the street, there was no cab to be found; they set out to look for one, calling to the drivers they saw passing in the distance.

60   They walked toward the Seine,[7] shivering and miserable. Finally, on the embankment, they found one of those ancient nocturnal broughams[8] which are only to be seen in Paris at night, as if they were ashamed to show their shabbiness in daylight.

61   It took them to their door in the Rue des Martyrs, and they went sadly upstairs to their apartment. For her, it was all over. And he was thinking that he had to be at the Ministry by ten.

62   She took off her wraps before the mirror so that she could see herself in all her glory once more. Then she cried out. The necklace was gone; there was nothing around her neck.

63   Her husband, already half undressed, asked:

64   "What's the matter?"

65   She turned toward him in a frenzy:

66   "The . . . the . . . necklace—it's gone."

67   He got up, thunderstruck.

68   "What did you say? . . . What! . . . Impossible!"

69   And they searched the folds of her dress, the folds of her wrap, the pockets, everywhere.

70   They didn't find it.

71   He asked:

72   "Are you sure you still had it when we left the ball?"

73   "Yes. I remember touching it in the hallway of the Ministry."

74   "But if you had lost it in the street, we would have heard it fall. It must be in the cab."

75   "Yes, most likely. Do you remember the number?"

76   "No. What about you—did you notice it?"

77   "No. "

78   They looked at each other in utter dejection. Finally Loisel got dressed again.

79   "I'm going to retrace the whole distance we covered on foot," he said, "and see if I can't find it."

80   And he left the house. She remained in her evening dress, too weak to go to bed, sitting crushed on a chair, lifeless and blank.

81   Her husband returned at about seven o'clock. He had found nothing.

82   He went to the police station, to the newspapers to offer a reward, to the offices of the cab companies—in a word, wherever there seemed to be the slightest hope of tracing it.

---

7. **Seine** (sayn) river flowing through Paris.
8. **broughams** (broomz) *n.* horse-drawn carriages.

> Then she cried out. The necklace was gone; there was nothing around her neck.

CLOSE READ

ANNOTATE: In paragraphs 66–68, mark the punctuation that suggests hesitation or speech that is broken up in some way.

QUESTION: Why does the author use these punctuation marks? What emotions do they convey?

CONCLUDE: How does the punctuation add to the effect of the dialogue?

83   She spent the whole day waiting, in a state of utter hopelessness before such an appalling catastrophe.

84   Loisel returned in the evening, his face lined and pale; he had learned nothing.

85   "You must write to your friend," he said, "and tell her that you've broken the clasp of the necklace and that you're getting it mended. That'll give us time to decide what to do."

86   She wrote the letter at his dictation.

87   By the end of the week, they had lost all hope.

88   Loisel, who had aged five years, declared:

89   "We'll have to replace the necklace."

90   The next day they took the case in which it had been kept and went to the jeweler whose name appeared inside it. He looked through his ledgers:

91   "I didn't sell this necklace, madame. I only supplied the case."

92   Then they went from one jeweler to the next, trying to find a necklace like the other, racking their memories, both of them sick with worry and distress.

93   In a fashionable shop near the Palais Royal, they found a diamond necklace which they decided was exactly like the other. It was worth 40,000 francs. They could have it for 36,000 francs.

94   They asked the jeweler to hold it for them for three days, and they stipulated that he should take it back for 34,000 francs if the other necklace was found before the end of February.

95   Loisel possessed 18,000 francs left him by his father. He would borrow the rest.

96   He borrowed, asking a thousand francs from one man, five hundred from another, a hundred here, fifty there. He signed promissory notes,[9] borrowed at exorbitant rates, dealt with usurers and the entire race of moneylenders. He compromised his whole career, gave his signature even when he wasn't sure he would be able to honor it, and horrified by the anxieties with which his future would be filled, by the black misery about to descend upon him, by the prospect of physical privation and moral suffering, went to get the new necklace, placing on the jeweler's counter 36,000 francs.

97   When Madame Loisel went to return the necklace, Madame Forestier said in a faintly waspish tone:

98   "You could have brought it back a little sooner! I might have needed it."

99   She didn't open the case as her friend had feared she might. If she had noticed the substitution, what would she have thought? What would she have said? Mightn't she have taken Madame Loisel for a thief?

---

9. **promissory** (PROM uh sawr ee) **notes** written promises to pay back borrowed money.

100   Madame Loisel came to know the awful life of the poverty-stricken. However, she resigned herself to it with unexpected fortitude. The crushing debt had to be paid. She would pay it. They dismissed the maid; they moved into an attic under the roof.

101   She came to know all the heavy household chores, the loathsome work of the kitchen. She washed the dishes, wearing down her pink nails on greasy casseroles and the bottoms of saucepans. She did the laundry, washing shirts and dishcloths which she hung on a line to dry; she took the garbage down to the street every morning, and carried water upstairs, stopping at every floor to get her breath. Dressed like a working-class woman, she went to the fruit store, the grocer, and the butcher with her basket on her arm, bargaining, outraged, contesting each sou[10] of her pitiful funds.

102   Every month some notes had to be honored and more time requested on others.

103   Her husband worked in the evenings, putting a shopkeeper's ledgers in order, and often at night as well, doing copying at twenty-five centimes a page.

104   And it went on like that for ten years.

105   After ten years, they had made good on everything, including the usurious rates and the compound interest.

106   Madame Loisel looked old now. She had become the sort of strong woman, hard and coarse, that one finds in poor families. Disheveled, her skirts askew, with reddened hands, she spoke in a loud voice, slopping water over the floors as she washed them. But sometimes, when her husband was at the office, she would sit down by the window and muse over that party long ago when she had been so beautiful, the belle of the ball.

107   How would things have turned out if she hadn't lost that necklace? Who could tell? How strange and fickle life is! How little it takes to make or break you!

108   Then one Sunday when she was strolling along the Champs-Élysées[11] to forget the week's chores for a while, she suddenly caught sight of a woman taking a child for a walk. It was Madame Forestier, still young, still beautiful, still charming.

109   Madame Loisel started to tremble. Should she speak to her? Yes, certainly she should. And now that she had paid everything back, why shouldn't she tell her the whole story?

110   She went up to her.

111   "Hello, Jeanne."

112   The other didn't recognize her and was surprised that this plainly dressed woman should speak to her so familiarly. She murmured:

113   "But . . . madame! . . . I'm sure . . . You must be mistaken."

---

10. **sou** (soo) *n.* former French coin, worth very little; the centime (SAHN teem), mentioned later, was also of little value.
11. **Champs-Élysées** (SHAHN zay lee ZAY) fashionable street in Paris.

CLOSE READ

ANNOTATE: Mark the shortest sentence in paragraph 100.

QUESTION: How is this sentence different from the others in the paragraph?

CONCLUDE: What effect does this short sentence create that a longer sentence might not?

CLOSE READ

ANNOTATE: Underline the repeated word in paragraph 108.

QUESTION: Why does the author repeat this word?

CONCLUDE: What is the effect of this repetition?

114   "No, I'm not. I am Mathilde Loisel."

115   Her friend gave a little cry.

116   "Oh! Oh, my poor Mathilde, how you've changed!"

117   "Yes, I've been through some pretty hard times since I last saw you and I've had plenty of trouble—and all because of you!"

118   "Because of me? What do you mean?"

119   "You remember the diamond necklace you lent me to wear to the party at the Ministry?"

120   "Yes. What about it?"

121   "Well, I lost it."

122   "What are you talking about? You returned it to me."

123   "What I gave back to you was another one just like it. And it took us ten years to pay for it. You can imagine it wasn't easy for us, since we were quite poor. . . . Anyway, I'm glad it's over and done with."

124   Madame Forestier stopped short.

125   "You say you bought a diamond necklace to replace that other one?"

126   "Yes. You didn't even notice then? They really were exactly alike."

127   And she smiled, full of a proud, simple joy.

128   Madame Forestier, profoundly moved, took Mathilde's hands in her own.

129   "Oh, my poor, poor Mathilde! Mine was false. It was worth five hundred francs at the most!" ❧

Comprehension Check

Complete the following items after you finish your first read.

1. At the beginning of the story, why is Madame Loisel unhappy with her life?

2. What steps does Madame Loisel take to dress for the party in a way she feels is appropriate?

3. What does Monsieur Loisel do to pay for the replacement necklace?

4. What does Madame Loisel learn about the borrowed necklace at the end of the story?

5. 🖉 **Notebook** To confirm your understanding, write a summary of "The Necklace."

- -

RESEARCH

Research to Clarify Choose at least one unfamiliar detail from the text. Briefly research that detail. In what way does the information you learned shed light on an aspect of the story?

Research to Explore Choose something from the text that interests you, and formulate a research question.

THE NECKLACE

Close Read the Text

1. This model, from paragraph 4 of the text, shows two sample annotations, along with questions and conclusions. Close read the passage, and find another detail to annotate. Then, write a question and your conclusion.

> **ANNOTATE:** These details are like those one would find in fairy tales.
>
> **QUESTION:** Why does Madame Loisel have fairy-tale fantasies?
>
> **CONCLUDE:** Madame Loisel is like a child dreaming of being a princess in a story.

ANNOTATE: This long sentence is two sentences connected by a semicolon.

QUESTION: Why does the author structure this fantasy sequence in this way?

CONCLUDE: The long, continuous sentence shows how immersed Madame Loisel is in her fantasy.

> . . . she would visualize elegant dinners with gleaming silver amid tapestried walls peopled by knights and ladies and exotic birds in a fairy forest; she would think of exquisite dishes served on gorgeous china, and of gallantries whispered and received with sphinx-like smiles while eating the pink flesh of trout or wings of grouse.

🔧 **Tool Kit**
Close-Read Guide and
Model Annotation

2. For more practice, go back into the text, and complete the close-read notes.

3. Revisit a section of the text you found important during your first read. Read this section closely, and **annotate** what you notice. Ask yourself **questions** such as "Why did the author make this choice?" What can you **conclude**?

Analyze the Text

CITE TEXTUAL EVIDENCE to support your answers.

📓 **Notebook** Respond to these questions.

1. (a) **Interpret** How do visits to her rich friend affect Mathilde?
   (b) **Analyze** Why does Mathilde react the way she does? Explain.

2. (a) **Compare and Contrast** What strengths do Mathilde and her husband, respectively, bring to their marriage? (b) **Speculate** Will Mathilde tell her husband the truth about the necklace? Explain.

3. **Make a Judgment** Which contributes more to Mathilde's misery—her circumstances or her desires? Explain.

4. **Essential Question:** *What do our possessions reveal about us?* What have you learned about materialism from reading this story?

Analyze Craft and Structure

Author's Choices: Literary Devices **Irony** is a discrepancy or contradiction between appearance and reality, between meaning and intention, or—as in "The Necklace"—between expectation and outcome. In **situational irony,** an event occurs that contradicts the expectations of the characters, the readers, or the audience.

Situational irony often involves a **surprise ending,** or an unexpected resolution to a story's plot. In all stories, writers plant clues that lead readers to have certain expectations of what characters will do or experience. In stories that have situational irony and surprise endings, some of those clues may be subtly false. When a surprise ending is effective, a story's resolution violates readers' expectations, but does so in a way that is both logical and believable. Readers may be startled by the ending but on reflection find that it makes sense.

Practice

CITE TEXTUAL EVIDENCE
to support your answers.

📓 **Notebook** Respond to these questions.

1. Fill in the chart to show how the story events lead to situational irony.

SITUATION	WHAT IS EXPECTED	WHAT HAPPENS
Mathilde's husband hands her an invitation to a glittering ball.		
Mathilde is a great success at the ball.		
The flighty Mathilde is faced with debt and hardship.		
Madame Forestier meets Mathilde on the street.		

2. How might Mathilde's life have been different if she had told Madame Forestier the truth right after the ball? Explain.

3. (a) How is the irony of the necklace symbolic of a larger irony in Mathilde's life?
   (b) How does Guy de Maupassant enhance this symbolism through the use of irony and surprise ending?

4. Is the surprise ending in "The Necklace" believable? Why or why not?

THE NECKLACE

Concept Vocabulary

refinement	exquisite	resplendent
suppleness	gallantries	homage

Why These Words? These concept vocabulary words are all related to elegance or high social status, which is what Mathilde Loisel desires. For example, she yearns for *refinement* and *suppleness* of wit as qualities of the "grandest ladies." In her daydreams, she visualizes the *exquisite* dishes served at elegant dinners.

1. How does the concept vocabulary sharpen the reader's understanding of Mathilde Loisel's character?

2. What other words in the selection connect to this concept?

Practice

📖 **Notebook** The concept vocabulary words appear in "The Necklace."

1. Use each concept word in a sentence in which sensory details reveal the word's meaning.

2. Challenge yourself to replace the concept word in three of the sentences you just wrote with a synonym. How does your word change affect the meaning of your sentence?

Word Study

Latin Root: -*splend*- In "The Necklace," to support the statement that Madame Loisel is the prettiest woman at the party, the narrator describes her as *resplendent*, or "dazzling." *Resplendent* is formed from the Latin root -*splend*-, which means "bright" or "shining."

1. Write the meanings of these words formed from the root -*splend*-: *splendor*, *splendid*, *splendiferous*. Consult a print or online dictionary if needed.

2. Use each of these three words in a sentence. Include context clues that reveal shades of meaning among the words.

WORD NETWORK

Add words related to materialism from the text to your Word Network.

Conventions

Punctuation Writers, such as Guy de Maupassant, use punctuation marks, including semicolons, to clarify the logical relationships between or among ideas. A **semicolon (;)** is used to join two closely related independent clauses that are not already joined by a coordinating conjunction. The second clause may or may not begin with a **conjunctive adverb**—such as *also*, *however*, *therefore*, or *furthermore*—or a **transitional expression**—such as *as a result*, *for instance*, or *on the other hand*.

Here are examples of correct use of semicolons, with and without a conjunctive adverb or a transitional phrase.

> **Example:** Madame Loisel desperately wants to attend the party; everyone worth impressing will be there.
>
> **Example / Conjunctive Adverb:** Her husband spends hours searching the streets; nevertheless, he comes home empty-handed.
>
> **Example / Transitional Expression:** The Loisels borrow 18,000 francs; as a result, they spend the next decade deep in debt.

Read It

1. Mark where a semicolon should be inserted in each of the following sentences based on "The Necklace."

   a. Everyone wants an invitation to the party they are in great demand.

   b. There are no cabs to be found outside in the street consequently, the Loisels set out to look for one.

   c. There is nothing around Madame Loisel's neck the necklace is gone.

   d. The necklace turns out to have been much less valuable than Madame Loisel thought in fact, it was merely a piece of cheap costume jewelry.

2. Reread paragraph 100 of "The Necklace." Mark the semicolon, as well as the two independent clauses it separates.

Write It

Write three sentences of your own to describe Madame Loisel—her character, her dreams, and her experiences in the story. Use a semicolon in each sentence.

TIP

CLARIFICATION
When the second independent clause begins with a conjunctive adverb or transitional expression, place a semicolon before the conjunctive adverb or transitional expression and a comma after it.

THE NECKLACE

Writing to Sources

A diary is a form of autobiographical writing because it describes the writer's own experiences and expresses his or her thoughts, feelings, and observations. Many diaries are composed as daily segments or entries. Most are not written for publication or even to be read by anyone else. However, some literary diaries are written with other readers in mind.

Assignment

Just before the final meeting between Mathilde Loisel and Madame Forestier, the narrator of "The Necklace" ponders what might have happened to Mathilde in other circumstances:

How would things have turned out if she hadn't lost that necklace? Who could tell? How strange and fickle life is! How little it takes to make or break you!

Adopt the perspective of Mathilde Loisel, and write a **diary entry** in which you explain how your life changed after the party. Use elements in the story, but also feel free to add new elements from your own imagination. Pay particular attention to the role that poverty and hardship begin to play in Mathilde's life. Be sure to mention the contributions Mathilde's husband makes.

Vocabulary and Conventions Connection Include several of the concept vocabulary words in your diary entry. Also, try to use at least one semicolon to join closely related independent clauses.

refinement	exquisite	resplendent
suppleness	gallantries	homage

- -

Reflect on Your Writing

After you have written your diary entry, answer these questions.

1. Have you written consistently from the perspective of Madame Loisel?

2. Is your portrayal of Madame Loisel's thought process consistent with the way it is portrayed in the story? Explain.

3. Why These Words? The words you choose make a difference in your writing. Which words did you specifically choose to make your diary entry consistent with Madame Loisel's personality?

Speaking and Listening

Assignment

In the character of Mathilde Loisel, deliver a **monologue** that might have taken place after the end of the story. In your monologue, tell your husband what you learned about the true value of the necklace, and explain how that makes you feel.

1. **Choose an Emotional Tone** Begin planning your monologue by considering how Madame Forestier's final revelation will affect Mathilde Loisel. Will Madame Loisel be shocked, angry, philosophical, despairing? What lessons, if any, will she draw from the news that the necklace was a fake?

2. **Plan Your Interpretation** Consider what the story shows about the Loisels' way of life for the past ten years. What will be Madame Loisel's attitude toward the poverty and hardship the couple has endured? How will she express her thoughts and feelings to her husband?

3. **Prepare Your Delivery** Practice your recitation before you present the monologue to your class. Include the following performance techniques to achieve the desired effect.

   - Speak clearly and comfortably without rushing.
   - Vary the tone and pitch of your voice to convey meaning and add interest. Avoid speaking in a flat, monotone style.
   - Use appropriate and effective body language. Maintain eye contact to keep your audience's attention.

4. **Evaluate Monologues** As your classmates deliver their monologues, listen attentively. Use an evaluation guide like the one shown to analyze their presentations.

EVALUATION GUIDE

Rate each statement on a scale of 1 (not demonstrated) to 4 (demonstrated).

☐ 1. The speaker presented a convincing interpretation of Mathilde Loisel.

☐ 2. The speaker communicated clearly and expressively.

☐ 3. The speaker used a variety of vocal tones and pitches.

☐ 4. The speaker used effective gestures and body language.

☐ 5. The speaker clearly explained Madame Loisel's thoughts and feelings about the true value of the necklace.

📝 EVIDENCE LOG

Before moving on to a new selection, go to your Evidence Log and record what you learned from "The Necklace."

About the Author

Chinua Achebe (1930–2013) is renowned for novels and stories that explore the conflicts of modern Africa. He was born into the Nigerian Igbo tribe and publicly supported the independence of the Igbo-dominated Biafra region from Nigeria. Considered the founding father of modern African literature in the English language, Achebe is read widely in Africa and around the world. His first and most celebrated novel, *Things Fall Apart*, portrays the disruption of Igbo tribal society by Western colonialism.

🔧 Tool Kit
First-Read Guide and Model Annotation

Civil Peace

Concept Vocabulary

You will encounter the following words as you read "Civil Peace." Before reading, note how familiar you are with each word. Then, rank the words in order from most familiar (1) to least familiar (6).

WORD	YOUR RANKING
inestimable	
blessings	
amenable	
influence	
surrender	
windfall	

After completing the first read, come back to the concept vocabulary and review your rankings. Mark changes to your original rankings as needed.

First Read FICTION

Apply these strategies as you conduct your first read. You will have an opportunity to complete the close-read notes after your first read.

NOTICE *whom* the story is about, *what* happens, *where* and *when* it happens, and *why* those involved react as they do.

ANNOTATE by marking vocabulary and key passages you want to revisit.

First Read

CONNECT ideas within the selection to what you already know and what you have already read.

RESPOND by completing the Comprehension Check and by writing a brief summary of the selection.

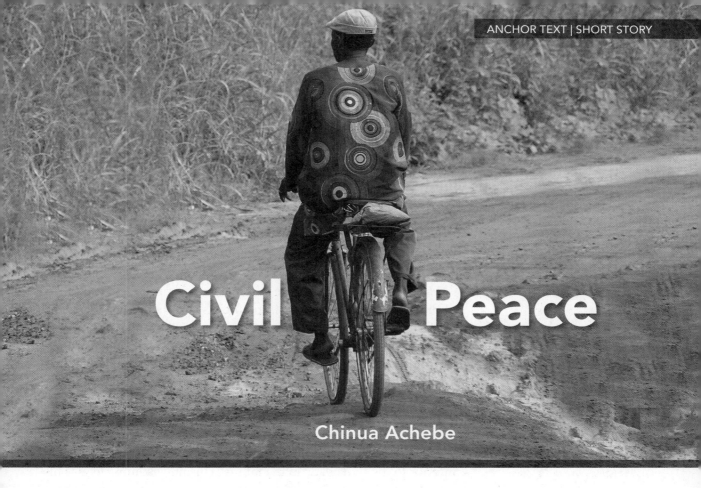

Civil Peace

Chinua Achebe

BACKGROUND

In 1967, Nigeria entered a civil war when the country's southeastern territories declared independence, calling themselves the Republic of Biafra. The Biafrans, most of whom belonged to the Igbo ethnic group, said they broke away from Nigeria because another ethnic group, called the Hausa, had massacred Igbo in the north. After nearly three years of war, the Biafrans surrendered. More than one million people had died in battle or from starvation. "Civil Peace" unfolds in the aftermath of this war.

1   Jonathan Iwegbu counted himself extraordinarily lucky. "Happy survival!" meant so much more to him than just a current fashion of greeting old friends in the first hazy days of peace. It went deep to his heart. He had come out of the war with five **inestimable blessings**—his head, his wife Maria's head, and the heads of three out of their four children. As a bonus he also had his old bicycle—a miracle too but naturally not to be compared to the safety of five human heads.

2   The bicycle had a little history of its own. One day at the height of the war it was commandeered "for urgent military action." Hard as its loss would have been to him he would still have let it go without a thought had he not had some doubts about the genuineness of the officer. It wasn't his disreputable rags, nor the toes peeping out of one blue and one brown canvas shoe, nor yet the two stars of

NOTES

inestimable (ihn EHS tuh muh buhl) *adj.* too great to count or measure

blessings (BLEHS ihngz) *n.* things that benefit or bring happiness

amenable (uh MEHN uh buhl)
adj. agreeable

influence (IHN floo uhns)
n. dishonest persuasion;
bribery

surrender (suh REHN duhr) *n.*
act of giving up

CLOSE READ

ANNOTATE: In paragraph 4,
mark words and phrases
related to luck or wonder.

QUESTION: Why do
references to luck and
wonder appear so
frequently?

CONCLUDE: What effect do
these repeated references
have, particularly on how
readers see Jonathan?

his rank done obviously in a hurry in biro,[1] that troubled Jonathan; many good and heroic soldiers looked the same or worse. It was rather a certain lack of grip and firmness in his manner. So Jonathan, suspecting he might be **amenable** to **influence**, rummaged in his raffia bag and produced the two pounds with which he had been going to buy firewood which his wife, Maria, retailed to camp officials for extra stock-fish and corn meal, and got his bicycle back. That night he buried it in the little clearing in the bush where the dead of the camp, including his own youngest son, were buried. When he dug it up again a year later after the **surrender** all it needed was a little palm-oil greasing. "Nothing puzzles God," he said in wonder.

3   He put it to immediate use as a taxi and accumulated a small pile of Biafran[2] money ferrying camp officials and their families across the four-mile stretch to the nearest tarred road. His standard charge per trip was six pounds and those who had the money were only glad to be rid of some of it in this way. At the end of a fortnight[3] he had made a small fortune of one hundred and fifteen pounds.

4   Then he made the journey to Enugu and found another miracle waiting for him. It was unbelievable. He rubbed his eyes and looked again and it was still standing there before him. But, needless to say, even that monumental blessing must be accounted also totally inferior to the five heads in the family. This newest miracle was his little house in Ogui Overside. Indeed nothing puzzles God! Only two houses away a huge concrete edifice some wealthy contractor had put up just before the war was a mountain of rubble. And here was Jonathan's little zinc house of no regrets built with mud blocks quite intact! Of course the doors and windows were missing and five sheets off the roof. But what was that? And anyhow he had returned to Enugu early enough to pick up bits of old zinc and wood and soggy sheets of cardboard lying around the neighborhood before thousands more came out of their forest holes looking for the same things. He got a destitute carpenter with one old hammer, a blunt plane and a few bent and rusty nails in his tool bag to turn this assortment of wood, paper, and metal into door and window shutters for five Nigerian shillings or fifty Biafran pounds. He paid the pounds, and moved in with his overjoyed family carrying five heads on their shoulders.

5   His children picked mangoes near the military cemetery and sold them to soldiers' wives for a few pennies—real pennies this time— and his wife started making breakfast akara balls[4] for neighbors in a hurry to start life again. With his family earnings he took his bicycle

1. **biro** (BY roh) informal British English for "ballpoint pen."
2. **Biafran** (bee AF ruhn) of the rebellious southeastern region of Nigeria, which declared itself the independent Republic of Biafra in the civil war of 1967.
3. **fortnight** two weeks.
4. **akara** (uh KAHR uh) **balls** deep-fried balls of ground beans.

to the villages around and bought fresh palm-wine which he mixed generously in his rooms with the water which had recently started running again in the public tap down the road, and opened up a bar for soldiers and other lucky people with good money.

6   At first he went daily, then every other day and finally once a week, to the offices of the Coal Corporation where he used to be a miner, to find out what was what. The only thing he did find out in the end was that that little house of his was even a greater blessing than he had thought. Some of his fellow ex-miners who had nowhere to return at the end of the day's waiting just slept outside the doors of the offices and cooked what meal they could scrounge together in Bournvita tins. As the weeks lengthened and still nobody could say what was what Jonathan discontinued his weekly visits altogether and faced his palm-wine bar.

7   But nothing puzzles God. Came the day of the **windfall** when after five days of endless scuffles in queues[5] and counter-queues in the sun outside the Treasury he had twenty pounds counted into his palms as ex-gratia[6] award for the rebel money he had turned in. It was like Christmas for him and for many others like him when the payments began. They called it (since few could manage its proper official name) *egg-rasher*.

8   As soon as the pound notes were placed in his palm Jonathan simply closed it tight over them and buried fist and money inside his trouser pocket. He had to be extra careful because he had seen a man a couple of days earlier collapse into near-madness in an instant before that oceanic crowd because no sooner had he got his twenty pounds than some heartless ruffian picked it off him. Though it was not right that a man in such an extremity of agony should be blamed yet many in the queues that day were able to remark quietly at the victim's carelessness, especially after he pulled out the innards of his pocket and revealed a hole in it big enough to pass a thief's head. But of course he had insisted that the money had been in the other pocket, pulling it out too to show its comparative wholeness. So one had to be careful.

9   Jonathan soon transferred the money to his left hand and pocket so as to leave his right free for shaking hands should the need arise, though by fixing his gaze at such an elevation as to miss all approaching human faces he made sure that the need did not arise, until he got home.

10   He was normally a heavy sleeper but that night he heard all the neighborhood noises die down one after another. Even the night watchman who knocked the hour on some metal somewhere in the distance had fallen silent after knocking one o'clock. That must have been the last thought in Jonathan's mind before he was finally carried

windfall (WIHND fawl) *n.* unexpected good fortune

---

5. **queues** (kyooz) *n.* British English for "lines."
6. **ex-gratia** (ehks GRAY shee uh) as a favor (Latin).

away himself. He couldn't have been gone for long, though, when he was violently awakened again.

11   "Who is knocking?" whispered his wife lying beside him on the floor.

12   "I don't know," he whispered back breathlessly.

13   The second time the knocking came it was so loud and imperious that the rickety old door could have fallen down.

14   "Who is knocking?" he asked them, his voice parched and trembling.

15   "Na tief-man and him people," came the cool reply. "Make you hopen de door."⁷ This was followed by the heaviest knocking of all.

16   Maria was the first to raise the alarm, then he followed and all their children.

17   *"Police-o! Thieves-o! Neighbors-o! Police-o! We are lost! We are dead! Neighbors, are you asleep? Wake up! Police-o!"*

18   This went on for a long time and then stopped suddenly. Perhaps they had scared the thief away. There was total silence. But only for a short while.

19   "You done finish?" asked the voice outside. "Make we help you small. Oya, everybody!"

20   *"Police-o! Tief-man-so! Neighbors-o! We done loss-o! Police-o! . . ."*

21   There were at least five other voices besides the leader's.

22   Jonathan and his family were now completely paralyzed by terror. Maria and the children sobbed inaudibly like lost souls. Jonathan groaned continuously.

23   The silence that followed the thieves' alarm vibrated horribly. Jonathan all but begged their leader to speak again and be done with it.

24   "My frien," said he at long last, "we don try our best for call dem but I tink say dem all done sleep-o … So wetin we go do now? Sometaim you wan call soja? Or you wan make we call dem for you? Soja better pass police. No be so?"

25   "Na so!" replied his men. Jonathan thought he heard even more voices now than before and groaned heavily. His legs were sagging under him and his throat felt like sandpaper.

26   "My frien, why you no de talk again. I de ask you say you wan make we call soja?"

27   "No."

28   "Awrighto. Now make we talk business. We no be bad tief. We no like for make trouble. Trouble done finish. War done finish and all the katakata wey de for inside. No Civil War again. This time na Civil Peace. No be so?"

29   "'Na so!" answered the horrible chorus.

CLOSE READ

ANNOTATE: In paragraphs 24–27, mark words and phrases that suggest a casual friendliness in the way the thief speaks to Jonathan.

QUESTION: Why does the thief address Jonathan with seeming friendliness and familiarity?

CONCLUDE: What is the effect of this seemingly friendly tone?

---

7. **"Na tief-man . . . hopen de door"** (dialect) "I am a thief with my accomplices. Open the door."

30   "What do you want from me? I am a poor man. Everything I had went with this war. Why do you come to me? You know people who have money. We . . ."

31   "Awright! We know say you no get plenty money. But we sef no get even anini. So derefore make you open dis window and give us one hundred pound and we go commot. Orderwise we de come for inside now to show you guitar-boy like dis . . ."

32   A volley of automatic fire rang through the sky. Maria and the children began to weep aloud again.

33   "Ah, missisi de cry again. No need for dat. We done talk say we na good tief. We just take our small money and go nwayorly. No molest. Abi we de molest?"

34   "At all!" sang the chorus.

35   "My friends," began Jonathan hoarsely. "I hear what you say and I thank you. If I had one hundred pounds . . ."

36   "Lookia my frien, no be play we come play for your house. If we make mistake and step for inside you no go like am-o. So derefore . . ."

CLOSE READ

ANNOTATE: A **simile** is a figure of speech that uses an explicit comparison word such as *like* or *as* to make a comparison between two dissimilar things. In paragraph 40, mark the simile.

QUESTION: Why does the author use this simile after the threats of violence that came earlier in the story?

CONCLUDE: What is the effect of this simile?

37 "To God who made me; if you come inside and find one hundred pounds, take it and shoot me and shoot my wife and children. I swear to God. The only money I have in this life is this twenty-pounds *egg-rasher* they gave me today . . ."

38 "Ok. Time de go. Make you open dis window and bring the twenty pound. We go manage am like dat."

39 There were now loud murmurs of dissent among the chorus: "Na lie de man de lie; e get plenty money . . . Make we go inside and search properly well . . . Wetin be twenty pound? . . ."

40 "Shurrup!" rang the leader's voice like a lone shot in the sky and silenced the murmuring at once. "Are you dere? Bring the money quick!"

41 "I am coming," said Jonathan fumbling in the darkness with the key of the small wooden box he kept by his side on the mat.

42 At the first sign of light as neighbors and others assembled to commiserate with him he was already strapping his five-gallon demijohn[8] to his bicycle carrier and his wife, sweating in the open fire, was turning over akara balls in a wide clay bowl of boiling oil. In the corner his eldest son was rinsing out dregs of yesterday's palm-wine from old beer bottles.

43 "I count it as nothing," he told his sympathizers, his eyes on the rope he was tying. "What is *egg-rasher*? Did I depend on it last week? Or is it greater than other things that went with the war? I say, let *egg-rasher* perish in the flames! Let it go where everything else has gone. Nothing puzzles God." ❧

---

8. **demijohn** (DEHM ee jon) *n.* large glass or earthenware bottle with a wicker cover.

Comprehension Check

Complete the following items after you finish your first read.

1. What conflict sets the scene for the story?

2. What does Jonathan get in exchange for the rebel money he had saved?

3. What type of people show up at Jonathan's door one night, and what do they demand?

4. What do Jonathan and his family do the morning after they are robbed?

5. 📓 **Notebook** To confirm your understanding, write a summary of "Civil Peace."

- -

RESEARCH

Research to Clarify Choose at least one unfamiliar detail from the text. Briefly research that detail. In what way does the information you learned shed light on an aspect of the story?

Research to Explore Choose something from the text that interests you, and formulate a research question.

CIVIL PEACE

Close Read the Text

1. This model, from paragraph 9 of the text, shows two sample annotations, along with questions and conclusions. Close read the passage, and find another detail to annotate. Then, write a question and your conclusion.

> **ANNOTATE:** This short clause comes at the end of a long sentence with multiple phrases and clauses.
>
> **QUESTION:** Why does the author structure this sentence in this way?
>
> **CONCLUDE:** The sentence structure captures the stress Jonathan feels—he cannot let down his guard until he gets home.

Close Read
ANNOTATE · QUESTION · CONCLUDE

> **ANNOTATE:** These details show that Jonathan carefully avoids contact with others.
>
> **QUESTION:** Why does the author include this point?
>
> **CONCLUDE:** This shows Jonathan's resourcefulness. With money in his pocket, contact with others is dangerous, so he quietly avoids it.

> Jonathan soon transferred the money to his left hand and pocket so as to leave his right free for shaking hands should the need arise, though by fixing his gaze at such an elevation as to miss all approaching human faces he made sure that the need did not arise, until he got home.

Tool Kit
Close-Read Guide and Model Annotation

2. For more practice, go back into the text, and complete the close-read notes.

3. Revisit a section of the text you found important during your first read. Read this section closely, and **annotate** what you notice. Ask yourself **questions** such as "Why did the author make this choice?" What can you **conclude**?

- -

Analyze the Text

CITE TEXTUAL EVIDENCE
to support your answers.

📓 **Notebook** Respond to these questions.

1. (a) What are the "five inestimable blessings" for which Jonathan is grateful? (b) **Interpret** What does Jonathan's attitude toward these blessings show you about the nature of the Nigerian civil war?

2. **Compare and Contrast** How is Jonathan's reaction to the loss of the *egg-rasher* different from that of the man robbed at the Treasury?

3. **Infer** After the robbery, Jonathan says, "Or is it greater than other things that went with the war?" To what is he referring? Explain.

4. **Connect** Why do you think the author chooses the term "Civil Peace" as the story's title? Explain your reasoning, using details from the story.

5. **Essential Question:** *What do our possessions reveal about us?* What have you learned about materialism from reading this story?

Analyze Craft and Structure

Development of Theme The **theme** of a literary work is the central message or insight into life it expresses. The theme may be stated directly or implied. When the theme is implied, readers must analyze elements of the text to determine the larger message the author is conveying. Thematic clues may appear in any story element, including the following:

- **setting,** or the time and place in which a story is set—key part of a setting is a work's **historical and cultural context**. The events, conflicts, and beliefs that affect the people in the society of the story may offer thematic clues.

- **characters,** or people in the story—Their statements, behavior, actions, and reactions may be clues to the theme.

- **plot development,** or the sequence of related events in a story—The relationships among events, including how one leads to the next, may be thematic clues.

- **description,** or the use of sensory details to show what a setting or characters are like—In particular, the use of **juxtaposition,** in which disparate ideas or details are shown side-by-side, may suggest themes. For example, in "Civil Peace," Jonathan's children pick mangoes from a cemetery. That juxtaposition shows how death is simply part of life for survivors of the civil war. Authors may use juxtaposition to call attention to important ideas.

Practice

CITE TEXTUAL EVIDENCE to support your answers.

📓 **Notebook** Respond to these questions.

1. (a) Find an example of the juxtaposition of two ideas in "Civil Peace." (b) What effect does Achebe create by pairing these two ideas?

2. (a) Describe the events in the story that prompt Jonathan to use the expression "Nothing puzzles God." (b) Judging from the circumstances of each event, explain what you think Jonathan means by this expression.

3. Using a chart like the one shown, analyze three episodes that spark a strong response in Jonathan.

EPISODE	JONATHAN'S RESPONSE	WHAT RESPONSE SHOWS ABOUT JONATHAN

4. How are the episodes you noted in your chart related? What do Jonathan's responses suggest about the story's theme? Explain.

5. What theme do Jonathan's actions and the events in the story develop? Support your answer with evidence from the text.

CIVIL PEACE

Concept Vocabulary

inestimable	amenable	surrender
blessings	influence	windfall

Why These Words? These concept vocabulary words all relate to fortune, good or bad. For example, Jonathan thinks of his five *blessings* as *inestimable*. Both of these words relate to Jonathan's perceptions of his life as being full of good fortune.

1. How do the concept words help the reader understand how Jonathan views his world?

2. What other words in the selection connect to this concept?

Practice

🖙 **Notebook** The concept vocabulary words appear in "Civil Peace."

1. With a partner, choose one of the concept words, and take turns naming as many related words as you can.
2. Find the sentences containing the concept words in the selection. With a partner, replace each concept word with a synonym. Discuss how your substitutions change the meanings of the sentences.

Word Study

Compound Nouns The concept vocabulary word *windfall* is an example of a compound noun. A **compound noun** is a noun formed by combining two or more separate words—in this case, the words *wind* and *fall*.

Compound nouns may be "open," as in *pizza parlor*; hyphenated, as in *meat-eater*; or "closed," as in *basketball*. Whether a given compound noun is open, hyphenated, or closed is a matter of convention, and writers sometimes deviate from the conventional spelling for effect. If you are unsure how to spell a particular compound noun, consult a dictionary.

Read this passage from paragraph 2 of "Civil Peace." Mark the three compound nouns, and label each one *open*, *hyphenated*, or *closed*. Then, write a meaning for each of them. Consult a dictionary as needed.

> So Jonathan . . . produced the two pounds with which he had been going to buy firewood which his wife, Maria, retailed . . . for extra stock-fish and corn meal, and got his bicycle back.

WORD NETWORK

Add words related to materialism from the text to your Word Network.

Author's Style

Character Development Fiction writers use a variety of techniques to create engaging, interesting, and believable characters. Sometimes writers give characters a voice with **dialect.** Dialect is a form of a language spoken by people in a particular region or group. It may involve changes to the pronunciation, vocabulary, and sentence structure of the standard form of the language. A writer's choice to have characters speak in dialect may add a sense of authenticity to a story.

Read It

1. Mark examples of dialect that appear in the two passages from "Civil Peace" that are shown in the chart. Then, revise each passage using standard English.

PASSAGE	REVISION IN STANDARD ENGLISH
Jonathan: *"What is egg-rasher? Did I depend on it last week? Or is it greater than other things that went with the war? I say, let egg-rasher perish in the flames! Let it go where everything else has gone. Nothing puzzles God."* (paragraph 43)	
Thief Leader: *"Awrighto. Now make we talk business. We no be bad tief. We no like for make trouble. Trouble done finish. War done finish and all the katakata wey de for inside. No Civil War again. This time na Civil Peace. No be so?"* (paragraph 28)	

2. Consider differences between the original passages and your revisions. What is lost and what is gained by the author's choice to use dialect? Explain.

Write It

📝 **Notebook** Dialect is one form of nonstandard language. There are other forms, including the language common to social media and texting. Write a brief paragraph in which you describe your morning routine. Use standard English. Then, write another paragraph on the same topic. Use nonstandard language variations with which you are familiar.

CIVIL PEACE

Writing to Sources

Informative writing presents evidence and explanations to help readers understand concepts and ideas. In informative writing about literary works—such as a character analysis—you present your interpretation of a text, use text evidence to illustrate that interpretation, and explain how the evidence and your interpretation connect.

Assignment

The fate of the main character in "Civil Peace" is determined in large part by his personality. Write a brief **character analysis** of Jonathan. In your analysis, identify Jonathan's main character traits, including his strengths and weaknesses. Then, explain how these traits help Jonathan overcome obstacles.

- First, review the story to analyze Jonathan in detail. Using a two-column chart, list his strengths and weaknesses.

- Identify specific examples in the story that demonstrate each trait.

- Consulting your chart, select the main ideas you want to convey and the order in which you will express them.

- Link supporting details to your main idea using phrases such as *for example*. Include transition words such as *instead* to connect ideas.

- End with a conclusion that logically follows from and completes the ideas you developed in the body of your essay.

Vocabulary Connection

Include several of the concept vocabulary words in your character analysis.

inestimable	amenable	surrender
blessings	influence	windfall

Reflect on Your Writing

After you have written your character analysis, answer these questions.

1. Did writing the character analysis deepen your understanding of "Civil Peace"? Why or why not?

2. What questions do you still have about the story after writing the character analysis?

3. **Why These Words?** The words you choose make a difference in your writing. Which transition words did you use in your writing to help move your reader from idea to idea?

Speaking and Listening

You can share your ideas about a piece of literature by delivering an oral interpretation for an audience. To do so, combine a careful analysis of the work with an expressive reading or performance that reveals your understanding and demonstrates your sensitivity to the author's choices.

Assignment

Deliver an **oral interpretation.** Choose an excerpt from "Civil Peace" you feel is especially meaningful. Read the excerpt aloud for the class. Then, briefly explain how that excerpt helps develop the story's theme.

---

1. **Identify the Excerpt** Review the story in your mind, and consider which part you remember most vividly.

2. **Connect to the Theme** Think about how your excerpt relates to the theme of the story as a whole. If you are having difficulty connecting your excerpt with the theme, consider choosing another part of the text. Make a few notes about this connection on a piece of paper or index card that you can refer to when you are speaking.

3. **Practice your Reading** Practice your oral interpretation with a partner. Use the following performance techniques to achieve a powerful effect.

   - Avoid speaking in a flat, monotone style. Instead, vary your tone, and allow your voice to reflect the emotions of the excerpt.

   - Avoid speaking too quickly or too slowly.

   - Use gestures to convey the text's meaning, but make sure they are not excessive or distracting.

   - Recite the text enough times that it becomes familiar. In that way, you can look up and make eye contact with your audience.

4. **Evaluate Oral Interpretations** As your classmates deliver their oral interpretations, listen attentively. Use an evaluation guide like the one shown to evaluate their deliveries.

EVALUATION GUIDE

Rate each statement on a scale of 1 (not demonstrated) to 4 (demonstrated).

☐ The reading was clear and understandable.

☐ The speaker read with energy and expression that conveyed the meaning of the text.

☐ The speaker clearly and effectively connected the excerpt to the theme of the story.

☐ The speaker made eye contact with the audience.

✎ EVIDENCE LOG

Before moving on to a new selection, go to your Evidence Log and record what you learned from "Civil Peace."

About Tutankhamun

Tutankhamun (circa 1341–1323 B.C.) was an Egyptian pharaoh, or monarch, who ruled from approximately 1332 to 1323 B.C. King Tut, as he has come to be known, was only nine or ten years old when he ascended to the throne. Evidence suggests that he suffered from a variety of health problems, including malaria and a rare bone disease, and probably walked with a cane. He died at the age of nineteen. Given his youth and health problems, it is likely that most of his political decisions were made by advisors. During Tutankhamun's reign, Egypt renewed neglected relationships with other kingdoms and states, and engaged in several military campaigns. (The image shown here is a mask that was found on Tutankhamun's mummy. It was made in his likeness out of gold and precious stones and was used to cover the king's mummified face.)

Fit for a King: Treasures of Tutankhamun

Technical Vocabulary

The following words or concepts will be useful to you as you analyze, discuss, and write about ancient objects.

Egyptology: study of the language, culture, and history of ancient Egypt	• Someone who studies Egyptology is called an Egyptologist. • In the United States, Egyptology is more associated with archaeology, or the scientific study of human history. In Europe, it is more associated with the study of language.
artifact: portable object made, modified, or used by people	• Rare artifacts often have great scientific, historic, and cultural value. • Artifacts that are very rare, made of precious materials, or culturally significant may have high monetary value.
iconography: system of symbolic images that conveys a subject, worldview, or concept	• Most cultures have iconography that is unique and recognizable. • Changes in a culture's iconography may signal shifts in its economy, religion, politics, or another fundamental aspect of a society.
context: position and immediate surroundings of an artifact or other feature in the location where it is found	• An artifact's context helps archaeologists understand its function and importance. • If the location has been undisturbed since the artifact was first placed there, it is called *primary context*. If the location has been changed by human or other activity, it is called *secondary context*.

First Review MEDIA: ART AND PHOTOGRAPHY

Apply these strategies as you conduct your first review. You will have an opportunity to complete a close review after your first review.

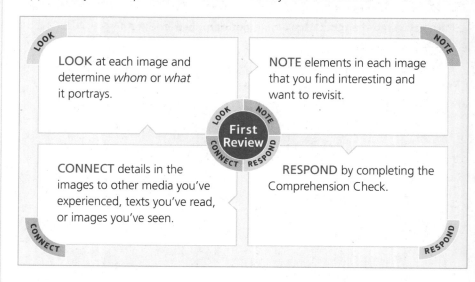

LOOK at each image and determine *whom* or *what* it portrays.

NOTE elements in each image that you find interesting and want to revisit.

CONNECT details in the images to other media you've experienced, texts you've read, or images you've seen.

RESPOND by completing the Comprehension Check.

First Review

Fit for a King:
Treasures of Tutankhamun

BACKGROUND

In 1922, a British archaeologist named Howard Carter discovered the tomb of King Tutankhamun in the Valley of the Kings near Luxor, Egypt. It had taken Carter more than ten years to locate the tomb, and the discovery changed the world. Unlike most Egyptian tombs that had been unearthed, Tutankhamun's was nearly undisturbed. For more than three thousand years, the four chambers of the tomb had protected the mummified remains of the pharaoh—the first intact mummy ever found—as well as a trove of nearly four thousand objects. The tomb held jewelry, beds, couches, chairs, vases, statues, chariots, thrones, weapons, and shrines. There were musical instruments, lamps, vessels containing ointments and oils, board games, fine clothing, fans, numerous bottles of wine, and food. The ancient Egyptians believed their pharaoh would need these items in the afterlife. The discovery of the glories within King Tut's tomb captured the world's imagination and sparked widespread interest in ancient Egypt that continues to this day.

PHOTO 1: Objects in the Antechamber Harry Burton was an archaeological photographer who was part of Howard Carter's team. Burton took this photo of objects in the tomb's Antechamber. These include a cow-headed couch and boxes containing joints of meat.

NOTES

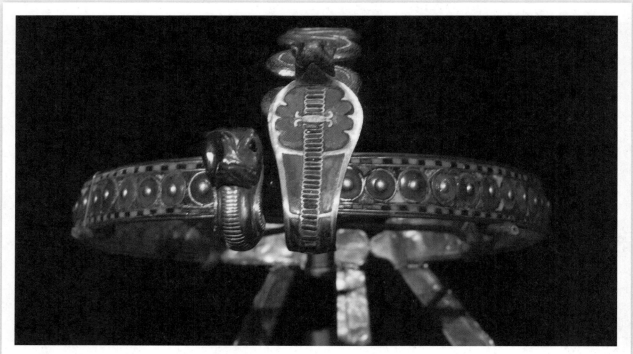

PHOTO 2: Cobra Uraeus Diadem This diadem, or crown, was found on Tutankhamun's mummy in the tomb's Burial Chamber. It features representations of a vulture and a cobra, both of which symbolize the power of the pharaoh. The vulture represents Upper Egypt, and the *cobra uraeus*—or rising cobra—represents Lower Egypt. The vulture's head is made of solid gold. The cobra is also gold inlaid with precious stones. Tutankhamun wore this diadem, or one like it, during his lifetime.

NOTES

PHOTO 3: Alabaster Funerary Barge This alabaster vessel was probably used to hold perfume. Egyptologists believe it is a replica of Tutankhamun's funerary barge. It is fourteen inches tall, highlighted with gold leaf, and inlaid with glass and semiprecious stones. The object was found in the tomb's Annex, a room that was originally used as a storage chamber.

NOTES

PHOTO 4: Golden Flabellum, or Fan Tutankhamun was buried with eight large fans, including the one shown here. This gold fan was originally mounted on a long pole and fitted with 42 ostrich feathers. One side shows a hunting scene with the figure of the young pharaoh in a chariot. The other side shows his return from the hunt. This object was found in the tomb's Burial Chamber.

NOTES

PHOTO 5: Canopic Chest Canopic jars were used to hold the internal organs of the deceased—the liver, lungs, stomach, and intestines—which were removed during the mummification process. Ancient Egyptians believed the dead would need these organs in the afterlife. This chest was found in the tomb's Treasury. It holds four canopic jars made of alabaster. The four lids (two of which are shown here) represent Tutankhamun wearing a headdress that features the vulture and cobra, symbols of the pharaoh's power.

NOTES

Comprehension Check

Complete the following items after you finish your first review.

1. What objects are represented in each of the four color photographs?

2. Cite three other types of objects that were found in Tutankhamun's tomb but do not appear in these five photographs.

3. What symbolism appears on the objects represented in both Photo 2 and Photo 5?

TECHNICAL VOCABULARY

Use these words as you discuss, analyze, and write about the photo essay.

Egyptology
artifact
iconography
context

Close Review

Look at the photo essay again. Write down any new observations that seem important. What **questions** do you have? What can you **conclude?**

Analyze the Media

⊟ **Notebook** Respond to these questions.

1. **Generalize** What do these objects suggest about the types of things ancient Egyptians felt were important?

2. **Infer** Photo 1 shows part of the tomb's Antechamber as Carter's team first found it. What does this image reveal about the organization of objects in the Antechamber? Explain.

3. **Analyze** The treasures with which Tutankhamun was buried were seen as necessary to his existence in the afterlife. What do these objects suggest about ancient Egyptians' views of both earthly life and the afterlife? Explain.

4. **Extend** The discovery of Tutankhamun's tomb and its treasures generated worldwide interest in ancient Egypt. Using your knowledge of the discovery, explain why you think this is so.

5. **Essential Question:** *What do our possessions reveal about us?* What have you learned about materialism from examining this photo essay?

⊞ WORD NETWORK

Add words related to materialism from the text to your Word Network.

Speaking and Listening

Photojournalism is a type of news reporting in which the photos tell most of the story. With today's technology, creating a work of photojournalism is technically much easier than it was in the past. However, the requirements for strong photojournalism remain the same as always—powerful pictures must tell an interesting story.

FIT FOR A KING:
TREASURES OF TUTANKHAMUN

Assignment

Create a work of **photojournalism**—either in a digital format or on a poster—reporting on possessions that you or others in your community find meaningful.

- Take photos of these objects, draw them, or use images from magazines or other sources.
- Write captions that describe the images, or pose questions for viewers to consider.
- You may choose to add text that explains each object's significance.

Plan It Decide what your medium will be, and organize the resources you need. If you're going to take photographs, you'll need a camera or smartphone. If you're going to make drawings or other personally created art, you'll need art supplies. If you're going to use images from print media or the Internet, you'll need scissors and a copier or a printer. Use the chart to keep track of your images.

IMAGE	WHERE, WHEN, WHO	SOURCE OR MEDIUM

Present It Publish your work of photojournalism by presenting it to the class. Use technology if possible. Be prepared to discuss your work and answer questions other students might have about it.

Tool Kit
Student Model of an Informative Text

ACADEMIC VOCABULARY

As you craft your essay, consider using some of the academic vocabulary you learned at the beginning of the unit.

paradox
chronicle
allocate
deduce
primary

Write an Informative Essay

You have read two short stories and viewed a photo essay. Each deals in its own way with the concept of value. In "The Necklace," Mathilde Loisel pays a heavy price for a moment of extravagance. In "Civil Peace," Jonathan Iwegbu loses a small fortune in much less time than it took to earn it. In the photo essay "Fit for a King: Treasures of Tutankhamun," the viewer can see the items Egyptians buried with their pharaoh for his voyage to the afterlife. Now, you will use your knowledge of the topic to write an informative essay about how people assign value.

Assignment

Think about how the characters or real people featured in this section decide what is valuable to them. Consider different reasons that objects either have or lack value. Then, write an **informative essay** in which you answer these questions:

> What makes something valuable? What makes something a treasure?

Elements of an Informative Essay

An **informative text** presents and explains information about a topic.

An effective informative essay includes these elements:

- a clear thesis statement
- facts and details drawn from a variety of reliable, credible sources
- a well-organized structure, including an introduction, a body, and a conclusion
- use of appropriate and varied transitions that clarify relationships among complex ideas
- correct grammar and usage
- an appropriately formal style and objective tone

Model Informative Text For a model of a well-crafted informative essay, see the Launch Text, "I Came, I Saw, I Shopped."

Challenge yourself to find all of the elements of an effective informative essay in the text. You will have an opportunity to review these elements as you prepare to write your own informative essay.

Prewriting/Planning

Write a Working Thesis Now that you have read and thought about the selections, write a rough thesis statement. This should be the main point you wish to make in response to the questions posed in this assignment. Your thesis statement should present an idea you will explain and support in greater detail in the body of your essay. As you continue to write, you may revise your thesis or even change it entirely. For now, it will help you choose evidence to develop and support your ideas.

Working Thesis: _____

_____.

Gather Evidence from Texts With your working thesis in mind, review the selections and your notes to identify details that you can use to support your ideas. Because two of the selections in this section of the unit are works of fiction, look for the following types of evidence:

- plot events from the stories that speak to issues of materialism
- descriptions of settings or objects in the stories that relate to ideas about possessions or materialism
- quotations from the stories that show how characters feel and think about material possessions

You may also use your observations of the photos in "Fit for a King," as well as information from the captions, as evidence. Use a chart to gather and organize meaningful details from the selections.

✎ EVIDENCE LOG

Review your Evidence Log and identify key details you may want to cite in your informative essay.

SELECTION	MEANINGFUL DETAILS
The Necklace	
Civil Peace	
Fit for a King: Treasures of Tutankhamun	

Connect Across Texts As you write your informative essay, you may use evidence from one text to develop ideas based on another. Include evidence from both the short stories and the photo essay to develop your thesis. It can be helpful to use one piece of evidence as your main point in a paragraph, and then reinforce it with another piece of evidence.

Drafting

Organize Your Ideas Informative essays generally include three parts:

- the **introduction,** in which you state your thesis
- the **body,** in which you develop the thesis
- the **conclusion,** in which you restate or readdress your thesis

Your introduction may be longer than a single paragraph. For example, in the Launch Text, "I Came, I Saw, I Shopped," the first three paragraphs serve as the introduction. A thesis statement appears in the fourth paragraph: "What drives our need to own the latest games, shoes, or phones? There are many notions." The body of the text provides different explanations for the urge to purchase. In addition, the writer uses headings to organize the sections and guide the reader through the information. In the concluding paragraph, the writer links examples from the body to the thesis: "All of the information we have about shopping and spending suggests that the desire for a particular item is not so simple."

Use the organizer to plan your draft.

INTRODUCTION	BODY	CONCLUSION
present the thesis	develop the thesis with varied evidence	restate or readdress the thesis

Write a First Draft Refer to your organizer as you write your first draft. Each part of your essay should lead logically to the next. Make sure that body paragraphs provide reasons and evidence that clearly support your thesis, and that your conclusion circles back to restate, summarize, or otherwise connect to your thesis. Keep the structure of your essay simple and logical so that readers can follow the flow of your ideas.

LANGUAGE DEVELOPMENT: CONVENTIONS

Create Cohesion: Conjunctive Adverbs

As you draft and revise your informative essay, use a variety of transitions to create cohesion and to clarify the relationships among your ideas. When two independent clauses are closely related, consider joining them together with a **semicolon (;)** and a **conjunctive adverb**—a word that indicates the precise logical relationship between the ideas the clauses express.

Read It

Each of these sentences from the Launch Text uses a semicolon and a conjunctive adverb to connect two closely related independent clauses.

- *It's possible, though, that you've lost track of these things;* <u>*consequently*</u>*, they are forgotten, but not gone, collecting dust in a closet somewhere.* (shows cause and effect)

- *It is the rare driver who uses an antique car for her daily commute;* <u>*likewise*</u>*, the collectible doll from 1959 that sold at auction in May 2006 for $27,450 did not become a child's favorite toy.* (shows similarity)

- *Some purchases of collectibles may be investments in items that will grow in value;* <u>*however*</u>*, others are driven largely by emotions, such as longing for a time past.* (shows contrast)

Write It

As you draft and revise your informative essay, look for independent clauses that have related ideas.

If you want to . . .	consider using one of these conjunctive adverbs:
show similarity	*equally, likewise, similarly*
show contrast	*instead, however, nevertheless*
show cause and effect	*consequently, therefore, thus*
show addition	*furthermore, also, moreover, additionally*

TIP

PUNCTUATION
Make sure to punctuate conjunctive adverbs correctly.

- Use a comma after a conjunctive adverb at the beginning of an independent clause.

- Use a comma before and after a conjunctive adverb in the middle of an independent clause.

Revising

Evaluating Your Draft

Use the following checklist to evaluate the effectiveness of your draft. Then, use your evaluation and the instructions on this page to guide your revision.

FOCUS AND ORGANIZATION	EVIDENCE AND ELABORATION	CONVENTIONS
☐ Provides an introduction that includes a clear thesis statement.	☐ Develops the thesis with textual evidence.	☐ Uses words, phrases, and clauses to clarify the relationships among ideas.
☐ Provides a conclusion that restates or revisits the thesis.	☐ Provides adequate examples for each major idea.	☐ Attends to the norms and conventions of the discipline, especially the correct use and punctuation of transitions.
☐ Establishes a logical organization and develops connections among ideas.	☐ Uses vocabulary and word choice that are appropriate for the audience and purpose.	
	☐ Establishes and maintains a formal style and an objective tone.	

WORD NETWORK

Include interesting words from your Word Network in your informative text.

Revising for Focus and Organization

Evaluate Logic and Coherence Reread your essay and consider the following questions:

- Does the introduction set forth a clear, specific thesis?
- Does each body paragraph add a distinct idea to that thesis?
- Does the essay end with a conclusion that readdresses the thesis?

If you have answered "no" to any of those questions, take action: Make your thesis more specific, clarify ideas or information presented in the body paragraphs, or revise your conclusion to make a clear connection back to your introduction.

Revising for Evidence and Elaboration

Evaluate Quality of Evidence Review your draft. Does each body paragraph include evidence that clearly supports your main ideas? If not, go back to the selections, and locate details, quotations, or examples that provide better support for the points you wish to make.

Evaluate Tone In academic writing such as an informative essay, your **tone**, or attitude, should be appropriately formal, authoritative, and neutral. Apply the following steps to create and maintain an appropriate tone:

- Avoid slang and abbreviations, and limit the use of contractions.
- Generally, avoid idioms, which tend to be less formal in tone.
- Refer to places, people, or formal concepts by their proper names.

Review your draft for any words or phrases that create an informal or otherwise unsuitable tone. Replace any such terms with more formal choices.

PEER REVIEW

Exchange essays with a classmate. Use the checklist to evaluate your classmate's informative essay and provide supportive feedback.

1. Is the thesis clear?

☐ yes   ☐ no   If no, explain what confused you.

2. Are key points developed with evidence?

☐ yes   ☐ no   If no, point out what needs more support.

3. Does the conclusion readdress the thesis in light of the evidence?

☐ yes   ☐ no   If no, write a brief note explaining what you thought was missing.

4. What is the strongest part of your classmate's essay? Why?

_____

_____

_____

_____

Editing and Proofreading

Edit for Conventions Reread your draft for accuracy and consistency. Correct errors in grammar and word usage. Check your use of transitions. Make sure you have placed them where they most effectively connect two ideas.

Proofread for Accuracy Read your draft carefully, looking for errors in spelling and punctuation. Check your use of commas around transitions. Use commas as necessary to set off conjunctive adverbs and transitional phrases.

Publishing and Presenting

Create a final version of your informative essay. Share it with your class so that your classmates can read it and make comments. In turn, review and comment on your classmates' work. Consider the ways in which other students' informative essays are both similar to and different from your own. Always maintain a polite and respectful tone when commenting.

Reflecting

Think about what you learned by writing your informative essay. What could you do differently the next time you need to write an informative essay to make the writing experience easier and to make your information more interesting?

ESSENTIAL QUESTION:

What do our possessions reveal about us?

The comfort and convenience that material objects provide help keep us safe, warm, and productive. But what happens when obtaining material wealth becomes a preoccupation or even an obsession? The selections you will read present various perspectives on these questions. You will work in a group to continue your exploration of materialism, identity, and personal values.

Small-Group Learning Strategies

Throughout your life, in school, in your community, and in your career, you will continue to learn and work with others.

Review these strategies and the actions you can take to practice them as you work in teams. Add ideas of your own for each step. Use these strategies during Small-Group Learning.

STRATEGY	ACTION PLAN
Prepare	• Complete your assignments so that you are prepared for group work. • Organize your thinking so you can contribute to your group's discussions. •
Participate fully	• Make eye contact to signal that you are listening and taking in what is being said. • Use text evidence when making a point. •
Support others	• Build on ideas from others in your group. • Invite others who have not yet spoken to do so. •
Clarify	• Paraphrase the ideas of others to ensure that your understanding is correct. • Ask follow-up questions. •

CONTENTS

PERFORMANCE TASK

SPEAKING AND LISTENING FOCUS
Present an Informative Text

The Small-Group readings explore how the human quest for material objects and wealth can make people both happy and miserable. After reading, your group will plan and deliver a multimedia presentation about these concepts.

Working as a Team

1. **Discuss the Topic** In your group, discuss the following question:

   Do you think one's happiness increases as one's wealth does?

   As you take turns sharing your responses, be sure to provide details to explain your position. After all group members have shared, discuss similarities and differences in your perspectives.

2. **List Your Rules** As a group, decide on the rules that you will follow as you work together. Samples are provided; add two more of your own. As you work together, you may add or revise rules based on your experience together.

   - Everyone should participate in group discussions.
   - People should not interrupt.

   - _____

     _____

   - _____

     _____

3. **Apply the Rules** Share what you have learned about what our possessions reveal about us. Make sure each person in the group contributes. Take notes on and be prepared to share with the class one thing that you heard from another member of your group.

4. **Name Your Group** Choose a name that reflects the unit topic.

   Our group's name: _____

5. **Create a Communication Plan** Decide how you want to communicate with one another. For example, you might use online collaboration tools, email, or instant messaging.

   Our group's decision: _____

   _____

Making a Schedule

First, find out the due dates for the small-group activities. Then, preview the texts and activities with your group, and make a schedule for completing the tasks.

SELECTION	ACTIVITIES	DUE DATE
In La Rinconada, Peru, Searching for Beauty in Ugliness		
Avarice The Good Life Money		
The Golden Touch		
from King Midas		
The Thrill of the Chase		

Working on Group Projects

As your group works together, you'll find it more effective if each person has a specific role. Different projects require different roles. Before beginning a project, discuss the necessary roles, and choose one for each group member. Here are some possible roles; add your own ideas.

Project Manager: monitors the schedule and keeps everyone on task

Researcher: organizes research activities

Recorder: takes notes during group meetings

_____

_____

_____

_____

About the Author

Originally from Lima, Peru, **Marie Arana** (b. 1949) is a journalist, an author, and the former chief editor of *Book World* for the *Washington Post*. Arana's memoir of growing up as an immigrant in the United States was a finalist for the National Book Award. Her novel *Cellophane* was a finalist for the John Sargent Prize. Arana has been the chairperson for committees that decide both the Pulitzer Prize and the American Book award. Her most recent project is a biography of the great liberator of South America, Simón Bolívar.

In La Rinconada, Peru, Searching for Beauty in Ugliness

Concept Vocabulary

As you perform your first read of "In La Rinconada, Peru, Searching for Beauty in Ugliness," you will encounter the following words.

marauding	intemperate	despoiled

Base Words If these words are unfamiliar to you, analyze each one to see whether it contains a base word you know. Then, use your knowledge of the "inside" word, along with context, to determine the meaning of the concept word. Here is an example of how to apply the strategy.

Unfamiliar Word: *habitation*

Familiar "Inside" Word: *habitat*, meaning "region where a plant or animal naturally grows or lives"

Context: . . . La Rinconada, the highest human **habitation** in the world.

Conclusion: Perhaps a habitation is a place or settlement in which *people* live.

Apply your knowledge of base words and other vocabulary strategies to determine the meanings of unfamiliar words you encounter during your first read.

First Read NONFICTION

Apply these strategies as you conduct your first read. You will have an opportunity to complete a close read after your first read.

NOTICE the general ideas of the text. *What* is it about? *Who* is involved?

ANNOTATE by marking vocabulary and key passages you want to revisit.

First Read
NOTICE · ANNOTATE · CONNECT · RESPOND

CONNECT ideas within the selection to what you already know and what you have already read.

RESPOND by completing the Comprehension Check and by writing a brief summary of the selection.

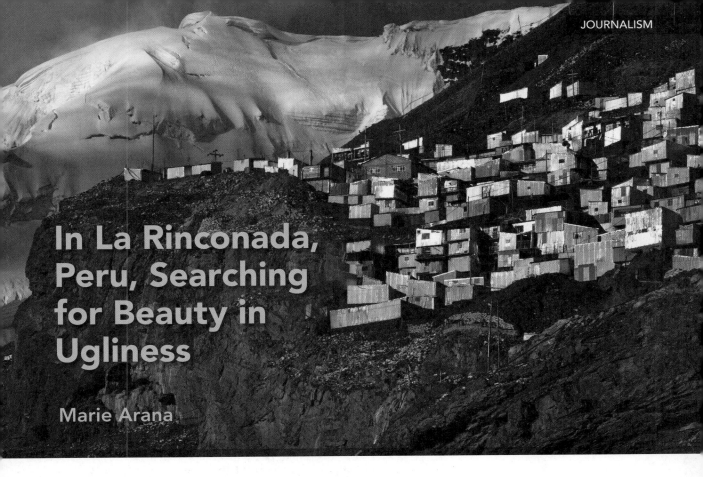

In La Rinconada, Peru, Searching for Beauty in Ugliness

Marie Arana

BACKGROUND

Fortune hunters have been searching for treasures in South America for centuries—and for good reason. Below the surface lie precious stones, as well as silver and gold. The mining for gold high in the Peruvian mountains has come at a high price for the environment and the people of these lands. In the barren region of La Rinconada, the mining companies use toxic chemicals as they search for gold.

1   Gold. The Aztecs killed for it. The Inca enslaved whole populations for it. Spain sent legions of **marauding** conquistadors up and down the Americas in a hallucinatory hunt, believing that gold was so abundant that chieftains rolled in it, washing away the glittering residue in their daily morning swims.

2   Down the centuries, the quest for El Dorado has held the South American continent in thrall, luring generations of fortune hunters to its far reaches, from 1st-century warlords to 21st-century adventurers. The earth beneath them has not disappointed. The geologic exuberance known as the Cordillera of the Andes has yielded a fount of treasure: the emeralds of Boyaca, the silver of Potosi, the gold of Cajamarca.

3   Indeed, when Pizarro[1] conquered Cajamarca in 1532, he demanded a roomful of gold from the emperor Atahualpa; when it was

NOTES

Mark base words or indicate another strategy you used that helped you determine meaning.

marauding (muh RAW dihng) *adj.*

MEANING:

---

1. **Pizarro** (pih ZAHR oh) Francisco Pizarro, Spanish conquistador who captured Peru from the Incas.

Mark base words or indicate another strategy you used that helped you determine meaning.

intemperate (ihn TEHM puhr iht) *adj.*

MEANING:

produced, he chopped off the Inca's head and established a new kind of Golden Rule. So it was that a mineral became king and a craze began.

4   Nowhere has Peru's frenzy for gold been so fevered as in the mountains that surround Lake Titicaca. And nowhere has that fever been so **intemperate** as in a town tucked into a glacial aerie: La Rinconada, the highest human habitation in the world.

5   It is a destination for only the most valiant. Clinging to the peak of Mount Ananea, with a cowl of glacier overhead, La Rinconada boasts few tourists, no hotel, no sights to speak of, apart from the endless snow, a dome of blue sky and a swarm of hard-bitten inhabitants. For the 50,000 souls who brave the subzero cold to pick rock on those hoary heights, there is no sewage system, no water, no paved roads, no sanitation whatsoever. It is a wilderness of ice, rock, and gold, perched more than 18,000 feet up in the Peruvian Andes.

6   Beside the gawping mine shafts that scar the mountain's face are huts of tin, built at capricious and precarious angles, with nothing to keep out the glacial wind but improvised sheets of metal; nothing to generate warmth but fetid heaps of garbage. The only convenience here is the electricity, brought in by overlords so that the machinery can grind and shuttle-cars can rumble through the mountain's black veins. At night, La Rinconada glitters like a cruel oasis.

7   Make no mistake: This is a trip for the armchair only. As Dante might say, let me guide you through a fascinating circle of hell.

To a Barren World

8   I would not have gone up to the peak the locals call "la Bella Durmiente"—Sleeping Beauty—had I not been accompanied by a team of professionals from CARE. I traveled there to write a script for "Girl Rising," a film directed by Richard Robbins, produced by the Documentary Group and poised for release next week.

9   It is a film about girls who live in desperately hard places, about how educating them could change their families, their communities, and very possibly the world. In the course of my journey up to La Rinconada, I had every expectation that I would find hunger and hardship. What I had not expected was to find beauty in ugliness—to see, as a mountain shaman might put it, the sacred in the profane.

10   Being a native of Lima, I knew what every schoolchild knows, that although Peru is small (slightly smaller than Alaska), it encompasses a virtual panoply[2] of landforms: mountain, jungle, desert, marshland, archipelago, coastline—all in defined geographic areas, and often in dramatic contiguity. Fly over Peru, and Mount Huascaran's majestic peak seems to hover over the foliage of the Amazon jungle; the green cliffs of Miraflores are just down the coast from the sands of Chan Chan.

11   But riding a truck from Puno to the little village of Putina—circling the northernmost bend of Lake Titicaca—I almost convinced myself

---

2. **panoply** (PAN uh plee) *n.* array.

that this trip would continue its happy, paved course into the horizon. The roads were good, the views of the so-called "highest navigable lake in the world" literally breathtaking, and at almost 13,000 feet, there was no malaise that a few cups of coca tea couldn't cure.

12   In fact, this part of the world is known for its pharmacological cornucopia. Every shrub or weed is a botanical miracle: *flores de Bach* for melancholy, *muña* for chills or bone pain, *pampanis* for intestinal gas, *yahuar chonca* for diarrhea. Fields of medicinal possibility rushed past as we raced along the highway. Looking out at the reed catamarans that skimmed the lake's dazzling surface or the grass islands that floated peacefully in the sun, I couldn't imagine that snows trickling into that paradise were anything but pristine.

13   Within a half-hour of leaving Putina, however, the road had become dirt, rock, soon frozen mud, and my crew was being pitched about, as it would be for two more hours of a difficult journey. The Altiplano, a stretch of high mesa only slightly lower than the Tibetan plateau, stretched before us, stippled with rough grass and stone. Trees were scarce, thatched huts more so, and the odd flowers—bright orange cantutas—had brought a herd of startled alpaca onto that frigid January plain. They stood at the limits of faded pasture, raising their delicate heads as we bounced over rut and rock, eyeing us with haughty scorn.

14   Before long, as broad swaths of arid plain gave way to scarred earth, we could see why La Rinconada is only rarely visited by government poobahs.[3] The air at 18,000 feet is stiflingly thin, the cold excruciating. Now and then, ramshackle trucks and vans rattled past, carrying miners and their families, stopping on the roadside to catch their breath, chew coca leaf, and leave offerings to the earth goddess, Pachamama, to whom altars had been erected along the way. All about, for as far as the eye could see, was a crazed landscape. What was once a region of sparkling lakes, leaping fish, and grassland is now a barren world that beggars the imagination.

15   The green is gone. The earth is turned. What you see as Mount Ananea looms into view is a lunar landscape, pitted with orange lakes that reek of cyanide. The birds that once flew over La Rinconada are nowhere to be seen; none flap overhead, save an occasional vulture. The odor is staggering; it is the putrid stench of chemicals, of rot, of human excrement. Even a whipping wind cannot sweep away the stink.

16   As you ascend toward the great white cap of Sleeping Beauty, all you see is garbage, a choking ruin, and ghostly shadows picking through it. Gigantic trucks shove at the earth. Whole families wade out into the toxic pools, fishing for gold. Along the perilously winding road that climbs to the summit, flocks of women in wide skirts scramble up cliffs, carrying heavy bags of ore, hoping to pound a fleck of gold from the waste that has spilled from the mine shafts; children stagger beside them, shouldering burdens of their own.

3. **poobahs** (POO boz) *n.* leaders who have a large amount of influence.

17   With so much poverty about, it is hard to believe that Sleeping Beauty harbors riches, that gold ripped from her entrails will glitter on Cartier and Tiffany counters around the world. But history books tell us that Mount Ananea has been offering up gold since the days of the Inca. According to travelers' journals, a block the size of a horse's head and weighing more than 100 pounds was pulled free in the 1500s and sent to the Spanish king. The region's rivers were said to be strewn with glittering nuggets.

18   El Inca Garcilaso de la Vega, a half-Indian, half-Spanish chronicler who lived in the 16th century, wrote that this tract of Peru contained gold beyond imagining. Chunks of shiny rock as large as a human head—and 24-karat pure—had rolled from the damp black stone.

19   Although the king's mines collapsed in the 1700s under the weight of the glacier and were abandoned for 200 years, interest in Ananea was rekindled in the 1960s, when teams of European and Japanese mountaineers scaled the stretch known as the Cordillera Real. Hordes of village boys followed, building huts, bringing families. With little more than small picks and big dreams, some defied the odds and struck gold. Today, there are just enough stories of random fortune to keep their children here.

A Bench of Gold

20   Peru is booming these days. Its restaurants are full; its cuisine has become all the rage. Cusco and Machu Picchu are world-class destinations. Peru's economy boasts one of the highest growth rates in the world. In the past six years, its annual growth has hovered between 6 and 9 percent, rivaling the colossal engines of China and India.

21   Peru is one of the world's leading producers of silver and one of Latin America's most exuberant founts of precious metals. It is an energetic producer of natural gas. It is one of the top five harvesters of fish on the planet. Its premier fashion photographer is the darling of *Vogue*. Walk Lima's streets and you can't fail to see the evidence of progress: Here is a country alive with investment and tourism, a hive of construction, home to a rising and robust middle class.

22   But it is gold that has brought multinational companies to the highlands of Puno, many of them installing sturdy, viable operations that promise to lift rural communities out of poverty. Peru is hoping that Atahualpa's curse is dead; that gold will be its salvation; that the country will no longer be—as the old saying has it—a beggar sitting on a bench of gold.

23   All the same, the wheels of progress that have sped Peru toward economic success and a burgeoning middle class have yet to climb

^ Elaborate golden bird, Mochica, Peru, ca. 200 B.C.–A.D. 650

NOTES

the pestilential[4] road to La Rinconada. There, in the shadow of Sleeping Beauty, every miner is on his own, and every woman and child who accompanies him a hostage to fickle fortune.

24   Gold no longer rolls from the mountain in chunks the size of a man's head (if indeed it ever did). But the present generation of miners has found that a manic pounding of rock can produce miracles. In 2011, 150 tons of gold were harvested in Peru, worth $6.8 billion. In order to produce it, almost 5 million tons of Peruvian rock were knocked free and ground down. Look at it this way: For every gold ring you see on a finger, miners have had to turn 250 tons of rock.

25   In La Rinconada, the ore that harbors those precious flecks is washed in ponds of cyanide, pounded with mercury in giant mortars of stone and burned clean in ovens that send mercury fumes coiling up onto the glacier's snows. The work outdoors is often done by women and children. The work in the damp, freezing shafts is done by men. At the end of the process, a miner working under the cachorreo system—a man who labors for 30 days and gets paid on the 31st day in the form of whatever rock he can carry—may walk away with a nugget worth $40. His neighbor, on the other hand, may be rich beyond his imagining.

26   One thing is sure: Every year, less and less is harvested from Sleeping Beauty. There is only so much gold on this planet. For all the

---

4. **pestilential** (pehs tuh LEHN shuhl) *adj.* dangerous; literally, disease-causing.

masks of Tutankhamun, for all the headdresses of the Lord of Sipan,[5] for all the bling and glitter of Fifth Avenue, the total amount of gold that humans have been able to pull from rock is a mere 170,000 metric tons, barely enough to fill two Olympic swimming pools. More than half of it has been mined in the last 50 years.

27   Some of this, mind you, has been done responsibly. But as earth is heaved and ore carved from the unruly cliffs of Ananea, the glacier and nearby lakes have sent toxic injections to the sparkling waters of Lake Titicaca.

A Sudden Awe

28   Wandering the ice-mud streets of La Rinconada, one can't help but hope that this gold town's days are numbered. The population that lives below—that has inhabited the shores of Lake Titicaca for centuries—made that hope known last year in a protest against all mining operations that didn't take into consideration the health and welfare of the locals. The Aymara, who are gentle by nature, were particularly vociferous on the subject, storming through Puno last May and unleashing their fury on everything in their way. The Peruvian military responded in kind.

29   The trickle-down of an economic boom can be surprising.

30   Even so, with all the antipathy a traveler might summon for a place so willfully **despoiled**, I found myself standing beside the road a good distance from La Rinconada, looking back at that promontory in wonder. With all my senses jangled, with the altitude making my every step as labored as an astronaut's, I found myself filled with sudden awe.

31   Like the Ancient Mariner, who stared at the leaden sea and its hideous slime and eventually beheld a rare, soul-lifting beauty, I suddenly saw the tin rooftops gleam like a mantle of diamonds. As the sun moved over the snow, the ravished mountain seemed to ripple with ribbons of color. In that happy trance, I recalled the kindness of a widow who offered me the shelter of her hut and a gourd of hot soup. I remembered the fiery spirit of Senna, a 14-year-old girl who could recite a string of verses by the great poet Vallejo. I heard the laughter of a child in yellow, who danced in a noonday cantina.

32   Even here, on this plundered peak, there are fleeting moments of joy. ❧

Mark base words or indicate another strategy you used that helped you determine meaning.

despoiled (dih SPOYLD) *v.*

MEANING:

_____

5. **Lord of Sipan** (see PON) Peruvian mummy discovered in 1987. The mummy's tomb contained many gold ornaments and articles of jewelry.

Comprehension Check

Complete the following items after you finish your first read. Review and clarify details with your group.

1. What is La Rinconada?

2. What basic facilities and services does La Rinconada lack?

3. What has drawn multinational corporations to the mountains around La Rinconada?

4. How are the miners who work under the cachorreo system paid?

5. **📰 Notebook** To confirm your understanding, write a summary of the article.

- -

RESEARCH

Research to Clarify Choose at least one unfamiliar detail from the text. Briefly research that detail. In what way does the information you learned shed light on an aspect of the article?

Research to Explore Conduct research on an aspect of the text you find interesting. For example, you may want to learn more about the history of the Incas or modern Peruvian culture. Share what you learn with your group.

Close Read the Text

With your group, revisit sections of the text you marked during your first read. **Annotate** details that you notice. What **questions** do you have? What can you **conclude**?

IN LA RINCONADA, PERU, SEARCHING FOR BEAUTY IN UGLINESS

Analyze the Text

CITE TEXTUAL EVIDENCE to support your answers.

Notebook Complete the activities.

1. **Review and Clarify** With your group, reread paragraph 23 of the article. What do you see as the "curse" of Atahualpa? In your opinion, has the curse been lifted, or does Peru still live under its influence? Explain.

2. **Present and Discuss** Now, work with your group to share the passages from the text that you found especially important. Take turns presenting your passages. Discuss what you noticed in the text, what questions you asked, and what conclusions you reached.

3. **Essential Question:** *What do our possessions reveal about us?* What has this article taught you about materialism? Discuss with your group.

TIP

GROUP DISCUSSION
If you do not fully understand a group member's comment, ask for clarification. To ensure an effective exchange, use a respectful and friendly tone.

WORD NETWORK
Add words related to materialism from the text to your Word Network.

LANGUAGE DEVELOPMENT

Concept Vocabulary

| marauding | intemperate | despoiled |

Why These Words? The three concept vocabulary words are related. With your group, determine what the words have in common. Write your ideas, and add another word that fits the category.

Practice

Notebook Confirm your understanding of these words by using them in a paragraph. Include context clues that hint at each word's meaning.

Word Study

Latin Root: -temp- The Latin root *-temp-* may have one of two meanings. In some words, such as the concept vocabulary word *intemperate*, it means "moderation," "restraint," or "calmness." In other words, such as the word *temporary*, it means "time."

Find and record the definitions of these words containing the root *-temp-*: *distemper*, *contemporary*, *temporal*. For each word, write which meaning the root contributes.

Analyze Craft and Structure

Literary Nonfiction Journalism is nonfiction that presents objective, or neutral, facts about a newsworthy story or situation. Works of journalism focus on current events or on situations with continuing relevance. **Literary journalism** presents the same types of fact-based information as regular journalism, but does not remain objective. Instead, it is subjective, or includes the writer's personal observations and feelings. Literary journalism often uses the following techniques that are usually associated with fiction:

- descriptive language and imagery
- the writer's personal observations, thoughts, and feelings
- a sense of story, with beginning, middle, and end

Practice

CITE TEXTUAL EVIDENCE to support your answers.

Work independently to identify passages in the article that exemplify literary journalism. Then, share and discuss your choices with your group.

ELEMENTS OF LITERARY JOURNALISM	EXAMPLES FROM THE ARTICLE
Newsworthy content	
Facts	
Journalist's personal observations, thoughts, and feelings	
Descriptive language and imagery	
Narrative elements that give a sense of beginning, middle, and end	

IN LA RINCONADA, PERU, SEARCHING FOR BEAUTY IN UGLINESS

Author's Style

Word Choice Writers often use **imagery**, or language that appeals to the senses and creates an image in the reader's mind, to build meaning in a text and to evoke emotion in readers. **Sensory details** are the building blocks of imagery. They appeal to the reader's five senses—sight, smell, hearing, taste, and touch—and create vivid images that help convey important ideas in a text.

> EXAMPLE: "It is a wilderness of ice, rock, and gold. . . ." Sensory details appeal to the reader's sense of *sight*.
>
> EXAMPLE: "The odor is staggering; it is the putrid stench of chemicals. . . ." Sensory details appeal to the reader's sense of *smell*.

Read It

Work individually. Find examples of imagery in the article. Identify the senses to which each example appeals, and explain how it improves your understanding of the text. After you've completed the chart, gather as a group and discuss your responses.

EXAMPLE OF IMAGERY	SENSES ENGAGED	EFFECT ON MEANING IN THE TEXT

Write It

📓 **Notebook** Imagine that you have won a free trip to visit La Rinconada, Peru. Using what you've learned about La Rinconada from the article, write a paragraph explaining why you would or would not go on this trip. Use at least three examples of imagery in your paragraph.

Research

Assignment

With your group, create and deliver a **multimedia presentation** that includes text, images, and data. Choose one of the following topics:

☐ Make plans for a **website** that focuses on the artwork of the Inca. Your website should include photos, facts about Inca art, quotations from experts, and descriptions of the artwork. Use the following questions to guide your research:

- In what kinds of art did the Inca specialize?
- How closely was Incan art connected to religion?
- How important was gold to Incan artwork?
- Where can people see Incan art today?

☐ Create an **annotated bibliography** of travel writings by journalists or photographers who have made the trip to La Rinconada. Include descriptions and evaluations of Arana's article and at least three other sources. Use the following questions to develop your description and evaluation of each text:

- Why did this author travel to La Rinconada?
- What is this author's impression of La Rinconada?
- How is this author's impression of La Rinconada similar to or different from Arana's impression?

☐ Create an **illustrated timeline** that focuses on Francisco Pizarro and the Battle of Cajamarca. Use the following questions to help guide your research and develop a timeline of key events:

- What events led up to the battle?
- What impact did Pizarro's actions have on the Incan Empire?
- Was the Incan Empire able to recover from its contact with the Europeans?

✎ EVIDENCE LOG

Before moving on to a new selection, go to your Evidence Log and record what you learned from "In La Rinconada, Peru, Searching for Beauty in Ugliness."

Project Plan Before you begin, make a list of tasks that the group will need to complete. Assign each group member a task.

Gather Information and Images If you choose the plan for a website or the illustrated timeline, you will likely review more material than you will need. Use a chart to organize information for each source you review, and use your notes to choose the best sources to include in your presentation.

FACT/IMAGE	SOURCE INFORMATION

Avarice

The Good Life

Money

Concept Vocabulary

As you perform your first read of these three poems, you will encounter the following words.

| avarice | desperate | needy |

Context Clues If these words are unfamiliar to you, try using **context clues**—other words and phrases that appear nearby in the text—to help you determine their meanings. There are various types of context clues that may help you as you read.

Synonyms: The **glimmer** of the candlelight reminded me of the twinkle of starlight.

Restatement: A **glimmer** caught my eye—a faint, flickering light reflecting off the surface of a diamond ring.

Contrast of Ideas: The mere **glimmer** from the dying light bulb was not enough to brighten the dark, shadowy room.

Apply your knowledge of context clues and other vocabulary strategies to determine the meanings of unfamiliar words you encounter during your first read. Confirm your definitions using a college-level dictionary.

First Read POETRY

Apply these strategies as you conduct your first read. You will have an opportunity to complete a close read after your first read.

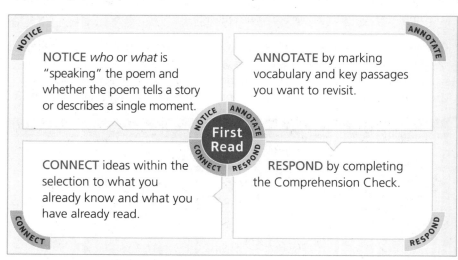

NOTICE *who* or *what* is "speaking" the poem and whether the poem tells a story or describes a single moment.

ANNOTATE by marking vocabulary and key passages you want to revisit.

CONNECT ideas within the selection to what you already know and what you have already read.

RESPOND by completing the Comprehension Check.

NOTICE ANNOTATE CONNECT RESPOND

First Read

About the Poets

Yusef Komunyakaa (b. 1947) grew up in New Orleans, where he was strongly influenced by the local culture including blues, jazz, and the Creole-influenced speech patterns of the city's inhabitants. As a young man, Komunyakaa served his country in Vietnam, and some of his best poems focus on this time, capturing both the physical and psychological toll of the war.

Tracy K. Smith (b. 1972) teaches creative writing at Princeton University. Prior to that, Smith held a prestigious Stegner fellowship at Stanford University. In 2012, Smith won a Pulitzer Prize for her book *Life on Mars*, which describes a futuristic world that nevertheless has a great deal to say about current times.

Reginald Gibbons (b. 1947) spent his early life in Houston, Texas, far from the literary world of which he would become a part. Gibbons studied Spanish and Portuguese at Princeton University, but he quickly took to poetry after earning a doctorate from Stanford in comparative literature. Gibbons has focused on social injustice throughout his career, attempting to use the platform of poetry to activate social awareness and change.

Backgrounds

Avarice

This selection is part of a series of seven poems by Yusef Komunyakaa. Each one is named after the seven deadly sins of medieval Christian theology, which were moral offenses that were considered particularly terrible. These sins were pride, avarice, lust, envy, gluttony, wrath, and sloth.

The Good Life

"The good life" is a stock phrase that can be traced back to the ancient Greek philosophers Epicurus and Aristotle. They both developed theories about what it means to live a good life and explored whether such a life would involve happiness, moral righteousness, wealth, useful work, or something else entirely.

Money

This poem features an element of American culture that is now almost entirely gone— door-to-door sales. Before the widespread use of media and telephones, salespeople would make unexpected stops at private homes in the hopes of selling their products or services. Many towns and cities have passed ordinances to regulate and restrict uninvited door-to-door solicitations.

Avarice

Yusef Komunyakaa

At six, she chewed off
The seven porcelain buttons
From her sister's christening gown
& hid them in a Prince Albert can

5 On a sill crisscrossing the house
In the spidery crawlspace.
She'd weigh a peach in her hands
Till it rotted. At sixteen,

She gazed at her little brother's
10 Junebugs pinned to a sheet of cork,
Assaying their glimmer, till she
Buried them beneath a fig tree's wide,

Green skirt. Now, twenty-six,
Locked in the beauty of her bones,
15 She counts eight engagement rings
At least twelve times a day.

"Avarice" by Yusef Komunyakaa. Copyright © 2000 by Yusef Komunyakaa. Reprinted by permission of
Farrar, Straus and Giroux, LLC. CAUTION: Users are warned that this work is protected under copyright
laws and downloading is strictly prohibited. The right to reproduce or transfer the work via any medium
must be secured with Farrar, Straus and Giroux, LLC.

NOTES

Mark context clues or indicate
another strategy you used that
helped you determine meaning.

avarice (AV uh rihs) *n.*

MEANING:

The Good Life

Tracy K. Smith

When some people talk about money
They speak as if it were a mysterious lover
Who went out to buy milk and never
Came back, and it makes me nostalgic
5 For the years I lived on coffee and bread,
Hungry all the time, walking to work on payday
Like a woman journeying for water
From a village without a well, then living
One or two nights like everyone else
10 On roast chicken and red wine.

Money

Reginald Gibbons

1 The children are eating lunch at home on a summer weekday when a man comes to the door and asks their mother if she has anything that needs fixing or carrying or any yardwork he can do. They chew their food a little dreamily as, with her back straight and her voice carefully polite, she says No, thank you, I'm sorry, and the man goes away. Who was that, Mama? they say. Oh, no one, she says.

2 They are sitting down to dinner but they have to wait because the doorbell rings and a thin young boy begins to tell their father about a Sales Program he's completing for a scholarship to be Supervisor, and he holds up a filthy tattered little booklet and lifts also his **desperate** guile[1] and heavily guarded hope, and the children's father says, No thank you, sorry but I can't help you out this time, and the boy goes away. The children start to eat and don't ask anything, because the

NOTES

Mark context clues or indicate another strategy you used that helped you determine meaning.

desperate (DEHS puhr iht) *adj.*
MEANING:

---

1. **guile** (gyl) *n.* sly or cunning intelligence.

boy was just a boy, but their father acts irritated and hasty when he sits back down.

3   Once a glassy-eyed heavy girl who almost seems asleep as she stands outside their door offers for sale some little handtowels stitched by the blind people at the Lighthouse for the Blind and the children are in the folds of their mother's full skirt listening to the girl's small voice and their mother says, Well, I bought some the last time.

4   She buys the children school supplies and food, she pays the two boys for mowing the yard together and weeding her flower bed. She gets a new sewing machine for her birthday from the children's father, and she buys fabric and thread and patterns and makes dresses for the girls, to save money. She tells the children each to put a dime or quarter into the collection plate at Church, and once a month she puts in a little sealed white envelope, and the ushers move slowly along the ends of the pews weaving the baskets through the congregation, and the organist plays a long piece of music.

5   Whisk brooms, magazine subscriptions, anything you need hauled away, little league raffle tickets, cookies, chocolate candy, can I do any yardwork again and again, hairbrushes, Christmas cards, do you need help with your ironing one time, and more, came calling at the front door while the children were sometimes eating, sometimes playing. Their faces would soften with a kind of comfort in the authority of mother or father, with a kind of wonder at the **needy** callers.

6   Their father left for work every day early, and came home for dinner, and almost always went again on Saturday; in his car. Their mother opened a savings account for each child and into each put the first five dollars. The children felt proud to see their names in the passbooks, and wanted to know when they could take the money out. But they were told they had to save their money not spend it. They felt a kind of pleasure in these mysteries, to know that there were things you would understand later when you grew up and had your own house and while your children were eating their dinner and making too much noise the way you did, you knew it was true, the doorbell would ring, the familiar surprise of it, who would it be, and someone would be holding a little worn book or a bundle of dishtowels or once an old man, but perhaps he only looked old, with his beard, came with bunches of carnations, white, red, and pink, and he too was turned away. ❧

Mark context clues or indicate another strategy you used that helped you determine meaning.

needy (NEED ee) *adj.*

MEANING:

Comprehension Check

Complete the following items after you finish your first read. Review and clarify details with your group.

AVARICE

1. What does the main character do at age six?

2. At the age of twenty-six, what does she count twelve times a day?

THE GOOD LIFE

1. For what is the speaker nostalgic?

2. What physical feeling dominated that period in the speaker's life?

MONEY

1. What repeatedly happens at the children's house?

2. What instructions about money do the parents give the children?

- -

RESEARCH

Research to Clarify Choose at least one unfamiliar detail from one of the poems. Briefly research that detail. In what way does the information you learned shed light on an aspect of the poem?

POETRY COLLECTION

TIP

GROUP DISCUSSION

When discussing these poems, be aware that group members may have a wide range of experiences with money. Focus your discussion on the texts, and do not make assumptions about other group members' perspectives.

WORD NETWORK

Add words related to materialism from the texts to your Word Network.

Close Read the Text

With your group, revisit sections of the text you marked during your first read. **Annotate** details that you notice. What **questions** do you have? What can you **conclude**?

Analyze the Text

CITE TEXTUAL EVIDENCE to support your answers.

Notebook Complete the activities.

1. **Review and Clarify** With your group, reread "The Good Life." Why might the speaker feel "nostalgic" for a time of life that may have been difficult? Explain.

2. **Present and Discuss** Now, work with your group to share other key passages from the poems. Take turns presenting your choices. Discuss what you noticed in the text, what questions you asked, and what conclusions you reached.

3. **Essential Question:** *What do our possessions reveal about us?* What have these poems taught you about materialism? Discuss with your group.

LANGUAGE DEVELOPMENT

Concept Vocabulary

avarice	needy	desperate

Why These Words? The three concept vocabulary words are related. With your group, determine what the words have in common. Write your ideas, and add another word that fits the category.

Practice

Notebook Use a print or online dictionary to confirm the definitions of the concept words. Write a sentence using each of the words. How did the concept words make your sentences more vivid? Discuss.

Word Study

Denotation and Connotation The literal dictionary meaning of a word is its **denotation**. The **connotation** of a word is the emotional and cultural meaning it suggests. Words can have positive, neutral, or negative connotations.

For example, to describe someone as greedy and cheap, you might refer to his or her *avarice*. On the other hand, to make the same person sound careful and smart about money, you might use the word *thrifty*. *Avarice* has a negative connotation, whereas *thrifty* has a positive one.

Identify one word from one of the poems that has a positive connotation and one word that has a negative connotation. With your group, discuss the effect of these word choices on the poem.

Analyze Craft and Structure

Author's Choices: Speaker and Point of View Like a narrator that relates the events of a story, the **speaker** is the voice that "tells" a poem. A speaker may seem like the poet, but the two are not one and the same. Like a narrator, a speaker is an imaginary voice. Also like a narrator, the speaker's point of view affects what readers learn or perceive.

- **First-Person Point of View:** The speaker uses first-person pronouns (*I* and *me)* and is part of the action of the poem.

- **Third-Person Point of View:** The speaker uses third-person pronouns (*he*, *she*, *they*, and so on) and seems to stand outside the action of the poem. There are two types of third-person points of view. An **omniscient** speaker is an all-knowing observer who can reveal the thoughts and feelings of all characters in a poem. A **limited third-person** speaker can reveal only what one character is thinking and feeling.

To understand a poem, it is important to identify who the speaker is, what he or she knows and does not know, and how he or she feels about the topic of the poem—his or her **tone.**

Practice

CITE TEXTUAL EVIDENCE to support your answers.

Work with your group to consider the identity of the speaker in each poem. Then, identify the points of view and tones each one uses. Collect your notes in the chart.

POEM	SPEAKER'S POINT OF VIEW	SPEAKER'S TONE
Avarice Speaker:		
The Good Life Speaker:		
Money Speaker:		

Notebook Answer these questions.

1. (a) In "Avarice," the speaker notes four different items "she" keeps. What is similar and different about those items? (b) What does the poem suggest about greed—is it useless, selfish, etc.? Explain.

2. In "The Good Life," which life does the speaker seem to feel is "good"— the one in which money is more available, or the one spent living on "coffee and bread"? Explain.

3. (a) In "Money," which details suggest the nature of the children's lives? (b) How do these details contrast with those that describe the people at the door? (c) Is the speaker simply describing a situation or is the speaker criticizing something? Explain.

Author's Style

Poetic Language Sound devices are patterns of words that emphasize the sound relationships in language. All sound devices create musical and emotional effects, heighten the sense of unity in a poem, and emphasize meaning. These devices include alliteration and consonance.

- **Alliteration** is the repetition of initial consonant sounds in the stressed syllables of nearby words.

  EXAMPLE: His soul swooned slowly as he heard the snow falling faintly. —from "The Dead," James Joyce

- **Consonance** is the repetition of final consonant sounds in stressed syllables with different vowel sounds, as in *hat* and *sit*.

  EXAMPLE: Where now he sat, concerned with he knew what, / A quiet light, and then not even that. —from "An Old Man's Winter Night," Robert Frost

Read It

Find examples of alliteration and consonance in each poem in this colleciton. Use the chart to list your examples. Then, discuss the effects of each example.

POEM	ALLITERATION	CONSONANCE
Avarice		
The Good Life		
Money		

Write It

🖹 **Notebook** Write four sentences describing a familiar scene or event in your school, city, or town. Use alliteration in two sentences, and consonance in the other two. Mark each example of alliteration and consonance that you use.

Writing to Sources

Assignment

With your group, plan and write a **short story** that answers a question left open by one of the poems. Choose from the following options.

☐ In "Avarice," how does the young woman acquire eight engagement rings?

☐ In "The Good Life," why does the speaker feel "nostalgic" about the past? What has changed in the speaker's life?

☐ In "Money," what has really happened to the thin young boy who claims to be completing a Sales Program?

Project Plan Before you begin to write, brainstorm for ideas about the setting and characters. Choose a main character, and decide on the conflict he or she will face. Determine how that conflict will begin, develop, and resolve. Capture ideas and notes in the chart.

STORY ELEMENTS	NOTES
Characters	
Setting	
Conflict and Plot Events	

✐ EVIDENCE LOG

Before moving on to a new selection, go to your Evidence Log and record what you learned from "Avarice," "The Good Life," and "Money."

Drafting and Revising Decide how you will organize the drafting stage. You may have everyone in the group write a version of the story, and then pull the best parts of each one into a final product. Alternatively, you may assign specific sections to individual group members. Make sure to divide the work up fairly. In addition, make sure that your story is consistent with the details and information in the poem. Once you have a completed first draft, read the story aloud. Consider how you can make it clearer, more vivid, or more faithful to the poem. Revise as needed and share your story with the class.

THE GOLDEN TOUCH

Comparing Texts

In this lesson, you will compare two versions of the King Midas myth. First, complete the first-read and close-read activities for "The Golden Touch." This work will help prepare you for the comparing task.

from KING MIDAS

About the Author

Nathaniel Hawthorne (1804–1864) was born in Salem, Massachusetts. After attending Bowdoin College in Maine, Hawthorne began a career as an author. Though Hawthorne's writings were well received, he continued to work at the local Custom House until his very successful publication of *The Scarlet Letter* in 1850. Hawthorne's works explore issues of good against evil and are heavily influenced by the Puritan culture of his hometown, which a century before his birth had been the site of the famous Salem witch trials.

The Golden Touch

Concept Vocabulary

As you perform your first read of the story, you will encounter these words.

burnished	lustrous	gilded

Context Clues If these words are unfamiliar to you, try using **context clues**—other words and phrases that appear nearby in the text—to help you determine their meanings. There are various types of context clues that may help you as you read.

> **Restatement:** The confrontation was **inevitable;** <u>every attempt to avoid it failed</u>.
>
> **Elaborating Details:** The <u>raging</u> fireplace **incinerated** the thin paper letter <u>instantly, leaving only ash</u>.
>
> **Contrast of Ideas:** He was as **lavish** with his friends as he was <u>stingy and ungiving</u> with strangers.

Apply your knowledge of context clues and other vocabulary strategies to determine the meanings of unfamiliar words you encounter during your first read.

First Read FICTION

Apply these strategies as you conduct your first read. You will have an opportunity to complete a close read after your first read.

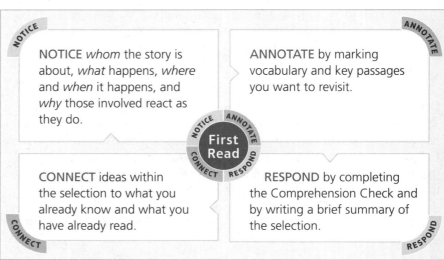

NOTICE *whom* the story is about, *what* happens, *where* and *when* it happens, and *why* those involved react as they do.

ANNOTATE by marking vocabulary and key passages you want to revisit.

First Read

CONNECT ideas within the selection to what you already know and what you have already read.

RESPOND by completing the Comprehension Check and by writing a brief summary of the selection.

The Golden Touch

Nathaniel Hawthorne

BACKGROUND

"The Golden Touch" is one of six stories that Hawthorne published as *A Wonder-Book for Girls and Boys* in 1851. Hawthorne's aim was to take the Greek myths out of their "classic coldness" and update them so that children of his time could enjoy them. To give the myths a friendlier tone, Hawthorne invented a narrator named Eustace Bright, a young man of great energy and imagination, who tells each tale to a group of lively children. With respect to the retelling of myths by Eustace, Hawthorne promised, "I shall purge out all the old heathen wickedness, and put in a moral wherever practicable."

1   Once upon a time, there lived a very rich man, and a king besides, whose name was Midas; and he had a little daughter, whom nobody but myself ever heard of, and whose name I either never knew, or have entirely forgotten. So, because I love odd names for little girls, I choose to call her Marygold.

2   This King Midas was fonder of gold than of anything else in the world. He valued his royal crown chiefly because it was composed of that precious metal. If he loved anything better, or half so well, it was the one little maiden who played so merrily around her father's footstool. But the more Midas loved his daughter, the more did he desire and seek for wealth. He thought, foolish man! that the best thing he could possibly do for this dear child would be to bequeath her the immensest pile of yellow, glistening coin, that had ever been

NOTES

heaped together since the world was made. Thus, he gave all his thoughts and all his time to this one purpose. If ever he happened to gaze for an instant at the gold-tinted clouds of sunset, he wished that they were real gold, and that they could be squeezed safely into his strong box. When little Marygold ran to meet him, with a bunch of buttercups and dandelions, he used to say, "Poh, poh, child! If these flowers were as golden as they look, they would be worth the plucking!"

3   And yet, in his earlier days, before he was so entirely possessed with this insane desire for riches, King Midas had shown a great taste for flowers. He had planted a garden, in which grew the biggest and beautifullest and sweetest roses that any mortal ever saw or smelt. These roses were still growing in the garden, as large, as lovely and as fragrant, as when Midas used to pass whole hours in gazing at them, and inhaling their perfume. But now, if he looked at them at all, it was only to calculate how much the garden would be worth, if each of the innumerable rose petals were a thin plate of gold. And though he once was fond of music (in spite of an idle story about his ears, which were said to resemble those of an ass), the only music for poor Midas, now, was the chink of one coin against another.

4   At length (as people always grow more and more foolish, unless they take care to grow wiser and wiser), Midas had got to be so exceedingly unreasonable, that he could scarcely bear to see or touch any object that was not gold. He made it his custom, therefore, to pass a large portion of every day in a dark and dreary apartment, under ground, at the basement of his palace. It was here that he kept his wealth. To this dismal hole—for it was little better than a dungeon—Midas betook himself, whenever he wanted to be particularly happy. Here, after carefully locking the door, he would take a bag of gold coin, or a gold cup as big as a washbowl, or a heavy golden bar, or a peck-measure of gold dust, and bring them from the obscure corners of the room into the one bright and narrow sunbeam that fell from the dungeonlike window. He valued the sunbeam for no other reason but that his treasure would not shine without its help. And then would he reckon over the coins in the bag; toss up the bar, and catch it as it came down; sift the gold dust through his fingers; look at the funny image of his own face, as reflected in the **burnished** circumference of the cup; and whisper to himself, "O Midas, rich King Midas, what a happy man art thou!" But it was laughable to see how the image of his face kept grinning at him, out of the polished surface of the cup. It seemed to be aware of his foolish behavior, and to have a naughty inclination to make fun of him.

5   Midas called himself a happy man, but felt that he was not yet quite so happy as he might be. The very tiptop of enjoyment would never be reached, unless the whole world were to become his

Mark context clues or indicate another strategy you used that helped you determine meaning.

burnished (BUR nihsht) *adj.*

MEANING:

treasure room, and be filled with yellow metal which should be all his own.

6   Now, I need hardly remind such wise little people as you are, that in the old, old times, when King Midas was alive, a great many things came to pass, which we should consider wonderful if they were to happen in our own day and country. And, on the other hand, a great many things take place nowadays, which seem not only wonderful to us, but at which the people of old times would have stared their eyes out. On the whole, I regard our own times as the strangest of the two; but, however that may be, I must go on with my story.

7   Midas was enjoying himself in his treasure room, one day, as usual, when he perceived a shadow fall over the heaps of gold; and, looking suddenly up, what should he behold but the figure of a stranger, standing in the bright and narrow sunbeam! It was a young man, with a cheerful and ruddy face. Whether it was that the imagination of King Midas threw a yellow tinge over everything, or whatever the cause might be, he could not help fancying that the smile with which the stranger regarded him had a kind of golden radiance in it. Certainly, although his figure intercepted the sunshine, there was now a brighter gleam upon all the piled-up treasures than before. Even the remotest corners had their share of it, and were lighted up, when the stranger smiled, as with tips of flame and sparkles of fire.

8   As Midas knew that he had carefully turned the key in the lock, and that no mortal strength could possibly break into his treasure-room, he, of course, concluded that his visitor must be something more than mortal. It is no matter about telling you who he was. In those days, when the earth was comparatively a new affair, it was supposed to be often the resort of beings endowed with supernatural powers, and who used to interest themselves in the joys and sorrows of men, women and children, half playfully and half seriously. Midas had met such beings before now, and was not sorry to meet one of them again. The stranger's aspect, indeed, was so good-humored and kindly, if not beneficent, that it would have been unreasonable to suspect him of intending any mischief. It was far more probable that he came to do Midas a favor. And what could that favor be, unless to multiply his heaps of treasure?

9   The stranger gazed about the room; and when his **lustrous** smile had glistened upon all the golden objects that were there, he turned again to Midas.

10   "You are a wealthy man, friend Midas!" he observed. "I doubt whether any other four walls, on earth, contain so much gold as you have contrived to pile up in this room."

11   "I have done pretty well—pretty well," answered Midas, in a discontented tone. "But, after all, it is but a trifle, when you consider

Mark context clues or indicate another strategy you used that helped you determine meaning.

lustrous (LUHS truhs) *adj.*

MEANING:

that it has taken me my whole life to get it together. If one could live a thousand years, he might have time to grow rich!"

12   "What!" exclaimed the stranger, "Then you are not satisfied?"

13   Midas shook his head.

14   "And pray what would satisfy you?" asked the stranger. "Merely for the curiosity of the thing, I should be glad to know."

15   Midas paused and meditated. He felt a presentiment[1] that this stranger, with such a golden luster in his good-humored smile, had come hither with both the power and the purpose of gratifying his utmost wishes. Now, therefore, was the fortunate moment, when he had but to speak, and obtain whatever possible, or seemingly impossible thing, it might come into his head to ask. So he thought, and thought, and thought, and heaped up one golden mountain upon another, in his imagination, without being able to imagine them big enough. At last, a bright idea occurred to King Midas. It seemed really as bright as the glistening metal which he loved so much.

16   Raising his head, he looked the lustrous stranger in the face.

17   "Well, Midas," observed his visitor, "I see that you have at length hit upon something that will satisfy you. Tell me your wish."

18   "It is only this," replied Midas. "I am weary of collecting my treasures with so much trouble, and beholding the heap so diminutive, after I have done my best. I wish everything that I touch to be changed to gold!"

19   The stranger's smile grew so very broad, that it seemed to fill the room like an outburst of the sun, gleaming into a shadowy dell, where the yellow autumnal leaves—for so looked the lumps and particles of gold—lie strewn in the glow of light.

20   "The Golden Touch!" exclaimed he. "You certainly deserve credit, friend Midas, for striking out so brilliant a conception. But are you quite sure that this will satisfy you?"

21   "How could it fail?" said Midas.

22   "And will you never regret the possession of it?"

23   "What could induce me?" asked Midas. "I ask nothing else, to render me perfectly happy."

24   "Be it as you wish, then," replied the stranger, waving his hand in token of farewell. "Tomorrow, at sunrise, you will find yourself gifted with the Golden Touch."

25   The figure of the stranger then became exceedingly bright, and Midas involuntarily closed his eyes. On opening them again, he beheld only one yellow sunbeam in the room, and, all around him, the glistening of the precious metal which he had spent his life in hoarding up.

26   Whether Midas slept as usual that night, the story does not say. Asleep or awake, however, his mind was probably in the state of a child's, to whom a beautiful new plaything has been promised in the

---

1. **presentiment** (prih ZEHN tuh muhnt) *n.* feeling that something is about to happen.

morning. At any rate, day had hardly peeped over the hills, when King Midas was broad awake, and, stretching his arms out of bed, began to touch the objects that were within reach. He was anxious to prove whether the Golden Touch had really come, according to the stranger's promise. So he laid his finger on a chair by the bedside, and on various other things, but was grievously disappointed to perceive that they remained of exactly the same substance as before. Indeed, he felt very much afraid that he had only dreamed about the lustrous stranger, or else that the latter had been making game of him. And what a miserable affair would it be, if, after all his hopes, Midas must content himself with what little gold he could scrape together by ordinary means, instead of creating it by a touch!

27   All this while, it was only the gray of the morning, with but a streak of brightness along the edge of the sky, where Midas could not see it. He lay in a very disconsolate mood, regretting the downfall

of his hopes, and kept growing sadder and sadder, until the earliest sunbeam shone through the window, and **gilded** the ceiling over his head. It seemed to Midas that this bright yellow sunbeam was reflected in rather a singular way on the white covering of the bed. Looking more closely, what was his astonishment and delight, when he found that this linen fabric had been transmuted to what seemed a woven texture of the purest and brightest gold! The Golden Touch had come to him, with the first sunbeam!

28   Midas started up, in a kind of joyful frenzy, and ran about the room, grasping at everything that happened to be in his way. He seized one of the bedposts, and it became immediately a fluted

NOTES

Mark context clues or indicate another strategy you used that helped you determine meaning.

gilded (GIHLD ihd) *v.*

MEANING:

golden pillar. He pulled aside a window curtain, in order to admit a clear spectacle of the wonders which he was performing; and the tassel grew heavy in his hand—a mass of gold. He took up a book from the table. At his first touch, it assumed the appearance of such a splendidly bound and gilt-edged volume as one often meets with, nowadays; but, on running his fingers through the leaves, behold! it was a bundle of thin golden plates, in which all the wisdom of the book had grown illegible. He hurriedly put on his clothes, and was enraptured to see himself in a magnificent suit of gold cloth, which retained its flexibility and softness, although it burdened him a little with its weight. He drew out his handkerchief, which little Marygold had hemmed for him. That was likewise gold, with the dear child's neat and pretty stitches running all along the border, in gold thread!

29   Somehow or other, this last transformation did not quite please King Midas. He would rather that his little daughter's handiwork should have remained just the same as when she climbed his knee, and put it into his hand.

30   But it was not worth while to vex himself about a trifle. Midas now took his spectacles from his pocket, and put them on his nose, in order that he might see more distinctly what he was about. In those days, spectacles for common people had not been invented, but were already worn by kings; else, how could Midas have had any? To his great perplexity, however, excellent as the glasses were, he discovered that he could not possibly see through them. But this was the most natural thing in the world; for, on taking them off, the transparent crystals turned out to be plates of yellow metal, and, of course, were worthless as spectacles, though valuable as gold. It struck Midas as rather inconvenient, that, with all his wealth, he could never again be rich enough to own a pair of serviceable spectacles.

> Somehow or other, this last transformation did not quite please King Midas.

31   "It is no great matter, nevertheless," said he to himself, very philosophically. "We cannot expect any great good, without its being accompanied with some small inconvenience. The Golden Touch is worth the sacrifice of a pair of spectacles, at least, if not of one's very eyesight. My own eyes will serve for ordinary purposes, and little Marygold will soon be old enough to read to me."

32   Wise King Midas was so exalted by his good fortune, that the palace seemed not sufficiently spacious to contain him. He therefore went down stairs, and smiled, on observing that the balustrade[2] of the staircase became a bar of burnished gold, as his hand passed over it, in his descent. He lifted the doorlatch (it was brass only a moment ago, but golden when his fingers quitted it), and emerged into the garden. Here, as it happened, he found a great number of beautiful roses in full bloom, and others in all the stages of lovely bud and

2. **balustrade** (BAL uhs trayd) *n.* railing.

blossom. Very delicious was their fragrance in the morning breeze. Their delicate blush was one of the fairest sights the world; so gentle, so modest, and so full of sweet tranquility, did these roses seem to be.

33   But Midas knew a way to make them far more precious, according to his way of thinking, than roses had ever been before. So he took great pains in going from bush to bush, and exercised his magic touch most indefatigably; until every individual flower and bud, and even the worms at the heart of some of them, were changed to gold. By the time this good work was completed, King Midas was summoned to breakfast; and, as the morning air had given him an excellent appetite, he made haste back to the palace.

34   What was usually a king's breakfast, in the days of Midas, I really do not know, and cannot stop now to investigate. To the best of my belief, however, on this particular morning, the breakfast consisted of hot cakes, some nice little brook trout, roasted potatoes, fresh boiled eggs, and coffee, for King Midas himself, and a bowl of bread and milk for his daughter Marygold. At all events, this is a breakfast fit to set before a king; and, whether he had it or not, King Midas could not have had a better.

35   Little Marygold had not yet made her appearance. Her father ordered her to be called, and, seating himself at table, awaited the child's coming, in order to begin his own breakfast. To do Midas justice, he really loved his daughter, and loved her so much the more this morning, on account of the good fortune which had befallen him. It was not a great while before he heard her coming along the passageway, crying bitterly. This circumstance surprised him, because Marygold was one of the cheerfullest little people whom you would see in a summer's day, and hardly shed a thimbleful of tears in a twelve-month. When Midas heard her sobs, he determined to put little Marygold into better spirits, by an agreeable surprise; so, leaning across the table, he touched his daughter's bowl (which was a China one, with pretty figures all around it), and transmuted it to gleaming gold.

36   Meanwhile, Marygold slowly and disconsolately opened the door, and showed herself with her apron at her eyes, still sobbing as if her heart would break.

37   "How now, my little lady! " cried Midas. "Pray what is the matter with you, this bright morning?"

38   Marygold, without taking the apron from her eyes, held out her hand, in which was one of the roses which Midas had so recently transmuted.

39   "Beautiful!" exclaimed her father. "And what is there in this magnificent golden rose to make you cry?"

40   "Ah, dear father!" answered the child, as well as her sobs would let her; "it is not beautiful, but the ugliest flower that ever grew! As soon as I was dressed, I ran into the garden to gather some roses for you; because I know you like them, and like them the better when gathered by your little daughter. But, oh dear, dear me! What do you

think has happened? Such a misfortune! All the beautiful roses, that smelled so sweetly and had so many lovely blushes, are blighted and spoilt! They are grown quite yellow, as you see this one, and have no longer any fragrance! What can have been the matter with them?"

41 "Poh, my dear little girl—pray don't cry about it!" said Midas, who was ashamed to confess that he himself had wrought the change which so greatly afflicted her. "Sit down and eat your bread and milk! You will find it easy enough to exchange a golden rose like that (which will last hundreds of years), for an ordinary one, which would wither in a day."

42 "I don't care for such roses as this!" cried Marygold, tossing it contemptuously away. "It has no smell, and the hard petals prick my nose!"

43 The child now sat down to table, but was so occupied with her grief for the blighted roses that she did not even notice the wonderful transmutation of her China bowl. Perhaps this was all the better; for Marygold was accustomed to take pleasure in looking at the queer figures, and strange trees and houses, that were painted on the circumference of the bowl; and these ornaments were now entirely lost in the yellow hue of the metal.

44 Midas, meanwhile, had poured out a cup of coffee; and, as a matter of course, the coffeepot, whatever metal it may have been when he took it up, was gold when he set it down. He thought to himself, that it was rather an extravagant style of splendor, in a king of his simple habits, to breakfast off a service of gold, and began to be puzzled with the difficulty of keeping his treasures safe. The cupboard and the kitchen would no longer be a secure place of deposit for articles so valuable as golden bowls and coffeepots.

45 Amid these thoughts, he lifted a spoonful of coffee to his lips, and, sipping it, was astonished to perceive that, the instant his lips touched the liquid, it became molten gold, and, the next moment, hardened into a lump!

46 "Ha!" exclaimed Midas, rather aghast.

47 "What is the matter, father?" asked little Marygold, gazing at him, with the tears still standing in her eyes.

48 "Nothing, child, nothing! " said Midas. "Eat your milk, before it gets quite cold."

49 He took one of the nice little trouts on his plate, and, by way of experiment, touched its tail with his finger. To his horror, it was immediately transmuted from an admirably fried brook trout into a gold fish, though not one of those goldfishes which people often keep in glass globes, as ornaments for the parlor. No; but it was really a metallic fish, and looked as if it had been very cunningly made by the nicest goldsmith in the world. Its little bones were now golden wires; its fins and tail wore thin plates of gold; and there were the marks of the fork in it, and all the delicate, frothy appearance of a nicely fried fish, exactly imitated in metal. A very pretty piece of work, as you may suppose; only King Midas, just at that moment, would

much rather have had a real trout in his dish than this elaborate and valuable imitation of one.

50 "I don't quite see," thought he to himself, "how I am to get any breakfast!"

51 He took one of the smoking hot cakes, and had scarcely broken it, when, to his cruel mortification, though, a moment before, it had been of the whitest wheat, it assumed the yellow hue of Indian meal. To say the truth, if it had really been a hot Indian cake, Midas would have prized it a good deal more than he now did, when its solidity and increased weight made him too bitterly sensible that it was gold. Almost in despair, he helped himself to a boiled egg, which immediately underwent a change similar to those of the trout and the cake. The egg, indeed, might have been mistaken for one of those which the famous goose, in the storybook, was in the habit of laying; but King Midas was the only goose that had had anything to do with the matter.

52 "Well, this is a quandary!" thought he, leaning back in his chair, and looking quite enviously at little Marygold, who was now eating her bread and milk with great satisfaction. "Such a costly breakfast before me, and nothing that can be eaten!"

53 Hoping that, by dint of great despatch, he might avoid what he now felt to be a considerable inconvenience, King Midas next snatched a hot potato, and attempted to cram it into his mouth, and swallow it in a hurry. But the Golden Touch was too nimble for him. He found his mouth full, not of mealy potato, but of solid metal, which so burnt his tongue that he roared aloud, and, jumping up from the table, began to dance and stamp about the room, both with pain and affright.

54   "Father, dear father!" cried little Marygold, who was a very affectionate child, "pray what is the matter? Have you burnt your mouth?"

55   "Ah, dear child," groaned Midas, dolefully, "I don't know what is to become of your poor father!"

56   And, truly, my dear little folks, did you ever hear of such a pitiable case, in all your lives? Here was literally the richest breakfast that could be set before a king, and its very richness made it absolutely good for nothing. The poorest laborer, sitting down to his crust of bread and cup of water, was far better off than King Midas, whose delicate food was really worth its weight in gold. And what was to be done? Already, at breakfast, Midas was excessively hungry. Would he be less so by dinnertime? And how ravenous would be his appetite for supper, which must undoubtedly consist of the same sort of indigestible dishes as those now before him! How many days, think you, would he survive a continuance of this rich fare?

57   These reflections so troubled wise King Midas, that he began to doubt whether, after all, riches are the one desirable thing in the world, or even the most desirable. But this was only a passing thought. So fascinated was Midas with the glitter of the yellow metal, that he would still have refused to give up the Golden Touch for so paltry a consideration as a breakfast. Just imagine what a price for one meal's victuals! It would have been the same as paying millions and millions of money (and as many millions more as would take forever to reckon up) for some fried trout, an egg, a potato, a hot cake, and a cup of coffee!

58   "It would be quite too dear," thought Midas.

59   Nevertheless, so great was his hunger, and the perplexity of his situation, that he again groaned aloud, and very grievously too. Our pretty Marygold could endure it no longer. She sat, a moment, gazing at her father, and trying, with all the might of her little wits, to find out what was the matter with him. Then, with a sweet and sorrowful impulse to comfort him, she started from her chair, and running to Midas, threw her arms affectionately about his knees. He bent down and kissed her. He felt that his little daughter's love was worth a thousand times more than he had gained by the Golden Touch.

60   "My precious, precious Marygold!" cried he.

61   But Marygold made no answer.

62   Alas, what had he done? How fatal was the gift which the stranger bestowed! The moment the lips of Midas touched Marygold's forehead, a change had taken place. Her sweet, rosy face, so full of affection as it had been, assumed a glittering yellow color, with yellow teardrops congealing on her cheeks. Her beautiful brown ringlets took the same tint. Her soft and tender little form grew hard and inflexible within her father's encircling arms. O, terrible misfortune! The victim of his insatiable desire for wealth, little Marygold was a human child no longer, but a golden statue!

63   Yes, there she was, with the questioning look of love, grief, and pity, hardened into her face. It was the prettiest and most woeful sight that ever mortal saw. All the features and tokens of Marygold were there; even the beloved little dimple remained in her golden chin. But, the more perfect was the resemblance, the greater was the father's agony at beholding this golden image, which was all that was left him of a daughter. It had been a favorite phrase of Midas, whenever he felt particularly fond of the child, to say that she was worth her weight in gold. And now the phrase had become literally true. And now, at last, when it was too late, he felt how infinitely a warm and tender heart, that loved him, exceeded in value all the wealth that could be piled up betwixt the earth and sky!

64   It would be too sad a story, if I were to tell you how Midas, in the fullness of his gratified desires, began to wring his hands and bemoan himself; and how he could neither bear to look at Marygold, nor yet to look away from her. Except when his eyes were fixed on the image, he could not possibly believe that she was changed to gold. But, stealing another glance, there was the precious little figure, with a yellow teardrop on its yellow cheek, and a look so piteous and tender, that it seemed as if that very expression must needs soften the gold, and make it flesh again. This, however, could not be. So Midas had only to wring his hands, and to wish that he were the poorest man in the wide world, if the loss of all his wealth might bring back the faintest rose color to his dear child's face.

> Except when his eyes were fixed on the image, he could not possibly believe that she was changed to gold.

65   While he was in this tumult of despair, he suddenly beheld a stranger, standing near the door. Midas bent down his head, without speaking; for he recognized the same figure which had appeared to him, the day before, in the treasure room, and had bestowed on him this disastrous faculty of the Golden Touch. The stranger's countenance still wore a smile, which seemed to shed a yellow luster all about the room, and gleamed on little Marygold's image, and on the other objects that had been transmuted by the touch of Midas.

66   "Well, friend Midas," said the stranger, "pray how do you succeed with the Golden Touch?"

67   Midas shook his head.

68   "I am very miserable," said he.

69   "Very miserable, indeed!" exclaimed the stranger. "And how happens that? Have I not faithfully kept my promise with you? Have you not everything that your heart desired?"

70   "Gold is not everything," answered Midas. "And I have lost all that my heart really cared for."

71   "Ah! So you have made a discovery, since yesterday?" observed the stranger. "Let us see, then. Which of these two things do you

think is really worth the most—the gift of the Golden Touch, or one cup of clear cold water?"

72   "O, blessed water!" exclaimed Midas. "It will never moisten my parched throat again!"

73   "The Golden Touch," continued the stranger, "or crust of bread?"

74   "A piece of bread," answered Midas, "is worth all the gold on earth!"

75   "The Golden Touch," asked the stranger, "or your own little Marygold, warm, soft, and loving, as she was an hour ago?"

76   "O, my child, my dear child!" cried poor Midas, wringing his hands. " I would not have given that one small dimple in her chin for the power of changing this whole big earth into a solid lump of gold!"

77   "You are wiser than you were, King Midas!" said the stranger, looking seriously at him. "Your own heart, I perceive, has not been entirely changed from flesh to gold. Were it so, your case would indeed be desperate. But you appear to be still capable of understanding that the commonest things, such as lie within everybody's grasp, are more valuable than the riches which so many mortals sigh and struggle after. Tell me, now, do you sincerely desire to rid yourself of this Golden Touch?"

78   "It is hateful to me!" replied Midas.

79   A fly settled on his nose, but immediately fell to the floor; for it, too, had become gold. Midas shuddered.

80   "Go, then," said the stranger, "and plunge into the river that glides past the bottom of your garden. Take likewise a vase of the same water, and sprinkle it over any object that you may desire to change back again from gold into its former substance. If you do this in earnestness and sincerity, it may possibly repair the mischief which your avarice has occasioned."

81   King Midas bowed low; and when he lifted his head, the lustrous stranger had vanished.

82   You will easily believe that Midas lost no time in snatching up a great earthen pitcher (but, alas me! it was no longer earthen after he touched it), and hastening to the riverside. As he scampered along, and forced his way through the shrubbery, it was positively marvelous to see how the foliage turned yellow behind him, as if the autumn had been there, and nowhere else. On reaching the river's brink, he plunged headlong in, without waiting so much as to pull off his shoes.

83   "Poof! poof! poof!" snorted King Midas, as his head emerged out of the water. "Well; this is really a refreshing bath, and I think it must have quite washed away the Golden Touch. And now for filling my pitcher!"

84   As he dipped the pitcher into the water, it gladdened his very heart to see it change from gold into the same good, honest earthen vessel which it had been before he touched it. He was conscious, also, of a change within himself. A cold, hard, and heavy weight seemed to

have gone out of his bosom. No doubt, his heart had been gradually losing its human substance, and transmuting itself into insensible metal, but had now softened back again into flesh. Perceiving a violet, that grew on the bank of the river, Midas touched it with his finger, and was overjoyed to find that the delicate flower retained its purple hue, instead of undergoing a yellow blight. The curse of the Golden Touch had, therefore, really been removed from him.

85   King Midas hastened back to the palace: and, I suppose, the servants knew not what to make of it when they saw their royal master so carefully bringing home an earthen pitcher of water. But that water, which was to undo all the mischief that his folly had wrought, was more precious to Midas than an ocean of molten gold could have been. The first thing he did, as you need hardly be told, was to sprinkle it by handfuls over the golden figure of little Marygold.

86   No sooner did it fall on her than you would have laughed to see how the rosy color came back to the dear child's cheek!—and how she began to sneeze and sputter!—and how astonished she was to find herself dripping wet, and her father still throwing more water over her!

87   "Pray do not, dear father!" cried she. " See how you have wet my nice frock, which I put on only this morning!"

88   For Marygold did not know that she had been a little golden statue; nor could she remember anything that had happened since the moment when she ran, with outstretched arms, to comfort poor King Midas.

89   Her father did not think it necessary to tell his beloved child how very foolish he had been, but contented himself with showing how much wiser he had now grown. For this purpose, he led little Marygold into the garden, where he sprinkled all the remainder of the water over the rosebushes, and with such good effect that above five thousand roses recovered their beautiful bloom. There were two circumstances, however, which, as long as he lived, used to put King Midas in mind of the Golden Touch. One was, that the sands of the river sparkled like gold; the other, that little Marygold's hair had now a golden tinge, which he had never observed in it before she had been transmuted by the effect of his kiss. This change of hue was really an improvement, and made Marygold's hair richer than in her babyhood.

90   When King Midas had grown quite an old man, and used to trot Marygold's children on his knee, he was fond of telling them this marvelous story, pretty much as I have now told it to you. And then would he stroke their glossy ringlets, and tell them that their hair, likewise, had a rich shade of gold, which they had inherited from their mother.

91   "And, to tell you the truth, my precious little folks," quoth King Midas, diligently trotting the children all the while, "ever since that morning, I have hated the very sight of all other gold, save this!" ❧

Comprehension Check

Complete the following items after you finish your first read. Review and clarify details with your group.

1. What type of person visits King Midas in his treasure room?

2. What wish does the stranger grant?

3. What happens to the king's daughter when she hugs her father?

4. How does the stranger help Midas reverse the curse of the golden touch?

5. 🗒 **Notebook** To confirm your understanding, write a summary of the story.

- -

RESEARCH

Research to Clarify Choose at least one unfamiliar detail from the text. Briefly research that detail. In what way does the information you learned shed light on an aspect of the story?

Research to Explore Find out more about Hawthorne's book *A Wonder-Book for Girls and Boys*. What other Greek myths does the volume retell?

Close Read

With your group, revisit sections of the text you marked during your first read. **Annotate** details that you notice. What **questions** do you have? What can you **conclude**?

THE GOLDEN TOUCH

Analyze the Text

> **CITE TEXTUAL EVIDENCE** to support your answers.

 **Notebook** Complete the activities.

1. **Review and Clarify** With your group, reread paragraph 2 of the text. What words and phrases would you use to describe King Midas, based on the details the author gives in this paragraph? Is the narrator's attitude toward the king positive or negative? How do you know?

2. **Present and Discuss** Now, work with your group to share the passages from the text that you found especially important. Take turns presenting your passages. Discuss what you noticed in the text, what questions you asked, and what conclusions you reached.

3. **Essential Question:** *What do our possessions reveal about us?* What has this selection taught you about how the desire for material objects can affect people's judgment? Discuss with your group.

 TIP

CLOSE READING

In your discussion, talk about how the narrator's tone, or attitude, and word choice affect your impressions of King Midas. As a group, decide whether you are sympathetic to the plight in which Midas finds himself.

LANGUAGE DEVELOPMENT

Concept Vocabulary

burnished	lustrous	gilded

Why These Words? The three concept vocabulary words are related. With your group, determine what the words have in common. Write your ideas, and add another word that fits the category.

Practice

 Notebook Copy the sentences from the text that include the concept words into your notebook. Then, rewrite each sentence using a synonym for the concept word. Finally, share your revisions with another group member, and discuss how the substitutions affect the sentences' meanings.

Word Study

Notebook **Latin Root: *-lus-*** The narrator of "The Golden Touch" describes the stranger's smile as lustrous. The word *lustrous* is formed from the Latin root *-lus-* (sometimes spelled *-luc-*), meaning "light" or "shining."

Write the meanings of these words formed from the root *-lus-*: *illustrative*, *lackluster*, *elucidate*. Consult a dictionary as needed.

WORD NETWORK

Add words related to materialism from the text to your Word Network.

Analyze Craft and Structure

Narrative Structure Every story is driven by a **conflict**, or problem, that sets the plot in motion. The **plot** is the sequence of related events that make up the action of the story. The sequence of events in a plot can be divided into five parts that trace the introduction, development, and ending of the conflict.

- **Exposition:** The characters, setting, and basic situation are introduced.
- **Rising Action:** The central conflict begins and develops. Usually, an **inciting incident**, which is a pivotal event or situation, triggers the story's conflict.
- **Climax:** The story's conflict reaches its highest point of drama or tension.
- **Falling Action:** The tension in the story decreases, and the conflict moves toward resolution.
- **Resolution:** The conflict ends and any remaining issues are settled.

TIP

GROUP DISCUSSION

Everyone in your group may not agree about where the point of highest tension or drama occurs in the story. Honor different points of view, but also make sure that you support your perceptions with textual evidence.

Practice

CITE TEXTUAL EVIDENCE
to support your answers.

With your group, analyze the plot of "The Golden Touch." Use the chart to identify when the different plot stages occur. Identify the action that happens in each stage.

STAGE OF PLOT	DETAILS
Exposition	• Midas is introduced as a rich king. • Marygold is introduced. • The king's obsession with gold is described.
Inciting Incident and Rising Action	
Climax	
Falling Action	
Resolution	

Conventions

Types of Clauses Writers use various types of clauses to convey specific meanings. A **noun clause** is a type of subordinate clause that functions as a noun in a sentence—as a subject, a direct object, an indirect object, a subject complement, an object of a preposition, or an appositive. Noun clauses frequently begin with one of the following: *that, which, who, whom, whose, what, where, when, why, whether, how,* or *how much.*

This box shows examples of noun clauses and some of the ways they may function in a sentence.

 TIP

CLARIFICATION
Refer to the Grammar Handbook to learn more about these terms.

> EXAMPLE: <u>What the stranger gave Midas</u> was more a curse than a gift.
> FUNCTION: subject of the verb *was*
>
> EXAMPLE: Midas didn't know <u>whether the stranger would return</u>.
> FUNCTION: direct object of the verb *know*
>
> EXAMPLE: Midas was afraid of <u>how much harm his "gift" might cause</u>.
> FUNCTION: object of the preposition *of*
>
> EXAMPLE: Midas' biggest regret was <u>that he had hurt his daughter</u>.
> FUNCTION: subject complement of the noun *regret*

Read It

Work individually. Read these sentences from "The Golden Touch." Mark each noun clause. Then, identify its function in the sentence.

1. But now, if he looked at them at all, it was only to calculate how much the garden would be worth. . . .

2. . . . this linen fabric had been transmuted to what seemed a woven texture of the purest and brightest gold!

3. One was that the sands of the river sparkled like gold. . . .

Write It

Complete each sentence by filling in a noun clause. Then, write whether that noun clause functions in the sentence as a direct object, a subject, or a subject complement.

1. Midas suspected _____ .

2. Marygold's death was _____ .

3. _____ was not expected.

THE GOLDEN TOUCH

Comparing Texts

Now, you will read a twentieth-century poem that takes the King Midas tale in a very different direction. After you complete the first-read and close-read activities, you will compare the poem to Hawthorne's short story.

from KING MIDAS

About the Poet

Howard Moss (1922–1987) is best known as the poetry editor for the *New Yorker* magazine, a position he held for almost forty years, beginning in 1950. The *New Yorker*'s poetry editor holds a unique position in America's literary world. As editor, Moss was responsible for discovering and nurturing the careers of many of the twentieth century's most important poets. In fact, Moss was an accomplished poet himself and produced fourteen highly praised books of poetry during his career. In 1972, Moss won a National Book Award for his book *Selected Poems*.

from King Midas

Concept Vocabulary

As you perform your first read of the poem, you will encounter these words.

mail	obdurate	ore

Context Clues If these words are unfamiliar to you, try using **context clues**—other words and phrases that appear nearby in the text—to help you determine their meanings.

> **Synonyms:** Midas rules over his **dominion,** a <u>kingdom</u> spanning a portion of modern-day Turkey.
>
> **Contrast of Ideas:** Though usually <u>well-behaved</u>, the toddler was **incorrigible** when it came to long car rides.

Apply your knowledge of context clues and other vocabulary strategies to determine the meanings of unfamiliar words you encounter during your first read.

First Read POETRY

Apply these strategies as you conduct your first read. You will have an opportunity to complete a close read after your first read.

NOTICE who or what is "speaking" the poem and whether the poem tells a story or describes a single moment.

ANNOTATE by marking vocabulary and key passages you want to revisit.

CONNECT ideas within the selection to what you already know and what you have already read.

RESPOND by completing the Comprehension Check.

First Read

from

King Midas

Howard Moss

BACKGROUND

The Greek myth of King Midas identifies Midas as King of Phrygia, a region that is currently part of Turkey. As the story goes, one day some local farmers find a part-man, part-goat *satyr* asleep in their field and bring him to the king. Midas recognizes the creature as Silenus, a close companion of Dionysus, the god of grapes, wine, and festive merriment. Midas gives food and comfort to the satyr. Soon, Dionysus arrives and is grateful to Midas for treating his companion so generously. In recognition of this hospitality, Dionysus offers to grant Midas a single wish.

I. THE KING'S SPEECH

The palace clocks are stiff as coats of **mail**.
Time stopped; I flicked it with my fingernail.
My taste is shattered on these works of art
It fathers by a touch: My bread's too rich,
5 My butter much too golden, and my meat
A nugget on my plate as cold as ice;

Fresh water in my throat turns precious there,
Where every drop becomes a millionaire.

I rather would be blind than see this world
10 All affluent in yellow, bought and sold
By Kings that hammer roses into gold:
I did not know I loved their warring thorns
Until they flowered into spikes so hard
My blood made **obdurate** the rose's stem.
15 My God was generous. O much too much!
The nearest rose is now beyond my reach.

My furry cat is sculpture, my dog dead;
They stare at me with four wild sparkling eyes
That used to sparkle with dry wit; instead,
20 Having no wit that they can profit by,
They are pure profit, and their silences
Might make a King go mad, for it was I
Who made their lively muscles stiffly pose—
This jaundice[1] is relentless, and it grows.

25 Princess, come no closer; my rigid kiss,
Though it is royal still, will make you this
Or that kind of a statue. And my Queen,
Be armed against this gold paralysis,
Or you will starve and thinly bed alone,
30 And when you dream, a gold mine in your brain
Will have both eyes release their golden **ore**
And cry for tears they could not cry before.

I would be nothing but the dirt made loud,
A ripeness of the weeds, a timid sun,
35 Or oppositely be entirely cloud,
Absolved of matter, dissolving in the rain,
Or any small, anonymous live thing
Than be the reigning King of this dominion
Where gold makes poor the richness of decay.
40 O Dionysus, change me back to clay!

Mark context clues or indicate another strategy you used that helped you determine meaning.
obdurate (OB duhr iht) *adj.*
MEANING:

Mark context clues or indicate another strategy you used that helped you determine meaning.
ore (awr) *n.*
MEANING:

---

1. **jaundice** (JAWN dihs) *n.* disease that causes one's skin to turn yellow.

II. THE PRINCESS'S SONG

I praise the bird, the river, and the tree.
If I were deaf or dumb, I could not see
Imagination is the heart of me.

A falling leaf in fall's a thing to mourn.
45 When river beds are dry, nothing is born.
Dear sparrow, sing your song this blessed morn.

Divided into two, I am a tree.
The branches are too high for me to see,
The roots too hidden from reality.

50 They say that veins of gold lie underground.
Beware, explorers, of the spoil you find:
Though you sail back and forth, you sail around.

The laurel grows upon the laurel tree.
Apollo[2] plucked the string of mystery
55 And made a golden echo in the sea.

III. THE QUEEN'S SPEECH

May every child of mine be barren, golden!
May every mammal turn to golden swine!
Here is a list, O gardeners and huntsmen,
Of what to kill and what to leave alone:
60 All natural things must go excepting those
That are by nature golden. Whatever grows
The King's touchy color let live, but close
Your nets upon the pink and crimson rose.

But I will save one rose tree in this pot
65 That I may gaze at it, and when he's not
About, I'll look and look till light is gone
At flower, petal, stem, and leaf. And then,
I'll ponder how a King became a fool!
Long live King Midas! And the Golden Rule!

---

2. **Apollo** (uh POL oh) Greek god of light and music.

Comprehension Check

Complete the following items after you finish your first read. Review and clarify details with your group.

1. What causes the palace clocks to stop at the beginning of the poem?

2. What has happened to the pets in the king's household?

3. At the end of "The King's Speech," what request does Midas make to the god that gave him the golden touch?

4. What orders does the Queen give to her gardeners and huntsmen?

5. How does the Queen view Midas and his wish?

- -

RESEARCH

Research to Clarify Choose at least one unfamiliar detail from the text. Briefly research that detail. In what way does the information you learned shed light on an aspect of the poem?

Research to Explore Find out more about retellings or adaptations of Greek myths. Which popular books and movies are based on these ancient stories?

MAKING MEANING

Close Read

With your group, revisit sections of the text you marked during your first read. **Annotate** details that you notice. What **questions** do you have? What can you **conclude**?

from KING MIDAS

Analyze the Text

Complete the activities.

1. **Review and Clarify** With your group, reread lines 1–8 of "The King's Speech." Based on the speaker's descriptions, what are some words and phrases you might use to describe Midas?

2. **Present and Discuss** Now, work with your group to share the passages from the text that you found especially important. Take turns presenting your passages. Discuss what you noticed in the text, what questions you asked and what conclusions you reached.

3. **Essential Question:** *What do our possessions reveal about us?* What has this selection taught you about materialism? Discuss with your group.

TIP

GROUP DISCUSSION
Hawthorne's story shows King Midas both before and after he gains "the golden touch." Moss's poem begins after Midas has received this gift. Consider how this change affects how you see the king and why the poet may have made this choice.

LANGUAGE DEVELOPMENT

Concept Vocabulary

mail	obdurate	ore

Why These Words? The three concept vocabulary words are related. With your group, determine what the words have in common. Write your ideas, and add another word that fits the category.

Practice

 Notebook Write a fill-in-the-blank sentence for each concept word, leaving a space where the word would be. Trade your work with another group member. Challenge each other to identify each missing word.

WORD NETWORK

Add words related to materialism from the text to your Word Network.

Word Study

Latin Root: -dur- In "King Midas," the speaker laments that his touch has made a rose's stem obdurate. The word *obdurate* is formed from the Latin root -*dur*-, meaning "hard," "strong," or "lasting." Write the meanings of these words formed from the root -*dur*-: *endure, duration, durable*. Use a print or online dictionary to verify your definitions.

from KING MIDAS

Analyze Craft and Structure

Author's Choices: Poetic Structure The way in which a poet organizes a poem is referred to as **poetic structure.** Two of the main building blocks of poetic structure are stanzas and rhyme.

- **Stanza:** A stanza is a group of lines, usually separated from other stanzas by space. Stanzas are named according to their number of lines, as follows: *couplet:* a two-line stanza; *tercet:* a three-line stanza; *quatrain:* a four-line stanza; *sestet:* a six-line stanza; *octave:* an eight-line stanza.

- **Rhyme:** Rhyme is the repetition of sounds at the ends of words. **Exact rhyme** is the use of identical sounds, as in *love* and *dove.* **Slant rhyme** is the use of similar sounds that do not match perfectly, as in *prove* and *glove.*

- **Rhyme Scheme:** A regular pattern of **end rhyme**—or rhyming words at the ends of lines—is called a rhyme scheme. Rhyme schemes are identified by the use of letters, with one letter assigned to each rhyming sound. For example, in "When You Are Old," William Butler Yeats uses the rhyme scheme *abba*:

When you are old and gray and full of *sleep,*	*a*
And nodding by the fire, take down this *book,*	*b*
And slowly read, and dream of the soft *look,*	*b*
Your eyes had once, and of their shadows *deep;*	*a*

Practice

CITE TEXTUAL EVIDENCE to support your answers.

In the chart, use the letters *a, b, c,* and so on to identify the rhyming sounds that end each line from "The Queen's Speech." Then, note whether each pair of rhymes is exact or slant.

LINE	RHYMING SOUND	EXACT OR SLANT
But I will save one rose tree in this pot		
That I may gaze at it, and when he's not		
About, I'll look and look till light is gone		
At flower, petal, stem, and leaf. And then,		
I'll ponder how a King became a fool!		
Long live King Midas! And the Golden Rule!		

📓 **Notebook** Respond to these questions.

1. Why do you think the poet chose to vary stanza lengths for each section of the poem? How do the different types of stanzas reflect the ways in which each speaker thinks and feels?

2. Note the rhyme schemes of "The King's Speech" and "The Princess's Song." How do the two rhyme schemes affect your reading of these sections? Why might the second section be called a "song"?

Author's Style

Author's Choices: Poetic Structure In poetry, the arrangement of stressed (´) and unstressed (˘) syllables is called **meter.** The basic unit of meter is the **foot,** which usually consists of one stressed and one or more unstressed syllables. The most frequently used foot in American poetry is the **iamb**—one unstressed syllable followed by a stressed syllable. The type and number of feet in the lines of a poem determine its meter. For example, a pattern of five iambs per line is known as *iambic pentameter* (the prefix *penta-* means "five"). The sections from "King Midas" are written in iambic pentameter.

Poets also use **enjambment,** or the continuation of a sentence past a line break. Enjambment allows the poet to continue the flow of ideas and also maintain a metrical pattern. For instance, in "The King's Speech," the sentence that begins in line 9 ends in line 11.

Read It

Work individually. Reread the first stanza of "The King's Speech." Use a vertical rule to separate individual feet. Then, mark the stressed (´) and unstressed (˘) syllables of each foot. Note: The poet may deviate from strict iambic pentameter, perhaps by including two stressed syllables or more than two syllables in a foot, or by using fewer than five feet per line. Identify these variations, and consider how they add to the poem's meaning. The first line has been marked for you. After all members of your group have finished marking the stanza, compare and discuss your work.

The pál | ace clocks | are still | as coats | of mail

Time stopped; I flicked it with my fingernail.

My taste is shattered on these works of art

It fathers by a touch: My bread's too rich,

My butter much too golden, and my meat

A nugget on my plate as cold as ice;

Fresh water in my throat turns precious there,

Where every drop becomes a millionaire.

Write It

Notebook Write a short poem based on the King Midas story, using iambic pentameter. You may choose whether to use either uniform or varied stanza lengths, as well as whether or not to use rhyme.

THE GOLDEN TOUCH

from KING MIDAS

Writing to Compare

You have read a short story and a poem, both of which retell the Midas myth. The myth of King Midas is one of the central cautionary tales of Western culture. Midas is blessed with the golden touch, only to discover that the power to create unlimited wealth might actually be worthless. Deepen your understanding of the ways in which the form of a work influences its meaning by comparing and writing about the presentation of the same story in different genres.

Assignment

Write a **compare-and-contrast essay** in which you analyze the portrayals of the characters in the two retellings of the Midas myth. Consider how the form of each text shapes the information the writer includes and contributes to readers' understanding of the characters and their conflicts. Work with your group to analyze the texts. Then, work independently to write your essay.

Prewriting

Notebook Complete the activity, and answer the questions that follow.

Analyze the Texts With your group, identify details about the characters that appear in both the short story and the poem. Then, identify details about characters that appear in only one text or the other.

DETAILS IN BOTH TEXTS	DETAILS IN POEM ONLY	DETAILS IN STORY ONLY

1. How does your understanding of King Midas change as you read the two texts? In which work do you learn more about what Midas feels and thinks? Explain.

2. How does your understanding of the princess change as you read the two texts? In which text is her character more developed?

3. What does the princess symbolize in the two texts? Does her character have the same meaning in the story that it does in the poem? Explain.

Drafting

Write a Statement of Purpose Determine the specific purpose, or goal, of your essay. Then, write a statement of purpose that you can use in your introduction. Include both the authors' names and the titles in your statement. Complete this sentence to get started:

Statement of Purpose: In this essay, I will analyze _____ _____ and show how _____.

Organize Ideas In this essay, you will identify similarities and differences in characters' portrayals in two works. Do you think the differences or the similarities are more important? Focus your essay by emphasizing the elements you feel matter the most.

Identify Passages Use your Prewriting notes to identify specific passages from the short story and the poem to use in your essay.

Example Passage: _____

Point It Will Support: _____

Example Passage: _____

Point It Will Support: _____

Example Passage: _____

Point It Will Support: _____

Example Passage: _____

Point It Will Support: _____

Write a Rough Draft Use your notes and evidence to produce a first draft. If you suspect something is not quite right, make a note in brackets: for example, "[find a more accurate transitional word]." Then, continue to write. You can go back later and clarify your meaning or fix any issues.

Review, Revise, and Edit

Read your draft aloud to your group. Take a moment to write down ideas that occur to you as you read. Then, ask your peers for feedback.

- Can they follow the logic of your ideas?
- Should any information be cut or replaced?
- Are any explanations vague or unconvincing?
- Is all the textual evidence on point, or does some fail to support the ideas?

Use the feedback to revise your draft. Then, finalize your essay by editing and proofreading it.

> **✎ EVIDENCE LOG**
>
> Before moving on to a new selection, go to your Evidence Log and record what you learned from "The Golden Touch," and the excerpts from "King Midas."

About the Author

Margie Goldsmith

(b. 1945) is a writer, an athlete, a filmmaker, and a novelist. Most of all, she is an adventurer who has traveled to 130 different countries to research the articles she has written. Writing for such publications as *National Geographic* and the *New York Times,* Goldsmith has reported on some of the world's most exotic locales, including Tibet, Antarctica, Easter Island, and Borneo. When she isn't trekking to some far-flung place, Goldsmith lives in New York City, where she likes to explore the wilds of Central Park.

The Thrill of the Chase

Concept Vocabulary

As you perform your first read of "The Thrill of the Chase," you will encounter the following words.

artifacts	legacy	marvel

Context Clues If these words are unfamiliar to you, try using **context clues**—other words or phrases that appear nearby in the text—to help you determine their meanings. There are various types of context clues that may help you as you read.

Restatement: With the boat caught in the teeth of the **tempest,** the crew buckled down against the raging storm.

Elaborating Details: Its wheels screeching and its pistons clattering, the train arrived with a **cacophony.**

Contrast of Ideas: It was quite a surprise to see how dull, slow, and miserable the flu had made Oliver, after his **effervescent** conversation of the night before.

Apply your knowledge of context clues and other vocabulary strategies to determine the meanings of unfamiliar words you encounter during your first read.

First Read NONFICTION

Apply these strategies as you conduct your first read. You will have an opportunity to complete a close read after your first read.

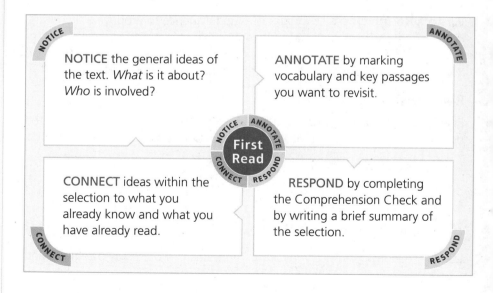

NOTICE the general ideas of the text. *What* is it about? *Who* is involved?

ANNOTATE by marking vocabulary and key passages you want to revisit.

CONNECT ideas within the selection to what you already know and what you have already read.

RESPOND by completing the Comprehension Check and by writing a brief summary of the selection.

The
Thrill
of the
Chase

Margie Goldsmith

BACKGROUND

This article chronicles the controversies surrounding a modern-day hunt for a real-life buried treasure. Fascination with buried treasure probably has its origin with the pirate William Kidd, who was said to have buried a chest full of gold doubloons somewhere on Long Island in the seventeenth century. Though Kidd's treasure was never found, it spawned a host of stories and legends. In the United States, pirate legends soon evolved into Wild West legends in which notorious bank robbers, outlaws, and prospectors hid their riches in remote mountain wilderness areas. Very few of these mysterious treasures have ever been found.

1   Blame Ralph Lauren. In 1996 the designer paid a visit to his friend Forrest Fenn, who lived in Santa Fe, NM. Fenn had recently undergone chemo and radiation for kidney cancer, and was told there was only a 20 percent chance for his survival. He sold his successful Santa Fe art gallery and settled in to await the inevitable. While he did, many friends stopped by to visit him and his wife at home.

2   The place was filled with more than 5,000 pieces of museum-quality Southwestern art and **artifacts**, from Sitting Bull's[1] pipe and an 18th-century painted buffalo skin to early Indian pottery and rare Plains Indian medicine bonnets. Lauren immediately fell in love with a Crow Indian hat covered in white ermine skins and carved antelope horns, and offered to buy it. Fenn refused, saying it was one of his favorites. Lauren said, "Well, you can't take it with you." To which Fenn replied, "Then I'm not going."

3   Though the hat remained safely ensconced in Fenn's collection, Lauren's visit gave the ailing art collector an idea. Inspired by the adventure stories he had devoured as a child, Fenn sat down to write a memoir, jotting down scenes and remembrances as they came to him. As an Air Force pilot during the Vietnam War, he flew 328 missions and was shot down twice. After the war he turned to art,

NOTES

Mark context clues or indicate another strategy you used that helped you determine meaning.

artifacts (AHR tuh fakts) *n.*

MEANING:

---

1. **Sitting Bull** (1831–1890) Native American chief of the Sioux tribe.

Mark context clues or indicate another strategy you used that helped you determine meaning.

legacy (LEHG uh see) *n.*

MEANING:

settling in Santa Fe with his wife, Peggy, and opening Fenn Gallery, which became the most successful art gallery in New Mexico. Fenn's holdings included Remingtons and Russells and O'Keeffes—every big name in Western art—and many of those works are now in museums ranging from the Buffalo Bill Historical Center in Cody, Wyo., to the Art Institute of Chicago. Buying and selling art was how Fenn came to know Lauren, yes, but also Robert Redford, Jacqueline Onassis, Sam Shepard, Jessica Lange, Steven Spielberg, and Donna Karan.[2]

4   And that's when things got interesting. As he wrote, Fenn was reminded of how much fun he'd had hunting down fine art pieces and building his collection over the decades. He felt it would be a shame if all that ended with his death. The memoir would help preserve his **legacy**, of course—but as he saw it, there was only one way to pass along that sense of delight, that thrill of the hunt.

5   So Fenn bought an antique bronze chest and started to fill it with treasures. The booty included a jar full of gold dust panned in Alaska, gold coins, large and small gold nuggets, pre-Columbian[3] gold animal figures, two ancient Chinese jade carvings, a 17th-century Spanish gold and emerald ring and a beloved bracelet of turquoise beads, excavated from a Mesa Verde[4] ruin in 1903, that Fenn had won in a game of pool. The total value amounted to about $3 million.

6   Fenn decided he would hide the chest with a copy of his book in the desert, maybe even as he walked out into the wilderness to die. That could trigger a hunt of its own, spark some excitement; one day an intrepid searcher would find his bones and his treasure and learn who he was, think kindly of him. His memory would live on.

7   It seemed like a perfect plan. Except for one hitch.

8   Fenn didn't die.

9   Forrest Fenn's cancer went into remission—and it stayed that way. As a result, he didn't quite get around to burying that treasure. More than a dozen years passed.

10 Then, in 2010, Fenn turned 80, and the milestone spurred him back into action. "I had this treasure chest full of gold and jewels just burning a hole in my vault," he says. "So I decided to go ahead and hide it somewhere in the mountains north of Santa Fe, leaving clues on how to find it for any searcher willing to try."

11 The clues are encoded in the memoir he self-published that year, *The Thrill of the Chase*. There are nine of them, all contained in a single poem Fenn wrote.

12   *As I have gone alone in there*
        And with my treasures bold,
        I can keep my secret where,
        And hint of riches new and old.

---

2. **Robert Redford . . . Donna Karan** American celebrities.
3. **pre-Columbian** of or relating to the history and cultures of the Americas before the arrival of Christopher Columbus in 1492.
4. **Mesa Verde** high plateau in southern Colorado.

13   *Begin it where warm waters halt*
      And take it in the canyons down,
      Not far, but too far to walk.
      Put in below the home of Brown.

14   *From there it's no place for the meek,*
      The end is ever drawing nigh;
      There'll be no paddle up your creek,
      Just heavy loads and water high.

15   *If you've been wise and found the blaze,*
      Look quickly down, your quest to cease,
      But tarry scant with marvel gaze,
      Just take the chest and go in peace.

16   *So why is it that I must go*
      And leave my trove for all to seek?
      The answer I already know,
      I've done it tired, and now I'm weak.

17   *So hear me all and listen good,*
      Your effort will be worth the cold.
      If you are brave and in the wood
      I give you title to the gold.

NOTES

Mark context clues or indicate another strategy you used that helped you determine meaning.

marvel (MAHR vuhl) *n.*

MEANING:

18   As word spread about what Fenn had done, treasure hunters rushed to Santa Fe. Based on the 5,000-plus emails he has received about the treasure, he estimates that more than 1,000 people have searched for it, though he assumes there must be others out there that he doesn't know about.

19   Many who contact Fenn are looking for a little extra help; others simply want to share their stories. "Dear Mr. Fenn," wrote one, "we don't think we will find the treasure chest but I just want to thank you for getting me and my family off of the couch and out into the mountains." Another man told of how he went out to look with his grown son. The two slept in a van and talked about their hopes for the future. They gave up the search after two days, but it wasn't a wasted effort, the father wrote. "If it hadn't been for the book, my son and I would never have had this time with each other."

20   Which isn't to say the quest should be undertaken lightly. "There are dangers involved," Fenn says." Things can complicate the search—earthquakes, mudslides, forest fires, floods, trees, falling rocks. There are those who have been at risk in water when they attempted to search someplace where it was not really safe to go. Some have not been prepared to face the elements after they parked their car and started walking. Some have lacked the proper clothing, food, and water."

21   One eager individual donned scuba gear and swam along the bottom of a murky lake until he almost ran out of air. Another "rode

28 miles on a bicycle in the snow and almost froze after getting wet," Fenn says.

22   Still, the treasure hunters keep coming. One Chicago couple, for instance, has traveled to New Mexico 14 times to look for Fenn's prize. (In an email, the wife told Fenn, "We are experts on where the treasure is not.")

23   "What serious adventurers should remember," Fenn says, "is to not believe anything that is not in my poem or otherwise in my book. There's some misinformation out there. For instance, I never said I buried the chest, I said only that I hid it. That is not to say it is not buried, so maybe we need to define the terms. Does 'hidden' mean in plain sight? What is the difference between 'buried,' 'entombed,' and 'sepultured'? What does the word 'blaze' in the poem mean? A horse can have a blaze on its forehead, a blaze can be scraped on a tree to mark one's way, a blaze can mean a flame or a scar on a rock. And what about 'water high'? Does it mean deep, or higher than normal?"

24   Fenn generally refuses to give additional clues, but he'll make the rare exception—of sorts. When one woman emailed him to complain that the clues were too difficult, he told her the treasure chest is located more than 300 miles west of Toledo.

25   Beyond queries from treasure seekers, Fenn has also received a number of letters from people simply wondering why on earth he would do this. "I wanted to create some intrigue and adventure and maybe a little mystery," Fenn explains.

26   Plus, he says, "Anyone who dies with over $50 is a failure."

27   Finding Fenn's treasure has proved so difficult that some are left questioning whether the whole thing is an elaborate hoax. But doubters need only ask Fenn's friend Douglas Preston, a bestselling author whose novel *The Codex* is based on Fenn's story.

28   "That gold is out there—I held it with my own hands," says Preston, one of the few to have seen the chest before Fenn hid it. "Some of the most wonderful things in the treasure are enormous gold nuggets the size of hen's eggs, weighing more than a pound each, and worth several times their bullion value. He included things that would survive a long time, and that would be interesting and unusual. And the chest itself is quite rare; it's a Romanesque lockbox from the 12th century, and with the gold and jewels inside, it weighs 42 pounds."

29   Surprisingly, there have been only a few items about the treasure in the local newspaper or on the news. But there are certainly other signs of it around Santa Fe. The Inn and Spa at Loretto offers guests a "Thrill of the Chase" package, which includes two nights' accommodations, a scavenger hunt, and an autographed copy of Fenn's book. There's also a "Thrill of the Chase" signature cocktail, a blend of light rum, sweet vermouth, and Amaretto di Saronno sprinkled with gold flakes, and a Forrest Fenn sandwich, consisting of pastrami with apple sauerkraut on marble rye (Fenn's favorite).

30   When Fenn himself walks down the street these days, locals constantly stop him; they want to know if anyone has found the

treasure. Others shake his hand and call him a hero. Local jeweler Marc Howard hails Fenn as a cross between Will Rogers[5] and Mark Twain. "He's a story-weaver, and has created a legacy that will reach out into the future."

31   Fenn is modest about the whole thing, though. "I was hoping the treasure chase would cause some excitement and get a few guys out into the mountains," he says. "I did not expect it to get so big so fast."

32   He hasn't gone back to his hiding place to see if the treasure is still there. He assumes it hasn't been found (though he knows of "more than a few people" who have searched within 500 feet of the site), and that suits him fine. "I think that I'll be a little disappointed when it is found, because the mystery will be gone."

33   One clue follower, Dal Neitzel, has been looking for the treasure for more than two years. He's already made five trips down from his home in Washington State, and plans to keep looking. Not that the booty is Neitzel's primary motivation: Fenn's treasure hunt has turned into something bigger, something more meaningful.

34   "Forrest Fenn is the hider of undiscovered dreams for thousands of folks who go looking for that treasure," he says, "and discover not the place where the treasure is hidden, but the place in their heart where adventure sleeps, and trails begin." ❧

---

5. **Will Rogers** (1879–1935) famous American cowboy, vaudeville performer, movie actor, and newspaper columnist during the 1920s and 1930s.

Comprehension Check

Complete the following items after you finish your first read. Review and clarify details with your group.

1. How did Forrest Fenn make a living in Santa Fe?

2. What did Fenn put in his treasure chest?

3. What clues does Fenn provide for the location of the treasure?

4. 📓 **Notebook** To confirm your understanding, write a summary of the article.

- -

RESEARCH

Research to Clarify Choose at least one unfamiliar detail from the text. Briefly research that detail. In what way does the information you learned shed light on an aspect of the article?

THE THRILL OF THE CHASE

TIP

GROUP DISCUSSION
Be an active listener. As members of your group share key passages and explain their choices, give them your full attention. Ask questions, such as "Could you say more about that?" or "What sentence or paragraph in the text led you to that conclusion?"

WORD NETWORK
Add words related to materialism from the text to your Word Network.

Close Read the Text

With your group, revisit sections of the text you marked during your first read. **Annotate** details that you notice. What **questions** do you have? What can you **conclude**?

Analyze the Text

CITE TEXTUAL EVIDENCE
to support your answers.

Notebook **Complete the activities.**

1. **Review and Clarify** With your group, reread paragraphs 25–28 of the selection. What would you say to someone who claims that Fenn's treasure is nothing more than a hoax? Explain.

2. **Present and Discuss** Work with your group to share other key passages from "The Thrill of the Chase." Take turns presenting your choices. Discuss what you noticed in the text, what questions you asked, and what conclusions you reached.

3. **Essential Question:** *What do our possessions reveal about us?* What has this article taught you about materialism? Discuss with your group.

LANGUAGE DEVELOPMENT

Concept Vocabulary

artifacts	legacy	marvel

Why These Words? The three concept vocabulary words are related. With your group, determine what the words have in common. Write your ideas, and add another word that fits the category.

Practice

Notebook Write a sentence using each of the concept words. Use a thesaurus to replace each concept word with a synonym. Discuss with your group how your substitutions affect the meanings of your sentences.

Word Study

Notebook **Latin Root:-fac-** In "The Thrill of the Chase," Goldsmith discusses a home filled with thousands of artifacts. The word *artifacts* is formed from the Latin root *-fac-* (sometimes spelled *-fic-*), meaning "to make" or "to do."

Write the meanings of these words formed from the root *-fac-: manufacture*, *artificial*, *edifice*. Use a print or online dictionary to verify your definitions.

Analyze Craft and Structure

Literary Nonfiction: Feature Story "The Thrill of the Chase" is an example of a **feature story**, a type of journalism that appears in magazines and other periodicals. A feature story typically covers a high-interest topic in an extended format that allows the author to explore ideas or events in depth. This form of nonfiction contains elements that are closely associated with fiction and often not found in news stories. For example, a feature story may contain description and imagery. A feature story may also include the author's own analysis of events and ideas, in contrast with more impersonal kinds of journalism.

Feature stories typically follow this organizational pattern:

- **Title:** The title captures readers' interest.
- **Introduction:** The first few paragraphs set the scene and identify the main idea.
- **Body:** The middle section presents facts, quotations, and examples to tell what happened and develop ideas. The extended format allows the writer to explore and refine information with more complexity than shorter-form journalism. The body may use subheadings or other formatting to clarify details and orient the reader.
- **Conclusion:** The story ends with a quotation or image that leaves readers with a lasting impression.

Practice

CITE TEXTUAL EVIDENCE
to support your answers.

With your group, review the article to identify how the author uses specific sentences, paragraphs, and sections to introduce, develop, and refine her ideas. Capture your observations in the chart.

SECTION OF ARTICLE	IDEA(S) INTRODUCED / DEVELOPED / REFINED
Title: "The Thrill of the Chase"	
Introduction: paragraphs 1–5	
Body: paragraphs 6–11	
Body: paragraphs 12–17	
Body: paragraphs 18–25	
Body: paragraphs 26–30	
Conclusion: paragraphs 31–34	

THE THRILL OF THE CHASE

Author's Style

Sentence Variety A skilled writer uses words the way a musician uses musical notes. In the same way that a musician will build and elaborate on a motif or melody, authors clarify and develop ideas and claims with **sentence variety.** Using sentences of different lengths allows an author to vary the effect of the text on the reader.

- **Long sentences** add rhythm, substance, complexity, and detail. Long sentences are often useful for explaining, comparing, and providing examples.
- **Short sentences** add drama and impact. They provide "punch" and directness.
- **Varied sentence lengths** give a text rhythm, musicality, and pace that keep the reader interested and make the text easier to understand.

Read It

Work together with your group to analyze sentence variety in the article by examining the paragraphs listed in the chart. Explain how the sentence variety in each paragraph enhances meaning, clarifies ideas, develops an image, or otherwise affects the reader's experience of the text.

PARAGRAPH	SENTENCE VARIETY/EFFECT ON READER
1	• Short sentence grabs your attention. • Long second sentence adds detail through explanation.
4	
10	
20	
23	

Write It

📝 **Notebook** Work on your own to write a paragraph explaining the steps you would take to find Forrest Fenn's treasure. Use sentence variety in your paragraph.

Speaking and Listening

Assignment

With your group, conduct a **debate** on one of the following questions.

☐ **Is Forrest Fenn's motivation for hiding the treasure and creating the mystery admirable?**

As you choose a position, consider the following: What is Fenn's stated goal in hiding the treasure? Does the goal seem credible? Does he back it up with his actions?

☐ **According to Fenn, "Anyone who dies with more than $50 is a failure." Do you agree with this statement?**

As you choose a position, consider the following: What about people who want to leave their money to their children or a good charity—are they failures?

☐ **Is it pointless to spend time looking for a treasure that might never be found?**

As you choose a position, consider the following: How would the treasure hunters feel if they found out there is no treasure? Would that change their feelings about the experience?

EVIDENCE LOG

Before moving on to a new selection, go to your Evidence Log and record what you learned from "The Thrill of the Chase."

1. **Support a Position** As a group, choose the question you will discuss. Then, work independently to decide your position. Identify at least three specific reasons for your position as well as passages from Goldsmith's article that you could use to illustrate your points. Collect your ideas in the chart.

SUPPORTING REASONS	SUPPORTING PASSAGES OR OTHER EVIDENCE
1.	
2.	
3.	

2. **Debate the Question** Gather with your group, and invite each group member to present his or her response and evidence. Take turns discussing and analyzing one another's positions. Ask questions, and clarify your responses. Work together to reach a conclusion that identifies the strongest argument. This may draw on points from several group members. Summarize your conclusion, and then share it with the class as a whole.

Deliver a Multimedia Presentation

Assignment

You have read about individuals, families, and societies who pursue material possessions in some form. Work with your group to develop and refine a **multimedia presentation** that addresses this question:

> **In what ways can material possessions create both a sense of comfort and a sense of anxiety?**

As you review the articles, poems, and short story you have read, remember to consider the positive and negative aspects of the hunt for material possessions. Incorporate media and information from outside sources to support your ideas.

Plan With Your Group

Analyze the Texts With your group, discuss the various ways in which material possessions affect the comfort level or anxiety level of the individuals, families, and nations in the texts you have read. Use the chart to list your ideas. For each selection, identify the emotional and physical effects created by material possessions. Then, write a thesis statement about the relationship between material possessions and a person's state of mind.

TITLE	EFFECTS OF MATERIAL POSSESSIONS
In La Rinconada, Peru, Searching for Beauty in Ugliness	
Avarice The Good Life Money	
The Golden Touch	
from King Midas	
The Thrill of the Chase	
Relationship between possessions and emotional state:	

Gather Evidence and Media Examples Scan the selections to record specific examples that support your group's thesis. Then, brainstorm and search for images and media you can use to illustrate each example. Consider photographs, illustrations, music, graphs, and videos. Allow each group member to make suggestions.

Organize Your Ideas Review your notes and media choices as a group, and choose the strongest examples to include in your presentation. Once you have reached a decision, assign roles for each part of the presentation.

Rehearse With Your Group

Practice With Your Group Use this checklist to evaluate the effectiveness of your group's first run-through. Then, use your evaluation and the instructions here to guide your revision.

CONTENT	USE OF MEDIA	PRESENTATION TECHNIQUES
☐ The presentation presents a clear thesis.	☐ The media support the thesis.	☐ Media are visible and audible.
☐ Main ideas are supported with evidence from the texts in Small-Group Learning.	☐ The media communicate key ideas.	☐ Transitions between media segments are smooth.
☐ The presentation conveys information coherently.	☐ Media are used evenly throughout the presentation.	☐ The speaker uses voice and gestures effectively.
	☐ Equipment functions properly.	

Fine-Tune the Content To make your presentation stronger, consider whether you have included sufficient details and examples to support your main ideas. You may need to add more information from your sources to ensure your key points are clear to listeners.

Improve Your Use of Media Make sure that you have used media effectively in your presentation. Remember that visuals help the audience draw connections among ideas in a presentation. Choose memorable and relevant media to best support your group's main ideas.

Brush Up on Your Presentation Techniques Demonstrate confidence in your ideas through your posture, bearing, and facial expression.

- Make eye contact with all your listeners, not just one or two people.
- Vary the volume, tone, and pacing of your voice to emphasize key points and to keep your audience engaged.
- Use appropriate gestures to support what you are saying.

Present and Evaluate

When you present as a group, be sure that each member has taken into account each of the checklist items. As you watch other groups, evaluate how well they meet the checklist requirements.

ESSENTIAL QUESTION:

What do our possessions reveal about us?

In this section, you will complete your study of materialism by exploring an additional selection related to the topic. You'll then share what you learn with classmates. To choose a text, follow these steps.

Look Back Think about the selections you have already studied. What more do you want to know about the topic of materialism?

Look Ahead Preview the texts by reading the descriptions. Which one seems more interesting and appealing to you?

Look Inside Take a few minutes to scan the text you chose. Choose a different one if this text doesn't meet your needs.

Independent Learning Strategies

Throughout your life, in school, in your community, and in your career, you will need to rely on yourself to learn and work on your own. Review these strategies and the actions you can take to practice them during Independent Learning. Add ideas of your own to each category.

STRATEGY	ACTION PLAN
Create a schedule	• Understand your goals and deadlines. • Make a plan for what to do each day. •
Practice what you have learned	• Use first-read and close-read strategies to deepen your understanding. • After you read, evaluate the usefulness of the evidence to help you understand the topic. • Consider the quality and reliability of the source. •
Take notes	• Record important ideas and information. • Review your notes before preparing to share with a group. •

Choose one selection. Selections are available online only.

First-Read Guide

Use this page to record your first-read ideas.

Tool Kit
First-Read Guide and
Model Annotation

Selection Title: _____

NOTICE new information or ideas you learn about the unit topic as you first read this text.

ANNOTATE by marking vocabulary and key passages you want to revisit.

First Read
NOTICE ANNOTATE
CONNECT RESPOND

CONNECT ideas within the selection to other knowledge and the selections you have read.

RESPOND by writing a brief summary of the selection.

Close-Read Guide

Use this page to record your close-read ideas.

Selection Title: _____

⊘ **Tool Kit**
Close-Read Guide and
Model Annotation

Close Read the Text

Revisit sections of the text you marked during your first read. Read these sections closely and **annotate** what you notice. Ask yourself **questions** about the text. What can you **conclude?** Write down your ideas.

Analyze the Text

Think about the author's choices of patterns, structure, techniques, and ideas included in the text. Select one and record your thoughts about what this choice conveys.

QuickWrite

Pick a paragraph from the text that grabbed your interest. Explain the power of this passage.

✏ EVIDENCE LOG

Go to your Evidence Log and record what you learned from the text you read.

Share Your Independent Learning

Prepare to Share

What do our possessions reveal about us?

Even when you read or learn something independently, you can continue to grow by sharing what you have learned with others. Reflect on the text you explored independently, and write notes about its connection to the unit. In your notes, consider why this text belongs in this unit.

Learn From Your Classmates

💬 **Discuss It** Share your ideas about the text you explored on your own. As you talk with your classmates, jot down ideas that you learn from them.

Reflect

Review your notes, and mark the most important insight you gained from these writing and discussion activities. Explain how this idea adds to your understanding of the topic of materialism.

Review Evidence for an Informative Essay

At the beginning of this unit, you responded to the following questions:

> How do we decide what we want versus what we need?
> What can result from an imbalance between want and need?

✎ EVIDENCE LOG

Review your Evidence Log and your QuickWrite from the beginning of the unit. What have you learned?

☐ NEW IDEAS	☐ REINFORCED IDEAS
Identify at least three pieces of evidence that showed you something new.	Identify at least three pieces of evidence that reinforced your initial perspective.
1.	**1.**
2.	**2.**
3.	**3.**

State your response to the prompt now in the form of a thesis statement: ___

_____

_____

Identify at least one way to develop your thesis: _____

_____

_____

Evaluate the Strength of Your Evidence Consider your informative essay. Do you have facts to support your thesis? Will you be able to use quotations from various sources? If not, make a plan.

☐ Conduct research   ☐ Talk with classmates

☐ Reread a selection   ☐ Ask an expert

☐ Other: _____

SOURCES

- WHOLE-CLASS SELECTIONS
- SMALL-GROUP SELECTIONS
- INDEPENDENT-LEARNING SELECTION

PART 1

Writing to Sources: Informative Essay

In this unit, you read about various characters, both real and fictional, who found themselves questioning what is valuable. Each had to make choices between what he or she needed and what he or she wanted.

Assignment

Write an **informative essay** in which you examine a topic and convey ideas, concepts, and information related to the following questions:

> How do we decide what we want versus what we need? What can result from an imbalance between want and need?

Use credible evidence from at least three of the selections you read and researched in this unit to support your ideas. Ensure that you introduce your topic; develop the topic with relevant facts, details, and quotations; establish a clear organization of both primary and secondary ideas; and use appropriate and varied transitions. Also, consider using headings or other formatting options to clarify the organization of your ideas and aid readers' comprehension.

Reread the Assignment Review the assignment to be sure you fully understand it. The task may reference some of the academic words presented at the beginning of the unit. Be sure you understand each of the words here in order to complete the assignment correctly.

Academic Vocabulary

paradox	allocate	primary
chronicle	deduce	

WORD NETWORK

As you write and revise your informative essay, use your Word Network to help vary your word choices.

Review the Elements of Effective Informative Texts Before you begin writing, read the Informative Rubric. Once you have completed your first draft, check it against the rubric. If one or more of the elements is missing or not as strong as it could be, revise your essay to add or strengthen that component.

Informative Rubric

	Focus and Organization	Evidence and Elaboration	Conventions
4	The introduction engages the reader and states a thesis in a very effective way. The essay includes formatting, graphics, and multimedia when useful to aiding comprehension. The conclusion summarizes ideas and readdresses the thesis.	The topic is developed with well-chosen, relevant, and sufficient facts, extended definitions, concrete details, quotations, or other information appropriate to the audience's knowledge of the topic. The language is always precise and appropriate for the audience and purpose. The tone of the essay is always formal and objective.	The essay intentionally uses standard English conventions of usage and mechanics. Transitions are appropriately varied to link major sections of the text, create cohesion, and clarify the relationships among complex ideas and concepts.
3	The introduction engages the reader and sets forth the thesis. The essay includes some formatting, graphics, and multimedia when useful to aiding comprehension. The conclusion offers some insight into the thesis and summarizes ideas.	The topic is mostly developed with well-chosen, relevant, and sufficient facts, extended definitions, concrete details, quotations, or other information appropriate to the audience's knowledge of the topic. The language is mostly precise and appropriate for the audience and purpose. The tone of the essay is mostly formal and objective.	The essay demonstrates general accuracy in standard English conventions of usage and mechanics. Transitions are mostly varied to link major sections of the text, create cohesion, and clarify the relationships among complex ideas and concepts.
2	The introduction states a thesis but does not engage the reader. The essay includes formatting, graphics, and multimedia, but they are not always used appropriately to aid comprehension. The conclusion restates information.	The topic is developed with some variety of facts, definitions, details, quotations, or other information appropriate to the audience's knowledge of the topic. The language is sometimes precise and appropriate for the audience and purpose. The tone of the essay switches from formal to informal at times.	The essay uses a mix of correct and incorrect standard English conventions of usage and mechanics. Transitions are sometimes used to link major sections of the text, create cohesion, and clarify the relationships among complex ideas and concepts, or are sometimes used incorrectly.
1	The introduction does not state a thesis. The essay does not include formatting, graphics, or multimedia. The conclusion does not summarize ideas or is missing completely.	The topic is not developed with well-chosen, relevant, and sufficient facts, extended definitions, concrete details, quotations, or other information appropriate to the audience's knowledge of the topic. The language is confusing. The tone of the essay is inappropriately informal.	The essay contains many mistakes in standard English conventions of usage and mechanics. The essay lacks appropriate transitions.

PART 2
Speaking and Listening: Oral Presentation

Assignment
After completing the final draft of your informative essay, use it as the foundation for a three- to five-minute **oral presentation.**

Instead of simply reading your essay aloud, take the following steps to make your oral presentation lively and engaging.

- Write a fresh introduction that grabs the audience's attention and establishes your thesis. Write a conclusion that summarizes your thesis and supporting points in a memorable way.
- Gather images that illustrate your ideas, and integrate them into the presentation so that they maintain audience interest, clarify points, and do not distract from the focus of the presentation.

Review the Oral Presentation Rubric The criteria by which your oral presentation will be evaluated appear in the rubric below. Review these criteria before presenting to ensure that you are prepared.

	Content	Organization	Presentation Technique
3	The introduction engages the listener and states a thesis in a very effective way. The presentation develops the thesis coherently with evidence from various sources. The language is always precise and appropriate for the audience and purpose. The conclusion offers fresh insight into the thesis.	The speaker uses time very effectively by spending the right amount of time on every part. Ideas progress logically, supported by a variety of transitions. Listeners can follow the presentation.	The speaker maintains effective eye contact. The speaker presents with strong conviction and energy.
2	The introduction states a thesis. The presentation develops the thesis with some evidence from several sources. The language is sometimes precise and appropriate for the audience and purpose. The conclusion restates the thesis.	The speaker uses some of the time effectively by spending the right amount of time on most parts. Ideas progress logically, supported by some transitions. Listeners can mostly follow the presentation.	The speaker mostly maintains effective eye contact. The speaker presents with some level of conviction and energy.
1	The introduction does not state a thesis. The presentation does not develop the thesis with evidence from multiple sources. The language is not precise and appropriate for the audience and purpose. The conclusion does not restate the thesis.	The speaker does not use time effectively. Most parts of the presentation are too long or too short. Ideas do not progress logically. Listeners have difficulty following the presentation.	The speaker does not establish eye contact. The speaker presents without conviction or energy.

Reflect on the Unit

Now that you've completed the unit, take a few moments to reflect on your learning. Use the questions below to think about where you succeeded, what skills and strategies helped you, and where you can continue to grow.

Reflect on the Unit Goals

Look back at the goals at the beginning of the unit. Use a different colored pen to rate yourself again. Think about readings and activities that contributed the most to the growth of your understanding. Record your thoughts.

Reflect on the Learning Strategies

Discuss It Write a reflection on whether you were able to improve your learning based on your Action Plans. Think about what worked, what didn't, and what you might do to keep working on these strategies. Record your ideas before a class discussion.

Reflect on the Text

Choose a selection that you found challenging, and explain what made it difficult.

Explain something that surprised you about a text in the unit.

Which activity taught you the most about what people find valuable? What did you learn?

Virtue and Vengeance

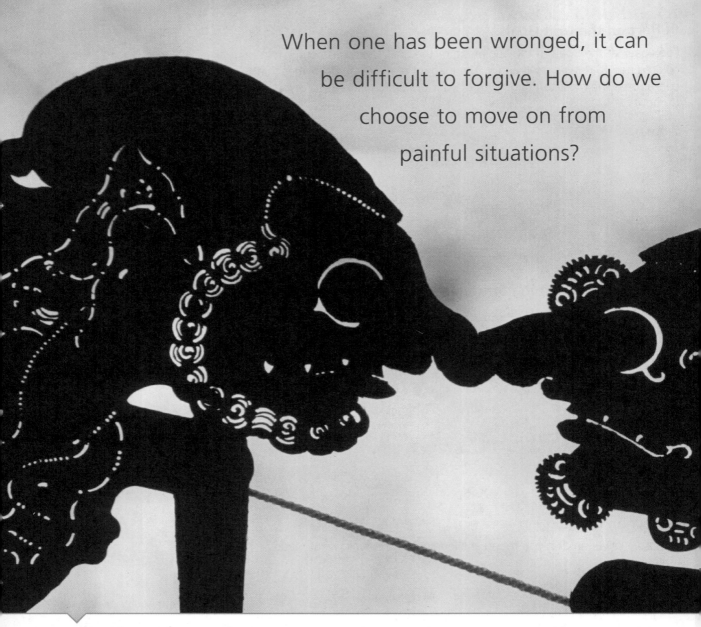

When one has been wronged, it can be difficult to forgive. How do we choose to move on from painful situations?

The Tempest 1: Rock the Ship

💬 Discuss It Why can it be difficult to forgive someone who has wronged you in some way?

Write your response before sharing your ideas.

UNIT INTRODUCTION

ESSENTIAL QUESTION:

What motivates us to forgive?

LAUNCH TEXT
ARGUMENT MODEL
Neither Justice nor
Forgetting: Defining
Forgiveness

 ## WHOLE-CLASS LEARNING

LITERATURE AND CULTURE

Historical Context
The Tempest

ANCHOR TEXT: DRAMA

The Tempest
William Shakespeare

Act I

Act II

Act III

Act IV

Act V

▶ MEDIA CONNECTION:
Dressing
The Tempest:
Slide Show,
The New York Times

COMPARE

ANCHOR TEXT: POETRY COLLECTION 1

*En el Jardín
de los Espejos
Quebrados,*
Caliban Catches
a Glimpse of His
Reflection
Virgil Suárez

Caliban
J. P. Dancing Bear

PERFORMANCE TASK

WRITING FOCUS:
Write an Argument

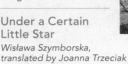 ## SMALL-GROUP LEARNING

POETRY COLLECTION 2

**They are
hostile nations**
Margaret Atwood

**Under a Certain
Little Star**
*Wisława Szymborska,
translated by Joanna Trzeciak*

SPEECH

**Let South Africa
Show the World How
to Forgive**
Desmond Tutu

PERFORMANCE TASK

SPEAKING AND LISTENING FOCUS:
Present an Argument

INDEPENDENT LEARNING

REFLECTIVE ESSAY

The Sun Parlor
Dorothy West

MEDIA: WEB ARTICLE

**The Forgiveness
Project: Eric Lomax**
The Forgiveness Project

BOOK REVIEW

**A Dish Best
Served Cold**
Aminatta Forna

CRITICISM

from **Shakespeare
and the French Poet**
*Yves Bonnefoy, translated
by John Naughton*

FOLKTALE

**What We Plant,
We Will Eat**
retold by S. E. Schlosser

INFORMATIONAL TEXT

**Understanding
Forgiveness**
PBS

PERFORMANCE-BASED ASSESSMENT PREP

Review Evidence for an Argument

PERFORMANCE-BASED ASSESSMENT

Argument: Essay and Informal Speech

PROMPT:

Can justice and forgiveness go hand in hand?

Unit Goals

Throughout the unit, you will deepen your perspective of forgiveness by reading, writing, speaking, listening, and presenting. These goals will help you succeed on the Unit Performance-Based Assessment.

Rate how well you meet these goals right now. You will revisit your ratings later when you reflect on your growth during this unit.

SCALE	1	2	3	4	5
	NOT AT ALL WELL	NOT VERY WELL	SOMEWHAT WELL	VERY WELL	EXTREMELY WELL

READING GOALS

	1	2	3	4	5
• Evaluate written arguments by analyzing how authors state and support claims.	○	○	○	○	○
• Expand your knowledge and use of academic and concept vocabulary.	○	○	○	○	○

WRITING AND RESEARCH GOALS

	1	2	3	4	5
• Write an argumentative essay in which you support claims using valid reasoning and relevant evidence.	○	○	○	○	○
• Conduct research projects of various lengths to explore a topic and clarify meaning.	○	○	○	○	○

LANGUAGE GOAL

	1	2	3	4	5
• Quote directly from the text with exact quotations; paraphrase an idea by restating it in your own words.	○	○	○	○	○

SPEAKING AND LISTENING GOALS

	1	2	3	4	5
• Collaborate with your team to build on the ideas of others, develop consensus, and communicate.	○	○	○	○	○
• Integrate audio, visuals, and text in presentations.	○	○	○	○	○

Academic Vocabulary: Argument

Academic terms appear in all subjects and can help you read, write, and discuss with more precision. Here are five academic words that will be useful to you in this unit as you analyze and write arguments.

Complete the chart.

1. Review each word, its root, and the mentor sentences.

2. Use the information and your own knowledge to predict the meaning of each word.

3. For each word, list at least two related words.

4. Refer to a dictionary or other resources if needed.

 TIP

FOLLOW THROUGH
Study the words in this chart, and mark them or their forms wherever they appear in the unit.

WORD	MENTOR SENTENCES	PREDICT MEANING	RELATED WORDS
allusion ROOT: **-lud-/-lus-** "play"	1. Because the audience did not understand the *allusion* to *The Tempest*, the joke fell flat. 2. The *allusion* to World War I helps readers understand the characters' anxiety.		allude; allusive
articulate ROOT: **-art-** "join"	1. If you *articulate* your ideas more clearly, people may be swayed to your point of view. 2. Each student was asked to *articulate* one concern.		
contentious ROOT: **-tend-/-tens-** "stretch"; "strain"	1. The candidate began with a *contentious* remark that angered her opponent. 2. The diplomat tries to resolve conflicts by taking a peacemaking rather than a *contentious* approach.		
vehement ROOT: **-veh-/-vect-** "carry"; "drag"	1. The winning debater's argument was both *vehement* and logical. 2. Despite *vehement* opposition, the council chose to make an unpopular budget cut.		
tolerate ROOT: **-tol-** "bear"; "carry"	1. The music was so loud we could barely *tolerate* it. 2. The referee warned both teams that she would not *tolerate* cheap fouls.		

LAUNCH TEXT | ARGUMENT MODEL

This selection is an example of an **argument**, a type of writing in which the author states and defends a position on a topic. This is the type of writing you will develop in the Performance-Based Assessment at the end of the unit.

As you read, think about how the writer builds a case. Mark the text to help you answer this question: What is the writer's position, and what evidence supports it?

Neither Justice nor Forgetting: Defining Forgiveness

NOTES

1   The concept of forgiveness is central to William Shakespeare's play *The Tempest*. Some readers maintain that its main character, Prospero, represents this noble virtue. However, a careful reading shows evidence to the contrary as Prospero's forgiveness always has a price.

2   From the beginning, Prospero seizes every opportunity fate brings him to get revenge. The storm from which the play takes its title puts his brother, Antonio, within Prospero's grasp. Twelve years earlier, Antonio took Prospero's land and power and exiled him to a distant island. Prospero's anger still burns.

3   Prospero's revenge is made possible by his own cunning. During his exile, he studied sorcery. The storm that batters Antonio's party is one that Prospero uses magic to create. He is sincere when he asks Ariel, his magical servant, "But are they, Ariel, safe?" However, he does not flinch at the miseries the sailors endure.

4   In this same exchange, Prospero taunts Ariel when the sprite requests his freedom. At length, Prospero reminds Ariel that he once rescued him from a magical prison. He browbeats Ariel until the sprite grovels. Then, before Prospero offers Ariel freedom, he makes him meek with a threat:

> If thou more murmur'st, I will rend an oak
> And peg thee in his knotty entrails till
> Thou hast howled away twelve winters.

5   At other times, Prospero savors victory, demonstrating his power and control before offering a change of heart. In this speech, he teases Antonio before accepting his brother's apology:

NOTES

> For you, most wicked sir, whom to call brother
> Would even infect my mouth, I do forgive
> Thy rankest fault—all of them; and require
> My dukedom of thee, which perforce, I know,
> Thou must restore.

If to forgive is to let go of anger and resentment, then Prospero cannot be called forgiving.

6   Caliban, Prospero's prisoner and servant, presents another example of forgiveness mixed with punishment. For all practical purposes, Prospero has enslaved Caliban because the creature once menaced his daughter Miranda. Later, in an effort to be free, Caliban plots to kill Prospero. Yet Prospero neither respects Caliban nor finds him threatening. Instead, he describes him as a "Dull thing . . . that Caliban / Whom now I keep in service."

7   Prospero ultimately shows Caliban mercy, which could be seen as forgiveness. But he first punishes Caliban thoroughly and continues to hold him in contempt. His forgiveness is less an emotional change than a simple dismissal of Caliban's importance.

8   As some critics interpret *The Tempest*, Prospero is moved to mercy by Ariel's sadness for the shipwreck victims. His anger softened, Prospero learns to forgive. But again, for Prospero, bygones cannot be bygones until he has received an apology:

> . . . The rarer action is
> In virtue than in vengeance. They being penitent,
> The sole drift of my purpose doth extend
> Not a frown further. . . .

9   Shakespeare is the foremost dramatist in the English language with good reason. In Prospero, he creates a complex portrait in which anger, the desire for control, the need for vengeance, and the will to forgive battle it out. In the end, Prospero does let go and forgive, but not before bringing his enemies to their knees. ❧

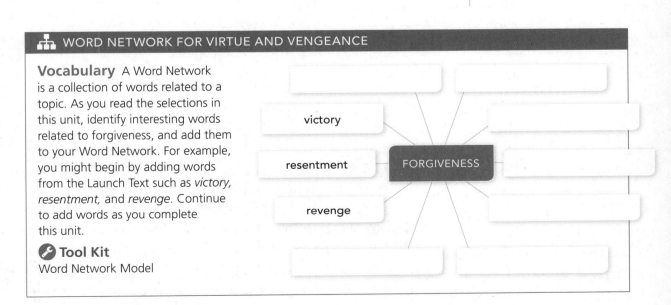

🕸 WORD NETWORK FOR VIRTUE AND VENGEANCE

Vocabulary A Word Network is a collection of words related to a topic. As you read the selections in this unit, identify interesting words related to forgiveness, and add them to your Word Network. For example, you might begin by adding words from the Launch Text such as *victory*, *resentment*, and *revenge*. Continue to add words as you complete this unit.

🔧 **Tool Kit**
Word Network Model

victory

resentment

revenge

FORGIVENESS

Summary

Write a summary of "Neither Justice nor Forgetting: Defining Forgiveness." A **summary** is a concise, complete, and accurate overview of a text. It should not include a statement of your opinion or an analysis.

Launch Activity

Four-Corner Debate Consider this statement: There are some misdeeds that should never be forgiven.

- Record your position on the statement.

  ☐ Strongly Agree ☐ Agree ☐ Disagree ☐ Strongly Disagree

  _____

  _____

- Form a group with like-minded students in one corner of the classroom. Discuss questions such as, "What examples from literature, movies, history, or your own observations of life lead you to take this position?"

- After your discussion, have a representative from each group present a two- to three-minute summary of the group's position.

- After all the groups have presented their views, move into the four corners again. If you change your corner, be ready to explain why.

QuickWrite

Consider class discussions, presentations, the video, and the Launch Text as you think about the prompt. Record your first thoughts here.

PROMPT: **Can justice and forgiveness go hand in hand?**

EVIDENCE LOG FOR VIRTUE AND VENGEANCE

Review your QuickWrite. Summarize your thoughts in one sentence to record in your Evidence Log. Then, record textual details or evidence from "Neither Justice nor Forgetting: Defining Forgiveness" that support your thinking.

Prepare for the Performance-Based Assessment at the end of the unit by completing the Evidence Log after each selection.

🔧 **Tool Kit**
Evidence Log Model

Title of Text: _____ Date: _____

CONNECTION TO PROMPT	TEXT EVIDENCE/DETAILS	ADDITIONAL NOTES/IDEAS

How does this text change or add to my thinking? Date: _____

ESSENTIAL QUESTION:

What motivates us to forgive?

It is impossible to go through life without somehow hurting others or being hurt by them. Can we forgive the offenses that wound us most deeply? How do we decide when—or whether—to forgive? You will work with your whole class to explore the concepts of virtue and vengeance. The selections you are going to read present insights into forgiveness.

Whole-Class Learning Strategies

Throughout your life, in school, in your community, and in your career, you will continue to learn and work in large-group environments.

Review these strategies and the actions you can take to practice them as you work with your whole class. Add ideas of your own for each step. Get ready to use these strategies during Whole-Class Learning.

STRATEGY	ACTION PLAN
Listen actively	• Eliminate distractions. For example, put your cellphone away. • Keep your eyes on the speaker. •
Clarify by asking questions	• If you're confused, other people probably are, too. Ask a question to help your whole class. • If you see that you are guessing, ask a question instead. •
Monitor understanding	• Notice what information you already know, and be ready to build on it. • Ask for help if you are struggling. •
Interact and share ideas	• Share your ideas and answer questions, even if you are unsure. • Build on the ideas of others by adding details or making a connection. •

CONTENTS

COMPARE

PERFORMANCE TASK

WRITING FOCUS

Write an Argument

The Whole-Class readings raise questions about vengeance and power, and ask us to consider forgiveness as being, possibly, a better choice. After reading, you will write an argument in the form of literary criticism in which you discuss the values of virtue and vengeance.

Historical Context

Elizabethan England

A Golden Age Queen Elizabeth I came to the throne following a tumultuous period in English history. During the reign of her father, King Henry VIII, thousands of people had been executed. Warfare had been frequent, and the royal treasury was drained. The brief reigns of Elizabeth's half-brother Edward and half-sister Mary were equally stormy. Elizabeth, by contrast, proved to be a strong and successful ruler, frugal with money and popular with her people. Her long reign (1558–1603) is often seen as a golden age in English history. The relative stability that Elizabeth created allowed commerce and culture to thrive.

The Renaissance Elizabeth ruled toward the end of a flowering of European learning known as the Renaissance (REHN uh sahns). The Renaissance began in Florence and other Italian city-states around 1350, and then spread throughout Europe. The word *renaissance* means "rebirth," and the era saw renewed interest in the arts and sciences that hearkened back to ancient Greece and Rome. The cultural pursuit of art and learning had diminished in Western Europe after the fall of the Roman Empire. Influenced by the achievements of the ancients, Renaissance writers and architects created new forms and designs that emphasized individual human expression. Painters and sculptors studied ancient Greek and Roman art to explore a new focus on the human form. Philosophers and religious reformers challenged old ideas, as did scientists who strove to unlock the hidden secrets of the natural world. With new knowledge of the skies, navigators sailed the globe, expanding trade and exploring distant lands.

∧ Elizabeth I was crowned at the age of 25. This painting by the Italian artist Federico Zuccaro is one of hundreds of portraits made of the queen during her reign.

Sixteenth-Century English Monarchs

King Edward VI ruled from 1547 to 1553

1500s

King Henry VIII ruled from 1509 to 1547

The English Renaissance Elizabeth I encouraged commercial enterprise and the efforts of English navigators, such as Sir Walter Raleigh, who tried to establish a colony in Virginia, and Sir Francis Drake, who sailed around the globe. Profiting particularly from the wool trade, a strong merchant class developed in England, narrowing the gap between rich and poor. London, with nearly 200,000 people, became Europe's largest city. It was a bustling if dirty cultural and political capital that attracted newcomers from overseas as well as from the English countryside. In 1588, the English army defeated the Spanish Armada, a fleet of warships sent by King Philip II of Spain to invade England. The victory contributed both to Elizabeth's legend and to the country's sense of national pride. It also set England firmly on the path to becoming ruler of the seas.

Elizabeth's reign was not only remarkable for its commercial and military successes. On the contrary, her court was a center for musicians and artists, both European and native born. The philosopher Sir Francis Bacon, who pioneered the informal essay as a literary form, became an unofficial member of the queen's group of advisors. Sir Philip Sidney, a popular courtier and diplomat, wrote a series of love sonnets that were much imitated. The poet Edmund Spenser wrote an adventure-packed epic called *The Faerie Queene* that he dedicated to Queen Elizabeth. The greatest Elizabethan literature, however, was written for the stage. The greatest of these voices were the playwrights Christopher Marlowe, Ben Jonson, and—greatest of them all—William Shakespeare.

The Concern for Stability Elizabeth's father, King Henry VIII, had married six times. He divorced three of his wives and executed two others, including Elizabeth's mother, Anne Boleyn. Queen Mary, Elizabeth's half-sister, infuriated the nation by wedding Phillip II of Spain, who abandoned her soon afterward. Perhaps because of these examples, or perhaps because she worried about sharing power, Elizabeth I never married.

> ### QUICK INSIGHT
> A sonnet, from the Italian for "little song," is a fourteen-line poem originally developed in Italy. Sidney's sonnets ushered in a sonnet-writing craze: Edmund Spenser, William Shakespeare, and just about every other Elizabethan poet produced a *sonnet sequence,* or series.

Queen Mary ruled from 1553 to 1558

Queen Elizabeth I ruled from 1558 to 1603

1600

Theater in Elizabethan England

London theaters drew crowds that are large even by today's standards.

During the Elizabethan era, the religious plays of the Middle Ages gave way to English tragedies and comedies modeled on those of ancient Greece and Rome. Scholars at Oxford and Cambridge universities studied and translated the ancient plays into English. The first great Elizabethan playwrights attended those universities, which is why they are sometimes called the University Wits. The most prominent of the Wits, Christopher Marlowe, pioneered the use of blank verse in drama.

For a time, Elizabethan acting companies still traveled the countryside as their medieval counterparts had done. They performed at festivals, inns, and castles. Gradually, however, the better acting companies acquired noble patrons, or sponsors, and began staging private performances in their patrons' homes. They also gave performances at court, where elaborate masques—productions featuring singing and dancing—were especially popular.

From the Theatre to the Globe England's first public theater opened in 1576. Known simply as the Theatre, it was built by the actor James Burbage, whose company would later attract the young William Shakespeare. Since the performance of plays was banned in London proper, Burbage built the Theatre just outside the city walls. When its lease expired, Richard Burbage, who took charge of the company after his father's death, decided to move operations to Southwark (SUHTH uhrk), just south across the River Thames (tehmz) from London. He built a new theater, called the Globe, which opened in 1599. Shakespeare's first play to be performed there was probably *The Tragedy of Julius Caesar*.

Theater Structure England's first theaters were two- to three-story structures with a central space open to the sky. The open space was surrounded by enclosed seating in two or three tiers, or galleries, that faced inward. On the ground floor, a stage projected into an area called the pit. Audience members called

‹ This illustration shows how the Globe might have looked as the audience arrived for a performance.

groundlings paid a small fee to stand in the pit and watch the play. Wealthier audience members, including aristocrats, occupied the more expensive sheltered gallery seats. Since artificial light was not used, performances generally took place in the afternoon. Audiences were boisterous, cheering and booing loudly. Most theaters could hold up to 3,000 people and drew the largest crowds on holidays.

Theater Stagecraft The portion of the building behind the stage was used to mount the production. This area included dressing rooms, storage rooms, and waiting areas from which actors could enter and exit the stage. The second-level gallery directly above the stage served as a performance space. There was no scenery; instead, settings were communicated through dialogue. Special effects were very simple—smoke might accompany a battle scene, for example. Actors playing members of the nobility or royalty wore elegant clothes. These were not really costumes as we think of them today, but simply the same types of clothing worn by high-ranking Elizabethans. Since acting was not considered proper for women, female roles were played by boys of about eleven or twelve, before their voices changed. Given the constraints of the era's stagecraft, the productions were unrealistic by modern standards. However, they were also fast paced, colorful, and highly entertaining.

The Blackfriars In 1609, Shakespeare's company, the King's Men, began staging plays at an indoor theater called the Blackfriars. They still used the Globe during the summer months. The Blackfriars was one of the first English theaters to include artificial lighting, which enabled nighttime performances. Designed to appeal to wealthy patrons only, the Blackfriars did not have inexpensive seats or a space set aside for groundlings. Indoor theaters of this sort, attracting a fashionable crowd, would become the norm in centuries to come.

> **QUICK INSIGHT**
> The upper stage could be used for particular scenes, or to stage a scene with actors on two levels. It was also the seating area for musicians, an important part of many productions. Several of Shakespeare's plays, particularly the comedies, contain songs.

Shakespeare's Globe, a reconstruction of the original theater, was completed in 1997 near the site of the original building. The modern convenience of artificial lighting allows for nighttime performances, such as the one shown in this photo.

William Shakespeare

Unlike other famed writers of his time, William Shakespeare (1564–1616) was neither a lofty aristocrat nor a university scholar. Nevertheless, he is widely regarded as the greatest writer in the English language.

"What's Past Is Prologue" Shakespeare was born in Stratford-upon-Avon, a market town on the Avon River about seventy-five miles northwest of London. His father, John, was a successful glove maker who served for a time as town mayor. His mother, born Mary Arden, was the daughter of a wealthy farmer who owned the land on which John Shakespeare's father lived. Although the records have been lost, it is believed that Shakespeare attended the Stratford Grammar School, where he would have studied logic, history, Latin grammar, some Greek, and works by the Roman poets Ovid, Horace, and Virgil and Roman playwrights Plautus and Terence. When he left school, he would thus have had a solid foundation in classical literature.

"All the World's a Stage" In 1582, when he was eighteen, Shakespeare married a woman named Anne Hathaway, who was twenty-six. The couple had a daughter, Susanna, in 1583 and twins, Judith and Hamnet, two years later. No one knows what Shakespeare did for the next several years, but in the early 1590s his name began to appear in the world of the London theater. Working first as an actor, Shakespeare soon began writing plays. By 1594, he was part owner and principal playwright of the Lord Chamberlain's Men, the acting company run by the Burbages. As the leading actor in most of Shakespeare's plays, Richard Burbage was also becoming famous. Soon he decided to move the company to the new theater district in Southwark. There, Burbage oversaw the construction of the Globe theater, which was larger than the company's old home in London. With bigger audiences, profits increased for Burbage, Shakespeare, and all the other co-owners.

The Lord Chamberlain's Men was named for its sponsors, first Henry Carey, Lord Hunsdon, and then his son George. Both men served in the high government post of Lord Chamberlain. After Queen Elizabeth I died in 1603, her successor, James I, became the company's patron. In his honor, the company changed its name to the King's Men.

"Parting Is Such Sweet Sorrow" In 1609, the King's Men began to perform year-round, using the Globe theater in summer and the Blackfriars during the colder months. Profits increased even more, and about a year later Shakespeare was able to retire. He returned to his childhood home of Stratford, where he bought the second-largest house in town, invested in land, and continued to write. Shakespeare died in 1616, leaving the bulk of his estate to his elder daughter, Susanna, and a smaller sum to Judith. (Hamnet had died in 1596.)

THERE IS NO DARKNESS BUT IGNORANCE

Shakespeare's Influence

Nearly four hundred years after his death, William Shakespeare remains the most influential writer in the English language. His characters are known by name around the world. Filmmakers, painters, novelists, and composers reuse his plots, and phrases he coined still slip into daily conversation. You have probably quoted Shakespeare without even knowing it. Here are just a few examples of expressions made famous in his plays.

EXPRESSION AND SOURCE	
All the world's a stage. (*As You Like It*)	Loved not wisely, but too well (*Othello*)
Brave new world (*The Tempest*)	More sinned against than sinning (*King Lear*)
Brevity is the soul of wit. (*Hamlet*)	Neither a borrower nor a lender be. (*Hamlet*)
Come full circle (*King Lear*)	Parting is such sweet sorrow. (*Romeo and Juliet*)
Dish fit for the gods (*Julius Caesar*)	Strange bedfellows (*The Tempest*)
A foregone conclusion (*Othello*)	Throw cold water on it. (*The Merry Wives of Windsor*)
It was Greek to me. (*Julius Caesar*)	Too much of a good thing (*As You Like It*)
Lend me your ears. (*Julius Caesar*)	What's past is prologue. (*The Tempest*)

The Authorship Question

Because the documentary evidence of Shakespeare's life is slim and his roots fairly humble, some have questioned whether he really wrote the plays with which he is credited. Shakespeare scholars believe that the surviving texts of the plays were edited and that a few late plays even had co-authors, but nearly all dismiss the notion that Shakespeare did not write them. Nevertheless, the theories persist. Several suggest that Will Shakespeare, actor and Burbage business partner, served as a front for some highborn person (the Earl of Oxford, the Countess of Pembroke, and so on). Some theories center on the philosopher and essayist Sir Francis Bacon as the true author—ignoring the fact that Bacon's writing style is completely different from Shakespeare's. The most interesting theories surround the playwright Christopher Marlowe, who was killed in a tavern brawl in 1593. According to these theories, Marlowe used Shakespeare as a front after faking his own death to escape retribution for blasphemous writings or his career as a government spy.

How to Read Shakespeare

Shakespeare wrote his plays in the language of his time. To the modern ear, however, that language can sound almost foreign. Certain words have changed meaning or fallen out of use. The idioms, slang, and humor of twenty-first-century America are very different from those of Elizabethan England. These differences present challenges for modern-day readers of Shakespeare. Here are some strategies for dealing with them.

CHALLENGE: Archaic Words

Many words Shakespeare used are now archaic, or outdated. Here are some examples:

TYPE OF WORD	CONTEMPORARY ENGLISH	ELIZABETHAN ENGLISH	EXAMPLES FROM *THE TEMPEST*
pronouns	*you, your, yours*	thou, thee, thy, thine	*Dost* **thou** *forget / From what a torment I did free* **thee**? (i.ii.250–251)
verbs	*come, will, do, has*	cometh, wilt, doth, hath	*. . . their tongues* **hath** *into bondage / Brought my . . . ear. . . .* (III.i.41–42)
familiar words used in unfamiliar ways	*handsome*	brave	*Believe me, sir, / It carries a* **brave** *form.* (I.ii.413–414)
	various	several	*Where, but even now, with strange and* **several** *noises . . .* (V.i.232, 235)

STRATEGIES

Familiarize yourself with the meanings of common archaic words in Shakespeare.

If a word is completely unfamiliar, look to the marginal notes for a translation or for clues to meaning in the surrounding text.

CHALLENGE: Inverted Word Order

The syntax, or word order, Shakespeare uses may also be archaic. In contemporary English, the subject (s) of a sentence usually appears before the verb (v). Shakespeare often inverts this order, placing the verb before the subject.

Contemporary English Syntax

s   v
What do **you say**?

Elizabethan English Syntax

v   s
What **say you**?

STRATEGY

If a sentence uses inverted syntax, identify its subject and verb. Then, rephrase the sentence, placing the subject before the verb.

CHALLENGE: Long Sentences

Many of Shakespeare's sentences span more than one line of verse. This is especially true when Shakespeare uses a semicolon to connect two or more clauses.

> *I am your wife, if you will marry me;*
> *If not, I'll die your maid. To be your fellow*
> *You may deny me; but I'll be your servant,*
> *Whether you will or no.* (*The Tempest*, III.i.83–86)

STRATEGIES

Look for capital letters and end marks to see where sentences begin and end.

When a sentence is made up of two clauses connected by a semicolon, consider how the ideas in the clauses relate.

CHALLENGE: Elizabethan Worldview

In Shakespeare's day, English society was rigidly organized. The nobility occupied the top rung of the social ladder, and the uneducated peasantry occupied the bottom. It was difficult, if not impossible, to advance from one social class to another.

The ladder of power also existed within families. Parents made life choices for their children. Within a marriage, the husband was the master of his wife.

Elizabethan people expected to live shorter, more difficult lives, and they understood the events of a life to be controlled by fate. They did not believe they had the power to shape their own destinies as we do today.

STRATEGY

Keep the Elizabethan worldview in mind as you read. If a character's attitude clashes with your own, try to view the situation through the character's eyes. This will help you understand why he or she is behaving or speaking in a certain way.

Close Read the Text

Annotating the text as you read can help you tackle the challenges of Shakespearean language. Here are two sample annotations of an excerpt from Act III, Scene ii, of *The Tempest*. In this scene, Caliban, the half-human slave of the magician Prospero, is carousing with two shipwreck survivors on the island that Prospero rules.

ANNOTATE: This is surprisingly gentle language for a "monster." And it is written in verse. Then, the spell breaks and the bloodthirsty Caliban returns, speaking again in prose.

QUESTION: What do these shifts show about Caliban?

CONCLUDE: Caliban is more than a brute—he is also sensitive and poetic. Maybe Shakespeare is suggesting that we all have within us both a monster and a poet.

Caliban. Art thou afeard?
Stephano. No, monster, not I.
Caliban. Be not afeard; the isle is full of noises,
Sounds and sweet airs that give delight and hurt not.
Sometimes a thousand twangling instruments
Will hum about mine ears; and sometimes voices
That, if I then had waked after long sleep,
Will make me sleep again: and then, in dreaming,
The clouds methought would open and show riches
Ready to drop upon me, that, when I waked,
I cried to dream again.
Stephano. This will prove a brave kingdom to me,
where I shall have my music for nothing.
Caliban. When Prospero is destroyed.

ANNOTATE: This long sentence is made up of several parts connected by a semicolon and a colon. Each part starts with a time-order word.

QUESTION: How are the ideas in each part connected?

CONCLUDE: A paraphrase of the first part might read: "Sometimes I hear noises." The second part might read: "Other times, I hear voices that lull me to sleep." In the third part, he is saying, "Once asleep, I dream of the clouds parting and riches raining down on me. It's a dream I never want to end." The punctuation threads the parts together. We are carried with Caliban into the dream state he is describing.

About the Playwright

William Shakespeare
(1564–1616) has long been
called one of the greatest
writers in the history of
the English language. He
was born in a town not
far from London. In his
twenties, he made his name
as an actor and playwright
and eventually became
part owner of the Globe
theater, where he wrote
and produced plays until
he was in his late forties.
He then retired to the
town where he grew up.
For more information, see
the Literature and Culture
feature.

🔧 **Tool Kit**
First-Read Guide and
Model Annotation

The Tempest, Act I

Concept Vocabulary

You will encounter the following words as you read Act I of *The Tempest*.
Before reading, note how familiar you are with each word. Then, rank the
words in order from most familiar (1) to least familiar (3).

WORD	YOUR RANKING
perfidious	
treacherous	
usurp	

After completing the first read, come back to the concept vocabulary and
review your rankings. Mark changes to your original rankings as needed.

First Read DRAMA

Apply these strategies as you conduct your first read. You will have an
opportunity to complete the close-read notes after your first read.

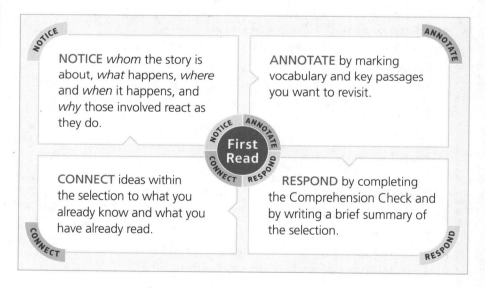

NOTICE *whom* the story is about, *what* happens, *where* and *when* it happens, and *why* those involved react as they do.

ANNOTATE by marking vocabulary and key passages you want to revisit.

CONNECT ideas within the selection to what you already know and what you have already read.

RESPOND by completing the Comprehension Check and by writing a brief summary of the selection.

First Read

BACKGROUND

The Bard's Last Play *The Tempest* is likely the last play that Shakespeare wrote as sole playwright. It was first performed in 1611, several years before his retirement to Stratford, leading some to hear in Prospero's speeches Shakespeare's farewell to the theater. A tale of exile, fairies, and magic, *The Tempest* enchants with its juxtapositions of civilization and nature, innocence and worldly wisdom, airy flights of fancy and earthly desire.

Shakespeare's Sources Shakespeare appears to have created the story of *The Tempest* out of his imagination. However, he was clearly influenced by reports of the Virginia Company's attempts to colonize America. In the summer of 1609, a fleet with 400 colonists encountered a terrible storm in which one of the ships was lost and another ran aground in the "far Bermoothes," the rugged coast of Bermuda. Reports that Shakespeare almost certainly read suggested that the island was a wonderful and magical place. Is Bermuda Prospero's magical island? Probably not, but it's an interesting thought. Certainly Shakespeare was influenced by survivors' reports of this tempest, and by the notion of the "brave new world" that lay over the horizon, ready for discovery and exploration.

The Play Through the Centuries In many ways, *The Tempest* is a beautiful meditation on creativity and art. Prospero's magical acts echo the magic that we are seeing in the theater, and the happiness that Prospero creates for the characters at the play's end duplicates the delight that theatergoers feel upon enjoying the play. We, too, are the beneficiaries of Prospero's art.

Modern audiences, however, have been interested in the theme of colonization in the play and have focused attention on the characters of Caliban and Ariel, both of whom are enslaved to the powerful Prospero. Is the play an allegory of New World colonization, and if so, what is Shakespeare's take on it? Is Prospero bringing a better life to the island and its inhabitants, or is he exploiting them for his own ends? What are the rights of Caliban, the "natural" inhabitant of the island? Does he benefit from Prospero's care, or was he better off alone on the island before Prospero's arrival?

A NOTE ABOUT THE IMAGES: The photographs that illustrate *The Tempest* in this program are from the 2010 film directed by Julie Taymor. In the film, Prospero is played by the noted English actress Dame Helen Mirren. The character's name is changed to Prospera, and Miranda addresses her parent as "Mother." As you read the play, consider whether this casting choice affects how audiences understand the play's characters and conflicts.

The Tempest Act I

William Shakespeare

CHARACTERS

The Scene: An uninhabited island.

Alonso, King of Naples

Sebastian, his brother

Prospero, the rightful Duke of Milan

Antonio, his brother, the usurping Duke of Milan

Ferdinand, son to the King of Naples

Gonzalo, an honest old councilor

Adrian and Francisco, lords

Caliban, a savage and deformed slave

Trinculo, a jester

Stephano, a drunken butler

Master of a ship

Boatswain

Mariners

Miranda, daughter to Prospero

Ariel, an airy spirit

Iris, Ceres, Juno, Nymphs, Reapers: [presented by] Spirits

[Other Spirits Attending on Prospero]

Scene i • *On a ship at sea.*

[*A tempestuous noise of thunder and lightning heard. Enter a* Shipmaster *and a* Boatswain.]

Master. Boatswain!

Boatswain. Here, master. What cheer?[1]

Master. Good,[2] speak to th' mariners! Fall to't, yarely,[3] or we run ourselves aground. Bestir, bestir!

                                           [*Exit.*]

[*Enter* Mariners.]

5 **Boatswain.** Heigh, my hearts! Cheerly, cheerly, my hearts! Yare, yare! Take in the topsail! Tend to th' master's whistle![4] Blow till thou burst thy wind, if room enough![5]

[*Enter* Alonso, Sebastian, Antonio, Ferdinand, Gonzalo, *and others.*]

 Alonso. Good boatswain, have care. Where's the master? Play the men.[6]

10 **Boatswain.** I pray now, keep below.

 Antonio. Where is the master, bos'n?

 Boatswain. Do you not hear him? You mar our labor. Keep your cabins; you do assist the storm.

 Gonzalo. Nay, good, be patient.

15 **Boatswain.** When the sea is. Hence! What cares these roarers[7] for the name of king? To cabin! Silence! Trouble us not!

 Gonzalo. Good, yet remember whom thou hast aboard.

 Boatswain. None that I more love than myself. You are a councilor; if you can command these elements to silence and
20 work the peace of the present,[8] we will not hand[9] a rope more. Use your authority. If you cannot, give thanks you have lived so long, and make yourself ready in your cabin for the mischance of the hour, if it so hap. Cheerly,[10] good hearts! Out of our way, I say.

                                           [*Exit.*]

 Gonzalo. I have great comfort from this fellow. Methinks he
25 hath no drowning mark upon him; his complexion is perfect gallows.[11] Stand fast, good Fate, to his hanging! Make the rope of his destiny our cable, for our own doth little advantage.[12] If he be not born to be hanged, our case is miserable.

                                       [*Exit with the rest.*]

[*Enter* Boatswain.]

---

1. **What cheer?** What is your will? What do you wish?
2. **Good** good fellow.
3. **yarely** *adv.* vigorously; briskly; quickly.
4. **whistle** *n.* high-pitched whistle used to give orders.
5. **Blow . . . enough** This is addressed to the wind and means "Blow until you split or burst as long as we are in the open sea and have room to maneuver."
6. **Play the men** Make the men work.
7. **roarers** *n.* loud, noisy characters (here, referring either to the waves or to Alonso, Antonio, and Gonzalo).
8. **command . . . present** order the raging storm to stop and bring peace to the present (as you are accustomed to doing in your job as king's councilor).
9. **hand** *v.* handle.
10. **cheerly** *adv.* quickly.
11. **no drowning . . . gallows** this alludes to a popular proverb, "He that's born to be hanged need fear no drowning."
12. **for . . . advantage** our own destiny will not save us from drowning.

13. **Bring . . . course** nautical term meaning "Bring the ship about to try to hold the course."

14. **They . . . office** The passengers are noisier than the storm or our work.

15. **give o'er** give up.

16. **pox . . . throat** a plague or curse on your throat.

17. **warrant him for** guarantee him against.

18. **unstanched** *adj.* not checked or stopped.

19. **Lay . . . off** Get control. Bring her back on course. Get the ship out to sea. Get her away from shore.

20. **merely** *adv.* totally; completely.

21. **wide-chopped** *adj.* big-mouthed; talkative.

22. **ten tides** Pirates were tied down on the shore and left to drown by the washing of tides over them, usually three.

23. **heath** *n.* heather, a shrub that grows on open wasteland.

24. **furze** *n.* gorse, a shrub that puts forth yellow flowers.

25. **fain** *adv.* rather.

Boatswain. Down with the topmast! Yare! Lower, lower! Bring
30 her to try with main course.[13] [*A cry within.*] A plague upon this
howling! They are louder than the weather or our office.[14]

[*Enter Sebastian, Antonio, and Gonzalo.*]

Yet again! What do you here? Shall we give o'er[15] and drown?
Have you a mind to sink?

Sebastian. A pox o' your throat,[16] you bawling, blasphemous,
35 incharitable dog!

Boatswain. Work you, then.

Antonio. Hang, cur! Hang, you insolent noisemaker! We are less
afraid to be drowned than thou art.

Gonzalo. I'll warrant him for[17] drowning, though the ship
40 were no stronger than a nutshell and as leaky as an unstanched[18]
wench.

Boatswain. Lay her ahold, ahold! Set her two courses! Off to sea
again! Lay her off![19]

[*Enter Mariners wet.*]

Mariners. All lost! To prayers, to prayers! All lost! [*Exit.*]

45 **Boatswain.** What, must our mouths be cold?

Gonzalo. The King and Prince at prayers! Let's assist them,
For our case is as theirs.

Sebastian. I'm out of patience.

Antonio. We are merely[20] cheated of our lives by drunkards.
This wide-chopped[21] rascal—would thou mightst lie drowning
50 The washing of ten tides![22]

Gonzalo. He'll be hanged yet,
Though every drop of water swear against it
And gape at wid'st to glut him.

[*A confused noise within*] "Mercy on us!"
"We split, we split!" "Farewell, my wife and children!"
"Farewell, brother!" "We split, we split, we split!"

[*Exit Boatswain.*]

55 **Antonio.** Let's all sink wi' th' king.

Sebastian. Let's take leave of him.

[*Exit with Antonio.*]

Gonzalo. Now would I give a thousand furlongs of sea for
an acre of barren ground—long heath,[23] brown furze,[24]
anything. The wills above be done, but I would fain[25] die a
dry death. [*Exit.*]

Scene ii • *The island. In front of Prospero's cell.*

[*Enter* Prospero *and* Miranda.]

Miranda. If by your art, my dearest father, you have
Put the wild waters in this roar, allay them.
The sky, it seems, would pour down stinking pitch
But that the sea, mounting to th' welkin's cheek,[1]
5 Dashes the fire out. O, I have suffered
With those that I saw suffer! A brave[2] vessel
(Who had no doubt some noble creature in her)
Dashed all to pieces! O, the cry did knock
Against my very heart! Poor souls, they perished!
10 Had I been any god of power, I would
Have sunk the sea within the earth or ere[3]
It should the good ship so have swallowed and
The fraughting[4] souls within her.

Prospero.   Be collected.
No more amazement.[5] Tell your piteous[6] heart
15 There's no harm done.

Miranda.   O, woe the day!

Prospero.   No harm.
I have done nothing but in care of thee,
Of thee my dear one, thee my daughter, who
Art ignorant of what thou art, naught knowing
Of whence I am, nor that I am more better[7]
20 Than Prospero, master of a full poor cell,
And thy no greater father.[8]

Miranda.   More to know
Did never meddle[9] with my thoughts.

Prospero.   'Tis time
I should inform thee farther. Lend thy hand
And pluck my magic garment from me. So.

                           [*Lays down his robe.*]

25 Lie there, my art. Wipe thou thine eyes; have comfort.
The direful spectacle of the wrack,[10] which touched
The very virtue[11] of compassion in thee,
I have with such provision[12] in mine art
So safely ordered that there is no soul—
30 No, not so much perdition[13] as an hair
Betid[14] to any creature in the vessel
Which thou heard'st cry, which thou saw'st sink.
   Sit down;
For thou must now know farther.

1. **welkin's cheek** sky's clouds.

2. **brave** *adj.* splendid.

3. **ere** *prep.* before.

4. **fraughting** *adj.* laden, referring back to the ship, which is loaded with a cargo of souls.
5. **amazement** *n.* bewilderment; alarm; consternation.
6. **piteous** *adj.* filled with pity; compassionate.

7. **more better** of higher rank.

8. **thy . . . father** your father, who is no greater than master of a poor cave.
9. **meddle** *v.* mix.

10. **wrack** *n.* wreck.
11. **virtue** *n.* essence.
12. **provision** *n.* foresight.

13. **perdition** *n.* loss.
14. **Betid** befallen; happened.

Miranda.   You have often
Begun to tell me what I am; but stopped

35 And left me to a bootless[15] inquisition,
Concluding, "Stay; not yet."

Prospero.   The hour's now come;
The very minute bids thee ope thine ear.
Obey, and be attentive. Canst thou remember
A time before we came unto this cell?

40 I do not think thou canst, for then thou wast not

16. Out beyond; past more than.

Out[16] three years old.

Miranda.   Certainly, sir, I can.

Prospero. By what? By any other house or person?
Of anything the image tell me that
Hath kept with thy remembrance.

Miranda.   'Tis far off,

45 And rather like a dream than an assurance
That my remembrance warrants. Had I not
Four or five women once that tended me?

Prospero. Thou hadst, and more, Miranda. But how is it
That this lives in thy mind? What seest thou else

17. abysm of time depths of the past.

50 In the dark backward and abysm of time?[17]
If thou rememb'rest aught ere thou cam'st here,
How thou cam'st here thou mayst.

Miranda.   But that I do not.

Prospero. Twelve year since, Miranda, twelve year since,
Thy father was the Duke of Milan and

55 A prince of power.

Miranda.   Sir, are not you my father?

18. piece of virtue example of perfection and purity.

Prospero. Thy mother was a piece of virtue,[18] and
She said thou wast my daughter; and thy father
Was Duke of Milan; and thou his only heir

19. no worse issued no less royal.

And princess, no worse issued.[19]

Miranda.   O the heavens!

60 What foul play had we that we came from thence?
Or blessèd was't we did?

Prospero.   Both, both, my girl!
By foul play, as thou say'st, were we heaved thence,

20. holp *v.* helped.

But blessedly holp[20] hither.

Miranda.   O, my heart bleeds
To think o' th' teen[21] that I have turned you to,

21. teen *n.* misery.
22. from gone from.

65 Which is from[22] my remembrance! Please you, farther.

Prospero. My brother and thy uncle, called Antonio—
I pray thee mark me—that a brother should
Be so **perfidious**!—he whom next thyself

perfidious (puhr FIHD ee uhs)
adj. unfaithful and dishonest

Of all the world I loved, and to him put
70 The manage of my state; as at that time
Through all the signories[23] it was the first,
And Prospero the prime duke, being so reputed
In dignity, and for the liberal arts
Without a parallel; those being all my study,
75 The government I cast upon my brother
And to my state grew stranger, being transported
And rapt in secret studies. Thy false uncle—
Dost thou attend me?

Miranda.   Sir, most heedfully.

Prospero. Being once perfected[24] how to grant suits,
80 How to deny them, who t' advance, and who
To trash for overtopping,[25] new-created
The creatures that were mine, I say—or changed 'em,
Or else new-formed 'em[26]—having both the key
Of officer and office, set all hearts i' th' state
85 To what tune pleased his ear, that now he was
The ivy which had hid my princely trunk
And sucked my verdure[27] out on't. Thou attend'st not?

Miranda. O, good sir, I do.

Prospero.   I pray thee mark me.
I thus neglecting worldly ends, all dedicated
90 To closeness[28] and the bettering of my mind—
With that which, but by being so retired,
O'erprized all popular rate, in my false brother
Awaked an evil nature,[29] and my trust,
Like a good parent, did beget of him
95 A falsehood in its contrary as great
As my trust was, which had indeed no limit,
A confidence sans bound. He being thus lorded—
Not only with what my revenue yielded
But what my power might else exact, like one
100 Who having into truth—by telling of it,[30]
Made such a sinner of his memory
To credit[31] his own lie, he did believe
He was indeed the Duke, out o' th' substitution
And executing th' outward face of royalty
105 With all prerogative.[32] Hence his ambition growing—
Dost thou hear?

Miranda.   Your tale, sir, would cure deafness.

Prospero. To have no screen between this part he played
And him he played it for, he needs will be
Absolute Milan.[33] Me (poor man) my library
110 Was dukedom large enough. Of temporal[34] royalties
He thinks me now incapable; confederates

NOTES

23. **signories** *n.* feudal authority; seigneuries; principalities.

24. **perfected** skilled at.

25. **trash for overtopping** hold back from going too fast or being too ambitious; "trash" refers to a cord or leash used in training dogs.

26. **new-created . . . 'em** remade my staff—either by replacing those I had chosen with others loyal to him or by turning my people against me.

27. **verdure** *n.* green vegetation; health and vigor.

28. **closeness** *n.* seclusion.

29. **with . . . nature** by devoting myself to higher things, which is beyond popular understanding, I aroused evil in my brother.

30. **like . . . it** like one truly entitled to what my power commanded by simply claiming the right.

31. **credit** *v.* believe.

32. **out . . . prerogative** by substituting for me and pretending he was royalty with all its rights and privileges.

33. **Absolute Milan** Duke in fact, not just in pretense.

34. **temporal** *adj.* in time; of this world.

(So dry he was for sway)³⁵ wi' th' King of Naples
To give him annual tribute, do him homage,
Subject his coronet to his crown, and bend

115 The dukedom, yet unbowed (alas, poor Milan!),
To most ignoble stooping.

Miranda.   O the heavens!

Prospero. Mark his condition,³⁶ and th' event;³⁷ then tell me
If this might be a brother.

Miranda.   I should sin
To think but nobly of my grandmother.

120 Good wombs have borne bad sons.

Prospero.   Now the condition.
The King of Naples, being an enemy
To me inveterate, hearkens my brother's suit;
Which was, that he, in lieu o' th' premises³⁸
Of homage and I know not how much tribute,

125 Should presently extirpate me and mine
Out of the dukedom and confer fair Milan
With all the honors, of my brother. Whereon,
A treacherous army levied, one midnight
Fated to th' purpose, did Antonio open

130 The gates of Milan; and, i' th' dead of darkness,
The ministers³⁹ for th' purpose hurried thence
Me and thy crying self.

Miranda.   Alack, for pity!
I, not rememb'ring how I cried out then,
Will cry it o'er again; it is a hint⁴⁰

135 That wrings mine eyes to't.

Prospero.   Hear a little further,
And then I'll bring thee to the present business
Which now's upon's; without the which this story
Were most impertinent.⁴¹

Miranda.   Wherefore did they not
That hour destroy us?

Prospero.   Well demanded, wench.

140 My tale provokes that question. Dear, they durst not,
So dear the love my people bore me; nor set
A mark so bloody on the business; but,
With colors fairer, painted their foul ends.
In few,⁴² they hurried us aboard a bark;

145 Bore us some leagues to sea, where they prepared
A rotten carcass of a butt,⁴³ not rigged,
Nor tackle, sail, nor mast; the very rats
Instinctively have quit it. There they hoist us,
To cry to th' sea that roared to us; to sigh

150 To th' winds, whose pity, sighing back again,
Did us but loving wrong.

Miranda.   Alack, what trouble
Was I then to you!

Prospero.   O, a cherubim
Thou was that did preserve me! Thou didst smile.
Infused with a fortitude from heaven,
155 When I have decked the sea with drops full salt,[44]
Under my burden groaned; which raised in me
An undergoing stomach,[45] to bear up
Against what should ensue.

Miranda.   How came we ashore?

Prospero. By providence divine.
160 Some food we had and some fresh water, that
A noble Neapolitan, Gonzalo,
Out of his charity, who being then appointed
Master of this design, did give us, with
Rich garments, linens, stuffs, and necessaries,
165 Which since have steaded much.[46] So, of his gentleness,
Knowing I loved my books, he furnished me
From mine own library with volumes that
I prize above my dukedom.

Miranda.   Would I might
But ever see that man!

Prospero.   Now I arise:
170 Sit still, and hear the last of our sea sorrow.
Here in this island we arrived; and here
Have I, thy schoolmaster, made thee more profit
Than other princess' can,[47] that have more time
For vainer hours, and tutors not so careful.

175 **Miranda.** Heavens thank you for't! And now I pray you, sir—
For still 'tis beating in my mind—your reason
For raising this sea storm?

Prospero.   Know thus far forth.
By accident most strange, bountiful Fortune
(Now my dear lady)[48] hath mine enemies
180 Brought to this shore; and by my prescience[49]
I find my zenith[50] doth depend upon
A most auspicious star, whose influence
If now I court not, but omit,[51] my fortunes
Will ever after droop. Here cease more questions.
185 Thou art inclined to sleep. 'Tis a good dullness,
And give it way: I know thou canst not choose.

[Miranda *sleeps*.]

NOTES

44. decked . . . salt decorated the sea with tears.

45. undergoing stomach underlying courage.

46. steaded much been of much use.

47. princess' can princesses have.

48. Now . . . lady now my supporter.

49. prescience *n.* knowledge before an event.

50. zenith *n.* highest fortune

51. omit *v.* ignore.

52. Come away come here.

53. quality *n.* others like Ariel who make up his band of spirits.

54. to point to the smallest detail; with absolute precision.

55. Now . . . deck now on the prow, now amidships, now on the rear deck or poop.

56. flamed amazement caused terror by appearing as fire.

57. boresprit *n.* bowsprit; a sailing term.

58. distinctly *adv.* in distinct or separate places.

Come away,[52] servant, come! I am ready now.
Approach, my Ariel! Come!

[*Enter* Ariel.]

Ariel. All hail, great master! Grave sir, hail! I come
190 To answer thy best pleasure; be't to fly,
To swim, to dive into the fire, to ride
On the curled clouds. To thy strong bidding task
Ariel and all his quality.[53]

Prospero.   Hast thou, spirit,
Performed to point,[54] the tempest that I bade thee?

195 **Ariel.** To every article.
I boarded the King's ship. Now on the beak,
Now in the waist, the deck,[55] in every cabin,
I flamed amazement.[56] Sometime I'd divide
And burn in many places; on the topmast,
200 The yards, and boresprit[57] would I flame distinctly,[58]
Then meet and join. Jove's lightnings, the precursors
O' th' dreadful thunderclaps, more momentary
And sight-outrunning were not. The fire and cracks
Of sulfurous roaring the most mighty Neptune
205 Seem to besiege, and make his bold waves tremble;

The sorcerer Prospera (played by Dame Helen Mirren) confers with her servant Ariel (played by Ben Whishaw).

Yea, his dread trident shake.

Prospero. My brave spirit!
Who was so firm, so constant, that this coil[59]
Would not infect his reason?

Ariel. Not a soul
But felt a fever of the mad and played
210 Some tricks of desperation. All but mariners
Plunged in the foaming brine and quit the vessel,
Then all afire with me. The King's son Ferdinand,
With hair up-staring[60] (then like reeds, not hair),
Was the first man that leapt; cried, "Hell is empty,
215 And all the devils are here!"

Prospero. Why that's my spirit!
But was not this nigh shore?

Ariel. Close by, my master.

Prospero. But are they, Ariel, safe?

Ariel. Not a hair perished.
On their sustaining[61] garments not a blemish,
But fresher than before; and as thou bad'st me,
220 In troops I have dispersed them 'bout the isle.
The King's son have I landed by himself,
Whom I left cooling of the air with sighs
In an odd angle of the isle, and sitting,
His arms in this sad knot. [*Illustrates with a gesture.*]

Prospero. Of the King's ship,
225 The mariners, say how thou hast disposed,
And all the rest o' th' fleet.

Ariel. Safely in harbor
Is the King's ship; in the deep nook where once
Thou call'dst me up at midnight to fetch dew
From the still-vexed Bermoothes,[62] there she's hid;
230 The mariners all under hatches stowed,
Who, with a charm joined to their suff'red labor,[63]
I have left asleep. And for the rest o' th' fleet,
Which I dispersed, they all have met again,
And are upon the Mediterranean flote[64]
235 Bound sadly home for Naples,
Supposing that they saw the King's ship wracked
And his great person perish.

Prospero. Ariel, thy charge
Exactly is performed; but there's more work.
What is the time o' th' day?

Ariel. Past the mid season.[65]

240 **Prospero.** At least two glasses.[66] The time 'twixt six and now
Must by us both be spent most preciously.

NOTES

59. **coil** *n.* tumult; uproar.
60. **up-staring** *adj.* standing up on end.

CLOSE READ
ANNOTATE: In lines 214–215, mark the words that Ariel quotes directly from Ferdinand.

QUESTION: Why does Ariel quote Ferdinand? What effect is he trying to achieve?

CONCLUDE: What does this passage show about Ariel's relationship to Prospero?

61. **sustaining** *adj.* supporting by keeping them afloat.

62. **Bermoothes** Bermudas.

63. **suff'red labor** work they had done.

64. **flote** *n.* sea.

65. **mid season** noon.

66. **two glasses** two o'clock; the turning of two hourglasses.

Ariel. Is there more toil? Since thou dost give me pains,[67]
Let me remember[68] thee what thou hast promised,
Which is not yet performed me.

Prospero.   How now? Moody?
245 What is't thou canst demand?

Ariel.   My liberty.

Prospero. Before the time be out? No more!

Ariel.   I prithee,
Remember I have done thee worthy service,
Told thee no lies, made thee no mistakings, served
Without or grudge or grumblings. Thou did promise
250 To bate me a full year.[69]

Prospero.   Dost thou forget
From what a torment I did free thee?

Ariel.   No.

Prospero. Thou dost; and think'st it much to tread the ooze
Of the salt deep,
To run upon the sharp wind of the North,
255 To do me business in the veins[70] o' th' earth
When it is baked[71] with frost.

Ariel.   I do not, sir.

Prospero. Thou liest, malignant thing! Hast thou forgot
The foul witch Sycorax,[72] who with age and envy[73]
Was grown into a hoop? Hast thou forgot her?

260 **Ariel.** No, sir.

72. Sycorax name of the witch,
possibly made up from two or
more Greek words.

73. envy *n.* spite.

Prospero.   Thou hast. Where was she born? Speak!
Tell me!

Ariel. Sir, in Argier.[74]

Prospero.   O, was she so? I must
Once in a month recount what thou hast been,
Which thou forget'st. This damned witch Sycorax,
For mischiefs manifold, and sorceries terrible
265 To enter human hearing, from Argier,
Thou know'st, was banished. For one thing she did
They would not take her life. Is not this true?

Ariel. Ay, sir.

Prospero. This blue-eyed hag was hither brought with child
270 And here was left by th' sailors. Thou, my slave,
As thou report'st thyself, wast then her servant.
And, for thou wast a spirit too delicate
To act her earthy and abhorred commands,
Refusing her grand hests,[75] she did confine thee,

75. hests *n.* orders.
76. more potent ministers more
powerful agents.

275 By help of her more potent ministers,[76]

And in her most unmitigable rage,
Into a cloven pine; within which rift
Imprisoned thou didst painfully remain
A dozen years; within which space she died
280 And left thee there, where thou didst vent thy groans
As fast as millwheels strike. Then was this island
(Save for the son that she did litter here,
A freckled whelp, hagborn) not honored with
A human shape.

    Ariel.   Yes, Caliban her son.

285 **Prospero.** Dull thing, I say so! He, that Caliban
Whom now I keep in service. Thou best know'st
What torment I did find thee in; thy groans
Did make wolves howl and penetrate the breasts
Of ever-angry bears. It was a torment
290 To lay upon the damned, which Sycorax
Could not again undo. It was mine art,
When I arrived and heard thee, that made gape
The pine, and let thee out.

    Ariel.   I thank thee, master.

    Prospero. If thou more murmur'st, I will rend an oak
295 And peg thee in his knotty entrails till
Thou hast howled away twelve winters.

    Ariel.   Pardon, master,
I will be correspondent[77] to command
And do my spiriting gently.[78]

    Prospero.   Do so; and after two days
I will discharge thee.

    Ariel.   That's my noble master!
300 What shall I do? Say what? What shall I do?

    Prospero. Go make thyself like a nymph o' th' sea. Be subject
To no sight but thine and mine, invisible
To every eyeball else. Go take this shape
And hither come in't. Go! Hence with diligence!   [*Exit* Ariel.]
305 Awake, dear heart, awake! Thou hast slept well.
Awake!

    Miranda.   The strangeness of your story put
Heaviness[79] in me.

    Prospero.   Shake it off. Come on.
We'll visit Caliban, my slave, who never
Yields us kind answer.

    Miranda.   'Tis a villain, sir,
310 I do not love to look on.

    Prospero.   But, as 'tis,

CLOSE READ
ANNOTATE: Mark all of Ariel's speeches in lines 251–293.

QUESTION: What is the main difference between Ariel's lines and Prospero's?

CONCLUDE: What does this difference suggest about the personalities of the two characters and the nature of their relationship?

77. correspondent *adj.* obedient.
78. gently *adj.* graciously.

79. Heaviness *n.* sleepiness.

We cannot miss[80] him. He does make our fire,
Fetch in our wood, and serves in offices
That profit us. What, ho! Slave! Caliban!
Thou earth, thou! Speak!

Caliban. [*Within*]   There's wood enough within.

315 **Prospero.** Come forth, I say! There's other business for thee.
Come, thou tortoise! When?

[*Enter* Ariel *like a water nymph.*]

81. quaint *adj.* clever; ingenious.

Fine apparition! My quaint[81] Ariel,
Hark in thine ear.   [*Whispers.*]

Ariel.   My lord it shall be done.   [*Exit.*]

Prospero. Thou poisonous slave, got by the devil himself
320 Upon thy wicked dam, come forth!

[*Enter* Caliban.]

Caliban. As wicked dew as e'er my mother brushed
With raven's feather from unwholesome fen

82. southwest wind believed to carry the plague.

83. blister *v.* give blisters or sores.

84. Urchins *n.* goblins.

85. vast . . . work the long period of the night when goblins are permitted to do what they wish.

Drop on you both! A southwest[82] blow on ye
And blister[83] you all o'er!

325 **Prospero.** For this, be sure, tonight thou shalt have cramps,
Side-stitches that shall pen thy breath up. Urchins[84]
Shall, for that vast of night that they may work,[85]
All exercise on thee; thou shalt be pinched
As thick as honeycomb, each pinch more stinging
330 Than bees that made 'em.

Caliban.   I must eat my dinner.
This island's mine by Sycorax my mother,
Which thou tak'st from me. When thou cam'st first,
Thou strok'st me and made much of me; wouldst give me
Water with berries in't; and teach me how
335 To name the bigger light, and how the less,
That burn by day and night. And then I loved thee
And showed thee all the qualities o' th' isle,
The fresh springs, brine pits, barren place and fertile.
Cursed be I that did so! All the charms
340 Of Sycorax—toads, beetles, bats, light on you!
For I am all the subjects that you have,
Which first was mine own king; and here you sty[86] me

86. sty *v.* lodge or pen up, as in a pigsty.

87. rock *n.* cave.

In this hard rock,[87] whiles you do keep from me
The rest o' th' island.

Prospero.   Thou most lying slave,

88. stripes *n.* whiplashes.

345 Whom stripes[88] may move, not kindness! I have used thee,
(Filth as thou art) with human care, and lodged thee
In mine own cell till thou didst seek to violate
The honor of my child.

Caliban, the native inhabitant of the island, is often depicted as poorly or not fully formed. In the 2010 film adaptation, this aspect of Caliban's character (here played by Djimon Hounsou) was made literal with the use of makeup and prosthetics.

Caliban. O ho, O ho! Would't had been done!
350 Thou didst prevent me; I had peopled else
This isle with Calibans.

    Miranda.   Abhorrèd slave,
Which any print of goodness wilt not take,
Being capable of all ill[89] I pitied thee,
Took pains to make thee speak, taught thee each hour
355 One thing or other. When thou didst not, savage,
Know thine own meaning, but wouldst gabble like
A thing most brutish, I endowed thy purposes
With words that made them known. But thy vile race,
Though thou didst learn, had that in't which good natures
360 Could not abide to be with. Therefore wast thou
Deservedly confined into this rock, who hadst
Deserved more than a prison.

    Caliban. You taught me language, and my profit on't
Is, I know how to curse. The red plague rid[90] you
365 For learning[91] me your language!

NOTES

89. **print . . . ill** impression of goodness will not take since you are capable only of making an evil impression.

90. **rid** *v.* destroy.
91. **learning** teaching.

Prospero.   Hagseed, hence!
Fetch us in fuel. And be quick, thou'rt best,[92]
To answer other business. Shrug'st thou, malice?
If thou neglect'st or dost unwillingly
What I command, I'll rack thee with old cramps,
370 Fill all thy bones with aches, make thee roar
That beasts shall tremble at thy din.

Caliban.   No, pray thee.
[*Aside*] I must obey. His art is of such pow'r
It would control my dam's god, Setebos,[93]
And make a vassal of him.

Prospero.   So, slave; hence!   [*Exit* Caliban.]

[*Enter* Ferdinand *and* Ariel (*invisible*), *playing and singing.*]

Ariel's song.

375   Come unto these yellow sands,
                 And then take hands:
            Curtsied when you have and kissed
                 The wild waves whist,[94]
            Foot it featly[95] here and there;
380   And, sweet sprites, the burden bear.
                 Hark, hark!
                      [*Burden, dispersedly*][96] Bow, wow!
                 The watchdogs bark.
                      [*Burden, dispersedly*] Bow, wow!
                 Hark, hark! I hear
                 The strain of strutting chanticleer[97]
385   Cry cock-a-diddle-dow.

Ferdinand. Where should this music be? I' th' air or th' earth?
It sounds no more; and sure it waits upon
Some god o' th' island. Sitting on a bank,
Weeping again the King my father's wrack,
390 This music crept by me upon the waters,
Allaying both their fury and my passion[98]
With its sweet air. Thence I have followed it,
Or it hath drawn me rather; but 'tis gone.
No, it begins again.

Ariel's song.

395   Full fathom five[99] thy father lies;
                 Of his bones are coral made;
            Those are pearls that were his eyes:
                 Nothing of him that doth fade
            But doth suffer a sea change
400   Into something rich and strange.
            Sea nymphs hourly ring his knell;
                      [*Burden*] Ding-dong

93. **Setebos** South American Indian god who was mentioned in a travel book by a sixteenth-century Englishman.

94. **kissed . . . whist** kissed the wild waves into silence.
95. **featly** *adv.* nimbly.

96. *Burden, dispersedly* stage direction calling for a background sound of dogs and later of a crowing rooster.
97. **chanticleer** *n.* rooster, originally the name of the rooster character in popular medieval fables.

98. **passion** *n.* emotion; sorrow.

99. **Full fathom five** fully or completely at a depth of thirty feet in water.

Hark! Now I hear them—ding-dong bell.

Ferdinand. The ditty does remember my drowned father.
This is no mortal business, nor no sound
405 That the earth owes.[100] I hear it now above me.

Prospero. The fringed curtains of thine eye advance[101]
And say what thou seest yond.

Miranda.   What is't? A spirit?
Lord, how it looks about! Believe me, sir,
It carries a brave form. But 'tis a spirit.

410 **Prospero.** No, wench; it eats, and sleeps, and hath such senses
As we have, such. This gallant which thou seest
Was in the wrack; and, but he's something stained
With grief (that's beauty's canker), thou mightst call him
A goodly person. He hath lost his fellows
415 And strays about to find 'em.

Miranda.   I might call him
A thing divine; for nothing natural
I ever saw so noble.

Prospero.   [*Aside*] It goes on, I see,
As my soul prompts it. Spirit, fine spirit, I'll free thee
Within two days for this.

Ferdinand.   Most sure, the goddess
420 On whom these airs attend! Vouchsafe my prayer
May know if you remain[102] upon this island,
And that you will some good instruction give
How I may bear me[103] here. My prime request,
Which I do last pronounce, is (O you wonder!)
425 If you be maid or no?

Miranda.   No wonder, sir,
But certainly a maid.

Ferdinand.   My language! Heavens!
I am the best of them that speak this speech,
Were I but where 'tis spoken.

Prospero.   How? The best?
What wert thou if the King of Naples heard thee?

430 **Ferdinand.** A single[104] thing, as I am now, that wonders
To hear thee speak of Naples. He does hear me;
And that he does I weep. Myself am Naples,
Who with mine eyes, never since at ebb, beheld
The King my father wracked.

Miranda.   Alack, for mercy!

435 **Ferdinand.** Yes, faith, and all his lords, the Duke of Milan
And his brave son being twain.[105]

NOTES

100. **owes** *v.* owns; possesses.
101. **advance** *v.* look up.

CLOSE READ
ANNOTATE: Mark the end punctuation in Miranda's dialogue in lines 407–409.

QUESTION: Which sentence might an actor emphasize most?

CONCLUDE: What effect does the punctuation have on the reader's and audience's understanding of Miranda?

102. **remain** *v.* live; dwell.

103. **bear me** behave; conduct myself.

104. **single** *adj.* helpless; alone; solitary.

105. **twain** two.

usurp (yoo ZURP) *v.* take over
without having authority

109. ow'st *v.* own.

110. gentle . . . fearful good birth
and courageous.

111. My . . . tutor? Am I to
be taught by one so far
below me?

112. ward *n.* position of defense.

113. stick *n.* Prospero's magic
wand.

Prospero. [*Aside*] The Duke of Milan
And his more braver daughter could control[106] thee,
If now 'twere fit to do 't. At the first sight
They have changed eyes.[107] Delicate Ariel,
440 I'll set thee free for this. [*To Ferdinand*] A word, good sir.
I fear you have done yourself some wrong.[108] A word!

Miranda. Why speaks my father so ungently? This
Is the third man that e'er I saw; the first
That e'er I sighed for. Pity move my father
445 To be inclined my way!

Ferdinand. O, if a virgin,
And your affection not gone forth, I'll make you
The Queen of Naples.

Prospero. Soft, sir! One word more.
[*Aside*] They are both in either's powers. But this swift business
I must uneasy make, lest too light winning
450 Make the prize light. [*To Ferdinand*] One word more! I charge thee
That thou attend me. Thou dost here **usurp**
The name thou ow'st[109] not, and hast put thyself
Upon this island as a spy, to win it
From me, the lord on't.

Ferdinand. No, as I am a man!

455 **Miranda.** There's nothing ill can dwell in such a temple.
If the ill spirit have so fair a house,
Good things will strive to dwell with't.

Prospero. Follow me.
[*To Miranda*] Speak not you for him; he's a traitor.
[*To Ferdinand*] Come!
460 I'll manacle thy neck and feet together:
Sea water shalt thou drink; thy food shall be
The fresh-brook mussels, withered roots, and husks
Wherein the acorn cradled. Follow!

Ferdinand. No.
I will resist such entertainment till
Mine enemy has more pow'r.

[*He draws, and is charmed from moving.*]

Miranda. O dear father,
465 Make not too rash a trial of him, for
He's gentle and not fearful.[110]

Prospero. What? I say,
My foot my tutor?[111] [*To Ferdinand*] Put thy sword up, traitor—
Who mak'st a show but dar'st not strike, thy conscience
Is so possessed with guilt! Come, from thy ward![112]
470 For I can here disarm thee with this stick[113]
And make thy weapon drop.

Miranda.   Beseech you, father!

Prospero. Hence! Hang not on my garments.

Miranda.   Sir, have pity.
I'll be his surety.

Prospero.   Silence! One word more
Shall make me chide thee, if not hate thee. What,
475 An advocate for an imposter! Hush!
Thou think'st there is no more such shapes as he,
Having seen but him and Caliban. Foolish wench!
To th' most of men this is a Caliban,
And they to him are angels.

Miranda.   My affections
480 Are then most humble. I have no ambition
To see a goodlier man.

Prospero. [*To* Ferdinand] Come on, obey!
Thy nerves[114] are in their infancy again
And have no vigor in them.

Ferdinand.   So they are.
My spirits, as in a dream, are all bound up.
485 My father's loss, the weakness which I feel,
The wrack of all my friends, nor this man's threats
To whom I am subdued, are but light to me,
Might I but through my prison once a day
Behold this maid. All corners else o' th' earth
490 Let liberty make use of.[115] Space enough
Have I in such a prison.

Prospero. [*Aside*]   It works. [*To* Ferdinand] Come on.
[*To* Ariel] Thou hast done well, fine Ariel! [*To* Ferdinand]
  Follow me.
[*To* Ariel] Hark what thou else shalt do me.

Miranda.   Be of comfort.
My father's of a better nature, sir,
495 Than he appears by speech. This is unwonted
Which now came from him.

Prospero.   Thou shalt be free
As mountain winds; but then[116] exactly do
All points of my command.

Ariel.   To th' syllable.

Prospero. [*To* Ferdinand] Come, follow. [*To* Miranda]
  Speak not for him.

                                        [*Exit.*]

NOTES

CLOSE READ
ANNOTATE: Mark the three shortest sentences in Prospero's dialogue in lines 473–479.

QUESTION: What is the pattern created by these short sentences combined with the longer sentences?

CONCLUDE: What is the effect of this pattern?

114. **nerves** *n.* sinews; muscles; strength.

115. **All . . . of** Let freedom be in all the rest of the world.

116. **but then** until then.

Comprehension Check

Complete the following items after you finish your first read.

1. How did Prospero and Miranda end up on the island years before the present action of the play?

2. What does Prospero do to bring the mariners to the island?

3. What happens when Miranda and Ferdinand meet each other for the first time?

4. Who is Caliban?

5. 🗐 **Notebook** Confirm your understanding of Act I by writing a summary.

RESEARCH

Research to Clarify Choose at least one unfamiliar detail from the text. Briefly research that detail. In what way does the information you learned shed light on an aspect of the play?

Research to Explore Choose something from the text that interests you, and formulate a research question. Write your question here.

Close Read the Text

Reread Act I, Scene ii, lines 386–394. Mark the verbs. What kinds of actions do they name? What do they suggest about the way in which Ferdinand came to the spot where Prospero and Miranda see him?

Close Read

ANNOTATE · QUESTION · CONCLUDE

THE TEMPEST, ACT I

Analyze the Text

CITE TEXTUAL EVIDENCE to support your answers.

 Notebook Respond to these questions.

1. (a) How does Miranda react to the shipwreck? (b) **Interpret** What does her reaction show about her character?

2. (a) Who causes the shipwreck, and on whose behalf? (b) **Connect** Why is this information revealed while Miranda is asleep?

3. (a) **Infer** Why does Prospero arrange for Ferdinand and Miranda to meet? (b) **Evaluate** What does Prospero achieve as a result of their first encounter?

Concept Vocabulary

perfidious	treacherous	usurp

Why These Words? The three concept vocabulary words all relate to betrayal. As you review the text, find other words that fit the category.

Practice

Notebook Confirm your understanding of these words by using each in a line of dialogue between two siblings in conflict. Write your lines. Trade lines with a partner, and read the dialogue aloud.

Word Study

Notebook **Latin Suffix: -ous** The concept vocabulary word *perfidious* ends with the Latin suffix -ous, which forms adjectives and means "full of," "characterized by," or "having the qualities of." *Perfidious*, then, means "characterized by perfidy, or disloyal behavior."

1. Find the word *tempestuous* in the first stage direction of Scene i, and find the word *blasphemous* in line 34 of Scene i. Using your knowledge of the noun from which it was formed, write the meaning of each word. Use a print or online dictionary to verify your definitions.

2. Find the following words in Scene ii: *auspicious* (line 182) and *poisonous* (line 319). Use context clues to write the meaning of each word. Check your definitions against a dictionary.

WORD NETWORK

Add words related to forgiveness from the text to your Word Network.

THE TEMPEST, ACT I

Analyze Craft and Structure

Shakespeare's Romances In Shakespeare's day, a play was either a **tragedy**, which ended in death and destruction, or a **comedy**, which ended in happiness and, often, a wedding. Comedies were not necessarily funny, but they were joyful. Toward the end of his career, Shakespeare began to write a different kind of play. Known as a **romance**, it incorporates elements of both tragedy and comedy. The ending is happy, but to reach it the characters must withstand many perils. The romances also share these other features:

- magical, supernatural, or otherwise unrealistic events
- a protagonist, or main character, who is an older man
- a subplot featuring young characters
- characters representing a variety of social levels, from laborers to nobility
- dark emotions with hints of violence

In Shakespeare's tragedies, threats of violence or suffering are fully realized. In the romances those threats are contained. However, this quality of dark forces straining to break through can make the romances unsettling. The plays end happily, but with a troubled edge to the joy.

Practice

CITE TEXTUAL EVIDENCE to support your answers.

Use the chart to note specific examples of the features of Shakespeare's romances that appear in *The Tempest*, Act I.

ELEMENT OF ROMANCE	EXAMPLE FROM ACT I
magical, supernatural, or otherwise unrealistic events	
a main character who is an older man	
a subplot featuring young characters	
dark emotions with hints of violence	
characters representing a variety of social levels	

Writing to Sources

A **paraphrase** is a restatement of another author's ideas in your own words. When writers include ideas from other texts in their arguments, they might choose to paraphrase portions rather than always use direct quotations. By paraphrasing, a writer both demonstrates his or her knowledge and provides evidence in a different way.

Assignment

In Shakespeare's plays, songs often sum up an entire situation. Analyze lines 395–402 of Ariel's song that appears near the end of Act I. Then, write a **paraphrase** of those lines.

Analyze the Song Before you paraphrase the song, make sure you understand it. Use the chart to analyze the lines. Then, write your paraphrase.

LINE(S) FROM THE SONG	MEANING
Full fathom five thy father lies;	
Of his bones are coral made;	
Those are pearls that were his eyes:	
Nothing of him that doth fade *But doth suffer a sea change* *Into something rich and strange.*	
Sea nymphs hourly ring his knell; *Ding-dong*	
Hark! Now I hear them—ding-dong bell.	

Reflect on Your Writing

Notebook After you have written your paraphrase, answer the following questions.

1. Do you think Ferdinand would respond to your paraphrase in the same way he responds to Ariel's song? Explain.

2. Using this exercise as an example, explain what is lost and what is gained by paraphrasing a text.

3. **Why These Words?** The words you choose make a difference in your writing. Which words did you specifically choose to capture the meaning of the song?

EVIDENCE LOG

Before moving on to a new selection, go to your Evidence Log, and record what you learned from *The Tempest,* Act I.

William Shakespeare

The Tempest, Act II

Concept Vocabulary

You will encounter the following words as you read Act II of *The Tempest*. Before reading, note how familiar you are with each word. Then, rank the words in order from most familiar (1) to least familiar (3).

WORD	YOUR RANKING
succession	
heir	
supplant	

After completing the first read, come back to the concept vocabulary and review your rankings. Mark changes to your original rankings as needed.

First Read DRAMA

Apply these strategies as you conduct your first read. You will have an opportunity to complete the close-read notes after your first read.

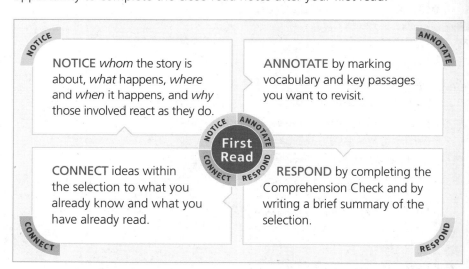

NOTICE *whom* the story is about, *what* happens, *where* and *when* it happens, and *why* those involved react as they do.

ANNOTATE by marking vocabulary and key passages you want to revisit.

CONNECT ideas within the selection to what you already know and what you have already read.

RESPOND by completing the Comprehension Check and by writing a brief summary of the selection.

The Tempest Act II

William Shakespeare

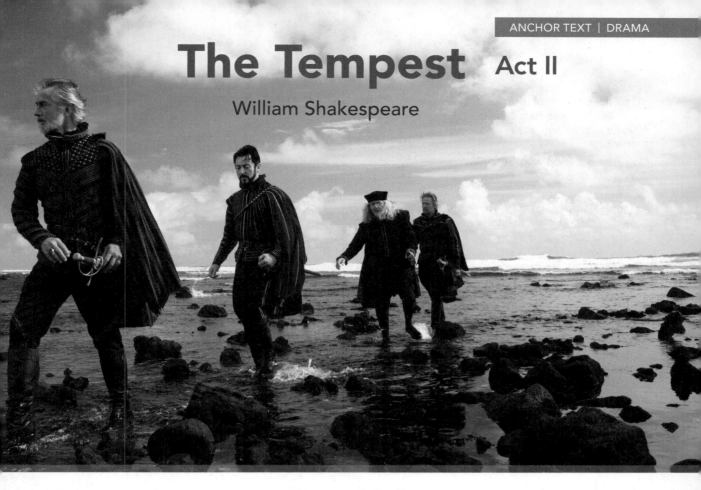

REVIEW AND ANTICIPATE

In Act I, a massive storm rocks a ship carrying King Alonso of Naples, his son Ferdinand, and others. The ship's passengers are thrown into the sea and wash up unharmed on Prospero's island. Prospero, the rightful Duke of Milan, has been living in exile on the island with his daughter, Miranda. Prospero tells Miranda that he has used magic to cause the storm. Furthermore, his brother, Antonio, is one of the passengers. Twelve years earlier, Antonio had stolen Prospero's dukedom, and had put Prospero and Miranda—who was then only three years old—to sea in a leaky boat. Now, Prospero's servant, the sprite Ariel, leads Ferdinand to Prospero. Miranda sees the prince and immediately falls in love. Prospero pretends to mistrust Ferdinand and takes him captive.

Scene i • *Another part of the island.*

[*Enter* Alonso, Sebastian, Antonio, Gonzalo, Adrian, Francisco, *and others*.]

Gonzalo. Beseech you, sir, be merry. You have cause
(So have we all) of joy; for our escape
Is much beyond our loss. Our hint of¹ woe
Is common; every day some sailor's wife,
5 The master of some merchant,² and the merchant,
Have just our theme of woe. But for the miracle,
I mean our preservation, few in millions
Can speak like us. Then wisely, good sir, weigh
Our sorrow with our comfort.

NOTES

1. **hint of** occasion for.

2. **master . . . merchant** captain of a ship owned by a merchant.

3. **porridge** *n.* kind of thick soup made with peas; hence, there is an indirect pun on the word *peace.*

4. **visitor** *n.* person who "visits" the sick or elderly and offers comfort.

5. **give . . . so** give up so easily; quickly stop offering unwanted comfort.

6. **One. Tell.** That's the first. Keep count.

7. **dollar** *n.* English pronunciation of the German *taler,* silver coin.

8. **Dolor** Latin word meaning "pain" or "grief." The word was pronounced very much like "dollar."

9. **wiselier** *adv.* more wittily; more cleverly.

10. **prithee, spare** please spare me all this cleverness; please shut up.

11. **old cock** old rooster, referring to Gonzalo.

12. **temperance** *n.* mild climate; also, moderation, and among Puritans, the name of a woman, as in the next line.

Alonso. Prithee, peace.

10 **Sebastian.** [*Aside to* Antonio] He receives comfort like cold porridge.[3]

Antonio. [*Aside to* Sebastian] The visitor[4] will not give him o'er so.[5]

Sebastian. Look, he's winding up the watch of his wit; by and 15 by it will strike.

Gonzalo. Sir—

Sebastian. [*Aside to* Antonio] One. Tell.[6]

Gonzalo. When every grief is entertained that's offered Comes to the entertainer—

20 **Sebastian.** A dollar.[7]

Gonzalo. Dolor[8] comes to him, indeed. You have spoken truer than you purposed.

Sebastian. You have taken it wiselier[9] than I meant you should.

Gonzalo. Therefore, my lord—

25 **Antonio.** Fie, what a spendthrift is he of his tongue!

Alonso. I prithee, spare.[10]

Gonzalo. Well, I have done. But yet—

Sebastian. He will be talking.

Antonio. Which, of he or Adrian, for a good wager, first begins 30 to crow?

Sebastian. The old cock.[11]

Antonio. The cock'rel.

Sebastian. Done! The wager?

Antonio. A laughter.

35 **Sebastian.** A match!

Adrian. Though this island seem to be desert—

Antonio. Ha, ha, ha!

Sebastian. So, you're paid.

Adrian. Uninhabitable and almost inaccessible—

40 **Sebastian.** Yet—

Adrian. Yet—

Antonio. He could not miss't.

Adrian. It must needs be of subtle, tender, and delicate temperance.[12]

45 **Antonio.** Temperance was a delicate wench.

Sebastian. Ay, and a subtle, as he most learnedly delivered.

Adrian. The air breathes upon us here most sweetly.

Sebastian. As if it had lungs, and rotten ones.

Antonio. Or as 'twere perfumed by a fen.

50 **Gonzalo.** Here is everything advantageous to life.

Antonio. True; save means to live.

Sebastian. Of that there's none, or little.

Gonzalo. How lush and lusty the grass looks! How green!

Antonio. The ground indeed is tawny.

55 **Sebastian.** With an eye of green[13] in't.

Antonio. He misses not much.

Sebastian. No; he doth but mistake the truth totally.

Gonzalo. But the rarity of it is—which is indeed almost beyond credit—

60 **Sebastian.** As many vouched rarities are.

Gonzalo. That our garments, being, as they were, drenched in the sea, hold, notwithstanding, their freshness and glosses, being rather new-dyed than stained with salt water.

Antonio. If but one of his pockets could speak, would it not say
65 he lies?[14]

Sebastian. Ay, or very falsely pocket up his report.[15]

Gonzalo. Methinks our garments are now as fresh as when we put them on first in Afric, at the marriage of the King's fair daughter Claribel to the King of Tunis.

70 **Sebastian.** 'Twas a sweet marriage, and we prosper well in our return.

Adrian. Tunis was never graced before with such a paragon to[16] their queen.

Gonzalo. Not since widow Dido's time.

75 **Antonio.** Widow! A pox o' that! How came that widow in? Widow Dido!

Sebastian. What if he had said "widower Aeneas"[17] too? Good Lord, how you take it!

Adrian. "Widow Dido" said you? You make me study of that.
80 She was of Carthage, not of Tunis.

Gonzalo. This Tunis, sir, was Carthage.

Adrian. Carthage?

Gonzalo. I assure you, Carthage.

Antonio. His word is more than the miraculous harp.[18]

85 **Sebastian.** He hath raised the wall and houses too.

Antonio. What impossible matter will he make easy next?

NOTES

13. **eye of green** patch of green here and there in the parched earth.

14. **If . . . lies?** If one of Gonzalo's pockets could speak, wouldn't it prove him a liar by being water stained?

15. **pocket . . . report** cover up Gonzalo's lie by not being stained. Gonzalo can't win either way.

16. **to** for.

17. **Widow Dido . . . "widower Aeneas"** allusion to a great love story in the national epic of Rome, the *Aeneid*, by Virgil.

18. **miraculous harp** harp of Amphion, son of the Greek god Zeus, played so perfectly that the stones for the walls of the city of Thebes slid into place by themselves. Gonzalo's words are more miraculous than the harp because they create a whole city by mistakenly identifying ancient Carthage with modern Tunis.

Sebastian. I think he will carry this island home in his pocket and give it his son for an apple.

Antonio. And, sowing the kernels of it in the sea, bring forth
90 more islands.

Gonzalo. Ay!

Antonio. Why, in good time.

Gonzalo. [*To* Alonso] Sir, we were talking that our garments seem now as fresh as when we were at Tunis at the marriage of
95 your daughter, who is now Queen.

Antonio. And the rarest that e'er came there.

19. Bate with the exception of.

Sebastian. Bate,[19] I beseech you, widow Dido.

Antonio. O, widow Dido! Ay, widow Dido!

Gonzalo. Is not, sir, my doublet as fresh as the first day I wore
100 it? I mean, in a sort.[20]

20. in a sort in a manner of speaking.

Antonio. That "sort" was well fished for.

Gonzalo. When I wore it at your daughter's marriage?

Alonso. You cram these words into mine ears against
The stomach of my sense.[21] Would I had never
105 Married my daughter there! For, coming thence,
My son is lost; and, in my rate,[22] she too,
Who is so far from Italy removed
I ne'er again shall see her. O thou mine heir
Of Naples and of Milan, what strange fish
110 Hath made his meal on thee?

21. You . . . sense You force comfort upon me so that it revolts against common sense.

22. rate *n.* view; opinion.

Francisco.   Sir, he may live.
I saw him beat the surges under him,
And ride upon their backs. He trod the water,
Whose enmity he flung aside, and breasted
The surge most swol'n that met him. His bold head
115 'Bove the contentious waves he kept, and oared
Himself with his good arms in lusty stroke
To th' shore, that o'er his wave-worn basis bowed,
As stooping to relieve him. I not doubt
He came alive to land.

Alonso.   No, no, he's gone.

120 **Sebastian.** [*To* Alonso] Sir, you may thank yourself for this
   great loss,
That would not bless our Europe with your daughter,
But rather loose her to an African,
Where she, at least, is banished from your eye,
Who hath cause to wet the grief on't.

Alonso.   Prithee, peace.

125 **Sebastian.** You were kneeled to and importuned otherwise

By all of us; and the fair soul herself
Weighed, between loathness and obedience, at
Which end o' th' beam should bow.[23] We have lost your son,
I fear, forever. Milan and Naples have
130 Moe[24] widows in them of this business' making
Than we bring men to comfort them.
The fault's your own.

Alonso.   So is the dear'st[25] o' th' loss.

Gonzalo. My Lord Sebastian,
The truth you speak doth lack some gentleness
135 And time to speak it in. You rub the sore,
When you should bring the plaster.

Sebastian.   Very well.

Antonio. And most chirurgeonly.[26]

Gonzalo. [*To* Alonso] It is foul weather in us all, good sir,
When you are cloudy.

Sebastian. [*Aside to* Antonio] Foul weather?

Antonio. [*Aside to* Sebastian]   Very foul.

140 **Gonzalo.** Had I plantation[27] of this isle, my lord—

Antonio. He'd sow't with nettle seed.

Sebastian.   Or docks, or mallows.

Gonzalo. And were the King on't, what would I do?

Sebastian. Scape being drunk for want of wine.

Gonzalo. I' th' commonwealth I would by contraries[28]
145 Execute all things. For no kind of traffic[29]
Would I admit; no name of magistrate;
Letters[30] should not be known; riches, poverty,
And use of service,[31] none; contract, **succession**,
Bourn, bound of land, tilth, vineyard, none;[32]
150 No use of metal, corn, or wine, or oil;
No occupation; all men idle, all;
And women too, but innocent and pure;
No sovereignty.[33]

Sebastian.   Yet he would be king on't.

Antonio. The latter end of his commonwealth forgets the
beginning.

155 **Gonzalo.** All things in common nature should produce
Without sweat or endeavor. Treason, felony,
Sword, pike, knife, gun, or need of any engine[34]
Would I not have; but nature should bring forth,
Of it[35] own kind, all foison,[36] all abundance,
160 To feed my innocent people.

Sebastian. No marrying 'mong his subjects?

Antonio. None, man; all idle—knaves.

Gonzalo. I would with such perfection govern, sir,
T' excel the Golden Age.

Sebastian. [*Loudly*]   Save his Majesty!

165 **Antonio.** [*Loudly*] Long live Gonzalo!

Gonzalo.   And—do you mark me, sir?

Alonso. Prithee, no more. Thou dost talk nothing to me.

Gonzalo. I do well believe your Highness; and did it to minister occasion[37] to these gentlemen, who are of such sensible[38] and nimble lungs that they always use to laugh at nothing.

170 **Antonio.** 'Twas you we laughed at.

Gonzalo. Who in this kind of merry fooling am nothing to you; so you may continue and laugh at nothing still.

Antonio. What a blow was there given!

Sebastian. An it had not fall'n flatlong.[39]

175 **Gonzalo.** You are gentlemen of brave mettle; you would lift the moon out of her sphere if she would continue in it five weeks without changing.
[*Enter* Ariel *(invisible) playing solemn music.*]

Sebastian. We would so, and then go a-batfowling.[40]

Antonio. Nay, good my lord, be not angry.

180 **Gonzalo.** No, I warrant you; I will not adventure my discretion so weakly.[41] Will you laugh me asleep? For I am very heavy.

Antonio. Go sleep, and hear us.
[*All sleep except* Alonso, Sebastian, *and* Antonio.]

Alonso. What, all so soon asleep? I wish mine eyes
Would, with themselves, shut up my thoughts. I find
185 They are inclined to do so.

Sebastian.   Please you, sir,
Do not omit the heavy offer of it.
It seldom visits sorrow; when it doth,
It is a comforter.

Antonio.   We too, my lord,
Will guard your person while you take your rest,
190 And watch your safety.

Alonso.   Thank you. Wondrous heavy.
                         [Alonso *sleeps. Exit* Ariel.]

Sebastian. What a strange drowsiness possesses them!

Antonio. It is the quality o' th' climate.

Sebastian.   Why

---

37. minister occasion offer an opportunity.
38. sensible *adj.* sensitive.

39. flatlong on the flat side of the sword.

40. We . . . a-batfowling We would use the light of the moon to hunt birds attracted to light at night and knock them down with bats or clubs.
41. not adventure . . . weakly not risk my reputation by responding to such weak wit.

Doth it not then our eyelids sink? I find not
Myself disposed to sleep.

Antonio.   Nor I: my spirits are nimble.
195 They fell together all, as by consent,
They dropped, as by a thunder-stroke. What might,
Worthy Sebastian—O, what might?—No more!
And yet methinks I see it in thy face,
What thou shouldst be. Th' occasion speaks thee,⁴² and
200 My strong imagination sees a crown
Dropping upon thy head.

Sebastian.   What? Art thou waking?

Antonio. Do you not hear me speak?

Sebastian.   I do; and surely
It is a sleepy language and thou speak'st
Out of thy sleep. What is it thou didst say?
205 This is a strange repose, to be asleep
With eyes wide open; standing, speaking, moving,
And yet so fast asleep.

Antonio.   Noble Sebastian,
Thou let'st thy fortune sleep—die, rather; wink'st⁴³
Whiles thou art waking.

Sebastian.   Thou dost snore distinctly;

NOTES

CLOSE READ
ANNOTATE: Mark the dialogue set off by dashes in Antonio's speech in lines 194–201.

QUESTION: Why does the playwright punctuate these lines in this way?

CONCLUDE: How does the punctuation affect readers' understanding of Antonio's emotions and thoughts?

42. **occasion speaks thee** opportunity offers you.

43. **wink'st** *v.* close your eyes.

Antonio (left, played by Chris Cooper) and Sebastian (right, played by Alan Cumming) hatch a plot against the king.

44. Trebles thee o'er triples your present power.

45. standing water still water; not moving water, as between the tides.

46. in stripping . . . invest it while seeming to deny ambition, you shape it all the more.

47. matter *n.* something of importance.

48. throes thee much gives you much pain.

49. earthed buried.

50. For . . . persuade for he (Gonzalo) is the very spirit of conviction and is nothing more than a professional persuader.

51. Ambition . . . there the eye of ambition cannot see beyond the present, and even doubts what it sees there.

heir (air) *n.* person who is legally entitled to inherit

52. Ten . . . life ten leagues farther than one could travel in a lifetime.

53. post *n.* mail courier.

54. till . . . razorable until newborn babes grow beards and have to shave.

55. cast *v.* cast up on shore; survive.

---

210 There's meaning in thy snores.

Antonio. I am more serious than my custom. You
Must be so too, if heed me; which to do
Trebles thee o'er.[44]

Sebastian.   Well, I am standing water.[45]

Antonio. I'll teach you how to flow.

Sebastian.   Do so: To ebb
215 Hereditary sloth instructs me.

Antonio.   O,
If you but knew how you the purpose cherish
Whiles thus you mock it; how, in stripping it,
You more invest it![46] Ebbing men, indeed,
Most often do so near the bottom run
220 By their own fear or sloth.

Sebastian.   Prithee, say on,
The setting of thine eye and cheek proclaim
A matter[47] from thee; and a birth indeed,
Which throes thee much[48] to yield.

Antonio.   Thus, sir:
Although this lord of weak remembrance, this
225 Who shall be of as little memory
When he is earthed,[49] hath here almost persuaded
(For he's a spirit of persuasion, only
Professes to persuade)[50] the King his son's alive,
'Tis as impossible that he's undrowned
230 And he that sleeps here swims.

Sebastian.   I have no hope
That he's undrowned.

Antonio.   O, out of that no hope
What great hope have you! No hope that way is
Another way so high a hope that even
Ambition cannot pierce a wink beyond,
235 But doubt discovery there.[51] Will you grant with me
That Ferdinand is drowned?

Sebastian.   He's gone.

Antonio.   Then, tell me,
Who's the next **heir** of Naples?

Sebastian.   Claribel.

Antonio. She that is Queen of Tunis; she that dwells
Ten leagues beyond man's life;[52] she that from Naples
240 Can have no note—unless the sun were post;[53]
The man i' th' moon's too slow—till newborn chins
Be rough and razorable;[54] she that from whom
We all were sea-swallowed, though some cast[55] again,

And by that destiny, to perform an act
245 Whereof what's past is prologue, what to come,
In yours and my discharge.

Sebastian.   What stuff is this? How say you?
'Tis true, my brother's daughter's Queen of Tunis;
So is she heir of Naples; 'twixt which regions
There is some space.

Antonio.   A space whose ev'ry cubit
250 Seems to cry out, "How shall that Claribel
Measure us back to Naples? Keep in Tunis,
And let Sebastian wake!" Say, this were death
That now hath seized them, why, they were no worse
Than now they are. There be that can rule Naples
255 As well as he that sleeps; lords that can prate
As amply and unnecessarily
As this Gonzalo; I myself could make
A chough of as deep chat.[56] O, that you bore
The mind that I do! What a sleep were this
260 For your advancement! Do you understand me?

Sebastian. Methinks I do.

Antonio.   And how does your content
Tender[57] your own good fortune?

Sebastian.   I remember
You did **supplant** your brother Prospero.

Antonio.   True.
And look how well my garments sit upon me,
265 Much feater[58] than before. My brother's servants
Were then my fellows; now they are my men.

Sebastian. But, for your conscience—

Antonio. Ay, sir, where lies that? If 'twere a kibe,[59]
'Twould put me to my slipper; but I feel not
270 This deity in my bosom. Twenty consciences
That stand 'twixt me and Milan, candied be they
And melt, ere they molest! Here lies your brother,
No better than the earth he lies upon—
If he were that which now he's like, that's dead—
275 Whom I with this obedient steel (three inches of it)
Can lay to bed forever; whiles you, doing thus,
To the perpetual wink for aye might put
This ancient morsel, this Sir Prudence, who
Should not upbraid our course. For all the rest,
280 They'll take suggestion as a cat laps milk;
They'll tell the clock[60] to any business that
We say befits the hour.

Sebastian.   Thy case, dear friend,
Shall be my precendent. As thou got'st Milan,

NOTES

56. I . . . chat I myself could make a crow sound as profound as Gonzalo.

57. Tender *v.* think of.

supplant (suh PLANT) *v.* replace by unethical means

58. feater more attractively; more fittingly.

59. kibe *n.* inflammation of the heel caused by cold.

60. tell the clock agree.

King Alonso (played by David Strathairn) sets out to search for the son he believes is dead.

CLOSE READ

ANNOTATE: Mark the clause set in parentheses in line 291.

QUESTION: Why does Shakespeare place this clause in parentheses?

CONCLUDE: How does this use of punctuation help to clarify Ariel's feelings?

I'll come by Naples. Draw thy sword. One stroke
285   Shall free thee from the tribute which thou payest,
      And I the King shall love thee.

Antonio.   Draw together;
And when I rear my hand, do you the like,
To fall it on Gonzalo.   [*They draw.*]

Sebastian.   O, but one word.
[*Enter Ariel (invisible) with music and song.*]

Ariel. My master through his art foresees the danger
290   That you, his friend, are in, and sends me forth
      (For else his project dies) to keep them living.
                              [*Sings in Gonzalo's ear.*]
            While you here do snoring lie,
            Open-eyed conspiracy

His time doth take.

295 If of life you keep a care,
Shake off slumber, and beware.
Awake, awake!

Antonio. Then let us both be sudden.

Gonzalo. [*Wakes.*]   Now, good angels
Preserve the King!   [*The others wake.*]

300 **Alonso.** Why, how now? Ho, awake! Why are you drawn?
Wherefore this ghastly looking?

Gonzalo.   What's the matter?

Sebastian. Whiles we stood here securing your repose,
Even now, we heard a hollow burst of bellowing
Like bulls, or rather lions. Did't not wake you?
305 It struck mine ear most terribly.

Alonso.   I heard nothing.

Antonio. O, 'twas a din to fright a monster's ear,
To make an earthquake! Sure it was the roar
Of a whole herd of lions.

Alonso.   Heard you this, Gonzalo?

Gonzalo. Upon mine honor, sir, I heard a humming,
310 And that a strange one, too, which did awake me.
I shaked you, sir, and cried. As mine eyes opened,
I saw their weapons drawn. There was a noise,
That's verily.[61] 'Tis best we stand upon our guard,
Or that we quit this place. Let's draw our weapons.

315 **Alonso.** Lead off this ground, and let's make further search
For my poor son.

Gonzalo.   Heavens keep him from these beasts!
For he is, sure, i' th' island.

Alonso.   Lead away.

Ariel. Prospero my lord shall know what I have done:
So, King, go safely on to seek thy son.   [*Exit.*]

⌘ ⌘ ⌘

Scene ii • *Another part of the island.*

[*Enter* Caliban *with a burden of wood. A noise of thunder heard.*]

Caliban. All the infections that the sun sucks up
From bogs, fens, flats, on Prosper fall, and make him
By inchmeal[1] a disease! His spirits hear me,
And yet I needs must curse. But they'll nor pinch,

61. That's verily that's the truth.

1. By inchmeal inch by inch

2. **urchin shows** visions of hobgoblins.

3. **Nor . . . firebrand** nor lead me astray with such illusions as the will-o'-the-wisp.

4. **mow** *v.* make faces.

5 Fright me with urchin shows,[2] pitch me i' th' mire,
   Nor lead me, like a firebrand,[3] in the dark
   Out of my way, unless he bid 'em. But
   For every trifle are they set upon me;
   Sometime like apes that mow[4] and chatter at me
10 And after bite me; then like hedgehogs which
   Lie tumbling in my barefoot way and mount
   Their pricks at my footfall; sometime am I
   All wound with adders, who with cloven tongues
   Do hiss me into madness.
   [*Enter* Trinculo.]
                          Lo, Now, lo!
15 Here comes a spirit of his, and to torment me
   For bringing wood in slowly. I'll fall flat.
   Perchance he will not mind me.   [*Lies down.*]

Trinculo. Here's neither bush nor shrub to bear off[5] any weather at all, and another storm brewing; I hear it sing i' th' wind. Yond
20 same black cloud, yond huge one, looks like a foul bombard[6] that would shed his liquor. If it should thunder as it did before, I know not where to hide my head. Yond same cloud cannot but fall by pailfuls. What have we here? A man or a fish? Dead or alive? A fish! He smells like a fish; a very ancient and fishlike
25 smell; a kind of not of the newest Poor John.[7] A strange fish! Were I in England now, as once I was, and had but this fish painted,[8] not a holiday fool there would but give a piece of silver. There would this monster make a man;[9] any strange beast there makes a man. When they will not give a doit[10] to relieve a
30 lame beggar, they will lazy out ten to see a dead Indian. Legged like a man! and his fins like arms! Warm o' my troth! I do now let loose my opinion, hold it no longer. This is no fish, but an islander, that hath lately suffered by a thunderbolt. [*Thunder.*] Alas, the storm is come again! My best way is to creep under his
35 gaberdine; there is no other shelter hereabout. Misery acquaints a man with strange bedfellows. I will here shroud[11] till the dregs of the storm be past.   [*Creeps under* Caliban's *garment.*]

[*Enter* Stephano, *singing (a bottle in his hand).*]

Stephano.   I shall no more to sea, to sea,
                       Here shall I die ashore.

40 This is a very scurvy[12] tune to sing at a man's funeral.
   Well, here's my comfort.   [*Drinks.*]

          The master, the swabber, the boatswain, and I,
                  The gunner, and his mate,
          Loved Mall, Meg, and Marian and Margery,
45   But none of us cared for Kate.
                  For she had a tongue with a tang,
                  Would cry to a sailor "Go hang!"
          She loved not the savor of tar nor of pitch;

5. **bear off** protect against.

6. **bombard** *n.* large jug made of leather.

7. **Poor John** type of fish similar to codfish.

8. **painted** The picture of a fish painted on a sign would advertise the show.

9. **make a man** make a person's fortune.

10. **doit** *n.* coin of the lowest value.

11. **shroud** *v.* cover myself.

12. **scurvy** *adj.* despicable.

50   Yet a tailor might scratch her where'er she did itch.
           Then to sea, boys, and let her go hang!

This is a scurvy tune too; but here's my comfort.   [*Drinks.*]

Caliban. Do not torment me! O!

Stephano. What's the matter? Have we devils here? Do you put
tricks upon 's with savages and men of Inde, ha? I have not
55 scaped drowning to be afeard now of your four legs. For it hath
been said, "As proper a man as ever went on four legs cannot
make him give ground"; and it shall be said so again, while
Stephano breathes at' nostrils.

Caliban. The spirit torments me. O!

60 **Stephano.** This is some monster of the isle with four legs, who
hath got, as I take it, an ague.[13] Where the devil should he learn
our language? I will give him some relief, if it be but for
that. If I can recover[14] him, and keep him tame, and get to
Naples with him, he's a present for any emperor that ever trod
65 on neat's leather.[15]

Caliban. Do not torment me, prithee; I'll bring my wood home
faster.

Stephano. He's in his fit now and does not talk after the wisest.
He shall taste of my bottle; if he have never drunk wine afore, it
70 will go near to remove his fit. If I can recover him and keep him
tame, I will not take too much for him.[16] He shall pay for him
that hath him, and that soundly.

Caliban. Thou dost me yet but little hurt. Thou wilt anon;[17] I
know it by thy trembling. Now Prosper works upon thee.

75 **Stephano.** Come on your ways, open your mouth; here is that
which will give language to you, cat.[18] Open your mouth. This
will shake your shaking, I can tell you, and that soundly. [*Gives
Caliban drink.*] You cannot tell who's your friend. Open your
chaps[19] again.

80 **Trinculo.** I should know that voice. It should be—but he is
drowned; and these are devils. O, defend me!

Stephano. Four legs and two voices—a most delicate monster!
His forward voice now is to speak well of his friend; his
backward voice is to utter foul speeches and to detract. If all the
85 wine in my bottle will recover him, I will help his ague. Come!
[*Gives drink.*] Amen! I will pour some in thy other mouth.

Trinculo. Stephano!

Stephano. Doth thy other mouth call me? Mercy, mercy! This is
a devil, and no monster. I will leave him; I have no long spoon.[20]

90 **Trinculo.** Stephano! If thou beest Stephano, touch me and speak
to me; for I am Trinculo—be not afeard—thy good friend
Trinculo.

NOTES

13. ague (AY gyoo) *n.* feverish ailment characterized by violent shivering, similar to malaria.

14. recover *v.* cure.

15. trod on neat's leather walked on cowhide; an ancient folk saying.

16. I . . . him however much I get for him will not be enough.

17. anon soon.

18. cat allusion to a popular saying of the day: "Ale will make a cat talk."

19. chaps slang for mouth.

20. long spoon another allusion to a proverb: "He who eats with the devil must have a long spoon."

NOTES

21. **siege** *n.* human waste; excrement.

22. **mooncalf** *n.* monster.

23. **butt** *n.* large cask of wine.

CLOSE READ

ANNOTATE: Alliteration is the repetition of initial consonant sounds in nearby stressed syllables. Mark examples of repeated words and alliteration in lines 115–119.

QUESTION: Why does Shakespeare use repetition and alliteration in this section of dialogue?

CONCLUDE: What is the effect of these sound devices?

24. **when time was** once upon a time; in time past.

25. **thee . . . bush** According to popular legend, the man in the moon was exiled there because he gathered firewood on Sunday, a day of rest and prayer. Gathering firewood was considered work. His dog was with him at the time.

Stephano. If thou beest Trinculo, come forth. I'll pull thee by the lesser legs. If any be Trinculo's legs, these are they. [*Draws him*
95 *out from under* Caliban's *garment.*] Thou art very Trinculo indeed! How cam'st thou to be the siege[21] of this mooncalf?[22] Can he vent Trinculos?

Trinculo. I took him to be killed with a thunderstroke. But art thou not drowned, Stephano? I hope now thou art not drowned.
100 Is the storm overblown? I hid me under the dead mooncalf's gaberdine for fear of the storm. And art thou living, Stephano? O, Stephano! Two Neapolitans scaped!

Stephano. Prithee do not turn me about; my stomach is not constant.

105 **Caliban.** [*Aside*] These be fine things, and if they be not sprites. That's a brave god and bears celestial liquor. I will kneel to him.

Stephano. How didst thou scape? How earnest thou hither? Swear by this bottle how thou cam'st hither. I escaped upon a
110 butt[23] of sack which the sailors heaved o'erboard—by this bottle which I made of the bark of a tree with mine own hands since I was cast ashore.

Caliban. I'll swear upon that bottle to be thy true subject, for the liquor is not earthly.

115 **Stephano.** Here! Swear then how thou escap'dst.

Trinculo. Swum ashore, man, like a duck. I can swim like a duck, I'll be sworn.

Stephano. Here, kiss the book. [*Gives him drink.*] Though thou canst swim like a duck, thou art made like a goose.

120 **Trinculo.** O Stephano, hast any more of this?

Stephano. The whole butt, man. My cellar is in a rock by th' seaside where my wine is hid. How now, mooncalf? How does thine ague?

Caliban. Hast thou not dropped from heaven?

125 **Stephano.** Out o' th' moon, I do assure thee: I was the Man i' th' Moon when time was.[24]

Caliban. I have seen thee in her, and I do adore thee. My mistress showed me thee and thy dog, and thy bush.[25]

Stephano. Come, swear to that; kiss the book. [*Gives him drink.*]
130 I will furnish it anon with new contents. Swear. [Caliban *drinks.*]

Trinculo. By this good light, this is a very shallow monster! I afeard of him? A very weak monster. The Man i' th' Moon!

A most poor credulous monster! Well drawn,[26] monster, in good
sooth!

135 **Caliban.** I'll show thee every fertile inch o' th' island; and I will
kiss thy foot. I prithee, be my god.

Trinculo. By this light, a most perfidious and drunken monster!
When's god's asleep, he'll rob his bottle.

Caliban. I'll kiss thy foot. I'll swear myself thy subject.

140 **Stephano.** Come on then. Down, and swear!

Trinculo. I shall laugh myself to death at this puppy-headed
monster. A most scurvy monster! I could find in my heart to
beat him—

Stephano. Come, kiss.

145 **Trinculo.** But that the poor monster's in drink. An abominable
monster!

Caliban. I'll show thee the best springs; I'll pluck thee berries;
I'll fish for thee, and get thee wood enough.
A plague upon the tyrant that I serve!
150 I'll bear him no more sticks, but follow thee,
Thou wondrous man.

Trinculo. A most ridiculous monster, to make a wonder of a poor
drunkard!

Caliban. I prithee let me bring thee where crabs[27] grow;
155 And I with my long nails will dig thee pignuts,[28]
Show thee a jay's nest, and instruct thee how
To snare the nimble marmoset.[29] I'll bring thee
To clust'ring filberts,[30] and sometimes I'll get thee
Young scamels[31] from the rock. Wilt thou go with me?

160 **Stephano.** I prithee now, lead the way without any more
talking. Trinculo, the King and all our company else being
drowned, we will inherit here. Here, bear my bottle. Fellow
Trinculo, we'll fill him by and by again.[Caliban *sings drunkenly.*]

Caliban. Farewell master; farewell, farewell!

165 **Trinculo.** A howling monster! A drunken monster!

Caliban.   No more dams I'll make for fish,
                Nor fetch in firing
                At requiring,
            Nor scrape trenchering,[32] nor wash dish
170   'Ban, 'Ban, Ca—Caliban
            Has a new master. Get a new man!
Freedom, high day! High day, freedom! High day, freedom!

Stephano. O brave monster! Lead the way.   [*Exit.*]

26. **Well drawn** good long drink of
wine.

27. **crabs** *n.* crabapples.
28. **pignuts** *n.* roots or other
underground tubers;
earthnuts.
29. **marmoset** *n.* small New World
monkey.
30. **filberts** *n.* hazel trees.
31. **scamels** unknown word;
perhaps a misspelling of
"seamels" or "sea mews," sea
gulls which often build their
nests on the rocks that line the
shore.

32. **trenchering** *n.* wooden platter
used as a dish for food.

Comprehension Check

Complete the following items after you finish your first read.

1. What do Alonso, Gonzalo, Sebastian, and Antonio believe has happened to Ferdinand?

2. In Scene i, why do most of the characters fall asleep?

3. What do Sebastian and Antonio plot while the others are asleep?

4. **📑 Notebook** Confirm your understanding of Act II by writing a summary.

- -

RESEARCH

Research to Clarify Choose at least one unfamiliar detail from the text. Briefly research that detail. In what way does the information you learned shed light on an aspect of the play?

Research to Explore Choose something from the text that interests you, and formulate a research question. Write your question here.

MAKING MEANING

Close Read the Text

Reread lines 268–283 of Act II, Scene i. Mark details that refer to things that are real and not real for Antonio. What is he saying about the reality of "conscience"? How is Antonio's point of view in direct conflict with the island setting?

THE TEMPEST, ACT II

- -

Analyze the Text

CITE TEXTUAL EVIDENCE to support your answers.

📓 **Notebook** Respond to these questions.

1. (a) In Scene i, lines 61–63, 67–69, and 99–100, Gonzalo remarks on his clothes. Why? (b) **Infer** What do Gonzalo's remarks imply about the shipwreck and the island?

2. (a) **Connect** What do Antonio and Sebastian have in common? (b) **Deduce** How does this similarity affect their conversations in Scene i?

3. (a) **Interpret** In Scene ii, why does Caliban promise to serve Stephano and Trinculo? (b) **Assess** What possible impact could the collaboration of Caliban, Stephano, and Trinculo have on the other characters?

LANGUAGE DEVELOPMENT

Concept Vocabulary

| heir | succession | supplant |

Why These Words? The three concept vocabulary words relate to the transfer of power from one generation to the next. As you review the text, find other words that fit the category.

Practice

📓 **Notebook** Confirm your understanding of these words by using them in a short paragraph. Use context clues that hint at each word's meaning.

Word Study

📓 **Notebook** **Latin Prefix: sub-** The Latin prefix *sub-* means "under," "beneath," "from beneath," or "less than." Often, the final *b* assimilates, or becomes more similar, to the first letter of the root to which the suffix attaches. For instance, it becomes a *p* in the concept word *supplant* and a *c* in the concept word *succession*.

Explain how the prefix *sub-* contributes to the meanings of these words: *substandard*, *subconscious*, *support*, *suppress*.

 WORD NETWORK

Add words related to forgiveness from the text to your Word Network.

THE TEMPEST, ACT II

Analyze Craft and Structure

Poetic Structures Unrhymed iambic pentameter, or **blank verse,** was invented during the English Renaissance to reflect natural speech. An **iamb** is a metrical foot, or unit, that consists of one unstressed syllable (˘) followed by one stressed syllable (´). The prefix *penta-* means "five." Thus, in iambic pentameter, there are five iambic feet to each line.

The following lines from "Birches," a poem by American poet Robert Frost, are written in iambic pentameter. Say the lines aloud, and notice the rise and fall of the stressed and unstressed syllables.

> When I see birches bend to left and right
>
> Across the lines of straighter darker trees,
>
> I like to think some boy's been swinging them.

In Shakespeare's plays, high-ranking, aristocratic characters usually speak in blank verse. By contrast, comic characters, joking aristocrats, and characters of low rank usually speak in prose, which does not follow any metrical pattern. The contrast of blank verse and prose clarifies characters' social status and contributes to the tone of their interactions. It is noteworthy, then, that Caliban speaks in both blank verse and prose.

Practice

> **CITE TEXTUAL EVIDENCE**
> to support your answers.

📓 **Notebook** **Answer these questions.**

1. Use the chart to identify examples of blank verse and prose in Act II of *The Tempest*.

LINES	CHARACTER	BLANK VERSE OR PROSE?
Scene i, 225–232		
Scene ii, 18–37		
Scene ii, 154–159		

2. Mark the stressed and unstressed syllables in this line from Act II, Scene i.

   All things in common nature should produce

3. Explain why some shipwreck survivors speak in prose in Act II, Scene i.

4. (a) In Act II, Scene ii, when does Caliban speak in blank verse, and when does he speak in prose? (b) How do these variations reflect Caliban's character?

Author's Style

Word Choice In any work of literature, a writer uses the tools of character development, or **characterization,** to reveal what characters are like. Since plays rely almost entirely on spoken dialogue, characters' **diction,** or word choice, is a key part of their portrayals. Shakespeare creates basic distinctions among characters by having aristocrats speak in blank verse and lower-ranking characters speak in prose; but he goes far beyond those divisions. In Shakespeare's plays, characters' diction reflects all aspect of their personalities, including their knowledge, experience, and desires. Their diction may be formal or informal, light-hearted or heavy, clever or plodding, clear or vague. It may be poetic and full of figurative language, or streamlined and direct. All of these choices reflect who the characters are.

Read It

Briefly describe the type of diction each character uses in these passages. To help your analysis, consider the knowledge and experience of the world the words reflect.

PASSAGE	DICTION
Gonzalo. Beseech you, sir, be merry. You have cause (So have we all) of joy; for our escape Is much beyond our loss….	
Ariel. If of life you keep a care, Shake off slumber, and beware. Awake, awake!	
Caliban. All the infections that the sun sucks up From bogs, fens, flats, on Prosper fall, and make him By inchmeal a disease! His spirits hear me, And yet I needs must curse.	
Trinculo. I shall laugh myself to death at this puppy-headed monster. A most scurvy monster! I could find in my heart to beat him—	

Write It

Write two brief passages about the same topic. In one passage, use diction that Caliban might use. In the other, use diction that Ariel might use.

EVIDENCE LOG

Before moving on to a new selection, go to your Evidence Log and record what you learned from *The Tempest,* Act II.

Playwright

William Shakespeare

🔧 **Tool Kit**
First-Read Guide and
Model Annotation

The Tempest, Act III

Concept Vocabulary

You will encounter the following words as you read Act III of *The Tempest*. Before reading, note how familiar you are with each word. Then, rank the words in order from most familiar (1) to least familiar (4).

WORD	YOUR RANKING
valiant	
vigilance	
valor	
invulnerable	

After completing the first read, come back to the concept vocabulary and review your rankings. Mark changes to your original rankings as needed.

First Read DRAMA

Apply these strategies as you conduct your first read. You will have an opportunity to complete the close-read notes after your first-read.

NOTICE *whom* the story is about, *what* happens, *where* and *when* it happens, and *why* those involved react as they do.

ANNOTATE by marking vocabulary and key passages you want to revisit.

First Read

CONNECT ideas within the selection to what you already know and what you have already read.

RESPOND by completing the Comprehension Check and by writing a brief summary of the selection.

The Tempest Act III

William Shakespeare

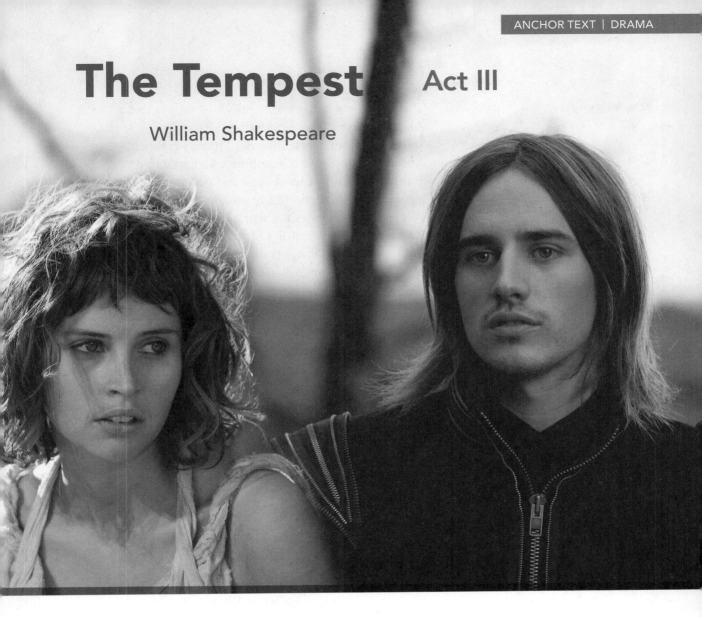

REVIEW AND ANTICIPATE

King Alonso and his entourage survive the storm and wash up on different parts the island. Alonso is mourning Ferdinand, whom he believes to be dead, and refuses to be cheered up by Gonzalo. Antonio and Sebastian plot to kill Alonso and make Sebastian king. Ariel foils their first attempt. Caliban encounters the court jester, Trinculo, and they are discovered by a sailor, Stephano, who has saved a barrel of wine from the wreckage. They drink a lot, and Caliban offers to be Stephano's subject.

Scene i • *In front of Prospero's cell.*

[*Enter* Ferdinand, *bearing a log*.]

Ferdinand. There be some sports are painful, and their labor
Delight in them sets off;[1] some kinds of baseness
Are nobly undergone, and most poor matters

NOTES

1. **sets off** *v.* cancels or balances the pain.

Point to rich ends. This my mean task

5　Would be as heavy to me as odious, but

The mistress which I serve quickens[2] what's dead

And makes my labors pleasures. O, she is

Ten times more gentle than her father's crabbed;

And he's composed of harshness. I must remove

10　Some thousands of these logs and pile them up.

Upon a sore injunction.[3] My sweet mistress

Weeps when she sees me work, and says such baseness

Had never like executor. I forget;[4]

But these sweet thoughts do even refresh my labors,

15　Most busiest, when I do it.[5]

[*Enter* Miranda; *and* Prospero (*behind, unseen*).]

Miranda.　　　　　　　　Alas, now, pray you,

Work not so hard! I would the lightning had

Burnt up those logs that you are enjoined to pile!

Pray, set it down and rest you. When this burns,

'Twill weep[6] for having wearied you. My father

20　Is hard at study; pray now rest yourself;

He's safe for these three hours.

Ferdinand.　　　　　　　O most dear mistress,

The sun will set before I shall discharge

What I must strive to do.

Miranda.　　　　　　If you'll sit down,

I'll bear your logs the while. Pray, give me that;

25　I'll carry it to the pile.

Ferdinand.　　　　　No, precious creature;

I had rather crack my sinews, break my back,

Than you should such dishonor undergo,

While I sit lazy by.

Miranda.　　　　It would become me

As well as it does you: and I should do it

30　With much more ease; for my good will is to it,

And yours it is against.

Prospero. [*Aside*]　　　Poor worm, thou art infected!

This visitation[7] shows it.

Miranda.　　　　　You look wearily.

Ferdinand. No, noble mistress, 'tis fresh morning with me

When you are by at night. I do beseech you,

35　Chiefly that I might set it in my prayers,

What is your name?

Miranda.　　　　Miranda. O my father,

I have broke your hest to say so!

Ferdinand.　　　　　Admired Miranda![8]

Indeed the top of admiration, worth

Miranda (played by Felicity Jones) stands in the doorway of the island home where she has lived since she was three years old.

What's dearest to the world! Full many a lady
40 I have eyed with best regard, and many a time
Th' harmony of their tongues hath into bondage
Brought my too diligent ear. For several virtues
Have I liked several women; never any
With so full soul but some defect in her
45 Did quarrel with the noblest grace she owed,
And put it to the foil.[9] But you, O you,
So perfect and so peerless, are created
Of every creature's best!

Miranda.   I do not know
One of my sex; no woman's face remember,
50 Save, from my glass, mine own. Nor have I seen
More that I may call men than you, good friend,
And my dear father. How features are abroad,
I am skilless[10] of; but, by my modesty
(The jewel in my dower), I would not wish
55 Any companion in the world but you;
Nor can imagination form a shape,
Besides yourself, to like of. But I prattle
Something too wildly, and my father's precepts
I therein do forget.

Ferdinand.   I am, in my condition
60 A prince, Miranda; I do think, a king
(I would not so), and would no more endure
This wooden slavery than to suffer
The fleshfly blow[11] my mouth. Hear my soul speak!
The very instant that I saw you, did
65 My heart fly to your service; there resides,
To make me slave to it; and for your sake
Am I this patient log-man.

Miranda.   Do you love me?

Ferdinand. O heaven, O earth, bear witness to this sound,
And crown what I profess with kind event
70 If I speak true! If hollowly, invert
What best is boded me[12] to mischief! I,
Beyond all limit of what else i' th' world,
Do love, prize, honor you.

Miranda.   I am a fool
To weep at what I am glad of.

Prospero. [*Aside*]   Fair encounter
75 Of two most rare affections! Heavens rain grace
On that which breeds between 'em!

Ferdinand.   Wherefore weep you?

Miranda. At mine unworthiness, that dare not offer

9. **put it to the foil** put it to the test, which it failed.

10. **skilless** ignorant.

11. **blow** *v.* befoul; contaminate; pollute.

12. **What . . . me** what good fortune will be given me.

What I desire to give, and much less take
What I shall die to want.[13] But this is trifling;[14]
80 And all the more it seeks to hide itself,
The bigger bulk it shows. Hence, bashful cunning,
And prompt me, plain and holy innocence!
I am your wife, if you will marry me;
If not, I'll die your maid. To be your fellow[15]
85 You may deny me; but I'll be your servant,
Whether you will or no.

Ferdinand. My mistress, dearest,
And I thus humble ever.

Miranda. My husband then?

Ferdinand. Ay, with a heart as willing
As bondage e'er of freedom.[16] Here's my hand.

90 **Miranda.** And mine, with my heart in't; and now farewell
Till half an hour hence.

Ferdinand. A thousand thousand!
[*Exit* (Ferdinand *and* Miranda *in different directions*).]

Prospero. So glad of this as they I cannot be,
Who are surprised withal;[17] but my rejoicing
At nothing can be more. I'll to my book;
95 For yet ere suppertime must I perform
Much business appertaining.[18] [*Exit.*]

Scene ii • *Another part of the island.*

[*Enter* Caliban, Stephano, *and* Trinculo.]

Stephano. Tell not me! When the butt is out, we will drink
water; not a drop before. Therefore bear up, and board 'em.[1]
Servant monster, drink to me.

Trinculo. Servant monster? The folly of this island! They say
5 there's but five upon this isle; we are three of them. If th' other
two be brained like us, the state totters.

Stephano. Drink, servant monster, when I bid thee; thy eyes are
almost set in thy head.

Trinculo. Where should they be set else? He were a brave
10 monster indeed if they were set in his tail.

Stephano. My man-monster hath drowned his tongue in sack.[2]
For my part, the sea cannot drown me. I swam, ere I could
recover the shore, five-and-thirty leagues off and on, by this
light. Thou shalt be my lieutenant, monster, or my standard.[3]

NOTES

13. **want** *v.* lack; be without.

14. **But . . . trifling** But words cannot express my feelings.

15. **fellow** *n.* partner.

16. **as willing . . . freedom** as eagerly as a prisoner is to gain his freedom.

17. **withal** by it all.

18. **appertaining** *adj.* relating (to my plans).

1. **bear . . . 'em** old seaman's expression meaning "drink up."

2. **sack** *n.* a white wine.

3. **standard** *n.* standard-bearer, but Caliban can barely stand.

4. if you list if you wish. In sailor's jargon, *list* means "lean to one side," as an injured ship or a drunken man.

valiant (VAL yuhnt) *adj.* brave; courageous

5. I am . . . constable I am in good enough condition to fight a policeman.

6. deboshed *adj.* drunken; debauched.

7. natural fool; idiot.

8. the next tree elliptical expression for "You'll hang from the next tree."

9. Marry exclamation meaning "By the Virgin Mary!"

CLOSE READ

ANNOTATE: In lines 31–53, mark words and phrases that reflect the types of behavior and language used by a king and his courtiers.

QUESTION: Why does Shakespeare include these references?

CONCLUDE: What effect do these references have?

10. this thing Trinculo.

15 **Trinculo.** Your lieutenant, if you list;⁴ he's no standard.

Stephano. We'll not run, Monsieur Monster.

Trinculo. Nor go neither; but you'll lie like dogs, and yet say nothing neither.

Stephano. Mooncalf, speak once in thy life, if thou beest a good
20 mooncalf.

Caliban. How does thy honor? Let me lick thy shoe. I'll not serve him; he's not **valiant**.

Trinculo. Thou liest, most ignorant monster; I am in case to justle a constable.⁵ Why, thou deboshed⁶ fish thou, was there ever man a
25 coward that hath drunk so much sack as I today? Wilt thou tell a monstrous lie, being but half a fish and half a monster?

Caliban. Lo, how he mocks me! Wilt thou let him, my lord?

Trinculo. "Lord" quoth he? That a monster should be such a natural!⁷

30 **Caliban.** Lo, lo, again! Bite him to death, I prithee.

Stephano. Trinculo, keep a good tongue in your head. If you prove a mutineer—the next tree!⁸ The poor monster's my subject, and he shall not suffer indignity.

Caliban. I thank my noble lord. Wilt thou be pleased to hearken
35 once again to the suit I made to thee?

Stephano. Marry,⁹ will I. Kneel and repeat it; I will stand, and so shall Trinculo.

[*Enter* Ariel, *invisible*.]

Caliban. As I told thee before, I am subject to a tyrant,
A sorcerer, that by his cunning hath
40 Cheated me of the island.

Ariel. Thou liest.

Caliban.   Thou liest, thou jesting monkey thou!
I would my valiant master would destroy thee.
I do not lie.

Stephano. Trinculo, if you trouble him any more in's tale, by
45 this hand, I will supplant some of your teeth.

Trinculo. Why, I said nothing.

Stephano. Mum then, and no more. Proceed.

Caliban. I say by sorcery he got this isle;
From me he got it. If thy greatness will
50 Revenge it on him—for I know thou dar'st,
But this thing¹⁰ dare not—

Stephano. That's most certain.

Caliban. Thou shalt be lord of it, and I'll serve thee.

Stephano. How now shall this be compassed? Canst thou bring
55 me to the party?

Caliban. Yea, yea, my lord! I'll yield him thee asleep,
Where thou mayst knock a nail into his head.

Ariel. Thou liest; thou canst not.

Caliban. What a pied[11] ninny's this! Thou scurvy patch![12]
60 I do beseech thy greatness, give him blows
And take his bottle from him. When that's gone,
He shall drink nought but brine, for I'll not show him
Where the quick freshes[13] are.

Stephano. Trinculo, run into no further danger! Interrupt the
65 monster one word further and, by this hand, I'll turn my mercy
out o' doors and make a stockfish[14] of thee.

Trinculo. Why, what did I? I did nothing. I'll go farther off.

Stephano. Didst thou not say he lied?

Ariel. Thou liest.

70 **Stephano.** Do I so? Take thou that. [*Strikes* Trinculo.] As you like
this, give me the lie another time.

Trinculo. I did not give the lie. Out o' your wits, and hearing
too? A pox o' your bottle! This can sack and drinking do. A
murrain[15] on your monster, and the devil take your fingers!

75 **Caliban.** Ha, ha, ha!

Stephano. Now, forward with your tale. [*To* Trinculo] Prithee,
stand farther off.

Caliban. Beat him enough. After a little time
I'll beat him too.

Stephano.   Stand farther. Come, proceed.

80 **Caliban.** Why, as I told thee, 'tis a custom with him
I' th' afternoon to sleep. There thou mayst brain him,
Having first seized his books, or with a log
Batter his skull, or paunch[16] him with a stake,
Or cut his wezand[17] with thy knife. Remember
85 First to possess his books; for without them
He's but a sot,[18] as I am, nor hath not
One spirit to command. They all do hate him
As rootedly as I. Burn but his books.
He has brave utensils[19] (for so he calls them)
90 Which, when he has a house, he'll deck withal.
And that most deeply to consider is
The beauty of his daughter. He himself
Calls her a nonpareil.[20] I never saw a woman
But only Sycorax my dam and she;
95 But she as far surpasseth Sycorax

NOTES

11. **pied** *adj.* many-colored.
12. **patch** *n.* jester.

13. **freshes** *n.* freshwater streams.

14. **stockfish** *n.* dried and salted codfish.

15. **murrain** *n.* cattle disease.

16. **paunch** *v.* stab in the belly.
17. **wezand** (WEE zuhnd) *n.* throat; windpipe.
18. **sot** *n.* fool.

19. **utensils** *n.* household furnishings.

20. **nonpareil** (non puhr EHL) *n.* from the French, meaning "without equal."

As great'st does least.

Stephano. Is it so brave a lass?

Caliban. Ay, lord. She will become thy bed, I warrant.
And bring thee forth brave brood.

Stephano. Monster, I will kill this man. His daughter and I will
100 be King and Queen—save our Graces!—And Trinculo and
thyself shall be viceroys. Dost thou like the plot, Trinculo?

Trinculo. Excellent.

Stephano. Give me thy hand. I am sorry I beat thee; but while
thou liv'st, keep a good tongue in thy head.

105 **Caliban.** Within this half hour will he be asleep.
Wilt thou destroy him then?

Stephano. Ay, on mine honor.

Ariel. This will I tell my master.

Caliban. Thou mak'st me merry; I am full of pleasure.
Let us be jocund. Will you troll the catch[21]
110 You taught me but whilere?[22]

Stephano. At thy request, monster, I will do reason, any reason.
Come on, Trinculo, let us sing. [*Sings.*]

Flout 'em and scout[23] 'em
And scout 'em and flout 'em!
115 Thought is free.

Caliban. That's not the tune.

[Ariel *plays the tune on a tabor[24] and pipe.*]

Stephano. What is this same?

Trinculo. This is the tune of our catch, played by the picture of
Nobody.[25]

120 **Stephano.** If thou beest a man, show thyself in thy likeness. If
thou beest a devil, take't as thou list.

Trinculo. O, forgive me my sins!

Stephano. He that dies pays all debts. I defy thee. Mercy
upon us!

125 **Caliban.** Art thou afeard?

Stephano. No, monster, not I.

Caliban. Be not afeard; the isle is full of noises,
Sounds and sweet airs that give delight and hurt not.
Sometimes a thousand twangling instruments
130 Will hum about mine ears; and sometime voices
That, if I then had waked after long sleep,
Will make me sleep again; and then, in dreaming,
The clouds methought would open and show riches
Ready to drop upon me, that, when I waked,

21. Will . . . catch Will you sing the tune?

22. but whilere just now.

23. scout *v.* mock.

24. *tabor* *n.* small drum.

25. picture of Nobody possibly an allusion to a comedy called *No-body and Some-body.*

CLOSE READ

ANNOTATE: In Caliban's speech, lines 127–135, mark all the words related to sound.

QUESTION: Why does Shakespeare give Caliban this varied, rich language?

CONCLUDE: What is the effect of this speech, particularly as it distinguishes Caliban from Stephano and Trinculo?

135   I cried to dream again.

Stephano. This will prove a brave kingdom to me, where I shall have my music for nothing.

Caliban. When Prospero is destroyed.

Stephano. That shall be by and by; I remember the story.

140 **Trinculo.** The sound is going away; let's follow it, and after do our work.

Stephano. Lead, monster; we'll follow. I would I could see this taborer; he lays it on.

Trinculo. [*To* Caliban] Wilt come? I will follow Stephano.

                              [*Exit.*]

⌘ ⌘ ⌘

Scene iii • *Another part of the island.*

[*Enter* Alonso, Sebastian, Antonio, Gonzalo, Adrian, Francisco, *and others.*]

Gonzalo. By'r Lakin,[1] I can go no further, sir;
My old bones aches. Here's a maze trod indeed
Through forthrights and meanders![2] By your patience,
I needs must rest me.

Alonso.   Old lord, I cannot blame thee,
5 Who am myself attached[3] with weariness
To th' dulling of my spirits. Sit down and rest.
Even here I will put off my hope, and keep it
No longer for my flatterer. He is drowned
Whom thus we stray to find; and the sea mocks
10 Our frustrate search on land. Well, let him go.

Antonio. [*Aside to* Sebastian] I am right glad that he's so out
  of hope.
Do not for one repulse forego the purpose
That you resolved t' effect.

Sebastian.   [*Aside to* Antonio] The next advantage
Will we take throughly.

Antonio.   [*Aside to* Sebastian] Let it be tonight;
15 For, now they are oppressed with travel, they
Will not nor cannot use such **vigilance**
As when they are fresh.

Sebastian.   [*Aside to* Antonio] I say tonight. No more.

[*Solemn and strange music; and* Prospero *on the top*[4] (*invisible*).
Enter several strange Shapes, *bringing in a banquet; and dance about
it with gentle actions of salutations; and, inviting the King etc. to eat,
they depart.*]

NOTES

1. **By'r Lakin** dialect, meaning "By our Lady."

2. **forthrights and meanders.** straight and wandering paths.

3. **attached** *adj.* afflicted; seized.

vigilance (VIHJ uh luhns) *n.* watchfulness

4. *on the top* stage direction indicating that Prospero is to stand at the rear of the stage or possibly on a structure above it so as to seem invisible to the characters onstage.

5. kind keepers good protectors or guardian angels.

6. living drollery puppet show, such as Punch 'n' Judy, but using live actors.

7. certes certain; sure.

Alonso. What harmony is this? My good friends, hark!

Gonzalo. Marvelous sweet music!

20 **Alonso.** Give us kind keepers,[5] heavens! What were these?

Sebastian. A living drollery.[6] Now I will believe
That there are unicorns; that in Arabia
There is one tree, the phoenix throne; one phoenix
At this hour reigning there.

Antonio. I'll believe both;
25 And what does else want credit, come to me,
And I'll be sworn 'tis true. Travelers ne'er did lie,
Though fools at home condemn 'em.

Gonzalo. If in Naples
I should report this now, would they believe me?
If I should say, I saw such islanders?
30 (For certes,[7] these are people of the island)
Who, though they are of monstrous shape, yet note,
Their manners are more gentle, kind, than of

Our human generation you shall find
Many—nay, almost any.

Prospero. [*Aside*] Honest lord.

35 Thou hast said well; for some of you there present
Are worse than devils.

Alonso. I cannot too much muse[8]
Such shapes, such gesture and such sound, expressing,
(Although they want the use of tongue) a kind
Of excellent dumb discourse.

Prospero. [*Aside*] Praise in departing.[9]

40 **Francisco.** They vanished strangely.

Sebastian. No matter, since
They have left their viands[10] behind; for we have stomachs.
Will't please you taste of what is here?

Alonso. Not I.

Gonzalo. Faith, sir, you need not fear. When we were boys,

8. **muse** *v.* wonder at; ponder.

9. **Praise in departing** Keep your praise until you leave.

10. **viands** *n.* food.

Lord Gonzalo (played by Tom Conti), King Alonso, and the others in the entourage, rest for a moment from their search for Ferdinand.

11. **Dewlapped** *adj.* having loose skin hanging from the neck like that of certain animals, such as cows and bulls.

12. **Each . . . warrant of** ordinary travelers (who take out insurance at which they are repaid five-to-one) confirm nowadays that such fanciful creatures actually exist.

13. *harpy* *n.* mythical figure from ancient Greece who pursued those guilty of wrongdoing.

14. *quaint device* stage mechanism, such as a puff of smoke and a trapdoor, that aids the banquet hidden by Ariel's harpy wings to "vanish."

15. **to instrument** as its instrument.

valor (VAL uhr) *n.* personal fortitude or bravery

16. **even with . . . selves** with courage granted by madness men kill themselves.

17. **tempered** made.

invulnerable (in VUHL nuhr uh buhl) *adj.* incapable of being harmed

18. **dowle . . . plume** fluffy little feather in my covering of feathers.

19. **My fellow . . . invulnerable** My companions are as incapable of being harmed (as I am).

20. **If you . . . strengths** But even if you could hurt us, your swords are too heavy for your strength.

21. **requit it** avenged that wrong.

22. **nothing . . . sorrow** nothing but sincere repentance (will protect you from the wrath of the avenging powers).

Who would believe that there were mountaineers
45 Dewlapped[11] like bulls, whose throats had hanging at 'em
Wallets of flesh? Or that there were such men
Whose heads stood in their breasts? Which now we find
Each putter-out of five for one will bring us
Good warrant of.[12]

   Alonso.   I will stand to, and feed;
50 Although my last, no matter, since I feel
The best is past. Brother, my lord the Duke,
Stand to, and do as we.

[*Thunder and lightning. Enter* Ariel, *like a harpy;*[13] *claps his wings upon the table; and with a quaint device* [14] *the banquet vanishes.*]

   Ariel. You are three men of sin, whom destiny—
That hath to instrument[15] this lower world
55 And what is in't—the never-surfeited sea
Hath caused to belch up you and on this island,
Where man doth not inhabit, you 'mongst men
Being most unfit to live. I have made you mad;
And even with suchlike **valor** men hang and drown
60 Their proper selves.[16]

                [Alonso, Sebastian, *etc. draw their swords.*]
             You fools! I and my fellows
Are ministers of Fate. The elements,
Of whom your swords are tempered,[17] may as well
Wound the loud winds, or with bemocked-at-stabs
Kill the still-closing waters, as diminish
65 One dowle that's in my plume.[18] My fellow ministers
Are like **invulnerable**.[19] If you could hurt,
Your swords are now too massy for your strengths[20]
And will not be uplifted. But remember
(For that's my business to you) that you three
70 From Milan did supplant good Prospero;
Exposed unto the sea, which hath requit it,[21]
Him and his innocent child; for which foul deed
The pow'rs delaying, not forgetting, have
Incensed the seas and shores, yea, all the creatures,
75 Against your peace. Thee of thy son, Alonso,
They have bereft; and do pronounce by me
Ling'ring perdition (worse than any death
Can be at once) shall step by step attend
You and your ways; whose wraths to guard you from,
80 Which here, in this most desolate isle, else falls
Upon your heads, is nothing but heart's sorrow[22]
And a clear life ensuing.

[*He vanishes in thunder; then, to soft music, enter the* Shapes *again, and dance with mocks and mows,*[23] *and carrying out the table.*]

Prospero. Bravely the figure of this harpy hast thou
Performed, my Ariel; a grace it had, devouring.[24]
85 Of my instruction hast thou nothing bated
In what thou hadst to say. So, with good life
And observation strange, my meaner ministers
Their several kinds have done.[25] My high charms work,
And these, mine enemies, are all knit up
90 In their distractions. They now are in my pow'r;
And in these fits I leave them, while I visit
Young Ferdinand, whom they suppose is drowned,
And his and mine loved darling.   [*Exit above.*]

Gonzalo. I' th' name of something holy, sir, why stand you
95 In this strange stare?

Alonso.   O, it is monstrous, monstrous!
Methought the billows spoke and told me of it;
The winds did sing it to me; and the thunder,
That deep and dreadful organ pipe, pronounced
The name of Prosper; it did bass my trespass.[26]
100 Therefore my son i' th' ooze is bedded; and
I'll seek him deeper than e'er plummet sounded
And with him there lie mudded.   [*Exit.*]

Sebastian.   But one fiend at a time,
I'll fight their legions o'er![27]

Antonio.   I'll be thy second.
                    [*Exit* Sebastian *and* Antonio.]

Gonzalo. All three of them are desperate; their great guilt,
105 Like poison given to work a great time after,
Now 'gins to bite the spirits. I do beseech you,
That are of suppler joints, follow them swiftly
And hinder them from what this ecstasy[28]
May now provoke them to.

Adrian.   Follow, I pray you.
                    [*Exit all.*]

NOTES

23. *mocks and mows* derisive gestures and grimaces.

24. **a grace . . . devouring** your performance had an all-consuming grace.

25. **with good life . . . done** with true-to-life acting and close attention to my wishes, your lower-ranking companions—my agents—have performed their parts according to their natures.

26. **bass my trespass** the bass part of nature's thunderous music made clear to me the wrong I did Prospero.

27. **But one fiend . . . o'er** If they put one devil against me at a time, I'll fight their armies to the last demon.

28. **ecstasy** *n.* insanity.

Comprehension Check

Complete the following items after you finish your first read.

1. What task does Prospero require of Ferdinand?

2. What decision do Ferdinand and Miranda make during their conversation?

3. What does Caliban want Stephano to do for him?

4. What does Ariel first provide and then take away from Alonso and his entourage?

5. 🗐 **Notebook** Confirm your understanding of Act III by writing a summary.

- -

RESEARCH

Research to Clarify Choose at least one unfamiliar detail from the text. Briefly research that detail. In what way does the information you learned shed light on an aspect of the play?

Research to Explore Choose something from the text that interests you, and formulate a research question.

Close Read the Text

Reread Ariel's speech in Act III, Scene iii, lines 65–82. Mark words that refer to death and suffering. How do these words help explain why Ariel says, "For that's my business to you" in line 69?

THE TEMPEST, ACT III

- -

Analyze the Text

CITE TEXTUAL EVIDENCE
to support your answers.

Notebook Complete the activities.

1. **Interpret** How do you know that Prospero approves of the growing love between Miranda and Ferdinand? Explain.

2. **(a)** How does Prospero haunt this act, even though he does not make a formal appearance in any scene? **(b)** In what ways is Prospero different from all the other characters?

3. **(a) Infer** What is the purpose of Ariel's speech after the banquet vanishes? **(b) Evaluate** What contribution does the speech make to the plot, or sequence of events? **(c) Evaluate** How do Gonzalo's lines at the end of the act build on the speech?

4. **Essential Question:** *What motivates us to forgive?* What have you learned about forgiveness by reading Act III of *The Tempest?*

LANGUAGE DEVELOPMENT

Concept Vocabulary

valiant	valor	invulnerable	vigilance

Why These Words? The four concept vocabulary words relate to strength and bravery. How does each word contribute to meaning in the text? What other words in the selection connect to this concept?

Practice

Notebook Use each concept vocabulary word in a sentence that describes a character from the play.

Word Study

Notebook Latin Root: -val- The root *-val-* is from a Latin word that means "to be of worth." It contributes that meaning to two of the concept vocabulary words. In Scene ii, Shakespeare uses the word *valiant* in reference to qualities that others value, such as strength and courage. *Valor* is a related word that means "great courage, especially when confronting danger."

Identify three other words that have the root *-val-*. Explain how the root contributes to the meaning of each word.

 WORD NETWORK

Add words related to forgiveness from the text to your Word Network.

THE TEMPEST, ACT III

Analyze Craft and Structure

Dramatic Structure Picture the workings of an old fashioned watch, with big gears and small gears intermeshed and precisely turning. This image conveys something of the way a drama works. The biggest gear is the main **plot**, or sequence of events. As it turns, it engages with one or more smaller gears, which are the **subplots**, or minor stories that complicate the plot. Playwrights often use plot and subplot to explore thematic ideas from different perspectives and to reveal complexities of character.

In *The Tempest*, Shakespeare links plot and subplot with care and precision. The main events of the play relate to Prospero's plan to test and teach Alonso, Sebastian, and Antonio. Several subplots explore related ideas, serving to reflect and comment on the main story.

Practice

Review Act III. Make notes in the chart about what is going on, at this point, in the main plot and in the subplots.

PLOT / SUBPLOT	EVENTS
Main Plot: Prospero, Alonso, Antonio, Sebastian	
Subplot: Prospero, Miranda, Ferdinand	
Subplot: Prospero, Ariel	
Subplot: Sebastian, Antonio	
Subplot: Caliban, Stephano, Trinculo	

Notebook Use the information you gathered in the chart to respond to these questions.

1. What do Prospero's remarks in Act III, Scene i, imply about his wishes for his daughter? Explain.

2. Act I made it clear that Ariel wants his freedom. **(a)** What does Ariel do in Act III to earn his freedom? **(b)** How does Prospero view Ariel's efforts?

3. Which conspirators are more dangerous, Sebastian and Antonio or Caliban and Stephano? Explain your answer using evidence from the subplots.

4. Considering all the subplots, do you think Prospero wants to harm other characters, help them, or something else? Explain.

Speaking and Listening

Assignment

With a partner, give a **dramatic reading** of a scene or part of a scene from Act III. Each of you may read lines for more than one character. Use your voice and gestures to make the change from one character to another clear to your audience.

1. **Choose Your Scene** With your partner, choose one of the three scenes, or part of a scene, to read. Choose a scene you especially enjoy for its humor, its emotion, its language, or another reason.

2. **Analyze the Scene** Read through the scene with your partner. Familiarize yourself with any words you have not encountered before. Review the scene for sentences that you do not immediately comprehend, and work out their meanings. Think about how your chosen scene develops its subplot and how that fits into the main plot of the play.

3. **Develop Your Characters** Talk with your partner about the traits of each character in your scene. Is this person innocent, treacherous, foolish, angry? How will you convey the character's qualities in your reading?

4. **Rehearse** Practice the scene several times with your partner. Look for ways to communicate your interpretation of each character. Help each other find ways to use your voices to express different feelings, shades of meaning, and comic or emotional elements. Suggest gestures, posture, or other body language that will help convey characters' traits.

5. **Evaluate Readings** As your classmates deliver their readings, listen and watch attentively. Use an evaluation guide like the one shown to analyze their deliveries.

EVALUATION GUIDE

Rate each statement on a scale of 1 (not demonstrated) to 4 (demonstrated).

☐ The scene demonstrated a convincing interpretation of the characters and the action.

☐ The speakers communicated clearly and expressively.

☐ The speakers used their voices effectively to convey characters' qualities.

☐ The speakers used gestures, posture, and body language to convey characters effectively.

EVIDENCE LOG

Before moving on to a new selection, go to your Evidence Log and record what you learned from *The Tempest,* Act III.

Playwright

William Shakespeare

🔧 **Tool Kit**
First-Read Guide and
Model Annotation

The Tempest, Act IV

You will encounter the following words as you read Act IV of *The Tempest*. Before reading, note how familiar you are with each word. Then, rank the words in order from most familiar (1) to least familiar (3).

WORD	YOUR RANKING
opportune	
industrious	
incite	

After completing the first read, come back to the concept vocabulary and review your rankings. Mark changes to your original rankings as needed.

First Read DRAMA

Apply these strategies as you conduct your first read. You will have an opportunity to complete the close-read notes after your first read.

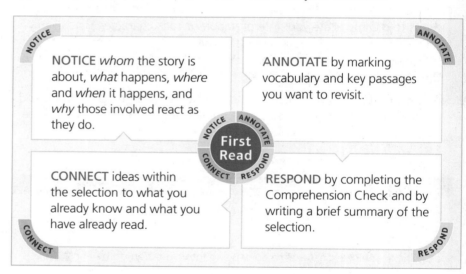

NOTICE *whom* the story is about, *what* happens, *where* and *when* it happens, and *why* those involved react as they do.

ANNOTATE by marking vocabulary and key passages you want to revisit.

CONNECT ideas within the selection to what you already know and what you have already read.

RESPOND by completing the Comprehension Check and by writing a brief summary of the selection.

First Read

The Tempest

Act IV

William Shakespeare

REVIEW AND ANTICIPATE

Ferdinand remains in captivity for a time, working as Prospero's servant and falling more in love with Miranda, who reciprocates. They declare their love and agree to marry. Prospero, eavesdropping, approves. Caliban proposes to Stephano that they kill Prospero and take over his island, his books, and his daughter. Stephano agrees. Ariel, overhearing this plot, runs to tell Prospero. Ariel presents a great banquet to King Alonso and his entourage, and then takes it away again, accusing them of their crimes against Prospero and warning them of a terrible future if they don't reform. Alonso goes looking for his son, followed by Antonio and Sebastian. Gonzalo follows all of them, fearing that they have gone mad.

Scene i • *In front of Prospero's cell.*

[*Enter* Prospero, Ferdinand, *and* Miranda.]

Prospero. If I have too austerely punished you,
Your compensation makes amends; for I
Have given you here a third of mine own life,
Or that for which I live; who once again

NOTES

1. strangely *adv.* wonderfully.

2. boast her off praise her to the sky.

3. halt *v.* limp.

4. I do . . . oracle I believe you even if a prophet should say otherwise.

5. sanctimonious *adj.* sacred; holy.

6. aspersion *n.* ritual sprinkling of water, as in a religious ceremony.

7. this contract grow this marriage develop into a family.

8. As . . . you as the lamps of the god of marriage burn clearly to light your way at the wedding ceremony.

opportune (op uhr TOON) *adj.* very favorable

9. worser genius can bad demon can make.

10. edge intense pleasure.

11. Phoebus' steeds the horses of the sun god Apollo, which pulled his chariot across the sky from dawn to dusk.

industrious (ihn DUHS tree uhs) *adj.* hard-working

12. foundered made lame.

13. below below the horizon.

14. What, Ariel! Here, Ariel! Come here, Ariel!

incite (ihn SYT) *v.* strongly encourage

15. rabble *n.* the lower-ranking spirits; mob or disorderly collection of lower-class individuals.

16. vanity *n.* trifle; small, unimportant thing.

5 I tender to thy hand. All thy vexations
Were but my trials of thy love, and thou
Hast strangely[1] stood the test. Here, afore heaven,
I ratify this my rich gift. O Ferdinand,
Do not smile at me that I boast her off,[2]
10 For thou shalt find she will outstrip all praise
And make it halt[3] behind her.

Ferdinand.   I do believe it
Against an oracle.[4]

Prospero. Then, as my gift, and thine own acquisition
Worthily purchased, take my daughter. But
15 If thou dost break her virgin-knot before
All sanctimonious[5] ceremonies may
With full and holy rite be minist'red,
No sweet aspersion[6] shall the heavens let fall
To make this contract grow;[7] but barren hate,
20 Sour-eyed disdain, and discord shall bestrew
The union of your bed with weeds so loathly
That you shall hate it both. Therefore take heed,
As Hymen's lamps shall light you.[8]

Ferdinand.   As I hope
For quiet days, fair issue and long life,
25 With such love as 'tis now, the murkiest den,
The most **opportune** place, the strong'st suggestion
Our worser genius can,[9] shall never melt
Mine honor into lust, to take away
The edge[10] of that day's celebration
30 When I shall think or Phoebus' steeds[11] are foundered[12]
Or Night kept chained below.[13]

Prospero.   Fairly spoke.
Sit then and talk with her; she is thine own.
What, Ariel![14] My **industrious** servant, Ariel!

[*Enter* Ariel.]

Ariel. What would my potent master? Here I am.

35 **Prospero.** Thou and thy meaner fellows your last service
Did worthily perform; and I must use you
In such another trick. Go bring the rabble,[15]
O'er whom I give thee pow'r, here to this place.
Incite them to quick motion; for I must
40 Bestow upon the eyes of this young couple
Some vanity[16] of mine art. It is my promise,
And they expect it from me.

Ariel.   Presently?

Prospero. Ay, with a twink.

Ariel. Before you can say "Come" and "Go,"

45 And breathe twice and cry, "So, so,"
Each one, tripping on his toe,
Will be here with mop[17] and mow.
Do you love me, master? No?

Prospero. Dearly, my delicate Ariel. Do not approach
50 Till thou dost hear me call.

Ariel.   Well; I conceive.[18]   [*Exit.*]

Prospero. Look thou be true.[19] Do not give dalliance[20]
Too much the rein; the strongest oaths are straw
To th' fire i' th' blood: be more abstemious,[21]
Or else good night your vow!

Ferdinand.   I warrant you sir.
55 The white cold virgin snow upon my heart
Abates the ardor of my liver.

Prospero.   Well.
Now come, my Ariel; bring a corollary[22]
Rather than want a spirit. Appear, and pertly!
No tongue! All eyes! Be silent.   [*Soft music*]

[*Enter* Iris.[23]]

60 **Iris.** Ceres,[24] most bounteous lady, thy rich leas[25]
Of wheat, rye, barley, fetches,[26] oats, and peas;
Thy turfy mountains, where live nibbling sheep,
And flat meads thatched with stover,[27] them to keep;
Thy banks with pionèd and twillèd-brims,[28]
65 Which spongy April at thy hest betrims
To make cold nymphs chaste crowns; and thy broom groves.
Whose shadow the dismissèd bachelor loves,
Being lasslorn; thy pole-clipt[29] vineyard;
And thy sea-marge,[30] sterile and rocky-hard,
70 Where thou thyself dost air[31]—the queen o' th' sky,[32]
Whose wat'ry arch and messenger am I,
Bids thee leave these, and with her sovereign grace,

[Juno *descends*.[33]]

Here on this grass plot, in this very place,
To come and sport; her peacocks fly amain.[34]
75 Approach, rich Ceres, her to entertain.

[*Enter* Ceres.]

Ceres. Hail, many-colored messenger, that ne'er
Dost disobey the wife of Jupiter,[35]
Who, with thy saffron wings, upon my flow'rs
Diffusest honey drops, refreshing show'rs,
80 And with each end of thy blue bow dost crown
My bosky[36] acres and my unshrubbed down,
Rich scarf to my proud earth. Why hath thy queen

NOTES

17. **mop** *n.* grin or gesture.

18. **conceive** *v.* comprehend; understand.

19. **Look . . . true** (addressed to Ferdinand and Miranda, who were embracing) Stop that! Be faithful to your promise.

20. **dalliance** *n.* amorous play; playful lovemaking.

21. **abstemious** *adj.* moderate; sparing.

22. **corollary** *n.* extra spirit.

23. **Iris** in classical mythology, a goddess who served as a messenger of the gods.

24. **Ceres** Roman goddess of the earth and agriculture.

25. **leas** *n.* meadows.

26. **fetches** *n.* vegetables; also clover, alfalfa, and soybeans.

27. **meads . . . stover** meadows having grasses used to feed cattle or sheep.

28. **pionèd and twillèd-brims** undercut by the stream and retained by interwoven branches.

29. **pole-clipt** *adj.* pruned.

30. **sea-marge** *n.* margins of the sea; ashore.

31. **Where . . . air** When you yourself stroll on holiday.

32. **queen o' th' sky** Roman goddess Juno, queen of the gods.

33. **Juno *descends*** stage direction indicating that Juno is slowly lowered from the ceiling of the stage.

34. **amain** *adv.* speedily. (Juno's chariot was drawn by peacocks.)

35. **Jupiter** in Roman mythology, ruler of the gods.

36. **bosky** *adj.* woodsy.

37. **estate** *v.* bestow.

38. **Venus** Roman goddess of love.

39. **her son** Cupid, the Roman god of love.

40. **Dis** Roman god of the underworld.

41. **my daughter got** allusion to the classical myth of the abduction of Proserpine. Proserpine, the daughter of Ceres, was carried off by Dis to his underworld kingdom, where he made her queen.

42. **blind boy's** Cupid's; he was often shown blindfolded.

43. **scandaled** *adj.* scandalous.

44. **Paphos** major center for the worship of Venus, on Cyprus.

45. **Mars' hot minion** Venus, who was the mistress of Mars, the Roman god of war.

46. **returned again** returned home to Paphos.

47. **waspish-headed son** Cupid, who was thought of as having a sharp sting like a wasp because of his arrows.

48. **boy right out** ordinary boy, like all other boys.

49. **still** forever, always.

50. **Spring . . . harvest** as summer ends may spring begin—in other words, may there never be a winter in your lives.

Summoned me hither to this short-grassed green?

Iris. A contract of true love to celebrate

85 And some donation freely to estate[37]
On the blest lovers.

Ceres.   Tell me, heavenly bow,
If Venus[38] or her son,[39] as thou dost know,
Do now attend the Queen? Since they did plot
The means that dusky Dis[40] my daughter got,[41]

90 Her and her blind boy's[42] scandaled[43] company
I have forsworn.

Iris.   Of her society
Be not afraid; I met her Deity
Cutting the clouds towards Paphos,[44] and her son
Dove-drawn with her. Here thought they to have done

95 Some wanton charm upon this man and maid,
Whose vows are, that no bed-right shall be paid
Till Hymen's torch be lighted. But in vain;
Mars' hot minion[45] is returned again;[46]
Her waspish-headed son[47] has broke his arrows,

100 Swears he will shoot no more, but play with sparrows
And be a boy right out.[48]

[*Juno alights.*]

Ceres.   Highest queen of state,
Great Juno, comes; I know her by her gait.

Juno. How does my bounteous sister? Go with me
To bless this twain, that they may prosperous be

105 And honored in their issue.

[*They sing.*]

Juno.   Honor, riches, marriage-blessing,
          Long continuance, and increasing,
          Hourly joys be still[49] upon you!
          Juno sings her blessings upon you.

110 **Ceres.**   Earth's increase, foison plenty,
          Barns and garners never empty,
          Vines and clust'ring bunches growing,
          Plants with goodly burthen bowing;
          Spring come to you at the farthest

115   In the very end of harvest.[50]
          Scarcity and want shall shun you,
          Ceres' blessing so is on you.

Ferdinand. This is a most majestic vision, and
Harmoniously charmingly. May I be bold

120 To think these spirits?

Prospero.   Spirits, which by mine art
I have from their confines called to enact

My present fancies.

Ferdinand.   Let me live here ever!
So rare a wond'red[51] father and a wise
Makes this place Paradise.

[Juno *and* Ceres *whisper, and send* Iris *on employment.*]

Prospero.   Sweet, now, silence!
125 Juno and Ceres whisper seriously.
There's something else to do. Hush and be mute,
Or else our spell is marred.

Iris. You nymphs, called Naiades,[52] of the windring[53] brooks,
With your sedged crowns and ever-harmless looks,
130 Leave your crisp[54] channels, and on this green land
Answer your summons; Juno does command.
Come, temperate nymphs, and help to celebrate
A contract of true love; be not too late.

[*Enter certain* Nymphs.]

You sunburnt sicklemen, of August weary,
135 Come hither from the furrow and be merry.
Make holiday; your rye-straw hats put on
And these fresh nymphs encounter everyone
In country footing.[55]

[*Enter certain* Reapers, *properly habited. They join with the* Nymphs
in a graceful dance; towards the end whereof Prospero *starts
suddenly, and speaks;*[56] *after which, to a strange, hollow, and confused
noise, they heavily*[57] *vanish.*]

Prospero. [*Aside*] I had forgot that foul conspiracy
140 Of the beast Caliban and his confederates
Against my life. The minute of their plot
Is almost come. [*To the* Spirits] Well done! Avoid![58] No more!

Ferdinand. This is strange: your father's in some passion
That works him strongly.

Miranda.   Never till this day
145 Saw I him touched with anger so distempered.[59]

Prospero. You do look, my son, in a movèd sort,[60]
As if you were dismayed; be cheerful, sir.
Our revels now are ended. These our actors,
As I foretold you, were all spirits and
150 Are melted into air, into thin air;
And, like the baseless fabric of this vision,
The cloud-capped towers, the gorgeous palaces,
The solemn temples, the great globe itself,
Yea, all which it inherit,[61] shall dissolve,
155 And, like this insubstantial pageant faded,
Leave not a rack[62] behind. We are such stuff

NOTES

51. **wond'red** *adj.* wonderful.

52. **Naiades** water nymphs,
minor goddesses of classical
mythology who were usually
represented as lovely young
women.

53. **windring** *adj.* wandering.

54. **crisp** *adj.* having little waves.

CLOSE READ
ANNOTATE: In lines 128–138,
mark rhyming words.

QUESTION: Why does
Shakespeare use rhyming verse
here rather than blank verse?

CONCLUDE: What is the effect
of this choice, especially when
compared to the rest of the
play's dialogue?

55. **footing** *n.* dancing.

56. *speaks* Prospero breaks the
spell, which required silence.

57. **heavily** *adv.* reluctantly.

58. **Avoid** *v.* Depart!

59. **distempered** *adj.* fierce;
intense.

60. **movèd sort** troubled state
of mind.

61. **it inherit** inhabit it.

62. **rack** *n.* windswept cloud.

ANNOTATE: In lines 146–163, mark the point at which Prospero's sentences, first long and flowing, suddenly become shorter and more abrupt.

QUESTION: Why does Prospero's speech change at this point?

CONCLUDE: What does this change signal in Prospero's emotions or understanding?

63. **presented** This is ambiguous. It could mean that Ariel acted the part of Ceres or, in the role of Iris, introduced Ceres and the entire pageant.

64. **varlets** *n.* low, vile rascals.

65. **bending** heading.

66. **unbacked** *adj.* unsaddled and hence unrestrained.

67. **Advanced** *v.* raised.

68. **goss** *n.* shrubs.

69. **mantled** *adj.* covered, as with a polluted foam or scum.

70. **trumpery** *n.* fancy-looking, gaudy, cheap clothes.

71. **stale** *n.* bait.

As dreams are made on, and our little life
Is rounded with a sleep. Sir, I am vexed.
Bear with my weakness; my old brain is troubled.
160 Be not disturbed with my infirmity.
If you be pleased, retire into my cell
And there repose. A turn or two I'll walk
To still my beating mind.

Ferdinand, Miranda.   We wish your peace.
[*Exit* Ferdinand *with* Miranda.]

Prospero. Come with a thought! I thank thee, Ariel. Come.
[*Enter* Ariel.]

165 **Ariel.** Thy thoughts I cleave to. What's thy pleasure?

Prospero.   Spirit,
We must prepare to meet with Caliban.

Ariel. Ay, my commander. When I presented⁶³ Ceres,
I thought to have told thee of it, but I feared
Lest I might anger thee.

170 **Prospero.** Say again, where didst thou leave these varlets?⁶⁴

Ariel. I told you, sir, they were red-hot with drinking;
So full of valor that they smote the air
For breathing in their faces, beat the ground
For kissing of their feet; yet always bending⁶⁵
175 Towards their project. Then I beat my tabor;
At which like unbacked⁶⁶ colts they pricked their ears,
Advanced⁶⁷ their eyelids, lifted up their noses
As they smelt music. So I charmed their ears
That calflike they my lowing followed through
180 Toothed briers, sharp furzes, pricking goss,⁶⁸ and thorns,
Which ent'red their frail shins. At last I left them
I' th' filthy mantled⁶⁹ pool beyond your cell,
There dancing up to th' chins, that the foul lake
O'erstunk their feet.

Prospero.   This was well done, my bird.
185 Thy shape invisible retain thou still.
The trumpery⁷⁰ in my house, go bring it hither
For stale⁷¹ to catch these thieves.

Ariel.   I go, I go.   [*Exit.*]

Prospero. A devil, a born devil, on whose nature
Nurture can never stick; on whom my pains,
190 Humanely taken, all, all lost, quite lost!
And as with age his body uglier grows,
So his mind cankers. I will plague them all,
Even to roaring.

[*Enter* Ariel, *loaden with glistering apparel, etc.*]

Trinculo, played by Russell Brand in the 2010 movie, tries on Prospera's clothes in a comic interlude.

72. line *n.* linden tree.

73. Jack knave; also will-o'-the-wisp.

74. hoodwink *v.* hide.

75. o'er ears underwater (in the polluted pool).

76. O King . . . peer alludes to a popular song.

77. frippery *n.* shop selling old, secondhand clothes.

78. dropsy *n.* ailment caused by excessive accumulation of fluid in the body.

79. luggage *n.* encumbrance; burdens.

Come, hang them on this line.[72]

[*Prospero and* Ariel *remain, invisible. Enter* Caliban, Stephano, *and* Trinculo, *all wet.*]

Caliban. Pray you tread softly, that the blind mole may not
195 Hear a foot fall. We now are near his cell.

Stephano. Monster, your fairy, which you say is a harmless fairy, has done little better than played the Jack[73] with us.

Trinculo. Monster, I do smell all horse piss, at which my nose is in great indignation.

200 **Stephano.** So is mine. Do you hear, monster? If I should take a displeasure against you, look you—

Trinculo. Thou wert but a lost monster.

Caliban. Good my lord, give me thy favor still.
Be patient, for the prize I'll bring thee to
205 Shall hoodwink[74] this mischance. Therefore speak softly.
All's hushed as midnight yet.

Trinculo. Ay, but to lose our bottles in the pool—

Stephano. There is not only disgrace and dishonor in that, monster, but an infinite loss.

210 **Trinculo.** That's more to me than my wetting. Yet this is your harmless fairy, monster.

Stephano. I will fetch off my bottle, though I be o'er ears[75] for my labor.

Caliban. Prithee, my king, be quiet. Seest thou here?
215 This is the mouth o' th' cell. No noise, and enter.
Do that good mischief which may make this island
Thine own forever, and I, thy Caliban,
For aye thy footlicker.

Stephano. Give me thy hand. I do begin to have bloody
220 thoughts.

Trinculo. O King Stephano! O peer![76] O worthy Stephano, look what a wardrobe here is for thee!

Caliban. Let it alone, thou fool! It is but trash.

Trinculo. O, ho, monster! We know what belongs to a frippery.[77]
225 O King Stephano!

Stephano. Put off that gown, Trinculo! By this hand, I'll have that gown.

Trinculo. Thy Grace shall have it.

Caliban. The dropsy[78] drown this fool! What do you mean
230 To dote thus on such luggage?[79] Let's alone,
And do the murder first. If he awake,

From toe to crown he'll fill our skins with pinches,
Make us strange stuff.

Stephano. Be you quiet, monster. Mistress line, is not this my
235 jerkin?[80] [*Takes it down.*] Now is the jerkin under the line.[81] Now,
jerkin, you are like to lose your hair and prove a bald jerkin.[82]

Trinculo. Do, do![83] We steal by line and level,[84] and't like[85]
your Grace.

Stephano. I thank thee for that jest. Here's a garment for't. Wit
240 shall not go unrewarded while I am king of this country. "Steal
by line and level" is an excellent pass of pate.[86] There's another
garment for't.

Trinculo. Monster, come, put some lime[87] upon your fingers, and
away with the rest.

245 **Caliban.** I will have none on't. We shall lose our time
And all be turned to barnacles,[88] or to apes
With foreheads villainous low.

Stephano. Monster, lay-to your fingers; help to bear this away
where my hogshead of wine is, or I'll turn you out of my
250 kingdom. Go to, carry this.

Trinculo. And this.

Stephano. Ay, and this.

[*A noise of hunters heard. Enter divers* Spirits, *in shape of dogs and hounds, and hunt them about;* Prospero *and* Ariel *setting them on.*]

Prospero. Hey, Mountain, hey!

Ariel. Silver! There it goes, Silver!

255 **Prospero.** Fury, Fury! There, Tyrant, there! Hark, hark!

[Caliban, Stephano, *and* Trinculo, *are driven out.*]

Go charge my goblins that they grind their joints
With dry convulsions,[89] shorten up their sinews
With agèd cramps,[90] and more pinch-spotted make them
Than pard or cat o' mountain.[91]

Ariel.   Hark, they roar!

260 **Prospero.** Let them be hunted soundly. At this hour
Lie at my mercy all mine enemies.
Shortly shall all my labors end, and thou
Shalt have the air at freedom. For a little,
Follow, and do me service.   [*Exit.*]

NOTES

80. jerkin *n.* sleeveless, hip-length jacket.

81. under the line under the linden tree. Also a play on the word *line*, which can refer to the line on maps marking the equator—see the next sentence.

82. Now . . . bald jerkin Sailors crossing the equator were believed to lose their hair from high fevers contracted in the tropics.

83. Do, do Fine, fine!

84. line and level plumb line and carpenter's level, tools used as rules for making straight lines.

85. and't like and if it please.

86. pass of pate thrust of wit.

87. lime *n.* birdlime, a sticky substance used to trap birds—thieves are supposed to have sticky fingers.

88. barnacles *n.* north European geese that breed in the frigid arctic.

89. dry convulsions vicious spasms that cause bones to grind against one another.

90. agèd cramps cramps such that the elderly might get.

91. pard . . . mountain leopard or wildcat.

CLOSE READ
ANNOTATE: In lines 253–255, mark the repeated words.

QUESTION: Why does Shakespeare repeat these words?

CONCLUDE: What is the effect of this repetition?

Comprehension Check

Complete the following items after you finish your first read.

1. At the beginning of Act IV, what arrangement between Ferdinand and Miranda does Prospero approve?

2. Why does Prospero have Ariel arrange a pageant?

3. Who are the actors in Ariel's show?

4. Why does Prospero stop the show?

5. What does Prospero command the spirits to do to Stephano, Trinculo, and Caliban?

6. 🗐 **Notebook** Confirm your understanding of Act IV by writing a summary.

- -

RESEARCH

Research to Clarify Choose at least one unfamiliar detail from the text. Briefly research that detail. In what way does the information you learned shed light on an aspect of the play?

Research to Explore Choose something from the text that interested you, and formulate a research question.

Close Read the Text

Reread Prospero's famous speech after the pageant (lines 146–163) and mark the adjectives. What feelings do these adjectives, as a group, create? What else could you describe using these adjectives?

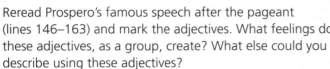

THE TEMPEST, ACT IV

Analyze the Text

CITE TEXTUAL EVIDENCE
to support your answers.

Respond to these questions.

1. (a) What services does Ariel perform for Prospero in Act IV? (b) **Compare and Contrast** How are these services similar, and how are they different?

2. **Evaluate** In Act IV, which of Prospero's words and actions are motivated mainly by his sense of responsibility as Miranda's father? Explain.

3. (a) **Analyze** What does Caliban understand or feel about Prospero that Stephano and Trinculo do not? (b) **Compare and Contrast** How does the behavior of the three characters in Prospero's cell emphasize these differences? Explain.

4. **Essential Question:** *What motivates us to forgive?* What have you learned about forgiveness by reading Act IV of *The Tempest*?

LANGUAGE DEVELOPMENT

Concept Vocabulary

incite	industrious	opportune

Why These Words? The three concept vocabulary words all relate to beginning something new and making an effort. What other words in the selection connect to this concept?

Practice

 Notebook To confirm your understanding of the concept vocabulary words, write one sentence about Ariel that includes all three words. Then, explain why each word works well in the sentence.

Word Study

Etymology: Words From Sailing Words often enter general vocabulary from specific fields of interest. Shakespeare uses the word *opportune*, which has been in the general vocabulary for centuries with the meaning "very favorable." Originally, *opportune* came from a Latin sailing term for a wind that blows in the direction of port.

Notebook Use a dictionary to look up these words from sailing: *overboard*, *jettison*, *figurehead*. Record both the original literal meanings and the contemporary figurative meanings.

WORD NETWORK

Add words related to forgiveness from the text to your Word Network.

THE TEMPEST, ACT IV

Analyze Craft and Structure

Dramatic Structures In plays, most of the information is expressed through characters' words—the dialogue—and actions. However, playwrights also use special forms of dialogue, called **dramatic speeches,** to advance the plot and provide insights into characters' emotions and motivations.

- **Soliloquy:** a lengthy speech in which a character—alone on the stage—expresses his or her true thoughts or feelings. An example of this occurs in Act III, Scene i, when Ferdinand describes how thoughts of Miranda help him tolerate hard labor.

- **Aside:** a brief remark, often addressed to the audience and meant to be kept from the other characters. For example, in Act III, Scene iii, Prospero uses a sarcastic aside to comment on the evil of those who plotted against him.

- **Monologue:** a lengthy speech by one character delivered to other characters who are on stage. In Act III, Scene ii, Caliban's monologue provides information about Prospero to his fellow conspirators.

Practice

CITE TEXTUAL EVIDENCE to support your answers.

Briefly review Act IV. Then, answer the questions.

1. Use the chart to identify the type of dramatic speech that appears in the listed passages. Then, explain who is the intended audience for the speech.

LINES	TYPE OF SPEECH	INTENDED AUDIENCE
Scene i, lines 60–75		
Scene i, lines 139–142		
Scene i, lines 171–184		

📓 **Notebook** Answer the questions.

2. (a) How does Prospero's role throughout the play make asides a natural choice for his character? (b) In what ways does Ariel's role also lend itself to the use of asides? Explain.

3. Prospero's speech in Act IV, Scene i, lines 146–163, is one of Shakespeare's most famous monologues. (a) Which details indicate that Prospero's first intention was to reassure Ferdinand? (b) At what point and in what ways does this emphasis change? (c) How does this shift seem to affect Prospero? Explain.

4. To whom is Prospero referring when he says, "We are such stuff / As dreams are made on, and our little life / is rounded with a sleep"? Explain.

Author's Style

Author's Choices: Motif Writers use recurring patterns of imagery, symbols, and language that are called **motifs**. In *The Tempest*, the repetition of language and imagery related to deception and magic creates a central motif that runs throughout the play. The play includes other motifs, as well, such as sleep and monsters. This use of motifs adds richness to the play's plot and language, and helps to develop its themes.

Shakespeare often repeats a single word throughout a play, so that it gains ever-deepening layers of meaning. In *The Tempest*, for example, he repeats the word *strange* (or variations of it, such as *strangeness* and *strangely*). The word—or its related forms— appears four times in Act I, seven times in Act II, five times in Act III, and three times in Act IV.

Read It

Explain what the word *strange* or *strangely* means as it is used in each passage presented in the chart. Then, tell whether its use relates to magic.

✐ EVIDENCE LOG

Before moving on to a new selection, go to your Evidence Log and record what you learned from *The Tempest,* Act IV.

PASSAGE	MEANING OF *STRANGE* OR *STRANGELY*
Prospero to Ferdinand: All thy vexations / Were but my trials of thy love, and thou / Hast strangely stood the test.	
Ferdinand to Miranda: This is strange: your father's in some passion / That works him strongly.	
Caliban to Stephano and Trinculo: If he awake, / From toe to crown he'll fill our skins with pinches, / Make us strange stuff.	

Write It

⊟ Notebook Look up the word *strange* in an unabridged dictionary. Read all of the possible meanings, and study the examples of how the word is used. Then, write a paragraph describing the meanings that are most closely related to *The Tempest*.

Playwright

William Shakespeare

The Tempest, Act V

Concept Vocabulary

You will encounter the following words as you read Act V of *The Tempest*. Before reading, note how familiar you are with each word. Then, rank the words in order from most familiar (1) to least familiar (4).

WORD	YOUR RANKING
penitent	
pardon	
merciful	
rectify	

After completing the first read, come back to the concept vocabulary and review your rankings. Mark changes to your original rankings as needed.

First Read DRAMA

Apply these strategies as you conduct your first read. You will have an opportunity to complete the close-read notes after your first read.

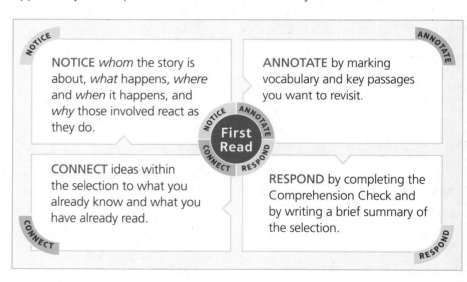

NOTICE *whom* the story is about, *what* happens, *where* and *when* it happens, and *why* those involved react as they do.

ANNOTATE by marking vocabulary and key passages you want to revisit.

CONNECT ideas within the selection to what you already know and what you have already read.

RESPOND by completing the Comprehension Check and by writing a brief summary of the selection.

First Read

NOTICE · ANNOTATE · CONNECT · RESPOND

Tool Kit
First-Read Guide and Model Annotation

The Tempest

Act V

William Shakespeare

REVIEW AND ANTICIPATE

Miranda and Ferdinand receive Prospero's blessing to marry, and
Prospero has Ariel gather spirits to present a pageant in honor of
the upcoming wedding. Three spirits appear as the mythological
figures Iris, Juno, and Ceres. They deliver monologues blessing the
wedding and call on other spirits to perform a dance, but Prospero
abruptly stops the show. He has remembered the plot against his life
by Caliban, Trinculo, and Stephano, and sends for Ariel to discuss it.
Ariel says that he has led the conspirators around the island and into
a dirty pond. Prospero sets a trap for them by having Ariel hang out
a line of fine clothing. The clothing distracts the conspirators. Then,
Ariel and Prospero set a pack of spirit hounds on them and chase
them away.

Scene i • *In front of Prospero's cell.*

[*Enter* Prospero *in his magic robes, and* Ariel.]

Prospero. Now does my project gather to a head.
My charms crack not, my spirits obey, and time
Goes upright with his carriage.[1] How's the day?

Ariel. On the sixth hour, at which time, my lord,
5 You said our work should cease.

Prospero.   I did say so,
When first I raised the tempest. Say, my spirit,

NOTES

1. carriage *n.* burden.

2. **weather-fends** protects from inclement weather.

3. **till your release** until you free them.

4. **eaves of reeds** thatched roofs.

CLOSE READ

ANNOTATE: In lines 21–24, mark details that relate to feeling, both emotional and physical.

QUESTION: Why does Prospero include so many feeling references in his question to Ariel?

CONCLUDE: With what conflict is Prospero struggling?

penitent (PEHN uh tuhnt) *adj.* sorry for one's wrongdoing

5. **fly him** race with him.

6. **green sour ringlets** small circles of darker grass that accompany circles of mushrooms.

7. **mushrumps** *n.* mushrooms.

8. **Weak masters** not powerful magicians.

9. **spurs** *n.* roots.

How fares the King and 's followers?

Ariel.   Confined together
In the same fashion as you gave in charge,
Just as you left them—all prisoners, sir,
10 In the line grove which weather-fends[2] your cell.
They cannot budge till your release.[3] The King,
His brother, and yours abide all three distracted,
And the remainder mourning over them,
Brimful of sorrow and dismay; but chiefly
15 Him that you termed, sir, the good old Lord Gonzalo.
His tears run down his beard like winter's drops
From eaves of reeds.[4] Your charm so strongly works 'em
That if you now beheld them, your affections
Would become tender.

Prospero.   Dost thou think so, spirit?

20 **Ariel.** Mine would, sir, were I human.

Prospero.   And mine shall.
Hast thou, which art but air, a touch, a feeling
Of their afflictions, and shall not myself,
One of their kind, that relish all as sharply,
Passion as they, be kindlier moved than thou art?
25 Though with their high wrongs I am struck to th' quick,
Yet with my nobler reason 'gainst my fury
Do I take part. The rarer action is
In virtue than in vengeance. They being **penitent**,
The sole drift of my purpose doth extend
30 Not a frown further. Go, release them, Ariel.
My charms I'll break, their senses I'll restore,
And they shall be themselves.

Ariel.   I'll fetch them, sir.   [*Exit.*]

Prospero. Ye elves of hills, brooks, standing lakes, and groves,
And ye that on the sands with printless foot
35 Do chase the ebbing Neptune, and do fly him[5]
When he comes back; you demi-puppets that
By moonshine do the green sour ringlets[6] make,
Whereof the ewe not bites; and you whose pastime
Is to make midnight mushrumps,[7] that rejoice
40 To hear the solemn curfew; by whose aid
(Weak masters[8] though ye be) I have bedimmed
The noontide sun, called forth the mutinous winds,
And 'twixt the green sea and the azured vault
Set roaring war; to the dread rattling thunder
45 Have I given fire and rifted Jove's stout oak
With his own bolt; the strong-based promontory
Have I made shake and by the spurs[9] plucked up
The pine and cedar; graves at my command

Have waked their sleepers, oped, and let 'em forth
50 By my so potent art. But this rough magic
I here abjure; and when I have required
Some heavenly music (which even now I do)
To work mine end upon their senses that[10]
This airy charm is for, I'll break my staff,
55 Bury it certain fathoms in the earth,
And deeper than did ever plummet sound
I'll drown my book.   [*Solemn music.*]

[*Here enter* Ariel *before; then* Alonso, *with a frantic gesture, attended
by* Gonzalo; Sebastian *and* Antonio *in like manner, attended by*
Adrian *and* Francisco. *They all enter the circle which* Prospero *had
made, and there stand charmed; which* Prospero *observing, speaks.*]

A solemn air and the best comforter
To an unsettled fancy, cure thy brains,
60 Now useless, boiled within thy skull! There stand,
For you are spell-stopped.
Holy Gonzalo, honorable man,
Mine eyes, ev'n sociable to the show of thine,
Fall fellowly drops.[11] The charm dissolves apace;
65 And as the morning steals upon the night,
Melting the darkness, so their rising senses
Begin to chase the ignorant fumes that mantle
Their clearer reason. O good Gonzalo,
My true preserver, and a loyal sir
70 To him you follow'st! I will pay thy graces
Home[12] both in word and deed. Most cruelly
Didst thou, Alonso, use me and my daughter.
Thy brother was a furtherer in the act.
Thou art pinched for't now, Sebastian. Flesh and blood,
75 You, brother mine, that entertained ambition,
Expelled remorse and nature;[13] whom, with Sebastian
(Whose inward pinches therefore are most strong),
Would here have killed your king, I do forgive thee,
Unnatural though thou art. Their understanding
80 Begins to swell, and the approaching tide
Will shortly fill the reasonable shore,
That now lies foul and muddy. Not one of them
That yet looks on me or would know me. Ariel,
Fetch me the hat and rapier in my cell.
85 I will discase[14] me, and myself present
As I was sometime Milan, Quickly, spirit!
Thou shalt ere long be free.
                           [*Exit* Ariel *and returns immediately.*]

[Ariel *sings and helps to attire him.*]

Where the bee sucks, there suck I;
In a cowslip's bell I lie;
90 There I couch when owls do cry.

NOTES

10. **their senses that** the senses of those whom.

11. **sociable . . . drops** identifying with the tears in your eyes, mine also drop tears in sympathy.

12. **pay . . . Home** repay your kindness fully.

13. **nature** *n.* natural feeling of brotherly affection and loyalty.

14. **discase** *v.* undress.

On the bat's back I do fly
After summer merrily.
Merrily, merrily shall I live now
Under the blossom that hangs on the bough.

95 **Prospero.** Why, that's my dainty Ariel! I shall miss thee,
But yet thou shalt have freedom; so, so, so.
To the King's ship, invisible as thou art!
There shalt thou find the mariners asleep
Under the hatches. The master and the boatswain
100 Being awake, enforce them to this place,
And presently,[15] I prithee.

Ariel. I drink the air before me, and return
Or ere your pulse twice beat.   [*Exit.*]

Gonzalo. All torment, trouble, wonder, and amazement
105 Inhabits here. Some heavenly power guide us
Out of this fearful country!

Prospero.   Behold, sir King,
The wrongèd Duke of Milan, Prospero.
For more assurance that a living prince
Does now speak to thee, I embrace thy body,
110 And to thee and thy company I bid
A hearty welcome.

Alonso.   Whe'r[16] thou be'st he or no,
Or some enchanted trifle[17] to abuse me,
As late I have been, I not know. Thy pulse
Beats, as of flesh and blood; and, since I saw thee,
115 Th' affliction of my mind amends, with which,
I fear, a madness held me. This must crave[18]
(And if this be at all[19]) a most strange story.
Thy dukedom I resign and do entreat
Thou pardon me my wrongs. But how should Prospero
120 Be living and be here?

Prospero.   First, noble friend,
Let me embrace thine age, whose honor cannot
Be measured or confined.

Gonzalo.   Whether this be
Or be not, I'll not swear.

Prospero.   You do yet taste
Some subtleties[20] o' th' isle, that will not let you
125 Believe things certain. Welcome, my friends all.
[*Aside to* Sebastian *and* Antonio] But you, my brace of lords,
   were I so minded,
I here could pluck his Highness' frown upon you
And justify[21] you traitors. At this time
I will tell no tales.

15. **presently** *adv.* quickly.

16. **Whe'r** whether.
17. **trifle** *n.* ghost.

18. **crave** *v.* yearn for; desire intensely.
19. **And . . . all** and if this be real.

pardon (PAHR duhn) *v.* forgive

20. **taste . . . subtleties** sense some deceptions—an allusion to popular pastries made to look like castles, ships, and the like.

21. **justify** *v.* prove.

Sebastian.   [*Aside*] The devil speaks in him.

Prospero.   No.

130 For you, most wicked sir, whom to call brother
Would even infect my mouth, I do forgive
Thy rankest fault—all of them; and require
My dukedom of thee, which perforce, I know,
Thou must restore.

Alonso.   If thou beest Prospero,
135 Give us particulars of thy preservation;
How thou hast met us here, who three hours since
Were wracked upon this shore; where I have lost
(How sharp the point of this remembrance is!)
My dear son Ferdinand.

Prospero.   I am woe[22] for't, sir.

140 **Alonso.** Irreparable is the loss, and patience
Says it is past her cure.

Prospero.   I rather think
You have not sought her help, of whose soft grace
For the like loss I have her sovereign aid
And rest myself content.

Alonso.   You the like loss?

145 **Prospero.** As great to me, as late,[23] and supportable
To make the dear loss, have I means much weaker
Than you may call to comfort you; for I
Have lost my daughter.

Alonso.   A daughter?
O heavens, that they were living both in Naples,
150 The King and Queen there! That they were, I wish
Myself were mudded in that oozy bed
Where my son lies. When did you lose your daughter?

Prospero. In this last tempest. I perceive these lords
At this encounter do so much admire
155 That they devour their reason, and scarce think
Their eyes do offices[24] of truth, their words
Are natural breath. But, howsoev'r you have
Been justled from your senses, know for certain
That I am Prospero, and that very duke
160 Which was thrust forth of Milan, who most strangely
Upon this shore, where you were wracked, was landed,
To be the lord on't. No more yet of this;
For 'tis a chronicle of day by day,
Not a relation for a breakfast, nor
165 Befitting this first meeting. Welcome, sir;
This cell's my court. Here have I few attendants,
And subjects none abroad.[25] Pray you, look in.

NOTES

22. woe *adj.* sorry.

CLOSE READ
ANNOTATE: In lines 142–148, mark Prospero's references to his having lost his daughter Miranda.

QUESTION: Why does Prospero describe Miranda this way?

CONCLUDE: What effect is Prospero trying to achieve?

23. As . . . late as great a loss to me as to you, and as recent a one.

24. do offices perform the functions.

25. abroad elsewhere on this island.

26. *discovers* v. reveals.

27. **for a score . . . play** if we were really playing for high stakes and you cheated me, I'd call it fair play.

merciful (MUR sih fuhl) *adj.* showing kindness

28. **eld'st** *adj.* longest.

CLOSE READ

ANNOTATE: Mark the two related adjectives used in lines 188 and 189.

QUESTION: Why does Shakespeare choose these words?

CONCLUDE: What effect do these adjectives create?

My dukedom since you have given me again,
I will requite you with as good a thing,
170 At least bring forth a wonder, to content ye
As much as me my dukedom.

[*Here* Prospero *discovers*²⁶ Ferdinand *and* Miranda *playing at chess.*]

Miranda. Sweet lord, you play me false.

Ferdinand.   No, my dearest love,
I would not for the world.

Miranda. Yes, for a score of kingdoms you should wrangle,
175 And I would call it, fair play.²⁷

Alonso.   If this prove
A vision of the island, one dear son
Shall I twice lose.

Sebastian.   A most high miracle!

Ferdinand. Though the seas threaten, they are **merciful**.
I have cursed them without cause.   [*Kneels.*]

Alonso.   Now all the blessings
180 Of a glad father compass thee about!
Arise, and say how thou cam'st here.

Miranda.   O, wonder!
How many goodly creatures are there here!
How beauteous mankind is! O brave new world,
That has such people in't!

Prospero.   'Tis new to thee.

185 **Alonso.** What is this maid with whom thou wast at play?
Your eld'st²⁸ acquaintance cannot be three hours.
Is she the goddess that hath severed us
And brought us thus together?

Ferdinand.   Sir, she is mortal;
But by immortal providence she's mine:
190 I chose her when I could not ask my father
For his advice, nor thought I had one. She
Is daughter to this famous Duke of Milan,
Of whom so often I have heard renown,
But never saw before; of whom I have
195 Received a second life; and second father
This lady makes him to me.

Alonso.   I am hers.
But, O, how oddly will it sound that I
Must ask my child forgiveness!

Prospero.   There, sir, stop.
Let us not burthen our remembrance with
200 A heaviness that's gone.

Gonzalo.   I have inly wept,

Or should have spoke ere this. Look down, you gods,
And on this couple drop a blessèd crown!
For it is you that have chalked forth the way
Which brought us hither.

Alonso.   I say, amen, Gonzalo.

205 **Gonzalo.** Was Milan thrust from Milan, that his issue
Should become kings of Naples? O, rejoice
Beyond a common joy, and set it down
With gold on lasting pillars. In one voyage
Did Claribel her husband find at Tunis,
210 And Ferdinand her brother found a wife
Where he himself was lost; Prospero his dukedom
In a poor isle; and all of us ourselves
When no man was his own.

Alonso.   [*To* Ferdinand *and* Miranda] Give me your hands.
Let grief and sorrow still embrace his heart
215 That doth not wish you joy!

Gonzalo.   Be it so! Amen!

[*Enter* Ariel, *with the* Master *and* Boatswain *amazedly following*.]

O, look, sir; look, sir! Here is more of us!
I prophesied, if a gallows were on land,
This fellow could not drown. Now, blasphemy,
That swear'st grace o'erboard,²⁹ not an oath on shore?
220 Hast thou no mouth by land? What is the news?

Boatswain. The best news is, that we have safely found
Our king and company; the next, our ship,
Which, but three glasses³⁰ since, we gave out split,
Is tight and yare³¹ and bravely rigged as when
225 We first put out to sea.

Ariel.   [*Aside to* Prospero] Sir, all this service
Have I done since I went.

Prospero.   [*Aside to* Ariel] My tricksy spirit!

Alonso. These are not natural events; they strengthen
From strange to stranger. Say, how came you hither?

Boatswain. If I did think, sir, I were well awake,
230 I'd strive to tell you. We were dead of sleep,
And (how we know not) all clapped under hatches;
Where, but even now, with strange and several noises
Of roaring, shrieking, howling, jingling chains,
And more diversity of sounds, all horrible,
235 We were awaked; straightway at liberty;
Where we, in all her trim, freshly beheld
Our royal, good, and gallant ship, our master
Cap'ring to eye her.³² On a trice, so please you,

29. blasphemy . . . o'erboard
irreverent curses that threw
salvation into the sea.

30. glasses *n.* hours.
31. yare *adj.* shipshape.

32. master . . . her captain dancing
to see her.

Even in a dream, were we divided from them
240 And were brought moping[33] hither.

Ariel. [*Aside to* Prospero]   Was't well done?

Prospero. [*Aside to* Ariel] Bravely, my diligence. Thou shalt be free.

Alonso. This is as strange a maze as e'er man trod,
And there is in this business more than nature
Was ever conduct[34] of. Some oracle
245 Must **rectify** our knowledge.

Prospero.   Sir, my liege,
Do not infest your mind with beating on
The strangeness of this business. At picked leisure,
Which shall be shortly, single I'll resolve you
(Which to you shall seem probable) of every
250 These happened accidents;[35] till when, be cheerful
And think of each thing well. [*Aside to* Ariel] Come hither, spirit.
Set Caliban and his companions free.
Untie the spell. [*Exit* Ariel.] How fares my gracious sir?
There are yet missing of your company
255 Some few odd lads that you remember not.

[*Enter* Ariel, *driving in* Caliban, Stephano *and* Trinculo,
in their stolen apparel.]

Stephano. Every man shift for all the rest, and let no man take
care of himself; for all is but fortune. *Coraggio,*[36] bully-monster,
coraggio!

Trinculo. If these be true spies which I wear in my head, here's a
260 goodly sight.

Caliban. O Setebos, these be brave spirits indeed!
How fine my master is! I am afraid
He will chastise me.

Sebastian.   Ha, ha!
What things are these, my Lord Antonio?
265 Will money buy 'em?

Antonio.   Very like. One of them
Is a plain fish and no doubt marketable.

Prospero. Mark but the badges[37] of these men, my lords,
Then say if they be true.[38] This misshapen knave,
His mother was a witch, and one so strong
270 That could control the moon, make flows and ebbs,
And deal in her command without her power.[39]
These three have robbed me, and this demi-devil
(For he's a bastard one) had plotted with them
To take my life. Two of these fellows you
275 Must know and own; this thing of darkness I
Acknowledge mine.

Caliban.   I shall be pinched to death.

Alonso. Is not this Stephano, my drunken butler?

Sebastian. He is drunk now. Where had he wine?

Alonso. And Trinculo is reeling ripe. Where should they
280 Find this grand liquor that hath gilded 'em?
How cam'st thou in this pickle?

Trinculo. I have been in such a pickle, since I saw you last, that I
fear me will never out of my bones. I shall not fear flyblowing.[40]

Sebastian. Why, how, now, Stephano?

285 **Stephano.** O, touch me not! I am not Stephano, but a cramp.

Prospero. You'd be king o' the isle, sirrah?

Stephano. I should have been a sore[41] one then.

Alonso. This is a strange thing as e'er I looked on.

Prospero. He is as disproportioned in his manners
290 As in his shape. Go, sirrah, to my cell;
Take with you your companions. As you look
To have my pardon, trim it handsomely.

Caliban. Ay, that I will; and I'll be wise hereafter,
And seek for grace. What a thrice-double ass
295 Was I, to take this drunkard for a god
And worship this dull fool!

Prospero.   Go to! Away!

Alonso. Hence, and bestow your luggage where you found it.

Sebastian. Or stole it rather.
               [*Exit* Caliban, Stephano, *and* Trinculo.]

Prospero. Sir, I invite your Highness and your train
300 To my poor cell, where you shall take your rest
For this one night; which, part of it, I'll waste[42]
With such discourse as, I not doubt, shall make it
Go quick away—the story of my life,
And the particular accidents gone by
305 Since I came to this isle. And in the morn
I'll bring you to your ship, and so to Naples,
Where I have hope to see the nuptial
Of these our dear-beloved solemnizèd;
And thence retire me to my Milan, where
310 Every third thought shall be my grave.

Alonso.   I long
To hear the story of your life, which must
Take[43] the ear strangely.

Prospero.   I'll deliver[44] all;
And promise you calm seas, auspicious gales

40. flyblowing *n*. infestation of maggots.

41. sore *adj*. pained or angry.

42. waste *v*. spend.

43. Take . . . strangely sound strange.
44. deliver *v*. tell.

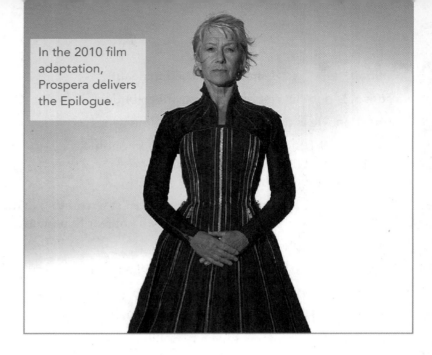

In the 2010 film adaptation, Prospera delivers the Epilogue.

And sail so expeditious that shall catch
315 Your royal fleet far off. [*Aside to* Ariel] My Ariel, chick,
That is thy charge. Then to the elements
Be free, and fare thou well! [*To the others*] Please you, draw near.

[*Exit all.*]

⌘ ⌘ ⌘

Epilogue

Spoken by Prospero

Now my charms are all o'erthrown,
And what strength I have's mine own,
Which is most faint. Now 'tis true,
I must be here confined by you,
5 Or sent to Naples. Let me not,
Since I have my dukedom got
And pardoned the deceiver, dwell
In this bare island by your spell;
But release me from my bands[1]
10 With the help of your good hands.[2]
Gentle breath[3] of yours my sails
Must fill, or else my project fails;
Which was to please. Now I want
Spirits to enforce, art to enchant;
15 And my ending is despair
Unless I be relieved by prayer,[4]
Which pierces so that it assaults
Mercy itself and frees all faults.
As you from crimes would pardoned be,
20 Let your indulgence[5] set me free.

[*Exit.*]

FINIS

CLOSE READ

ANNOTATE: In lines 1–20, mark the rhyming words.

QUESTION: Why does Shakespeare end the play in rhyming verse?

CONCLUDE: What is the effect of this final passage?

1. **bands** *n*. pledges; promises.
2. **hands** *n*. applause.
3. **Gentle breath** approving comments.

4. **prayer** my plea, request, or petition.

5. **indulgence** *n*. generosity; also, remission from sins according to Roman Catholic doctrine.

Discuss It Do the costumes in the slide show fit your sense of what the characters should be wearing?

Write your response before sharing your ideas.

Dressing *The Tempest*: Slide Show,
The New York Times

Comprehension Check

Complete the following items after you finish your first read.

1. What are Ferdinand and Miranda doing when we first see them in Act V?

2. What does Alonso immediately resign when he sees Prospero?

3. What is Prospero's last command to Ariel?

4. **Notebook** Confirm your understanding of Act V by writing a summary.

- -

RESEARCH

Research to Clarify Choose at least one unfamiliar detail from the text. Briefly research that detail. In what way does the information you learned shed light on an aspect of the play?

THE TEMPEST, ACT V

Close Read the Text

1. This model, from lines 16–20 of Act V, Scene i, shows two sample annotations, along with questions and conclusions. Close read the passage, and find another detail to annotate. Then, write a question and your conclusion.

Close Read — ANNOTATE • QUESTION • CONCLUDE

ANNOTATE: These sentences are much shorter than those before them.

QUESTION: Why are these lines so short and simple?

CONCLUDE: The sentences express straightforward and sincere feeling.

ANNOTATE: These words compare Gonzalo's tears to water dripping from a roof in winter.

QUESTION: Why does Shakespeare use this image?

CONCLUDE: The image could relate to Gonzalo's age, to his tenderness, or to the melting of hardened feelings.

Ariel. His tears run down his beard like winter's drops
From eaves of reeds. Your charm so strongly works 'em
That if you now beheld them, your affections
Would become tender.
Prospero.   Dost thou think so, spirit?
Ariel. Mine would, sir, were I human.
Prospero.   And mine shall.

2. For more practice, go back into the text, and complete the close-read notes.

3. Revisit a section of the text you found important during your first read. Read this section closely, and **annotate** what you notice. Ask yourself **questions** such as "Why did the author make this choice?" What can you **conclude**?

 Tool Kit
Close-Read Guide and Model Annotation

Analyze the Text

CITE TEXTUAL EVIDENCE to support your answers.

Notebook Respond to these questions.

1. **Interpret** Why does Prospero decide to forgive the conspirators?

2. (a) When the audience knows something that a character does not, the effect is called **dramatic irony.** Where in Act V does Alonso express a wish that is ironic in this way? (b) **Support** What makes the wish ironic? (c) **Make a Judgment** Is Prospero justified in placing Alonso in the circumstances that evoke this wish?

3. (a) What does Prospero do for Ariel and Caliban in the final scene? (b) **Synthesize** How does Prospero's final soliloquy, in the Epilogue, reflect these actions?

4. **Essential Question:** *What motivates us to forgive?* What have you learned about forgiveness from reading *The Tempest*?

Analyze Craft and Structure

Plot Structure In Shakespearean comedies, the **resolution** of a play occurs in its final section, when all conflicts are resolved and all characters come together. Order is restored. The rightful king returns. Those who should lose ill-gotten gains lose them. Justice is served with mercy. *The Tempest* follows this pattern, but the resolution is not so tidy. It is colored by Prospero's mixed feelings and his sorrow at giving up magic.

Shakespeare adds an **epilogue** after the resolution. In a typical epilogue, a character adds final comments on the conflict and resolution of the play. Prospero's epilogue is different; it is a request to the audience to grant him his freedom. Over the centuries, some critics have seen this speech as a request from Shakespeare himself—the magician of the stage—to release him from his duties and let him retire.

Practice

CITE TEXTUAL EVIDENCE to support your answers.

Use the chart to record how the resolution of the plot affects each character in *The Tempest*.

CHARACTER	WHAT IS RESOLVED IN ACT V
Prospero	
Miranda	
Ferdinand	
Alonso	
Sebastian	
Antonio	
Gonzalo	
Ariel	
Caliban	
Stephano	
Trinculo	

Notebook Reread the Epilogue aloud. Then, answer the questions.

1. (a) What emotions does Prospero convey in this passage? (b) Which lines express these emotions most strongly? Explain.
2. If Shakespeare intended the Epilogue as a personal farewell to his audiences, is this speech appropriate? Explain.

THE TEMPEST, ACT V

Concept Vocabulary

| penitent | pardon | merciful | rectify |

Why These Words? These concept words relate to forgiveness and putting things right, the main emphasis of Act V of *The Tempest*. For example, Prospero says that because King Alonso and his companions are *penitent*, he will not punish them further.

1. How does the concept vocabulary reinforce the resolution of the play?

2. What other words in Act V connect to this concept?

Practice

🖙 **Notebook** The concept vocabulary words appear in Act V of *The Tempest*.

1. Write a sentence for each concept vocabulary word that clearly conveys its meaning.
2. Revise each sentence you wrote using a synonym for the concept vocabulary word. After each sentence, note whether the synonym means precisely what the vocabulary word does, or whether the synonym has a slightly different **denotation**—the literal dictionary meaning—or **connotation**—the feeling it elicits.

Word Study

Latin Root: *-pen-* English words containing the root *-pen-* may derive from one of two sources. Some words, such as *penalize*, meaning "to make illegal," come from the Latin word *poena*, meaning "punishment." Other words, such as *penultimate*, meaning "next to last," come from the Latin word *paene*, meaning "almost."

1. Infer whether each of the following words derives from the Latin word *poena* or the Latin word *paene*. Write your inference. Then, use a college-level dictionary to verify your answers.

   • *penology*, meaning "study of the rehabilitation of criminals"

   • *peninsula*, meaning "land area nearly surrounded by water"

   • *penumbra*, meaning "partly shadowed area"

   • *penalty*, meaning "negative legal consequence"

2. 🖙 **Notebook** The word *pain* also derives from the Latin *poena*. Explain how the meaning of *poena* contributes to the meaning of *pain*. Use a specialized resource such as an etymological dictionary to verify your answer.

Author's Style

Poetic Structure Until about the middle of the 1500s, all English plays were written in rhymed verse. By the time Shakespeare started writing plays in the 1590s, blank verse had become the fashion. The young playwright used this unrhymed form brilliantly, but he did not abandon the powerful tool of rhyme. Throughout his work, rhyming couplets set apart significant moments from the rest of the action.

A **rhyming couplet** is a pair of lines that have the same meter and end words that rhyme. The rhyme is **full rhyme**, which means that the final stressed vowel sounds of the words are identical, as are any consonant sounds that follow. For example, *blameless* and *shameless* are full rhymes. Shakespeare uses rhyming couplets in iambic pentameter, but for special occasions such as songs and chants, he uses a shorter line with a different meter.

Read It

Review three points in the play in which rhyming couplets are used—the first line of each passage appears in the chart. Then, explain the effects of the change in rhyme and meter. What moment, idea, feeling, or characters do these passages set apart from the rest of the play's action?

PASSAGE	EFFECTS OF RHYMING COUPLETS
Come unto these yellow sands . . . (Act I, Scene ii, lines 375–385)	
Ceres, most bounteous lady, thy rich leas . . . (Act IV, Scene i, lines 60–75)	
Now my charms are all o'erthrown . . . (Act V, Epilogue, lines 1–20)	

Write It

📓 **Notebook** Imagine that you are Prospero. Write two rhyming couplets, about either your daughter (Miranda) or your brother (Antonio). Make sure to use full rhymes and the same meter in each couplet.

THE TEMPEST, ACT V

Writing to Sources

Literary criticism is any writing that examines and evaluates a literary work. A critic can explore a work in many different ways, including the following:

- explain its form or structure
- consider how readers respond to it
- examine it as a product of a specific culture
- link it to its author's life and personal influences

Assignment

Write a brief **critical essay** in which you analyze *The Tempest*'s uneasy ending. Remember that this is a romance, in which a happy ending comes only after characters have faced daunting challenges. The ending restores order and seems happy, but there are strains in that happiness. For example, consider these elements of discord:

- Prospero is giving up his powers. See the "farewell to magic" speech. (Act V, Scene i, lines 33–57)
- Prospero "forgives" Antonio, while reminding him of his treachery. See their exchange. (Act V, Scene i, lines 129–141)

In your essay, explain how one of these two elements complicates the happy ending.

Vocabulary and Conventions Connection In your essay consider including several of the concept vocabulary words.

penitent	pardon	merciful	rectify

- -

Reflect on Your Writing

After you have written your literary criticism, answer the following questions:

1. How did writing about the resolution of the play help you understand it?

2. What evidence and specific details did you use in your writing? How did they help you make your points?

3. Why These Words? The words you choose make a difference in your writing. Which words did you specifically choose to add clarity to your literary criticism?

Speaking and Listening

Assignment

With a partner, deliver an **oral presentation** on the question of which is more powerful, "nature," a person's inborn identity, or "nurture," a person's upbringing. Take a position on the question, and use evidence from the play to support your ideas. Consider the following questions:

- If Caliban and Miranda were both brought up under the watchful eye of Prospero, why are they so different?
- What caused Antonio to betray his brother Prospero?
- What is Shakespeare saying about the relative impact of nature and nurture on a person's attitude and behavior?

Prepare for the presentation by planning your arguments, considering possible counterarguments, and drafting an opening statement.

1. **Outline Your Argument** With your partner, discuss the arguments in favor of your position. Decide which ideas are the strongest. Then, use a chart to make notes about your arguments and supporting points.

ARGUMENT	SUPPORT

2. **Anticipate Counterarguments** Discuss arguments that could be made against your position. Consider how you can effectively answer them.

3. **Draft and Practice** Use the ideas and evidence you organized in your chart to craft a logical, persuasive introduction to your presentation. Practice your delivery and make adjustments to strengthen it.

4. **Deliver and Evaluate Presentations** As your classmates deliver their presentations, listen attentively. Use an evaluation guide like the one shown to analyze their deliveries.

PRESENTATION EVALUATION GUIDE

Rate each statement on a scale of 1 (not demonstrated) to 4 (demonstrated).

☐ The introduction states a clear position.

☐ The presentation includes well-supported arguments.

☐ Ideas are supported with evidence from the play.

☐ The presentation anticipates and addresses a counterargument.

✎ EVIDENCE LOG

Before moving on to a new selection, go to your Evidence Log and record what you learned from *The Tempest*.

THE TEMPEST

Comparing Texts

In this lesson, you will compare two poems inspired by Shakespeare's *The Tempest* with the play itself. First, you will complete the first-read and close-read activities for the two poems.

POETRY COLLECTION 1

En el Jardín de los Espejos Quebrados, Caliban Catches a Glimpse of His Reflection
Caliban

Concept Vocabulary

You will encounter the following words as you read the poems. Before reading, note how familiar you are with each word. Then, rank the words in order from most familiar (1) to least familiar (6).

WORD	YOUR RANKING
swollen	
scarred	
welt	
sliver	
cartilage	
clench	

After completing the first read, come back to the concept vocabulary and review your rankings. Mark changes to your original rankings as needed.

First Read POETRY

Apply these strategies as you conduct your first read. You will have the opportunity to complete a close read after your first read.

Tool Kit
First-Read Guide and
Model Annotation

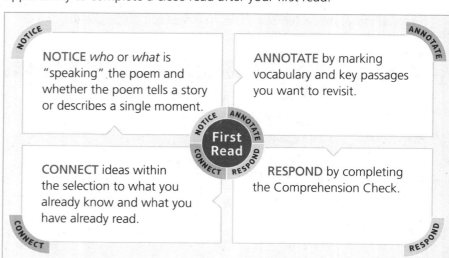

NOTICE *who* or *what* is "speaking" the poem and whether the poem tells a story or describes a single moment.

ANNOTATE by marking vocabulary and key passages you want to revisit.

CONNECT ideas within the selection to what you already know and what you have already read.

RESPOND by completing the Comprehension Check.

About the Poets

When **Virgil Suárez** (b. 1962) and his family moved to the United States from Cuba, his parents worked difficult jobs in sweatshops and factories producing fabric. As a distinguished Latino poet, Suárez uses his personal immigration experience to tell stories of refuge and immigrant identity. He continues to write poetry and teach creative writing at Florida State University.

J. P. Dancing Bear (b. 1961) is the author of thousands of poems, founding editor of *The American Poetry Journal*, and owner of Dream Horse Press. He lives in the Monterey Bay area of California. J. P. Dancing Bear is the host of the weekly hour-long poetry show called *Out of Our Minds*, which airs on public radio. Among his most recent works is *Cephalopodic*, a collection of love poems.

Backgrounds

En el Jardín de los Espejos Quebrados, Caliban Catches a Glimpse of His Reflection

The works of Shakespeare have been referenced and reinterpreted by many other authors. This poem comes from a collection by Virgil Suárez that uses the character of Caliban from *The Tempest* to explore the experience of growing up in Cuba.

Caliban

In 2005, a collection of poetry called *In a Fine Frenzy* was published in which many different poets wrote poems responding to various aspects of Shakespeare's plays. This poem by J. P. Dancing Bear is part of that collection.

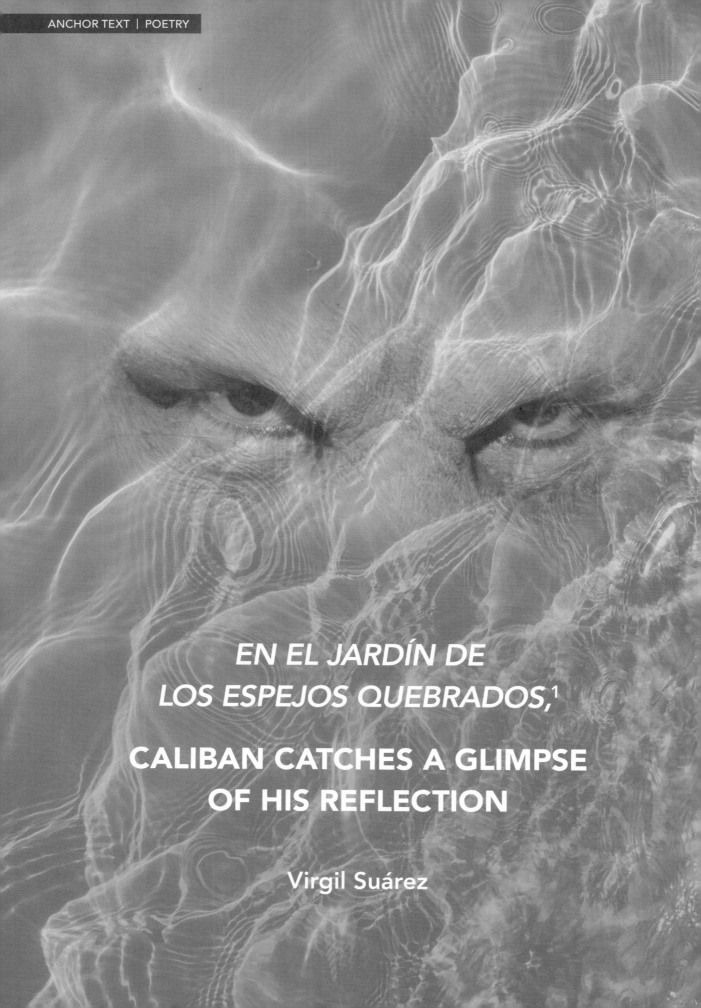

*EN EL JARDÍN DE
LOS ESPEJOS QUEBRADOS,*[1]

CALIBAN CATCHES A GLIMPSE
OF HIS REFLECTION

Virgil Suárez

To call a man a beast, one must see into his heart,
this much he knows is true in this garden of shadow
and light. When he cuts through it, leaving tracks

on the bone-white sands, he often stops to catch
5   his breath, rest from the day's delivery of wood
to Prospero's house. He thinks of the old man's

daughter, her feather-soft hands, the way she'll smile
up at her dresser mirror, as if she knows this secret
of slatted images on a pond's surface. He hunches

10 close to the ground, where the warmth from the day's
heat coils about his naked, **swollen** feet. He feels
his **scarred** face, this empty promise of healing.

*Yo soy el hombre sin rumbo, el hombre en las tinieblas
de los días y las noches*[2] . . . aimless and uprooted,
15 the way a porpoise frolics on the crest of the waves,

a manatee's weight sinks it into the wavering penumbra
of a river's depth. Fourteen scars on his scalp, his fingers
know the story, each **welt**, the piece of his right ear

missing, **sliver** of **cartilage**, a nose broken too often.
20 How could he be the man in love with such a woman?
"*¿Por qué no?*"[3] he calls out. In this island of all things

broken, shifted, he isn't the only one damaged by history,
by the way storms surge and ravage, uprooted royal
palms everywhere, roof shingles like buried hands,

25 so red, so blue, to call this man a beast you must bow.

NOTES

swollen (SWOH luhn) *adj.*
puffed up

scarred (skahrd) *adj.* marked
by healed wounds

welt (wehlt) *n.* ridge on the
skin caused by a blow

sliver (SLIHV uhr) *n.* small,
slender piece of a hard
material

cartilage (KAHR tuh lihj) *n.*
firm, flexible tissue almost as
hard as bone

---

1. ***EN EL JARDÍN DE LOS ESPEJOS QUEBRADOS*** "In the Garden of Broken Mirrors" (Spanish).
2. ***Yo soy . . . las noches*** "I am the man without direction, the man in the darkness of the days and the nights" (Spanish).
3. ***"¿Por qué no?"*** "Why not?" (Spanish).

Caliban

J. P. Dancing Bear

NOTES

Before hatred ate my heart
there was music:
my mother's willow music,
her dark willow music of wind and wave.
5 There was water singing over
the roots of ash, over stones.

Mother, I am a dead thing
with a voice trained for anything but song,

shackled in magic and pushed down,
10 taught to speak with a tongue
that damns with bellyaches.

Mother, your songs will die within me.
Mother, I am shaped an evil thing.
My tears run for the loss of song.
15 My fists **clench** for you.

clench (klehnch) *v.* close
tightly

Comprehension Check

Complete the following items after you finish your first read.

1. In *"En el Jardín de los Espejos Quebrados . . .,"* what is Caliban doing?

2. In *"En el Jardín de los Espejos Quebrados . . .,"* of whom is Caliban thinking?

3. Who is the speaker of "Caliban"?

4. In "Caliban," of whom is the speaker thinking?

5. In "Caliban," what did the speaker's mother use to make music?

- -

RESEARCH

Research to Clarify Choose at least one unfamiliar detail from one of the poems. Briefly research that detail. In what way does the information you learned shed light on an aspect of the poem?

Research to Explore Choose something from one of the poems that interested you, and formulate a research question.

Close Read the Text

1. Revisit sections of the text you marked during your first read. **Annotate** what you notice. What **questions** do you have? What can you **conclude**?

- -

Analyze the Text

> **CITE TEXTUAL EVIDENCE** to support your answers.

📓 **Notebook** Respond to these questions.

1. Interpret What does the speaker of "*En el Jardín De Los Espejos Quebrados*, Caliban Catches a Glimpse of His Reflection" mean when he says, "To call a man a beast, one must see within his heart"?

2. (a) In "*En el Jardín De Los Espejos Quebrados . . . ,*" what kinds of marks disfigure Caliban's body? **(b) Analyze** What do these marks suggest about Caliban's supposed ugliness?

3. Interpet When the speaker of "Caliban" says, "Before hatred ate my heart," what does he mean?

4. Essential Question: *What motivates us to forgive?* What have you learned about forgiveness from reading these poems?

LANGUAGE DEVELOPMENT

Concept Vocabulary

swollen	cartilage	sliver
scarred	welt	clench

Why These Words? The concept vocabulary words all relate to physical damage, especially wounds and the signs they leave behind. The speaker of "*En el Jardín de los Espejos Quebrados . . .*" mentions Caliban's "swollen feet" and "scarred face." Both *swollen* and *scarred* refer to physical ways in which a person's body shows signs of injury.

1. How does the concept vocabulary help readers understand the sorrow of Caliban?

2. What other words in the poems connect to this concept?

> 🔗 **WORD NETWORK**
>
> Add words related to forgiveness from the texts to your Word Network.

THE TEMPEST

POETRY COLLECTION 1

Writing to Compare

In Shakespeare's *The Tempest,* Caliban is one of the darker mysteries of the island. The child of a powerful sorceress whom Prospero defeated, Caliban is belittled and enslaved. Although he gets to tell part of his story in the play, he is ultimately silenced. In these poems, he is given a new voice.

Assignment

Write a **comparison-and-contrast essay** in which you analyze Caliban's character as portrayed in the play and in one of the poems. In addition, express a judgment about the value of reading new works based on old characters. To do so, consider these questions:

- Does the poem show Caliban in a new way while remaining true to the play? Alternatively, is the change so profound that Caliban is now a different character?

- Does the poem have a deeper or different message about oppressed people than does the play?

- Does the poem help you see the play in a fresh way?

Support your analysis with evidence from both the play and the poem.

Prewriting

Analyze the Texts Review the sections of the play noted in the chart. Identify details related to Caliban's birth, experiences, appearance, thoughts, feelings, and actions. Then, choose one of the poems, and identify mirror details—those that reflect or comment on elements you noted in the play. Choose the poem you find most intriguing.

Poem you will compare: _____

	THE TEMPEST	THE POEM
Act I, Scene ii, lines 261–286		
Act I, Scene ii, lines 309–374		
Act II, Scene ii, lines 59–74		
Act III, Scene ii, lines 38–138		

Drafting

Organize Textual Details This assignment requires you to show similarities and differences in how Caliban is portrayed in two works. Use the chart to organize your notes.

ELEMENT	SIMILARITIES	DIFFERENCES
Experiences		
Appearance		
Thoughts and Feelings		
Behavior and Actions		

Choose a Structure Choose one of these formats to organize your essay.

- **Block format:** Discuss the portrayal of Caliban in the play, and then his portrayal in the poem.

- **Point-by-point format:** Discuss specific aspects of Caliban's portrayal in each text, alternating between the two.

Conclude your essay by addressing the broader question about the value of new literature based on older characters or stories.

Use Varied Support Details from the text are your best forms of evidence, but you should also weave in other types of support.

- **Summaries,** or brief retellings of the events of a plot, can give readers useful information. Be sure not to confuse a summary with deeper analysis.

- **Paraphrases,** or restatements in your own words, can help you clarify complex ideas. In this essay, you may want to paraphrase some Shakespearean language.

Review, Revise, and Edit

Once you are done drafting, reread your essay. Make sure you have supported your ideas with clear reasons and evidence. Review each paragraph, marking its main idea. Then, mark sentences that support that idea. If there are sentences that do not support or develop the main idea, consider deleting or rewriting them. If there are too few sentences supporting a main idea, add them. Be sure to proofread textual details cited in your essay against the original text to ensure your transcription is accurate.

✐ EVIDENCE LOG

Before moving on to a new selection, go to your Evidence Log and record what you learned from *The Tempest,* "*En el Jardín De Los Espejos Quebrados,* Caliban Catches a Glimpse of His Reflection," and "Caliban."

Tool Kit

Student Model of an Argument

ACADEMIC VOCABULARY

As you craft your argument, consider using some of the academic vocabulary you learned in the beginning of this unit.

allusion
articulate
contentious
vehement
tolerate

Write an Argument

You have read a play that deals with the concepts of virtue and vengeance. You have also read two poems based on a character in the play. In *The Tempest,* a man in exile seeks revenge against those who displaced him. In "*En el Jardín de los Espejos Quebrados,* Caliban Catches a Glimpse of His Reflection" and "Caliban," poets consider the feelings of a character trapped in slavery. Now, you will use your knowledge of these texts to write an argument.

> **Assignment**
>
> Consider Prospero's realization at the end of *The Tempest*: "The rarer action is / In virtue than in vengeance" (Act V, Scene i, lines 27–28). Also consider your understanding of the poems reinterpreting Caliban. Then, take and defend a position on the topics of virtue and vengeance. Write a brief **argumentative essay** in which you state and support your position on this question:
>
> **Is there more value in vengeance or virtue (forgiveness)?**

Elements of Argument

Argumentative writing provides the opportunity to present and defend your ideas about a topic. Although arguments often use nonfiction texts, facts, and data as evidence, you can also use interpretations of literature to support your ideas. Any argument, including one about literature, requires the development of a logical line of reasoning and the support of ideas with strong, persuasive evidence.

An effective argument contains these elements:

- a thesis statement, or precise claim, that expresses your position on a topic or question
- the inclusion of a counterclaim, or opposing position, and a discussion of why it is less convincing than your position
- textual evidence that supports your position
- a logical organization, including a conclusion that follows from and supports your thesis
- a formal style and objective tone appropriate for the purpose and audience
- error-free grammar, including the correct use of colons when introducing lists or quotations

Model Argument For a model of a well-crafted argument, see the Launch Text, "Neither Justice nor Forgetting: Defining Forgiveness."

Challenge yourself to find all of the elements of effective argument in the text. You will have an opportunity to review these elements as you prepare to write your own argument.

Prewriting / Planning

Write a Preliminary Claim Now that you have read and thought about the selections, write a sentence in which you state your working **claim**, or main position on the question posed in this assignment. Your claim should be a debatable response to the assignment question. For example, you might argue that vengeance focuses and motivates some people more than forgiveness does—or vice versa. As you continue to write, you may revise your claim or even change it entirely. For now, it will help you develop your supporting reasons and evidence.

Working Claim: _____

_____ .

Consider Possible Counterclaims Remember that part of your essay should address **counterclaims**, or opposing positions. Complete these sentences to address a counterclaim. Think about reasons and evidence you can use to defend your position.

Another reader might say that _____ .

The reason he or she might think this is because _____ .

However, my position is stronger because _____ .

The evidence that supports this is _____ .

Gather Evidence From Sources There are many different types of evidence you can use to support your argument:

- **personal thoughts:** ideas you have formed through your reading

- **quotations from the texts:** evidence from the texts you just read that illustrate your points

- **analysis of text passages:** interpretations of key passages from the text that support your argument about virtue or vengeance

- **quotations from authorities:** statements from leading experts that support your points

- **historical context:** key information about the social and cultural setting of a selection

Connect Across Texts As you write your argument, you will be using evidence from the literature in Whole-Class learning to support your claim, while also acknowledging counterclaims. You can also do a limited amount of research to find ideas and quotations from credible sources that support your ideas. Keep your purpose in mind, as well as the background of your intended audience, while selecting source materials and forming your argument.

EVIDENCE LOG

Review your Evidence Log and identify key details you may want to cite in your argument.

Drafting

Organize Your Ideas Once you have gathered evidence that you will use in your argument, create an organizational plan. You may use a standard outline or a graphic organizer to set up a logical sequence for your ideas. Revise your working claim as necessary.

Organize Your Evidence Before you begin drafting, consider using the following structure to organize evidence in each body paragraph of your essay.

- Introduce the evidence by providing context for its place in the source text.
- Present the evidence, which may consist of quotations or paraphrases.
- Explain the evidence—what it means and why it is important.
- Connect the evidence to your claim.

Your evidence should build toward the main claim. It should be organized so that your audience can follow your reasoning and understand how your ideas support your position on the assignment topic. In the chart, you can see a breakdown of how the Launch Text uses evidence to support the claim that Prospero's motives for granting or withholding forgiveness are complex.

INTRODUCTION OF EVIDENCE	QUOTATION	EXPLANATION OF EVIDENCE	RELATE EVIDENCE TO THE THESIS
At other times, Prospero savors victory before he shows forgiveness ... In this speech, he teases Antonio before accepting his brother's apology:	For you, most wicked sir, whom to call brother / Would even infect my mouth, I do forgive / Thy rankest fault—all of them; and require / My dukedom of thee, which perforce, I know, / Thou must restore.	He demonstrates his power and control before he offers a change of heart.	If to forgive is to let go of anger and resentment, then Prospero cannot be called forgiving.

Deal With Counterclaims When you are deciding how to organize your evidence and analysis, remember to address counterclaims. The logical place to analyze counterclaims is after you have strongly established your own position. Develop a strong argument with evidence that shows the limitations of each counterclaim you anticipated during prewriting. Remember that you also build up your own argument by knocking others down.

Write a First Draft Use your organizational plan to write your first draft. Remember to clearly state your claim and to address possible counterclaims. Use a variety of evidence from the literary texts and from secondary sources, and make clear connections to your thesis and counterclaims.

LANGUAGE DEVELOPMENT: CONVENTIONS

Create Cohesion: Quotations and Paraphrases

When you want to use an idea from a text to develop your thesis, you can either quote directly from the text with exact quotations, or you can paraphrase an idea by restating it in your own words.

- Exact quotations can highlight a character's attitude, a writer's word choice, or an essayist's opinion.
- Paraphrases can help you clarify key ideas. Make sure that your paraphrases accurately reflect the original text.

Read It

These sentences from the Launch Text use exact quotations and paraphrases to develop the thesis.

- *He is sincere when he asks Ariel, his magical servant, "But are they, Ariel, safe?"* (introduces exact quotation with a comma)
- *At length, Prospero reminds Ariel that he once rescued him from a magical prison.* (uses paraphrase to help make a point about the mixed messages sent by Propero's treatment of Ariel)

Write It

As you draft your argument, use appropriate transitions and punctuation to smoothly incorporate quotations and paraphrases into your writing.

IF YOU WANT TO . . .	DO THE FOLLOWING:
introduce an exact quotation	Use descriptive words such as *says*, *comments*, and *remarks*. You can also use a colon after an introductory sentence to introduce a longer quotation. Surround the quotation in quotation marks, including all punctuation used in the source text.
introduce a block quotation (when quoted text is longer than four lines of prose or three lines of verse)	Introduce the longer quotation, then use a colon. Note that a block quotation does not have quotation marks surrounding it.
introduce paraphrased text	Give credit to the source of the ideas by mentioning its title, author, or both. Do not use quotation marks around phrases and sentences that are in your own words.

PUNCTUATION

Make sure to correctly punctuate quotations in your writing.

- Use punctuation inside the quotation marks. For example, if you end a sentence with a quotation, the period should appear before the ending quotation mark.
- Use a colon to introduce longer quotations.

Revising
Evaluating Your Draft

Use the following checklist to evaluate the effectiveness of your first draft. Then, use your evaluation and the instruction on this page to guide your revision.

FOCUS AND ORGANIZATION	EVIDENCE AND ELABORATION	CONVENTIONS
☐ Introduces a claim, or position on a topic.	☐ Develops the claim and opposing claims fairly, supplying evidence for each, while pointing out the strengths and limitations of both.	☐ Attends to the norms and conventions of the discipline, especially the correct use and punctuation of quotations.
☐ Distinguishes the claim from opposing claims.		
☐ Provides a conclusion that follows from and supports the claim.	☐ Provides adequate examples for each major idea.	
☐ Establishes a logical organization and develops a progression throughout the argument.	☐ Uses vocabulary that is appropriate for the audience and purpose.	
☐ Uses transitional words, phrases, and clauses to clarify the relationships between and among ideas.	☐ Establishes and maintains a formal style and an objective tone.	

Revising for Focus and Organization

Logical Argument and Conclusion Reread your argument, paying attention to the flow of ideas. Are they presented in a logical order? Have you made the connections between your ideas, exact quotations, and paraphrases clear? Does your conclusion follow naturally from the claim and evidence that you presented, and does it end your essay memorably?

Revising for Evidence and Elaboration

Tone When you write about literature, use an objective tone and, in general, avoid "I statements." For example, do not use language such as "I believe that the quotation shows. . . ." Instead, replace such language with direct statements, such as "This evidence shows. . . ."

Revise to Eliminate Unnecessary Information Reread your draft, looking for any words or phrases that are either not precise or not essential. Here are some steps to help you revise ideas to support your claim:

- Underline your claim and the main idea of each paragraph.
- Highlight sentences that do not support your claim.
- Add or revise text evidence and transitional phrases to make a tighter connection to your claim.
- Eliminate any paragraphs or details that do not clearly contribute to your argument.

🔗 WORD NETWORK

Include interesting words from your Word Network in your argument.

Exchange essays with a classmate. Use the checklist to evaluate your classmate's argument and provide supportive feedback.

1. Is the claim clear?

☐ yes   ☐ no   If no, explain what confused you.

2. Is a counterclaim clearly stated? Is there sufficient evidence to counter it?

☐ yes   ☐ no   If no, point out what is missing.

3. Did you find the argument convincing?

☐ yes   ☐ no   If no, write a brief note explaining what you thought was missing.

4. What is the strongest part of your classmate's essay? Why?

_____

_____

_____

_____

Editing and Proofreading

Edit for Conventions Reread your draft for accuracy and consistency. Correct errors in grammar and word usage. When using a direct quotation, make sure that punctuation such as periods or commas are used within the quotation marks.

Proofread for Accuracy Read your draft carefully, looking for errors in spelling and punctuation. Check the spelling of words in direct quotations. Because *The Tempest* is an older text, the spelling of the words may be different from the modern spelling. Check the source material for the exact spelling used.

Publishing and Presenting

Create a final version of your essay. Share it with your class so that your classmates can read it and make comments. In turn, review and comment on your classmates' work. Consider the ways in which other students' arguments are both similar to and different from your own. Always maintain a polite and respectful tone when commenting.

Reflecting

Think about what you learned by writing your argument. What could you do differently the next time to make the writing experience easier and your argument stronger? For example, you might ask more questions and hold more discussions about the selections to get other points of view about the topic.

ESSENTIAL QUESTION:

What motivates us to forgive?

Many of the wrongs we experience are personal—small insults or slights. Some, however, are much bigger. How should we react when issues of guilt and forgiveness affect whole countries? You will work in a group to continue your exploration of the concepts of virtue and vengeance.

Small-Group Learning Strategies

Throughout your life, in school, in your community, and in your career, you will continue to learn and work with others.

Review these strategies and the actions you can take to practice them as you work in teams. Add ideas of your own for each step. Use these strategies during Small-Group Learning.

STRATEGY	ACTION PLAN
Prepare	• Complete your assignments so that you are prepared for group work. • Organize your thinking so you can contribute to your group's discussions. •
Participate fully	• Make eye contact to signal that you are listening and taking in what is being said. • Use text evidence when making a point. •
Support others	• Build off ideas from others in your group. • Invite others who have not yet spoken to join the discussion. •
Clarify	• Paraphrase the ideas of others to ensure that your understanding is correct. • Ask follow-up questions. •

CONTENTS

Working as a Team

1. **Take a Position** In your group, discuss the following question:

   Why do you think people have difficulty making apologies?

   As you take turns sharing your positions, be sure to provide reasons for your choice. After all group members have shared, discuss some of the personal attributes that might be required to make a sincere apology.

2. **List Your Rules** As a group, decide on the rules that you will follow as you work together. Samples are provided; add two more of your own. You may add or revise rules based on your experience together.

   - Everyone should participate in group discussions.
   - People should not interrupt.

   - _____

     _____

   - _____

     _____

3. **Apply the Rules** Practice working as a group. Share what you have learned about forgiveness and vengeance. Make sure each person in the group contributes. Take notes and be prepared to share with the class one thing that you heard from another member of your group.

4. **Name Your Group** Choose a name that reflects the unit topic.

   Our group's name: _____

5. **Create a Communication Plan** Decide how you want to communicate with one another. For example, you might use online collaboration tools, email, or instant messaging.

   Our group's decision: _____

   _____

Making a Schedule

First, find out the due dates for the small-group activities. Then, preview the texts and activities with your group, and make a schedule for completing the tasks.

SELECTION	ACTIVITIES	DUE DATE
They are hostile nations Under a Certain Little Star		
Let South Africa Show the World How to Forgive		

Working on Group Projects

As your group works together, you'll find it more effective if each person has a specific role. Different projects require different roles. Before beginning a project, discuss the necessary roles, and choose one for each group member. Some possible roles are listed here. Add your own ideas to the list.

Project Manager: monitors the schedule and keeps everyone on task

Researcher: organizes research activities

Recorder: takes notes during group meetings

_____

_____

_____

_____

_____

POETRY COLLECTION 2

They are hostile nations

Under a Certain Little Star

Concept Vocabulary

As you perform your first read of the poems, you will encounter these words.

target	vulnerable	hounded

Context Clues If these words are unfamiliar to you, try using **context clues**—other words and phrases in the surrounding text—to help you determine their meanings. There are various types of context clues that may help you as you read.

Synonyms: The disappearance of the red fox from these woods reminds us how many other species have been hunted to the point of **extinction**.

Restatement of Ideas: We should be **compassionate** to those who lost their homes in the wildfire because kindness and understanding will help them through this difficult time.

Contrast of Ideas: Even though they feel **isolated**, we should remind them that they are in the company of others who care about them.

Apply your knowledge of context clues and other vocabulary strategies to determine the meanings of unfamiliar words you encounter during your first read.

First Read POETRY

Apply these strategies as you conduct your first read. You will have an opportunity to complete a close read after your first read.

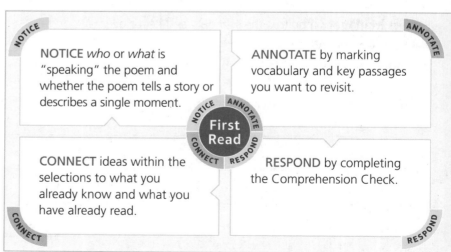

NOTICE who or what is "speaking" the poem and whether the poem tells a story or describes a single moment.

ANNOTATE by marking vocabulary and key passages you want to revisit.

CONNECT ideas within the selections to what you already know and what you have already read.

RESPOND by completing the Comprehension Check.

About the Poets

Margaret Atwood (b. 1939) is widely regarded as one of North America's leading writers. Atwood enjoys both acclaim from prestigious literary critics and commercial success. Many of her novels, including such works as *The Handmaid's Tale, Cat's Eye*, and the Booker Prize–winning *The Blind Assassin,* have been both bestsellers and prize-winners. Atwood has always defied inclusion in any neat category. Her work is intensely personal, but it has also become increasingly political over the years. Her poems and novels range from the familiar contemporary scene to descriptions of strange future worlds.

Wisława Szymborska (1923–2012) lived her entire life in her native Poland. After World War II, she supported a socialist government for Poland, but by the mid-1950s, Szymborska had grown disillusioned with Soviet-style socialism. She gradually became an outspoken critic of the Soviets. Szymborska began her career as a visual artist, and only after World War II did she begin writing poems. Szymborska's poetry gathered avid supporters beginning in the 1960s and ultimately earned her the Nobel Prize in Literature in 1996.

Backgrounds

They are hostile nations

In the 1970s, when this poem was written, the threat of nuclear war between the United States and the Soviet Union created a fear of worldwide extinction. One danger of such a catastrophe would be nuclear winter—the ash clouds and smoke from nuclear war would blot out the sun and freeze the planet. These concerns are echoed in this poem.

Under a Certain Little Star

The concept of *apology* is central to this poem. In its most familiar usage, an *apology* is a statement expressing regret. The word comes from the Greek term for "a speech in defense." It originally described a literary genre dating back to the Greek philosopher Plato and his *Apology* in the fourth century B.C. In an *apology*, an author defends or explains beliefs that other people have criticized.

They are hostile nations

Margaret Atwood

i

In view of the fading animals
the proliferation of sewers and fears
the sea clogging, the air
nearing extinction

5 we should be kind, we should
take warning, we should forgive each other

Instead we are opposite, we
touch as though attacking,

the gifts we bring
10 even in good faith maybe
warp in our hands to
implements, to maneuvers

ii

Put down the **target** of me
you guard inside your binoculars,
15 in turn I will surrender

this aerial photograph
(your **vulnerable**
sections marked in red)
I have found so useful

20 See, we are alone in
the dormant field, the snow
that cannot be eaten or captured

iii

Here there are no armies
here there is no money

25 It is cold and getting colder

We need each others'
breathing, warmth, surviving
is the only war
we can afford, stay

30 walking with me, there is almost
time / if we can only
make it as far as

the (possibly) last summer

Mark context clues or indicate another strategy you used that helped you determine meaning.

target (TAHR giht) *n.*

MEANING:

vulnerable (VUHL nuhr uh buhl) *adj.*

MEANING:

Under a Certain Little Star

Wisława Szymborska
translated by Joanna Trzeciak

Mark context clues or indicate another strategy you used that helped you determine meaning.

hounded (HOWN dihd) *adj.*

MEANING:

My apologies to chance for calling it necessity.
My apologies to necessity in case I'm mistaken.
Don't be angry, happiness, that I take you for my own.
May the dead forgive me that their memory's but a flicker.
5 My apologies to time for the quantity of world overlooked per second.
My apologies to an old love for treating a new one as the first.
Forgive me, far-off wars, for carrying my flowers home.
Forgive me, open wounds, for pricking my finger.
My apologies for the minuet[1] record, to those calling out from the abyss.
10 My apologies to those in train stations for sleeping soundly at five in
    the morning.
Pardon me, **hounded** hope, for laughing sometimes.
Pardon me, deserts, for not rushing in with a spoonful of water.
And you, O hawk, the same bird for years in the same cage,
staring, motionless, always at the same spot,
15 absolve me even if you happen to be stuffed.
My apologies to the tree felled for four table legs.
My apologies to large questions for small answers.
Truth, do not pay me too much attention.

---

1. **minuet** (mihn yoo EHT) *n.* music for a slow dance for groups of couples, originating in France in the seventeenth century.

Solemnity, be magnanimous[2] toward me.
20 Bear with me, O mystery of being, for pulling threads from your veil.
Soul, don't blame me that I've got you so seldom.
My apologies to everything that I can't be everywhere.
My apologies to all for not knowing how to be every man and woman.
I know that as long as I live nothing can excuse me,
25 since I am my own obstacle.
Do not hold it against me, O speech, that I borrow weighty words,
and then labor to make them light.

---

2. **magnanimous** (mag NAN uh muhs) *adj.* generous; rising above pettiness or meanness.

Comprehension Check

Complete the following items after you finish your first read. Review and clarify details with your group.

THEY ARE HOSTILE NATIONS

1. According to the speaker, what is happening to the animals, the sea, and the air?

2. In the second section of the poem, what deal does the speaker try to make with the enemy?

3. According to the speaker, what is the "only war we can afford"?

UNDER A CERTAIN LITTLE STAR

4. What does the speaker spend most of the poem doing?

5. What does the speaker ask of "Truth"?

- -

RESEARCH

Research to Clarify Choose at least one unfamiliar detail from one of the poems. Briefly research that detail. In what way does the information you learned shed light on an aspect of the poem?

POETRY COLLECTION 2

Close Read the Text

With your group, revisit sections of the texts you marked during your first read. **Annotate** details that you notice. What **questions** do you have? What can you **conclude**?

Analyze the Text

> **CITE TEXTUAL EVIDENCE**
> to support your answers.

Complete the activities.

1. **Review and Clarify** With your group, reread "They are hostile nations." What two enemies does the speaker identify? Which enemy does the speaker view as more of a threat? Discuss with your group.

2. **Present and Discuss** Now, work with your group to share the passages from the text that you found especially important. Take turns presenting your passages. Discuss what you noticed in the text, what questions you asked, and what conclusions you reached.

3. **Essential Question:** *What motivates us to forgive?* What have these poems taught you about virtue and vengeance? Discuss with your group.

TIP

GROUP DISCUSSION
Keep in mind that members of your group will have different ideas about the individual's relationship with and responsibility for other people and the environment. Take the time to understand one another's perspectives as you discuss the poems.

WORD NETWORK

Add words related to forgiveness from the text to your Word Network.

LANGUAGE DEVELOPMENT

Concept Vocabulary

target	vulnerable	hounded

Why These Words? The three concept vocabulary words are related. With your group, determine what the words have in common. Write your ideas, and add another word that fits the category.

Practice

📓 **Notebook** Confirm your understanding of each vocabulary word by using it in a sentence. Include context clues that hint at the word's meaning.

Word Study

📓 **Notebook** **Animal Words** In "Under a Certain Little Star," the speaker addresses her "hounded hope." The word *hounded* comes from *hound*—a dog used for hunting. It provides a vivid image of how bothersome, persistent, and even threatening a hunting dog can be.

There are many words that derive their meanings from the characteristics we associate with certain animals. Find and record the definitions for each of the following animal words: *dogged, kittenish, lionize, sheepish.*

Analyze Craft and Structure

Speaker The **speaker** in a poem serves the same function as the narrator in a story—it is the "voice" that tells, observes, explains, and describes. The speaker may seem like the poet, but the two are not one and the same. Rather, the speaker is an imagined voice that the poet creates. The speaker's traits, circumstances, actions, and **tone**, or attitude, help develop the **themes**, or messages, in poetry.

Generally, an **audience** is simply the people who read a literary work. However, in some poetry, the speaker addresses a specific audience directly. The speaker might name such a figure, or readers may need to use details to infer that figure's identity. Look for personal pronouns, such as *I, you,* and *we,* and other key words and phrases to determine who the speaker is, whom he or she is addressing, and how the two are related.

Practice

CITE TEXTUAL EVIDENCE to support your answers.

Work on your own to complete the chart. Then, discuss your responses with your group.

SPEAKER IN "THEY ARE HOSTILE NATIONS"
What is the speaker doing in the poem? How does the speaker view his or her situation?
What is the speaker's tone, or emotional attitude? Which details suggest this tone?
Whom is the speaker addressing? Explain.

SPEAKER IN "UNDER A CERTAIN LITTLE STAR"
What does the speaker do throughout the poem?
What is the speaker's tone, or emotional attitude? Which details suggest this tone?
What audiences does the speaker address directly?

⬤ **Notebook** Write a brief explanation of a deeper meaning, or theme, each poem expresses.

POETRY COLLECTION 2

Author's Style

In literature, **apostrophe** is a rhetorical device in which the speaker directly addresses a person who is dead or absent, an object, or an abstract concept. Because it is so direct, the use of apostrophe helps convey the speaker's ideas and feelings about the person, object, or concept with greater impact and emotion. In one memorable example from *Hamlet*, the main character uses apostrophe when he asks despairingly, "O Death, where is thy sting?"

> Szymborska's poem, "Under a Certain Little Star," uses a great deal of apostrophe:
>
> *Don't be angry, <u>happiness,</u> that I take you for my own.*
>
> *And you, <u>O hawk,</u> the same bird for years in the same cage.*
>
> *Forgive me, open <u>wounds,</u> for pricking my finger.*

Read It

Work individually. Find three other examples of apostrophe in "Under a Certain Little Star." Mark whom or what is being addressed in each example and how it affects the tone and meaning of that part of the poem.

1.

2.

3.

Write It

📝 **Notebook** Rewrite a stanza of "They are hostile nations" to include apostrophe. Then, write a few sentences that describe the effect of adding apostrophe to the stanza.

Writing to Sources

Assignment

With your group, write a **poem** that is modeled after Atwood's "They are hostile nations" or Szymborska's "Under a Certain Little Star." Choose one of the following assignments:

☐ Using Szymborska's "Under a Certain Little Star" as your model, write a poem in which you apologize to various people, objects, and ideas.

☐ Write a four-stanza poem based on Atwood's "They are hostile nations." Begin your stanzas with the same phrases that begin the stanzas in Atwood's poem. You may write more or fewer lines than Atwood uses in her first four stanzas. Use the following model to begin your poem:

In view of _____,

we should _____.

Instead we are _____,

the gifts we bring _____.

☐ Take on the identity of something that the speaker addresses in "Under A Certain Little Star." Then, write a poem from the concept's or object's perspective that responds to the apology the speaker offers. For example, the speaker in your poem might be happiness or the felled tree.

✎ EVIDENCE LOG

Before moving on to a new selection, go to your log and record what you learned from "They are hostile nations" and "Under A Certain Little Star."

Project Plan With your group, brainstorm ideas for your poem, and decide how to incorporate them into your poem. Use the chart to organize your ideas. Assign each group member particular lines or a particular stanza.

Revise Your Poem As a group, decide how to revise your poem to ensure that the lines and stanzas work well together and that the finished poem meets the requirements for the assignment.

LINES OR STANZA	IDEAS	WRITER

About the Author

Desmond Tutu
(1931–2021) was born under
the *apartheid* system in
South Africa that assigned
blacks to a second-class
status with limited rights and
economic opportunity. Tutu
gradually worked his way
up through the hierarchy
of the Anglican Church to
become Archbishop of Cape
Town. From this position,
he applied pressure on the
South African government to
end apartheid. For his efforts,
which eventually helped end
apartheid in South Africa,
Tutu was awarded the 1984
Nobel Peace Prize. In 1995,
he was appointed chair of
South Africa's Truth and
Reconciliation Commission,
which investigated human
rights violations during
the apartheid era. From
2007 to 2013, Archbishop
Tutu was the founding chair
of The Elders, a group of
independent global leaders
working together for peace
and human rights.

Let South Africa Show the World How to Forgive

Concept Vocabulary

As you perform your first read of the speech, you will encounter these words.

democratic	interdependence	communal

Familiar Word Parts When determining the meaning of an unfamiliar word, look for word parts, such as roots, prefixes, and suffixes, that you know. Doing so may help you unlock word meanings.

Familiar Prefix: The prefix *inter-* appears at the beginning of such words as *intertwine*, *interfere*, and *interruption*. It means "between." So the word *interaction* means "action taking place between people."

Familiar Suffix: The suffix *-al* appears at the end of words such as *national* and *regional*. It means "of," "like," "related to," or "pertaining to." So the word *autumnal* means "pertaining to autumn."

Apply your knowledge of familiar word parts and other vocabulary strategies to determine the meanings of unfamiliar words you encounter during your first read.

First Read NONFICTION

Apply these strategies as you conduct your first read. You will have an opportunity to complete a close read after your first read.

NOTICE

NOTICE the general ideas of the text. *What* is it about? *Who* is involved?

ANNOTATE

ANNOTATE by marking vocabulary and key passages you want to revisit.

First Read

CONNECT ideas within the selections to what you already know and what you have already read.

RESPOND by completing the Comprehension Check and by writing a brief summary of the selection.

Let South Africa Show the World How to Forgive

Desmond Tutu

Anti-apartheid activist Nelson Mandela served as South Africa's first black president from 1994 to 1999. Here, he is shown (center, wearing suit and tie) at an election rally in Johannesburg, South Africa, in 1994.

BACKGROUND

Apartheid was the system of legal racial segregation in South Africa put into place by the country's white government in 1948. Apartheid imposed repressive restrictions upon black South Africans, including denying them the right to vote. Apartheid ended in 1994 after years of negotiations. In the following speech given at the University of Toronto in 2000, Desmond Tutu reflects on the injustices of apartheid and the work of Nelson Mandela, who fought against the system for 40 years.

1   If you asked even the most sober students of South African affairs what they thought was going to happen to South Africa a few years ago, almost universally they predicted that the most ghastly catastrophe would befall us; that as sure as anything, we would be devastated by a comprehensive bloodbath.

2   It did not happen. Instead, the world watched with amazement, indeed awe, at the long lines of South Africans of all races, snaking their way to their polling booths on April 27, 1994. And they thrilled as they witnessed Nelson Mandela being inaugurated as the first democratically elected president of South Africa on May 10, 1994.

NOTES

Nearly everyone described what they were witnessing—a virtually bloodless, reasonably peaceful transition from injustice and oppression to freedom and democracy—as a miracle.

3   When the disaster did not overtake us, there were those who said, "Wait until a black-led government takes over. Then these blacks who have suffered so grievously in the past will engage in the most fearful orgy of revenge and retribution against the whites."

4   Well, that prediction too was not fulfilled. Instead the world saw something quite unprecedented. They saw the process of the Truth and Reconciliation Commission,[1] when perpetrators of some of the most gruesome atrocities were given amnesty in exchange for a full disclosure of the facts of the offense. Instead of revenge and retribution, this new nation chose to tread the difficult path of confession, forgiveness, and reconciliation.

5   We South Africans have not done too badly. It is sometimes said of newly **democratic** countries that their first elections too frequently end up being their last. Well, we have already had a fairly uneventful second general election and have witnessed the transition from a charismatic, first democratically elected president, Nelson Mandela, to the more pragmatic, pipe-smoking Thabo Mbeki. The turmoil and instability that many feared would accompany these crucial events have not occurred. Why? Well, first, you have prayed for us and, if miracles had to happen anywhere, South Africa was a prime site for a miracle.

6   And we have been richly blessed to have had at such a critical time in our history a Nelson Mandela. He was imprisoned for 27 years; most expected that when he emerged, he would be riddled with a lust for retribution. But the world has been amazed; instead of spewing calls for revenge, he urged his own people to work for reconciliation—and invited his former jailer to attend his presidential inauguration as a VIP guest.

7   Wonderfully, Mr. Mandela has not been the only person committed to forgiveness and reconciliation. Less well-known people (in my theology no one is "ordinary," for each one of us is created in the image of God) are the real heroes and heroines of our struggle.

8   There was a Mrs. Savage who was injured in a hand-grenade attack by one of the liberation movements. She was so badly injured that her children bathed her, clothed her, and fed her. She could not go through a security checkpoint at the airport because she still had shrapnel in her and all sorts of alarms would have been set off. She told us [at the Truth and Reconciliation Commission] that she would like to meet the perpetrator—she, a white woman, and he almost certainly, a black perpetrator, in the spirit of forgiveness. She would

Mark familiar word parts or indicate another strategy you used that helped you determine meaning.

democratic (dehm uh KRAT ihk) *adj.*

MEANING:

---

1. **Truth and Reconciliation Commission** court-like organization established in South Africa after the end of apartheid to hear testimony from both victims of apartheid and those who committed crimes in its name. Desmond Tutu was the commission's chairman.

like to forgive him and then extraordinarily she added, "And I hope he forgives me." Now that is almost mind-boggling.

9   The daughter of one of four African National Congress[2] activists, whom the police ambushed and then killed gruesomely—their mutilated bodies were found in their burnt-out car—came to tell her story. She said the police were still harassing her mother and her children, even after their father had died. When she finished, I asked her whether she would be able to forgive those who had done this. We were meeting in a city hall packed to the rafters. You could hear the proverbial pin drop, as she replied, "We would like to forgive. We just want to know whom to forgive."

10   Our country did not go the way of Nuremberg,[3] to bring the perpetrators of such crimes to trial. After the Second World War, the Allies had defeated the Germans and could apply so-called "victor's justice." In our case, neither the apartheid government nor the liberation movements had defeated their adversary. Our country could not afford the exorbitant cost of trials, even if we could have held them and had the evidence to satisfy a court of law.

11   Our country rejected the other extreme of a blanket amnesty, as happened in General Augusto Pinochet's Chile.[4] It victimized the victims a second time around and was really trying to let bygones be bygones, when in fact they never become bygones. Certainly, Gen. Pinochet now knows you can't act with reckless impunity and hope to get away with it forever. This is a moral universe.

12   Our country chose a middle way of individual amnesty for truth. Some would say, what about justice? And we say retributive justice is not the only kind of justice. There is also restorative justice, because we believe in Ubuntu—the essence of being human, that idea that we are all caught up in a delicate network of **interdependence**. We say, "A person is a person through other persons." I need you in order to be me and you need me in order to be you.

13   The greatest good is **communal** corporate harmony, and resentment, anger, revenge are corrosive of this harmony. To nurse grudges and resentment is bad for your blood pressure. Psychologists have now found that to forgive is good for our personal, physical, psychic health, as well as our health as a community, as a society. We discovered that people experienced healing through telling their stories. The process opened wounds that were festering. We cleansed them, poured ointment on them, and knew they would heal. A young man who had been blinded by police action in his township came to tell us the story of that event. When he finished he was asked how he felt now, and he said, "You have given me back my eyes."

NOTES

Mark familiar word parts or indicate another strategy you used that helped you determine meaning.

interdependence (ihn tuhr dih PEHN duhns) *n.*

MEANING:

communal (kuh MYOON uhl) *adj.*

MEANING:

---

2. **African National Congress** South African political party and black nationalist organization led by Nelson Mandela.
3. **Nuremberg** city in Southern Germany where Nazi war criminals were tried by an international military tribunal.
4. **General Augusto Pinochet's Chile** Pinochet took over Chile in a 1973 military coup that killed thousands of Chileans. Afterward, his government passed a law granting amnesty to the military officers responsible for the violence.

14   Retribution leads to a cycle of reprisal, leading to counter-reprisal in an inexorable movement, as in Rwanda, Northern Ireland, and in the former Yugoslavia. The only thing that can break that cycle, making possible a new beginning, is forgiveness. Without forgiveness there is no future.

15   We have been appalled at the depths of depravity revealed by the testimonies before the Truth and Reconciliation Commission. Yes, we human beings have a remarkable capacity for evil—we have refined ways of being mean and nasty to one another. There have been genocides, holocausts, slavery, racism, wars, oppression, and injustice.

16   But that, mercifully, is not the whole story about us. We were exhilarated as we heard people who had suffered grievously, who by rights should have been baying for the blood of their tormentors, utter words of forgiveness, reveal an extraordinary willingness to work for reconciliation, demonstrating magnanimity and nobility of spirit.

17   Yes, wonderfully, exhilaratingly, we have this extraordinary capacity for good. Fundamentally, we are good; we are made for love, for compassion, for caring, for sharing, for peace and reconciliation, for transcendence, for the beautiful, for the true and the good.

18   Who could have imagined that South Africa would be an example of anything but the most awful ghastliness? And now we see God's sense of humor, for God has chosen this unlikely lot and set us up as some kind of paradigm, as some kind of model that just might provide the world with a viable way of dealing with post-conflict, post-repression periods. We have not been particularly virtuous, anything but. We are not particularly smart—precisely. God wants to point at us as this unlikely bunch and say to the trouble spots of the world, "Look at them. They had a nightmare called apartheid. It has ended. Your nightmare, too, will end. They used to have what people regarded as an intractable problem. They are now resolving it. Nowhere in the world can people ever again claim that their problems are intractable." There is hope for all of us. ❧

Comprehension Check

Complete the following items after you finish your first read. Review and clarify details with your group.

1. According to Desmond Tutu, what did most people predict would happen after the end of apartheid in South Africa?

2. According to Tutu, what happened after elections were held that surprised the world?

3. What role did the Truth and Reconciliation Commission play after the end of apartheid?

4. What does Tutu see as the most important element in South Africa's success so far?

5. 📓 **Notebook** Confirm your understanding by writing a summary of the speech.

- -

RESEARCH

Research to Clarify Choose at least one unfamiliar detail from the text. Briefly research that detail. In what way does the information you learned shed light on an aspect of the speech?

Research to Explore Choose something from the text that interests you, and formulate a research question.

LET SOUTH AFRICA SHOW THE
WORLD HOW TO FORGIVE

Close Read the Text

With your group, revisit sections of the speech you marked during your first read. **Annotate** details that you notice. What **questions** do you have? What can you **conclude**?

Close Read

ANNOTATE · QUESTION · CONCLUDE

- -

Analyze the Text

CITE TEXTUAL EVIDENCE
to support your answers.

Complete the activities.

1. **Review and Clarify** With your group, reread paragraph 6 of the selection. What does inviting his former jailer to his presidential inauguration indicate about Mandela's character and his ability to lead?

2. **Present and Discuss** Now, work with your group to share passages from the text that you found especially important. Take turns presenting your passages. Discuss what you notice in the text, what questions you asked, and what conclusions you reached.

3. **Essential Question:** *What motivates us to forgive?* What has this speech taught you about forgiveness? Discuss this idea with your group.

LANGUAGE DEVELOPMENT

Concept Vocabulary

democratic	interdependence	communal

Why These Words? The three concept vocabulary words are related. With your group, determine what the words have in common. Write your ideas, and add another word that fits the category.

Practice

📝 **Notebook** Confirm your understanding of the concept vocabulary words by using them in sentences. Be sure to include context clues to hint at each word's meaning.

Word Study

📝 **Notebook** **Greek Root Word:** *kratos* The endings of the concept vocabulary word *democratic* and the related noun *democracy* derive from the Greek word *kratos*, meaning "rule" or "power." Like *democratic*, other English words ending in -*cracy* or -*cratic* tend to describe particular forms of government.

Use a college-level dictionary to look up these words derived from *kratos*: *aristocracy*, *plutocratic*. Write their definitions.

Analyze Craft and Structure

Persuasive Techniques This speech is an example of a persuasive text, one that attempts to convince listeners to take a certain position or action. Persuasive writers and speakers use many techniques to move and convince audiences. These techniques include the use of **anecdotes,** or brief meaningful stories, to achieve certain persuasive effects:

- to provide a specific example or illustration of a general idea or concept
- to make an abstract idea more tangible and concrete
- to make a text more personal and memorable, thus engaging listeners' or readers' emotions

TIP

To make sure everyone in the group understands what an anecdote is and does, try telling anecdotes. Pick a topic, such as standing up for yourself, and then ask group members to suggest anecdotes that would support a speech on that topic.

Practice

CITE TEXTUAL EVIDENCE to support your answers.

Reread the paragraphs from the speech identified in the chart, and summarize the anecdotes they present. Then, explain the purpose and persuasive effect of each anecdote. Work on your own, and then share your responses with your group.

ANECDOTE	EFFECT
paragraph 6:	
paragraph 8:	
paragraph 9:	

LET SOUTH AFRICA SHOW THE
WORLD HOW TO FORGIVE

Conventions

Types of Clauses A **relative clause** is a type of dependent clause that acts as an adjective in a sentence. It modifies a noun or pronoun by telling *what kind* or *which one*. A relative clause often begins with one of these **relative pronouns**: *who, whom, whose, which,* or *that.* The chart shows examples of relative clauses from Desmond Tutu's speech.

SENTENCE	RELATIVE PRONOUN	WORD(S) MODIFIED
When she finished, I asked her whether she would be able to forgive those <u>who had done this</u>. (paragraph 9)	who	the demonstrative pronoun *those*
The daughter of one of four African National Congress activists, <u>whom the police ambushed and then killed gruesomely</u> . . . came to tell her story. (paragraph 9)	whom	the noun *activists*
The turmoil and instability <u>that many feared would accompany these crucial events</u> have not occurred. (paragraph 5)	that	the nouns *turmoil* and *instability*

Read It

Work individually. In each of these sentences from Desmond Tutu's speech, mark the relative pronoun and the relative clause. Write the noun or pronoun it modifies. When you have finished, discuss your answers with your group.

1. The process opened wounds that were festering.

2. A young man who had been blinded by police action in his township came to tell us the story of that event.

3. The only thing that can break that cycle, making possible a new beginning, is forgiveness.

Write It

📓 **Notebook** In the example, the original sentences have been combined, using a relative clause, to create the revision.

> EXAMPLE
>
> **Original:** We humans have a remarkable capacity for evil. We have refined ways of being nasty to one another.
>
> **Revised:** We humans, who have a remarkable capacity for evil, have refined ways of being nasty to one another.

Use a relative clause to combine these sentence pairs.

1. South Africa operated under the apartheid system. The system has ended.

2. Mandela was its first black president. Mandela had been imprisoned for 27 years.

Research

Assignment

Research, prepare, and deliver a **multimedia presentation** in which you incorporate text, images, and, if possible, audio or video to express and support your ideas. Incorporate quotations and examples from the speech by Desmond Tutu. Choose from the following options:

☐ Create an **informational slideshow** that explains the conditions of life for both blacks and whites under apartheid in South Africa.
- What rights did each group have under apartheid?
- How did each group view the system?

☐ Create an **illustrated timeline** of events that led to the ending of apartheid in South Africa.
- What key events took place during the apartheid era? What effect did they have on politics and social issues in South Africa?
- What organizations and leaders around the world joined the protests against apartheid? How did their actions help bring about the end of apartheid in South Africa?

☐ Create a plan for the design and content for a **website** about the Truth and Reconciliation Commission.
- How and when was the commission formed? What were its official goals?
- Who ran the committee? How were decisions made?
- How effective has the commission been in helping to heal South Africa?

☑ EVIDENCE LOG

Before moving on to a new selection, go to your Evidence Log and record what you learned from "Let South Africa Show the World How to Forgive."

Project Plan Before you begin, make a list of tasks you will need to complete in order to create your multimedia presentation. Then, assign tasks to individual group members.

Organize Text, Visuals, and Source Information Use a chart to organize the different parts of your presentation. Make sure each image, video, or audio track supports your ideas. Also, be sure to record the source for each element.

TEXT	IMAGE	VIDEO/AUDIO	SOURCE

SOURCES

- THEY ARE HOSTILE NATIONS

- UNDER A CERTAIN LITTLE STAR

- LET SOUTH AFRICA SHOW THE WORLD HOW TO FORGIVE

Present an Argument

Assignment

You have read about both individuals and nations that have wrestled with decisions involving forgiveness. Work with your group to plan a **talk show segment** that addresses this question:

> Does forgiveness first require an apology?

Plan With Your Group

Analyze the Text As a group, review the texts in this section and your notes, keeping the prompt question in mind: Does forgiveness first require an apology? Use the chart to identify how you think the speakers in these texts would respond to the question. Cite textual details that support that position.

SPEAKER	POSITION ON APOLOGY AND FORGIVENESS
Atwood's speaker in "They are hostile nations"	
Szymborska's speaker in "Under a Certain Little Star"	
Desmond Tutu	

Choose Your Roles Each group member should choose a role to play in the talk show. Three people should represent the speakers of the texts in this section. Another should play the host. If you have additional group members, choose characters from *The Tempest*.

Gather Evidence Brainstorm for the types of questions a talk show host would ask to elicit responses on issues related to the prompt. Consider how each personality would respond and the types of follow-up questions and discussions their responses would generate.

Choose Order and Format Model your presentation on talk shows you've seen. For instance, some shows invite guests out one by one, but then have them interact with one another as well as the host. Select the format of the show and the order in which the guests will appear. Remember that each speaker will have to present an argument that addresses the question in the prompt.

Rehearse With Your Group

Practice With Your Group Do a dry run of your talk show without a live audience. Use this checklist to evaluate the effectiveness of your group's first run-through. Then, use your evaluation and the instructions provided to guide your final presentation.

CONTENT	PRESENTATION TECHNIQUES
☐ The questions and follow-ups flow in a way that makes sense.	☐ The format is clear and understandable.
☐ Arguments are supported with evidence.	☐ Transitions between guests' perspectives and new lines of questioning are smooth.
☐ Each speaker's perspective is clearly represented.	☐ Interactions between talk show host and guests are engaging for an audience.

Preparing the Presentation An effective presentation is the result of planning and practice. Use these tips to prepare to deliver your talk show to the class:

- If possible, rehearse your talk show presentation in the room where it will take place. Check sight lines to make sure that all guests will be visible to the entire audience. Do a sound check as well to ensure that the interactions between host and guests can be heard.

- Practice shifting from the show's opening, to the entrance of the host, to the introductions of each speaker. Work to make these transitions smooth and to keep the pace of the show lively.

Know Your Audience Understanding your audience will help you present your ideas effectively.

- Adjust word choice, evidence, and rhetoric to the interest, backgrounds, and knowledge level of your listeners.

- Anticipate counterarguments. The host can make the show more lively by drawing out areas of disagreement between guests.

- Respond to the interests of your listeners by staking out strong positions and capturing them in an engaging way.

Present and Evaluate

When you present as a group, be sure that each member has taken into account each of the checklist items. As you watch other groups, evaluate how well they meet the checklist requirements.

ESSENTIAL QUESTION:

What motivates us to forgive?

Guilt, revenge, and forgiveness are fundamental issues in both literature and real life. In this section, you will complete your study of virtue and vengeance by exploring an additional selection related to the topic. You'll then share what you learn with classmates. To choose a text, follow these steps.

Look Back Think about the selections you have already studied. What more do you want to know about the topics of virtue, or forgiveness, and vengeance?

Look Ahead Preview the texts by reading the descriptions. Which one seems most interesting and appealing to you?

Look Inside Take a few minutes to scan the text you chose. Choose a different one if this text doesn't meet your needs.

Independent Learning Strategies

Throughout your life, in school, in your community, and in your career, you will need to rely on yourself to learn and work on your own. Review these strategies and the actions you can take to practice them during Independent Learning. Add ideas of your own to each category.

STRATEGY	ACTION PLAN
Create a schedule	• Understand your goals and deadlines. • Make a plan for what to do each day. •
Practice what you have learned	• Use first-read and close-read strategies to deepen your understanding. • After you read, evaluate the usefulness of the evidence to help you understand the topic. • Consider the quality and reliability of the source. •
Take notes	• Record important ideas and information • Review your notes before preparing to share with a group. •

CONTENTS

Choose one selection. Selections are available online only.

PERFORMANCE-BASED ASSESSMENT PREP

Review Evidence for an Argument

Complete your Evidence Log for the unit by evaluating what you have learned and synthesizing the information you have recorded.

First-Read Guide

Use this page to record your first-read ideas.

Tool Kit
First-Read Guide and
Model Annotation

Selection Title: _____

NOTICE

NOTICE new information or ideas you learn about the unit topic as you first read this text.

ANNOTATE

ANNOTATE by marking vocabulary and key passages you want to revisit.

First Read
NOTICE ANNOTATE
CONNECT RESPOND

CONNECT

CONNECT ideas within the selection to other knowledge and the selections you have read.

RESPOND

RESPOND by writing a brief summary of the selection.

Close-Read Guide

Use this page to record your close-read ideas.

Selection Title: _____

Close Read the Text

Revisit sections of the text you marked during your first read. Read these sections closely and **annotate** what you notice. Ask yourself **questions** about the text. What can you **conclude?** Write down your ideas.

Analyze the Text

Think about the author's choices of patterns, structure, techniques, and ideas included in the text. Select one, and record your thoughts about what this choice conveys.

QuickWrite

Pick a paragraph from the text that grabbed your interest. Explain the power of this passage.

_____

_____

_____

_____

_____

_____

_____

_____

Share Your Independent Learning

Prepare to Share

What motivates us to forgive?

Even when you read something independently, your understanding continues to grow when you share what you have learned with others. Reflect on the text you explored independently, and write notes about its connection to the unit. In your notes, consider why this text belongs in this unit.

Learn from Your Classmates

💬 **Discuss It** Share your ideas about the text you explored on your own. As you talk with your classmates, jot down ideas that you learn from them.

Reflect

Mark the most important insight you gained from these writing and discussion activities. Explain how this idea adds to your understanding of the topic of virtue and vengeance.

Review Evidence for an Argument

At the beginning of this unit, you took a position on the following question:

> Can justice and forgiveness go hand in hand?

✐ EVIDENCE LOG

Review your Evidence Log and your QuickWrite from the beginning of the unit. Has your position changed?

☐ YES	☐ NO
Identify at least three pieces of evidence that convinced you to change your mind.	Identify at least three pieces of evidence that reinforced your initial position.
1.	1.
2.	2.
3.	3.

State your position now: _____

_____

_____

Identify a possible counterargument: _____

_____

_____

Evaluate the Strength of Your Evidence Consider your argument. Do you have enough evidence to support your claim? Do you have enough evidence to refute a counterargument? If not, make a plan.

☐ Do more research   ☐ Talk with my classmates

☐ Reread a selection   ☐ Ask an expert

☐ Other:_____

SOURCES

- WHOLE-CLASS SELECTIONS

- SMALL-GROUP SELECTIONS

- INDEPENDENT-LEARNING SELECTION

PART 1

Writing to Sources: Argument

In this unit, you read about various characters, both real and fictional, who found themselves questioning the value of forgiveness. Each had to make a choice about what to do after they were wronged by another.

Assignment

Write an **argumentative essay** in which you state and defend a claim responding to the following question:

Can justice and forgiveness go hand in hand?

Propose and defend a claim related to the topics of justice and forgiveness. Use credible evidence from at least three of the selections you read and researched in this unit to support your claim. Acknowledge and address a counterclaim, or claim that contradicts your claim, on the topics of justice and forgiveness. Articulate the reasons that support your point of view.

Reread the Assignment Review the assignment to be sure you fully understand it. The task may reference some of the academic words presented at the beginning of the unit. Be sure you understand each of the words here in order to complete the assignment correctly.

Academic Vocabulary

allusion	articulate	contentious
vehement	tolerate	

⟁ WORD NETWORK

As your write and revise your argument, use your Word Network to help vary your word choices.

Review the Elements of Effective Argument Before you begin writing, read the Argument Rubric. Once you have completed your first draft, check it against the rubric. If one or more of the elements is missing or not as strong as it could be, revise your essay to add or strengthen that component.

Argument Rubric

	Focus and Organization	Evidence and Elaboration	Conventions
4	The introduction states the thesis, or main claim, in a compelling way. Establishes a clear relationship between the texts and the topic of the assignment. Writer's claims and text analysis progress logically, and include a variety of sentence transitions. The conclusion demonstrates deep comprehension and evaluation of the texts.	Varied sources of evidence are comprehensive and specific, and contain relevant information. Textual analysis is supported with appropriate use of exact quotations and paraphrases. Acknowledges and refutes a valid counterclaim.	The conventions of standard English are used consistently throughout the entire essay. Correctly and consistently indicates exact quotations from the text.
3	The introduction states the thesis, or main claim. Establishes some relationship between the texts and the topic of the assignment. Writer's claims and text analysis progress logically, and include appropriate sentence transitions. The conclusion demonstrates deep comprehension of the texts.	Sources of evidence are somewhat varied, and contain mostly relevant information. Some exact quotations and paraphrases are supplied to support textual analysis. Acknowledges and mostly refutes a valid counterclaim.	The conventions of standard English are used throughout most of the essay. Correctly indicates exact quotations from the text most of the time.
2	The introduction states the thesis, or main claim. Establishes some similarities or differences between the texts. Writer's claims and text analysis progress logically. Transition words and phrases are used. The conclusion demonstrates comprehension of the texts.	Some relevant evidence is used to support textual analysis. Textual analysis is somewhat supported with an exact quotation and paraphrase. Acknowledges and partially refutes a counterclaim.	The conventions of standard English are sometimes used in the essay. Correctly indicates exact quotations from the text some of the time.
1	The thesis, or main claim, is not clearly stated. Relationship between the texts, or between the texts and the topic, is not established. Writer's claims and text analysis are unclear or hard to follow. Transition words and phrases are not present. The conclusion does not demonstrate comprehension of the texts.	Does not include significant analysis of the texts. Does not include supporting evidence for analysis. Does not acknowledge or does not refute a counterclaim.	The conventions of standard English are rarely or never used in the essay. Does not correctly indicate exact quotations from the text.

PART 2
Speaking and Listening: Informal Speech

Assignment

After completing the final draft of your argument, use it as the foundation for a three- to five-minute **informal speech**.

Transform your written argument into a clear and engaging informal speech. Think about the following elements as you prepare.

- Consider your audience. Present evidence that will convince them of your claim.
- Include relevant media or visuals to capture and maintain your audience's interest.
- Make eye contact with your audience, and vary the volume, tone, and pacing of your voice to emphasize key points.

Review the Rubric Before you deliver your presentation, check your plans against this rubric. If one or more of the elements is missing or not as strong as it could be, revise your presentation.

	Content	Use of Media	Presentation Technique
3	Presentation establishes a claim in a compelling way. Presentation has strong valid reasons and evidence that support the claim while clearly acknowledging counterclaims.	Media has obvious connection to the topic and provides support for the speaker's claim.	The speaker maintains effective eye contact. The speaker presents with strong conviction and energy.
2	Presentation establishes a claim. Presentation has valid reasons and evidence that support the claim while acknowledging counterclaims.	Media is relevant to the claim.	The speaker mostly maintains effective eye contact. The speaker presents with some level of conviction and energy.
1	Presentation does not clearly state a claim. Presentation does not have reasons or evidence to support a claim or acknowledge counterclaims.	Media is not present, or is irrelevant.	The speaker does not establish eye contact. The speaker presents without conviction or energy.

Reflect on the Unit

Now that you've completed the unit, take a few moments to reflect on your learning.

Reflect on the Unit Goals

Look back at the goals at the beginning of the unit. Use a different colored pen to rate yourself again. Think about readings and activities that contributed the most to the growth of your understanding. Record your thoughts.

Reflect on the Learning Strategies

Discuss It Write a reflection on whether you were able to improve your learning based on your Action Plans. Think about what worked, what didn't, and what you might do to keep working on these strategies. Record your ideas before a class discussion.

Reflect on the Text

Choose a selection that you found challenging, and explain what made it difficult.

Explain something that surprised you about a text in the unit.

Which activity taught you the most about virtue and vengeance? What did you learn?

Blindness and Sight

When we say, "I see," what do we mean? How many ways are there to see—or fail to see—the world?

Blind Teen Ben Underwood

💬 **Discuss It** How do Ben's experiences and attitudes redefine what it means to have vision?

Write your response before sharing your ideas.

UNIT INTRODUCTION

ESSENTIAL QUESTION:

What does it mean to see?

LAUNCH TEXT
NONFICTION NARRATIVE
Just Six Dots

WHOLE-CLASS LEARNING

LITERATURE AND CULTURE

Historical Context
Oedipus the King

ANCHOR TEXT: DRAMA

Oedipus the King, Part I
Sophocles, translated by Nicholas Rudall

ANCHOR TEXT: DRAMA

Oedipus the King, Part II
Sophocles, translated by Nicholas Rudall

▶ MEDIA CONNECTION:
Oedipus the King

PERFORMANCE TASK

WRITING FOCUS:
Write a Nonfiction Narrative

SMALL-GROUP LEARNING

LETTER

View From the Empire State Building
Helen Keller

POETRY COLLECTION

Blind
Fatima Naoot, translated by Kees Nijland

The Blind Seer of Ambon
W. S. Merwin

On His Blindness
Jorge Luis Borges, translated by Robert Mezey

SHORT STORY

The Country of the Blind
H. G. Wells

MEMOIR

The Neglected Senses
from For the Benefit of Those Who See
Rosemary Mahoney

PERFORMANCE TASK

SPEAKING AND LISTENING FOCUS:
Present an Oral Retelling

INDEPENDENT LEARNING

NOVEL EXCERPT

from **Blindness**
José Saramago, translated by Giovanni Pontiero

MEDIA: NEWSCAST

Dr. Geoffrey Tabin Helps Blind Ethiopians Gain Sight
ABC News

MEDIA: INFORMATIONAL GRAPHIC

How Your Eyes Trick Your Mind
Melissa Hogenboom

SCIENCE ARTICLE

Blind, Yet Seeing: The Brain's Subconscious Visual Sense
Benedict Carey

ORAL HISTORY

Experience: I First Saw My Wife Ten Years After We Married
Shandar Herian

SCIENCE ARTICLE

Visual Neuroscience: Look and Learn
Apoorva Mandavilli

PERFORMANCE-BASED ASSESSMENT PREP

Review Notes for a Nonfiction Narrative

PERFORMANCE-BASED ASSESSMENT

Narrative: Nonfiction Narrative and Storytelling Session

PROMPT:

Is there a difference between seeing and knowing?

Unit Goals

Throughout the unit, you will deepen your perspective of blindness and sight by reading, writing, speaking, listening, and presenting. These goals will help you succeed on the Unit Performance-Based Assessment.

Rate how well you meet these goals right now. You will revisit your ratings later when you reflect on your growth during this unit.

SCALE	1	2	3	4	5
	NOT AT ALL WELL	NOT VERY WELL	SOMEWHAT WELL	VERY WELL	EXTREMELY WELL

READING GOALS

	1	2	3	4	5
• Evaluate written narrative texts by analyzing how authors introduce and develop central ideas or themes.	○	○	○	○	○
• Expand your knowledge and use of academic and concept vocabulary.	○	○	○	○	○

WRITING AND RESEARCH GOALS

	1	2	3	4	5
• Write a narrative in which you convey experiences or events using effective technique, well-chosen details, and well-structured event sequences.	○	○	○	○	○
• Conduct research projects of various lengths to clarify meaning and to explore topics in greater depth.	○	○	○	○	○

LANGUAGE GOALS

	1	2	3	4	5
• Correctly use varied sentence structures to add interest to writing and presentations.	○	○	○	○	○

SPEAKING AND LISTENING GOALS

	1	2	3	4	5
• Collaborate with your team to build on the ideas of others, develop consensus, and communicate.	○	○	○	○	○
• Integrate audio, visuals, and text in presentations.	○	○	○	○	○

Academic Vocabulary: Nonfiction Narrative

Academic terms appear in all subjects and can help you read, write, and discuss with more precision. Here are five academic words that will be useful to you in this unit as you analyze and write nonfiction narratives.

Complete the chart.

1. Review each word, its root, and the mentor sentences.

2. Use the information and your own knowledge to predict the meaning of each word.

3. For each word, list at least two related words.

4. Refer to a dictionary or other resources if needed.

TIP

FOLLOW THROUGH
Study the words in this chart, and mark them or their forms wherever they appear in the unit.

WORD	MENTOR SENTENCES	PREDICT MEANING	RELATED WORDS
integrate ROOT: **-teg-** "touch"	1. If your day is too busy for a long workout, try to *integrate* exercise a few minutes at a time. 2. I like how you *integrate* comic details into an otherwise sad story.		integration; integral
delineate ROOT: **-lin-** "line"	1. On the map, the red lines *delineate* national borders and the blue lines indicate bodies of water. 2. With only a few brush strokes, the artist was able to *delineate* her subject's features clearly.		
volition ROOT: **-vol-** "wish"; "will"	1. Did you do that of your own *volition* or did someone pressure you into it? 2. Pearl made the decision instinctively, without conscious thought or *volition*.		
vivid ROOT: **-viv-** "live"	1. Even though it happened long ago, my memory of that day is incredibly precise and *vivid*. 2. Henri Matisse is a French painter who was known for his *vivid* use of color.		
altercation ROOT: **-alter-** "other"	1. In our school, there is zero tolerance for fighting or any type of *altercation*. 2. Sam and Rick got into a disagreement that nearly became an *altercation*.		

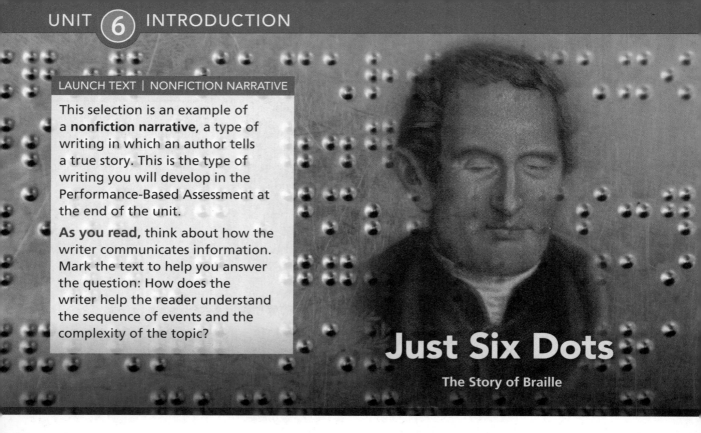

This selection is an example of a **nonfiction narrative**, a type of writing in which an author tells a true story. This is the type of writing you will develop in the Performance-Based Assessment at the end of the unit.

As you read, think about how the writer communicates information. Mark the text to help you answer the question: How does the writer help the reader understand the sequence of events and the complexity of the topic?

Just Six Dots
The Story of Braille

NOTES

1   A system of just six raised dots can tell any story. Six dots can spin out tales of romance or relate accounts of historic events. They can even tell the story of the man who invented them: Louis Braille.

2   As a young boy, Louis loved to observe his father, a leather worker, in his workshop near Paris. Louis would gaze with eager attention as Simon-René Braille transformed unfinished leather into fine harnesses for horses. One day when he was three, Louis grabbed an awl and a strip of leather. He jabbed the sharp tool down, hoping to copy his father's masterful movements and punch the strip with a perfect hole. Instead, the awl slipped and pierced his right eye. The Iinjury and resulting infection left Louis completely blind by the age of five.

3   Simon-René was determined not to let Louis's blindness end his education. Returning to the workshop, he pounded nails into wooden strips, arranging them to form letters. Soon, Louis attended the local school, where he excelled. However, his parents realized that he needed specialized instruction to truly succeed. At the age of ten, Louis went to Paris to study at the world's only school for the blind.

4   There, Louis met the founder of the school, Valentin Haüy, a sighted man who was deeply committed to educating the blind. Recognizing the importance of independence in learning, he developed a new way of printing books with thickly embossed letters. The system worked, but the books were heavy and slow to read. On top of that, it took both sight and skill to make them.

5   When Louis was eleven, army captain Charles Barbier visited the school. He had devised a different system, which he called "night

NOTES

writing," that allowed soldiers to read orders in the dark. It used raised dots in sets of twelve. Barbier's code inspired Louis to create his own, easier and faster system.

6   Louis worked on his code for years. By the time he was fifteen, he had perfected the code that would bear his name. Unlike Barbier's code, braille uses cells of just six dots. By arranging six dots in two parallel rows with three dots in each, he created a cell that can be instantly sensed by one fingertip. With sixty-four possible combinations of dots, each cell names a letter, number, punctuation mark, or word.

7   The director of Louis's school was so impressed with the invention that he encouraged all of the students to learn it. Louis published the first braille book in 1829. Blind students could now read with ease. They could also write, using a pointed tool called a dot stylus.

8   However, braille did not gain wider acceptance right away. The school's next director, Pierre-Armand Dufau, was opposed to braille code. He worried that once blind people could read there would be no need for sighted teachers, so he banned the use of braille. Dufau's assistant, Joseph Gaudet, did not agree. After many years, he convinced Dufau to accept Braille's system. They decided to introduce the new invention when the school moved into a new building.

9   At the dedication ceremony on February 22, 1844, Gaudet read aloud a 15-page book that told the crowd about Louis Braille's accomplishment. Then, he sent one student out of the room and asked another to use the code to write down a poem. The first student came back into the room and read the poem perfectly. The crowd was amazed, and some suspected a trick. One man guessed that the first student had memorized the poem before the ceremony. He took a theater ticket out of his pocket and challenged the students to repeat the demonstration with information from that paper. When they performed the task one more time, even he was convinced.

10   On that day, the world accepted what Louis Braille already knew: Just six raised dots can contain the passion and power of language.

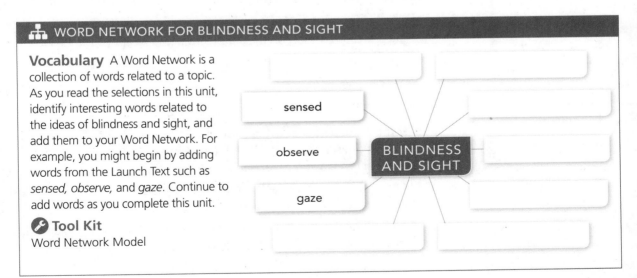

🔀 WORD NETWORK FOR BLINDNESS AND SIGHT

Vocabulary A Word Network is a collection of words related to a topic. As you read the selections in this unit, identify interesting words related to the ideas of blindness and sight, and add them to your Word Network. For example, you might begin by adding words from the Launch Text such as *sensed, observe,* and *gaze.* Continue to add words as you complete this unit.

sensed

observe

gaze

BLINDNESS AND SIGHT

🔧 **Tool Kit**
Word Network Model

Summary

Write a summary of "Just Six Dots." A **summary** is a concise, complete, and accurate overview of a text. It should not include a statement of your opinion or an analysis.

Launch Activity

Conduct a Four-Corner Debate Consider this statement: **Seeing is believing.**

- Record your position on the statement, and explain your thinking.

  ☐ Strongly Agree   ☐ Agree   ☐ Disagree   ☐ Strongly Disagree

  _____

  _____

- Form a group of like-minded students in one corner of the classroom. Discuss questions such as "What details from the text or your own experience lead you to take this position?"

- After your discussion, have a representative deliver a two- to three-minute summary of your group's position.

- After all groups have presented, move into the four corners again. If you change your corner, be prepared to explain why.

QuickWrite

Consider class discussions, presentations, the video, and the Launch Text as you think about the prompt. Record your first thoughts here.

PROMPT: **Is there a difference between seeing and knowing?**

EVIDENCE LOG FOR BLINDNESS AND SIGHT

Review your QuickWrite. Summarize your thoughts in one sentence to record in your Evidence Log. Then, record textual details or evidence from "Just Six Dots" that support your thinking.

Prepare for the Performance-Based Assessment at the end of the unit by completing the Evidence Log after each selection.

Tool Kit
Evidence Log Model

Title of Text: _____   Date: _____

CONNECTION TO PROMPT	TEXT EVIDENCE/DETAILS	ADDITIONAL NOTES/IDEAS

How does this text change or add to my thinking?   Date: _____

ESSENTIAL QUESTION:

What does it mean to see?

We can see a beautiful sight, but we can also see the truth in something. When we say, "I see," do we really mean "I understand"? You will work with your whole class to explore the concepts of blindness and sight. The play you are going to read presents insights into the many ways we can see—or not see—ourselves and the world around us.

Whole-Class Learning Strategies

Throughout your life, in school, in your community, and in your career, you will continue to learn and work in large-group environments.

Review these strategies and the actions you can take to practice them as you work with your whole class. Add ideas of your own for each step. Get ready to use these strategies during Whole-Class Learning.

STRATEGY	ACTION PLAN
Listen actively	• Eliminate distractions. For example, put your cell phone away. • Keep your eyes on the speaker. •
Clarify by asking questions	• If you're confused, other people probably are, too. Ask a question to help your whole class. • If you see that you are guessing, ask a question instead. •
Monitor understanding	• Notice what information you already know and be ready to build on it. • Ask for help if you are struggling. •
Interact and share ideas	• Share your ideas and answer questions, even if you are unsure. • Build on the ideas of others by adding details or making a connection. •

CONTENTS

^ This fresco depicting the Prince of Lilies is a beautiful example of Minoan art. It appears on a wall in the Minoan Palace of Knossos on the Greek island of Crete.

Historical Context
Ancient Greece

The cultural and political influence of ancient Greece extended throughout the Mediterranean and into central Asia.

The Earliest Greeks More than one thousand years before the birth of Sophocles, the playwright who wrote *Oedipus the King*, a people that we call the Mycenaeans (my suh NEE uhnz) began to settle throughout the Greek mainland, which juts down from Europe into the Mediterranean Sea. They established strongholds in Thebes, Pylos, Athens, Mycenae, and elsewhere, building thick-walled palaces decorated with bronze metalwork. From the Minoans (mih NOH uhnz), a sophisticated people who lived on the southern Greek island of Crete, they learned about writing, and they recorded palace business and other transactions on clay tablets. Many of these tablets have survived. The writings reveal a complex society that included administrative officials, priests, slaves, tradesmen, craftsmen and artisans, and an active warrior class. At the top of the social pyramid in each stronghold was a wanax, or king.

In about 1450 B.C., Minoan civilization collapsed, and the Mycenaeans became the dominant culture on Crete. Their influence spread throughout the Mediterranean islands and into western Asia Minor, or present-day Asian Turkey. On one of their most famous military ventures, the Mycenaeans successfully attacked the city of Troy in northern Asia Minor. We know that conflict as the Trojan War, which later became the subject of Homer's epic poems the *Iliad* and the *Odyssey*. It was among the last of the Mycenaean military successes. Soon afterward, Mycenaean civilization collapsed into a period called the Greek Dark Ages. The art of writing was lost, and the kingdoms broke down into small tribal units.

Reemerging From Darkness In about 850 B.C., a vibrant Greek culture began to reemerge, spurred by flourishing trade throughout the Mediterranean. Along with the economic boom came a resurgence of arts and learning capped by

Homer's masterful epics. Although Homer composed in the oral tradition, the Greeks soon began writing again, this time adapting the Phoenician writing system into the first true alphabet. They also began regrouping into city-states, or cities that functioned independently, just as countries do. By 500 B.C., the two most powerful city-states were Sparta, on Greece's Peloponnesian (pehl uh puh NEE shuhn) peninsula, and Athens, which stood east of Sparta in an area called Attica. Sparta was a monarchy with a powerful ruling council and a strong military tradition. Athens developed a government in which decision-making was shared by all adult males (other than slaves). It was, in short, the world's first democracy.

The Rise and Fall of Athens From 490 to 479 B.C., Athens and Sparta fought as allies in the Persian Wars, when the powerful Persian Empire (present-day Iran) twice tried to invade Greece. Despite Sparta's military prowess, it was Athens that led two important victories: the Battle of Marathon in the beginning and the Battle of Salamis later. These victories helped usher in a Golden Age of prosperity and achievement for Athens. Led by the statesman Pericles (PEHR uh kleez), Athens became a great intellectual center, attracting artists, poets, scientists, and philosophers. Impressive new buildings were constructed, and civic festivals grew more splendid. Among those who contributed greatly to this cultural flowering was Sophocles: playwright, government official, and—briefly—general in the Athenian military.

Unfortunately, Pericles' foreign policy aroused the resentment of other Greek city-states. In 432 B.C., Sparta and its allies joined against Athens and its allies in what became known as the Peloponnesian War. Athens was defeated, and for a time, Sparta, and later Thebes, exerted control over the Greek world. In the end, however, it was Philip of Macedon, a monarch from a kingdom to the north of Greece, who rose to ascendancy. Philip's son Alexander would embark on an amazing series of military conquests that would spread Greek influence all the way into central Asia. His exploits would earn him the title by which he is still known today: Alexander the Great.

> **QUICK INSIGHT**
> According to legend, after the Battle of Marathon, an Athenian soldier raced 26 miles back to Athens to share news of the victory. He then collapsed and died. The 26-mile race known as a marathon originated in his honor.

∨ The Parthenon, a temple dedicated to the goddess Athena, appears in the foreground of this photo of the Acropolis in Athens. The temple is among the most important surviving structures from Greece's Golden Age.

Ancient Greek Theater

An art form rooted in religious ritual gave rise to plays of enduring power.

Religious Foundations Greek theater was rooted in Greek religion, which was based on a belief in many gods. Each god was associated with one or more aspects of nature or human behavior. Poseidon (puh SY duhn), for example, was the god of the seas, while Apollo was the god of light. Athena (uh THEE nuh) was the goddess of wisdom, while Aphrodite (af ruh DY tee) was the goddess of love. Zeus (zoos) ruled over all the gods, yet even he was not all-powerful. Like human beings and lesser gods, Zeus could not alter fate.

The gods are key characters in Greek mythology, the set of stories the Greeks told to explain the world around them. In these myths, the gods often behave like human beings at our worst—they are angry, jealous, and petty. They are even deceitful and often vengeful. They are especially quick to punish human beings guilty of hubris (HYOO brihs), or excessive pride.

From Ritual to Art Theater in ancient Greece originated at annual festivals called Dionysia (dy uh NY see uh), which were dedicated to Dionysus, the god of wine. At these festivals, a **chorus,** or group of singers, honored Dionysus by chanting hymns called dithyrambs (DIHTH uh ramz). According to legend, at one festival a poet named Thespis stepped away from the chorus. He began a dialogue with the chorus leader while role-playing figures from the Greek myths. Thus, drama was born. The playwright Aeschylus developed the dramatic form further by adding a second actor, and the playwright Sophocles later introduced a third player to the stage.

By the time Sophocles was writing, plays had become great spectacles performed in a large outdoor amphitheater with thousands in attendance. The amphitheater was built on a slope with seating that rose in a semicircle from the performing area, or **orchestra**. There was no curtain, but painted scenery could be hung at the back. Performers wore large masks that allowed the same actor to perform different roles.

At the Dionysia, prizes were awarded to the best playwright. By 501 B.C., the three-day festival featured work by three competitors. Each playwright presented a **tetralogy,** or group of four plays, on a different day. The plays usually included a bawdy drama called a **satyr** (SAYT uhr) **play,** as well as three tragedies. About fifteen years later, a separate competition for comedies was added.

Dramatic Structure Greek plays are verse drama, in which the dialogue takes the form of poetry. Typically, the plays follow a consistent format. They open with a **prologue,** or exposition, that presents the background of the conflict. The chorus then performs a **parados** (PAR uhd uhs), or opening song. This is followed by the first scene. Additional songs, called **odes,** divide scenes, as a curtain does

∧ This mask depicts Dionysus, the god of wine, adorned with full beard and a grapevine crown.

QUICK INSIGHT

From the name of Thespis, the first actor, comes the English word *thespian,* an elegant term for an actor. The Greek word for an actor, however, was *hypokrites,* meaning "someone acting a part." That term, of course, is the origin of our word *hypocrite.*

in most modern theater. At the end of a tragedy, the chorus performs a **paean** (PEE uhn) of thanksgiving to Dionysus. The tragedy then concludes with an **exodus** (EHKS uh duhs), or final scene.

The chorus is central to the production, providing key background information and commentary on the action. Chorus recitals often divide into a **strophe** (STROH fee) and an answering **antistrophe** (an TIHS truh fee). During the strophe, the chorus sings while twisting or dancing from right to left. During the antistrophe, the chorus moves in the opposite direction. Some odes have a concluding stanza, or **epode** (EHP ohd), when the chorus may have stood still. To help propel the plot, the chorus leader, or **choragos** (koh RAY guhs; also spelled *choragus*), often exchanges thoughts with the rest of the chorus as well as with the actors.

QUICK INSIGHT
Strophe is Greek for "twist." Originally, a catastrophe was simply the ending, or final plot twist, of a play. Because the endings of Greek tragedies involved disastrous events, the word has come to have its current meaning of a disastrous outcome.

The Theater of Dionysus in Athens

The earliest dramas were likely performed in the Agora, or marketplace, in Athens. Later, the Theater of Dionysus (shown here as it appears today) was built on the slope of the Acropolis, the upper part of the city where other important buildings also stood. Stone seating was not used at first; instead, theater-goers probably sat on wooden benches.

^ This Roman bust of Aristotle is based on a fourth–century B.C. Greek bronze.

Aristotle and Greek Tragedy

In *Poetics*, Aristotle examined the mechanisms that make tragedy so compelling for audiences. His work remains the most influential discussion of drama the world has seen.

Fundamentals of Tragedy In his landmark work *Poetics*, the Greek philosopher Aristotle (ar ih STOT uhl; 384–322 B.C.) provides a famous examination of tragedy. He describes a *tragedy* as a serious play recounting related events in the life of a person of high rank or importance who is brought low and often meets his or her doom. The main character, called the *tragic hero* or *protagonist*, experiences this reversal of fortune as a result of what the Greeks called *hamartia* (hah mahr TEE uh), a *tragic flaw* or profound error in judgment. When a tragic flaw is involved, it usually takes form as *hubris*, or excessive pride. Fate, too, plays a decisive role in ensuring the tragic hero's downfall. In addition, the protagonist may face an *antagonist*, a rival character whose opposition contributes to his or her downfall.

Although the plot and its outcome are central to a tragedy, the events come as no surprise to most audience members. Greek audiences knew the myths upon which the plays were based; they knew what would happen. Nevertheless—according to Aristotle—the audience becomes caught up in the action because the play arouses their feelings of pity and fear. At the end of the play, explains Aristotle, the audience experiences a *catharsis* (kuh THAHR sihs), a cleansing or release of these emotions. Aristotle believed that the best plays engender fear and pity through the story and characters, not through the spectacle of the production itself.

Three Masters Three playwrights are considered the grand masters of Greek tragedy: Aeschylus (EHS kih luhs; c. 525–456 B.C.), Sophocles (SOF uh kleez; 496–406 B.C.), and Euripides (yoo RIHP uh deez; 480–406 B.C.). Between them, the three won first prize forty-two times in the annual drama competitions at Athens. Aeschylus, the pioneer of tragedy, is praised especially for his poetic language. Sophocles is most famous for his character development and insight into human nature. Euripides is noted for his efforts to address social concerns and humanitarian themes in his plays.

Sophocles (496–406 B.C.) Although he lived and wrote more than two thousand years ago, Sophocles is still considered one of the finest and most influential playwrights who ever lived. He won first prize at the annual Dionysia in Athens twenty-four times; never once did he place below second.

QUICK INSIGHT

Aristotle was the pupil of another famous Greek philosopher, Plato (PLAYT oh; c. 427–c. 347 B.C.), who himself studied under yet another famous Greek philosopher, Socrates (SOK ruh teez; c. 470–399 B.C.). Aristotle had a famous pupil too—Alexander the Great, whose conquests spread Greek culture throughout Europe, North Africa, and much of Asia.

A Golden Time to Live Sophocles grew up in a prosperous family in Colonus, near Athens. At sixteen, he was one of the young men chosen to perform in a choral ode celebrating the Athenian victory over the Persians at Salamis, the event that marks the beginning of Athens's golden age. Throughout his long life, he remained a leading figure of that era. Admired for his good looks and athleticism, he was also a talented musician and a frequent contributor to Athenian public life. He served for a time as a city treasurer and also as a general in the conflict with Samos, an island that revolted against Athens in 441 B.C. Late in life, he was elected to a special committee to investigate the disastrous failure of the Athenian military expedition to Sicily.

A Leading Light It was in theater, however, that Sophocles truly shone. His career as a dramatist began in 468 B.C., when he entered the annual Dionysia and beat the celebrated dramatist Aeschylus to take first prize. Over the next 62 years he wrote more than 120 plays, seven of which have survived. Among the most celebrated are *Oedipus the King*, the tragedy Aristotle considered the best example of the form, and *Antigone*, the story of Oedipus' daughter. Sophocles is known for strong female characters and for his insight into human nature. He is credited with introducing a third actor to drama and also with the practice of using painted scenery. He died two years before Athens surrendered to Sparta in the Peloponnesian War, the event that marks the end of Athens's Golden Age.

‹ This painting by the nineteenth-century French artist Jean-Auguste-Dominique Ingres depicts Aeschylus (with scroll) Sophocles, and Euripides. The work is a study for a much larger work entitled *The Apotheosis of Homer.*

About the Playwright

Sophocles (496–406 B.C.) was one of three Classical Athenian playwrights who together created the basic theatrical conventions of Greek tragedy, the foundation of drama in Western civilization. The other two were Aeschylus and Euripides. Before these three great dramatists, Greek theater consisted of static recitations performed by a chorus and a single actor. Aeschylus added a second actor, creating the possibility of true dialogue. When Sophocles added a third actor, complex relationships emerged in Greek drama.

🔧 **Tool Kit**
First-Read Guide and Model Annotation

Oedipus the King, Part I

You will encounter the following words as you read *Oedipus the King*, Part I. Before reading, note how familiar you are with each word. Then, rank the words in order from most familiar (1) to least familiar (3).

WORD	YOUR RANKING
proclamation	
decree	
edicts	

After completing the first read, come back to the concept vocabulary and review your rankings. Mark changes to your original rankings as needed.

First Read DRAMA

Apply these strategies as you conduct your first read. You will have an opportunity to complete the close-read notes after your first read.

NOTICE *whom* the story is about, *what* happens, *where* and *when* it happens, and *why* those involved react as they do.

ANNOTATE by marking vocabulary and key passages you want to revisit.

First Read

CONNECT ideas within the selection to what you already know and what you have already read.

RESPOND by completing the Comprehension Check and by writing a brief summary of the selection.

BACKGROUND FOR THE PLAY

The Theban Plays *Oedipus the King* (or *Oedipus Rex*) is one of three surviving plays by Sophocles centering on the Greek myth of Oedipus (EHD ih puhs), king of Thebes; the other two are *Oedipus at Colonus* and *Antigone*. Known as the Theban plays, they are now often published as a chronological trilogy, with *Antigone* last. However, Sophocles did not write the plays for the same Dionysia, and he apparently wrote *Antigone* first.

The Oedipus Myth The myth of Oedipus was well known to Greek audiences; in fact, Aeschylus wrote several earlier plays about it, although only his *Seven Against Thebes* has survived. In the myth, a prophecy informs Laius (LAY uhs; also spelled *Laïos*), king of Thebes, and his wife Jocasta (yoh KOS tuh; also spelled *Iocaste*) that their son will grow up to kill his father and marry his mother. Horrified, they send the infant off to be destroyed, but he is instead saved and adopted by a couple from Corinth. When the child, called Oedipus, grows up, he learns of the prophecy. Believing the warning refers to his adoptive parents, he flees in order to protect them. At a crossroads, he quarrels with and kills a stranger. Then, on the road to Thebes, he discovers the city is being plagued by a monstrous sphinx. In Greek mythology, the sphinx is a creature with a lion's body, bird's wings, and a woman's head. Waiting near the entrance to the city, the sphinx poses a riddle to all those who approach and eats anyone who cannot answer. The sphinx refuses to abandon its hold on the city until someone can solve the riddle. Oedipus does so, thereby saving the city and becoming a hero. As compensation, the recently widowed queen marries him, and he becomes king. It is several years after this point in the larger story that the play *Oedipus the King* begins.

> ### QUICK INSIGHT
> The famous riddle that Oedipus answered was "What has four legs in the morning, two at noon, and three in the evening?" The answer is a human being—crawling as a child, walking upright as an adult, and using a cane in old age.

Oedipus the King

Sophocles
translated by Nicholas Rudall

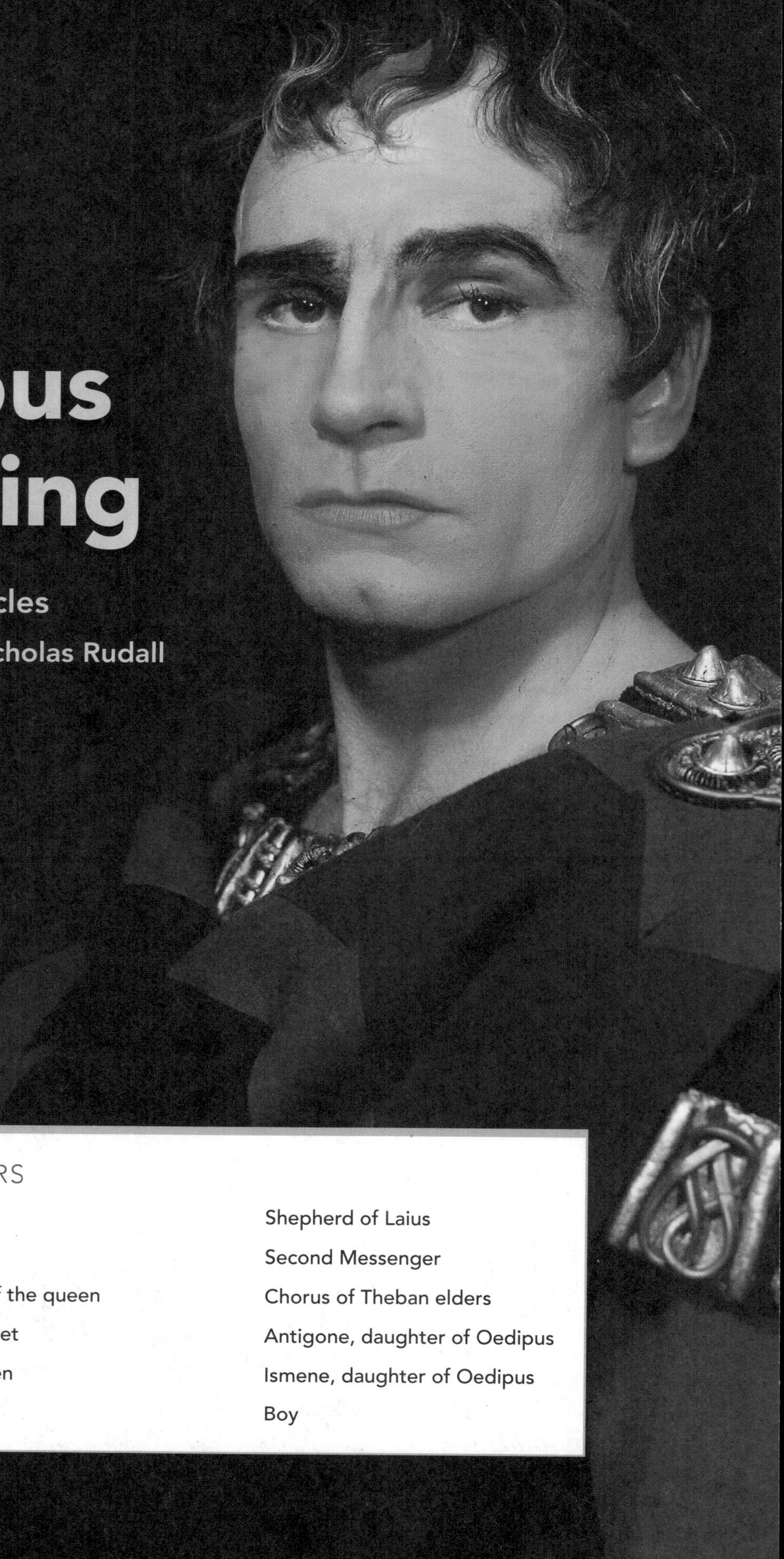

CHARACTERS

Oedipus

Priest of Zeus

Creon, brother of the queen

Teiresias, a prophet

Jocasta, the queen

Messenger

Shepherd of Laius

Second Messenger

Chorus of Theban elders

Antigone, daughter of Oedipus

Ismene, daughter of Oedipus

Boy

Oedipus. My children, you who live in the heart of this our city, living sons of ancient Cadmus,[1] why have you come to these sacred altars? Why do you bring garlands[2] and kneel in supplication[3] to the gods?

5 The city is laced with the breath of incense.
The air quivers with lamentation and with prayer.
My children, I did not want to hear your desires from messengers.
Therefore I have come in person to hear you speak—I, Oedipus your king.
10 (*to a Priest*) You there, since you are the eldest, speak on their behalf.
Tell me what is troubling you. Do you come in fear?
Do you seek a blessing from the gods?
Tell me. Never doubt that I will help you in every way I can.
15 I am moved and touched to find you suppliant here.

Priest. Oedipus, great king of Thebes! You see before you clinging to the altar's steps men of all ages. Here are boys too young to be alone. Here are priests weighed down with time, priests of Zeus[4]—as I am. Here are young men as yet unmarried.
20 And thousands more, olive wreaths in their hair, throng the public squares. They huddle before the two shrines of Athena[5] and at Apollo's[6] temple where the god speaks in the glowing embers of his fire. Your eyes see the truth: Thebes is drowning in a deadly sea, is sinking beneath the waves of death.
25 There is a blight that eats the budding fruits of the earth.
Our cattle die. Women give birth to stillborn children. A deadly plague consumes our city, strikes like bolts of lightning, burns our flesh, and ravages the house of Cadmus. My lord, we are plunged into darkness. Death alone grows fat upon our agony.
30 We have come to you to offer our prayers.
We know you are no god.
But of all men you are the most wise in the ways of god.
You saved us from the Sphinx,[7] who sang her doom from the stone of her breast.
35 You saved us from her plague. You knew no more than we, we could not teach you.
But you saved us when a god touched your mind.
Therefore, great King of Thebes, we turn to you.
Save us. Heal us. Listen to the gods. Listen to the minds of mortals.
40 Your wisdom saved us long ago.
It can save us now when troubles seethe again.
You are the pinnacle of nobility, give us back our lives.
Remember that we call you the Liberator.
Remember that we love you for your courage long ago. Let not
45 the world remember you as the king who once was great but then fell from greatness.

Save the ship of state from the storm.
Once, years ago, you turned our unhappiness to joy.
You can do it once more.
50 You rule this land. No man disputes your power.
But rule over the living, not the dead.
When no men throng the streets, the city walls are nothing and
our proud ships mere empty shells.

Oedipus. Oh my poor children. I understand the passions that
55 brought you here.
I know that you are plagued with sickness. Yet sick as you are,
not as sick as I.
What each of you suffers is your own pain, no one else's.
But I suffer for you, for my city, and for myself.
60 I was not asleep. You are not waking me.
I have been weeping for a long time.
I have paced my restless room thinking, thinking.
In the end I found a remedy and I have put it to work:
I have sent Creon, son of Menoeceus,[8] brother of the queen, to
65 Delphi. There at Apollo's oracle he will learn, if he can, what
I must do or promise to do to save the city.
I have been counting the days and I am troubled. For he should
have returned.
What can be keeping him? This is the day! He should be here.
70 But whenever he returns I will do what the god orders.

Priest. Your promise is given in good time. They say that Creon
is here.

Oedipus. Oh Lord Apollo, may his news shine as bright as the
hope on his face.

75 **Priest.** The news must be good. He is crowned with laurel,[9] a
wreath thick with berries.

Oedipus. We shall soon know. See where he comes.

(Creon enters)

Oedipus. Oh brother, Prince of Thebes, what answer do you
bring us from Apollo?

80 **Creon.** A powerful answer. Our deep agonies will be healed if
they are treated right.

Oedipus. What did the oracle say? Your words are ambiguous. I
still hover between hope and fear.

Creon. Do you wish me to speak in public in front of all these
85 men? I will of course. But should we not go inside?

Oedipus. Let them hear. For I suffer for them more than for myself.

Creon. Then I will tell you what I heard. In plain words, the
oracle commands us to expel from Thebes an old pollution. We
are sheltering a thing that is killing us and is beyond cure.
90 We cannot let it feed upon us any longer.

8. **Menoeceus** (meh NIH see uhs)
Theban statesman and soldier
of renown.

9. **laurel** (LAWR uhl) *n.* leaves
of the laurel tree, used to
show honor.

Oedipus. What pollution? How are we to expel it from our midst?

Creon. By exile or by death. Blood must answer for blood.
A murder blew the deadly plague breath on our city.

Oedipus. A murder? Whose? Did the god not name the man?

95 **Creon.** My lord, Laius once was our king before you came to rule over us.

Oedipus. I know. I never saw the man, but others told me of him.

Creon. He was murdered. Apollo demands that we take revenge upon the man who killed him.

100 **Oedipus.** Where are the killers? How, after so many years, can we find a clue to solve the crime?

Creon. Apollo said the killer is amongst us. We must search and be aware of everything.

Oedipus. Where was he killed? In the palace or outside the city
105 or in some other country?

Creon. He told us that he was going to the shrine of a god. He never came home again.

Oedipus. Was there no witness . . . some attendant to tell what happened?

110 **Creon.** They were all killed. Except for one.
He escaped, but his terror made him forget all but one thing.

Oedipus. What was that? That one thing may be the key that unlocks this whole mystery.

Creon. He said a band of highwaymen[10] attacked them.
115 They were outnumbered and the king was killed.

Oedipus. Strange that highwaymen should be so bold . . . unless they were bribed by some faction from the city.

Creon. We considered that. But when Laius was killed the city was besieged with other troubles. There was no time for
120 vengeance.

Oedipus. What troubles could have stopped you from finding the killer of your king?

Creon. The Sphinx. Her riddles stopped our ears and brought destruction.

125 **Oedipus.** Once again I must bring the darkness into the light.
Apollo is right to show, as you do, this concern for the dead.
I will obey his command. I will stand by your side. I will avenge this country's loss.
It is my duty. I do it not for some unknown friend but for myself.
130 We must expel this evil.
Whoever killed King Laius might be the death of me—who knows?
It might happen even now.
It is in my own interest to avenge your slaughtered king.

NOTES

CLOSE READ
ANNOTATE: In line 93, mark the words Creon uses to describe how the murder affected the city.

QUESTION: Why does the playwright use a metaphor, or imaginative comparison, to describe the arrival of the plague?

CONCLUDE: What is the effect of Creon's describing the plague in this way?

10. **highwaymen** *n.* robbers.

Oedipus and the Sphinx

My children, leave the altar's steps. Raise the olive branches to
135   the sun.
Call the elders of Thebes to gather here. Tell them I will do all
that is in my power.
With the god's help we will be saved. Without it we are lost.

Priest. Rise up, my children. We came to hear just this. And our
140   king has given his word.
Apollo has sent us an oracle.
May he walk among us and heal us and drive this plague from
our city.

(all exit)

Chorus. Oh sweet voice of Apollo
145   You bring the truth of Zeus
To Thebes from your shrine of gold.
What do you say to us?
My heart trembles with fear.

Apollo, God of Healing, hear us!
150   Do you cast upon us a grief unknown before
Or in the circle of time awaken a remembered doom?
Immortal voice, golden child of Hope, speak to us.

We pray to Athena. Daughter of Zeus, defend us.
We pray to Artemis[11] of Thebes, her sister.
155   Come to us now, throned on high above your people.
We pray to Apollo, distant archer.
Once, when we were in the jaws of death,
You drove the burning plague from us.
Come to us now, defend us.
160   You three powers of heaven,
Descend and save us.

Ah what griefs uncountable are ours.
Our people are sick and dying.
No man has the will to fight the god of death.
165   The gentle earth lies barren.
Women in labor groan in vain.

Body falls upon body
Swifter than the flight of birds
Swifter than the wave of fire
170   Racing to the shores of Night.

Corpses litter the city streets.
Death feeds upon death.
Infection breeds,[12] and there is
No time to mourn the uncountable dead.

175   Old gray women flock to the altars,
Weep, and rend the air with prayers
And cries of grief:
Apollo, heal us!

11. **Artemis** (AHR tuh mihs) Greek
goddess of the moon and the
hunt, twin sister of Apollo.

12. **Infection breeds** disease
multiplies and spreads.

Athena, golden child of Zeus,
180 Turn your shining face upon our pain.

The War god stalks our streets,
No sword in hand and yet we die.
Fire encircles our screams.
Send him to the Ocean's depths
185 Into the waves that kill the flames.
What life survives the night
Dies in tomorrow's sun.
Zeus turn your fire upon him,
With lightning strike the god of War.
190 Apollo, stretch tight your golden bow
Loose your arrows in our defense.
Artemis, race across our hills
In a blaze of saving light.
Dionysus,[13] God of Thebes,
195 Come to us with your shock of golden curls,
Flushed with wine in the whirlwind
Ecstasy of your followers.
Destroy the loathsome god of Death
In the conflagration of your joy.

(enter Oedipus)

200 **Oedipus.** I hear your prayer. Listen to me and I will teach you
how to heal.
You will find comfort and relief.
I knew nothing of this story of Laius's death, knew nothing of
the deed itself.
205 How could I therefore solve a crime alone?
But now, since I became a citizen after the murder, I make this
proclamation to all my fellow Thebans: If anyone knows the
man who killed King Laius, I order him to tell me everything.
He must not be afraid for his long silence. No, I promise that he
210 will not be punished with death but may leave this land in
safety. If any man knows that the killer was a foreigner, let him
speak out at once.
He shall have my thanks and a rich reward. But if you remain
silent and attempt to protect yourself or a friend and ignore my
215 commands, hear what I will do:
I forbid the people of this country, where I am king, ever to
harbor the killer or speak to him. Give him no place at your
prayers or sacrifices. Hound him from your homes. For he it is
who defiles our city. This the oracle has shown to me.
220 And I hereby join with the god as champion of our murdered king.
I lay this curse upon the killer, whether he acted alone or with
accomplices:
May your life be a searing agony!

13. **Dionysus** (dy uh NY suhs) Greek god of ecstasy, the theater, and wine.

proclamation (prok luh MAY shuhn) *n.* official announcement

This curse I even turn upon myself. For if it turns out that the
225 killer breaks my bread and shares my hearth,[14] I too must suffer.
This is my command. Obey it for my sake, for Apollo, and for
our country, which lies barren and diseased through the anger
of heaven.
Let us suppose the oracle had not spoken.
230 Should the murder of your king, your noble king, go unavenged?
This pollution had to be purged clean.
And now that I sit upon that great man's throne, possess his
wife, his bed, fathering children as would he if he had lived,
I will be his avenger. For had not fate cut him down he might
235 have produced a son, a brother to my children.
I now will become that son, as though in truth I were, and I will
hunt the killer down.
Vengeance for Laius, son of Labdacus, descendant of great
Cadmus and King Agenor![15]
240 If any men disobey my commands, may the gods make their
crops wither in the fields, may they never see the fruit of their
loins, may they rot on earth. But to you who are loyal to me and
approve what I have done, I pray that Justice and all the gods
look kindly upon you forever more.

245 **Chorus.** I swear to you my lord that I accept your commands.
I did not kill the king nor do I know who did.
My advice is this . . . Apollo posed the question . . . he should
give the answer and tell us who the murderer is.

Oedipus. Your advice is well taken. But no man can force the
250 gods to speak against their will.

Chorus. May I then suggest a second plan.

Oedipus. And a third if need be.

Chorus. My lord, if any man can speak with the god it is
Teiresias. He might bring us to the light.

255 **Oedipus.** I have already done it. Creon suggested it. And I have
sent for him. I am surprised he is not here.

Chorus. My mind is stirring now. Rumors from long ago. Mere
gossip.

Oedipus. Tell me. I want to know everything.

260 **Chorus.** It was said that he was killed by travelers.

Oedipus. That is what I heard. But no one knows the man who
saw him die.

Chorus. Well, if he knows what fear is, he will run in terror of
your curse.

265 **Oedipus.** A man who can do a thing like that is not afraid of
words.

NOTES

14. **hearth** (hahrth) *n.* home.

15. **King Agenor** (uh GEE nawr)
mythical king of Phoenicia,
believed to have trained the
Greek hero Achilles.

CLOSE READ
ANNOTATE: Mark the
punctuation that suggests
hesitation in lines 245–248.

QUESTION: Why does the
playwright, or translator,
indicate that these words
should be spoken with
hesitation?

CONCLUDE: What effect
do these lines have on
the reader? On a viewing
audience?

This eighteenth-century drawing depicts the blind seer Teiresias being led by a boy.

Chorus. But here comes one who can capture him.
Here is Teiresias, whose mind is fired by the god and in whom truth lives and breathes.

(*enter Teiresias, led by a boy*)

270 **Oedipus.** Teiresias our prophet, you understand all things—the hidden mysteries of the wise, the high things of heaven, and the low things of the earth.
Though your eyes cannot see, you know of this plague that infects our city.
275 We turn to you—our one defense—our shield.

No doubt the messengers told you what Apollo said in his reply to us:
One course alone can free us from this plague . . . we must find the murderers of King Laius.

280 We must execute them or expel them from this land.
Therefore give us freely of your gift of prophecy.
Save yourself, your country, and your king.
Save all the people from this pollution of spilled blood. We are in your hands.

285 There is no greater honor than for a man to serve his fellow men.

Teiresias. Alas! It is a miserable thing to be wise when wisdom brings no reward. I had forgotten that ancient truth. Otherwise I would not be here.

Oedipus. What is wrong? Why this melancholy mood?

290 **Teiresias.** Let me go home. Do not keep me here. It would be best if you bear your burden and I mine.

Oedipus. For shame!
No true-born Theban would withhold his gift of prophecy from the country that he loves.

295 **Teiresias.** Your words, my king, lie far from the truth. I am afraid that I, like you, will not speak true.

Oedipus. Oh speak! Hold nothing back. I order you to tell us what you know.
We are your suppliants.

300 **Teiresias.** Yes . . but you do not know what you are asking me. I will never reveal my miseries . . . or yours.

Oedipus. What!! You know something but will not speak?
Will you betray us and destroy the state?

Teiresias. I will not hurt myself or you. Why ask from me what I
305 will never tell?

Oedipus. You are a wicked man. Your silence would anger a lifeless stone.
Will nothing loosen your tongue, melt your heart, shake you out of this implacable silence?

310 **Teiresias.** You blame me but you do not see yourself. In your anger you turn on me.

Oedipus. Who could be calm when he heard you scorn the desperation of our city?

Teiresias. Well, whether I will speak or not, what will be will be.

315 **Oedipus.** That is true. And your duty is to tell me.

Teiresias. I have nothing more to say. You can rage to your heart's content.

decree (dih KREE) *n.* decision made by an authority

ANNOTATE: Mark the repeated word in lines 339 and 340.

QUESTION: Why does the playwright repeat this word?

CONCLUDE: What effect does this repetition have?

Oedipus. Yes, I am angry and *I* will not be silent! I will speak what is on my mind.

320   I think it was you, yes you, who planned the murder.
Yes—and did it all—except the actual killing.
And if you were not blind you would have done that too.

Teiresias. Is that so? Then hear me! I call upon you to obey the words of your own **decree**.

325   From this day on do not speak to me or to these citizens.
You are the killer. *You* bring the pollution upon Thebes.

Oedipus. Hold your slanderous tongue.
You taunt me and think because you are a prophet you will go scot-free.

330 **Teiresias.** I *am* free. For my strength lies in the truth.

Oedipus. Who made you say this? You didn't find this accusation through your art.

Teiresias. You made me speak. You provoked me against my will.

Oedipus. I made you speak?? Then speak again. Make clear
335   your charges.

Teiresias. Did you not understand the first time? Will you provoke me yet again?

Oedipus. I half understood your meaning. Speak again.

Teiresias. I say you are the murderer of the man whose
340   murderer you seek.

Oedipus. You will regret repeating so foul a slander.

Teiresias. Must I go on and inflame your anger even more?

Oedipus. You can say all you want. It will be a waste of breath.

Teiresias. I say that you are living in darkest shame with the
345   closest of your family.
And you know nothing of your sin.

Oedipus. Do you think that you can keep on spewing out your filth and get away with it?

Teiresias. Yes, if there is strength in truth and truth does not die.

350 **Oedipus.** Truth lives in other men but not in you.
For you, in ear, in mind, in eye, in everything are blind.

Teiresias. Poor fool! You lay words upon me which soon all men will lay upon you.

Oedipus. You are a child of endless darkness, and you have no
355   power over me or any man who can see the light of the sun.

Teiresias. True, I have no such power over you. Your fate is in the hands of Apollo.

Oedipus. Is this plot yours alone or was it Creon's idea?

Teiresias. Not Creon. You bring destruction upon yourself.

Oedipus. Wealth! Power! The art of being a ruler!
Kingship! The admiration of one's subjects!
What envy these things breed—if Creon, Creon whom I trusted,
who was my friend, seeks in secret to overthrow me.
All for this position of majesty which the city gave to me though
365 I did not seek it.
He has bought the services of this charlatan, this fraud, this
scheming beggar-priest.
With *money* in his hands his eyes can see. But his art is stone blind.
You there! Tell me! When did you ever prove that you were a
370 true prophet? When the Sphinx was destroying the city with her
riddles, why could you not save these people?
The riddle could not be solved by guessing.
It needed the true art of prophecy. And you were found wanting.
Neither the birds of the air nor the configurations of the stars[16]
375 could help you.
It was I, I who came here, Oedipus, an ordinary simple man.
I stopped the mouth of the Sphinx. I did not need omens.
I needed only my native wit. And you seek to overthrow me?

16. **the birds . . . the stars** Augury, the study of the flights of birds, and astrology, the study of the movements of stars and planets, were believed to tell the future to those who practiced them.

In a 1945 stage production, Oedipus, played by Laurence Olivier, accuses the prophet Teiresias. The chorus watches in the background.

You hope to reign with Creon in my place?

380 You will regret it, you and your friend Creon.
If it weren't for your age you would feel the pain that your treachery deserves.

Chorus. You both are angry. But now is not the time for fury.
We must decide how we can best obey the oracle.

385 **Teiresias.** You are the king. But I have the right to speak my mind freely.
In this I too am a king. I have no master but Apollo. I am his servant.
You cannot accuse me of being allied with Creon.

390 This is my answer: since you mocked my blindness, know that though you have eyes you cannot see how low you have fallen.
You do not know in whose house you live, no, nor with whom.
Who is your father, who is your mother? You do not know.
In ignorance you live as an enemy to the living and the dead.

395 But the curse of your parents one day will drive you wounded from this land.
Those eyes that now see clear day will be covered with darkest night.
Your cries will echo on every hill. Cithaeron[17] will ring with

400 your moans. For you will know that the marriage hymns that welcomed you to Thebes were a dirge of mourning for your ill-fated return.
All this will come to pass—and more—before you find your children and yourself.

405 Curse me then. Curse Creon. No mortal will be punished more horribly than you.

Oedipus. Must I endure his insolence? Damnation fall upon you! Get out of my sight!
Never set foot in my house again!

410 **Teiresias.** I would never have come if you had not ordered it.

Oedipus. I did not know you would play the fool.
Otherwise you would have waited a long time to be called.

Teiresias. The fool? Ha! Your parents thought me wise enough.

Oedipus. My parents? Who were they? Speak.

415 **Teiresias.** This day will give you a father and lead you to your grave.

Oedipus. You know only how to speak in the darkness of riddles.

Teiresias. I thought you were the man who could unlock a riddle's secret.

420 **Oedipus.** Yes! Mock me for the skill that made me great.

Teiresias. A greatness that will be your ruin.

Oedipus. I saved this city!

17. **Cithaeron** (suh THEE ruhn) mountain range in Greece.

Teiresias. It is time to leave. Come boy.

Oedipus. Yes, take him away. Leave me in peace.
425 Your presence here disturbs my world.

Teiresias. I go. But first I will tell you why I came. I am not afraid of you.
You cannot do me harm.
Hear me: the man you seek with your edicts warrants and
430 decrees—the man who killed the king—that man is here.
You think of him as foreign-born. But he is a Theban.
His good fortune will turn to sorrow. Though he has eyes, he will be blind.
Though he wear purple,[18] he will wear beggar's rags.
435 Leaning upon his staff, he will tap the earth that leads him into exile.
To his children he will be both brother and father.
To her who gave him birth both son and husband.
And to his father he will be both killer and the man who shared
440 his bed.
Go in now and think upon my words.
If you find that I have not spoken truth, then you can say I have no gift for prophecy.

(exit Oedipus, Teiresias, and Boy)

Chorus. The Oracle at Delphi has spoken.
445 But who is the man who took the blood of kings?
Who is this man of unspeakable darkness?
He must fly like the wind's swift steeds.
For on his heels Apollo races
In the blinding light of his father's fire.
450 And ever on his track the Furies[19] follow hard
Like hounds scenting blood.
Parnassus![20] Blinding peak of snow!
You flash to earth the icy will of the gods.
Find the killer. Find the man who roams
455 Like a bull in the forest's shadow,
Raging in the haunting dark as his doom hovers,
Ready to strike.
There is nowhere to hide from the light
Of Apollo's shrine,
460 When voices divine hunt him down.
The man skilled in the beating of the wings of birds
Troubles me deeply. Is there truth in his art?
I am lost. I have no words. I can see neither
Past nor future. I am adrift on the wind.
465 There was no quarrel ever that I knew
Between our royal house and Polybus, father of our king.
There is no proof. How then can I question his honor

NOTES

edicts (EE dihkts) *n.* commands from a public authority

18. **purple** color worn by the rich and important, especially royalty.

19. **the Furies** feared Greek goddesses of vengeance; punishers of the guilty.

20. **Parnassus** (pahr NAS uhs) sacred mountain within sight of the oracle at Delphi.

And in a feud of blood pursue this untracked murder?
Zeus and Apollo know all things,
470 Know the ways of mortal men.
But that a prophet knows more than I,
What proof is there? One man may possess
More wisdom than another. So how can I—
Without the truth before my eyes—cast blame
475 Upon my king?
He saved our city from the Sphinx
Was tested hard and shone like gold.
To my mind he is wise and guilt-free.

(enter Creon)

Creon. My fellow citizens, I have come here to lodge a protest.
480 I have heard that Oedipus has accused me of a grievous charge.
If he thinks that I have harmed him—by my actions or in
words—in this present crisis then I put no value on my life in
face of this dishonor. For I am not being accused of some minor
private mistake.
485 I am charged with being a traitor to the state and to you, my
friends.

Chorus. The king was angry. His words were rash. He was not
thinking when he spoke.

Creon. Did anyone dare to suggest that I had urged the seer to
490 bring false charges?

Chorus. Such things were mentioned. I do not know why.

Creon. How did he look? Surely he must have been
out of his senses when he made this hideous accusation?

Chorus. I do not know. It is not for me to judge the behavior of
495 my king.

(enter Oedipus)

Oedipus. You there! What are you doing here?
Do you have the gall to come near my palace?
There is no doubt in my mind that you planned to kill me and
usurp the throne.
500 Tell me, did you think I was a fool or a coward?
Is that why you hatched this plot against me?
Did you think I was too stupid to see your slithering
treachery—too frightened not to fight back?
You are the fool if you think you can get the crown without the
505 support of friends.
A crown must be fought for or bought.

Creon. Now you listen to me. You have spoken. It is your turn
to hear me.

Oedipus. Oh yes, you have a silver tongue.

510 But how can I learn anything from my deadliest enemy?

Creon. First, I would prove that those words are not true.

Oedipus. That you are not my enemy?

Creon. You are headstrong and stubborn. Change your ways.

Oedipus. And you are a fool if you think a man can betray his
515 family and get away with it.

Creon. That is a fair statement. But what betrayal are you
talking about?

Oedipus. Did you or did you not advise me to summon Teiresias?

Creon. I did. I would do it again.

520 **Oedipus.** How long has it been since Laius . . .

Creon. Laius . . . ? What are you talking about?

Oedipus. . . . since Laius left this earth in bloody violence?

Creon. I don't know . . . It was many years ago.

Oedipus. Was Teiresias the city's prophet at the time?

525 **Creon.** Yes. Skilled then as now, and deserving his reputation.

Oedipus. Did he speak of me then in any way?

Creon. Not to my knowledge. No.

Oedipus. Was there no search, no formal inquiry?

Creon. Of course. But nothing was discovered.

530 **Oedipus.** Why did our prophet not tell his story then?

Creon. I do not know. And since I don't, I will hold my tongue.

Oedipus. There is one thing you know and could speak of.

Creon. What is that? I will tell you everything.

Oedipus. That it was *you* who made Teiresias accuse me of
535 Laius's death.

Creon. If he accused you, you are the only one who knows of it.
But let me question you now.

Oedipus. Proceed. Prove me a killer if you can.

Creon. You married my sister. Is that correct?

540 **Oedipus.** Why would I deny it?

Creon. And as your wife and queen, she shares the throne?

Oedipus. She has all her heart's desires.

Creon. And with the two of you I have a third share of power?

Oedipus. Yes. And it is that which makes you a traitor.

545 **Creon.** Not true. Now begin to reason logically as I have. Would
any man choose the troubles, the anxiety of power if he had that
power but without the responsibility? I certainly would not.
I have no longing for the *name* of king. I prefer to *live* like one.

NOTES

CLOSE READ

ANNOTATE: Mark the italicized words in lines 545–550.

QUESTION: Why does the playwright, or translator, emphasize these words?

CONCLUDE: What is the effect of this emphasis, especially in clarifying Creon's reasoning?

This 2002 stage production of the play presents another vision of the Chorus.

NOTES

Any sensible man would feel the same way. All my needs, all
550 that I want, *you* provide.
I have nothing to fear.
But if I were king I would have to do things which I did not want.
So why should I seek the crown rather than the pleasant,
untroubled life I now lead?
555 I am not mad. I need no greater honors than I have now.
I am welcome everywhere . . . people greet me everywhere.
Those who want a favor from you are kind to me.
I know how to get what they ask of me.
So should I exchange this comfortable life for one like yours?
560 That would be insane. And I am not mad.
Nor was I ever tempted by the thought or shared in any intrigue.
If you doubt me, go to Delphi, learn if what I have said is true.
The god will speak the truth.
If you find that I conspired with Teiresias, then condemn me to
565 death.
I will join with you in my own condemnation.
But do not find me guilty on mere suspicion, without appeal.
You cannot on a whim judge a good man bad, a bad man good.
A man should offer up his precious life rather than betray a
570 friend.
In time you will know the truth. Time alone unlocks the secrets
of true justice.
A wicked man is discovered in the passing light of a single day.

Chorus. His words are carefully chosen. This demands discretion.
575 There should be no rush to judgment.

Oedipus. But he . . . did he not rush into his schemes, his plots? I must be as quick to counter him. If I do nothing, he will overthrow me.

Creon. So what is your intent . . . to send me into exile?

580 **Oedipus.** Exile? *No!* I want you dead.
I want the world to see the punishment that treason brings.

Creon. You still resist the truth? You will not believe me?

Oedipus. Why should I?

Creon. Then you are a fool.

585 **Oedipus.** For protecting myself?

Creon. In the name of justice, believe me!

Oedipus. You are a wicked, evil man.

Creon. What if you are wrong?

Oedipus. I must still be king.

590 **Creon.** Even if you are wrong?

Oedipus. Oh my city, my city.

Creon. It is my city too!

Chorus. My lords, keep your peace. I see the queen.
Jocasta is coming from her chambers. It is time, oh it is time.
595 For she alone can resolve this quarrel.

(enter Jocasta)

Jocasta. You are fools! Why do you shout in anger like this?

NOTES

Do you have no shame? The city is dying, and here you fight like petulant children.

(to Oedipus) Come into the house.

600 And you, Creon . . . go now.
No more of this quarreling over nothing!

Creon. Over nothing? You are wrong, my sister.
Your husband will send me into exile or to my death.

Oedipus. That is what I will do. For I have caught him, caught
605 him plotting against my life.

Creon. *No!* Let me die amongst the damned if I ever wished you
harm!

Jocasta. Oh believe him, Oedipus!
In the name of the gods, believe him when he swears.
610 For my sake and for these our citizens.

Chorus. Listen to her, my lord. I beg you listen to her.

Oedipus. What do you want me to do?

Chorus. Trust Creon. He has never spoken like a fool.
And now he has sworn before the gods.

615 **Oedipus.** Do you know what you are asking of me?

Chorus. I do.

Oedipus. Then speak on.

Chorus. Creon has been your friend. He has sworn an oath.
You should not mistrust his words.
620 You should not seem to be blinded by malice toward him.

Oedipus. You understand that what you say means death or
exile for me . . . ?

Chorus. *No! No!* I swear by Apollo, may I die alone and cursed
by the gods if ever meant that!
625 My heart is dying, withering fast when I hear your anger, hear
your hate.

Oedipus. Then let him go.
And let me die if that is what must be . . . or wander into exile in
shame, leaving this Thebes that I love. You, you citizens, you
630 move me to this change of heart. Not he . . . for wherever he
goes he will be hated.

Creon. You make peace, but your words are full of hate.
Your anger still seethes within your heart.
It will come back, this anger, to haunt you.

635 **Oedipus.** Leave me in peace. Go now.

Creon. I go. You misjudged me—these men did not.

(exit)

Chorus. Lady, take your husband into the palace.

Jocasta. Tell me first, what started this quarrel?

Chorus. There were rumors. And lies breed anger.

640 **Jocasta.** Were both to blame?

Chorus. Both.

Jocasta. What was said?

Chorus. Ask me no more. Thebes is dying.
Let sleeping griefs lie in their beds.

645 **Oedipus.** That is strange advice, my friend. I know you are
thinking of me.
But why would you try to stop me from doing what I must do?

Chorus. My king, I will say this once more.
I would be called a fool if I abandoned you now. You made this
650 country great.
And when the winds lashed our city, you brought our ship of
state into safe harbor.
There is no one but you . . . no one who can save us.

Jocasta. I must ask you, my husband and my king, what made
655 you so violently angry?

Oedipus. I love you . . . love you more than all these citizens. So
I will tell you.
Your brother Creon conspired against me.

Jocasta. Why? Why? What was the cause?

660 **Oedipus.** He accuses me of murdering Laius.

Jocasta. Does he know this or is it some rumor?

Oedipus. He is too clever to accuse himself.
He speaks through the mouth of a prophet . . . one that he has
bought.

665 **Jocasta.** Then let your conscience rest. Hear me. I have no belief
in the prophetic art.
I know. I *know.*
Let me tell you. Once long ago word came to Laius from the
Oracle at Delphi—I will not say it was from the god himself . . .
670 probably from his priests.
The word was that Laius would die at the hand of his own
son . . . my child and his.
Laius . . . at least this was the story . . . was killed by
highwaymen in broad daylight.
675 He was killed where three roads meet.
We had a son, but when he was only three days old Laius
pierced his ankles, left him on a hill to die. He gave the child to
others, of course, to do this. We knew then that Apollo had
changed the course of fate.

CLOSE READ
ANNOTATE: Mark the word
Jocasta repeats in line 659. Mark
the sentence she repeats in
line 667.

QUESTION: Why does the
playwright have her repeat this
word and phrase?

CONCLUDE: How does this
repetition relate to one of the
play's key ideas?

Laurence Olivier as Oedipus and Sybil Thorndike as Jocasta in a famous 1945 stage production.

680 The son would never kill his father.
The terror of the prophecy would die there on the hills.
That is what the prophet said, my king.
Pay it no mind. God alone shows us the truth.

Oedipus. A shadow crossed my mind as you spoke. And the
685 shadow chilled my mind.

Jocasta. What was it that touched you?

Oedipus. You said that Laius was killed where three roads meet.

Jocasta. That was what we were told at the time.

Oedipus. Where?

690 **Jocasta.** Phocis . . . that is the name of the town . . .
It is where the road to Thebes divides, and you can go to Delphi
or Daulia.

Oedipus. When?

Jocasta. We heard about it just before you came. Just before you
695 won this kingdom.

Oedipus. Oh what a net of death have the gods been weaving
for me!

Jocasta. Oedipus, why are you so troubled?

Oedipus. Do not ask me. Not yet. Tell me about Laius—how old
was he?

Jocasta. He was tall. His hair was becoming gray. He was about
your height.

Oedipus. I feel that my own curse now begins to descend on me.

Jocasta. I am afraid. When I look on you I am afraid.

Oedipus. Perhaps the seer who has no eyes can see the truth.
But tell me, tell me all you know.

Jocasta. I will tell you everything. But now fear grips my soul.

Oedipus. Was the king accompanied by many men—as befitting
his office or . . . ?

Jocasta. There were just five men. One was a messenger. There
was a single chariot.
He was driving.

Oedipus. Aaagh, that is enough, enough.
Who told you what happened?

Jocasta. A servant. He was the only one to escape.

Oedipus. Is he still one of ours?

Jocasta. No. When he came back here and found that you were
now our king . . . he came to me. He touched my hand . . . he
begged me to send him to the countryside where the shepherds
tend their flocks. Far from here, he said. I granted him his wish.
He was a slave, but he had earned this simple gift.

Oedipus. Can you get him back here quickly?

Jocasta. Of course. But why?

Oedipus. I have been too much alone. I have asked too few
questions. I need to talk to him.

Jocasta. Then he will be here. But you must talk to me too . . .
tell me of your fears.

Oedipus. I owe you that—oh I owe you that. For I have climbed
a mountain of fear.
And I need to talk to someone. I need to talk to you.
Polybus of Corinth[21] is my father. My mother is Merope. I grew
up in Corinth.
I was a prince.
One day a strange thing happened . . . it affected me deeply . . .
perhaps it should not.
There was a feast.
A man got drunk and shouted to the world that I was not my
father's son.
I kept quiet that night . . . though it hurt. And I was angry.

21. **Corinth** (KAWR ihnth) city-state
in ancient Greece.

740 The next day I went to see my father and my mother. I asked them about this.

They too were very angry. They said it was the mindless ranting of a drunken fool.

I found peace in that. But the suspicion lay there. Always. In my 745 mind.

I knew that people talked. I could not be still. I had to leave.

I said nothing to my parents. I went straight to Delphi, to the oracle. I questioned him.

The god was silent. He answered not a word. But then he spoke. 750 He spoke of other things.

His words were sometimes as clear as the burning sun, full of terror, pain, and things unbearable.

He said that I would bed my own mother, that I would breed children from that womb, and that the world would turn away 755 in horror.

He said that I would kill my own father.

I listened. And I fled.

From that day Corinth was but a distant land touched by the Western stars.

760 I moved onward, ever onward.

I never wanted to set eyes upon the horror spoken by the god.

And I came here . . . here where Laius was killed.

I will tell you all that happened.

There were three roads that met where I was traveling. A herald 765 came toward me.

There was a chariot, horses, and a man who looked like the man you described.

He was seated there within it.

The groom—who was leading the horses by the reins—forced 770 me off the road.

The man in the chariot ordered him to do so.

As the man lurched toward me I struck him. I was angry.

The old man saw this and hit me hard with his scepter.

I hit him back! Oh I hit him back! I knocked him out of the chariot.

775 He rolled on the ground. I beat him to death. I killed them all!

Now if that man . . . if Laius were part of my family . . . where then can I hide . . . escape from my misery? The gods must hate me. No citizen here must shelter me. No man must speak to me. I am anathema.[22]

780 I have cursed my pitiful self.

Oh think, oh think . . . I have touched you with these hands . . . these hands that killed your husband!

I am polluted. I am the embodiment of evil.

So I must run . . . run from this city of Thebes.

785 But I can never go home to the land that I love . . . never see Corinth again.

22. anathema (uh NATH uh muh) *adj.* detested or cursed.

I live in terror of killing my father and lying with my mother.
Ah, this was my destiny when I was born. The gods are cruel,
savage in their anger.

790 You gods, pity me. You are all powerful. But let me never see
that day. Oh let me vanish without trace from this earth rather
than know the fate that makes me loathed amongst mankind.

Chorus. We feel your anguish, my lord.
But until you have questioned the survivor, keep your hopes alive.

795 **Oedipus.** My hopes are dying, but they will await the coming of
this shepherd.

Jocasta. What do you expect from him when he comes?

Oedipus. Only this: if his account matches yours, I am cleared.

Jocasta. What was it I said that you find important?

800 **Oedipus.** You used the word "highwaymen." He said that
highwaymen had killed the king.
If he still speaks of several killers, then I was not the murderer.
I was alone.
There was no one else. But if he says there was only one, my
805 guilt is inescapable.

Jocasta. Then take heart. For this is indeed what he said. He
cannot change his tune now.
I heard it from his mouth as did the rest of Thebes.
But even if his story were to change, he cannot make the death
810 of Laius conform with the oracle.
Apollo said explicitly that Laius would die at the hands of my son.
But he, poor child, never shed any blood. He died too soon.
No, from now on I will give not a second's thought to the words
of the oracles.

815 **Oedipus.** You may indeed be right. But send for the shepherd
right away.

Jocasta. It is as good as done. Let us go in. I wish only to
please you.

(exit Oedipus and Jocasta)

Comprehension Check

Complete the following items after you finish your first read.

1. As the play opens, what disaster has befallen Thebes?

2. How did Oedipus become king of Thebes?

3. According to the Oracle, what is the solution to the problems Thebes faces?

4. What does Oedipus accuse Creon of doing?

5. 🗐 **Notebook** Confirm your understanding of the text by writing a summary.

- -

Research

Research to Clarify Choose at least one unfamiliar detail from the text. Briefly research that detail. In what way does the information you learned shed light on an aspect of the play?

Research to Explore Research some of the places mentioned in the play (Corinth, Cithaeron, Thebes, etc.). You may want to share what you learn with the class.

Close Read the Text

Reread lines 347–351 in the argument between Teiresias and Oedipus. Mark the nouns. What word is repeated? What is the effect of that repetition?

OEDIPUS THE KING, PART I

Analyze the Text

CITE TEXTUAL EVIDENCE to support your answers.

 **Notebook** Respond to these questions.

1. (a) Why does Oedipus feel he is the person most affected by the plague that has stricken Thebes? (b) **Interpret** How does this fact affect Oedipus' reception of Creon when Creon returns from Apollo's oracle?

2. (a) **Interpret** Why have the leaders of Thebes failed to pursue Laius' killers? (b) **Connect** How does this fact strengthen Oedipus' belief that he can find the murderers? (c) **Analyze** Why does the chorus appeal to Apollo after Oedipus promises to avenge Laius?

3. (a) **Classify** Which details in Teiresias' speech in lines 385–406 refer to darkness, vision, and insight? (b) **Compare and Contrast** At the end of Part I, in what different ways are Oedipus and Teiresias both blind? In what ways can both see?

4. (a) In lines 665–683, what reasons does Jocasta give for not having faith in prophecy? (b) **Compare and Contrast** At this point in the play, what do both Jocasta and Oedipus seem to believe about their abilities to control their own fates? Explain.

LANGUAGE DEVELOPMENT

Concept Vocabulary

proclamation	decree	edicts

 WORD NETWORK

Add words related to blindness and sight from the text to your Word Network.

Why These Words? The three concept vocabulary words relate to official pronouncements. Find other words in Part I that relate to this concept.

Practice

 **Notebook** To demonstrate your understanding of the concept vocabulary words, write a definition for each one. Then, list one or two synonyms for each word. Refer to a dictionary or a thesaurus as needed.

Word Study

 **Notebook** **Latin Root: -dict-** The word *edicts* is formed from the Latin root -*dict*-, meaning "say" or "speak."

Record three other words that are formed from the root -*dict*-. Write a definition for each word. Then, explain how the root -*dict*- contributes to each word's meaning.

OEDIPUS THE KING, PART I

Analyze Craft and Structure

Structure of Greek Plays Greek plays are **verse drama**, in which the dialogue takes the form of poetry. Greek tragedies follow a consistent format. Note that some modern translations deviate from strict classical form, observing some—but not all—these conventions.

- They open with a **prologue** that presents background information and describes the conflict.

- The **chorus**, a group of performers who speak and move together as they comment on the play, then enters and performs a **parados**, or opening song.

- The parados is followed by the first scene, which is called an **episode** and contains dialogue among characters.

- Additional songs, called **odes**, are presented at the end of each scene. They serve a function similar to that of the curtain coming down at the ends of scenes in modern theatrical productions.

- Before the final scene, the chorus performs a **paean,** or song of thanksgiving, to Dionysus, the Greek god at whose festivals classical drama originated.

- The tragedy concludes with an **exodos**, or final scene.

Practice

CITE TEXTUAL EVIDENCE to support your answers.

🖵 **Notebook** Respond to these questions.

1. Scan or reread Part I of *Oedipus the King*. Then, use the chart to record information that is provided or action that takes place in each section listed.

SECTION OF PLAY	INFORMATION AND/OR ACTION
prologue, lines 1–143	
parados, lines 144–199	
episode, lines 200–443	
ode, lines 444–478	

2. In addition to singing odes, the chorus may interact with the characters. (a) Reread lines 479–596. How does the chorus intervene in the dialogue between Oedipus and Creon? (b) Review the remainder of the scene that concludes Part I. What is different about the chorus's words after Jocasta arrives? (c) In what ways does the chorus heighten the dramatic tension?

Author's Style

The Greek Chorus The chorus (a group of performers who speak and move together as they comment on the play) is central to Greek drama. Between each scene or episode of dialogue among characters, the chorus provides key background information and commentary on the action. The chorus's recitals, or odes, often divide into two parts—a **strophe** and an answering **antistrophe**.

- During the strophe, the chorus expresses an initial position on the play's action. The chorus sings while twisting and dancing from right to left.
- During the antistrophe, the chorus responds to the message of the strophe while moving in the opposite direction.
- Some odes have a concluding stanza, or **epode**, when the chorus stands still.
- To help propel the plot, the chorus leader, or **choragos** (also spelled *choragus*), often exchanges thoughts with the rest of the chorus, as well as with the actors. In ancient Greece, the choragos was often a patron who helped pay the costs of producing a play.

Read It

Reread the ode that begins with line 444. Then, answer the questions.

1. Record your answers in the chart. **(a)** Which lines make up the strophe? Which lines make up the antistrophe? **(b)** In the strophe, what main idea does the chorus express about the king's killer? **(c)** What main idea does the chorus express in the antistrophe?

STROPHE	ANTISTROPHE
Lines:	Lines:
Main Idea:	Main Idea:

2. In which character does the chorus decide to put its faith—Oedipus or Teiresias? Why?

Write It

📓 **Notebook** Write a paragraph in which you describe how this ode offers "commentary" on the action of the play.

📝 EVIDENCE LOG

Before moving on to a new selection, go to your Evidence Log and record what you learned from *Oedipus the King,* Part I.

Playwright

Sophocles

Oedipus the King, Part II

Concept Vocabulary

You will encounter the following words as you read *Oedipus the King*, Part II. Before reading, note how familiar you are with each word. Then, rank the words in order from most familiar (1) to least familiar (3).

WORD	YOUR RANKING
oracles	
prophecy	
inexorable	

After completing the first read, come back to the concept vocabulary and review your rankings. Mark changes to your original rankings as needed.

First Read DRAMA

Apply these strategies as you conduct your first read. You will have an opportunity to complete the close-read notes after your first read.

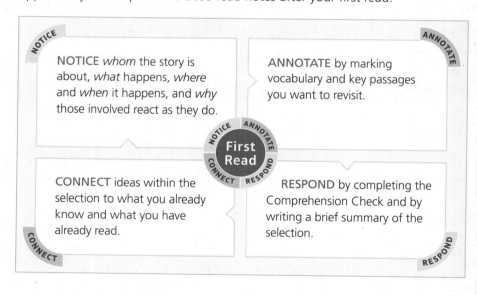

NOTICE *whom* the story is about, *what* happens, *where* and *when* it happens, and *why* those involved react as they do.

ANNOTATE by marking vocabulary and key passages you want to revisit.

CONNECT ideas within the selection to what you already know and what you have already read.

RESPOND by completing the Comprehension Check and by writing a brief summary of the selection.

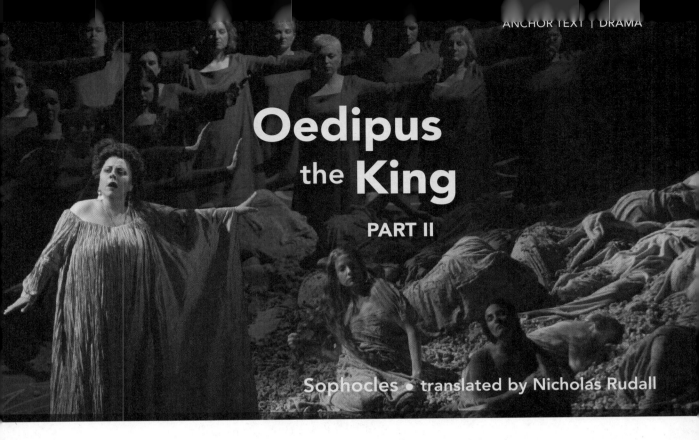

Oedipus the King

PART II

Sophocles • translated by Nicholas Rudall

Chorus. Let me walk humble in the paths of righteousness.
Let my life be simple and full of awe for things divine.
Let my tongue be free of arrogance.
Let me never seek too much.
5 For the gods live high in their imperial grace.
We alone are frail and mortal.
They live forever. Oblivion[1] will not cloud
Their everlasting power.
A tyrant is born from a womb of arrogance.
10 And insolence grows fat,
Fed by empty riches.
He scales the dizzying cliffs and grasps the crown.
But then his foot falters, falters,
And he will fall, fall and lie crumpled in the dust.
15 May the gods protect the man
Who loves his country,
Burns with the flame
Of his love for the state.

God is my eternal hope.
20 In god I trust. In god I wait for death.

But the proud man,
The man who spits in the face of justice,
The man who scorns the altars of the gods,
That man will lose his empty dreams in the whirlwind of god's fire.
25 Greed will cut him down.

NOTES

1. **Oblivion** (uh BLIHV ee uhn) *n.* condition of being entirely forgotten, especially in death.

CLOSE READ

ANNOTATE: In lines 1–14, mark details related to humility. Mark other details related to excessive pride.

QUESTION: Why does the playwright include these reminders of divine power and human frailty?

CONCLUDE: How do the concepts presented in this speech set up a context for the rest of the play's action?

2. **Elis** (EE lihs) renowned Greek city-state.

3. **Olympus** (uh LIHM puhs) Greek mountain believed to be the throne of the gods and the location of their palaces.

For he will never freely touch the divine
With hands that are sullied with money.
God's lightning will strike,
Strike the arrogant, strike the sinner.

30 In cities where there is no chorus
That will sing god's truth,
Fools will ever honor the wicked.

No more will I seek the mystery
Buried in the earth's deep core.

35 No more will I respect Delphi, Elis,[2] or Olympus[3]
If god's truth is not fulfilled on earth.

O Zeus, reveal your power!
O king, O lord of all, if that be true,
Reveal your eternal power to us!

40 The prophecies of Laius wither
And they die. Apollo is forsaken.
Faith and reverence are no more.

(enter Jocasta)

Jocasta. My lords of Thebes, I have come here with wreaths and incense to visit the shrines of the gods.

45 Oedipus is deeply troubled, haunted by images of terror.
He will not trust his reason as before. The new prophecies frighten him as did the old.
He listens to anyone who speaks of disaster for our house.
Nothing I say will comfort him, and so I turn to you, Lord

50 Apollo, since you are closest to our grief.
I bring my prayers and petitions to you. Grant us deliverance from this curse.
We are like sailors in a storm when they see their helmsman's[4] terror.

55 Oh help us, lord!

(enter Messenger)

Messenger. Friends, can you direct me to the palace of the king, or better yet to the king himself?

Chorus. This is his palace. The king is inside. This is his wife, the mother of his children.

60 **Messenger.** May the gods bless her and all her house and bring happiness to everyone.

Jocasta. Greetings to you! Your kind words deserve a kind reply. Why have you come? What is your news?

Messenger. It is good both for the king and the royal house.

65 **Jocasta.** Then speak. Who sent you?

Messenger. I come from Corinth. The words I bring may bring you joy . . . though they are not without some pain.

Jocasta. What is it? How can there be both joy and pain?

Messenger. The people of Corinth have resolved to make
70 Oedipus their king.

Jocasta. Is not the aged Polybus still king?

Messenger. No, my lady, he is dead and in his grave.

Jocasta. The father of Oedipus is dead?

Messenger. If I tell a lie may I die myself.

75 **Jocasta.** Quick! Take this news to my lord.
You **oracles** of the gods, where are you now?
Oedipus spent his life running from his father. He was in terror
that he would kill him.
And now not his son's hand but the hand of fate has cut him down.

(enter Oedipus)

80 **Oedipus.** My queen, Jocasta, why have you summoned me from
the palace?

Jocasta. Hear this man, and as he speaks think of what has
become of the solemn prophecies!

Oedipus. Who is he? What is his news?

85 **Jocasta.** He has come from Corinth, and his news is this: Your
father, Polybus, is dead.

Oedipus. What? Let me hear it, stranger, from your mouth.

Messenger. It cannot be said more plainly. Polybus is dead.

Oedipus. Did he die by treachery or from disease?

90 **Messenger.** It takes so little to send an old man to his rest.

Oedipus. Then the poor man died of sickness.

Messenger. Yes. He had lived a long life.

Oedipus. Ha! Oh my wife, where are the oracles now?
Why believe in the screams of whirling birds?
95 The Delphic god[5] had sworn that I would kill my father.
But he is dead and in his grave! And here I stand, I never drew
my sword.
Perhaps they might argue that he died of grief for his long
absent son.
100 But only in that sense could I have killed him. But no . . . the
oracles are dead.
Like Polybus, their words are turned to dust.

Jocasta. Did I not say that this is how it would be?

Oedipus. You did. But my own fear betrayed me.

105 **Jocasta.** Then never think on it again!

Oedipus. But yet . . . I am afraid of my mother's bed.

Jocasta. You are a mere man . . . the plaything of fate. You
cannot know the future.

NOTES

oracles (AWR uh kuhlz)
n. people who deliver
messages from the gods

5. **Delphic** (DEHL fihk) **god** Apollo,
whose temple was in the
Greek city of Delphi.

So why be afraid? Live your life from day to day. Have no more
110 cares.
Do not fear this marriage with your mother.
How many times have men lain with their mother in their dreams!
If you have sense in that head of yours, you will not be troubled
by such thoughts.

115 **Oedipus.** I want to be as confident as you. But my mother is still
alive.
And so I harbor still some fear.

Jocasta. But your father's death is filled with light.

Oedipus. Yes. But I am afraid of the living.

120 **Messenger.** Who is this woman that you fear?

Oedipus. Merope, Polybus's wife.

Messenger. Why should you fear her?

Oedipus. An oracle from the gods filled with terror.

Messenger. It is a secret or may a stranger hear of it?

125 **Oedipus.** It is no secret.
Apollo once prophesied that I would lie with my own mother
and with these hands kill my father.
That is why for all these years I have stayed away from Corinth.
I traveled far but always longed to see my parents' faces.

130 **Messenger.** This was the fear that turned you into an exile?

Oedipus. And the fear of killing my own father.

Messenger. Well, since I came to bring you pleasure, why
should I not free you from this fear?

Oedipus. You would be well rewarded.

135 **Messenger.** I confess I hoped to profit when you returned to
Corinth.

Oedipus. I will never go near my parents' home.

Messenger. Then, my son, you do not know what you are doing.

Oedipus. How so, old man? Tell me all you know.

140 **Messenger.** Is this why you are afraid to come home?

Oedipus. Yes. In case the word of the gods comes true.

Messenger. You are afraid that you will be cursed through your
parents?

Oedipus. I fear it now—I have feared it always.

145 **Messenger.** My son, your fears are baseless.

Oedipus. How baseless?

Messenger. Polybus had no blood ties to you.

Oedipus. Are you saying that Polybus was not my father?

Messenger. No more your father than I am.

CLOSE READ
ANNOTATE: Mark the
questions in lines 138–153.

QUESTION: Why does the
playwright include so many
questions in this section of
dialogue?

CONCLUDE: What is the
effect of this dialogue,
especially in reflecting
Oedipus' perspective?

150 **Oedipus.** But you are nothing to me.

Messenger. Nor was he.

Oedipus. Why then did he call me his son?

Messenger. Long ago I gave you to him as a gift.

Oedipus. What! But he loved me like a son.

155 **Messenger.** He had no children of his own. You touched his heart.

Oedipus. Was I a foundling[6] . . . did you buy me?

Messenger. I found you in the woods of Cithaeron.

Oedipus. What were you doing there?

Messenger. I was a shepherd. I tended the mountain flocks.

160 **Oedipus.** A wandering shepherd . . . a hired hand?

Messenger. Yes—but the man who saved your life.

Oedipus. Saved my life? How? From what?

Messenger. Your ankles will tell the story.

Oedipus. Why remind me of my childhood pain?

165 **Messenger.** I removed the pin that bolted your feet[7] together.

Oedipus. Yes . . . from my earliest memory I have had that mark.

Messenger. That is why you were given your name.

Oedipus. Who did it? My father, my mother? Tell me.

Messenger. I do not know. The man who gave you to me may
170 know more.

Oedipus. I thought it was you who had found me.

Messenger. No, another shepherd gave you to me.

Oedipus. Who was he? Can you tell me who he was?

Messenger. He was one of Laius's household.

175 **Oedipus.** The man who was once the king?

Messenger. Yes. He was a herdsman for King Laius.

Oedipus. Do you know if he is still alive?

Messenger. These Thebans here could better answer that.

Oedipus. Does any one of you know this shepherd?
180 Have you seen him in the fields or in the city? Answer me
right away.
It is time to clear this matter up.

Chorus. I think he is talking about the very man that we have
sent for.
185 But Queen Jocasta would know better than I.

Oedipus. Do you know this man we sent for? Is this the man the
stranger speaks of?

Jocasta. What man? Why does it matter? Leave it alone.

NOTES

6. **foundling** (FOWND lihng)
n. baby or small child
found deserted.

7. **pin that bolted your feet**
Laius pierced his baby's
feet and put a metal pin
through them before
sending him to be left
on a mountainside to
die. The name *Oedipus*
means "swollen foot."

It is a waste of time to worry about such trivial things.

190 **Oedipus.** Trivial? I cannot find out the secret of my birth!

Jocasta. If you care for your life . . . stop now. No more! My pain is hard enough.

Oedipus. You need not worry.
Even if my mother were a slave and the daughter of slaves, my
195 baseness[8] cannot touch you.

Jocasta. Oh listen to me. I am begging you. Seek no further.

Oedipus. I must go on. I must find the truth.

Jocasta. I am only thinking of your own good.

Oedipus. This breaks my patience!

200 **Jocasta.** May you never learn who you are!

Oedipus. Bring the man to me. Let her ever boast of her royal name.

Jocasta. I pity you. Pity is the only word I know. The rest is nothing.

(exit Jocasta)

205 **Chorus.** Oedipus, why has the queen left in such anguish? I am afraid of this silence.
There is something terrifying hanging over us.

Oedipus. Let it hang there. I have made up my mind.
I will find out who my parents were even if they were slaves.
210 Perhaps, with her woman's pride, the queen scorns my parentage.
But I cannot be dishonored. Fortune is my mother.
As the moons change, so do my fortunes.
If I am her child, why should I fear to trace my birth.
I am who I am.

215 **Chorus.** If I am a prophet, if wisdom lives in me,
Then in all reverence I proclaim that you,
Mount Cithaeron—you are the nurse and mother
Of our king!
Before the next full moon we will worship you,
220 Cithaeron! We will dance in your honor,
Protector of our royal house.
Apollo, Lord, join in the dance!

Who gave birth to you, child?
Who of the immortals was your mother?
225 Pan, roaming god of the hills . . . was he your father?
Or Apollo who haunts the woodland meadows?
Or was it Hermes of Cylene?[9] Or Dionysus
Who lives among the mountain peaks?
Did he take you from the arms of one
230 Of his dancing worshipers
And smile the smile of a god?

---

8. **baseness** (BAYS nihs) *n.* inferiority; lowness.

9. **Hermes** (HUR meez) **of Cylene** Greek god who acted as the messenger of the gods to humanity.

Oedipus, beginning to see the truth

(enter Shepherd and Servants)

Oedipus. You elders of Thebes, though I have never seen him, I would guess that this is the man we have been waiting for. His age matches well with the messenger there.

235 And I recognize the men who are bringing him as my servants. But you perhaps have seen him before and know him. I yield to you.

Chorus. I recognize him. He is one of Laius's servants . . . a simple herdsman but honest.

240 **Oedipus.** Let me ask you . . . you from Corinth . . . is this the man you meant?

Messenger. It is.

Oedipus. Now . . . old man . . . look into my eyes and answer me all that I ask.

245 Were you once a servant here?

Shepherd. I was. A slave . . . not bought but born on the estate.

Oedipus. What was your occupation . . . your livelihood?

Shepherd. For the best part of my life I tended sheep.

Oedipus. What pastures did you use the most?

250 **Shepherd.** Cithaeron and neighboring hills.

Oedipus. There you must have known this man.

Shepherd. Why would I . . . Which man??

Oedipus. This man here . . . since you met him years ago.

Shepherd. Offhand I . . . I can't remember.

255 **Messenger.** My king, I'm not surprised . . . but I will awaken his memory.
I'm sure he remembers when we both herded our flocks on Cithaeron.
He had two flocks, I one. Three long summers we were friends.
260 Then when winter came I drove my flock home, and he drove his to Laius's folds.
Isn't that what happened?

Shepherd. It was a long time ago, but that is all true.

Messenger. Then do you remember giving me a child to bring
265 up as my own?

Shepherd. Why do you ask me this question?

Messenger. Because this man who stands before you was that child.

Shepherd. Damnation take you! Hold your tongue!

270 **Oedipus.** Old man! Do not curse him.
What *you* said deserved our displeasure far more than he.

CLOSE READ

ANNOTATE: In lines 251–266, mark the questions the Shepherd asks.

QUESTION: What do the questions suggest about the Shepherd's knowledge and fears?

CONCLUDE: What is the effect of these questions?

Shepherd. Oh my king . . . what did I say that was wrong?

Oedipus. You refused to answer about the child.

Shepherd. He made no sense!!! He talks like a fool.

275 **Oedipus.** If you won't do it voluntarily, I'll *make* you talk.

Shepherd. I beg you . . . do not treat an old man like this.

Oedipus. Arrest this man. Seize him and put him in irons.

Shepherd. Alas . . . what have I done? What is it you want to know?

280 **Oedipus.** Did you give this man the child?

Shepherd. I did. And I wish I had died that very day.

Oedipus. And die you will unless you tell the truth.

Shepherd. If I tell the truth, I lose twice over.

Oedipus. This wicked man is still being evasive.

285 **Shepherd.** *No!* I have confessed I gave him the child a long time ago.

Oedipus. Whose child was it? Was it yours, or was it given to you?

Shepherd. Not mine . . . it was given to me.

Oedipus. Which of our citizens gave it, and from what family?

290 **Shepherd.** Oh for god's sake, master, ask no more!

Oedipus. If I have to question you again . . . you are finished.

Shepherd. Well then . . . it was a child of the house Laius.

Oedipus. Was he born of a slave or one of Laius's own children?

Shepherd. *Ahhh,* I stand upon the razor's edge. What must I say?

295 **Oedipus.** What must I hear? . . . But hear I must.

Shepherd. Know that the . . . the child . . . so people said . . . was his.
But the lady in the palace, your wife, she could tell you best.

Oedipus. What? She . . . she gave it to you?

300 **Shepherd.** My king, she did.

Oedipus. For what reason?

Shepherd. To put it to death.

Oedipus. The child's own mother?

Shepherd. She was afraid of a terrible **prophecy**.

305 **Oedipus.** What prophecy?

Shepherd. It was said that he would kill his father.

Oedipus. Did you then give it to this old man?

Shepherd. I felt such pity for the child. I thought he'd take it to the safety of the country.

310 But he saved it for the worst of griefs.

prophecy (PROF uh see) *n.* prediction about the future

For if you are indeed who this man says . . . god have mercy on you.
You were born into a life of misery.

Oedipus. Aaah, all has come to pass. All is true!
315 Light of the sun, let me never look on you again. I stand here, the most cursed of men.
Cursed in my birth. Cursed in an incestuous marriage.
Cursed in the murder of my father.

(exit Oedipus)

Chorus. Oh you generations of men,
320 Your life is as nothing.
A man is bathed in Fortune's light
And then he fades, fades, and fades into the dark.
Your fate I pity, Oedipus, your sad fall,
Your birth, your very birth into this world.

325 Oh Zeus! His was the greatest mind of all.
He defeated the riddling sharp-clawed Sphinx
And won glory, happiness, and power.
He saved us, was our tower and strength.
We made him our lord, our King of Thebes.

10. abased (uh BAYST) *adj.* brought down or lowered.

330 Now who is more abased,[10] more lost than he?
Whose life more desolate, whose grief more deep?
Oh Oedipus! In the same safe bed
You were both son and father!
How could the palace walls have so long kept their silence?

335 Time, that sees all things, has found you Oedipus,
Condemned the incest and the guilt.
Oh son of Laius! I wish that I had never
Looked on you. On you I pour my grief
As on the dead. From you I found new life.
340 In you I close my eyes in grief.

(enter Second Messenger)

Second Messenger. Oh you mighty lords of Thebes!
Oh! What you must now hear, now see!
Oh! How you will mourn if still you respect this house of Labdacus.[11]

11. house of Labdacus (LAB duh kuhs) the family that includes Laius, Jocasta, and their descendants, including Oedipus and his children.

345 No river could wash the bloodstains from this house. What now lies dark will soon be brought to light—anguish inflicted—all with full intent! Self-inflicted wounds cut deepest of all.

Chorus. Our past pains were deep enough. What more can you bring?

350 **Second Messenger.** My story is quickly told and quickly heard. Our queen Jocasta is dead.

Chorus. Alas! Poor lady, how did she die?

Second Messenger. By her own hand. I was not there to see the horror taking place.

355　But I will tell you, as best I can, of the wretched lady's suffering.
She ran into the forecourt of the palace. She was in a frenzy.
Then she raced towards her bridal chamber. She was tearing her hair with both hands.
Once she was in the room, she slammed the huge doors shut.

360　Laius! Oh Laius! she cried, called on her husband dead so long ago. She cast her mind upon the child that he had fathered . . . the child that had cut him down . . . the child who lay with his own mother and fathered the most monstrous brood. She cursed the bed that had fathered a husband by a husband and children
365　by a child.
What happened after that I cannot tell. For Oedipus burst in on us screaming loud.
All of us fixed our gaze upon him as he ran about in all directions.
We did not witness the last agony of her life.

370　For he ran up to us and demanded a sword, called on the wife that was no wife . . . the mother of his children and of his cursed self.
Some god must have entered him then in his madness.
It surely was no mortal . . . not one of us . . .

375　With a terrifying scream . . . as though someone called him from the other side . . . he hurled himself against the doors of her chamber.
The hinges buckled, snapped—and he rushed inside. That's when we saw her.

380　She was hanging there with a noose around her neck.
When he saw her he roared like a mad man and unhooked the noose.
Her poor body lay there on the ground and then, oh then . . . oh the terror . . . he tore the brooches from her robe and raised
385　them and plunged them into the sockets of his eyes.
He shouted aloud, "No longer shall these eyes see such agony as this!
No longer see the things that I have done . . . the things that I have suffered. Those whom you should never have seen will
390　now be shrouded in darkness, nor will you know those whom you love." And as he cried these words . . . not once but many times . . . he stabbed his eyes until the blood ran down his cheeks and matted his beard . . . Aahhh, not drop by drop but in a stream of black rain.
395　This is the horror that has struck them both, man and wife alike.
Till now this house was blessed with fortune. But from this day—
Grief, ruin, death, and shame . . . all ills that have a name . . . all are theirs.

Chorus. Is there no respite from his pain?

400 **Second Messenger.** He cries aloud to unlock the doors and let all Thebes look upon him—his father's killer—his mother's . . . I cannot speak the word. He swears that he will exile himself from this land.

He will not stay to bring upon the house the curse he himself
405 pronounced.

But his strength has left him. He has no one to guide him.

The torture that he suffers is more than any man can bear.

He will show himself to you. Even now they are opening the palace gates.

410 And you will see a sight that would provoke his bitterest enemy to tears.

Chorus. Oh pitiful, pitiful!! Never have these eyes seen such a terrible sight.

Sir, what madness descended on you?

415 What god has cursed you with this ungodly fate . . . you who were the most blessed of men?

Oh wretched, wretched Oedipus, I cannot look upon you.

Though I yearn to question and to learn, I must turn my eyes away in horror.

(enter Oedipus)

420 **Oedipus.** Ahhhh. Ahhhhhh. Pity me, pity me!

Where upon this earth am I to go in my pain?

Where will my voice be carried on the wind?

Oh god, where will it end?

Chorus. A place too terrible to tell, too dark to see.

425 **Oedipus.** Yes, even now the dark holds me in its grip.

Inexorable, unspeakable, eternal darkness.

The pain . . . yet again the pain. I am racked with spasms, tormented by memory.

Chorus. The past weighs heavy on the present.

430 **Oedipus.** My true and constant friend!

You are still beside me. You do not forget me nor spurn my blindness.

In my private dark I still know your voice.

Chorus. You have done terrible things. But why did you put out
435 your eyes?

What demon set you on?

Oedipus. It was Apollo, my friends, Apollo.

He did this to me. He buried me in this pain.

But it was this hand, no other's, that struck my eyes.

440 For why should I have eyes when there is nothing that I yearn to see?

Chorus. It is all that you say. It is true.

inexorable (ihn EHK suhr uh buhl) *adj.* impossible to prevent or stop

Oedipus. What could I look on to delight my heart?
What hear or touch to bring me joy?
445 Now take me from this place!
My friends, do not delay.
I am, of all men, the most accursed, most hated by the gods.

Chorus. I hear the depths of your despair but wish I had never
looked upon your face.

450 **Oedipus.** I curse the man who pulled the bolt from my feet.
He saved my life but should have left me on the hills to die.
This heavy grief would not now lie upon me and those I love.

Chorus. I share your sad wish.

Oedipus. Then I would never have killed my father
455 Nor married the woman who gave me birth.
But now my name will live on as the child unholy,
The child who defiled his mother's womb.
Was ever man more doomed than Oedipus?

Chorus. You have chosen a painful path.
460 It were better to be no more than live in darkness.

Oedipus. No! What I have done is right. You cannot change
my mind.
If I had eyes . . . how could I look upon my father down below?
How look upon my mother? I have sinned against them both.
465 To hang myself would not wash clean that sin.
You might say that the sight of children warms the heart.
But children born as mine were born?
My heart could not feel joy to look on them . . . nor on the walls
and temple statues of great Thebes.
470 No! Once I was its king—now I am nothing. I have condemned
myself to this my fate.
I have put the brand of murderer upon my own head.
How could I have looked my people in the face?
No . . . if I had known how to stop the spring of listening, I
475 would have done so.
I would have made this body a prison bereft of sight and sound.
Happiness lives only where sorrow cannot reach.
Cithaeron, why did you keep me safe . . . why did you not kill me?
Then I would never have had to bare my shame unto the world.
480 Polybus! Corinth! Oh my home!
For that is what I called you then . . . home of my ancestors,
home to my infant innocence.
Now all is turned to filth and evil.
Oh place where three roads meet, oh hidden pathway of doom!
485 You drank my blood!
Drank the blood that these hands shed . . . my father's blood!
You were the silent witnesses to my crime. You drove me here to
save the city.

CLOSE READ
ANNOTATE: In lines 476–491,
mark the places that Oedipus
addresses directly.

QUESTION: Why would the
playwright have Oedipus speak
to these places instead of to the
chorus?

CONCLUDE: What is the effect
of this use of direct address?

The blinded Oedipus

Oh marriage, fatal marriage . . . you gave me birth, and having
490 spawned you sowed the seed again and placed upon this earth
for all to see the mingled blood of fathers, brothers, children,
brides, wives, and mothers.
These horrors are the worst that mankind can ever know! Take
me then . . . for to speak of them is living death . . . Take me from
495 here with all speed—I beg you by the gods. Hide me in the
earth. Kill me.
Hurl me to the bottom of the sea . . . anywhere so long as you
never see my face again.
Come to me. Do not fear to touch this wretched body. Please . . .
500 do not be afraid.
I must bear the burden of my guilt alone.

(enter Creon)

Chorus. Here is Creon. He alone can grant your wishes.
He is now sole ruler and guardian of the state.

Oedipus. Ahh! what words can I find to speak? Why should he
505 trust me?
I have treated him like a bitter enemy.

Creon. I have not come here to mock you, Oedipus, nor to
reproach you for what happened in the past.
(he speaks to the Chorus) You should feel nothing but shame.
If you have no sense of human decency, at least show your
510 respect for the Sun, the god that gives us light and gives us life.
Do not let this man stand here when the heavens and the earth
cannot bear the sight of him.
Take him to the palace. Only his family should see the pain.

Oedipus. Hear me . . . please, Creon. You are here, and it fills
515 my heart with hope.
You are so noble—I so low. I ask of you one thing . . . not for me
but for you.

Creon. What is it?

Oedipus. Send me into exile now!
520 Put me in some desert where I will never again hear a
human voice.

Creon. This I had already decided. But first I had to consult
the god.

Oedipus. The decision was made . . . death to the father-killer,
525 the murderer. I am he.

Creon. Yes, that is what Apollo decreed.
But now, in our sudden present grief, we should consult him again.

Oedipus. How can you ask him about such a man as I?

Creon. I can. For even you would believe him now.

530 **Oedipus.** Yes. I am humbled now. But I ask you this one thing:

Grace the woman who lies within with a burial that only you can command.

You are her brother, touch her with your love.

For me . . . Oh never let this city—this Thebes—be cursed with
535 my living body.

No! Let me live in the hills . . . on Cithaeron. For that is where my name will ever live.

Cithaeron was to be my tomb. My father and my mother wished to bury me there.

540 Now let me find my death upon her slopes. For that is what they wished.

This much I know . . . disease will not cut me down, nor any common accident.

I was saved from death so I might die in grief beyond all mortal
545 knowing.

So be it. I care no longer how fate treats me.

But my children. Oh Creon . . . for my sons I have less concern. They are men, and they will survive.

But my daughters . . . two sweet innocents . . . ohhhh . . .
550 I can see them now . . . stealing a little of my food, sipping my wine. Laughing.

Oh look after them.

And one last request . . . let me hold them in my arms once more. Let me touch them and let me weep.
555 Oh Creon, let your noble heart break.

I have no eyes. But I have hands. Let me touch them, let me feel what once I saw.

(enter Antigone and Ismene)

Oedipus. I have no words! I touch you . . . I touch you my pretty ones.
560 I hear your tears. Can this be . . . can Creon have given you to me?

Creon. I have. I know how much you loved them.

Oedipus. God bless you . . . may the fates shine warm upon you for your kindness.

Not like me! Oh my children, where are you? Let me take you in
565 my arms.

I am your brother and your father.

Ahh, these hands that touch you now took the light from my eyes. These hands touched the mother that was both yours and mine!

I cannot see you, but my eyes still weep. My life to come will be
570 a path of pain.

For you there will be only grief.

At festivals, at feasts you will skulk in the shadows. You will burst into sudden tears. And when you are ready to marry—oh god, no man will woo you, no man will brook the shame. For
575 this shame will cling forever to our house. It will never die.

Their father killed his father, spewed the seed where he himself

< Oedipus, played by the French tragic actor Jean Mounet-Sully, with his daughters, Antigone and Ismene.

found life, and was the father of these children here . . . That is what they will say.

So no one will marry you . . . no one . . . you will be alone forever.

580 Creon, I turn to you now. You must be their father.

We who gave them life are dead. They are your family. . . .

Do not let them wander forever.

They are young. Pity them. Let them live in peace as I wander on the earth.

585 You must be their father now.

Do not let them be orphans of the dark . . . unmarried, beggar children. Oh pity them.

They are so young. And now they have nothing. Oh touch my hand, Lord Creon.

590 Swear pity.

My children, my heart is breaking.

Give me your word, Creon.

Oh my children, I wanted to talk to you.

But you are so young . . . so young.

595 My last words . . . find a home, find happiness, and be more fortunate than I.

Creon. Weep no more . . . go inside.

Oedipus. I will—but the pain lies heavy.

Creon. Weep no more. Time comes. Time comes.

600 **Oedipus.** I go but I have a last request.

Creon. Tell me.

Oedipus. Exile me, oh send me from this land!

Creon. That is what the gods will choose—not I.

Oedipus. But the gods loathe my very being!

605 **Creon.** Then they will grant your wish.

Oedipus. Take me from this place. I am ready.

Creon. Come. But you must let your children go.

Oedipus. Ohhhh, do not take my children from me!!!

Creon. You have nothing now. The power that made you great
610 was your destruction.

Chorus. Look on this man, you citizens of Thebes. . . . Mankind look hard.
This is and was Oedipus.
The man who defeated the Sphinx . . .
615 The man who became our great and brilliant king,
We envied him, we loved him, we admired him.
Now he is drowned in a sea of eternal pain.
Count no man happy till he dies.
Then, free from pain and sorrow—he may lie in peace.

MEDIA CONNECTION

Oedipus the King

💬 **Discuss It** How does listening to this audio performance, by L. A. Theatre Works, enhance your understanding of the characters and events featured in *Oedipus the King*?

Write your response before sharing your ideas.

Comprehension Check

Complete the following items after you finish your first read.

1. What news does the messenger bring Oedipus from Corinth?

2. What fear drove Jocasta to give her child to the shepherd?

3. What is the literal meaning of Oedipus' name? How does this name connect him to his past?

4. Why does Oedipus curse the man who saved him when he was an infant?

5. What injury does Oedipus inflict upon himself after he sees Jocasta dead?

6. 🗐 **Notebook** Confirm your understanding of the text by writing a summary.

- -

RESEARCH

Research to Clarify Choose at least one unfamiliar detail from the text. Briefly research that detail. In what way does the information you learned shed light on an aspect of the play?

Research to Explore Conduct research on the way various artists have portrayed Oedipus over the centuries. You may want to share what you learn with the class.

OEDIPUS THE KING, PART II

🔧 Tool Kit
Close-Read Guide and
Model Annotation

Close Read the Text

1. This model, from lines 146–153, shows two sample annotations, along with questions and conclusions. Close read the passage, and find another detail to annotate. Then, write a question and your conclusion.

> ANNOTATE: Oedipus does not understand what the messenger is saying.
>
> QUESTION: Why is Oedipus so confused?
>
> CONCLUDE: Everything he understands about his life is being challenged.

> ANNOTATE: The messenger turns out to be a person from Oedipus' past.
>
> QUESTION: Why didn't the messenger identify himself earlier?
>
> CONCLUDE: The delay suggests that the messenger is afraid to reveal this information.

Messenger. Polybus had no blood ties to you.
Oedipus. Are you saying that Polybus was not my father?
Messenger. No more your father than I am.
Oedipus. But you are nothing to me.
Messenger. Nor was he.
Oedipus. Why then did he call me his son?
Messenger. Long ago I gave you to him as a gift.

2. For more practice, go back into the play, and complete the close-read notes.

3. Revisit a section of the play you found important during your first read. Read this section closely, and **annotate** what you notice. Ask yourself **questions** such as "Why did the author make this choice?" What can you **conclude**?

Analyze the Text

CITE TEXTUAL EVIDENCE
to support your answers.

📓 **Notebook** Respond to these questions.

1. (a) What facts does Oedipus establish by questioning the old shepherd? (b) **Draw Conclusions** Why might this scene be considered the **climax,** or point of highest tension, in the tragedy? Explain.

2. (a) Why do you think Oedipus continues his investigation despite Jocasta's strong objections? (b) **Extend** What might the playwright be saying about the importance of knowing oneself?

3. (a) At the end of the play, what does Oedipus want Creon to do? (b) **Analyze** Why does Oedipus insist that he should remain blind and living rather than dead? (c) **Make a Judgment** At the end of the play, is Oedipus ennobled by his suffering? Explain.

4. **Essential Question:** *What does it mean to see?* What have you learned about seeing and knowing from reading this play?

Analyze Craft and Structure

Elements of Greek Tragedy In *Poetics*, the Greek philosopher Aristotle describes a **tragedy** as a serious play recounting related events in the life of a renowned and prosperous person who experiences a downfall. The main character, called the **tragic hero** or **protagonist**, undergoes this reversal of fortune as a result of **hamartia**, which is often translated as "a tragic flaw." This flaw may be an innate character weakness. However, it may simply be a terrible mistake, an error in judgment, or the result of incomplete knowledge or ignorance. In addition, the protagonist may face an **antagonist**, a rival character or a force that is in conflict with the protagonist and contributes to his or her downfall.

The events in Greek tragedies came as no surprise to their first audiences. Greek audiences knew the myths on which the plays were based. The result was **dramatic irony**, a contradiction between what a character thinks and what the audience knows to be true. Dramatic irony engages an audience emotionally. Tension and suspense build as the audience waits for the characters to realize the truth. Dramatic irony helps produce the result that Aristotle said defines a tragedy: inspiring fear and pity in the audience.

Practice

CITE TEXTUAL EVIDENCE to support your answers.

📝 **Notebook** **Respond to these questions.**

1. In what ways does Oedipus fit the definition of a tragic hero?

2. Is there an antagonist in the play? If so, who or what is it? Use the chart to explore the possibilities. Then, write a paragraph making an argument for your choice.

	CREON	TEIRESIAS	FATE
Whom or what does Oedipus struggle against most strongly?			
Who or what causes Oedipus the most harm?			
Who or what eventually destroys Oedipus?			

3. How does the dramatic irony of the play build as Oedipus learns about his past?

4. Some scholars have stated that Oedipus' tragic flaw is anger, whereas others suggest it is excessive pride. Do you think Oedipus has a tragic flaw? If so, explain whether you believe it to be anger, excessive pride, or another quality. If you do not think he has a specific tragic flaw, explain your reasoning. Support your answer with text evidence.

OEDIPUS THE KING, PART II

Concept Vocabulary

| oracle | prophecy | inexorable |

Why These Words? These concept vocabulary words relate to predicting and experiencing the future. For example, when the ancient Greeks wanted to know what the gods had planned for them, they consulted an *oracle*, a religious figure who spoke for the gods. In *Oedipus the King,* the Oracle at Delphi issues a *prophecy*, or prediction about the future, that sets the events of the play in motion.

1. How does the concept vocabulary sharpen a reader's understanding of the role that predictions played in Greek culture?

2. What other words from *Oedipus the King* relate to this concept?

WORD NETWORK

Add words related to blindness and sight from the text to your Word Network.

Practice

Notebook The concept words appear in *Oedipus the King,* Part II.

1. Use each concept word in a sentence that demonstrates your understanding of the word's meaning. Then, write a sentence about Oedipus using all three words.

2. Use a dictionary or etymology reference to compare the origins of the words *oracle* and *inexorable*. What do the words have in common?

Word Study

Denotation and Connotation A word's **denotation** is its dictionary meaning, independent of any associations the word may have. Synonyms have nearly identical denotations. A word's **connotation** is the idea or emotion associated with the word. Often, words have positive or negative connotations that affect how people respond to them in both writing and speech. Synonyms often have different connotations. For example, the concept vocabulary word *inexorable* means "impossible to stop or prevent." A synonym would be *unstoppable*. In most contexts, *inexorable* has negative connotations, while *unstoppable* has positive connotations.

1. Using a thesaurus, find other synonyms for *inexorable*. Write down three synonyms that have positive connotations and three that have negative connotations.

2. Choose three of the synonyms you found, and use each one in a separate sentence. Make the context of each sentence fit the connotation of the synonym.

Author's Style

Rhetorical Devices: Anaphora In *Oedipus the King,* the translator uses a variety of rhetorical devices, or patterns of language, to create dramatic effects. One of these rhetorical devices is **anaphora**, the repetition of a word or group of words at the beginning of two or more successive clauses or sentences. This is an ancient literary device that makes longer passages easier to remember, emphasizes key ideas, and adds emotional intensity. For example, consider the effect of anaphora when Oedipus expresses his grief and fear:

> **Oedipus.** <u>Where</u> upon this earth am I to go in my pain?
>
> <u>Where</u> will my voice be carried on the wind?

Read It

Read aloud the passages from Part II of *Oedipus the King* to get a sense of the sound of each example of anaphora. Mark the repeated wording in each passage. Then, note the effect of the anaphora. Consider, for example, how it establishes a rhythm, lends dialogue a certain majesty, emphasizes certain ideas, or creates a combination of these effects.

PASSAGE	EFFECT
Chorus. Let me walk humble in the paths of righteousness. Let my life be simple and full of awe for things divine. Let my tongue be free of arrogance. Let me never seek too much.	
Chorus. The man who spits in the face of justice, The man who scorns the altars of the gods, That man will lose his empty dreams in the whirlwind of god's fire.	
Oedipus. . . . I stand here, the most cursed of men. Cursed in my birth. Cursed in an incestuous marriage. Cursed in the murder of my father.	

Write It

🖉 **Notebook** Write a paragraph in which you describe a scene from *Oedipus the King*. Use anaphora in your paragraph.

OEDIPUS THE KING, PART II

Writing to Sources

Plays differ from other forms of fiction because they are made almost entirely of **dialogue**, the conversation between or among characters. Along with stage directions, dialogue advances the action of the plot and reveals character traits and relationships. In a play, the name of the character who is speaking precedes each passage of dialogue.

Assignment

Write a **dialogue** that might have taken place among members of the Theban community after the events of the play. The characters in the dialogue should explain what they think and feel about the events, including answers to these questions:

- Was Oedipus a good king?
- Does he deserve his punishment?
- What does it mean that Oedipus solved the riddle of the Sphinx but suspected nothing of his own true origins?

Vocabulary Connection Consider including several of the concept vocabulary words in your dialogue.

| oracle | prophecy | inexorable |

Reflect on Your Writing

After you have written your dialogue, answer these questions.

1. How did writing your dialogue help you understand Oedipus' dilemma?

2. What advice would you give to another student writing a dialogue?

3. Why These Words? The words you choose make a difference in your writing. Which words did you specifically choose to add power or clarity to your dialogue?

Speaking and Listening

Assignment

In the audio performance included with Part II of the play, the prophet Teiresias speaks with Oedipus. Listen to the performance, and consider the quality of the production and how well it interprets the text. Then, write a brief **critique** of the performance.

📝 EVIDENCE LOG

Before moving on to a new selection, go to your Evidence Log and record what you learned from *Oedipus the King,* Part II.

1. **Analyze the Performance** As you listen, consider elements of the production listed in the chart. Take notes about your observations. Include specific references and details as evidence.

PRODUCTION ELEMENTS	NOTES
Actors' Delivery: *Do the actors use their voices well? (Consider the tempo, or speed, at which they speak; variations in pitch; clarity of pronunciations; and uses of pauses or silences.)*	
Interpretation of the Text: *Does the production clarify the story, show it in a new way, or obscure it? Do actors' choices emphasize or mute qualities in the characters?*	
Production Values: *Do sound effects and music contribute to the power of the production or distract from it?*	

2. **Write Your Critique** Include a general claim, or statement of your position, on the quality of the production. Then, support your position with references to specific performance elements.

3. **Share and Discuss** When you have finished writing, exchange critiques with a partner, and discuss similarities and differences in your points of view. Then, consider how well you each met the criteria for the assignment. Share your feedback about what worked well, and suggest ways to strengthen any weaknesses. Use the evaluation guide to organize your thoughts.

EVALUATION GUIDE

Rate each statement on a scale of 1 (not demonstrated) to 6 (demonstrated).

☐ 1. The critique demonstrates careful listening and thought.

☐ 2. The critique states a clear claim, or position.

☐ 3. The critique takes into account the actors' deliveries, the interpretation of the text, and the production values.

☐ 4. The critique cites specific examples to support ideas.

WRITING TO SOURCES

• OEDIPUS THE KING, PART I

• OEDIPUS THE KING, PART II

🔧 **Tool Kit**
Student Model of a
Nonfiction Narrative

**ACADEMIC
VOCABULARY**

As you craft your
nonfiction narrative,
consider using some
of the academic
vocabulary you learned
in the beginning of this
unit.

**integrate
delineate
volition
vivid
altercation**

Write a Nonfiction Narrative

You have read *Oedipus the King,* a classic exploration of the explosive power
and dangers of self-knowledge—of seeing oneself and the world truly. Now,
you will use your ideas and reflections on the subject of seeing oneself clearly
to write a nonfiction narrative.

> **Assignment**
>
> Using information you have gathered through reading and your own
> life experiences, consider the differences between how people see
> themselves and how they are perceived by others. Write a **nonfiction
> narrative** about a time when one person's self-perception was unclear or
> incomplete, but someone else saw him or her clearly. Tell a true story that
> suggests an answer to the following question:
>
> > Can we see ourselves as clearly as others see us?

Elements of a Nonfiction Narrative

A **nonfiction narrative** describes a real experience in story form.
A well-written nonfiction narrative has the ability to inform, instruct,
persuade, or entertain.

Effective narrative nonfiction includes storytelling elements like those found
in fiction:

- details that establish a setting, or clear time and place
- a well-developed point of view and descriptions of people
- a problem or situation that is introduced, developed, and resolved
- a clearly delineated sequence of events that make up the action of
  the story
- use of varied narrative techniques to develop experiences, events,
  and/or characters
- a concluding message or reflection on the meaning of the story

Model Nonfiction Narrative For a model of a
well-crafted nonfiction narrative, see the Launch Text,
"Just Six Dots."

Note that nonfiction narratives can take many forms.
You may have read a memoir in which an author
tells a true story about his or her life. Some types
of journalism include the reporter's actions and
viewpoint as part of the story. The Launch Text, "Just
Six Dots," is a biographical account of Louis Braille.
You will have an opportunity to review storytelling
elements as you prepare to write your own nonfiction narrative.

Prewriting/Planning

Choose a Situation to Explore Your nonfiction narrative should relate a true and meaningful story in which someone's self-perception differs from how others see him or her. The event may have been instructive and positive, revealing strengths the person did not know he or she possessed. You may choose to write about yourself, someone you know, or someone you have observed or read about. Jot down some situations.

Situations: _____

_____

_____.

Develop the Situation Think about the people you will describe in your narrative. Consider what the reader needs to know about each person's character, distinguishing traits, and relationships. Then, use both **direct** and **indirect characterization** to provide that information: *Tell* readers what people are like, and *show* readers what people are like through descriptive details and dialogue.

Plan the Sequence of Events Structure your narrative so that individual events build on one another and create a logical sequence. Consider using narrative techniques that add interest. For example, a **flashback** is a scene that interrupts the chronological flow of a story to present an event from the past. A flashback can take the form of a memory, or even a dream. It can provide information that explains a situation in an interesting way. If you choose to use a flashback, make a timeline to clarify the order of events as they occurred in real life. Then, make an outline that includes the flashback and ensures that switches from present to past and back again do not cause confusion.

Gather Evidence Before you draft, collect ideas for descriptions you want to include in your narrative:

- **sensory details**, words that appeal to the senses of sight, smell, taste, touch, and hearing
- words and phrases that express how different people look and speak
- precise language to convey actions and gestures
- natural-sounding dialogue that moves the narrative along

Using vivid details adds interest and depth to your writing. For example, the Launch Text uses sensory details about touch to give Braille's accident a sense of immediacy.

> *He jabbed the sharp tool down, hoping to copy his father's masterful movements and punch the strip with a perfect hole. Instead, the awl slipped and pierced his right eye. The injury and resulting infection left Louis completely blind by age five.*
>
> —"Just Six Dots"

✔ EVIDENCE LOG

Review your Evidence Log and identify key details you may want to cite in your nonfiction narrative.

Drafting

Write With Purpose As the writer, you control the reader's perceptions of the people, places, and events you present. Choose details that address what is most significant for your specific purpose and audience. Keep in mind the special insight or knowledge that you would like to convey to the reader by the end of the narrative.

Adopt a Style Use a natural style, and write in your own voice. Ask yourself: *What attitude toward the subject do I want to express?* Also, use caution when writing dialogue. Because this is nonfiction, any conversation that you attribute to a speaker must have actually taken place.

You may use **first-person point of view**, using pronouns such as *I* and *my* to tell the story from your own perspective. Alternatively, you may attempt **third-person point of view**, which uses pronouns such as *he*, *she*, and *they* to describe all the people in a story from a more objective or neutral viewpoint.

Organize Your Narrative Narratives can be more interesting if they deviate from a strict chronological sequence. Consider pulling in elements that add useful complexity. This might involve describing events that happen at the same time as other events or adding commentary from a later point in time. Think about the story you are telling. Then, use the chart to consider ways you might add interest with a second plot line or commentary.

Meanwhile	Earlier that month	At the same time, in another room
Later, I discovered		

Write a First Draft Refer to your notes as you write a first draft. Remember to use descriptive details to paint word pictures that help readers see settings and people. Once you feel you have told the story vividly and well, reflect on its deeper meaning. Add a conclusion in which you share your reflection with readers.

Add Variety: Sentence Structure

As you draft and revise your narrative, add precision and liveliness to your writing by varying your **sentence structure**. The structure of a sentence is defined by the number of independent and dependent clauses it contains. There are four basic sentence structures: simple, compound, complex, and compound-complex.

- A **simple sentence** consists of a single independent clause.
- A **compound sentence** consists of two or more independent clauses.
- A **complex sentence** consists of one independent clause and one or more dependent clauses.
- A **compound-complex sentence** consists of two or more independent clauses and one or more dependent clauses.

The structure of a sentence conveys specific meaning to your audience. For instance, a compound sentence indicates that the ideas you are expressing are related and of equal importance. In a complex sentence, the subordinating conjunction you choose shows the specific logical relationship between your ideas.

Varying your sentence structure not only improves clarity but also adds interest to your writing. For instance, following a long, richly detailed compound-complex sentence with a short simple sentence may create a sense of urgency, excitement, or conviction.

Read It

The author of the Launch Text makes use of all four sentence structures.

- *Louis would gaze with eager attention as Simon-René Braille transformed unfinished leather into fine harnesses for horses.* (complex)
- *The crowd was amazed, and some suspected a trick.* (compound)
- *He worried that once blind people could read there would be no need for sighted teachers, so he banned the use of braille.* (compound-complex)
- *Dufau's assistant, Joseph Gaudet, did not agree.* (simple)

Write It

As you draft and revise your narrative, choose sentence structures that convey specific meanings, and vary them for effect.

TIP

PUNCTUATION
When punctuating a compound sentence, separate the independent clauses either with a comma and a coordinating conjunction or with a semicolon.

Revising

Evaluating Your Draft

Use the following checklist to evaluate the effectiveness of your draft. Then, use your evaluation and the instruction on this page to guide your revision.

FOCUS AND ORGANIZATION	DEVELOPMENT OF IDEAS/ ELABORATION	CONVENTIONS
☐ Provides an introduction that establishes a clear setting and point of view.	☐ Effectively uses narrative techniques, such as dialogue, pacing, and description.	☐ Attends to the norms and conventions of the discipline, especially the correct use and punctuation of phrases and clauses.
☐ Presents a coherent sequence of events.	☐ Uses descriptive details, sensory language, and precise words and phrases.	☐ Consulted a dictionary to check correct spelling and meaning.
☐ Provides a conclusion that follows from and reflects on the events and experiences in the narrative.		☐ Consulted a thesaurus to find effective language.

Revising for Focus and Organization

Clarify Insights Review your draft to make sure that you have clearly communicated the importance of the events developed in your narrative. Mark sentences that show the reader what you, or the people in your story, have learned. If necessary, add more of those sentences to better explain your insights. Make sure your conclusion follows from those insights and leaves readers with a lasting impression.

WORD NETWORK

Include interesting words from your Word Network in your narrative.

Revising for Evidence and Elaboration

Use Precise Language In order to craft a strong narrative that engages readers, choose words and phrases that are vivid, precise, and lively. Review your draft, identifying vague, imprecise, or weak language.

Vague: They went into the clear water.

Precise: They dove into the crystalline water.

Consider using a thesaurus to broaden your word choices. However, make sure to take into account subtle differences in the meanings of synonyms. Those differences can alter your meaning significantly. To prevent errors, double-check the definitions and consider the connotations of any replacement word choices you find in a thesaurus.

Exchange narratives with a classmate. Use the checklist to evaluate your classmate's narrative and provide supportive feedback.

1. Is the problem or situation clearly introduced and developed?

☐ yes   ☐ no   If no, explain what details could be added.

2. Are the people and events developed through dialogue and description?

☐ yes   ☐ no   If no, point out what is missing.

3. Does the narrative follow a well-structured sequence of events?

☐ yes   ☐ no   If no, write a brief note explaining what you thought was missing.

4. What is the strongest part of your classmate's narrative? Why?

_____

_____

_____

_____

Editing and Proofreading

Edit for Conventions Reread your draft for accuracy and consistency. Correct errors in grammar and word usage. Consider adding subordinate clauses to vary structure, add interest, or include relevant details. Consult a grammar handbook or online tools if you need support.

Proofread for Accuracy Read your draft carefully, looking for errors in spelling and punctuation. Check the punctuation of all compound, complex, and compound-complex sentences.

Publishing and Presenting

Create a final version of your nonfiction narrative. Share it with your class so that your classmates can read it and make comments. In turn, review and comment on your classmates' work. Consider the ways in which other students' narratives are both similar to and different from your own. Always maintain a polite and respectful tone when commenting.

Reflecting

Think about what you learned by writing your narrative. What could you do differently the next time you need to write a narrative to make the writing experience easier and to make your final product stronger? For example, you might read your narrative aloud and annotate passages that are especially difficult to follow.

ESSENTIAL QUESTION:

What does it mean to see?

Through sight, touch, taste, smell, and hearing, people discover and learn about their surroundings. When one or more of those senses is missing, does our knowledge or understanding of the world change? You will read selections that examine lives experienced without physical sight. You will work in a group to continue your exploration of blindness and sight.

Small-Group Learning Strategies

Throughout your life, in school, in your community, and in your career, you will continue to learn and work with others.

Review these strategies and the actions you can take to practice them as you work in teams. Add ideas of your own for each step. Use these strategies during Small-Group Learning.

STRATEGY	ACTION PLAN
Prepare	• Complete your assignments so that you are prepared for group work. • Organize your thinking so you can contribute to your group's discussions. •
Participate fully	• Make eye contact to signal that you are listening and taking in what is being said. • Use text evidence when making a point. •
Support others	• Build off ideas from others in your group. • Invite others who have not yet spoken to do so. •
Clarify	• Paraphrase the ideas of others to ensure that your understanding is correct. • Ask follow-up questions. •

CONTENTS

PERFORMANCE TASK

SPEAKING AND LISTENING FOCUS
Present an Oral Retelling

The Small-Group readings feature people who do not have the physical ability to see but who perhaps "see" in other ways. After reading, your group will plan and deliver an oral retelling about vision and sight.

Working as a Team

1. Take a Position In your group, discuss the following question:

Which of our senses is most important?

As you take turns sharing your ideas, be sure to provide reasons that support them. After all group members have shared, discuss some of the ways in which our senses help us understand or—perhaps— misunderstand our world.

2. List Your Rules As a group, decide on the rules that you will follow as you work together. Samples are provided; add two more of your own. You may add or revise rules based on your experience together.

- Everyone should participate in group discussions.
- People should not interrupt.

- _____

  _____

- _____

  _____

3. Apply the Rules Practice working as a group. Share what you have learned about blindness and sight. Make sure each person in the group contributes. Take notes, and be prepared to share with the class one thing that you heard from another member of your group.

4. Name Your Group Choose a name that reflects the unit topic.

Our group's name: _____

5. Create a Communication Plan Decide how you want to communicate with one another. For example, you might use online collaboration tools, email, or instant messaging.

Our group's decision: _____

_____

Making a Schedule

First, find out the due dates for the small-group activities. Then, preview the texts and activities with your group, and make a schedule for completing the tasks.

SELECTION	ACTIVITIES	DUE DATE
View From the Empire State Building		
Blind The Blind Seer of Ambon On His Blindness		
The Country of the Blind		
The Neglected Senses		

Working on Group Projects

As your group works together, you'll find it more effective if each person has a specific role. Different projects require different roles. Before beginning a project, discuss the necessary roles, and choose one for each group member. Here are some possible roles; add your own ideas.

Project Manager: monitors the schedule and keeps everyone on task

Researcher: organizes research activities

Recorder: takes notes during group meetings

_____

_____

_____

_____

_____

About the Author

When she was nineteen months old, **Helen Keller** (1880–1968) became seriously ill with an infection that left her blind and deaf. Limited to hand signals that only the immediate members of her household understood, Keller lived for six years in a world without language. Finally, with the help of Anne Sullivan, her teacher and friend, Keller broke through the barriers of blindness and deafness to learn language and communicate with others. Eventually, she became an accomplished author, social activist, and campaigner for women's rights. Her amazing journey is documented in the award-winning play and movie *The Miracle Worker*.

View From the Empire State Building

Concept Vocabulary

As you perform your first read of the letter, you will encounter these words.

unconquerable	indomitable	dominating

Familiar Word Parts When determining the meaning of an unfamiliar word, look for word parts—such as roots, prefixes, and suffixes—that you know. Doing so can help you unlock meaning. Here are two examples of using the strategy.

Familiar Roots: If the word *luminary* is unfamiliar to you, notice that it contains the root *-lum-*, meaning "light," which you may recognize from words such as *illuminate* or *luminous*. The definition of *luminary* probably has something to do with light.

Familiar Suffixes: If the word *meteoric* is unfamiliar to you, notice that it ends with the suffix *-ic*, meaning "having the characteristics of," which you may recognize from such words as *romantic* and *fantastic*. Something *meteoric* probably has the characteristics of a meteor— perhaps it is huge, is impressive, or makes a big impact.

Apply your knowledge of familiar word parts and other vocabulary strategies to determine the meanings of unfamiliar words you encounter during your first read.

First Read NONFICTION

Apply these strategies as you conduct your first read. You will have an opportunity to complete a close read after your first read.

NOTICE the general ideas of the text. *What* is it about? *Who* is involved?

ANNOTATE by marking vocabulary and key passages you want to revisit.

First Read

CONNECT ideas within the selection to what you already know and what you have already read.

RESPOND by completing the Comprehension Check and by writing a brief summary of the selection.

View From the Empire State Building

Helen Keller

BACKGROUND

When the Empire State Building was completed in 1931, it stood as the tallest skyscraper in the world. Helen Keller visited the building shortly after its opening, and images of her were captured by the *New York Times*. Fascinated by the photographs, Dr. John Finley wrote to Keller, who was both blind and deaf, asking her what she "saw" from so high up. Keller's response follows.

1   January 13, 1932

2   Dear Dr. Finley:

3   After many days and many tribulations which are inseparable from existence here below, I sit down to the pleasure of writing to you and answering your delightful question, "What Did You Think 'of the Sight' When You Were on the Top of the Empire Building?"

4   Frankly, I was so entranced "seeing" that I did not think about the sight. If there was a subconscious thought of it, it was in the nature of gratitude to God for having given the blind seeing minds. As I now recall the view I had from the Empire Tower, I am convinced that, until we have looked into darkness, we cannot know what a divine thing vision is.

5   Perhaps I beheld a brighter prospect than my companions with two good eyes. Anyway, a blind friend gave me the best description I had of the Empire Building until I saw it myself.

6   Do I hear you reply, "I suppose to you it is a reasonable thesis that the universe is all a dream, and that the blind only are awake?" Yes— no doubt I shall be left at the Last Day on the other bank defending the incredible prodigies of the unseen world, and, more incredible still, the strange grass and skies the blind behold are greener grass and bluer skies than ordinary eyes see. I will concede that my guides saw a thousand things that escaped me from the top of the Empire

NOTES

Building, but I am not envious. For imagination creates distances and horizons that reach to the end of the world. It is as easy for the mind to think in stars as in cobblestones. Sightless Milton[1] dreamed visions no one else could see. Radiant with an inward light, he sent forth rays by which mankind beholds the realms of Paradise.

7   But what of the Empire Building? It was a thrilling experience to be whizzed in a "lift" a quarter of a mile heavenward, and to see New York spread out like a marvelous tapestry beneath us.

8   There was the Hudson—more like the flash of a sword-blade than a noble river. The little island of Manhattan, set like a jewel in its nest of rainbow waters, stared up into my face, and the solar system circled about my head! Why, I thought, the sun and the stars are suburbs of New York, and I never knew it! I had a sort of wild desire to invest in a bit of real estate on one of the planets. All sense of depression and hard times vanished, I felt like being frivolous with the stars. But that was only for a moment. I am too static to feel quite natural in a Star View cottage on the Milky Way, which must be something of a merry-go-round even on quiet days.

9   I was pleasantly surprised to find the Empire Building so poetical. From every one except my blind friend I had received an impression of sordid[2] materialism—the piling up of one steel honeycomb upon another with no real purpose but to satisfy the American craving for the superlative in everything. A Frenchman has said, in his exalted moments the American fancies himself a demigod, nay, a god; for only gods never tire of the prodigious. The highest, the largest, the most costly is the breath of his vanity.

10   Well, I see in the Empire Building something else—passionate skill, arduous and fearless idealism. The tallest building is a victory of imagination. Instead of crouching close to earth like a beast, the spirit of man soars to higher regions, and from this new point of vantage he looks upon the impossible with fortified courage and dreams yet more magnificent enterprises.

11   What did I "see and hear" from the Empire Tower? As I stood there 'twixt earth and sky, I saw a romantic structure wrought by human brains and hands that is to the burning eye of the sun a rival luminary.[3] I saw it stand erect and serene in the midst of storm and the tumult of elemental commotion. I heard the hammer of Thor[4] ring when the shaft began to rise upward. I saw the **unconquerable** steel, the flash of testing flames, the sword-like rivets. I heard the steam drills in pandemonium. I saw countless skilled workers welding together that mighty symmetry. I looked upon the marvel of frail, yet **indomitable** hands that lifted the tower to its **dominating** height.

Mark familiar word parts or indicate another strategy you used that helped you determine meaning.

unconquerable (uhn KONG kuhr uh buhl) *adj.*

MEANING:

indomitable (ihn DOM uh tuh buhl) *adj.*

MEANING:

dominating (DOM uh nay ting) *adj.*

MEANING:

----

1. **Sightless Milton** Seventeenth-century poet John Milton went blind in the 1650s, years before completing some of his greatest works.
2. **sordid** (SAWR dihd) *adj.* distasteful; dishonorable.
3. **luminary** (LOO muh nehr ee) *n.* something that gives light.
4. **hammer of Thor** Thor, the Norse god of thunder, carried a hammer that could crush mountains.

12   Let cynics and supersensitive souls say what they will about American materialism and machine civilization. Beneath the surface are poetry, mysticism, and inspiration that the Empire Building somehow symbolizes. In that giant shaft I see a groping toward beauty and spiritual vision. I am one of those who see and yet believe.

13   I hope I have not wearied you with my "screed"[5] about sight and seeing. The length of this letter is a sign of long, long thoughts that bring me happiness. I am, with every good wish for the New Year,

14   Sincerely yours,

15   Helen Keller

_____

5. **screed** (skreed) *n.* long piece of writing.

Comprehension Check

Complete the following items after you finish your first read. Review and clarify details with your group.

1. What question is Helen Keller answering in her letter?

2. Who accompanies Keller to the top of the Empire State Building?

3. According to Keller, how does a Frenchman describe the way Americans imagine themselves?

4. What symbolic meaning does Keller find in the Empire State Building?

5. **Notebook** Write a summary of the letter.

- -

RESEARCH

Research to Clarify Choose at least one unfamiliar detail from the text. Briefly research that detail. In what way does the information you learned shed light on an aspect of the letter?

VIEW FROM THE EMPIRE
STATE BUILDING

⊹ WORD NETWORK

Add words related to
blindness and sight from the
text to your Word Network.

Close Read the Text

With your group, revisit sections of the letter you marked
during your first read. **Annotate** details that you notice.
What **questions** do you have? What can you **conclude**?

**Close
Read**

ANNOTATE · QUESTION · CONCLUDE

Analyze the Text

CITE TEXTUAL EVIDENCE
to support your answers

📓 **Notebook** Complete the activities.

1. **Review and Clarify** With your group, reread paragraph 6 of "View From
the Empire State Building." How does Helen Keller describe the way blind
people see such things as grass and sky? How do you interpret Keller's
description of grass and sky? Does she mean her remark literally? Explain.

2. **Present and Discuss** Now, work with your group to share passages from
the selection that you found especially important. Take turns presenting
your passages. Discuss what details you noticed, what questions you
asked, and what conclusions you reached.

3. **Essential Question:** *What does it mean to see?* What has this
selection taught you about ways in which people see?

LANGUAGE DEVELOPMENT

Concept Vocabulary

| unconquerable | indomitable | dominating |

Why These Words? The three concept vocabulary words are related. With
your group, determine what the words have in common. Write your ideas,
and add another word that fits the category.

Practice

📓 **Notebook** Use a print or online dictionary to confirm the definitions
for the three concept vocabulary words. Write a sentence using each of the
words. How did the concept vocabulary words contribute to the clarity and
meaning of the sentences you wrote? Discuss.

Word Study

Latin Root: -dom- The Latin root *-dom-* means "house," "home," or
"master of the house." The word *indomitable*, for example, is an adjective
that means "unable to be ruled or defeated." Find several other words that
contain the root *-dom-*. Record the words and their meanings.

Analyze Craft and Structure

Author's Choices: Word Choice Any language that is not meant to be understood literally is **figurative language**. Figurative language includes figures of speech such as metaphors, similes, hyperbole, and personification.

A **metaphor** directly compares two unlike items, thus demonstrating a surprising similarity.
Example: The sun is a red-hot coal blazing down on us.

A **simile** uses an explicit comparison word such as *like* or *as* to compare two unlike items.
Example: The sun is like a red-hot coal in the sky.

Hyperbole is the deliberate use of exaggeration to express heightened emotion or add humor.
Example: My anger burned hotter than the light of ten thousand suns.

Personification gives a non-human thing the characteristics of a person.
Example: The red-hot eye of the sun stares down on us.

In addition to figurative language, writers also use precise, vivid words and phrases to provide accurate and engaging descriptions for their readers.

TIP

GROUP DISCUSSION
Keep in mind that members of your group might have different impressions of the effects of word choice and figurative language. There's no right impression or conclusion, but discussing opinions and the reasons for them will help you clarify your thoughts and learn from one another.

Practice

CITE TEXTUAL EVIDENCE to support your answers.

Work on your own to complete the chart. Identify examples of figurative language and precise word choice in Keller's letter. Then, discuss your choices with your group, and consider how each example adds to the vividness, beauty, or clarity of Keller's writing.

TYPE OF LANGUAGE	EXAMPLE FROM THE SELECTION
Simile	*The little island of Manhattan, set like a jewel in its nest of rainbow waters, . . .* (paragraph 8)

VIEW FROM THE EMPIRE
STATE BUILDING

Conventions

Types of Phrases Writers use various types of phrases, such as prepositional phrases, to convey specific meanings. A **prepositional phrase** consists of a preposition, the object of the preposition, and any modifiers of the object. An **adverbial phrase** is any prepositional phrase that acts as an adverb in a sentence, by modifying a verb, an adjective, or another adverb. Adverbial phrases tell *where*, *why*, *when*, *in what way*, or *to what extent*.

The chart shows examples of adverbial phrases. The prepositions are italicized, the adverbial phrases are highlighted, and the words they modify are underlined. Note that more than one adverbial phrase may modify a single word.

SENTENCE	FUNCTION(S) OF ADVERBIAL PHRASE(S)
One speaker drove *for* ninety miles to reach the conference.	tells *to what extent*
With apparent reluctance, he approached the podium.	tells *in what way*
After his speech, he retreated *to* the auditorium's rearmost row.	tell *when* and *where*

Read It

1. Working individually, read these passages from "View From the Empire State Building." Mark each adverbial phrase, and write whether it tells *where*, *why*, *when*, *in what way*, or *to what extent*. Then, discuss your answers with your group.

   a. A Frenchman has said, in his exalted moments the American fancies himself a demigod. . . .

   b. Well, I see in the Empire Building something else—passionate skill, arduous and fearless idealism.

2. Working individually, read this passage from paragraph 10 of "View From the Empire State Building." Identify the word that each underlined adverbial phrase is modifying. Recall that more than one adverbial phrase may modify a single word.

   . . . crouching close to earth like a beast, the spirit of man soars to higher regions, and from this new point of vantage he looks upon the impossible with fortified courage and dreams yet more magnificent enterprises.

Write It

📓 **Notebook** Write a paragraph that summarizes Keller's account of her experience at the top of the Empire State Building. Use at least three adverbial phrases in your paragraph, and mark them.

Research

Assignment

With your group, research, prepare, and deliver a **group presentation**. Choose one of these options:

☐ Create a **photo essay** on the construction of the Empire State Building. Include photos or illustrations that show the building in all of its stages of construction, from planning to completion. Add captions quoting primary sources, including Keller's letter. Consider the following questions:

- Who was the building's architect? How was the project financed? How did the designers of the building describe the project?

- What was it like for workers to stand on narrow girders 1,000 feet from the ground? How did the workers prepare to work at that height?

☐ An **allusion** is an unexplained reference within a text to a well-known person, place, event, art work, or literary work. The writer assumes readers know what the reference means. Select an allusion from Keller's letter, and create a **digital presentation** explaining it. Include images or audio clips to help your audience understand the allusion. Consider these questions:

- To whom or what is the allusion referring?

- In what way does the allusion reinforce Keller's message?

☐ The Empire State Building was constructed during the Great Depression, a period of prolonged economic hardship. Role-play a **radio interview** with Helen Keller about what the construction of the building meant to Americans living at that time. Record the interview, and publish it to your class as a podcast. Research to answer these questions:

- What did the typical American family experience during the Depression?

- How did the unemployment rate climb?

- What did the government do to help? How effective were these efforts?

✎ EVIDENCE LOG

Before moving on to a new selection, go to your Evidence Log and record what you learned from "View From the Empire State Building."

Project Plan Before you begin, make a list of tasks that need to be completed for the research and presentation. Assign individual group members to each task.

Presentation Plan Before you begin the presentation, make decisions about the roles and responsibilities each group member will assume. Also, make decisions about technology and props you will use. After all groups have delivered their presentations, hold a class discussion. Compare the presentation your group gave with those of the other small groups in the class.

POETRY COLLECTION

Blind

The Blind Seer of Ambon

On His Blindness

Concept Vocabulary

As you perform your first read of these poems, you will encounter the following words.

transcend	luminous	elemental

Context Clues If these words are unfamiliar to you, try using context clues to help you determine their meanings. There are various types of context clues that may help you as you read.

> **Restatement, or Synonyms:** Many **unfortunate** events, including two interceptions and three injuries, resulted in our <u>unlucky</u> loss in the state championships.
>
> **Elaborating Details:** After a <u>detailed article came out in the Health and Nutrition section of the newspaper</u>, it became even more **evident** that exercise extends one's life.
>
> **Contrast of Ideas:** The recent **shortage** of oil around the world has resulted in a <u>sharp increase</u> in gas prices in the United States.

Apply your knowledge of context clues and other vocabulary strategies to determine the meanings of unfamiliar words you encounter during your first read.

First Read POETRY

Apply these strategies as you conduct your first read. You will have an opportunity to complete a close read after your first read.

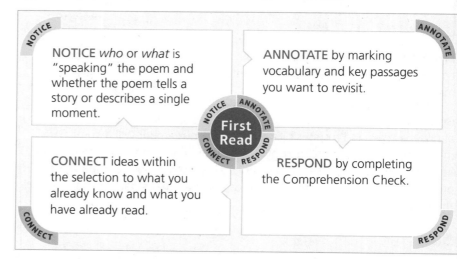

NOTICE who or what is "speaking" the poem and whether the poem tells a story or describes a single moment.

ANNOTATE by marking vocabulary and key passages you want to revisit.

CONNECT ideas within the selection to what you already know and what you have already read.

RESPOND by completing the Comprehension Check.

First Read

About the Poets

Fatima Naoot (b. 1964) was born in Cairo, Egypt, trained as an engineer, and became a writer after working as an architect for ten years. Naoot, who has published five books of poetry, and whose prize-winning work has been translated into seven different languages, was charged with "contempt of religion" in an Egyptian court in 2015 for a reference she made in one of her poems.

W. S. Merwin (b. 1927) has enjoyed a celebrated career in poetry for more than seven decades. Merwin has won almost every honor that a poet can receive, including the Bollingen Prize, two Pulitzer Prizes, and the Aiken Taylor Award. He has twice served as the Poet Laureate of the United States.

Jorge Luis Borges (1899–1986) is one of the giants of world literature. Born in Argentina, Borges helped establish the literary style known as magical realism. Borges's work is considered essential in universities and literary circles around the world. His unique style and point of view have inspired dozens of prominent authors, including Nobel Prize winners Gabriel García Márquez and J. M. Coetzee.

Backgrounds

Blind

Childhood blindness can occur for a number of reasons, including damage to the retina, a part of the eye that is sensitive to light, and cataracts, cloudy areas that form in the lens of the eye. For much of history, no form of blindness was curable. With today's medical techniques, however, some cases can be cured—especially cataracts, which can be removed with a rapid, if delicate, surgery.

The Blind Seer of Ambon

This poem honors Georg Eberhard Rumphius, a botanist who devoted fifty years of his life to the study of the plants, animals, climate, geography, and native culture of Ambon, an island in present-day Indonesia. During his stay in Ambon, Rumphius was plagued with misfortunes—he lost his eyesight, his wife and daughter were killed in an earthquake, and much of his work was either lost or destroyed.

On His Blindness

The title of this poem alludes to a sonnet by the seventeenth-century poet John Milton—an autobiographical meditation on his lost eyesight. Though Milton had become completely blind by the mid-1650s, he wrote his greatest works, including the epic poem *Paradise Lost*, without his sight. In his version of "On His Blindness," Borges reflects on his own experience of going blind.

Blind

Fatima Naoot

translated by Kees Nijland

All of a sudden she could see
After an intricate operation performed in a hurry
More in line with committing criminal poetry

A long time she had listened to dozens of books
5 Her empty eyes
Staring upwards
But
When she danced with Lama
On the hillside,
10 He told her that the soul can **transcend** earthly life
If freed from the retina.

She was illiterate
The pain on her face
While in trance
15 Spoilt the text
The pen bent
Before completing the story.

No way of return, now
Knowledge is coming
20 And ignorance is
A lost paradise

Therefore,
The thought of a drained memory
Stayed with her
25 Whenever her eye tried to see.
Silently
She poured out two shadows standing
In a breathless, dark hall,
Prepared for tea,
30 At the end of the show.

Two shadows,
One a lighting technician
And the other
Did his utmost to read
35 But
Utterly stunned
Could not complete the lesson.

Reading does not require eyes
So much was certain
40 When she suddenly regained sight
But did not find books

Mark context clues or indicate
another strategy you used that
helped you determine meaning.

transcend (tran SEHND) *v.*

MEANING:

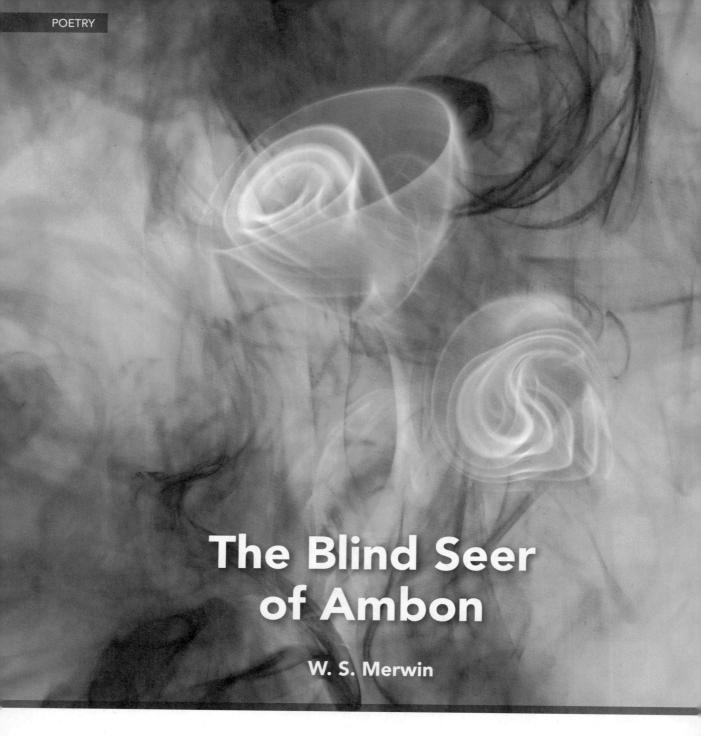

The Blind Seer of Ambon

W. S. Merwin

I always knew that I came from
another language

and now even when I can no longer see
I continue to arrive at words

5 but the leaves
and the shells were already here
and my fingers finding them echo
the untold light and depth

I was betrayed into my true calling
10 and denied in my advancement
I may have seemed somewhat strange
caring in my own time for living things
with no value that we know
languages wash over them one wave at a time

15 when the houses fell
in the earthquake
I lost my wife
and my daughter
it all roared and stood still
20 falling
where they were in the daylight

I named for my wife a flower
as though I could name a flower
my wife dark and **luminous**
25 and not there

I lost the drawings of the flowers
in fire

I lost the studies
of the flowers
30 my first six books in the sea

then I saw that the flowers themselves
were gone
they were indeed gone
I saw
35 that my wife was gone
then I saw that my daughter was gone
afterward my eyes themselves were gone

one day I was looking
at infinite small creatures
40 on the bright sand
and the next day is this
hearing after music
so this is the way I see now

I take a shell in my hand
45 new to itself and to me
I feel the thinness the warmth and the cold
I listen to the water
which is the story welling up
I remember the colors and their lives
50 everything takes me by surprise
it is all awake in the darkness

NOTES

Mark context clues or indicate
another strategy you used that
helped you determine meaning.

luminous (LOO muh nuhs) *adj.*

MEANING:

On His Blindness

Jorge Luis Borges

translated by Robert Mezey

In the fullness of the years, like it or not,
a luminous mist surrounds me, unvarying,
that breaks things down into a single thing,
colorless, formless. Almost into a thought.
5 The **elemental**, vast night and the day
teeming with people have become that fog
of constant, tentative light that does not flag,
and lies in wait at dawn. I longed to see
just once a human face. Unknown to me
10 the closed encyclopedia, the sweet play
in volumes I can do no more than hold,
the tiny soaring birds, the moons of gold.
Others have the world, for better or worse;
I have this half-dark, and the toil of verse.

Comprehension Check

Complete the following items after you finish your first read. Review and clarify details with your group.

BLIND

1. According to the speaker, how does the poem's main character ("she") gain the sense of sight?

2. After she regains her sight, what does she find missing from the world?

THE BLIND SEER OF AMBON

3. What happens to the speaker's houses?

4. Whom does the speaker lose?

ON HIS BLINDNESS

5. What does the speaker long to see just once?

6. Having lost sight, what does the speaker still have?

- -

RESEARCH

Research to Clarify Choose at least one unfamiliar detail from one of the poems. Briefly research that detail. In what way does the information you found shed light on an aspect of the poem?

POETRY COLLECTION

Close Read the Text

With your group, revisit sections of the text you marked during your first read. **Annotate** details that you notice. What **questions** do you have? What can you **conclude**?

- -

Analyze the Text

CITE TEXTUAL EVIDENCE to support your answers.

📓 **Notebook** Complete the activities.

1. **Review and Clarify** With your group, reread the final stanza of "The Blind Seer of Ambon." What does the shell symbolize? Why is the shell so important to the speaker?

2. **Present and Discuss** Now, work with your group to share the passages from the poems that you found especially important. Take turns presenting your passages. Discuss what details you noticed, what questions you asked, and what conclusions you reached.

3. **Essential Question:** *What does it mean to see?* What has this selection taught you about the meaning of seeing? Discuss with your group.

TIP

GROUP DISCUSSION

Keep in mind that personal experience can affect how a reader perceives a poem. For some, the poem's imagery and context will seem familiar. Others will be less comfortable with the poem's approach. Be aware and supportive of the impressions of others as your group discusses the poetry.

⛓ WORD NETWORK

Add words related to blindness and sight from the texts to your Word Network.

LANGUAGE DEVELOPMENT

Concept Vocabulary

transcend	luminous	elemental

Why These Words? The three concept vocabulary words are related. With your group, determine what the words have in common. Write your ideas, and add another word that fits the category.

Practice

📓 **Notebook** Use a print or online dictionary to confirm the definitions of the three concept vocabulary words. Write a sentence using each of the words. How did the concept vocabulary words contribute to the clarity and meaning of the sentences you wrote? Discuss.

Word Study

Latin Root: -lum- The speaker of "The Blind Seer of Ambon" refers to his wife as simultaneously "dark and luminous." This description may at first seem contradictory because the word *luminous* is formed from the Latin root *-lum-*, which means "light."

1. Write a definition of *luminous* that demonstrates your understanding of the root *-lum-*.

2. Identify two other words that are formed from the root *-lum-*. Record the words and their meanings.

Analyze Craft and Structure

Poet's Choices: Figurative Language While writers in all genres use figurative language, poets rely on it because it allows them to express ideas with extra vividness and precision. **Figurative language** is language that carries meanings beyond a literal level. Often, figurative language involves unexpected comparisons. This is the case with analogy.

- An **analogy** is a comparison that shows similarities between two things that are otherwise not alike.
- Often, an analogy explains something unfamiliar by likening it to something familiar.

Clearing up confusion is one use of analogy. However, analogies also provide a new way of looking at a subject that you thought you understood. It is this fresh view of a topic that makes analogy so useful in poetry, which often seeks to reveal hidden truths. To appreciate this use of analogy in poetry, you have to determine what is being compared. Then, consider how seeing one thing in terms of another creates a fresh understanding or insight. Doing so can help you figure out the message, or **theme**, that the poet is using the analogy to develop.

Practice

CITE TEXTUAL EVIDENCE
to support your answers.

Notebook Each of the poems in this collection is about loss of some sort, but also about gain. To arrive at an understanding of the poems and their themes, respond to the questions. Then, discuss your answers with the group.

1. (a) In the third stanza of "Blind," what situation is compared to a pen being bent before a story is completed? (b) How does the woman described by the speaker expect this situation to change?

2. (a) In "Blind," why is ignorance a "lost paradise"? (b) What has "she" lost by gaining sight?

3. (a) With what are the "leaves and shells" compared in the third stanza of "The Blind Seer of Ambon"? (b) In the final stanza, a different analogy involving a shell appears. What is being compared, and what does the shell represent to the speaker? (c) What message is the speaker conveying about what is lost and gained?

4. (a) In "On His Blindness," to what is blindness compared? (b) How do the analogies illustrate the speaker's attitude toward his blindness and his work? (c) What do the speaker's feelings of longing mixed with acceptance suggest about the poem's message?

POETRY COLLECTION

Author's Style

Word Choice and Meaning It is a general rule that the best writing *shows* rather than *tells*. In other words, rather than merely stating a message, a writer leads readers through the experience of a story or poem. Sensory details, imagery, and surprising juxtaposition are some of the many tools writers use to do this.

- **Sensory details** are words and phrases that relate to the five senses of sight, hearing, smell, taste, and touch.
- **Imagery** is the combining of sensory details to build word pictures in readers' minds.
- **Juxtaposition** involves the placement of ideas or details side by side. Often, juxtapositions involve surprising contrasts. For example, an **oxymoron** is a type of figurative language that expressly juxtaposes contrasting or contradictory ideas. The result is an expression that sheds new light on an idea. For example, a "deafening silence" is a stock, or common, oxymoron. It suggests a silence that is actually "loud" with unspoken meanings or feelings.

Sensory details, imagery, and surprising juxtapositions can be used in straightforward ways to describe a person or set a scene. However, they can also be used in imaginative ways to suggest deeper ideas.

Read It

1. Work individually. Find three examples of imagery in the poems. Explain the idea each image helps convey.

    a.

    b.

    c.

2. Explain in what way lines 23–24 from "Blind," shown here, are an example of an oxymoron.

    The thought of a drained memory / Stayed with her

Write It

📓 **Notebook** Write a brief paragraph in which you describe a person or a scene. Use at least two images and one oxymoron.

Speaking and Listening

Assignment

Choose one of the options, and create an **oral presentation** with your group.

☐ Prepare and perform a **recitation** of one of the poems. After your recitation, conduct a class discussion in which you consider the following questions:

- How does hearing the poem differ from simply reading it?
- What poetic devices are most effective when read aloud? Why?

☐ With your group, **paraphrase** one of the poems, rewriting it in your own words. You need not follow poetic form. Then, read aloud both the original poem and the paraphrased version. Hold a discussion about the following questions:

- How are the original poem and the paraphrase similar in meaning?
- Is the theme more evident in one? If so, which one and why?
- What does the absence of poetic devices in the paraphrase show you about the effects of those elements?

☐ Conduct a **round-table discussion** in which three students role-play the poets and answer questions about the themes and styles of their poems.

- Have a discussion moderator pose questions to the "poets" about how they use imagery and juxtaposition to develop meaning in their poems.
- The "poets" should respond by citing specific examples and evidence from their poems.

🖉 EVIDENCE LOG

Before moving on to a new selection, go to your Evidence Log and record what you learned from "Blind," "The Blind Seer of Ambon," and "On His Blindness."

Project Plan Before you begin, make a list of the tasks you will need to accomplish to complete the project. Use this chart to plan.

GROUP MEMBER	ROLE	QUESTIONS TO CONSIDER

Classroom Discussion While other groups are performing their presentations, pay close attention to the ideas expressed. Evaluate the use of evidence, and ask follow-up questions to clarify the speakers' reasoning. Carry out a final classroom discussion in which you discuss the group presentations. Make sure that all group members get a chance to voice their views.

About the Author

H. G. Wells (1866–1946) was an English novelist, journalist, sociologist, and historian. One of the founding writers of science fiction, Wells is remembered for such influential works as *The Time Machine, The War of the Worlds,* and *The First Men in the Moon.* His ideas helped shape popular conceptions of science and the colonization of space.

The Country of the Blind

Concept Vocabulary

As you perform your first read of "The Country of the Blind," you will encounter these words.

> incoherent   perplexity   delusions

Base Words If these words are unfamiliar to you, consider whether part of the word looks like a word you already know. Two or more words may have the same **base word,** with different prefixes and suffixes added. If you know one word, you may be able to determine the meaning of the other, even if the spellings vary. You can consult a dictionary to verify the word's meaning.

> **Unfamiliar Word:** *systematic*
>
> **Familiar Base Word:** *system*, meaning "organized method of doing something"
>
> **Preliminary Determination:** *Systematic* may mean "done according to a system, or organized method."
>
> **Verification:** The dictionary defines *systematic* as "methodical; done according to a plan."

Apply your knowledge of base words and other vocabulary strategies to determine the meanings of unfamiliar words you encounter during your first read.

First Read FICTION

Apply these strategies as you conduct your first read. You will have an opportunity to complete a close read after your first read.

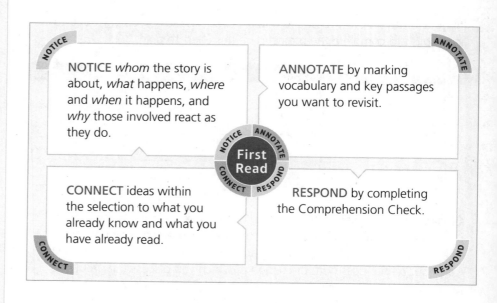

NOTICE *whom* the story is about, *what* happens, *where* and *when* it happens, and *why* those involved react as they do.

ANNOTATE by marking vocabulary and key passages you want to revisit.

CONNECT ideas within the selection to what you already know and what you have already read.

RESPOND by completing the Comprehension Check.

The Country of The Blind

H. G. Wells

BACKGROUND

"The Country of the Blind" was first published in 1904 and became one of H. G. Wells's best-known short stories. It is one of a number of popular science-fiction stories from the early 1900s that feature a community of people cut off from the outside world. These stories describe extraordinary societies with unique qualities, and the main characters are often outsiders exploring these new worlds.

1 Three hundred miles and more from Chimborazo, one hundred from the snows of Cotopaxi,[1] in the wildest wastes of Ecuador's Andes, there lies that mysterious mountain valley, cut off from the world of men, the Country of the Blind. Long years ago that valley lay so far open to the world that men might come at last through frightful gorges and over an icy pass into its equable meadows; and thither indeed men came, a family or so of Peruvians fleeing

NOTES

1. **Chimborazo . . . Cotopaxi** names of particular peaks in the Andes Mountains, the world's longest mountain range, located in South America.

from the lust and tyranny of an evil Spanish ruler. Then came the stupendous outbreak of Mindobamba, when it was night in Quito for seventeen days, and the water was boiling at Yaguachi and all the fish floating dying even as far as Guayaquil; everywhere along the Pacific slopes there were land-slips and swift thawings and sudden floods, and one whole side of the old Arauca crest slipped and came down in thunder, and cut off the Country of the Blind for ever from the exploring feet of men. But one of these early settlers had chanced to be on the hither side of the gorges when the world had so terribly shaken itself, and he perforce had to forget his wife and his child and all the friends and possessions he had left up there, and start life over again in the lower world. He started it again but ill, blindness overtook him, and he died of punishment in the mines; but the story he told begot a legend that lingers along the length of the Cordilleras of the Andes to this day.

2   He told of his reason for venturing back from that fastness, into which he had first been carried lashed to a llama, beside a vast bale of gear, when he was a child. The valley, he said, had in it all that the heart of man could desire—sweet water, pasture, and even climate, slopes of rich brown soil with tangles of a shrub that bore an excellent fruit, and on one side great hanging forests of pine that held the avalanches high. Far overhead, on three sides, vast cliffs of grey-green rock were capped by cliffs of ice; but the glacier stream came not to them but flowed away by the farther slopes, and only now and then huge ice masses fell on the valley side. In this valley it neither rained nor snowed, but the abundant springs gave a rich green pasture, that irrigation would spread over all the valley space. The settlers did well indeed there. Their beasts did well and multiplied, and but one thing marred their happiness. Yet it was enough to mar it greatly. A strange disease had come upon them, and had made all the children born to them there—and indeed, several older children also—blind. It was to seek some charm or antidote against this plague of blindness that he had with fatigue and danger and difficulty returned down the gorge. In those days, in such cases, men did not think of germs and infections but of sins; and it seemed to him that the reason of this affliction must lie in the negligence of these priestless immigrants to set up a shrine so soon as they entered the valley. He wanted a shrine—a handsome, cheap, effectual shrine—to be erected in the valley; he wanted relics and such-like potent things of faith, blessed objects and mysterious medals and prayers. In his wallet he had a bar of native silver for which he would not account; he insisted there was none in the valley with something of the insistence of an inexpert liar. They had all clubbed their money and ornaments together, having little need for such treasure up there, he said, to buy them holy help against their ill. I figure this dim-eyed young mountaineer, sunburnt, gaunt, and anxious, hat-brim clutched feverishly, a man all unused to the ways of the lower world, telling this story to some keen-

eyed, attentive priest before the great convulsion; I can picture him presently seeking to return with pious and infallible remedies against that trouble, and the infinite dismay with which he must have faced the tumbled vastness where the gorge had once come out. But the rest of his story of mischances is lost to me, save that I know of his evil death after several years. Poor stray from that remoteness! The stream that had once made the gorge now bursts from the mouth of a rocky cave, and the legend his poor, ill-told story set going developed into the legend of a race of blind men somewhere "over there" one may still hear today.

3 And amidst the little population of that now isolated and forgotten valley the disease ran its course. The old became groping and purblind,[2] the young saw but dimly, and the children that were born to them saw never at all. But life was very easy in that snow-rimmed basin, lost to all the world, with neither thorns nor briars, with no evil insects nor any beasts save the gentle breed of llamas they had lugged and thrust and followed up the beds of the shrunken rivers in the gorges up which they had come. The seeing had become purblind so gradually that they scarcely noted their loss. They guided the sightless youngsters hither and thither until they knew the whole Valley marvelously, and when at last sight died out among them the race lived on. They had even time to adapt themselves to the blind control of fire, which they made carefully in stoves of stone. They were a simple strain of people at the first, unlettered, only slightly touched with the Spanish civilization, but with something of a tradition of the arts of old Peru and of its lost philosophy. Generation followed generation. They forgot many things; they devised many things. Their tradition of the greater world they came from became mythical in color and uncertain. In all things save sight they were strong and able, and presently the chance of birth and heredity sent one who had an original mind and who could talk and persuade among them, and then afterwards another. These two passed, leaving their effects, and the little community grew in numbers and in understanding, and met and settled social and economic problems that arose. Generation followed generation. Generation followed generation. There came a time when a child was born who was fifteen generations from that ancestor who went out of the valley with a bar of silver to seek God's aid, and who never returned. Thereabouts it chanced that a man came into this community from the outer world. And this is the story of that man.

4 He was a mountaineer from the country near Quito, a man who had been down to the sea and had seen the world, a reader of books in an original way, an acute and enterprising man, and he was taken on by a party of Englishmen who had come out to Ecuador to climb mountains, to replace one of their three Swiss guides who had fallen ill. He climbed here and he climbed there, and then came the attempt

---

2. **purblind** (PUR blynd) *adj.* partly blind.

on Parascotopetl, the Matterhorn of the Andes,[3] in which he was lost to the outer world. The story of the accident has been written a dozen times. Pointer's narrative is the best. He tells how the little party worked their difficult and almost vertical way up to the very foot of the last and greatest precipice, and how they built a night shelter amidst the snow upon a little shelf of rock, and, with a touch of real dramatic power, how presently they found Nunez had gone from them. They shouted, and there was no reply; shouted and whistled, and for the rest of that night they slept no more.

5   As the morning broke they saw the traces of his fall. It seems impossible he could have uttered a sound. He had slipped eastward toward the unknown side of the mountain; far below he had struck a steep slope of snow, and ploughed his way down it in the midst of a snow avalanche. His track went straight to the edge of a frightful precipice, and beyond that everything was hidden. Far, far below, and hazy with distance, they could see trees rising out of a narrow, shut-in valley—the lost Country of the Blind. But they did not know it was the lost Country of the Blind, nor distinguish it in any way from any other narrow streak of upland valley. Unnerved by this disaster, they abandoned their attempt in the afternoon, and Pointer was called away to the war before he could make another attack. To this day Parascotopetl lifts an unconquered crest, and Pointer's shelter crumbles unvisited amidst the snows.

6   And the man who fell survived.

7   At the end of the slope he fell a thousand feet, and came down in the midst of a cloud of snow upon a snow slope even steeper than the one above. Down this he was whirled, stunned and insensible, but without a bone broken in his body; and then at last came to gentler slopes, and at last rolled out and lay still, buried amidst a softening heap of the white masses that had accompanied and saved him. He came to himself with a dim fancy that he was ill in bed; then realized his position with a mountaineer's intelligence, and worked himself loose and, after a rest or so, out until he saw the stars. He rested flat upon his chest for a space, wondering where he was and what had happened to him. He explored his limbs, and discovered that several of his buttons were gone and his coat turned over his head. His knife had gone from his pocket and his hat was lost, though he had tied it under his chin. He recalled that he had been looking for loose stones to raise his piece of the shelter wall. His ice-axe had disappeared.

8   He decided he must have fallen, and looked up to see, exaggerated by the ghastly light of the rising moon, the tremendous flight he had taken. For a while he lay, gazing blankly at that vast pale cliff towering above, rising moment by moment out of a subsiding tide of darkness. Its phantasmal, mysterious beauty held him for a space, and then he was seized with a paroxysm of sobbing laughter . . .

---

3. **Parascotopetl, the Matterhorn of the Andes** fictional mountain, which is compared to the most famous and iconic mountain in the Alps, the Matterhorn.

9   After a great interval of time he became aware that he was near the lower edge of the snow. Below, down what was now a moonlit and practicable slope, he saw the dark and broken appearance of rock-strewn turf. He struggled to his feet, aching in every joint and limb, got down painfully from the heaped loose snow about him, went downward until he was on the turf, and there dropped rather than lay beside a boulder, drank deep from the flask in his inner pocket, and instantly fell asleep . . .

10   He was awakened by the singing of birds in the trees far below.

11   He sat up and perceived he was on a little alp at the foot of a vast precipice, that was grooved by the gully down which he and his snow had come. Over against him another wall of rock reared itself against the sky. The gorge between these precipices ran east and west and was full of the morning sunlight, which lit to the westward the mass of fallen mountain that closed the descending gorge. Below him it seemed there was a precipice equally steep, but behind the snow in the gully he found a sort of chimney-cleft dripping with snow-water down which a desperate man might venture. He found it easier than it seemed, and came at last to another desolate alp, and then after a rock climb of no particular difficulty to a steep slope of trees. He took his bearings and turned his face up the gorge, for he saw it opened out above upon green meadows, among which he now glimpsed quite distinctly a cluster of stone huts of unfamiliar fashion. At times his progress was like clambering along the face of a wall, and after a time the rising sun ceased to strike along the gorge, the voices of the singing birds died away, and the air grew cold and dark about him. But the distant valley with its houses was all the brighter for that. He came presently to talus,[4] and among the rocks he noted—for he was an observant man—an unfamiliar fern that seemed to clutch out of the crevices with intense green hands. He picked a frond or so and gnawed its stalk and found it helpful.

12   About midday he came at last out of the throat of the gorge into the plain and the sunlight. He was stiff and weary; he sat down in the shadow of a rock, filled up his flask with water from a spring and drank it down, and remained for a time resting before he went on to the houses.

13   They were very strange to his eyes, and indeed the whole aspect of that valley became, as he regarded it, queerer and more unfamiliar. The greater part of its surface was lush green meadow, starred with many beautiful flowers, irrigated with extraordinary care, and bearing evidence of systematic cropping piece by piece. High up and ringing the valley about was a wall, and what appeared to be a circumferential water-channel, from which the little trickles of water that fed the meadow plants came, and on the higher slopes above this flocks of llamas cropped the scanty herbage. Sheds, apparently shelters or feeding-places for the llamas, stood against the boundary wall here and there. The irrigation streams ran together into a main

4. **talus** (TAY luhs) *n.* slope made of rock fragments.

channel down the center of the valley, and this was enclosed on either side by a wall breast high. This gave a singularly urban quality to this secluded place, a quality that was greatly enhanced by the fact that a number of paths paved with black and white stones, and each with a curious little curb at the side, ran hither and thither in an orderly manner. The houses of the central village were quite unlike the casual and higgledy-piggledy agglomeration of the mountain villages he knew; they stood in a continuous row on either side of a central street of astonishing cleanness; here and there their particolored facade was pierced by a door, and not a solitary window broke their even frontage. They were particolored with extraordinary irregularity, smeared with a sort of plaster that was sometimes grey, sometimes drab, sometimes slate-colored or dark brown; and it was the sight of this wild plastering first brought the word "blind" into the thoughts of the explorer. "The good man who did that," he thought, "must have been as blind as a bat."

14 He descended a steep place, and so came to the wall and channel that ran about the valley, near where the latter spouted out its surplus contents into the deeps of the gorge in a thin and wavering thread of cascade. He could now see a number of men and women resting on piled heaps of grass, as if taking a siesta, in the remoter part of the meadow, and nearer the village a number of recumbent children, and

then nearer at hand three men carrying pails on yokes along a little path that ran from the encircling wall toward the houses. These latter were clad in garments of llama cloth and boots and belts of leather, and they wore caps of cloth with back and ear flaps. They followed one another in single file, walking slowly and yawning as they walked, like men who have been up all night. There was something so reassuringly prosperous and respectable in their bearing that after a moment's hesitation Nunez stood forward as conspicuously as possible upon his rock, and gave vent to a mighty shout that echoed round the valley.

15   The three men stopped, and moved their heads as though they were looking about them. They turned their faces this way and that, and Nunez gesticulated with freedom. But they did not appear to see him for all his gestures, and after a time, directing themselves toward the mountains far away to the right, they shouted as if in answer. Nunez bawled again, and then once more, and as he gestured ineffectually the word "blind" came up to the top of his thoughts. "The fools must be blind," he said.

16   When at last, after much shouting and wrath, Nunez crossed the stream by a little bridge, came through a gate in the wall, and approached them, he was sure that they were blind. He was sure that this was the Country of the Blind of which the legends told. Conviction had sprung upon him, and a sense of great and rather enviable adventure. The three stood side by side, not looking at him, but with their ears directed toward him, judging him by his unfamiliar steps. They stood close together like men a little afraid, and he could see their eyelids closed and sunken, as though the very balls beneath had shrunk away. There was an expression near awe on their faces.

17   "A man," one said, in hardly recognizable Spanish—"a man it is—a man or a spirit—coming down from the rocks."

18   But Nunez advanced with the confident steps of a youth who enters upon life. All the old stories of the lost valley and the Country of the Blind had come back to his mind, and through his thoughts ran this old proverb, as if it were a refrain—

19   "In the Country of the Blind the One-eyed Man is King."

20   "In the Country of the Blind the One-eyed Man is King."

21   And very civilly he gave them greeting. He talked to them and used his eyes.

22   "Where does he come from, brother Pedro?" asked one.

23   "Down out of the rocks."

24   "Over the mountains I come," said Nunez, "out of the country beyond there—where men can see. From near Bogota,[5] where there are a hundred thousands of people, and where the city passes out of sight."

25   "Sight?" muttered Pedro. "Sight?"

5. **Bogota** (boh goh TAH) capital city of Colombia.

26   "He comes," said the second blind man, "out of the rocks."

27   The cloth of their coats Nunez saw was curiously fashioned, each with a different sort of stitching.

28   They startled him by a simultaneous movement toward him, each with a hand outstretched. He stepped back from the advance of these spread fingers.

29   "Come hither," said the third blind man, following his motion and clutching him neatly.

30   And they held Nunez and felt him over, saying no word further until they had done so.

31   "Carefully," he cried, with a finger in his eye, and found they thought that organ, with its fluttering lids, a queer thing in him. They went over it again.

32   "A strange creature, Correa," said the one called Pedro. "Feel the coarseness of his hair. Like a llama's hair."

33   "Rough he is as the rocks that begot him," said Correa, investigating Nunez's unshaven chin with a soft and slightly moist hand. "Perhaps he will grow finer." Nunez struggled a little under their examination, but they gripped him firm.

34   "Carefully," he said again.

35   "He speaks," said the third man. "Certainly he is a man."

36   "Ugh!" said Pedro, at the roughness of his coat.

37   "And you have come into the world?" asked Pedro.

38   "*Out* of the world. Over mountains and glaciers; right over above there, half-way to the sun. Out of the great big world that goes down, twelve days' journey to the sea."

39   They scarcely seemed to heed him. "Our fathers have told us men may be made by the forces of Nature," said Correa. "It is the warmth of things and moisture, and rottenness—rottenness."

40   "Let us lead him to the elders," said Pedro.

41   "Shout first," said Correa, "lest the children be afraid . . . This is a marvelous occasion."

42   So they shouted, and Pedro went first and took Nunez by the hand to lead him to the houses.

43   He drew his hand away. "I can see," he said.

44   "See?" said Correa.

45   "Yes, see," said Nunez, turning toward him, and stumbled against Pedro's pail.

46   "His senses are still imperfect," said the third blind man. "He stumbles, and talks unmeaning words. Lead him by the hand."

48   "As you will," said Nunez, and was led along, laughing.

49   It seemed they knew nothing of sight.

50   Well, all in good time he would teach them.

51   He heard people shouting, and saw a number of figures gathering together in the middle roadway of the village.

52   He found it tax his nerve and patience more than he had anticipated, that first encounter with the population of the Country of the Blind. The place seemed larger as he drew near to it, and the

smeared plasterings queerer, and a crowd of children and men and women (the women and girls, he was pleased to note, had some of them quite sweet faces, for all that their eyes were shut and sunken) came about him, holding on to him, touching him with soft, sensitive hands, smelling at him, and listening at every word he spoke. Some of the maidens and children, however, kept aloof as if afraid, and indeed his voice seemed coarse and rude beside their softer notes. They mobbed him. His three guides kept close to him with an effect of proprietorship, and said again and again, "A wild man out of the rock."

53   "Bogota," he said. "Bogota. Over the mountain crests."

54   "A wild man—using wild words," said Pedro. "Did you hear that—*Bogota*? His mind is hardly formed yet. He has only the beginnings of speech."

56   A little boy nipped his hand. "Bogota!" he said mockingly.

57   "Ay! A city to your village. I come from the great world—where men have eyes and see."

58   "His name's Bogota," they said.

59   "He stumbled," said Correa, "stumbled twice as we came hither."

60   "Bring him to the elders."

61   And they thrust him suddenly through a doorway into a room as black as pitch, save at the end there faintly glowed a fire. The crowd closed in behind him and shut out all but the faintest glimmer of day, and before he could arrest himself he had fallen headlong over the feet of a seated man. His arm, outflung, struck the face of someone else as he went down; he felt the soft impact of features and heard a cry of anger, and for a moment he struggled against a number of hands that clutched him. It was a one-sided fight. An inkling of the situation came to him, and he lay quiet.

62   "I fell down," he said; "I couldn't see in this pitchy darkness."

63   There was a pause as if the unseen persons about him tried to understand his words. Then the voice of Correa said: "He is but newly formed. He stumbles as he walks and mingles words that mean nothing with his speech."

64   Others also said things about him that he heard or understood imperfectly.

65   "May I sit up?" he asked, in a pause. "I will not struggle against you again."

66   They consulted and let him rise.

67   The voice of an older man began to question him, and Nunez found himself trying to explain the great world out of which he had fallen, and the sky and mountains and sight and such-like marvels, to these elders who sat in darkness in the Country of the Blind. And they would believe and understand nothing whatever he told them, a thing quite outside his expectation. They would not even understand many of his words. For fourteen generations these people had been blind and cut off from all the seeing world; the names for all the things of sight had faded and changed; the story of the outer world

Mark base words or indicate another strategy you used that helped you determine meaning.

incoherent (ihn koh HIHR uhnt) *adj.*

MEANING:

was faded and changed to a child's story; and they had ceased to concern themselves with anything beyond the rocky slopes above their circling wall. Blind men of genius had arisen among them and questioned the shreds of belief and tradition they had brought with them from their seeing days, and had dismissed all these things as idle fancies, and replaced them with new and saner explanations. Much of their imagination had shriveled with their eyes, and they had made for themselves new imaginations with their ever more sensitive ears and finger-tips. Slowly Nunez realized this; that his expectation of wonder and reverence at his origin and his gifts was not to be borne out; and after his poor attempt to explain sight to them had been set aside as the confused version of a new-made being describing the marvels of his **incoherent** sensations, he subsided, a little dashed, into listening to their instruction. And the eldest of the blind men explained to him life and philosophy and religion, how that the world (meaning their valley) had been first an empty hollow in the rocks, and then had come, first, inanimate things without the gift of touch, and llamas and a few other creatures that had little sense, and then men, and at last angels, whom one could hear singing and making fluttering sounds, but whom no one could touch at all, which puzzled Nunez greatly until he thought of the birds.

68   He went on to tell Nunez how this time had been divided into the warm and the cold, which are the blind equivalents of day and night, and how it was good to sleep in the warm and work during the cold, so that now, but for his advent, the whole town of the blind would have been asleep. He said Nunez must have been specially created to learn and serve the wisdom they had acquired, and that for all his mental incoherency and stumbling behavior he must have courage, and do his best to learn, and at that all the people in the doorway murmured encouragingly. He said the night—for the blind call their day night—was now far gone, and it behooved every one to go back to sleep. He asked Nunez if he knew how to sleep, and Nunez said he did, but that before sleep he wanted food.

69   They brought him food—llama's milk in a bowl, and rough salted bread—and led him into a lonely place, to eat out of their hearing, and afterwards to slumber until the chill of the mountain evening roused them to begin their day again. But Nunez slumbered not at all.

70   Instead, he sat up in the place where they had left him, resting his limbs and turning the unanticipated circumstances of his arrival over and over in his mind.

71   Every now and then he laughed, sometimes with amusement, and sometimes with indignation.

72   "Unformed mind!" he said. "Got no senses yet! They little know they've been insulting their heaven-sent king and master. I see I must bring them to reason. Let me think—let me think."

73   He was still thinking when the sun set.

74   Nunez had an eye for all beautiful things, and it seemed to him that the glow upon the snowfields and glaciers that rose about the

valley on every side was the most beautiful thing he had ever seen. His eyes went from that inaccessible glory to the village and irrigated fields, fast sinking into the twilight, and suddenly a wave of emotion took him, and he thanked God from the bottom of his heart that the power of sight had been given him.

75   He heard a voice calling to him from out of the village. "Ya ho there, Bogota! Come hither!"

76   At that he stood up smiling. He would show these people once and for all what sight would do for a man. They would seek him, but not find him.

77   "You move not, Bogota," said the voice.

78   He laughed noiselessly, and made two stealthy steps aside from the path.

79   "Trample not on the grass, Bogota; that is not allowed."

80   Nunez had scarcely heard the sound he made himself. He stopped amazed.

81   The owner of the voice came running up the piebald[6] path toward him.

82   He stepped back into the pathway. "Here I am," he said.

83   "Why did you not come when I called you?" said the blind man. "Must you be led like a child? Cannot you hear the path as you walk?"

84   Nunez laughed. "I can see it," he said.

85   "There is no such word as *see*," said the blind man, after a pause. "Cease this folly, and follow the sound of my feet."

86   Nunez followed, a little annoyed.

87   "My time will come," he said.

88   "You'll learn," the blind man answered. "There is much to learn in the world."

89   "Has no one told you, 'In the Country of the Blind the One-eyed Man is King'?"

90   "What is blind?" asked the blind man carelessly over his shoulder.

91   Four days passed, and the fifth found the King of the Blind still incognito, as a clumsy and useless stranger among his subjects.

92   It was, he found, much more difficult to proclaim himself than he had supposed, and in the meantime, while he meditated his *coup d'état*,[7] he did what he was told and learned the manners and customs of the Country of the Blind. He found working and going about at night a particularly irksome thing, and he decided that that should be the first thing he would change.

93   They led a simple, laborious life, these people, with all the elements of virtue and happiness, as these things can be understood by men. They toiled, but not oppressively; they had food and clothing sufficient for their needs; they had days and seasons of rest; they made much of music and singing, and there was love among them, and little children.

---

6. **piebald** (PY bawld) *adj.* covered with patches and spots.
7. *coup d'état* (KOO day TAH) *n.* sudden overthrow of a government by force.

94   It was marvelous with what confidence and precision they went about their ordered world. Everything, you see, had been made to fit their needs; each of the radiating paths of the valley area had a constant angle to the others, and was distinguished by a special notch upon its curbing; all obstacles and irregularities of path or meadow had long since been cleared away; all their methods and procedure arose naturally from their special needs. Their senses had become marvelously acute; they could hear and judge the slightest gesture of a man a dozen paces away—could hear the very beating of his heart. Intonation had long replaced expression with them, and touches gesture, and their work with hoe and spade and fork was as free and confident as garden work can be. Their sense of smell was extraordinarily fine; they could distinguish individual differences as readily as a dog can, and they went about the tending of the llamas, who lived among the rocks above and came to the wall for food and shelter, with ease and confidence. It was only when at last Nunez sought to assert himself that he found how easy and confident their movements could be.

95   He rebelled only after he had tried persuasion.

96   He tried at first on several occasions to tell them of sight. "Look you here, you people," he said. "There are things you do not understand in me."

97   Once or twice one or two of them attended to him; they sat with faces downcast and ears turned intelligently toward him, and he did his best to tell them what it was to see. Among his hearers was a girl, with eyelids less red and sunken than the others, so that

one could almost fancy she was hiding eyes, whom especially he hoped to persuade. He spoke of the beauties of sight, of watching the mountains, of the sky and the sunrise, and they heard him with amused incredulity that presently became condemnatory. They told him there were indeed no mountains at all, but that the end of the rocks where the llamas grazed was indeed the end of the world; thence sprang a cavernous roof of the universe, from which the dew and the avalanches fell; and when he maintained stoutly the world had neither end nor roof such as they supposed, they said his thoughts were wicked. So far as he could describe sky and clouds and stars to them it seemed to them a hideous void, a terrible blankness in the place of the smooth roof to things in which they believed—it was an article of faith with them that the cavern roof was exquisitely smooth to the touch. He saw that in some manner he shocked them, and gave up that aspect of the matter altogether, and tried to show them the practical value of sight. One morning he saw Pedro in the path called Seventeen and coming toward the central houses, but still too far off for hearing or scent, and he told them as much. "In a little while," he prophesied, "Pedro will be here." An old man remarked that Pedro had no business on path Seventeen, and then, as if in confirmation, that individual as he drew near turned and went transversely into path Ten, and so back with nimble paces toward the outer wall. They mocked Nunez when Pedro did not arrive, and afterwards, when he asked Pedro questions to clear his character, Pedro denied and outfaced him, and was afterwards hostile to him.

98   Then he induced them to let him go a long way up the sloping meadows toward the wall with one complacent individual, and to him he promised to describe all that happened among the houses. He noted certain goings and comings, but the things that really seemed to signify to these people happened inside of or behind the windowless houses—the only things they took note of to test him by—and of these he could see or tell nothing; and it was after the failure of this attempt, and the ridicule they could not repress, that he resorted to force. He thought of seizing a spade and suddenly smiting one or two of them to earth, and so in fair combat showing the advantage of eyes. He went so far with that resolution as to seize his spade, and then he discovered a new thing about himself, and that was that it was impossible for him to hit a blind man in cold blood.

99   He hesitated, and found them all aware that he had snatched up the spade. They stood alert, with their heads on one side, and bent ears toward him for what he would do next.

100   "Put that spade down," said one, and he felt a sort of helpless horror. He came near obedience.

101   Then he thrust one backwards against a house wall, and fled past him and out of the village.

102   He went athwart one of their meadows, leaving a track of trampled grass behind his feet, and presently sat down by the side of one of their ways. He felt something of the buoyancy that comes to all men in the beginning of a fight, but more perplexity. He began to realize that you cannot even fight happily with creatures who stand upon a different mental basis to yourself. Far away he saw a number of men carrying spades and sticks come out of the street of houses, and advance in a spreading line along the several paths toward him. They advanced slowly, speaking frequently to one another, and ever and again the whole cordon would halt and sniff the air and listen.

103   The first time they did this Nunez laughed. But afterwards he did not laugh.

104   One struck his trail in the meadow grass, and came stooping and feeling his way along it.

105   For five minutes he watched the slow extension of the cordon, and then his vague disposition to do something forthwith became frantic. He stood up, went a pace or so toward the circumferential wall, turned, and went back a little way. There they all stood in a crescent, still and listening.

106   He also stood still, gripping his spade very tightly in both hands. Should he charge them?

107   The pulse in his ears ran into the rhythm of "In the Country of the Blind the One-eyed Man is King!"

108   Should he charge them?

109   He looked back at the high and unclimbable wall behind— unclimbable because of its smooth plastering, but withal pierced with many little doors, and at the approaching line of seekers. Behind these others were now coming out of the street of houses.

Mark base words or indicate another strategy you used that helped you determine meaning.

perplexity (puhr PLEHK suh tee) *n.*

MEANING:

110   Should he charge them?

111   "Bogota!" called one. "Bogota! where are you?"

112   He gripped his spade still tighter, and advanced down the meadows toward the place of habitations, and directly he moved they converged upon him. "I'll hit them if they touch me," he swore; "by Heaven, I will. I'll hit." He called aloud, "Look here, I'm going to do what I like in this valley. Do you hear? I'm going to do what I like and go where I like!"

113   They were moving in upon him quickly, groping, yet moving rapidly. It was like playing blind man's buff, with everyone blindfolded except one. "Get hold of him!" cried one. He found himself in the arc of a loose curve of pursuers. He felt suddenly he must be active and resolute.

114   "You don't understand," he cried in a voice that was meant to be great and resolute, and which broke. "You are blind, and I can see. Leave me alone!"

115   "Bogota! Put down that spade, and come off the grass!"

116   The last order, grotesque in its urban familiarity, produced a gust of anger.

117   "I'll hurt you," he said, sobbing with emotion. "By Heaven, I'll hurt you. Leave me alone!"

118   He began to run, not knowing clearly where to run. He ran from the nearest blind man, because it was a horror to hit him. He stopped, and then made a dash to escape from their closing ranks. He made for where a gap was wide, and the men on either side, with a quick perception of the approach of his paces, rushed in on one another. He sprang forward, and then saw he must be caught, and *swish!* the spade had struck. He felt the soft thud of hand and arm, and the man was down with a yell of pain, and he was through.

119   Through! And then he was close to the street of houses again, and blind men, whirling spades and stakes, were running with a sort of reasoned swiftness hither and thither.

120   He heard steps behind him just in time, and found a tall man rushing forward and swiping at the sound of him. He lost his nerve, hurled his spade a yard wide at his antagonist, and whirled about and fled, fairly yelling as he dodged another.

121   He was panic-stricken. He ran furiously to and fro, dodging when there was no need to dodge, and in his anxiety to see on every side of him at once, stumbling. For a moment he was down and they heard his fall. Far away in the circumferential wall a little doorway looked like heaven, and he set off in a wild rush for it. He did not even look round at his pursuers until it was gained, and he had stumbled across the bridge, clambered a little way among the rocks, to the surprise and dismay of a young llama, who went leaping out of sight, and lay down sobbing for breath.

122   And so his *coup d'état* came to an end.

123   He stayed outside the wall of the valley of the Blind for two nights and days without food or shelter, and meditated upon the

unexpected. During these meditations he repeated very frequently and always with a profounder note of derision the exploded proverb: "In the Country of the Blind the One-Eyed Man is King." He thought chiefly of ways of fighting and conquering these people, and it grew clear that for him no practicable way was possible. He had no weapons, and now it would be hard to get one.

124   The canker[8] of civilization had got to him even in Bogota, and he could not find it in himself to go down and assassinate a blind man. Of course, if he did that, he might then dictate terms on the threat of assassinating them all. But—sooner or later he must sleep! . . .

125   He tried also to find food among the pine trees, to be comfortable under pine boughs while the frost fell at night, and—with less confidence—to catch a llama by artifice in order to try to kill it— perhaps by hammering it with a stone—and so finally, perhaps, to eat some of it. But the llamas had a doubt of him and regarded him with distrustful brown eyes, and spat when he drew near. Fear came on him the second day and fits of shivering. Finally he crawled down to the wall of the Country of the Blind and tried to make terms. He crawled along by the stream, shouting, until two blind men came out to the gate and talked to him.

126   "I was mad," he said. "But I was only newly made."

127   They said that was better.

128   He told them he was wiser now, and repented of all he had done.

129   Then he wept without intention, for he was very weak and ill now, and they took that as a favorable sign.

130   They asked him if he still thought he could "see."

131   "No," he said. "That was folly. The word means nothing—less than nothing!"

132   They asked him what was overhead.

133   "About ten times ten the height of a man there is a roof above the world—of rock—and very, very smooth." . . . He burst again into hysterical tears. "Before you ask me any more, give me some food or I shall die."

134   He expected dire punishments, but these blind people were capable of toleration. They regarded his rebellion as but one more proof of his general idiocy and inferiority; and after they had whipped him they appointed him to do the simplest and heaviest work they had for anyone to do, and he, seeing no other way of living, did submissively what he was told.

135   He was ill for some days, and they nursed him kindly. That refined his submission. But they insisted on his lying in the dark, and that was a great misery. And blind philosophers came and talked to him of the wicked levity of his mind, and reproved him so impressively for his doubts about the lid of rock that covered their cosmic casserole that he almost doubted whether indeed he was not the victim of hallucination in not seeing it overhead.

---

8. **canker** (KANG kuhr) *n.* something that causes rot or decay.

136   So Nunez became a citizen of the Country of the Blind, and these people ceased to be a generalized people and became individualities and familiar to him, while the world beyond the mountains became more and more remote and unreal. There was Yacob, his master, a kindly man when not annoyed; there was Pedro, Yacob's nephew; and there was Medina-saroté, who was the youngest daughter of Yacob. She was little esteemed in the world of the blind, because she had a clear-cut face, and lacked that satisfying, glossy smoothness that is the blind man's ideal of feminine beauty; but Nunez thought her beautiful at first, and presently the most beautiful thing in the whole creation. Her closed eyelids were not sunken and red after the common way of the valley, but lay as though they might open again at any moment; and she had long eyelashes, which were considered a grave disfigurement. And her voice was strong, and did not satisfy the acute hearing of the valley swains.[9] So that she had no lover.

137   There came a time when Nunez thought that, could he win her, he would be resigned to live in the valley for all the rest of his days.

138   He watched her; he sought opportunities of doing her little services, and presently he found that she observed him. Once at a rest-day gathering they sat side by side in the dim starlight, and the music was sweet. His hand came upon hers and he dared to clasp it. Then very tenderly she returned his pressure. And one day, as they were at their meal in the darkness, he felt her hand very softly seeking him, and as it chanced the fire leapt then and he saw the tenderness of her face.

139   He sought to speak to her.

140   He went to her one day when she was sitting in the summer moonlight spinning. The light made her a thing of silver and mystery. He sat down at her feet and told her he loved her, and told her how beautiful she seemed to him. He had a lover's voice, he spoke with a tender reverence that came near to awe, and she had never before been touched by adoration. She made him no definite answer, but it was clear his words pleased her.

141   After that he talked to her whenever he could take an opportunity. The valley became the world for him, and the world beyond the mountains where men lived in sunlight seemed no more than a fairy tale he would some day pour into her ears. Very tentatively and timidly he spoke to her of sight.

142   Sight seemed to her the most poetical of fancies, and she listened to his description of the stars and the mountains and her own sweet white-lit beauty as though it was a guilty indulgence. She did not believe, she could only half understand, but she was mysteriously delighted, and it seemed to him that she completely understood.

143   His love lost its awe and took courage. Presently he was for demanding her of Yacob and the elders in marriage, but she became fearful and delayed. And it was one of her elder sisters who first told Yacob that Medina-saroté and Nunez were in love.

---

9. **swains** (swaynz) *n.* males interested in seeking the affection of a woman.

Mark base words or indicate
another strategy you used that
helped you determine meaning.

delusions (dih LOO zhuhnz) *n.*

MEANING:

144   There was from the first very great opposition to the marriage of Nunez and Medina-saroté; not so much because they valued her as because they held him as a being apart, an idiot, incompetent thing below the permissible level of a man. Her sisters opposed it bitterly as bringing discredit on them all; and old Yacob, though he had formed a sort of liking for his clumsy, obedient serf, shook his head and said the thing could not be. The young men were all angry at the idea of corrupting the race, and one went so far as to revile and strike Nunez. He struck back. Then for the first time he found an advantage in seeing, even by twilight, and after that fight was over no one was disposed to raise a hand against him. But they still found his marriage impossible.

145   Old Yacob had a tenderness for his last little daughter, and was grieved to have her weep upon his shoulder.

146   "You see, my dear, he's an idiot. He has **delusions**; he can't do anything right."

147   "I know," wept Medina-saroté. "But he's better than he was. He's getting better. And he's strong, dear father, and kind—stronger and kinder than any other man in the world. And he loves me—and, father, I love him."

148   Old Yacob was greatly distressed to find her inconsolable, and, besides— what made it more distressing—he liked Nunez for many things. So he went and sat in the windowless council-chamber with the other elders and watched the trend of the talk, and said, at the proper time, "He's better than he was. Very likely, some day, we shall find him as sane as ourselves."

149   Then afterwards one of the elders, who thought deeply, had an idea. He was the great doctor among these people, their medicine-man, and he had a very philosophical and inventive mind, and the idea of curing Nunez of his peculiarities appealed to him. One day when Yacob was present he returned to the topic of Nunez.

150   "I have examined Bogota," he said, "and the case is clearer to me. I think very probably he might be cured."

151   "That is what I have always hoped," said old Yacob.

152   "His brain is affected," said the blind doctor.

153   The elders murmured assent.

154   "Now, *what* affects it?"

155   "Ah!" said old Yacob.

156   "*This,*" said the doctor, answering his own question. "Those queer things that are called the eyes, and which exist to make an agreeable soft depression in the face, are diseased, in the case of Bogota, in such a way as to affect his brain. They are greatly distended, he has eyelashes, and his eyelids move, and consequently his brain is in a state of constant irritation and distraction."

157   "Yes?" said old Yacob. "Yes?"

158   "And I think I may say with reasonable certainty that, in order to cure him completely, all that we need do is a simple and easy surgical operation—namely, to remove these irritant bodies."

159 "And then he will be sane?"

160 "Then he will be perfectly sane, and a quite admirable citizen."

161 "Thank Heaven for science!" said old Yacob, and went forth at once to tell Nunez of his happy hopes.

162 But Nunez's manner of receiving the good news struck him as being cold and disappointing.

163 "One might think," he said, "from the tone you take, that you did not care for my daughter."

164 It was Medina-saroté who persuaded Nunez to face the blind surgeons.

165 "*You* do not want me," he said, "to lose my gift of sight?"

166 She shook her head.

167 "My world is sight."

168 Her head drooped lower.

169 "There are the beautiful things, the beautiful little things—the flowers, the lichens among the rocks, the lightness and softness on a piece of fur, the far sky with its drifting down of clouds, the sunsets and the stars. And there is *you*. For you alone it is good to have sight, to see your sweet, serene face, your kindly lips, your dear, beautiful hands folded together . . . It is these eyes of mine you won, these eyes that hold me to you, that these idiots seek. Instead, I must touch you, hear you, and never see you again. I must come under that roof of

rock and stone and darkness, that horrible roof under which your imagination stoops . . . No; you would not have me do that?"

170   A disagreeable doubt had arisen in him. He stopped, and left the thing a question.

171   "I wish," she said, "sometimes——" She paused.

172   "Yes," said he, a little apprehensively.

173   "I wish sometimes—you would not talk like that."

174   "Like what?"

175   "I know it's pretty—it's your imagination. I love it, but now——"

176   He felt cold. *"Now?"* he said faintly.

177   She sat quite still.

178   "You mean—you think—I should be better, better perhaps——"

179   He was realizing things very swiftly. He felt anger, indeed, anger at the dull course of fate, but also sympathy for her lack of understanding—a sympathy near akin to pity.

180   *"Dear,"* he said, and he could see by her whiteness how intensely her spirit pressed against the things she could not say. He put his arms about her, he kissed her ear, and they sat for a time in silence.

181   "If I were to consent to this?" he said at last, in a voice that was very gentle.

182   She flung her arms about him, weeping wildly. "Oh, if you would," she sobbed, "if only you would!"

✳ ✳ ✳ ✳ ✳

183   For a week before the operation that was to raise him from his servitude and inferiority to the level of a blind citizen, Nunez knew nothing of sleep, and all through the warm sunlit hours, while the others slumbered happily, he sat brooding or wandered aimlessly, trying to bring his mind to bear on his dilemma. He had given his answer, he had given his consent, and still he was not sure. And at last work-time was over, the sun rose in splendor over the golden crests, and his last day of vision began for him. He had a few minutes with Medina-saroté before she went apart to sleep.

184   "Tomorrow," he said, "I shall see no more."

185   "Dear heart!" she answered, and pressed his hands with all her strength.

186   "They will hurt you but little," she said; "and you are going through this pain—you are going through it, dear lover, for *me* . . . Dear, if a woman's heart and life can do it, I will repay you. My dearest one, my dearest with the tender voice, I will repay."

187   He was drenched in pity for himself and her.

188   He held her in his arms, and pressed his lips to hers, and looked on her sweet face for the last time. "Good-bye!" he whispered at that dear sight, "good-bye!"

189   And then in silence he turned away from her.

190   She could hear his slow retreating footsteps, and something in the rhythm of them threw her into a passion of weeping.

191   He had fully meant to go to a lonely place where the meadows were beautiful with white narcissus, and there remain until the hour of his sacrifice should come, but as he went he lifted up his eyes and saw the morning, the morning like an angel in golden armor, marching down the steeps . . .

192   It seemed to him that before this splendor he, and this blind world in the valley, and his love, and all, were no more than a pit of sin.

193   He did not turn aside as he had meant to do, but went on, and passed through the wall of the circumference and out upon the rocks, and his eyes were always upon the sunlit ice and snow.

194   He saw their infinite beauty, and his imagination soared over them to the things beyond he was now to resign forever.

195   He thought of that great free world he was parted from, the world that was his own, and he had a vision of those further slopes, distance beyond distance, with Bogota, a place of multitudinous stirring beauty, a glory by day, a luminous mystery by night, a place of palaces and fountains and statues and white houses, lying beautifully in the middle distance. He thought how for a day or so one might come down through passes, drawing ever nearer and nearer to its busy streets and ways. He thought of the river journey, day by day, from great Bogota to the still vaster world beyond, through towns and villages, forest and desert places, the rushing river day by day, until its banks receded and the big steamers came splashing by, and one had reached the sea—the limitless sea, with its thousand islands, its thousands of islands, and its ships seen dimly far away in their incessant journeyings round and about that greater world. And there, unpent by mountains, one saw the sky—the sky, not such a disc as one saw it here, but an arch of immeasurable blue, a deep of deeps in which the circling stars were floating . . .

196   His eyes scrutinized the great curtain of the mountains with a keener inquiry.

197   For example, if one went so, up that gully and to that chimney[10] there, then one might come out high among those stunted pines that ran round in a sort of shelf and rose still higher and higher as it passed above the gorge. And then? That talus might be managed. Thence perhaps a climb might be found to take him up to the precipice that came below the snow; and if that chimney failed, then another farther to the east might serve his purpose better. And then? Then one would be out upon the amber-lit snow there, and halfway up to the crest of those beautiful desolations.

198   He glanced back at the village, then turned right round and regarded it steadfastly.

---

10. **chimney** (CHIHM nee) *n.* narrow column of rock.

199   He thought of Medina-saroté, and she had become small and remote.

200   He turned again towards the mountain wall, down which the day had come to him.

201   Then very circumspectly he began to climb.

202   When sunset came he was no longer climbing, but he was far and high. He had been higher, but he was still very high. His clothes were torn, his limbs were blood-stained, he was bruised in many places, but he lay as if he were at his ease, and there was a smile on his face.

203   From where he rested the valley seemed as if it were in a pit and nearly a mile below. Already it was dim with haze and shadow, though the mountain summits around him were things of light and fire. The mountain summits around him were things of light and fire, and the little details of the rocks near at hand were drenched with subtle beauty—a vein of green mineral piercing the grey, the flash of crystal faces here and there, a minute, minutely-beautiful orange lichen close beside his face. There were deep mysterious shadows in the gorge, blue deepening into purple, and purple into a luminous darkness, and overhead was the illimitable vastness of the sky. But he heeded these things no longer, but lay quite inactive there, smiling as if he were satisfied merely to have escaped from the valley of the Blind in which he had thought to be King.

204   The glow of the sunset passed, and the night came, and still he lay peacefully contented under the cold clear stars. ✦

Comprehension Check

Complete the following items after you finish your first read. Review and clarify details with your group.

1. How do the people who live in the Country of the Blind lose their sight?

2. How does Nunez end up in the Country of the Blind?

3. What unusual qualities does Nunez notice about the villagers' houses?

4. How do the villagers regard Nunez's ability to see, and what do they propose to do to him as a result?

5. ⊟ **Notebook** Confirm your understanding of the text by writing a timeline of events in the story.

- -

RESEARCH

Research to Clarify Choose at least one unfamiliar detail from the text. Briefly research that detail. In what way does the information you learned shed light on an aspect of the story?

Research to Explore This story may spark your curiosity to learn more. Briefly research a topic that interests you. You may want to share what you discover with your group.

Close Read the Text

With your group, revisit sections of the text you marked during your first read. **Annotate** details that you notice. What **questions** do you have? What can you **conclude**?

Analyze the Text

CITE TEXTUAL EVIDENCE
to support your answers.

📝 **Notebook** Complete the activities.

1. **Review and Clarify** With your group, reread paragraph 63 of the selection. Discuss how the people in the hidden valley have gradually created a place and a society in which sight is unnecessary.

2. **Present and Discuss** Now, work with your group to share passages from the selection that you found especially important. Take turns presenting your passages. Discuss what you noticed, what questions you asked, and what conclusions you reached.

3. **Essential Question:** *What does it mean to see?* What has the story taught you about blindness and sight? Discuss with your group.

Concept Vocabulary

| incoherent | perplexity | delusions |

Why These Words? The three concept vocabulary words are related. With your group, discuss the words, and determine what they have in common. Write another word related to this concept.

Practice

📝 **Notebook** Confirm your understanding of these words by using them in sentences. Include context clues that hint at meaning.

Word Study

📝 **Notebook** **Latin Root: -lud- / -lus-** In "The Country of the Blind," the father of a girl Nunez loves says, "He has delusions; he can't do anything right." The word *delusions* can be traced back to the Latin verb *ludere*, meaning "to play." English words derived from *ludere* contain the root *-lud-* or *-lus-* and tend to have meanings related to silliness, trickery, or deception. Explain how the root contributes to the meanings of *ludicrous* and *illusion*. Consult an etymological dictionary if needed.

Analyze Craft and Structure

Narrative Structure A **plot** is the sequence of related events in a story. All plots are driven by a **conflict,** or struggle between opposing forces. Likewise, every plot follows a basic sequence that involves how the conflict is introduced, developed, and resolved.

- **Exposition:** The characters, setting, and basic situation are introduced.
- **Rising action:** The central conflict is established and begins to intensify.
- **Climax:** The conflict reaches its highest point of drama or tension.
- **Falling action:** The tension in the story decreases.
- **Resolution:** The conflict ends, and any remaining issues are resolved.

Actions or external changes to a conflict or a character's situation are plot events. However, it is important to note that a character's change of feeling, new understanding, or realization can also be a plot event.

Practice

CITE TEXTUAL EVIDENCE to support your answers.

📓 **Notebook** Work together as a group to answer these questions.

1. Identify the distinct stages of the plot of "The Country of the Blind."

    (a) What information does the exposition provide? At what point does the exposition end?

    (b) What is the story's main conflict? At what point in the story is that conflict first introduced?

    (c) Cite one event and one character that add complications to the story's main conflict. Explain your choices.

    (d) At what point in the story does the conflict reach its point of greatest intensity? Explain, citing story details that support your choice.

    (e) What happens during the story's falling action? How does the conflict resolve?

2. Using your answers to questions 1 (a)–(e), fill in the details of the plot diagram for this story.

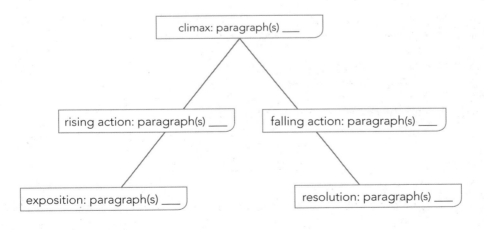

climax: paragraph(s) ___

rising action: paragraph(s) ___

falling action: paragraph(s) ___

exposition: paragraph(s) ___

resolution: paragraph(s) ___

THE COUNTRY OF THE BLIND

Author's Style

Author's Choices: Narrative Pacing Authors choose to speed a story up or slow it down by controlling sentence length, adding description or dialogue, and changing the frequency of plot events. How quickly or slowly a story moves is called its **pace**.

A slow-paced section of a story may focus on descriptions of the setting, characters, and events. Long descriptive passages help readers visualize details and may contribute to a particular **mood**, or emotional atmosphere. A fast-paced section of a story usually has a lot of movement, with one action following another in rapid succession. This may have the effect of increasing tension and moving the plot forward. Fast-paced sections may feature short, punchy sentences. However, in writing of Wells's era, action-packed clauses can also be embedded in longer sentences.

Read It

Work individually. Read each passage in the chart, and describe its pacing. Make notes about the characteristics of the passage that contribute to its pacing. Discuss your responses with your group. During your discussion, support your ideas by including examples from other parts of the story, as well. One example has been done for you.

SELECTION PASSAGE	PACE	EFFECTS
Three hundred miles and more from Chimborazo, one hundred from the snows of Cotopaxi, in the wildest wastes of Ecuador's Andes, there lies that mysterious mountain valley, cut off from the world of men, the Country of the Blind. (paragraph 1)	slow	introduces the setting; long sentence with many clauses conveys the setting's majesty and remoteness
"See?" said Correa. *"Yes, see," said Nunez, turning toward him, and stumbled against Pedro's pail.* *"His senses are still imperfect," said the third blind man. "He stumbles, and talks unmeaning words. Lead him by the hand."* *"As you will," said Nunez, and was led along, laughing.* *It seemed they knew nothing of sight.* *Well, all in good time he would teach them.* (paragraphs 44–50)		
He stopped, and then made a dash to escape from their closing ranks. He made for where a gap was wide, and the men on either side, with a quick perception of the approach of his paces, rushed in on one another. He sprang forward, and then saw he must be caught, and swish! the spade had struck. (paragraph 118)		

Write It

📓 **Notebook** Write two sections of a narrative. In one section, describe the setting. In the other, describe the action. Use techniques, such as longer or shorter sentences, to vary the pacing in the two sections. Then, explain how your choices created specific effects.

Writing to Sources

Assignment

Write a **response to the story**. Work together as a group to brainstorm for ideas and gather evidence, but work independently to write your own response. Choose from these options.

☐ **Retelling** Rewrite a portion of the story as a flashback, as though it is a memory being recalled by Nunez or another character. Explain how the pace and mood of the story change with the manipulation of time.

☐ **Character Description** Write a description of Nunez from another character's point of view. Include thoughts that this character has about Nunez at specific moments in the story. Cite lines of dialogue and other details from the story in your description.

☐ **Dialogue** Write a dialogue in which Nunez describes his experiences in "The Country of the Blind" to an outsider. The dialogue should take place after all the events of the story, when Nunez has returned to his own culture. Include all the major plot points of the story.

Project Plan Before you begin, get together as a group and review the notes you have taken as you analyzed different aspects of the story. Decide which notes might be useful to the project option you have chosen, and determine an equitable way to share the information.

Clarifying Ideas Brainstorm for ideas or story elements you will include in your writing assignment. These may involve important characters, plot points, or key shifts in the pace of the narrative. Refer to the text to clarify your ideas. Use the chart to gather your notes.

STORY DETAIL	HOW I WILL USE IT

Present After you have completed your writing, present the finished work to your group. Take turns reading one another's work and offering constructive feedback. Explain what you think worked well and what might be improved. Using the feedback from your peers, revise your writing.

✎ EVIDENCE LOG

Before moving on to a new selection, go to your Evidence Log and record what you learned from "The Country of the Blind."

About the Author

Rosemary Mahoney (b. 1961) is a citizen of both Ireland and the United States. Her writing has appeared in the *Wall Street Journal, National Geographic Traveler,* the *London Observer*, and many other publications. Regarding her book *For the Benefit of Those Who See, Entertainment Weekly* writes that it is as if Mahoney has "turned on the lights in a dark room, revealing how the world appears to those who experience it with their other four senses."

The Neglected Senses

Concept Vocabulary

As you perform your first read of "The Neglected Senses," you will encounter these words.

> traversed   periphery   navigating

Context Clues If these words are unfamiliar to you, try using **context clues**—other words and phrases that appear nearby in a text—to help you determine their meanings. There are various types of context clues that you may help you as you read.

> **Restatement:** The very tall teacher standing beside her tiny first graders was an **incongruous** sight indeed, a stark contrast that made the students' parents grin.
>
> **Contrast of Ideas:** The seemingly **relentless** blizzard brought such blinding snow and wind that it was hard to believe when it finally ended.

Apply your knowledge of context clues and other vocabulary strategies to determine the meanings of unfamiliar words you encounter during your first read.

First Read NONFICTION

Apply these strategies as you conduct your first read. You will have an opportunity to complete a close read after your first read.

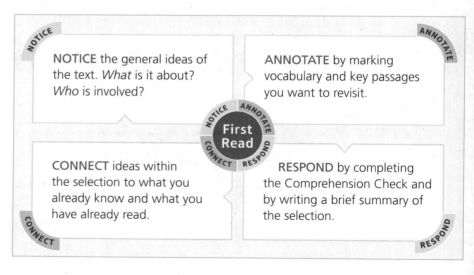

NOTICE the general ideas of the text. *What* is it about? *Who* is involved?

ANNOTATE by marking vocabulary and key passages you want to revisit.

CONNECT ideas within the selection to what you already know and what you have already read.

RESPOND by completing the Comprehension Check and by writing a brief summary of the selection.

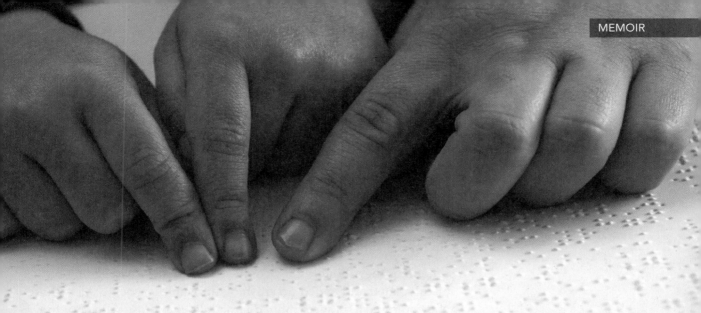

The Neglected Senses
from For the Benefit of Those Who See

Rosemary Mahoney

BACKGROUND
Due to a punishing climate and lack of medical care, Tibet has an unusually high population of blind people—thirty thousand of the 2.5 million Tibetans are either completely blind or significantly sight-impaired. Beginning in the 1990s, Braille Without Borders, a charitable organization founded by Sabriye Tenberken and Paul Kronenberg in Lhasa, Tibet, has opened schools to help blind Tibetans integrate into society and gain valuable skills.

1 At Braille Without Borders, you learn quickly not to stand idly in doorways or on staircases or in narrow hallways, for the consequence is that eventually somebody blind will slam into you. In settings familiar to the blind, the unobstructed navigability of transitional passageways is something they quite reasonably take for granted. A doorway exists solely to be passed through, a staircase solely to be ascended or descended, a hallway solely to be **traversed** on the way from one room to another. Unable to see that a two-hundred-pound man is sitting in the middle of a staircase, a pack of blind students will most likely fail to anticipate his anomalous presence and fall headlong over him as they attempt to skip down the stairs. The students at BWB race around their school, sprinting down the hallways, turning corners crisply at five miles per hour, skirting tables and chairs, opening doors without groping for the knobs, reaching for objects on shelves with surprising precision. They kick soccer balls, rearrange furniture, zip their own zippers, throw

Mark context clues or indicate another strategy you used that helped you determine meaning.

traversed (truh VURST) *v.*

MEANING:

things and catch things (yes, sometimes they miss the catch and the things end up hitting them in the face), fill their own soup bowls, go for walks downtown alone, make purchases without getting shortchanged. They know their realm so well that after a few days at the school, I began to forget that they were blind and would not have been entirely surprised to find a blind child successfully juggling three apples or using the banister as a balance beam. I realized that those who had some vision actually moved more hesitantly than those who were completely blind. The slightly sighted, still depending on their weakened eyes, had to take time to make out what they were seeing—to locate a doorknob, for example—and sometimes they thought they could see where they were going but miscalculated and ended up crashing into tables or posts. Also, those who could see a bit were more distractible than those who couldn't see at all, and they occasionally tried to read their Braille with whatever sight they had left, holding the embossed pages an inch from their eyes, a habit that Paul and Sabriye adamantly discouraged, because it taxes whatever vision remains and because it is much less efficient than tactile reading.

2   I was surprised by the ease and harmony the blind students had with their physical realm and was eager enough to understand it that at Sabriye's suggestion I agreed to let myself be blindfolded and led through the streets of Lhasa by two blind teenage girls, Choden and Yangchen.

3   The girls and I set off from the school and as soon as we crossed the big boulevard, Chingdol Dong Lu, I took a blindfold out of my pocket. Yangchen and Choden stood on either side of me, waiting expectantly, holding their white canes before them, clearly amused by the challenge. Yangchen, a shy, round-faced, cross-eyed sixteen-year-old with her hair in a ponytail, was completely blind in one eye and saw only faint impressions of light with the other. She wore a baseball cap, clodhopper boots, a plaid flannel shirt buttoned up to the throat, denim trousers, and a jean jacket. Yangchen's perpetually crossed eyes gave her the appearance of slapstick confusion. I came to learn, however, that Yangchen was a level-headed, sober, practical girl and possessed of considerable poise. Choden, a year younger than Yangchen, was pink-cheeked and ever smiling. She too wore a ponytail, plaid flannel shirt, denim jacket and pants, baseball cap, and hiking boots. Side by side in their rough-and-ready attire, the girls brought to mind a pair of lumberjacks ready to chop their way through a forest. Choden's eyes were pinched shut most of the time, but her left eye occasionally opened and seemed to range around in its orbit taking in some light and color.

4   The girls' blindness, their white canes, and my foreign presence with them had drawn a group of onlookers on the city sidewalk. As I pulled the blindfold over my eyes, I said to the girls, "We have a lot of people looking at us."

5   Excited and embarrassed, they hooted "Heeoo!" into their fingertips.

6   "And," I added, "one of the people looking at us is a tall Chinese policeman with a gun."[1]

7   To that dire piece of information they responded with a moment of shocked silence. And then they lowered their heads and muttered gravely, "Tchah!"

8   "But," I said, "never mind the people. I have put the blindfold on and cannot see them anymore. I am now putting my sunglasses on over the blindfold so that I can see even less."

9   "Good," Yangchen said. "Now you are blind?"

10   My eyes were sufficiently bound that I could see nothing at all—no light, no forms, nothing. The bright and varied colors of the buildings of Lhasa had disappeared, and I was presented with nothing but the backs of my own eyelids onto which my heartbeat was projected in rhythmic flashes of orange. In the high altitude and resultant low atmospheric pressure of Lhasa, I was often aware that my heart was struggling to do its job. Nowhere else in the world had I been so conscious of my own pulse. At night when I lay in bed, my heart pounded in my chest, ears, and eyes and I felt short of breath to the point that I slept with my mouth open and occasionally woke up feeling that I might actually be suffocating, whereupon I had to get up and walk around my enormous hotel room. Sometimes I even had to stand by an open window and inhale deeply (which only gave me the comforting *illusion* that I was getting more air when of course the reality was that the atmospheric pressure outside the room was exactly the same as it was inside it) until the suffocating feeling passed.

11   "I can't see a thing, I assure you," I said. "Now, listen, girls, you won't let me get lost in Lhasa, will you? You know I don't speak Tibetan."

12   With a hint of gloating pleasure Choden said, "Yah. We know it." Then she took my hand and thrust her white cane into it.

13   "Oh, am I taking a cane too?"

14   Yangchen, the older of the two, interjected nervously, "Cane? Well, no. Maybe no cane. Choden must have her own cane. Otherwise she can lose her road."

15   I passed the cane clumsily back to Choden. "Take your cane, Choden. God forbid you should lose your road while you're leading me."

16   The girls positioned themselves on either side of me, hooked their arms through mine, and we headed up the street. Immediately I had the sensation that the ground beneath my feet was tilting. Sound seemed to become louder, smells became stronger, and the breeze on my face felt more forceful and distracting. I tripped on a raised lip of pavement, and the girls quickly tightened their grip on my elbows to keep me from falling. The dragging clicking of one of the canes

---

1. **Chinese policeman with a gun** Tibet is currently under the control of China.

on the pavement sounded for all the world like the jittering ball in a spinning roulette wheel. I asked Choden if it was her cane that was making all that noise.

17   "Yah. Very nizey is my cane." Compelled to imitate the gravelly sound of her cane, Choden said with relish, "Zaaaarrrrr!"

18   Sensing that I was nervous, Yangchen said, "Rose, how you are feeling?"

19   "Well, I'm not really afraid," I said, "but I feel as though I'm in a boat that's moving. You know that feeling when you're in a boat and the water is moving beneath you and you're a little bit unsteady on your feet?"

20   "Oh, yah, I know it! Funny," Choden said. "You are a little bit nervous, is that right, Rose?"

21   I confessed that I was indeed a little bit nervous.

22   This seemed to please Choden. "Oh, ha!" she said, audibly smiling.

23   "Have you ever been in a boat?" I asked her.

24   "No, I never."

25   "Well, then how can you say you know how it feels?"

26   "Oh, ha! You are right."

27   "Tell me, girls, how do you feel? Does the ground feel steady to you?"

28   "Yah," Yangchen said, "is always steady. No problem. And now we must turn left."

29   "How do you know that?"

30   "Because the sound of many televisions."

31   Until Yangchen mentioned it, I had not noticed the sound of many televisions. I had vaguely heard some background noise beyond us, an insignificant presence at the **periphery** of my attention, but distracted by my nervousness, I had not identified it. Now, focusing on it, I realized that the sound of many televisions was quite loud; riotous, in fact—it was that unmistakably tinny television sound, a counterfeit, thinner version of firsthand sound. What I was hearing was the many-times-multiplied voices of two people having a tense dialogue in Chinese; they spoke with the razor-sharp accent of Beijing. And then I heard rapid gunfire; filtered and squeezed through the many televisions, the gunfire sounded feeble and fake, like plastic popguns in a penny arcade. I was disturbed that I hadn't noticed these sounds from a distance.

32   "That is men always selling televisions in a shop," Yangchen said. "Sometimes it is war films. When we hear the televisions, we know we must turn left."

33   It was a matter of familiarity, then, a recognizable constant in the girls' journey into the city.

34   We carried on at an alarmingly brisk pace. I expected at any moment to crack my forehead on a lamppost or go plummeting into an open manhole. I felt terribly vulnerable and had to fight the impulse to lift the blindfold off my face. As I walked I realized that I was holding my chin much higher in the air than I normally would,

---

Mark context clues or indicate another strategy you used that helped you determine meaning.

periphery (puh RIHF uhr ee) *n.*

MEANING:

the way I do when I'm swimming and trying to keep my head dry, and each step I took had the same quality of awkward anticipation as those last few exploratory, drop-footed steps taken toward the bottom of a staircase one is descending in the pitch-dark. I couldn't help lifting my hands in front of me in self-defense, like a pathetic caricature of a blind person. Linked at the elbows with the two girls, I found it difficult to lift my hands; nevertheless, I kept trying to lift them, and Yangchen kept gently pressing them down to show me I had nothing to fear.

35   "I shouldn't lift my hands, Yangchen?" I said.

36   "Umm. Maybe it is better to trust," Yangchen said. She was much too patient and polite a girl to just come out and say *No, you shouldn't*.

37   "Girls," I said, "I wouldn't be able to do this alone."

38   "You would be afraid?" Choden said.

39   "I would be very afraid."

40   "Oh, ha," Choden said.

41   "Do not be afraid," Yangchen said. "We are watching you."

42   All the blind students spoke this way—*We are watching you. Nice to see you. See you again. Please let me see that book.* For them, the vocabulary of vision was metaphorical, a symbolic representation of human connection, interest, and concern.

43   The girls coaxed me forward with their slender arms, never breaking their stride. I heard passing voices speaking Tibetan and Chinese, the sound of a small spluttering engine like that of a generator or an idling motorbike, the distant shrieks of children, a horn that sounded like a loud fart, something metallic scraping briefly on the pavement behind us, someone sneezing richly nearby, and all the while Choden's noisy cane rattling along in front of us like a yapping little dog leading the way.

44   Yangchen had a habit of humming as she walked. Each time she spoke, she had to interrupt her own humming, putting it on hold until there was silence between us again, whereupon she would resume the tune approximately where she had left off. I asked the girls how long they had been blind; both said from a very young age. I asked them what they had been doing before they came to Braille Without Borders in Lhasa.

45   Yangchen said, "I was only at home. Just praying something and helping my mother."

46   Choden said, "I'm too home. Praying and helping."

47   "Were there any other blind kids where you lived?"

48   "My country don't have blind kids," Choden said. "Only me."

49   "Not my country either," Yangchen said.

50   I knew that what they meant by "my country" were the villages they had come from, small mountain hamlets with mud-brick houses, muttering flocks of chickens, some goats, shaggy yaks with matted hair, and little else but the biggest sky in the world, an all-engulfing sunlight, and a distant backdrop of seriously jagged snowcapped mountains.

51   Yangchen informed me out of the blue that her father died when she was young and that her mother was, at present, dying. I was so taken aback that I couldn't bring myself to ask what her mother was dying of. Prompted by the mention of parents, Choden said, "My mother was pregnant with me, and a cow kick her in the stomach one time, and so that is why I got blind."

52   I thought about the physics of this. "Are you sure that's why you're blind, Choden?" I said.

53   "Yah. Sure," she said cheerfully, and she gave my arm a little squeeze, as if to assure me that it really was quite all right to have the future of your eyesight mystically predetermined by a wayward, mud-encrusted cow's hoof even before you were born. Like most Tibetans, the blind students were deeply conscious of reincarnation and karmic retribution.[2] The widespread Tibetan impulse to go to the temple and pray was not just an effort to achieve a higher spirituality but also a warding-off of the malign and omnipresent supernatural forces believed to be pressing upon each individual's life and destiny.

54   I asked the girls if they still prayed now that they were in Lhasa. Yes, every morning at seven they went to the temple to pray. What exactly were they praying for? For the goodness, they said, and good things and to make up for sins.

55   What kind of sins?

56   There was a silence while they thought about this. "Mmm, sometimes we broke some things at school," Choden said.

57   What things?

58   "Everythings! Braille machines and desks and—"

59   "And windows," Yangchen interjected.

60   "Because we cannot see and we make an accident sometimes."

61   I pointed out that these were not sins but forgivable mistakes. They thought about it, then agreed with me. A long silence followed while they searched their souls for real and purposive sins. I knew that the silence was due not to their reluctance to tell me their sins but to their inability to find anything really worthy to confess.

62   "Okay," I said, "never mind the sins."

63   "And anyway now we go right," Yangchen said, gently steering me with her arm.

64   "How do you know that?"

65   "You feel the ground got different here under your feet?"

66   I had felt nothing. But now that Yangchen had brought it to my attention, I realized that the ground we were walking on was very uneven. When I told the girls that I had felt nothing different, that the ground had seemed to me to be always uneven, they stopped, turned me around, and took me back to the start of the street.

67   "Rose, now we show you. You must go and feel the street here." Yangchen tapped my shin firmly with her cane to indicate that I

---

2. **reincarnation and karmic retribution** belief that the spirit of a person who dies is born into a new body, and that a person's actions in this life affect his or her next life.

^ School for the blind in Lhasa, Tibet

should try the street out with my foot; the gesture was surprisingly authoritative. It was also intimate in the way the gestures of a good teacher often are. "You feel how it feels."

68   I smeared the soles of my shoes around. "It feels smooth, like concrete pavement."

69   "Yah, smooth. Now come and you walk." We walked ten paces on the smooth pavement and then, very abruptly, the pavement changed and became something like cobblestone or roughly hewn brick. The first time around, I hadn't registered the change, which astonished me, because the contrast was in fact sudden and marked. I had simply not been paying attention to what was under my feet. Why would I? When one is in the habit of anticipating the path ahead by sight, one rarely makes conscious note of or even actually *feels* in any lasting way the texture of that path.

70   "When we feel the ground coming different under our feet, we know where we find ourselves," Yangchen said.

71   "Do you know when a person is walking close to you?"

72   "Yes, because we can hear them. And also sometimes can smell them. And also our cane can describe to us whatever is near us."

73   I told the girls their English was quite good and asked them if they were continuing to study the language.

NOTES

The Neglected Senses **793**

74　"Yah. Now we are learning how to speak in a restaurant," Yangchen said.

75　I wasn't sure what she meant by that. By way of explanation, Choden said in the tone of an extremely nervous, extremely unctuous[3] waitress, "Hello, madam. You are so very welcome. Good evening, can I help you, please? What would you like to please eat?"

76　In the voice of a customer who had memorized the entire menu and was bored stiff by it, Yangchen responded, "Yes, please. I would like to have please one yak s-t-e-a-k."

77　"Oh, very fine," Choden said. "Please, how would you like your yak s-t-e-a-k to be cooked?"

78　"I would like to have my yak steak to be cooked m-e-d-i-u-m rare, please."

79　"What would you please like to drink, please? Would you like to drink some of coffee?"

80　"Please," Yangchen said, "I would like a bottle of white w-i-n-d."

81　"Yangchen," I said, "w-i-n-d spells wind. A bottle of white wind would be something very rare, if not completely impossible."

82　Yangchen stopped in her tracks and positively guffawed at her mistake. "Oh, ha-ha-ha! No! Please, a bottle of white wine, please, I mean."

83　I told the girls that it was not necessary for them to use the word *please* every time they opened their mouths in a restaurant.

84　"No?"

85　"No. Once or twice is really enough. Otherwise you will become quite annoying."

86　"What does it mean, *annoying*?" Yangchen asked.

87　I explained that being annoying meant that soon enough the person you were serving in the restaurant would have a strong desire to slap you. Immediately they understood. True to Tibetan form, the girls did not let the word *annoying* go by without asking me how to spell it.

88　We walked on, listening to the sounds passing by—hammering, a squeaky wheel, birds chittering, voices speaking in Chinese and Tibetan, a horn being blown—and suddenly at my right shoulder, Yangchen interrupted her humming to ask me, "Rose, what is your hoppy?"

89　This question always surprises me and makes me uneasy, perhaps because I never have a plausible-sounding answer to the question. If a hobby is something one pursues purely for pleasure, then reading the Greek-English dictionary and another excellent book called *600 Modern Greek Verbs: Fully Conjugated in All the Tenses* is my hobby. I can become engrossed in those books so deeply—one word leading to another—that I fail to notice an entire hour passing. But how to explain this in an offhand way to a person you don't know well? As a hobby, it sounds not only pointless and dull but pretentious

---

3. **unctuous** (UHNGK choo uhs) *adj.* excessively and insincerely polite.

and pedantic as well. I have no desire to explain it. Anything I could truly claim as a hobby I am always reluctant to reveal. And the very concept of the hobby strikes me as too parochial, too specific, by definition too distinctly separate from life's main activities.

90   I told Yangchen that in general I liked rowing a boat, riding a bicycle, and making things out of wood—all the activities I liked that seemed to need no explanation or defense.

91   Yangchen said, "I like sing a song and learn some song and I also like rotten."

92   "Rotten? What's that?"

93   "Rotten. Rotten."

94   "Can you spell the word for me?"

95   "I cannot."

96   Choden tried to spell it for her. "Rot. R-o-t. R-o-t-e-n."

97   "Well, I hear what you're saying, but I'm not sure what you mean by it," I said. "*Rotten* is an adjective. It cannot be a hobby."

98   "Tchah! I am wrong." Yangchen tittered and laid the side of her face against my upper arm, half in embarrassment and half in apology.

99   I felt a soft breeze on my cheek. "Now it's a little windy," I said.

100   "Windy, yah."

101   "How come all of a sudden?" I guessed the answer. "Are we out of the closed street and in an open place?"

102   "You are right," Yangchen said. "We are in open and it is wind and there is a cloud."

103   "How do you know there's a cloud?"

104   "I do not feel the sun on my nose."

105   "I didn't notice that," I said.

106   "Oh, ha," Choden said.

107   By now I had learned that this was Choden's default response. When she didn't know what to say but wanted to maintain active participation in the conversation, she said encouragingly, *Oh, ha.*

108   I heard the sound of water splashing, like a hose or a downspout pouring onto a pavement. "Where is that splashing water coming from?" I said.

109   "Not water," Yangchen said. "That noise is frying of dumplings. Here is a small restaurant in the street."

110   Before long I heard the crashing sound of thunder.

111   "No," Choden said. "Not thunder. That is only the door of the marketplace. They are closing it. It makes a big noise."

112   The closing door sounded so much like thunder that I wanted to pull off my blindfold and look around to be sure that Choden wasn't tricking me. I asked Choden if she was sure it wasn't thunder.

113   "Yah, Rose, sure. Don't worry."

114   "Now I smell gasoline," I said.

115   "No. That is shoes smell."

116   "What?"

117   "Shoes smell. *Hongo*." The two girls conferred in Tibetan, trying to figure out how to explain to me what I was smelling. "It is the smell of shoes. They are selling the shoes here in the street."

118   I heard birdsong coming from somewhere behind us, a clear wandering whistle like that of a robin. I remarked on it, and Choden said, "No, it is not a bird. It is . . ." She said something to Yangchen in Tibetan, looking again for a word.

119   "Alarm. It is the alarm for a car in case a person tries to steal it."

120   They knew everything about their city. They knew what everything was and where it was and how it sounded and smelled and felt. They knew it by heart and with their eyes closed. It seemed to me that they knew the city every bit as well as its sighted residents, and I was beginning to wonder whether I too couldn't benefit from knowing my environment from this different perspective.

121   "Now the cloud went and the sun came shining," Yangchen said, and as soon as she said it I felt the sun on my head.

122   "Now we turn left," Choden said.

123   "How do you know we turn left?"

124   "We smell the incense. That smells very nice. It means we are nearly in Jokhang Temple."

125   The moment Choden mentioned it, the air was full of the smell of incense. Again, I hadn't noticed it until she alerted me to it. The girls were always one step ahead of me, maybe two. I had detected very little of what was taking place around me on this walk, perhaps because I was nervous and disoriented, but also because I was so used to **navigating** with my eyes that my other senses, relative to the senses of the blind girls, were atrophied. I stumbled along uncomfortably, feeling out of control and disliking that I was so slow in grasping and noticing what they noticed.

126   Sight is a slick and overbearing autocrat, trumpeting its prodigal knowledge and perceptions so forcefully that it drowns out the other, subtler senses. We go through our day semi-oblivious to a whole range of sensory information because we are distracted and enslaved by our eyes. Taste, touch, smell, and hearing can hardly get a word in edgewise to the brain. Those of us who have sight do not realize that our experience of life and the world is overpowered by our vision. In this sense, we too are handicapped. I began to envy Choden's and Yangchen's skills a little. In their presence, I saw that I had been missing a great deal of what was happening in my daily life, and I realized that it was not the blind person's deficiency that was drawing me into this subject but the revelation of my own. ❧

Mark context clues or indicate another strategy you used that helped you determine meaning.

navigating (NAV uh gayt ihng) *n.*

MEANING:

Comprehension Check

Complete the following items after you finish your first read. Review and clarify details with your group.

1. Where is the author, Mahoney, visiting?

2. What does Mahoney do to experience being blind?

3. What does Choden think caused her blindness?

4. What conclusion about her reliance on sight does Mahoney draw at the end of the excerpt?

5. 🖻 **Notebook** Confirm your understanding of the text by writing a summary.

- -

RESEARCH

Research to Clarify Choose at least one unfamiliar detail from the text. Briefly research that detail. In what way does the information you learned shed light on an aspect of the memoir?

Research to Explore This memoir may spark your curiosity to learn more. Briefly research a topic that interests you. You may want to share what you discover with your group.

THE NEGLECTED SENSES

Close Read the Text

With your group, revisit sections of the text you marked during your first read. **Annotate** details that you notice. What **questions** do you have? What can you **conclude**?

Analyze the Text

CITE TEXTUAL EVIDENCE
to support your answers.

Notebook Complete the activities.

1. **Review and Clarify** With your group, discuss Mahoney's claim in paragraph 42 that for Yangchen and Choden the "vocabulary of vision was metaphorical." How do you interpret Mahoney's remark?

2. **Present and Discuss** Now, work with your group to share the passages from the text that you found especially important. Take turns presenting your passages. Discuss what details you noticed, what questions you asked, and what conclusions you reached.

3. **Essential Question:** *What does it mean to see?* What has this selection taught you about how the blind define seeing? Discuss with your group.

TIP

GROUP DISCUSSION
Keep in mind that group members will have different interpretations of the text. These different perspectives enable group members to learn from one another and to clarify their own thoughts. Very often there is no single interpretation or conclusion.

WORD NETWORK

Add words related to blindness and sight from the text to your Word Network.

LANGUAGE DEVELOPMENT

Concept Vocabulary

traversed	periphery	navigating

Why These Words? The three concept vocabulary words are related. With your group, determine what the words have in common. Write your ideas, and add another word that fits the category.

Practice

Confirm your understanding of these words by using them in a brief conversation with your group members. Use each word at least once, in a way that demonstrates its meaning.

Word Study

Latin Root: -vers- / -vert- The Latin root *-vers-* or *-vert-* comes from a Latin verb meaning "to turn." Sometimes, it carries this meaning in English, as in the word *invert*. Other times, it indicates motion more generally, as in the word *traversed*. Find several other words that feature this root. Record the words and their meanings.

Analyze Craft and Structure

Development of Ideas Nonfiction is writing that is based in facts. It provides information, explains topics, or tells real-life stories. **Literary nonfiction** is writing that employs many of the same literary devices as fiction while still remaining factual. It may develop a plot, use sensory details, incorporate dialogue, and even use figurative language. A **memoir** is a type of literary nonfiction in which an author relates events from a specific period or about a specific aspect of his or her life. A form of autobiography, a memoir is usually written in the first-person point of view, using pronouns such as *I* and *my*. One unique aspect of a memoir is its **reflective standpoint,** or the way the author describes his or her thoughts or feelings in relation to past events. By looking back on events with fresh insight, the writer expresses an understanding of their deeper meaning. Literary elements help reveal that meaning.

 TIP

CLOSE READING

Even though Mahoney's text is a work of nonfiction, she uses literary techniques such as description and dialogue to engage readers. Consider the choices the author has made and discuss the effect they have on readers.

Practice

CITE TEXTUAL EVIDENCE to support your answers.

Use the chart to analyze the use of literary elements in "The Neglected Senses." Then, share and discuss your responses with your group.

LITERARY ELEMENT	EXPLANATION
Who is telling the story?	
What is the setting? How are different elements of the setting described?	
What conversations does the author capture in dialogue? What does her use of dialogue convey that explanations might not?	
How does the sequence of events lead to an insight? What is that insight?	
How do sensory details help bring events to life?	

THE NEGLECTED SENSES

Conventions

Types of Phrases Writers use various types of phrases to convey specific meanings. A **prepositional phrase** consists of a preposition, the object of the preposition, and any modifiers of the object. An **adjectival phrase** is any prepositional phrase that acts as an adjective in a sentence, by modifying a noun or a pronoun. Adjectival phrases tell *what kind* or *which one*.

The chart shows examples of adjectival phrases. The prepositions are italicized, the adjectival phrases are highlighted, and the words they modify are underlined.

SENTENCE	FUNCTION(S) OF ADJECTIVAL PHRASE(S)
The board members chose a chairperson *with* great credentials.	tells *what kind* of chairperson
I finally bought tickets *for* our trip *to* San Salvador.	one tells *what kind* of tickets; one tells *which* trip
The statue *of* the rearing horse *in* the park was huge.	both tell *which* statue

Read It

1. Working individually, read these passages from "The Neglected Senses." Mark each adjectival phrase, and write the word it modifies. Then, discuss your answers with your group.

   a. Yangchen's perpetually crossed eyes gave her the appearance of slapstick confusion.

   b. Immediately I had the sensation that the ground beneath my feet was tilting.

   c. Until Yangchen mentioned it, I had not noticed the sound of many televisions.

2. Reread paragraph 33 of "The Neglected Senses." Mark each adjectival phrase, and write the word it modifies.

Write It

Write a paragraph in which you explain what you have learned by reading this memoir, and identify a passage that was especially meaningful to you. Use at least one adjectival phrase in your paragraph.

Speaking and Listening

Assignment

With your group, prepare and deliver an **oral presentation**. Conduct brief Internet research for information and images to include in your presentation. Choose from the following options:

☐ Prepare an oral **summary** of what you have learned from "The Neglected Senses." Consider the following questions: What did you learn about how people use their senses to experience the world? What surprised you most about the interaction between Yangchen and Choden and the author? Why?

☐ Imagine that Yangchen and Choden are on a book tour with the author, Rosemary Mahoney. Role-play a **question-and-answer session** in which journalists question the two teens. Write out the questions, and have students role-play to provide answers. Consider the following questions: What is your school like? What are some of your interests and hobbies? What did you learn from leading the author through the city of Lhasa?

☐ Use information from the selection and the Internet to create a map of the part of the city that the author and the girls visited. Give a **virtual tour**, pointing out different features on the map to the class. Include images such as photographs.

Presentation Plan Deliver the presentation as a group. Have different group members present different sections of your work. Be sure to refer to specific information from the memoir, as well as from other sources. End your presentation with a conclusion that your audience will remember.

Use the chart to help organize your presentation.

IDEA	INFORMATION FROM MEMOIR	INFORMATION FROM OUTSIDE SOURCE	IMAGE

📝 EVIDENCE LOG

Before moving on to a new selection, go to your Evidence Log and record what you learned from "The Neglected Senses."

SOURCES

- VIEW FROM THE EMPIRE STATE BUILDING
- BLIND
- THE BLIND SEER OF AMBON
- ON HIS BLINDNESS
- THE COUNTRY OF THE BLIND
- THE NEGLECTED SENSES

Present an Oral Retelling

Assignment
You have read about different ways of seeing the world with and without eyesight. Work with your group to develop and refine an **oral retelling** of one of the selections that attempts to answer the following question:

Can one have sight but no vision, or vision but no sight?

Plan With Your Group

Analyze the Texts With your group, discuss different ways in which the writers—or the people or characters they present—see the world in the selections from Small-Group Learning. Consider both physical and symbolic or metaphorical ways of seeing. Also, discuss nuances in the meanings of sight and vision. Use the chart to list your ideas.

TITLE	WAYS TO SEE THE WORLD
View from the Empire State Building	
Blind The Blind Seer of Ambon On His Blindness	
The Country of the Blind	
The Neglected Senses	
Differences and Similarities Between Sight and Vision	

Gather Evidence and Media Examples Scan the selections to record specific examples that support your group's ideas. Then, brainstorm for ways that you can use the evidence to retell one of the selections from a point of view different from that of the original narrator or speaker. Remember to use a combination of dialogue, description, and reflection to present the experiences, events, and people or characters. Consider including photographs, illustrations, music, charts, graphs, or video clips to add interest and depth to your retelling. Allow each group member to make suggestions.

Organize Your Ideas Use a graphic organizer like this one to organize the script for your oral retelling. Assign roles for each part of the retelling, and record what the presenter will say.

ORAL RETELLING SCRIPT		
	Role	Script
Presenter 1		
Presenter 2		
Presenter 3		

Rehearse With Your Group

Practice With Your Group Use this checklist to evaluate your group's first run-through of your oral retelling. Then, use your evaluation and the instructions here to guide your revision.

CONTENT	USE OF MEDIA	PRESENTATION TECHNIQUES
☐ The retelling presents a clear point of view and answer to the question. ☐ Events are organized in a clear chronological sequence and linked by logical transitions.	☐ The media support the oral retelling. ☐ The media help communicate key ideas. ☐ Media are used evenly throughout the presentation. ☐ Equipment functions properly.	☐ Media are visible and audible. ☐ Transitions between media segments are smooth. ☐ The speaker varies pitch and tone to match meaning and mood.

Fine-Tune the Content To make your oral retelling stronger, use words and expressions that are consistent with the character of the narrator or speaker you have chosen. These details will be especially important in helping your audience understand your thoughts and ideas about sight and vision.

Improve Your Use of Media Practice shifting from spoken content to media elements. Plan what you will do and say if any piece of equipment fails.

Brush Up on Your Presentation Techniques If possible, rehearse your oral retelling in the room where it will take place. Check sight lines to make sure that your digital media will be visible to the entire audience. Do a sound check.

Present and Evaluate

When you present as a group, be sure that each member has taken into account each of the checklist items. As you watch other groups, evaluate how well they meet the checklist requirements.

ESSENTIAL QUESTION:

What does it mean to see?

The ability to see involves much more than our eyes; it involves our brains and our life experiences. In this section, you will complete your study of blindness and sight by exploring an additional selection related to the topic. You'll then share what you learn with classmates. To choose a text, follow these steps.

Look Back Think about the selections you have already studied. What more do you want to know about the topics of blindness and sight?

Look Ahead Preview the texts by reading the descriptions. Which one seems more interesting and appealing to you?

Look Inside Take a few minutes to scan the text you chose. Choose a different one if this text doesn't meet your needs.

Independent Learning Strategies

Throughout your life, in school, in your community, and in your career, you will need to rely on yourself to learn and work on your own. Review these strategies and the actions you can take to practice them during Independent Learning. Add ideas of your own to each category.

STRATEGY	ACTION PLAN
Create a schedule	• Understand your goals and deadlines. • Make a plan for what to do each day. •
Practice what you have learned	• Use first-read and close-read strategies to deepen your understanding. • After you read, evaluate the usefulness of the evidence to help you understand the topic. • Consider the quality and reliability of the source. •
Take notes	• Record important ideas and information. • Review your notes before preparing to share with a group. •

CONTENTS

Choose one selection. Selections are available online only.

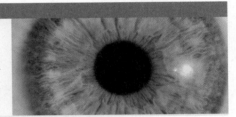
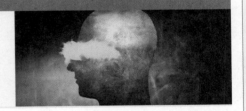

First-Read Guide

Use this page to record your first-read ideas.

Selection Title: _____

Tool Kit
First-Read Guide and
Model Annotation

NOTICE new information or ideas you learn about the unit topic as you first read this text.

ANNOTATE by marking vocabulary and key passages you want to revisit.

NOTICE ANNOTATE
First Read
CONNECT RESPOND

CONNECT ideas within the selection to other knowledge and the selections you have read.

RESPOND by writing a brief summary of the selection.

Close-Read Guide

Tool Kit
Close-Read Guide and
Model Annotation

Use this page to record your close-read ideas.

Selection Title: _____

Close Read the Text

Revisit sections of the text you marked during your first read. Read these sections closely and **annotate** what you notice. Ask yourself **questions** about the text. What can you **conclude?** Write down your ideas.

Analyze the Text

Think about the author's choices of patterns, structure, techniques, and ideas included in the text. Select one, and record your thoughts about what this choice conveys.

QuickWrite

Pick a paragraph from the text that grabbed your interest. Explain the power of this passage.

Share Your Independent Learning

Prepare to Share

What does it mean to see?

Even when you read or learn something independently, you can continue to grow by sharing what you have learned with others. Reflect on the text you explored independently and write notes about its connection to the unit. In your notes, consider why this text belongs in this unit.

Learn From Your Classmates

💬 **Discuss It** Share your ideas about the text you explored on your own. As you talk with your classmates, jot down ideas that you learn from them.

Reflect

Review your notes, and mark the most important insight you gained from these writing and discussion activities. Explain how this idea adds to your understanding of the topics of blindness and sight.

Review Notes for a Nonfiction Narrative

At the beginning of this unit, you wrote an initial response to this question:

Is there a difference between seeing and knowing?

✎ EVIDENCE LOG

Review your Evidence Log and your QuickWrite from the beginning of the unit. Have your ideas grown or changed?

☐ YES	☐ NO
Identify at least three ideas or descriptions that changed your mind or added to your knowledge.	Identify at least three ideas or descriptions that reinforced your initial position.
1.	**1.**
2.	**2.**
3.	**3.**

Which person or character that you read about had the greatest impact on your thinking? Explain, using text evidence.

_____

_____

_____

_____

_____

_____

Evaluate the Strength of Your Details Consider your nonfiction narrative. Do you have enough details to write a well-developed and engaging narrative about real-life events? Will you be able to tell a story that develops a theme related to the difference between seeing and knowing? If not, make a plan.

☐ Brainstorm for details to add   ☐ Talk with classmates

☐ Reread a selection   ☐ Ask an expert

☐ Other: _____

SOURCES

- WHOLE-CLASS SELECTIONS
- SMALL-GROUP SELECTIONS
- INDEPENDENT-LEARNING SELECTION

PART 1
Writing to Sources: Nonfiction Narrative

In this unit, you read about various people and characters, real and fictional, who are unable to see in one way or another.

Assignment

Write a **nonfiction narrative** in which you tell a true story related to the following question:

Is there a difference between seeing and knowing?

In your narrative, present both clearly delineated characters—the people who are involved in the action of the story—and settings. Include a logically sequenced series of events that show the choices people make and their reasons for making them. As you write, use sensory language to convey events vividly. Engage the reader, build to a climax, and close your narrative with a reflective conclusion. Integrate ideas from the texts in this unit to develop details in your story.

Reread the Assignment Review the assignment to be sure you fully understand it. You may choose to write an autobiographical narrative about your own personal experiences. You may also choose to interview someone else and write a narrative based on that person's experiences. The task may refer to some of the academic words presented at the beginning of the unit. Be sure you understand each of the words here in order to complete the assignment correctly.

Academic Vocabulary

integrate	volition	altercation
delineate	vivid	

⊹ WORD NETWORK

As your write and revise your nonfiction narrative, use your Word Network to help vary your word choices.

Review the Elements of an Effective Nonfiction Narrative Before you begin writing, read the Nonfiction Narrative Rubric. Once you have completed your first draft, check it against the rubric. If one or more of the elements is missing or not as strong as it could be, revise your essay to add or strengthen that component.

Narrative Rubric

	Focus and Organization	Evidence and Elaboration	Language Conventions
4	The introduction establishes a clear context and point of view. Events are presented in a clear sequence, building to a climax, and then moving toward the conclusion. The conclusion follows from and reflects on the events and experiences in the narrative and provides insightful reflection on the experiences related in the narrative.	Narrative techniques such as dialogue, pacing, and description are used effectively to develop people, events, and settings. Descriptive details, sensory language, and precise words and phrases are used effectively to convey the experiences in the narrative and to help the reader imagine the people and setting. Voice is established through word choice, sentence structure, and tone.	The narrative uses standard English conventions of usage and mechanics. Spelling and meaning are checked with the aid of a dictionary. Effective language is used with the aid of a thesaurus.
3	The introduction gives the reader some context and sets the point of view. Events are presented logically, though there are some jumps in time. The conclusion logically ends the story, but it only provides some reflection on the experiences related in the story.	Narrative techniques such as dialogue, pacing, and description are used occasionally. Descriptive details, sensory language, and precise words and phrases are used occasionally. Voice is established through word choice, sentence structure, and tone occasionally, though not evenly.	The narrative mostly uses standard English conventions of usage and mechanics, though there are some errors. Spelling and meaning are mostly checked with the aid of a dictionary, though there are a few errors. Effective language is mostly used with the aid of a thesaurus, though there are some lapses.
2	The introduction provides some description of a place. The point of view can be unclear at times. Transitions between events are occasionally unclear. The conclusion comes abruptly and provides only a small amount of reflection on the experiences related in the narrative.	Narrative techniques such as dialogue, pacing, and description are used sparingly. The story contains few examples of descriptive details and sensory language. People are not clearly distinguishable from one another.	The narrative contains some errors in standard English conventions of usage and mechanics. Some spelling and meaning errors appear throughout the narrative. The language appears basic.
1	The introduction does not introduce place and point of view. Events do not follow logically. The narrative lacks a conclusion.	The narrative is not developed with dialogue, pacing, and description. The narrative lacks descriptive details and sensory language. People speak in the same manner and do not have unique characteristics.	The narrative contains many errors in standard English conventions of usage and mechanics. Spelling and meaning errors appear throughout the narrative. The language appears basic and repetitive.

PART 2
Speaking and Listening: Storytelling

Assignment
After completing the final draft of your nonfiction narrative, use it as the basis for a three- to five-minute **storytelling session**.

Instead of simply reading your narrative aloud, take the following steps to make your storytelling lively and engaging:

- Grab your audience's attention by starting with an exciting scene or a vivid description of the people in your true story.
- Tell your story in a logical sequence that establishes a clear setting, describes characters, and sets up and develops the conflict.
- Vary the tone, pitch, and inflection of your voice to mirror the emotions and actions you describe.
- Use body language and gestures to add emphasis or to illustrate how characters behave or perform a particular action.
- Make eye contact with your audience.
- Use media, such as pictures and sound effects, to enhance your narrative.

Review the Rubric The criteria by which your storytelling will be evaluated appear in the rubric below. Review these criteria before presenting to ensure that you are prepared.

	Content	Use of Media	Presentation Techniques
3	Storyteller engages the audience by describing real people, a defined conflict, and a clear resolution.	Included media are appropriate and add interest.	The speaker's word choice, volume, pitch, and eye contact are engaging and appropriate.
2	Storyteller describes real people, a conflict, and a resolution.	Included media are dull or only tangentially relevant.	The speaker's word choice, volume, pitch, and eye contact are somewhat engaging and appropriate.
1	Storyteller does not clearly describe people or establish a defined conflict and resolution.	Included media are irrelevant or inappropriate to narrative.	The speaker's word choice, volume, pitch, and eye contact are neither engaging nor appropriate.

Reflect on the Unit

Now that you've completed the unit, take a few moments to reflect on your learning. Use the questions below to think about where you succeeded, what skills and strategies helped you, and where you can continue to grow in the future.

Reflect on the Unit Goals

Look back at the goals at the beginning of the unit. Use a different colored pen to rate yourself again. Think about readings and activities that contributed the most to the growth of your understanding. Record your thoughts.

Reflect on the Learning Strategies

Discuss It Write a reflection on whether you were able to improve your learning based on your Action Plans. Think about what worked, what didn't, and what you might do to keep working on these strategies. Record your ideas before joining a class discussion.

Reflect on the Text

Choose a selection that you found challenging, and explain what made it difficult.

Describe something that surprised you about a text in the unit.

Which activity taught you the most about blindness and sight? What did you learn?

RESOURCES

CONTENTS

Marking the Text: Strategies and Tips for Annotation

When you close read a text, you read for comprehension and then reread to unlock layers of meaning and to analyze a writer's style and techniques. Marking a text as you read it enables you to participate more fully in the close-reading process.

Following are some strategies for text mark-ups, along with samples of how the strategies can be applied. These mark-ups are suggestions; you and your teacher may want to use other mark-up strategies.

✱	Key Idea
!	I love it!
?	I have questions
◯	Unfamiliar or important word
- - - -	Context Clues

Suggested Mark-Up Notations

WHAT I NOTICE	HOW TO MARK UP	QUESTIONS TO ASK
Key Ideas and Details	• Highlight key ideas or claims. • Underline supporting details or evidence.	• What does the text say? What does it leave unsaid? • What inferences do you need to make? • What details lead you to make your inferences?
Word Choice	• Circle unfamiliar words. • Put a dotted line under context clues, if any exist. • Put an exclamation point beside especially rich or poetic passages.	• What inferences about word meaning can you make? • What tone and mood are created by word choice? • What alternate word choices might the author have made?
Text Structure	• Highlight passages that show key details supporting the main idea. • Use arrows to indicate how sentences and paragraphs work together to build ideas. • Use a right-facing arrow to indicate foreshadowing. • Use a left-facing arrow to indicate flashback.	• Is the text logically structured? • What emotional impact do the structural choices create?
Author's Craft	• Circle or highlight instances of repetition, either of words, phrases, consonants, or vowel sounds. • Mark rhythmic beats in poetry using checkmarks and slashes. • Underline instances of symbolism or figurative language.	• Does the author's style enrich or detract from the reading experience? • What levels of meaning are created by the author's techniques?

CLOSE READING

First Read

* Key Idea
! I love it!
? I have questions
◯ Unfamiliar or important word
---- Context Clues

NOTES

In a first read, work to get a sense of the main idea of a text. Look for key details and ideas that help you understand what the author conveys to you. Mark passages that prompt a strong response from you.

Here is how one reader marked up this text.

MODEL

INFORMATIONAL TEXT

from Classifying the Stars

Cecilia H. Payne

1   Sunlight and starlight are composed of waves of various lengths, which the eye, even aided by a telescope, is unable to separate. We must use more than a telescope. In order to sort out the component colors, the light must be dispersed by a prism, or split up by some other means. For instance, sunbeams passing through rain drops, are transformed into the myriad-tinted rainbow. The familiar rainbow spanning the sky is Nature's most glorious demonstration that light is composed of many colors.

2   The very beginning of our knowledge of the nature of a star dates back to 1672, when Isaac Newton gave to the world the results of his experiments on passing sunlight through a prism. To describe the beautiful band of rainbow tints, produced when sunlight was dispersed by his three-cornered piece of glass, he took from the Latin the word *spectrum*, meaning an appearance. The rainbow is the spectrum of the Sun. . . .

3   In 1814, more than a century after Newton, the spectrum of the Sun was obtained in such purity that an amazing detail was seen and studied by the German optician, Fraunhofer. He saw that the multiple spectral tints, ranging from delicate violet to deep red, were crossed by hundreds of fine dark lines. In other words, there were narrow gaps in the spectrum where certain shades were wholly blotted out. We must remember that the word spectrum is applied not only to sunlight, but also to the light of any glowing substance when its rays are sorted out by a prism or a grating.

First-Read Guide

Use this page to record your first-read ideas.

You may want to use a guide like this to organize your thoughts after you read. Here is how a reader completed a First-Read Guide.

Selection Title: _____Classifying the Stars_____

NOTICE

NOTICE new information or ideas you learned about the unit topic as you first read this text.

Light = different waves of colors. (Spectrum)

Newton - the first person to observe these waves using a prism.

Faunhofer saw gaps in the spectrum.

ANNOTATE

ANNOTATE by marking vocabulary and key passages you want to revisit.

Vocabulary
   myriad
   grating
   component colors

Different light types = different lengths

Isaac Newton also worked theories of gravity.

Multiple spectral tints? "colors of various appearance"

Key Passage:
Paragraph 3 shows that Fraunhofer discovered more about the nature of light spectrums: he saw the spaces in between the tints.

First Read
NOTICE ANNOTATE CONNECT RESPOND

CONNECT ideas within the selection to other knowledge and the selections you have read.

I remember learning about prisms in science class.

Double rainbows! My favorite. How are they made?

RESPOND by writing a brief summary of the selection.

Science allows us to see things not visible to the naked eye. What we see as sunlight is really a spectrum of colors. By using tools, such as prisms, we can see the components of sunlight and other light. They appear as single colors or as multiple colors separated by gaps of no color. White light contains a rainbow of colors.

CONNECT

RESPOND

TOOL KIT: CLOSE READING

CLOSE READING

ANNOTATE · QUESTION · Close Read · CONCLUDE

* Key Idea

! I love it!

? I have questions

◯ Unfamiliar or important word

---- Context Clues

In a close read, go back into the text to study it in greater detail. Take the time to analyze not only the author's ideas but the way that those ideas are conveyed. Consider the genre of the text, the author's word choice, the writer's unique style, and the message of the text.

Here is how one reader close read this text.

NOTES

MODEL

INFORMATIONAL TEXT

from Classifying the Stars
Cecilia H. Payne

explanation of sunlight and starlight

What is light and where do the colors come from?

1 * Sunlight and starlight are composed of waves of various lengths, which the eye, even aided by a telescope, is unable to separate. We must use more than a telescope. In order to sort out the **?** component colors, the light must be dispersed by a prism, or split up by some other means. For instance, sunbeams passing through rain drops, are transformed into the ◯myriad◯-tinted rainbow. **!** The familiar rainbow spanning the sky is Nature's most glorious demonstration that light is composed of many colors.

This paragraph is about Newton and the prism.

What discoveries helped us understand light?

2 * The very beginning of our knowledge of the nature of a star dates back to 1672, when Isaac Newton gave to the world the results of his experiments on passing sunlight through a prism. To describe the beautiful band of rainbow tints, produced when sunlight was dispersed by his three-cornered piece of glass, he took from the Latin the word *spectrum*, meaning an appearance. The rainbow is the ◯spectrum◯ of the Sun. . . .

Fraunhofer and gaps in spectrum

3 * In 1814, more than a century after Newton, the spectrum of the Sun was obtained in such purity that an amazing detail was seen and studied by the German optician, Fraunhofer. He saw that the multiple spectral tints, ranging from delicate violet to deep red, were crossed by hundreds of fine dark lines. In other words, there were narrow gaps in the spectrum where certain shades were wholly blotted out. We must remember that the word spectrum is applied not only to sunlight, but also to the light of any glowing substance when its rays are sorted out by a prism or a ◯grating.◯

Close-Read Guide

Use this page to record your close-read ideas.

You can use the Close-Read Guide to help you dig deeper into the text. Here is how a reader completed a Close-Read Guide.

Selection Title: _Classifying the Stars_

Close Read the Text

Revisit sections of the text you marked during your first read. Read these sections closely and **annotate** what you notice. Ask yourself **questions** about the text. What can you **conclude?** Write down your ideas.

ANNOTATE QUESTION
Close Read
CONCLUDE

Paragraph 3: Light is composed of waves of various lengths. Prisms let us see different colors in light. This is called the spectrum. Fraunhofer proved that there are gaps in the spectrum, where certain shades are blotted out.

More than one researcher studied this and each built off the ideas that were already discovered.

Analyze the Text

Think about the author's choices of patterns, structure, techniques, and ideas included in the text. Select one, and record your thoughts about what this choice conveys.

The author showed the development of human knowledge of the spectrum chronologically. Helped me see how ideas were built upon earlier understandings. Used dates and "more than a century after Newton" to show time.

QuickWrite

Pick a paragraph from the text that grabbed your interest. Explain the power of this passage.

The first paragraph grabbed my attention, specifically the sentence "The familiar rainbow spanning the sky is Nature's most glorious demonstration that light is composed of many colors." The paragraph began as a straightforward scientific explanation. When I read the word "glorious," I had to stop and deeply consider what was being said. It is a word loaded with personal feelings. With that one word, the author let the reader know what was important to her.

Argument

When you think of the word *argument*, you might think of a disagreement between two people, but an argument is more than that. An argument is a logical way of presenting a belief, conclusion, or stance. A good argument is supported with reasoning and evidence.

Argument writing can be used for many purposes, such as to change a reader's point of view or opinion or to bring about an action or a response from a reader.

Elements of an Argumentative Text

An **argument** is a logical way of presenting a viewpoint, belief, or stand on an issue. A well-written argument may convince the reader, change the reader's mind, or motivate the reader to take a certain action.

An effective argument contains these elements:

- a precise claim
- consideration of counterclaims, or opposing positions, and a discussion of their strengths and weaknesses
- logical organization that makes clear connections among claim, counterclaim, reasons, and evidence
- valid reasoning and evidence
- a concluding statement or section that logically completes the argument
- formal and objective language and tone
- error-free grammar, including accurate use of transitions

ARGUMENT: SCORE 1

Selfies, Photoshop, and You: Superficial Image Culture is Hurtful for Teens

Selfies are kind of cool, also kind of annoying, and some say they might be bad for you if you take too many. Selfies of celebrities and ordinary people are everywhere. People always try to smile and look good, and they take a lot of selfies when they are somewhere special, like at the zoo or at a fair. Some people spend so much time taking selfies they forget to just go ahead and have fun.

TV and other media are full of beautiful people. Looking at all those model's and celebrities can make kids feel bad about their one bodies, even when they are actually totally normal and fine and beautiful they way they are. Kids start to think they should look like the folks on TV which is mostly impossible. It's also a cheat because lots of the photos we see of celebrities and model's have been edited so they look even better.

Selfies make people feel even worse about the way they look. They're always comparing themselves and feeling that maybe they aren't as good as they should be. Selfies can make teens feel bad about their faces and bodies, and the stuff they are doing every day.

Regular people edit and change things before they post their pictures. That means, the pictures are kind of fake and it's impossible to compete with something that is fake. It's sad to think that teens can start to hate themselves and feel depressed just because they don't and can't look like a faked photo of a movie star.

Kids and teens post selfies to hear what others think about them, to show off, and to see how they compare with others. It can be kind of full of pressure always having to look great and smile. Even if you get positive comments about a selfie that you post, and everyone says you look beautiful, that feeling only lasts for a few minutes. After all, what you look like is just something on the outside. What's more important is what you are on the inside and what you do.

It's great for those few minutes, but then what? If you keep posting, people will not want to keep writing nice comments. Kids and teens should take a break from posting selfies all the time. It's better to go out and have fun rather than always keeping on posting selfies.

The writer does not clearly state the claim in the introduction.

The argument contains mistakes in standard English conventions of usage and mechanics.

The tone of the argument is informal, and the vocabulary is limited or ineffective.

The writer does not address counterclaims.

The conclusion does not restate any information that is important.

TOOL KIT: WRITING

ARGUMENT: SCORE 2

Selfies and You: Superficial Image Culture is Hurtful for Teens

Selfies are bad for teens and everyone else. Selfies of celebrities and ordinary people are everywhere. It seems like taking and posting selfies is not such a big deal and not harmful, but that's not really true. Actually, taking too many selfies can be really bad.

TV and other media are full of beautiful people. Looking at all those models and celebrities can make kids feel bad about their own bodies. Kids start to think they should look like the folks on TV which is mostly impossible. It's also a cheat because lots of the photos we see of celebrities and model's have been edited so they look even better.

Regular people use image editing software as well. They edit and change things before they post their pictures. That means, the pictures are kind of fake and it's impossible to compete with something that is fake.

Selfies make people feel even worse about the way they look. They're always comparing themselves and feeling that maybe they aren't as good as they should be. Selfies can make teens feel bad about their faces and bodies.

But maybe selfies are just a fun way to stay in touch, but that's not really how people use selfies, I don't think. Kids and teens post selfies show off. It can be full of pressure always having to look great and smile.

Sometimes posting a selfie can make you feel good if it gets lots of 'likes' and positive comments. But you can never tell. Someone also might say something mean. Also, even if you get positive comments and everyone says you look beautiful, that feeling only lasts for a few minutes. It's great for those few minutes, but then what? If you keep posting and posting, people will not want to keep writing nice comments.

The selfie culture today is just too much. Kids and teens can't be happy when they are always comparing themselves and worrying about what they look like. It's better to go out and have fun rather than always keeping on posting selfies.

The introduction establishes the writer's claim.

The tone of the argument is occasionally formal and objective.

The writer briefly acknowledges one counterclaim.

The conclusion offers some insight into the claim and restates information.

Selfies and You: Superficial Image Culture is Hurtful for Teens

Selfies are everywhere. Check out any social media site and you'll see an endless parade of perfect smiles on both celebrities and ordinary people. It may seem as if this flood of seflies is harmless, but sadly that is not true. Selfies promote a superficial image culture that is harmful and dangerous for teens.

The argument's claim is clearly stated.

The problem starts with the unrealistic: idealized images teens are exposed to in the media. Most models and celebrities are impossibly beautiful and thin. Even young children can feel that there is something wrong with they way they look. According to one research group, more than half of girls and one third of boys ages 6-8 feel their ideal body is thinner than their current body weight. Negative body image can result in serious physical and mental health problems.

The tone of the argument is mostly formal and objective.

The writer includes reasons and evidence that address and support claims.

When teens look at selfies they automatically make comparisons with the idealized images they have in their minds. This can make them feel inadequate and sad about themselves, their bodies, and their lives. And with social media sites accessible 24/7, it's difficult to get a break from the constant comparisons, competition, and judgment.

Image editing software plays a role too. A recent study carried out by the Renfrew Center Foundation said that about 50% of people edit pictures of themselves before posting. They take away blemishes, change skin tone, maybe even make themselves look thinner. And why not? Even the photos of models and celebrities are heavily edited. Teens can start to hate themselves and feel depressed just because they don't and can't look like a faked photo of a movie star.

Some say that posting a selfie is like sending a postcard to your friends and family, but that's not how selfies are used: teens post selfies to get feedback, to compare themselves with others, and to present a false image to the world. There is a lot of pressure to look great and appear happy.

The ideas progress logically, and the writer includes sentence transitions that connect the reader to the argument.

It's true that sometimes a selfie posted on social media gets 'likes' and positive comments that can make a person feel pretty. However, the boost you get from feeling pretty for five minutes doesn't last.

A million selfies are posted every day—and that's way too many. Selfies promote a superficial image culture that is harmful to teens. In the end, the selfie life is not a healthy way to have fun. Let's hope the fad will fade.

The conclusion restates important information.

TOOL KIT: WRITING

WRITING

ARGUMENT: SCORE 4

Selfies and You: Superficial Image Culture Is Hurtful for Teens

Smile, Snap, Edit, Post—Repeat! That's the selfie life, and it's everywhere. A million selfies are posted every day. But this **tsunami** of self-portraits is not as harmless as it appears. Selfies promote a superficial image culture that is hurtful and dangerous for teens.

It all starts with the unrealistic: When teens look at selfies they automatically make comparisons with the idealized images they have in their minds. This can cause them to feel inadequate and sad about themselves, their bodies, and their lives. According to Common Sense Media, more than half of girls and one third of boys ages 6-8 feel their ideal body is thinner than their current body weight. Negative body image can result in serious physical and mental health problems such as anorexia and other eating disorders.

To make matter worse, many or even most selfies have been edited. A recent study carried out by the Renfrew Center Foundation concluded that about 50% of people edit their own images before posting. They use image-editing software to take away blemishes, change skin tone, maybe even make themselves look thinner. And why not? Even the photos of models and celebrities are heavily edited.

Some say that selfies are a harmless and enjoyable way to communicate: posting a selfie is like sending a postcard to your friends and family, inviting them to share in your fun. But that is not how selfies are used: teens post selfies to get feedback, to compare themselves with others, and to present an (often false) image to the world.

It's true that posting a selfie on social media can generate 'likes' and positive comments that can make a person feel good.

However, the boost one gets from feeling pretty for five minutes is like junk food: it tastes good but it is not nourishing.

The selfie culture that is the norm today is out of control. The superficial image culture promoted by selfies is probably behind the recent 20 percent increase in plastic surgery—something with its own dangers and drawbacks. Let's hope the fad will fade, and look forward to a future where people are too busy enjoying life to spend so much time taking, editing, and posting pictures of themselves.

The introduction is engaging, and the writer's claim is clearly stated at the end of the paragraph.

The writer has included a variety of sentence transitions such as "To make matters worse…" "Some say…" "Another claim…" "It is true that…"

The sources of evidence are specific and contain relevant information.

The writer clearly acknowledges counterclaims.

The conclusion offers fresh insights into the claim.

TOOL KIT: WRITING

Argument Rubric

	Focus and Organization	Evidence and Elaboration	Conventions
4	The introduction engages the reader and establishes a claim in a compelling way. The argument includes valid reasons and evidence that address and support the claim while clearly acknowledging counterclaims. The ideas progress logically, and transitions make connections among ideas clear. The conclusion offers fresh insight into the claim.	The sources of evidence are comprehensive and specific and contain relevant information. The tone of the argument is always formal and objective. The vocabulary is always appropriate for the audience and purpose.	The argument intentionally uses standard English conventions of usage and mechanics.
3	The introduction engages the reader and establishes the claim. The argument includes reasons and evidence that address and support my claim while acknowledging counterclaims. The ideas progress logically, and some transitions are used to help make connections among ideas clear. The conclusion restates the claim and important information.	The sources of evidence contain relevant information. The tone of the argument is mostly formal and objective. The vocabulary is generally appropriate for the audience and purpose.	The argument demonstrates general accuracy in standard English conventions of usage and mechanics.
2	The introduction establishes a claim. The argument includes some reasons and evidence that address and support the claim while briefly acknowledging counterclaims. The ideas progress somewhat logically. A few sentence transitions are used that connect readers to the argument. The conclusion offers some insight into the claim and restates information.	The sources of evidence contain some relevant information. The tone of the argument is occasionally formal and objective. The vocabulary is somewhat appropriate for the audience and purpose.	The argument demonstrates some accuracy in standard English conventions of usage and mechanics.
1	The introduction does not clearly state the claim. The argument does not include reasons or evidence for the claim. No counterclaims are acknowledged. The ideas do not progress logically. Transitions are not included to connect ideas. The conclusion does not restate any information that is important.	Reliable and relevant evidence is not included. The vocabulary used is limited or ineffective. The tone of the argument is not objective or formal.	The argument contains mistakes in standard English conventions of usage and mechanics.

Informative/Explanatory Texts

Informative and explanatory writing should rely on facts to inform or explain. Informative writing can serve several purposes: to increase readers' knowledge of a subject, to help readers better understand a procedure or process, or to provide readers with an enhanced comprehension of a concept. It should also feature a clear introduction, body, and conclusion.

Elements of Informative/Explanatory Texts

Informative/explanatory texts present facts, details, data, and other kinds of evidence to give information about a topic. Readers turn to informational and explanatory texts when they wish to learn about a specific idea, concept, or subject area, or if they want to learn how to do something.

An effective informative/explanatory text contains these elements:

- a topic sentence or thesis statement that introduces the concept or subject
- relevant facts, examples, and details that expand upon a topic
- definitions, quotations, and/or graphics that support the information given
- headings (if desired) to separate sections of the essay
- a structure that presents information in a direct, clear manner
- clear transitions that link sections of the essay
- precise words and technical vocabulary where appropriate
- formal and object language and tone
- a conclusion that supports the information given and provides fresh insights

INFORMATIVE/EXPLANATORY: SCORE 1

Moai: The Giant Statues of Easter Island

Easter Island is a tiny Island. It's far out in the middle of the pacific ocean, 2200 miles off the coast. The closest country is Chile, in south america. The nearest island where people live is called Pitcairn, and that's about 1,300 miles away, and only about 60 people live so their most of the time. Easter island is much bigger than Pitcairn, and lots more people live there now—about 5,000-6,000. Although in the past there were times when only about 111 people lived there.

Even if you don't really know what it is, you've probably seen pictures of the easter island Statues. You'd recognize one if you saw it, with big heads and no smiles. Their lots of them on the island. Almost 900 of them. But some were never finished They're called *moai.* They are all different sizes. All the sizes together average out to about 13 feet tall and 14 tons of heavy.

Scientists know that Polynesians settled Easter Island (it's also called Rapa Nui, and the people are called the Rapanui people). Polynesians were very good at boats. And they went big distances across the Pacific. When these Polynesians arrived was probably 300, but it was probably 900 or 1200.

The island was covered with forests. They can tell by looking at pollin in lakes. The Rapanui people cut trees, to build houses. They didn't know that they wood run out of wood). They also carved *moai.*

The *moai* were made for important chiefs. They were made with only stone tools. They have large heads and narrow bodies. No 2 are the same. Although they look the same as far as their faces are concerned. They are very big and impressive and special.

Over the years, many of the statues were tipped over and broken. But some years ago scientists began to fix some of them and stand them up again. They look more better like that. The ones that have been fixed up are probably the ones you remember seeing in photographs.

The essay does not include a thesis statement.

The writer includes many details that are not relevant to the topic of the essay.

The essay has many errors in grammar, spelling, capitalization, punctuation. The errors detract from the fluency and effectiveness of the essay.

The sentences are often not purposeful, varied, or well controlled.

The essay ends abruptly and lacks a conclusion.

TOOL KIT: WRITING

MODEL

INFORMATIVE/EXPLANATORY: SCORE 2

Moai: The Giant Statues of Easter Island

Easter Island is a tiny Island. It's far out in the middle of the pacific ocean, 2200 miles off the coast. The closest South American country is Chile. The nearest island where people live is called Pitcairn, and that's almost 1,300 miles away. Even if don't know much about it, you've probably seen pictures of the Easter Island statues. You'd recognize one if you saw it. They're almost 900 of them. They're called *moai.* The average one is about 13 feet high (that's tall) and weighs a lot— almost 14 tons.

> The writer does not include a thesis statement.

Scientists know that Polynesians settled Easter Island (it's also called Rapa Nui, and the people are called the Rapanui). Polynesians were very good sailers. And they traveled big distances across the Pacific. Even so, nobody really can say exactly *when* these Polynesians arrived and settled on the Island. Some say 300 A.D., while others say maybe as late as 900 or even 1200 A.D.

> Some of the ideas are reasonably well developed.

Scientists can tell that when the settlers first arrived, the island was covered with forests of palm and hardwood. They can tell by looking at pollin deposits in lakes on the island. The Rapanui people cut trees, built houses, planted crops, and a thriving culture. They didn't know that cutting so many trees would cause problems later on (like running out of wood). They also began to carve *moai.*

> The essay has many errors in grammar, spelling, capitalization, punctuation. The errors decrease the effectiveness of the essay.

The *moai* were built to honor important Rapanui ancestors or chiefs. The statutes all have large heads and narrow bodies, but no too are exactly the same. There faces are all similar. Some have places where eyes could be inserted.

Why did the Rapanui stopped making *moai*? Part of it might have been because there were no more trees and no more of the wood needed to transport them. Part of it was maybe because the people were busy fighting each other because food and other necessary things were running out. In any case, they stopped making moai and started tipping over and breaking the ones that were there already. Later on, archeologists began to try to restore some of the statues and set them up again. But even now that some have been set up again, we still don't know a lot about them. I guess some things just have to remain a mystery!

> The writer's word choice shows that he is not fully aware of the essay's purpose and tone.

> The writer does not include a clear conclusion.

INFORMATIVE/EXPLANATORY: SCORE 3

Moai: The Giant Statues of Easter Island

Easter Island is a tiny place, far out in the middle of the Pacific Ocean, 2200 miles off the coast of South America. Another name for the island is Rapa Nui. Even if you don't know much about it, you would probably recognize the colossal head-and-torso carvings known as *moai*. Even after years of research by scientists, many questions about these extraordinary statues remain unanswered.

> The thesis statement is clearly stated.

Scientists now agree that it was Polynesians who settled Easter Island. Earlier some argued South American voyagers were the first. But the Polynesians were expert sailors and navigators known to have traveled huge distances across the Pacific Ocean. However, scientists do not agree about *when* the settlers arrived. Some say A.D. 300, while others suggest as late as between A.D. 900 and 1200.

Scientists say that when the settlers first arrived on Rapa Nui, the island was covered with forests of palm and hardwood. They can tell by looking at the layers of pollen deposited over the years in the lakes on the island. The Rapa Nui began to carve *moai*. They developed a unique artistic and architectural tradition all of their own.

> The essay has many interesting details, but some do not relate directly to the topic.

Archeologists agree that the *moai* were created to honor ancestor's or chief's. Most *moai* are made from a soft rock called *tuff* that's formed from hardened volcanic ash. The statues all have large heads on top of narrow bodies, but no two are exactly the same. Some have indented eye sockets where eyes could be inserted.

> There are very few errors in grammar, usage, and punctuation. These errors do not interrupt the fluency and effectiveness of the essay.

At some point, the Rapanui stopped making *moai*. Why? Was it because there were no more trees and no longer enough wood needed to transport them? Was it because the people were too busy fighting each other over resources which had begun to run out? No one can say for sure. Rival groups began toppling their enemys' *moai* and breaking them. By the 19th century, most of the statues were tipped over, and many were destroyed. It wasn't until many years later that archeologists began to restore some of the statues.

The *moai* of Easter Island are one of the most awe-inspiring human achievements ever. Thanks to scientific studies, we know much more about the *moai, ahu,* and Rapanui people than we ever did in the past. But some questions remain unanswered. At least for now, the *moai* are keeping their mouths shut, doing a good job of guarding their secrets.

> The writer's conclusion sums up the main points of the essay and supports the thesis statement.

TOOL KIT: WRITING

WRITING

MODEL

INFORMATIVE/EXPLANATORY: SCORE 4

Moai: The Giant Statues of Easter Island

Easter Island, 2200 miles off the coast of South America, is "the most remote inhabited island on the planet." Few have visited this speck in the middle of the vast Pacific Ocean, but we all recognize the colossal statues that bring this tiny island its fame: the head-and-torso carvings known as *moai*. Yet even after years of research by scientists, many questions about the *moai* remain unanswered.

Scientists now agree that it was Polynesians, not South Americans, who settled Easter Island (also known as Rapa Nui). Polynesians were expert sailors and navigators known to have traveled huge distances across the Pacific Ocean. Even so, there is little agreement about *when* the settlers arrived. Some say A.D. 300, while others suggest as late as between A.D. 900 and 1200.

Most archeologists agree that the *moai* were created to honor ancestors, chiefs, or other important people. Most *moai* are made from a soft rock called *tuff* that's formed from hardened volcanic ash. The statues have large heads atop narrow torsos, with eyes wide open and lips tightly closed. While the moai share these basic characteristics, no two are exactly the same: while all are huge, some are bigger than others. Some are decorated with carvings. Some have indented eye sockets where white coral eyes could be inserted. It's possible that the eyes were only put in for special occasions.

In the late 1600s, the Rapanui stopped carving *moai*. Was it because the forests had been depleted and there was no longer enough wood needed to transport them? Was it because they were too busy fighting each other over dwindling resources? No one can say for sure. What is known is that rival groups began toppling their enemies' *moai* and breaking them. By the 19th century, most of the statues were tipped over, and many were destroyed. It wasn't until many years later that archeologists began restoration efforts.

The *moai* of Easter Island are one of humanity's most awe-inspiring cultural and artistic achievements. Part of Rapa Nui was designated as a World Heritage Site in 1995 to recognize and protect these extraordinary creations. Thanks to scientific studies, we know much more about the *moai* than we ever did in the past. But some questions remain unanswered, some mysteries unsolved. Don't bother asking the *moai*: their lips are sealed.

The thesis statement of is clearly stated in an engaging manner.

The ideas in the essay relate to the thesis statement and focus on the topic.

The writer includes many specific and well-chosen details that add substance to the essay.

The fluency of the writing and effectiveness of the essay are unaffected by errors.

The conclusion relates to the thesis statement and is creative and memorable.

Informative/Explanatory Rubric

	Focus and Organization	Evidence and Elaboration	Conventions
4	The introduction engages the reader and states a thesis in a compelling way. The essay includes a clear introduction, body, and conclusion. The conclusion summarizes ideas and offers fresh insight into the thesis.	The essay includes specific reasons, details, facts, and quotations from selections and outside resources to support the thesis. The tone of the essay is always formal and objective. The language is always precise and appropriate for the audience and purpose.	The essay uses standard English conventions of usage and mechanics. The essay contains no spelling errors.
3	The introduction engages the reader and sets forth the thesis. The essay includes an introduction, body, and conclusion. The conclusion summarizes ideas and supports the thesis.	The essay includes some specific reasons, details, facts, and quotations from selections and outside resources to support the thesis. The tone of the essay is mostly formal and objective. The language is generally precise and appropriate for the audience and purpose.	The essay demonstrates general accuracy in standard English conventions of usage and mechanics. The essay contains few spelling errors.
2	The introduction sets forth the thesis. The essay includes an introduction, body, and conclusion, but one or more parts are weak. The conclusion partially summarizes ideas but may not provide strong support of the thesis.	The essay includes a few reasons, details, facts, and quotations from selections and outside resources to support the thesis. The tone of the essay is occasionally formal and objective. The language is somewhat precise and appropriate for the audience and purpose.	The essay demonstrates some accuracy in standard English conventions of usage and mechanics. The essay contains some spelling errors.
1	The introduction does not state the thesis clearly. The essay does not include an introduction, body, and conclusion. The conclusion does not summarize ideas and may not relate to the thesis.	Reliable and relevant evidence is not included. The tone of the essay is not objective or formal. The language used is imprecise and not appropriate for the audience and purpose.	The essay contains mistakes in standard English conventions of usage and mechanics. The essay contains many spelling errors.

Narration

Narrative writing conveys experience, either real or imaginary, and uses time to provide structure. It can be used to inform, instruct, persuade, or entertain. Whenever writers tell a story, they are using narrative writing. Most types of narrative writing share certain elements, such as characters, setting, a sequence of events, and, often, a theme.

Elements of a Narrative Text

A **narrative** is any type of writing that tells a story, whether it is fiction, nonfiction, poetry, or drama.

An effective nonfiction narrative usually contains these elements:

- an engaging beginning in which characters and setting are established
- characters who participate in the story events
- a well-structured, logical sequence of events
- details that show time and place
- effective story elements such as dialogue, description, and reflection
- the narrator's thoughts, feelings, or views about the significance of events
- use of language that brings the characters and setting to life

An effective fictional narrative usually contains these elements:

- an engaging beginning in which characters, setting, or a main conflict is introduced
- a main character and supporting characters who participate in the story events
- a narrator who relates the events of the plot from a particular point of view
- details that show time and place
- conflict that is resolved in the course of the narrative
- narrative techniques such as dialogue, description, and suspense
- use of language that vividly brings to life characters and events

NARRATIVE: SCORE 1

The Remark-a-Ball

Eddie decided to invent a Remark-a-Ball. Eddie thought Barnaby should be able to speak to him.

That's when he invited the Remark-a-Ball.

Barnaby had a rubber ball. It could make a bunchs of sounds that made Barnaby bark. It had always seemed that Barnaby was using his squeaky toy to talk, almost.

This was before Barnaby got hit by a car and died. This was a big deal. He took his chemistry set and worked real hard to created a thing that would make the toy ball talk for Barnaby, his dog.

Eddie made a Remark-a-Ball that worked a little too well, tho. Barnaby could say anything he wanted too. And now he said complaints—his bed didn't feel good, he wanted to be walks, he wanted to eat food.

Barnaby became bossy to Eddy to take him on walks or wake up. It was like he became his boss. Like my dad's boss. Eddy didn't like having a mean boss for a dog.

Eddy wished he hadn't invented the Remark-a-Ball.

The story's beginning is choppy and vague.

The sequence of events is unclear and hard to follow.

The narrative lacks descriptive details and sensory language.

The narrative contains many errors in standard English conventions of usage and mechanics.

The conclusion is abrupt and unsatisfying.

TOOL KIT: WRITING

Narrative (Score 1) **R19**

MODEL

NARRATIVE: SCORE 2

The Remark-a-Ball

Eddie couldn't understand what his dog was barking about, so he decided to invent a Remark-a-Ball. Eddie thought Barnaby should be able to speak to him.

That's when he invented the Remark-a-Ball.

Barnaby had a rubber ball the size of an orange. It could make a bunch of sounds that made Barnaby bark. It had always seemed to Eddie that Barnaby was almost talking with his squeaky toy.

This was a big deal. Eddy would be the first human ever to talk to a dog, which was a big deal! He took his chemistry set and worked real hard to created a thing that would make the toy ball talk for Barnaby, his dog.

Eddie made a Remark-a-Ball that worked a little too well, tho. Barnaby could say anything he wanted now. And now he mostly said complaints—his bed didn't feel good, he wanted to be walked all the time, he wanted to eat people food.

Barnaby became bossy to Eddy to take him on walks or wake him up. It was like he became his boss. His really mean boss, like my dad's boss. Eddy didn't like having a mean boss for a dog.

Eddy started to ignore his best friend, which used to be his dog named Barnaby. He started tot think maybe dogs shouldn't be able to talk.

Things were much better when Barnaby went back to barking

> The story's beginning provides few details to establish the situation.

> Narrative techniques such as dialogue, pacing, and description are used sparingly.

> The narrative contains some errors in standard English conventions of usage and mechanics.

> The conclusion comes abruptly and provides little insight about the story's meaning.

NARRATIVE: SCORE 3

The Remark-a-Ball

Any bark could mean anything: *I'm hungry*, *Take me outside*, or *There's that dog again*. Eddie thought Barnaby should be able to speak to him.

And that's how the Remark-a-Ball was born.

Barnaby had a rubber ball the size of an orange. It could make a wide range of sounds that made Barnaby howl. It had always seemed to Eddie that Barnaby was almost communicating with his squeaky toy.

This was big. This was epic. He would be the first human ever to bridge the communication gap between species! He dusted off his old chemistry set and, through trial and error, created a liquid bath that would greatly increase the toy's flexibility, resilience, and mouth-feel.

Eddie had a prototype that worked—perhaps too well. Barnaby was ready to speak his mind. This unleashed a torrent of complaints— his bed was lumpy, he couldn't *possibly* exist on just three walks a day, he wanted table food like the poodle next door.

Barnaby made increasingly specific demands to Eddie to take him on walks or wake him up. This kind of conversation did not bring them closer, as Eddie had thought, but instead it drove them apart.

Eddie started to avoid his former best friend, and he came to the realization that there is a good reason different species don't have a common language.

So Eddie quit letting Barnaby use the toy.

"Hey, Barn, want to go outside?" Eddie would say, and the dog, as if a switch was turned on, would shake, wag, pant, run in circles, and bark—just like he used to.

The story's beginning establishes the situation and the narrator's point of view but leaves some details unclear.

The narrative consistently uses standard English conventions of usage and mechanics.

Narrative techniques such as dialogue and description are used occasionally.

The conclusion resolves the situation or problem, but does not clearly convey the significance of the events in the story.

MODEL

NARRATIVE: SCORE 4

The Remark-a-Ball

Barnaby, for no apparent reason, leapt up and began to bark like a maniac. "Why are you barking?" asked Eddie, holding the leash tight. But Barnaby, being a dog, couldn't say. It could have been anything—a dead bird, a half-eaten sandwich, the Taj Mahal.

The story's beginning is engaging, sets up a point of view, and establishes characters and tone.

This was one of those times Eddie wished that Barnaby could talk. Any bark could mean anything: *I'm hungry, Take me outside,* or *There's that dog again.* Eddie thought, as buddies, they should be able to understand each other.

And that's how the Remark-a-Ball was born.

The narrative uses standard English conventions of usage and mechanics, except where language is manipulated for effect.

Barnaby had a squeaky toy—a rubber ball the size of an orange. It could emit a wide range of sounds. It made Barnaby howl even as he was squeaking it. And it had always seemed to Eddie that through this process Barnaby was almost communicating.

This was big. This was epic. He, Edward C. Reyes III, would be the first human ever to bridge the communication gap between species! He dusted off his old chemistry set and, through trial and error, created a liquid bath that would greatly increase the toy's flexibility, resilience, and mouth-feel.

By the end of the week Eddie had a prototype that worked— perhaps too well. Barnaby was ready to speak his mind. This unleashed a torrent of complaints—his bed was lumpy, he couldn't *possibly* exist on just three walks a day, he wanted table food like the poodle next door.

Events are presented in a logical sequence, and the progression from one even to another is smooth.

Barnaby made increasingly specific demands, such as "Wake me in ten minutes," and "I want filtered water." This kind of conversation did not bring them closer, as Eddie had thought, but instead it drove them apart.

Narrative techniques are used effectively to develop characters and events.

Eddie started to avoid his former best friend, and he came to the realization that there is a good reason different species don't have a common language. It didn't take long for the invention to be relegated to the very bottom of Barnaby's toy chest, too far down for him to get.

There followed a period of transition, after which Eddie and Barnaby returned to their former mode of communication, which worked out just fine.

"Hey, Barn, want to go outside?" Eddie would say, and the dog, as if a switch was turned on, would shake, wag, pant, run in circles, and bark—just like he used to.

The conclusion resolves the situation or problem and clearly conveys the significance of the events in the story.

"You're a good boy, Barnaby," Eddie would say, scratching him behind the ears.

Narrative Rubric

	Focus and Organization	Development of Ideas/ Elaboration	Conventions
4	The introduction establishes a clear context and point of view. Events are presented in a clear sequence, building to a climax, then moving toward the conclusion. The conclusion follows from and reflects on the events and experiences in the narrative.	Narrative techniques such as dialogue, pacing, and description are used effectively to develop characters, events, and setting. Descriptive details, sensory language, and precise words and phrases are used to convey the experiences in the narrative and to help the reader imagine the characters and setting. Voice is established through word choice, sentence structure, and tone.	The narrative uses standard English conventions of usage and mechanics. Deviations from standard English are intentional and serve the purpose of the narrative. Rules of spelling and punctuation are followed.
3	The introduction gives the reader some context and sets the point of view. Events are presented logically, though there are some jumps in time. The conclusion logically ends the story, but provides only some reflection on the experiences related in the story.	Narrative techniques such as dialogue, pacing, and description are used occasionally. Descriptive details, sensory language, and precise words and phrases are used occasionally. Voice is established through word choice, sentence structure, and tone occasionally, though not evenly.	The narrative mostly uses standard English conventions of usage and mechanics, though there are some errors. There are few errors in spelling and punctuation.
2	The introduction provides some description of a place. The point of view can be unclear at times. Transitions between events are occasionally unclear. The conclusion comes abruptly and provides only a small amount of reflection on the experiences related in the narrative.	Narrative techniques such as dialogue, pacing, and description are used sparingly. The story contains few examples of descriptive details and sensory language. Voice is not established for characters, so that it becomes difficult to determine who is speaking.	The narrative contains some errors in standard English conventions of usage and mechanics. There are many errors in spelling and punctuation.
1	The introduction fails to set a scene or is omitted altogether. The point of view is not always clear. The events are not in a clear sequence, and events that would clarify the narrative may not appear. The conclusion does not follow from the narrative or is omitted altogether.	Narrative techniques such as dialogue, pacing, and description are not used. Descriptive details are vague or missing. No sensory language is included. Voice has not been developed.	The text contains mistakes in standard English conventions of usage and mechanics. Rules of spelling and punctuation have not been followed.

Conducting Research

We are lucky to live in an age when information is accessible and plentiful. However, not all information is equally useful, or even accurate. Strong research skills will help you locate and evaluate information.

Narrowing or Broadening a Topic

The first step of any research project is determining your topic. Consider the scope of your project and choose a topic that is narrow enough to address completely and effectively. If you can name your topic in just one or two words, it is probably too broad. Topics such as Shakespeare, jazz, or science fiction are too broad to cover in a single report. Narrow a broad topic into smaller subcategories.

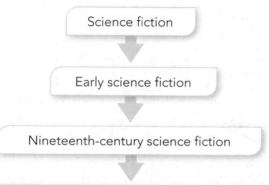

Science fiction

↓

Early science fiction

↓

Nineteenth-century science fiction

↓

Nineteenth-century science fiction that predicted the future accurately

When you begin to research a topic, pay attention to the amount of information available. If you feel overwhelmed by the number of relevant sources, you may need to narrow your topic further.

If there isn't enough information available as your research, you might need to broaden your topic. A topic is too narrow when it can be thoroughly presented in less space than the required size of your assignment. It might also be too narrow if you can find little or no information in library and media sources, so consider broadening your topic to include other related ideas.

Generating Research Questions

Use research questions to focus your research. Specific questions can help you avoid time-wasting digressions. For example, instead of simply hunting for information about Mark Twain, you might ask, "What jobs did Mark Twain have, other than being a writer?" or "Which of Twain's books was most popular during his lifetime?"

In a research report, your research question often becomes your thesis statement, or may lead up to it. The question will also help you focus your research into a comprehensive but flexible search plan, as well as prevent you from gathering unnecessary details. As your research teaches you more about your topic, you may find it necessary to refocus your original question.

Consulting Print and Digital Sources

Effective research combines information from several sources, and does not rely too heavily on a single source. The creativity and originality of your research depends on how you combine ideas from multiple sources. Plan to consult a variety of resources, such as the following:

- **Primary and Secondary Sources:** To get a thorough view of your topic, use primary sources (firsthand or original accounts, such as interview transcripts, eyewitness reports, and newspaper articles) and secondary sources (accounts, created after an event occurred, such as encyclopedia entries).

- **Print and Digital Resources:** The Internet allows fast access to data, but print resources are often edited more carefully. Use both print and digital resources in order to guarantee the accuracy of your findings.

- **Media Resources:** You can find valuable information in media resources such as documentaries, television programs, podcasts, and museum exhibitions. Consider attending public lectures given by experts to gain an even more in-depth view of your topic.

- **Original Research:** Depending on your topic, you may wish to conduct original research to include among your sources. For example, you might interview experts or eyewitnesses, or conduct a survey of people in your community.

Evaluating Sources It is important to evaluate the credibility, validity, and accuracy of any information you find, as well as its appropriateness for your purpose and audience. You may find the information you need to answer your research question in specialized and authoritative sources, such as almanacs (for social, cultural, and natural statistics), government publications (for law, government programs, and subjects such as agriculture), and information services. Also, consider consumer, workplace, and public documents.

Ask yourself questions such as these to evaluate these additional sources:

- **Authority:** Is the author well known? What are the author's credentials? Does the source include references to other reliable sources? Does the author's tone win your confidence? Why or why not?

- **Bias:** Does the author have any obvious biases? What is the author's purpose for writing? Who is the target audience?

- **Currency:** When was the work created? Has it been revised? Is there more current information available?

Using Online Encyclopedias

Online encyclopedias are often written by anonymous contributors who are not required to fact-check information. These sites can be very useful as a launching point for research, but should not be considered accurate. Look for footnotes, endnotes, or hyperlinks that support facts with reliable sources that have been carefully checked by editors.

RESEARCH

Using Search Terms

Finding information on the Internet can be both easy and challenging. Type a word or phrase into a general search engine and you will probably get hundreds—or thousands—of results. However, those results are not guaranteed to be relevant or accurate.

These strategies can help you find information from the Internet:

- Create a list of keywords that apply to your topic before you begin using a search engine. Consult a thesaurus to expand your list.
- Enter six to eight keywords.
- Choose precise nouns. Most search engines ignore articles and prepositions. Verbs may be used in multiple contexts, leading to sources that are not relevant. Use modifiers, such as adjectives, when necessary to specify a category.
- Use quotation marks to focus a search. Place a phrase in quotation marks to find pages that include exactly that phrase. Add several phrases in quotation marks to narrow your results.
- Spell carefully. Many search engines autocorrect spelling, but they cannot produce accurate results for all spelling errors.
- Scan search results before you click them. The first result isn't always the most relevant. Read the text and consider the domain before make a choice.
- Utilize more than one search engine.

Evaluating Internet Domains

Not everything you read on the Internet is true, so you have to evaluate sources carefully. The last three letters of an Internet URL identify the Website's domain, which can help you evaluate the information of the site.

- **.gov**—Government sites are sponsored by a branch of the United States federal government, such as the Census Bureau, Supreme Court, or Congress. These sites are considered reliable.
- **.edu**—Education domains include schools from kindergartens to universities. Information from an educational research center or department is likely to be carefully checked. However, education domains can also include student pages that are not edited or monitored.
- **.org**—Organizations are nonprofit groups and usually maintain a high level of credibility. Keep in mind that some organizations may express strong biases.
- **.com** and **.net**—Commercial sites exist to make a profit. Information may be biased to show a product or service in a good light. The company may be providing information to encourage sales or promote a positive image.

Taking Notes

Take notes as you locate and connect useful information from multiple sources, and keep a reference list of every source you use. This will help you make distinctions between the relative value and significance of specific data, facts, and ideas.

For long-term research projects, create source cards and notecards to keep track of information gathered from multiple resources.

Source Cards
Create a card that identifies each source.

- For print materials, list the author, title, publisher, date of publication, and relevant page numbers.
- For Internet sources, record the name and Web address of the site, and the date you accessed the information.
- For media sources, list the title, person, or group credited with creating the media, and the year of production.

Notecards
Create a separate notecard for each item of information.

- Include the fact or idea, the letter of the related source card, and the specific page(s) on which the fact or idea appears.
- Use quotation marks around words and phrases taken directly from print or media resources.
- Mark particularly useful or relevant details using your own annotation method, such as stars, underlining, or colored highlighting.

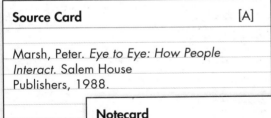

Source Card   [A]

Marsh, Peter. *Eye to Eye: How People Interact.* Salem House Publishers, 1988.

Notecard

Gestures vary from culture to culture. The American "OK" symbol (thumb and forefinger) is considered insulting in Greece and Turkey.

Source Card: A, p. 54.

Quote Accurately Responsible research begins with the first note you take. Be sure to quote and paraphrase your sources accurately so you can identify these sources later. In your notes, circle all quotations and paraphrases to distinguish them from your own comments. When photocopying from a source, include the copyright information. When printing out information from an online source, include the Web address.

Reviewing Research Findings

While conducting research, you will need to review your findings, checking that you have collected enough accurate and appropriate information.

Considering Audience and Purpose

Always keep your audience in mind as you gather information, since different audiences may have very different needs. For example, if you are writing an in-depth analysis of a text that your entire class has read together and you are writing for your audience, you will not need to gather background information that has been thoroughly discussed in class. However, if you are writing the same analysis for a national student magazine, you cannot assume that all of your readers have the same background information. You will need to provide facts from reliable sources to help orient these readers to your subject. When considering whether or not your research will satisfy your audience, ask yourself:

- Who are my readers? For whom am I writing?
- Have I collected enough information to explain my topic to this audience?
- Are there details in my research that I can omit because they are already familiar to my audience?

Your purpose for writing will also influence your review of research. If you are researching a question to satisfy your own curiosity, you can stop researching when you feel you understand the answer completely. If you are writing a research report that will be graded, you need to consider the criteria of the assignment. When considering whether or not you have enough information, ask yourself:

- What is my purpose for writing?
- Will the information I have gathered be enough to achieve my purpose?
- If I need more information, where might I find it?

Synthesizing Sources

Effective research writing does not merely present facts and details; it synthesizes—gathers, orders, and interprets—them. These strategies will help you synthesize information effectively:

- Review your notes and look for connections and patterns among the details you have collected.
- Arrange notes or notecards in different ways to help you decide how to best combine related details and present them in a logical way.
- Pay close attention to details that support one other, emphasizing the same main idea.
- Also look for details that challenge each other, highlighting ideas about which there is no single, or consensus, opinion. You might decide to conduct additional research to help you decide which side of the issue has more support.

Types of Evidence

When reviewing your research, also consider the kinds of evidence you have collected. The strongest writing contains a variety of evidence effectively. This chart describes three of the most common types of evidence: statistical, testimonial, and anecdotal.

TYPE OF EVIDENCE	DESCRIPTION	EXAMPLE
Statistical evidence includes facts and other numerical data used to support a claim or explain a topic.	Examples of statistical evidence include historical dates and information, quantitative analyses, poll results, and quantitative descriptions.	"Although it went on to become a hugely popular novel, the first edition of William Goldman's book sold fewer than 3,000 copies."
Testimonial evidence includes any ideas or opinions presented by others, especially experts in a field.	Firsthand testimonies present ideas from eyewitnesses to events or subjects being discussed.	"The ground rose and fell like an ocean at ebb tide." —Fred J. Hewitt, eyewitness to the 1906 San Francisco earthquake
	Secondary testimonies include commentaries on events by people who were not involved. You might quote a well-known literary critic when discussing a writer's most famous novel, or a prominent historian when discussing the effects of an important event	Gladys Hansen insists that "there was plenty of water in hydrants throughout [San Francisco] . . . The problem was this fire got away."
Anecdotal evidence presents one person's view of the world, often by describing specific events or incidents.	Compelling research should not rely solely on this form of evidence, but it can be very useful for adding personal insights and refuting inaccurate generalizations. An individual's experience can be used with other forms of evidence to present complete and persuasive support.	Although many critics claim the novel is universally beloved, at least one reader "threw the book against a wall because it made me so angry."

Incorporating Research Into Writing

Avoiding Plagiarism

Plagiarism is the unethical presentation of someone else's ideas as your own. You must cite sources for direct quotations, paraphrased information, or facts that are specific to a single source. When you are drafting and revising, circle any words or ideas that are not your own. Follow the instructions on pages R32 and R33 to correctly cite those passages.

Review for Plagiarism Always take time to review your writing for unintentional plagiarism. Read what you have written and take note of any phrases or sentences that do not have your personal writing voice. Compare those passages with your resource materials. You might have copied them without remembering the exact source. Add a correct citation to give credit to the original author. If you cannot find the questionable phrase in your notes, revise it to ensure that your final report reflects your own thinking and not someone else's work.

Quoting and Paraphrasing

When including ideas from research into your writing, you will decide to quote directly or paraphrase.

Direct Quotation Use the author's exact words when they are interesting or persuasive. You might decide to include direct quotations for these reasons:

- to share an especially clear and relevant statement
- to reference a historically significant passage
- to show that an expert agrees with your position
- to present an argument that you will counter in your writing.

Include complete quotations, without deleting or changing words. If you need to omit words for space or clarity, use ellipsis points to indicate the omission. Enclose direct quotations in quotation marks and indicate the author's name.

Paraphrase A paraphrase restates an author's ideas in your own words. Be careful to paraphrase accurately. Beware of making sweeping generalizations in a paraphrase that were not made by the original author. You may use some words from the original source, but a legitimate paraphrase does more than simply rearrange an author's phrases, or replace a few words with synonyms.

Original Text	"*The Tempest* was written as a farewell to art and the artist's life, just before the completion of his forty-ninth year, and everything in the play bespeaks the touch of autumn." Brandes, Georg. "Analogies Between *The Tempest* and *A Midsummer Night's Dream.*" *The Tempest*, by William Shakespeare, William Heinemann, 1904, p. 668.
Patchwork Plagiarism phrases from the original are rearranged, but too closely follows the original text.	A farewell to art, Shakespeare's play, *The Tempest*, was finished just before the completion of his forty-ninth year. The artist's life was to end within three years. The touch of autumn is apparent in nearly everything in the play.
Good Paraphrase	Images of autumn occur throughout *The Tempest*, which Shakespeare wrote as a way of saying goodbye to both his craft and his own life.

Maintaining the Flow of Ideas

Effective research writing is much more that just a list of facts. Be sure to maintain the flow of ideas by connecting research information to your own ideas. Instead of simply stating a piece of evidence, use transition words and phrases to explain the connection between information you found from outside resources and your own ideas and purpose for writing. The following transitions can be used to introduce, compare, contrast, and clarify.

Useful Transitions

When providing examples:

for example   for instance   to illustrate   in [name of resource], [author]

When comparing and contrasting ideas or information:

in the same way   similarly   however   on the other hand

When clarifying ideas or opinions:

in other words   that is   to explain   to put it another way

Choosing an effective organizational structure for your writing will help you create a logical flow of ideas. Once you have established a clear organizational structure, insert facts and details from your research in appropriate places to provide evidence and support for your writing.

ORGANIZATIONAL STRUCTURE	USES
Chronological order presents information in the sequence in which it happens.	historical topics; science experiments; analysis of narratives
Part-to-whole order examines how several categories affect a larger subject.	analysis of social issues; historical topics
Order of importance presents information in order of increasing or decreasing importance.	persuasive arguments; supporting a bold or challenging thesis
Comparison-and-contrast organization outlines the similarities and differences of a given topic.	addressing two or more subjects

RESEARCH

Formats for Citing Sources

In research writing, cite your sources. In the body of your paper, provide a footnote, an endnote, or a parenthetical citation, identifying the sources of facts, opinions, or quotations. At the end of your paper, provide a bibliography or a Works Cited list, a list of all the sources referred to in your research. Follow an established format, such as Modern Language Association (MLA) style.

Parenthetical Citations (MLA Style)

A parenthetical citation briefly identifies the source from which you have taken a specific quotation, factual claim, or opinion. It refers readers to one of the entries on your Works Cited list. A parenthetical citation has the following features:

- It appears in parentheses.
- It identifies the source by the last name of the author, editor, or translator, or by the title (for a lengthy title, list the first word only).
- It provides a page reference, the page(s) of the source on which the information cited can be found.

A parenthetical citation generally falls outside a closing quotation mark but within the final punctuation of a clause or sentence. For a long quotation set off from the rest of your text, place the citation at the end of the excerpt without any punctuation following.

Sample Parenthetical Citations

It makes sense that baleen whales such as the blue whale, the bowhead whale, the humpback whale, and the sei whale (to name just a few) grow to immense sizes (Carwardine et al. 19–21). The blue whale has grooves running from under its chin to partway along the length of its underbelly. As in some other whales, these grooves expand and allow even more food and water to be taken in (Ellis 18–21).

Authors' last names

Page numbers where information can be found

Works Cited List (MLA Style)

A Works Cited list must contain accurate information to enable a reader to locate each source you cite. The basic components of an entry are as follows:

- name of the author, editor, translator, and/or group responsible for the work
- title of the work
- publisher
- date of publication

For print materials, the information for a citation generally appears on the copyright and title pages. For the format of a Works Cited list, consult the examples on this page and in the MLA Style for Listing Sources chart.

Sample Works Cited List (MLA 8th Edition)

Carwardine, Mark, et al. *The Nature Company Guides: Whales, Dolphins, and Porpoises.* Time-Life, 1998.

"Discovering Whales." *Whales on the Net.* Whales in Danger, 1998, www.whales.org.au/discover/index.html. Accessed 11 Apr. 2017.

Neruda, Pablo. "Ode to Spring." *Odes to Opposites,* translated by Ken Krabbenhoft, edited and illustrated by Ferris Cook, Little, 1995, p. 16.

The Saga of the Volsungs. Translated by Jesse L. Byock, Penguin, 1990.

List an anonymous work by title.

List both the title of the work and the collection in which it is found.

Works Cited List or Bibliography?

A Works Cited list includes only those sources you paraphrased or quoted directly in your research paper. By contrast, a bibliography lists all the sources you consulted during research—even those you did not cite.

MLA (8th Edition) Style for Listing Sources

Book with one author	Pyles, Thomas. *The Origins and Development of the English Language.* 2nd ed., Harcourt Brace Jovanovich, 1971. [Indicate the edition or version number when relevant.]
Book with two authors	Pyles, Thomas, and John Algeo. *The Origins and Development of the English Language.* 5th ed., Cengage Learning, 2004.
Book with three or more authors	Donald, Robert B., et al. *Writing Clear Essays.* Prentice Hall, 1983.
Book with an editor	Truth, Sojourner. *Narrative of Sojourner Truth.* Edited by Margaret Washington, Vintage Books, 1993.
Introduction to a work in a published edition	Washington, Margaret. Introduction. *Narrative of Sojourner Truth,* by Sojourner Truth, edited by Washington, Vintage Books, 1993, pp. v–xi.
Single work in an anthology	Hawthorne, Nathaniel. "Young Goodman Brown." *Literature: An Introduction to Reading and Writing,* edited by Edgar V. Roberts and Henry E. Jacobs, 5th ed., Prentice Hall, 1998, pp. 376–385. [Indicate pages for the entire selection.]
Signed article from an encyclopedia	Askeland, Donald R. "Welding." *World Book Encyclopedia,* vol. 21, World Book, 1991, p. 58.
Signed article in a weekly magazine	Wallace, Charles. "A Vodacious Deal." *Time,* 14 Feb. 2000, p. 63.
Signed article in a monthly magazine	Gustaitis, Joseph. "The Sticky History of Chewing Gum." *American History,* Oct. 1998, pp. 30–38.
Newspaper article	Thurow, Roger. "South Africans Who Fought for Sanctions Now Scrap for Investors." *Wall Street Journal,* 11 Feb. 2000, pp. A1+. [For a multipage article that does not appear on consecutive pages, write only the first page number on which it appears, followed by the plus sign.]
Unsigned editorial or story	"Selective Silence." Editorial. *Wall Street Journal,* 11 Feb. 2000, p. A14. [If the editorial or story is signed, begin with the author's name.]
Signed pamphlet or brochure	[Treat the pamphlet as though it were a book.]
Work from a library subscription service	Ertman, Earl L. "Nefertiti's Eyes." *Archaeology,* Mar.–Apr. 2008, pp. 28–32. *Kids Search,* EBSCO, New York Public Library. Accessed 7 Jan. 2017. [Indicating the date you accessed the information is optional but recommended.]
Filmstrips, slide programs, videocassettes, DVDs, and other audiovisual media	*The Diary of Anne Frank.* 1959. Directed by George Stevens, performances by Millie Perkins, Shelley Winters, Joseph Schildkraut, Lou Jacobi, and Richard Beymer, Twentieth Century Fox, 2004. [Indicating the original release date after the title is optional but recommended.]
CD-ROM (with multiple publishers)	Simms, James, editor. *Romeo and Juliet.* By William Shakespeare, Attica Cybernetics / BBC Education / Harper, 1995.
Radio or television program transcript	"Washington's Crossing of the Delaware." *Weekend Edition Sunday,* National Public Radio, 23 Dec. 2013. Transcript.
Web page	"Fun Facts About Gum." ICGA, 2005–2017, www.gumassociation.org/index.cfm/facts-figures/fun-facts-about-gum. Accessed 19 Feb. 2017. [Indicating the date you accessed the information is optional but recommended.]
Personal interview	Smith, Jane. Personal interview, 10 Feb. 2017.

All examples follow the style given in the MLA Handbook, 8th edition, published in 2016.

MODEL

Evidence Log

Unit Title: Discovery

Perfomance-Based Assessment Prompt:
Do all discoveries benefit humanity?

My initial thoughts:
Yes - all knowledge moves us forward.

As you read multiple texts about a topic, your thinking may change. Use an Evidence Log like this one to record your thoughts, to track details you might use in later writing or discussion, and to make further connections.

Here is a sample to show how one reader's ideas deepened as she read two texts.

Title of Text: Classifying the Stars   Date: Sept. 17

CONNECTION TO THE PROMPT	TEXT EVIDENCE/DETAILS	ADDITIONAL NOTES/IDEAS
Newton shared his discoveries and then other scientists built on his discoveries.	Paragraph 2: "Isaac Newton gave to the world the results of his experiments on passing sunlight through a prism." Paragraph 3: "In 1814 . . . the German optician, Fraunhofer . . . saw that the multiple spectral tints . . . were crossed by hundreds of fine dark lines."	It's not always clear how a discovery might benefit humanity in the future.

How does this text change or add to my thinking? This confirms what I think.   Date: Sept. 20

Title of Text: Cell Phone Mania   Date: Sept. 21

CONNECTION TO THE PROMPT	TEXT EVIDENCE/DETAILS	ADDITIONAL NOTES/IDEAS
Cell phones have made some forms of communication easier, but people don't talk to each other as much as they did in the past.	Paragraph 7: "Over 80% of young adults state that texting is their primary method of communicating with friends. This contrasts with older adults who state that they prefer a phone call."	Is it good that we don't talk to each other as much? Look for article about social media to learn more about this question.

How does this text change or add to my thinking?   Date: Sept. 25
Maybe there are some downsides to discoveries. I still think that knowledge moves us forward, but there are sometimes unintended negative effects.

MODEL

Word Network

A word network is a collection of words related to a topic. As you read the selections in a unit, identify interesting theme-related words and build your vocabulary by adding them to your Word Network.

Use your Word Network as a resource for your discussions and writings. Here is an example:

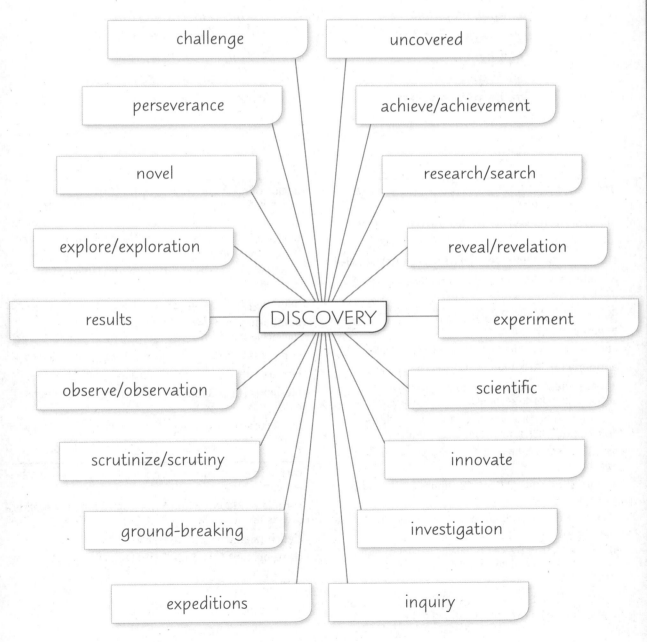

ACADEMIC / CONCEPT VOCABULARY

Academic vocabulary appears in **blue type**.

Pronunciation Key

Symbol	Sample Words	Symbol	Sample Words
a	*at, catapult, Alabama*	oo	*boot, soup, crucial*
ah	*father, charms, argue*	ow	*now, stout, flounder*
ai	*care, various, hair*	oy	*boy, toil, oyster*
aw	*law, maraud, caution*	s	*say, nice, press*
awr	*pour, organism, forewarn*	sh	*she, abolition, motion*
ay	*ape, sails, implication*	u	*full, put, book*
ee	*even, teeth, really*	uh	*ago, focus, contemplation*
eh	*ten, repel, elephant*	ur	*bird, urgent. perforation*
ehr	*merry, verify, terribly*	y	*by, delight, identify*
ih	*it, pin, hymn*	yoo	*music, confuse, few*
o	*shot, hopscotch, condo*	zh	*pleasure, treasure, vision*
oh	*own, parole, rowboat*		

A

advocate (AD vuh kiht) *n.* supporter; (AD vuh kayt) *v.* represent or support publicly

allocate (AL uh kayt) *v.* set aside; assign or portion

allusion (uh LOO zhuhn) *n.* indirect reference

altercation (awl tuhr KAY shuhn) *n.* angry dispute; quarrel

amelioration (uh meel yuh RAY shuhn) *n.* act of making something better or less painful

amenable (uh MEH nuh buhl) *adj.* agreeable

amiably (AY mee uh blee) *adv.* pleasantly

annihilate (uh NY uh layt) *v.* destroy completely

antiquity (an TIHK wuh tee) *n.* very great age

appeasement (uh PEEZ muhnt) *n.* giving in to demands in order to keep peace

articulate (ahr TIHK yuh liht) *adj.* spoken clearly; distinct; (ahr TIHK yuh layt) *v.* clearly express

artifact (AHR tuh fakt) *n.* object made, modified, or used by people

asphyxiation (uhs fihk see AY shuhn) *n.* state of being unable to breathe

asunder (uh SUHN duhr) *adv.* divided; torn into separate pieces

attribute (A truh byoot) *n.* quality or characteristic; (uh TRIHB yoot) *v.* think of as belonging to; to think of as caused by

avarice (AV uh rihs) *n.* great greed

aversion (uh VUR zhuhn) *n.* strong dislike

B

background music (BAK grownd) (MYOO zihk) *n.* music that is not the focus of a show but is added for effect

bar graph (bahr) (graf) *n.* representation of data points using rectangular bars

beachhead (BEECH hehd) *n.* secure starting point; foothold

beguiling (bih GY lihng) *adj.* influencing through charm

belaboring (bih LAY buhr ihng) *v.* focusing on something too much

beneficent (buh NEHF uh suhnt) *adj.* kind and good

bigotry (BIHG uh tree) *n.* intolerance; prejudice

blessings (BLEHS ihngz) *n.* things that benefit or bring happiness

burnished (BUR nihsht) *adj.* shiny; polished to a shine

C

cartilage (KAHR tuh lihj) *n.* firm, flexible tissue almost as hard as bone

chronicle (KRON uh kuhl) *n.* recorded history; narrative *v.* write the history of

clench (klehnch) *v.* close tightly

close-up shot (KLOS uhp) (shot) *n.* close-range view of the subject

cognitive (KOG nuh tihv) *adj.* relating to the process of thinking

commentators (KOM uhn tay tuhrz) *n.* people who discuss or write about events for film, television, radio, or newspapers

communal (kuh MYOON uhl) *adj.* belonging to all in a community or group

composition (kom puh ZIHSH uhn) *n.* arrangement of the parts of a photograph

contentious (kuhn TEHN shuhs) *adj.* fond of arguing; quarrelsome; controversial

context (KON tehkst) *n.* position and immediate surroundings of an artifact or other feature in the location where it is found

contradict (kon truh DIHKT) *v.* do, say, or mean the opposite of; disagree with

current (KUR uhnt) *n.* flow of liquid, air, electricity, etc.

D

decree (dih KREE) *n.* decision made by an authority

deduce (dih DOOS) *v.* reach a conclusion by reasoning

delineate (dih LIHN ee ayt) *v.* trace an outline; draw or sketch out; describe

delusions (dih LOO zhuhnz) *n.* false beliefs

demarcate (DEE mahr kayt) *v.* set the limits of

democracy (dih MOK ruh see) *n.* government that is run by the people

democratic (dehm uh KRAT ihk) *adj.* belonging to a democracy; of, by, and for the people

desperate (DEHS puhr iht) *adj.* extremely bad; reckless; without hope

despoiled (dih SPOYLD) *v.* robbed; stripped of possessions

dimension (duh MEHN shuhn) *n.* measurement of length, width, or depth; quality or part

disarmament (dihs AHR muh muhnt) *n.* limiting or getting rid of weapons

dissolution (dihs uh LOO shuhn) *n.* ending or downfall

dissonance (DIHS uh nuhns) *n.* lack of agreement or harmony

distress (dihs TREHS) *n.* unhappiness or pain

doctrine (DOK truhn) *n.* set of principles or beliefs

dominating (DOM uh nay ting) *adj.* rising high above; towering over

E

edicts (EE dihkts) *n.* commands from a public authority

editing (EHD iht ihng) *v.* taking pieces of film or video and putting them together in a new way.

Egyptology (ee jihp TOL uh jee) *n.* study of the language, culture, and history of ancient Egypt

elemental (ehl uh MEHN tuhl) *adj.* basic; necessary; as found in nature

entitled (ehn TY tuhld) *adj.* having the rights to something; having privileges

entreating (ehn TREET ihng) *adj.* asking; pleading

enunciation (ih nuhn see AY shuhn) *n.* manner in which a speaker pronounces words

envoy (EHN voy) *n.* messenger

ethereal (ih THIHR ee uhl) *adj.* extremely delicate and light in a way that seems too perfect for this world

exquisite (EHKS kwihz iht) *adj.* very beautiful or lovely

F

fissure (FIHSH uhr) *n.* long, narrow crack or opening

flurry (FLUR ee) *n.* sudden burst of activity or excitement

fundamental (fuhn duh MEHN tuhl) *adj.* basic; essential; most important

G

gallantries (GAL uhn treez) *n.* acts of polite attention to the needs of women

gesture (JEHS chuhr) *n.* movement of the body that conveys meaning

gilded (GIHLD ihd) *v.* covered in a thin layer of gold; *adj.* golden

gregarious (gruh GAIR ee uhs) *adj.* sociable

H

heir (air) *n.* person who is legally entitled to inherit

hierarchy (HY uh rahr kee) *n.* people or things organized in higher and lower ranks or classes

homage (OM ihj) *n.* something done to honor someone

hounded (HOWN dihd) *v.* chased; hunted; urged

I

iconography (y kuh NOG ruh fee) *n.* system of symbolic images that conveys a subject, worldview, or concept

ideologies (y dee OL uh jeez) *n.* sets of beliefs of a people, groups, or cultures

implore (ihm PLAWR) *v.* beg or plead

incite (ihn SYT) *v.* strongly encourage

incoherent (ihn koh HIHR uhnt) *adj.* not understandable; confused

indomitable (ihn DOM uh tuh buhl) *adj.* bravely or stubbornly unyielding

industrious (ihn DUHS tree uhs) *adj.* hard-working

inestimable (ihn EHS tuh muh buhl) *adj.* too great to count or measure

inexorable (ihn EHK suhr uh buhl) *adj.* impossible to prevent or stop

inflection (ihn FLEHK shuhn) *n.* changes to pitch or volume within a single word or between words

influence (IHN floo uhns) *n.* dishonest persuasion; bribery

infographic (ihn foh GRAF ihk) *n.* display that combines text with visual elements and design to represent data

initiative (ih NIHSH ee uh tihv) *n.* readiness and abillity to start something; lead

integrate (IHN tuh grayt) *v.* make public facilities availabe to people of all races; bring parts together to make a whole

intemperate (ihn TEHM puhr iht) *adj.* lacking self-control; excessive

interactions (ihn tuhr AK shuhnz) *n.* actions with each other

intercept (ihn tuhr SEHPT) *v.* stop or seize something before it gets to its destination

interdependence (ihn tuhr dih PEHN duhns) *n.* reliance on each other

invective (ihn VEHK tihv) *n.* negative, aggressive language that seeks to harm

invoke (ihn VOHK) *v.* call on

invulnerable (in VUHL nuhr uh buhl) *adj.* incapable of being harmed

L

lead-in (LEED ihn) *n.* in a newscast, the short preliminary section that is used to set up the main story or interview

legacy (LEHG uh see) *n.* something handed down from an ancestor or prior generation

lighting and color (LYT ihng) (KUHL uhr) *n.* use of light, shadow, and color in a photograph

line graph (lyn) (graf) *n.* representation of data points using a line that connects points

listlessly (LIHST lihs lee) *adv.* without energy or interest

location (loh KAY shuhn) *n.* place or scene in which a photograph is taken

luminous (LOO muh nuhs) *adj.* glowing; shining with its own light

lustrous (LUHS truhs) *adj.* shiny; brilliant

M

mail (mayl) *n.* flexible armor

manipulate (muh NIHP yuh layt) *v.* handle or operate; unfairly influence or change

marauding (muh RAW dihng) *adj.* killing and using violence to steal precious items

marginalize (MAHR juh nuh lyz) *v.* treat as unimportant

marvel (MAHR vuhl) *n.* astonishment; used poetically as an adjective meaning "astonished" or "full of wonder"

merciful (MUR sih fuhl) *adj.* showing kindness

motivate (MOH tuh vayt) *v.* provide with an incentive

muffled (MUH fuhld) *adj.* difficult to hear because something is covering and softening the sound

N

navigating (NAV uh gayt ihng) *n.* finding one's way

needy (NEE dee) *adj.* very poor; requiring help

negate (nih GAYT) *v.* make invalid; deny the truth of

O

obdurate (OB duhr iht) *adj.* stubborn; unyielding

objection (uhb JEHK shuhn) *n.* reason or argument against something

obscure (uhb SKYAWR) *adj.* not well-known

opportune (op uhr TOON) *adj.* very favorable

oracles (AWR uh kuhlz) *n.* people who deliver messages from the gods

ore (awr) *n.* any type of mineral, rock, or metal found in the earth

P

pacification (pas uh fuh KAY shuhn) *n.* state of peace put in place through diplomacy, or political negotiation; also, use of force to suppress a hostile or resistent population

paradox (PAR uh doks) *n.* seeming contradiction

pardon (PAHR duhn) *v.* forgive

pariah (puh RY uh) *n.* someone who is despised; social outcast

penitent (PEHN uh tuhnt) *adj.* sorry for one's wrongdoing

perfidious (puhr FIHD ee uhs) *adj.* unfaithful and dishonest

periphery (puh RIHF uhr ee) *n.* outer boundary; edge

perplexity (puhr PLEHK suh tee) *n.* confusion; being in a puzzled state

perspective (puhr SPEHK tihv) *n.* particular way of looking at something; point of view

perspective or angle (puhr SPEHK tihv) (ANG guhl) *n.* vantage point from which a photograph is taken

pie chart (py) (chahrt) *n.* representation of data points using a circle cut into segments

primary (PRY mehr ee) *adj.* first in importance

proclamation (prok luh MAY shuhn) *n.* official announcement

propaganda (prop uh GAN duh) *n.* information, often of a false or misleading nature, used to promote a cause

prophecy (PROF uh see) *n.* prediction about the future

psychological (sy kuh LOJ uh kuhl) *adj.* of the mind

R

recessed (rih SEHST) *adj.* remote; set back

reclusive (rih KLOO sihv) *adj.* solitary; avoiding the company of others

rectify (REHK tuh fy) *v.* correct

refinement (rih FYN muhnt) *n.* politeness; good manners

rending (REHN dihng) *n.* violent or forceful pulling apart of something

resplendent (rih SPLEHN duhnt) *adj.* dazzling; gorgeous

revolution (rehv uh LOO shuhn) *n.* overthrow of a government that is replaced by a new system

S

sabotage (SAB uh tozh) *v.* intentionally ruin or destroy

scarred (skahrd) *adj.* marked by healed wounds

shunned (shuhnd) *v.* rejected; avoided

silhouette (sihl uh WEHT) *n.* dark figure that is seen as a filled-in shape against a light background

sinister (SIHN uh stuhr) *adj.* giving the impression that something harmful or evil is happening or will happen

slant (slant) *n.* attitude or opinion that a reporter takes toward a story

sliver (SLIHV uhr) *n.* small, slender piece of a hard material

sneered (sneerd) *v.* showed dislike with a mean smile

spacious (SPAY shuhs) *adj.* large; roomy

spitefully (SPYT fuhl ee) *adv.* in a way that purposely harms someone or something

stimulus (STIHM yoo luhs) *n.* something that causes a response or reaction

stock footage (stok) (FUT ihj) *n.* film or video that has been shot for one purpose and is available for use in other projects

stoical (STOH ih kuhl) *adj.* keeping strong emotions in check

subject (SUHB jehkt) *n.* primary figure(s), object(s), or other content in a photograph

subversive (suhb VUR sihv) *adj.* causing ruin; destructive

succession (suhk SEHSH uhn) *n.* process by which one is entitled to a privilege, rank or inheritance

supplant (suh PLANT) *v.* replace by unethical means

suppleness (SUHP uhl nihs) *n.* smoothness; fluidity; ability to adapt easily to different situations

surrender (suh REHN duhr) *n.* act of giving up

swollen (SWOH luhn) *adj.* puffed up

T

target (TAHR giht) *n.* object to be hit or shot at

tolerate (TOL uh rayt) *v.* endure; allow to happen without interference

tone (tohn) *n.* sound of a voice with respect to pitch, volume, and overall quality

totalitarian (toh tal uh TAIR ee uhn) *adj.* ruled or governed by a single person or group

transcend (tran SEHND) *v.* go beyond the limits of; be higher or greater than

travail (truh VAYL) *n.* difficult situation or work

traversed (truh VURST) *v.* crossed; traveled across; moved sideways

treacherous (TREHCH uhr uhs) *adj.* not trustworthy

treachery (TREHCH uhr ee) *n.* act of betrayal

trill (trihl) *n.* high-pitched vibrating sound

tumultuous (too MUHL choo uhs) *adj.* loud, excited, and emotional

tyranny (TEER uh nee) *n.* harsh rule over a nation or people

U

unconquerable (uhn KAHNG kuh ruh buhl) *adj.* unable to be defeated

unvoiced (uhn VOYST) *adj.* not spoken out loud or expressed

usurp (yoo ZURP) *v.* take over without having authority

V

valiant (VAL yuhnt) *adj.* brave; courageous

valor (VAL uhr) *n.* personal fortitude or bravery

vehement (VEE uh muhnt) *adj.* showing stong feeling; passionate

verify (VEHR uh fy) *v.* prove to be true

vestibule (VEHS tuh byool) *n.* entrance room

vigilance (VIHJ uh luhns) *n.* watchfulness

vivid (VIHV ihd) *adj.* bright and brilliant; strong and distinct; very intense

volition (voh LIHSH uhn) *n.* act of choosing

vulnerable (VUHL nuhr uh buhl) *adj.* able to be wounded or hurt

W

welt (wehlt) *n.* ridge on the skin caused by a blow

windfall (WIHND fawl) *n.* unexpected good fortune

VOCABULARIO ACADÉMICO/ VOCABULARIO DE CONCEPTOS

El vocabulario académico está en **letra azul**.

A

advocate / abogar *v.* representar o apoyar públicamente

allocate / asignar *v.* apartar; repartir o dividir

allusion / alusión *s.* referencia indirecta

altercation / altercado *s.* disputa; pelea

amelioration / mejoramiento *s.* acto de mejorar algo, o de hacerlo menos doloroso

amenable / dispuesto *adj.* agradable

amiably / amablemente *adv.* cordialmente, afablemente

annihilate / aniquilar *v.* destruir por completo

antiquity / antigüedad *s.* de muchos años; de hace mucho tiempo

appeasement / apaciguamiento *s.* el acto de aceptar exigencias con el fin de mantener la paz

articulate / articular *v.* expresar claramente

articulate / elocuente *adj.* claramente expresado

artifacts / artefactos *s.* objetos de interés histórico hechos por los seres humanos

asphyxiation / asfixia *s.* estado en el que resulta imposible respirar

asunder / dividido *adj.* separado; desarmado en distintas partes

attribute / atribuir *v.* pensar que algo es de la competencia de alguien o algo, o que fue causado por esa persona o hecho

avarice / avaricia *s.* avidez o codicia desmedida

aversion / aversión *s.* fuerte rechazo

B

background music / música de fondo *s.* música que no es el centro de un espectáculo, pero que se incluye para producir un efecto

bar chart / gráfica de barras *s.* representación de datos en la que se usa barras rectangulares

beachhead / cabeza de puente *s.* posición militar; asidero o punto de apoyo

beguiling / encantador *adj.* que influye por medio de su encanto

belaboring / concentrarse *v.* centrarse en algo con mucha intensidad

benificent / bienhechor *adj.* amable, bueno, caritativo

bigotry / intolerancia *s.* prejuicio; fanatismo

blessings / bendiciones *s.* cosas que benefician o que producen felicidad

burnished / bruñido *adj.* brilloso; pulido

C

caption / pie de foto *s.* texto breve que acompaña a una imagen

cartilage / cartílago *s.* tejido fuerte y flexible, casi tan duro como un hueso

chronicle / crónica *s.* relato histórico; narración

clench / apretar *v.* cerrar con fuerza

close-up shot / toma de primer plano *s.* imagen del sujeto tomada muy de cerca

cognitive / cognitivo *adj.* relacionado con el proceso de pensar

commentators / comentaristas *s.* personas que comentan o escriben sobre ciertos eventos para el cine, la televisión, la radio o los periódicos

communal / comunal *adj.* que pertenece a todos los miembros de una comunidad o grupo

composition / composición *s.* distribución o arreglo de las partes de una fotografía

contentious / peleador *adj.* que le gusta discutir o buscar pelea

context / contexto *s.* posición y entorno inmediato de un artefacto u otro elemento en el lugar donde es encontrado

contradict / contradecir *v.* negar que un enunciado sea cierto; discrepar

current / corriente *s.* flujo de líquido, aire, electricidad, etc; *adj.* actual, relativo al tiempo presente

D

decree / decreto *s.* decisión tomada por una autoridad

deduce / deducir *v.* llegar a una conclusión a través del razonamiento

delineate / delinear *v.* trazar un bosquejo; dibujar o esbozar; describir

delusions / delirios *s.* creencias falsas; engaños, ilusiones

demarcate / demarcar *v.* establecer los límites de algo

democracy / democracia *s.* gobierno conducido por el pueblo

democratic / democrático *adj.* que pertenece a una democracia; que es de, por y para el pueblo

desperate / desesperado *adj.* extremadamente mal; sin esperanza

despoiled / depojado *adj.* robado; privado de sus posesiones

dimension / dimensión *s.* medición de la longitud, el ancho o la profundidad; una cualidad o parte

disarmament / desarme *s.* acción de limitar o eliminar las armas

dissolution / disolución *s.* final o ruina

dissonance / disonancia *s.* falta de acuerdo o de armonía

distress / aflicción *s.* infelicidad o dolor

doctrine / doctrina *s.* conjunto de principios o creencias

dominating / dominante *adj.* que se alza por encima; que se destaca de los demás

E

edicts / edictos *s.* mandatos

editing / editar *v.* tomar partes de una película o video y volver a juntarlas de otra manera

Egyptology / egiptología *s.* estudio del lenguaje, la cultura y la historia del Egipto antiguo

elemental / elemental *adj.* básico; necesario; como se encuentra en la naturaleza

entitled / autorizado *adj.* que tiene el derecho a algo; que tiene ciertos privilegios

entreating / suplicante *adj.* que pide o ruega

enunciation / enunciación *s.* la manera en que un hablante expone las palabras

envoy / enviado *s.* mensajero

ethereal / etéreo *adj.* sumamente delicado y ligero

exquisite / exquisito *adj.* muy bello o agradable

F

fissure / fisura *s.* abertura o grieta larga y estrecha

flurry / frenesí *s.* explosión repentina de actividad o entusiasmo

fundamental / fundamental *adj.* que forma el fundamento o base; parte esencial

G

gallantries / galanterías *s.* gestos corteses de atención hacia las mujeres

gesture / gesto *s.* movimiento del cuerpo que transmite un mensaje

gilded / dorado *adj.* cubierto con una ligera capa de oro; de color oro

gregarious / gregario *adj.* sociable

H

heir / heredero *s.* persona que está legalmente autorizada a heredar determinados bienes

hierarchy / jerarquía *s.* personas o cosas organizadas en rangos o clases, del más alto al más bajo

homage / homenaje *s.* algo que se hace para honrar a una persona

hounded / acosado *adj.* perseguido; urgido

I

iconography / iconografía *s.* sistema de imágenes simbólicas que representa a un personaje, tema, visión del mundo o concepto

ideologies / ideologías *s.* conjuntos de creencias de una persona, un grupo o una cultura

implore / implorar *v.* rogar, suplicar

incite / incitar *v.* estimular con firmeza a alguien para que haga algo

incoherent / incoherente *adj.* confuso; difícil de entender

indomitable / indomable *adj.* difícil de dominar, bravío; inflexible

industrious / industrioso *adj.* trabajador

inestimable / inestimable *adj.* tan importante que no se puede estimar o medir

inexorable / inexorable *adj.* imposible de prever o impedir

inflection / inflección *s.* cambios en el tono o volumen dentro de una misma palabra o entre palabras

influence / influencia *s.* persuasión, a veces deshonesta, como cuando se usa de "enchufe" o "palanca", es decir, como contacto para lograr algo

infographic / infografía *s.* representación gráfica de información que incluye símbolos, fotos, mapas, textos y elementos de diseño visuales

initiative / iniciativa *s.* disponibilidad o habilidad para iniciar algo

integrate / integrar *v.* hacer los servicios públicos accesibles a todas las razas; unir las partes de un todo

intemperate / desmedido *adj.* descontrolado; excesivo

interactions / interacciones *s.* acciones de unos con otros

intercept / interceptar *v.* detener o apropiarse de algo antes de que llegue a su destino

interdependence / interdependencia *s.* dependencia o confianza mutua

invective / invectiva *s.* discurso negativo y agresivo que intenta herir

invoke / invocar *v.* llamar, convocar

invulnerable / invulnerable *adj.* que no se puede dañar

L

lead-in / entradilla *s.* introducción a una noticia o entrevista

legacy / legado *s.* algo que se transmite o pasa de un ancestro a sus descendientes, o de una generación a otra

lighting and color / luz y color *s.* modo de usar las luces, las sombras y los colores en una fotografía

line graph / gráfica de líneas *s.* representación de datos mediante una línea para conectar puntos

listlessly / lánguidamente *adv.* sin energía ni interés

location / ubicación *s.* lugar donde se toma una fotografía

luminous / luminoso *adj.* brillante; que brilla con su propia luz

lustrous / lustroso *adj.* brilloso, brillante

M

mail / cota de malla *s.* armadura flexible

manipulate / manipular *v.* manejar u operar; cambiar o influir de manera injusta

marauding / saqueador *adj.* que mata y usa la violencia para robar objetos de valor

marginalize / marginalizar *v.* tratar a alguien como si no fuera importante

marvel / maravilla / maravillarse *s.* algo asombroso; *v.* estar sumamente asombrado

merciful / compasivo *adj.* clemente, misericordioso

motivate / motivar *v.* proporcionar un incentivo para que alguien se interese en algo

muffled / sofocado *adj.* difícil de oír porque algo cubre y suaviza el sonido

N

navigating / navegar *v.* dirigir, guiar

needy / necesitado *adj.* muy pobre; que precisa ayuda

negate / negar *v.* invalidar; negarle razón a algo

O

obdurate / obstinado *adj.* terco; inflexible

objection / objeción *s.* razón o argumento contra algo

obscure / oscuro *adj.* desconocido

opportune / oportuno *adj.* muy conveniente; que sucede en el momento apropiado

oracle / oráculo *s.* persona que da mensajes de los dioses

ore / mineral *s.* cualquier tipo de sustancia inorgánica sólida, piedra o metal que se encuentra en la tierra

P

pacification / pacificación *s.* estado de calma o paz como resultado de la acción de la diplomacia o de la negociación política

paradox / paradoja *s.* enunciado, dato o situación inconsistente con las creencias aceptadas

pardon / perdonar *v.* disculpar

pariah / paria *s.* alguien que es despreciado; un marginado

penitent / penitente *adj.* alguien que se arrepiente de sus malas acciones

perfidious / pérfido *adj.* infiel y deshonesto

periphery / periferia *s.* límite exterior; borde

perplexity / perplejidad *s.* confusión; estado de desconcierto

perspective / perspectiva *s.* punto de vista

perspective / perspectiva *s.* en un cuadro o foto, la ilusión o efecto de profundidad

perspective or angle / perspectiva o ángulo *s.* punto o lugar desde el cual se toma una fotografía

photojournalism / fotoperiodismo *s.* tipo de periodismo en el que las fotos constituyen gran parte del artículo

pie chart / gráfico circular *s.* representación de los datos mediante un círculo dividido en segmentos

portrait / retrato *s.* imagen de una persona o de un grupo de personas

primary / primario / primarias *adj.* primero en importancia; *s.* elección en la que se escoge el candidato de un partido político

proclamation / proclamación *s.* anuncio oficia

propaganda / propaganda *s.* información, por lo general falsa, que se usa para promover una causa

prophecy / profecía *s.* predicción acerca del futuro

psychological / psicológico *adj.* relativo a la mente

R

recessed / retirado *adj.* lejano; oculto

reclusive / aislado *adj.* solitario; que evita la compañía de otros

rectify / rectificar *v.* corregir

refinement / refinamiento *s.* gentileza; buenas maneras

rending / desgarrar *v.* rasgar o romper algo con violencia o por la fuerza

resplendent / resplandeciente *adj.* deslumbrante; espléndido

revolution / revolución *s.* derrocamiento de un gobierno con el fin de reemplazarlo por otro sistema

S

sabotage / sabotear *v.* arruinar; hacer daño

scarred / marcado *adj.* que tiene cicatrices de antiguas heridas

shun / evitar *v.* rechazar; rehuir

silhouette / silueta *s.* figura oscura que se ve como un recorte contra un fondo claro

sinister / siniestro *adj.* malévolo; amenazador

slant / sesgo (ideológico) *s.* actitud u opinión del reportero acerca de una noticia

sliver / astilla *s.* trozo pequeño y fino de un material duro

sneered / se burló *v.* mostró disgusto haciendo una mueca

social documentary / foto documental *s.* género fotográfico que muestra a la gente en su entorno habitual

spacious / espacioso *adj.* grande; amplio

spitefully / maliciosamente *adv.* con el propósito de hacerle daño a alguien o algo

stimulus / estímulo *s.* algo que provoca una respuesta o reacción

stock footage / filmación de archivo *s.* película o video que se ha grabado con un propósito y está disponible para usarse en otros proyectos

stoical / estoico *adj.* de manera que controla las emociones fuertes

subject / sujeto *s.* figura(s), objeto(s) u otro contenido de una fotografía

subversive / subversivo *adj.* que intenta cambiar el orden establecido; destructivo o causante de ruina

succession / sucesión *s.* proceso por el cual una persona adquiere el derecho a un privilegio, rango o herencia

supplant / suplantar *v.* reemplazar a alguien por medios ilegítimos o poco éticos

suppleness / flexibilidad *s.* la habilidad de adaptarse con facilidad a distintas situaciones

surrender / rendirse *s.* darse por vencido

swollen / inflamado *adj.* hinchado

T

target / blanco *s.* objeto al que se debe disparar o tirar

tolerate / tolerar *v.* soportar; permitir que algo suceda, sin interferir

tone / tono *s.* sonido de una voz con respecto a la modulación, volumen y timbre general

totalitarian / totalitario *adj.* dominado o gobernado por un solo grupo o persona

transcend / trascender *v.* traspasar los límites de algo; ser más alto o más grande que algo

travail / esfuerzo *s.* trabajo o situación difícil

traversed / atravesado *adj.* cruzado; recorrido; que se movió de lado

treacherous / traicionero *adj.* que no es digno de confianza

treachery / traición *s.* acción desleal

trill / gorjeo *s.* sonido muy alto y vibrante; *v.* gorjear, producir un sonido muy alto y vibrante

tumultuous / tumultuoso *adj.* fuerte, alterado y emocional

tyranny / tiranía *s.* gobierno cruel de un pueblo o nación

U

unconquerable / inconquistable *adj.* que no puede ser vencido

unvoiced / tácito *adj.* no dicho, implícito

usurp / usurpar *v.* tomar algo por la fuerza, sin tener autoridad para hacerlo

V

valiant / valiente *adj.* bravo; aguerrido

valor / valor *s.* valentía o fortaleza personal

vehement / vehemente *adj.* que demuestra tener sentimientos intensos; apasionado

verify / verificar *v.* comprobar que algo es cierto

vestibule / vestíbulo *s.* entrada o recibidor

vigilance / vigilancia *s.* supervisión, custodia, alerta

vivid / vívido *adj.* luminoso y brillante; fuerte y distinto; muy intenso

volition / volición *s.* acto o capacidad de escoger

vulnerable / vulnerable *adj.* que puede ser herido o dañado

W

welt / verdugón *s.* marca en la piel causada por un golpe

windfall / ganancia inesperada *s.* golpe de suerte; beneficios caídos del cielo

LITERARY TERMS HANDBOOK

ABSURDISM *Absurdism*, or a*bsurdist literature*, is a form of modernism that includes fantastic or dreamlike elements that blur the boundary between what is real and unreal.

ALLITERATION *Alliteration* is the repetition of initial consonant sounds. Writers use alliteration to give emphasis to words, to imitate sounds, and to create musical effects.

ALLUSION An *allusion* is a reference to a well-known person, place, event, literary work, or work of art.

ANALOGY An *analogy* makes a comparison between two or more things that are similar in some ways but otherwise unalike.

ANAPHORA *Anaphora* is a type of parallel structure in which a word or phrase is repeated at the beginning of successive clauses for emphasis.

ANECDOTE An *anecdote* is a brief story told to entertain or to make a point.

ANTAGONIST An *antagonist* is a character or force in conflict with a main character, or protagonist.

APOSTROPHE An *apostrophe* is a figure of speech in which a speaker directly addresses an absent person or a personified quality, object, or idea.

APPEAL An *appeal* is a rhetorical device used in argumentative writing to persuade an audience.

An appeal to ethics (Ethos) shows that an argument is just or fair.

An appeal to logic (Logos) shows that an argument is well reasoned.

An appeal to authority shows that a higher power supports the ideas.

An appeal to emotion (Pathos) is designed to influence readers.

ARGUMENT An *argument* is writing or speech that attempts to convince a reader to think or act in a particular way. An argument is a logical way of presenting a belief, conclusion, or stance. A good argument is supported with reasoning and evidence.

ASIDE An *aside* is a short speech delivered by a character in a play in order to express his or her thoughts and feelings. Traditionally, the aside is directed to the audience and is presumed not to be heard by the other characters.

AUTOBIOGRAPHY An *autobiography* is a form of nonfiction in which a writer tells his or her own life story. An autobiography may tell about the person's whole life or only a part of it.

BIOGRAPHY A *biography* is a form of nonfiction in which a writer tells the life story of another person.

Biographies have been written about many famous people, historical and contemporary, but they can also be written about "ordinary" people.

BLANK VERSE *Blank verse* is poetry written in unrhymed iambic pentameter lines. This verse form was widely used by William Shakespeare.

CHARACTER A *character* is a person or an animal who takes part in the action of a literary work. The main character, or protagonist, is the most important character in a story. This character often changes in some important way as a result of the story's events.

Characters are sometimes classified as round or flat, dynamic or static. A *round character* shows many different traits—faults as well as virtues. A *flat character* shows only one trait. A *dynamic character* develops and grows during the course of the story; a *static character* does not change.

CHARACTERIZATION *Characterization* is the act of creating and developing a character. In *direct characterization*, the author directly states a character's traits.

In *indirect characterization*, an author gives clues about a character by describing what a character looks like, does, and says, as well as how other characters react to him or her. It is up to the reader to draw conclusions about the character based on this indirect information.

The most effective indirect characterizations usually result from showing characters acting or speaking.

CLIMAX The *climax* of a story, novel, or play is the high point of interest or suspense. The events that make up the rising action lead up to the climax. The events that make up the falling action follow the climax.

COMEDY A *comedy* is a literary work, especially a play, that has a happy ending. Comedies often show ordinary characters in conflict with society. These conflicts are introduced through misunderstandings, deceptions, and concealed identities. When the conflict is resolved, the result is the correction of moral faults or social wrongs. Types of comedy include *romantic comedy*, which involves problems among lovers, and the *comedy of manners*, which satirically challenges the social customs of a sophisticated society. Comedy is often contrasted with tragedy, in which the protagonist meets an unfortunate end.

COMIC RELIEF *Comic relief* is a technique that is used to interrupt a serious part of a literary work by introducing a humorous character or situation.

CONFLICT A *conflict* is a struggle between opposing forces. Characters in conflict form the basis of stories, novels, and plays.

There are two kinds of conflict: **external** and **internal**. In an external conflict, the main character struggles against an outside force. The outside force may be nature itself.

An *internal conflict* involves a character in conflict with himself or herself.

CONNOTATION The ***connotation*** of a word is the set of ideas associated with it in addition to its explicit meaning.

CONSONANCE *Consonance* is the repetition of final consonant sounds in stressed syllables with different vowel sounds, as in *hat* and *sit*.

COUPLET A ***couplet*** is a pair of rhyming lines, usually of the same length and meter.

DENOTATION The ***denotation*** of a word is its dictionary meaning, independent of other associations that the word may have. The denotation of the word *lake*, for example, is "an inland body of water."

DESCRIPTION A ***description*** is a portrait in words of a person, place, or object. Descriptive writing uses sensory details, those that appeal to the senses: sight, hearing, taste, smell, and touch. Description can be found in all types of writing.

DIALECT *Dialect* is a special form of a language, spoken by people in a particular region or group. It may involve changes to the pronunciation, vocabulary, and sentence structure of the standard form of the language. Rudyard Kipling's "Danny Deever" is a poem written in the Cockney dialect of English, used by working-class Londoners.

DIALOGUE A ***dialogue*** is a conversation between characters that may reveal their traits and advance the action of a narrative. In fiction or nonfiction, quotation marks indicate a speaker's exact words, and a new paragraph usually indicates a change of speaker.

Quotation marks are not used in *script*, the printed copy of a play. Instead, the dialogue follows the name of the speaker:

DICTION *Diction* refers to an author's choice of words, especially with regard to range of vocabulary, use of slang and colloquial language, and level of formality.

DRAMA A ***drama*** is a story written to be performed by actors. The script of a drama is made up of ***dialogue***—the words the actors say—and ***stage directions,*** which are descriptions of how and where action happens.

The drama's ***setting*** is the time and place in which the action occurs. It is indicated by one or more sets, including furniture and backdrops, that suggest interior or exterior scenes. *Props* are objects, such as a sword or a cup of tea, that are used onstage.

At the beginning of most plays, a brief ***exposition*** gives the audience some background information about the characters and the situation. Just as in a story or novel, the plot of a drama is built around characters in conflict.

Dramas are divided into large units called *acts*, which are divided into smaller units called *scenes*. A long play may include many sets that change with the scenes, or it may indicate a change of scene with lighting.

ESSAY An ***essay*** is a short nonfiction work about a particular subject. While classification is difficult, five types of essays are sometimes identified.

A *descriptive essay* seeks to convey an impression about a person, place, or object.

An *explanatory essay* describes and summarizes information gathered from a number of sources on a concept.

A *narrative essay* tells a true story. An autobiographical essay is a narrative essay in which the writer tells a story from his or her own life.

A *persuasive essay* tries to convince readers to do something or to accept the writer's point of view.

EXPOSITION *Exposition* is writing or speech that explains a process or presents information. In the plot of a story or drama, the exposition is the part of the work that introduces the characters, the setting, and the basic situation.

EXTENDED METAPHOR In an ***extended metaphor,*** as in regular metaphor, a writer speaks or writes of a subject as though it were something else. An extended metaphor sustains the comparison for several lines or for an entire poem.

FANTASY A ***fantasy*** is a work of highly imaginative writing that contains elements not found in real life. Examples of fantasy include stories that involve supernatural elements, such as fairy tales, and stories that deal with imaginary places and creatures.

FICTION *Fiction* is prose writing that tells about imaginary characters and events. The term is usually used for novels and short stories, but it also applies to dramas and narrative poetry. Some writers rely on their imaginations alone to create their works of fiction. Others base their fiction on actual events and people, to which they add invented characters, dialogue, and plot situations.

FIGURATIVE LANGUAGE *Figurative language* is writing or speech not meant to be interpreted literally. It is often used to create vivid impressions by setting up comparisons between dissimilar things.

Some frequently used figures of speech are ***metaphor, simile,*** and ***personification.***

FLASHBACK A ***flashback*** is a means by which authors present material that occurred earlier than the present time of the narrative. Authors may include this material in the form of a characters' memories, dreams, or accounts of past events, or they may simply shift their narrative back to the earlier time.

FORESHADOWING *Foreshadowing* is the use in a literary work of clues that suggest events that have yet to occur. This technique helps to create suspense, keeping readers wondering about what will happen next.

FREE VERSE *Free verse* is poetry not written in a regular pattern of meter or rhyme.

GENRE A *genre* is a category or form of literature. Literature is commonly divided into three major types of writing: poetry, prose, and drama. For each type, there are several distinct genres, as follows:
1. **Poetry:** Lyric Poetry, Concrete Poetry, Dramatic Poetry, Narrative Poetry, and Epic Poetry
2. **Prose**: Fiction (Novels and Short Stories) and Nonfiction (Biography, Autobiography, Letters, Essays, and Reports)
3. **Drama:** Serious Drama and Tragedy, Comedy, Melodrama, and Farce

GOTHIC LITERATURE A genre that began in England in the late 1700s, *Gothic literature* features bleak or remote settings, characters in psychological torment, plots that include violence or the supernatural, strongly dramatic and intensely descriptive language, and a gloomy, melancholy, or eerie mood.

HYPERBOLE A *hyperbole* is a deliberate exaggeration or overstatement. Hyperboles are often used for comic effect.

IMAGERY *Imagery* is the descriptive or figurative language used in literature to create word pictures for the reader. These pictures, or images, are created by details of sight, sound, taste, touch, smell, or movement.

INFORMATIONAL GRAPHICS *Informational graphics* or *infographics* use images, symbols, graphs, and text to explain and depict the complexities of a topic in a clear and engaging way.

INTERVIEW An *interview* is a structured conversation between two people. In an interview, one person is trying to gain information from another in a question and answer format.

IRONY *Irony* is the general term for literary techniques that portray differences between appearance and reality, or expectation and result. In *verbal irony,* words are used to suggest the opposite of what is meant. In *dramatic irony,* there is a contradiction between what a character thinks and what the reader or audience knows to be true. In *irony of situation,* an event occurs that directly contradicts readers' expectations.

JUXTAPOSITION *Juxtaposition* is setting ideas or details side by side. This effectively helps readers analyze the similarities and differences between two ideas.

LITERARY NONFICTION *Literary nonfiction* is writing that employs many of the same literary devices as fiction while still remaining factual. It may develop a plot,

use sensory details, incorporate dialogue, and even use figurative language. Memoirs, autobiographies, speeches, and lectures are often considered literary nonfiction.

LYRIC POEM A *lyric poem* is a poem written in highly musical language that expresses the thoughts, observations, and feelings of a single speaker.

MAGICAL REALISM *Magical realism* incorporates elements of fantasy and myth into otherwise realistic narratives.

METAPHOR A *metaphor* is a figure of speech in which one thing is spoken of as though it were something else. Unlike a simile, which compares two things using *like* or *as,* a metaphor implies a comparison between them.

METER The *meter* of a poem is its rhythmical pattern. This pattern is determined by the number and arrangements of stressed syllables, or beats, in each line. To describe the meter of a poem, you must scan its lines. Scanning involves marking the stressed and unstressed syllables:

Each stressed syllable is marked with a slanted line (´) and each unstressed syllable with a horseshoe symbol (˘). The stressed and unstressed syllables are then divided by vertical lines (|) into groups called *feet.* The following types of feet are common in English poetry:
1. *Iamb:* a foot with one unstressed syllable followed by a stressed syllable, as in the word "again"
2. *Trochee:* a foot with one stressed syllable followed by an unstressed syllable, as in the word "wonder"
3. *Anapest:* a foot with two unstressed syllables followed by one strong stress, as in the phrase "on the beach"
4. *Dactyl:* a foot with one strong stress followed by two unstressed syllables, as in the word "wonderful"
5. *Spondee:* a foot with two strong stresses, as in the word "spacewalk"

Depending on the type of foot that is most common in them, lines of poetry are described as *iambic, trochaic, anapestic,* and so forth.

Lines are also described in terms of the number of feet that occur in them, as follows:
1. *Monometer:* verse written in one-foot lines
2. *Dimeter:* verse written in two-foot lines
3. *Trimeter:* verse written in three-foot lines
4. *Tetrameter:* verse written in four-foot lines
5. *Pentameter:* verse written in five-foot lines
6. *Hexameter:* verse written in six-foot lines
7. *Heptameter:* verse written in seven-foot lines

Blank verse is poetry written in unrhymed iambic pentameter.

Free verse is poetry that does not follow a regular pattern of meter and rhyme.

MODERNISM *Modernism* is a form of creative expression that developed during the early twentieth century. Modernism developed in response to the rapid rise of industry, the shift from rural to urban societies, and the horrors or war. Ambiguity, blurred boundaries between reality and fantasy, and themes of alienation are elements of modernism.

MONOLOGUE A *monologue* in a play is a long speech by one character that, unlike a soliloquy, is addressed to another character or characters.

MOOD *Mood,* or *atmosphere,* is the feeling created in the reader by a literary work or passage. The mood is often suggested by descriptive details. Often the mood can be described in a single word, such as *lighthearted, frightening,* or *despairing*.

NARRATION *Narration* is writing that tells a story. The act of telling a story in speech is also called *narration.* Novels and short stories are fictional narratives. Nonfiction works—such as news stories, biographies, and autobiographies—are also narratives. A narrative poem tells a story in verse.

NARRATIVE A *narrative* is a story told in fiction, nonfiction, poetry, or drama.

NARRATIVE POEM A *narrative poem* is one that tells a story.

NARRATOR A *narrator* is a speaker or character who tells a story. The writer's choice of narrator determines the story's *point of view,* or the perspective from which the story is told. By using a consistent point of view, a writer controls the amount and type of information revealed to the reader.

When a character in the story tells the story, that character is a *first-person narrator.* This narrator may be a major character, a minor character, or just a witness. Readers see only what this character sees, hear only what he or she hears, and so on. Viewing unfolding events from this character's perspective, the reader shares in his discoveries and feels more suspense than another point of view would provide.

When a voice outside the story narrates, the story has a *third-person narrator.* An *omniscient,* or all-knowing, third-person narrator can tell readers what any character thinks and feels. A *limited third-person narrator* sees the world through one character's eyes and reveals only that character's thoughts.

NONFICTION *Nonfiction* is prose writing that presents and explains ideas or that tells about real people, places, ideas, or events. To be classified as nonfiction, a work must be true.

NOVEL A *novel* is a long work of fiction. It has a plot that explores characters in conflict. A novel may also have one or more subplots, or minor stories, and several themes.

ONOMATOPOEIA *Onomatopoeia* is the use of words that imitate sounds. *Whirr, thud, sizzle,* and *hiss* are typical examples. Writers can deliberately choose words that contribute to a desired sound effect.

OXYMORON An *oxymoron* is a combination of words that contradict each other. Examples are "deafening silence," "honest thief," "wise fool," and "bittersweet." This device is effective when the apparent contradiction reveals a deeper truth.

PERSONIFICATION *Personification* is a type of figurative language in which a nonhuman subject is given human characteristics: *The moss embraced the tree.*

PERSUASION *Persuasion* is writing or speech that attempts to convince the reader to adopt a particular opinion or course of action.

An *argument* is a logical way of presenting a belief, conclusion, or stance. A good argument is supported with reasoning and evidence.

PLOT *Plot* is the sequence of events in a literary work. In most novels, dramas, short stories, and narrative poems, the plot involves both characters and a central conflict. The plot usually begins with an *exposition* that introduces the setting, the characters, and the basic situation. This is followed by the *inciting incident,* which introduces the central conflict. The conflict then increases during the *development* until it reaches a high point of interest or suspense, the *climax.* All the events leading up to the climax make up the *rising action.* The climax is followed by the *falling action,* which leads to the *denouement,* or *resolution,* in which the conflict is resolved and in which a general insight may be conveyed.

POETIC STRUCTURE The basic structures of poetry are lines and stanzas. A *line* is a group of words arranged in a row. A line of poetry may break, or end, in different ways. Varied *line lengths* can create unpredictable rhythms.

An *end-stopped line* is one in which both the grammatical structure and sense are complete at the end of the line.

A *run-on,* or *enjambed, line* is one in which both the grammatical structure and sense continue past the end of the line.

POETRY *Poetry* is one of the three major types of literature, the others being prose and drama. Most poems make use of highly concise, musical, and emotionally charged language. Many also make use of imagery, figurative language, and special devices of sound such as rhyme. Poems are often divided into lines and stanzas and often employ regular rhythmical patterns, or meters. Poetry that does not follow a regular metrical pattern is called *free verse.*

POINT OF VIEW *Point of view* is the perspective, or vantage point, from which a story is told. By using a consistent point of view, a writer controls the amount and type of information revealed to the reader. When a character in the story tells the story, that character is a **first-person narrator** and has a **limited point of view.** When a voice outside the story narrates and is all-knowing, the story has an **omniscient point of view.** A narrator that uses the **third-person point of view** sees the world through one character's eyes and reveals only that character's thoughts.

PROSE *Prose* is the ordinary form of written language. Most writing that is not poetry, drama, or song is considered prose. Prose is one of the major categories of literature and occurs in two forms: fiction and nonfiction.

PROSE POEM A **prose poem** is a poetic form that looks like prose, or a non-poetic work, but reads like poetry. Prose poems lack the line breaks most often found in poetry, but they contain other poetic techniques such as repetition or rhyme.

REPETITION *Repetition* is the use of any element of language—a sound, a word, a phrase, a clause, or a sentence—more than once within a passage of text.

Poets use many kinds of repetition. **Alliteration, assonance, consonance, rhyme,** and **rhythm** are repetitions of certain sounds and sound patterns. A *refrain* is a repeated line or group of lines. In both prose and poetry, repetition is used for musical effects and for emphasis.

RHETORICAL DEVICES Rhetorical devices are special patterns of words and ideas that create emphasis and stir emotion, especially in speeches or other oral presentations. **Parallelism,** for example, is the repetition of a grammatical structure in order to create a rhythm and make words more memorable.

Other common rhetorical devices include:
analogy: drawing comparisons between two unlike things
charged language: words that appeal to the emotions
concession: an acknowledgment of the opposition's argument
humor: use of language and details that make characters or situations funny
paradox: statement that seems to contradict but actually presents a truth
restatement: an expression of the same idea in different words
rhetorical questions: questions not meant to be answered because the answers are obvious. For example, *Is freedom a basic human right?* is a rhetorical question.
tone: the author's attitude toward the topic

RHYME *Rhyme* is the repetition of sounds at the end of words. End rhyme occurs when the rhyming words come at the ends of lines.

Internal rhyme occurs when one of the rhyming words appears within a line.

Exact rhyme involves the repetition of the same final vowel and consonant sounds in words like *ball* and *hall. Slant*

rhyme involves the repetition of words that sound alike but do not rhyme exactly, like *grove* and *love.*

RHYME SCHEME A **rhyme scheme** is a regular pattern of rhyming words in a poem. The rhyme scheme of a poem is indicated by using different letters of the alphabet for each new rhyme. In an *aabb* stanza, for example, line 1 rhymes with line 2 and line 3 rhymes with line 4.

Many poems use the same pattern of rhymes, though not the same rhymes, in each stanza.

SATIRE A **satire** is a literary work that ridicules the foolishness and faults of individuals, an institution, society, or even humanity in general.

SENSORY LANGUAGE *Sensory language* is writing or speech that appeals to one or more of the senses.

SEQUENCE OF EVENTS Authors often use **sequence of events,** or the order in which things happened, to structure nonfiction pieces that describe historical events or explain a change over time. Authors frequently describe important events in **chronological order,** or time order.

SETTING The **setting** of a literary work is the time and place of the action. Time can include not only the historical period—past, present, or future—but also a specific year, season, or time of day. Place may involve not only the geographical place—a region, country, state, or town—but also the social, economic, or cultural environment.

In some stories, setting serves merely as a backdrop for action, a context in which the characters move and speak. In others, however, setting is a crucial element.

SHORT STORY A **short story** is a brief work of fiction. In most short stories, one main character faces a conflict that is resolved in the plot of the story. Great craftsmanship must go into the writing of a good story, for it has to accomplish its purpose in relatively few words.

SIMILE A **simile** is a figure of speech in which the words like or as are used to compare two apparently dissimilar items. The comparison, however, surprises the reader into a fresh perception by finding an unexpected likeness.

SOCIAL COMMENTARY In works of **social commentary**, an author seeks to highlight, usually in a critical way, an aspect of society. Social commentary is often the point of **satire**, in which the author points out the absurdity of a practice, custom, or institution.

SOLILOQUY A **soliloquy** is a long speech expressing thethoughts of a character alone on stage.

SONNET A **sonnet** is a fourteen-line lyric poem, usually written in rhymed iambic pentameter. The *English,* or *Shakespearean,* sonnet consists of three quatrains (four-line stanzas) and a couplet (two lines), usually rhyming *abab cdcd efef gg.* The couplet usually comments on the ideas contained in the preceding twelve lines. The sonnet is usually not printed with the stanzas divided, but a reader can see distinct ideas in each.

The *Italian*, or *Petrarchan*, sonnet consists of an octave (eight-line stanza) and a sestet (six-line stanza). Often, the octave rhymes *abbaabba* and the sestet rhymes *cdecde*. The octave states a theme or asks a question. The sestet comments on the theme or answers the question.

SPEAKER The ***speaker*** is the imaginary voice assumed by the writer of a poem. In many poems, the speaker is not identified by name. When reading a poem, remember that the speaker of a poem may be a person, an animal, a thing, or an abstraction.

STAGE DIRECTIONS ***Stage directions*** are notes included in a drama to describe how the work is to be performed or staged. These instructions are printed in italics and are not spoken aloud. They are used to describe sets, lighting, sound effects, and the appearance, personalities, and movements of characters.

STANZA A ***stanza*** is a repeated grouping of two or more lines in a poem that often share a pattern of rhythm and rhyme. Stanzas are sometimes named according to the number of lines they have—for example, a *couplet*, two lines; a *quatrain*, four lines; a *sestet*, six lines; and an *octave*, eight lines.

STYLE ***Style*** refers to an author's unique way of writing. Elements determining style include diction; tone; characteristic use of figurative language, dialect, or rhythmic devices; and typical grammatical structures and patterns.

SURPRISE ENDING A ***surprise ending*** is a conclusion that violates the expectations of the reader but in a way that is both logical and believable.

SYMBOL A ***symbol*** is a character, place, thing or event that stands for something else, often an abstract idea. For example, a flag is a piece of cloth, but it also represents the idea of a country. Writers sometimes use conventional symbols like flags. Frequently, however, they create symbols of their own through emphasis or repetition.

SYNTAX ***Syntax*** is the structure of sentences.

THEME A ***theme*** is a central message or insight into life revealed through a literary work.

The theme of a literary work may be stated directly or implied. When the theme of a work is implied, readers infer what the work suggests about people or life.

Archetypal themes are those that occur in folklore and literature across the world and throughout history.

TONE The ***tone*** of a literary work is the writer's attitude toward his or her audience and subject. The tone can often be described by a single adjective, such as *formal* or *informal*, *serious* or *playful*, *bitter* or *ironic*.

TRAGEDY A ***tragedy*** is a work of literature, especially a play, that tells of a catastrophe, a disaster or great misfortune, for the main character. In ancient Greek drama, the main character was always a significant person—a king or a hero—and the cause of the tragedy was often a tragic flaw, or weakness, in his or her character. In modern drama, the main character can be an ordinary person, and the cause of the tragedy can be some evil in society itself. Tragedy not only arouses fear and pity in the audience, but also, in some cases, conveys a sense of the grandeur and nobility of the human spirit.

VOICE ***Voice*** is a writer's distinctive "sound" or way of "speaking" on the page. It is related to such elements as word choice, sentence structure, and tone. It is similar to an individual's speech style and can be described in the same way—fast, slow, blunt, meandering, breathless, and so on.

Voice resembles ***style***, an author's typical way of writing, but style usually refers to a quality that can be found throughout an author's body of work, while an author's voice may sometimes vary from work to work.

MANUAL DE TÉRMINOS LITERARIOS

ABSURDISM / LITERATURA DEL ABSURDO La *literatura del absurdo* es un tipo de *modernismo* que incluye elementos de fantasía o surreales que borran el límite entre lo real y lo irreal.

ALLITERATION / ALITERACIÓN La *aliteración* es la repetición de los sonidos consonantes iniciales. Los escritores usan la aliteración para dar énfasis a las palabras, para imitar sonidos y para crear efectos de musicalidad.

ALLUSION / ALUSIÓN Una *alusión* es una referencia a una persona, lugar, hecho, obra literaria u obra de arte muy conocida.

ANALOGY / ANALOGÍA Una *analogía* establece una comparación entre dos o más cosas que son parecidas en algunos aspectos pero se diferencian en otros.

ANAPHORA / ANÁFORA La *anáfora* es un tipo de paralelismo en el que una palabra o frase se repite al principio de varias cláusulas para hacer énfasis.

ANECDOTE / ANÉCDOTA Una *anécdota* es un relato breve que se narra con el fin de entretener o decir algo importante.

ANTAGONIST / ANTAGONISTA Un *antagonista* es un personaje o fuerza en conflicto con el personaje principal o protagonista.

APOSTROPHE / APÓSTROFE El *apóstrofe* es una figura retórica en la que el hablante se dirige directante a una persona ausente o a una idea, objeto o cualidad personificada.

APPEAL / APELACIÓN Una *apelación* es un recurso retórico que se usa en los escritos de argumentación para persuadir al público. Una apelación a la ética (Ethos) muestra que un argumento es justo. Una apelación a la lógica (Logos) muestra que un argumento está bien razonado. Una apelación a la autoridad muestra que las ideas que se presentan están respaldadas por un poder más alto. Una apelación a las emociones (Pathos) se usa con el propósito de influir en los lectores.

ARGUMENT / ARGUMENTO Un *argumento* es un escrito o discurso que trata de convencer al lector para que siga una acción o adopte una opinión en particular. Un argumento es una manera lógica de presentar una creencia, una conclusión, o una postura. Un buen argumento se respalda con razonamientos y pruebas.

ASIDE / APARTE Un *aparte* es un parlamento breve en boca de un personaje en una obra de teatro, en el que expresa sus verdaderos pensamientos y sentimientos. Tradicionalmente, los apartes se dirigen a la audiencia y se suponen inaudibles a los otros personajes.

AUTOBIOGRAPHY / AUTOBIOGRAFÍA Una *autobiografía* es una forma de no-ficción en la que el escritor cuenta su propia vida. Una autobiografía puede contar toda la vida de una persona o solo una parte de ella.

BIOGRAPHY / BIOGRAFÍA Una *biografía* es una forma de no-ficción en la que un escritor cuenta la vida de otra persona. Se han escrito biografías de muchas personas famosas, ya de la historia o del mundo contemporáneo, pero también pueden escribirse biografías de personas comunes.

BLANK VERSE / VERSO BLANCO El *verso blanco* es poesía escrita en líneas de pentámetros yámbicos sin rima. Esta forma de verso fue muy utilizada por William Shakespeare.

CHARACTER / PERSONAJE Un *personaje* es una persona o animal que participa de la acción en una obra literaria. El personaje principal, o protagonista, es el personaje más importante del relato. Este personaje a menudo cambia de una manera importante como resultado de los eventos que se suceden en el cuento.

Los personajes a veces son clasificados como complejos o chatos, dinámicos o estáticos. Un *personaje complejo* muestra muchos rasgos diferentes, tanto faltas como virtudes. *Un personaje chato* muestra solo un rasgo. Un *personaje dinámico* se desarrolla y crece en el curso del relato; mientras que un *personaje estático* no cambia.

CHARACTERIZATION / CARACTERIZACIÓN La *caracterización* es el acto de crear y desarrollar un personaje. En una *caracterización directa,* el autor expresa explícitamente los rasgos de un personaje. En una *caracterización indirecta,* el autor proporciona claves sobre el personaje, describiendo el aspecto del personaje, qué hace, qué dice, así como la manera en que otros personajes lo ven y reaccionan a él. Depende del lector qué conclusiones saque sobre los personajes basándose en información indirecta.

La caracterización indirecta más efectiva resulta por lo general de mostrar cómo hablan y actúan los personajes.

CLIMAX / CLÍMAX El *clímax* de un relato, de una novela o de un drama es el punto de mayor interés o suspenso. Los sucesos que forman el desarrollo de la acción anteceden al clímax. Los sucesos que conducen al desenlace son posteriores al clímax.

COMEDY / COMEDIA Una *comedia* es una obra literaria, por lo general una obra de teatro, que tiene un final feliz. Las comedias a menudo presentan personajes comunes en conflicto con la sociedad. Estos conflictos se producen a partir de malentendidos, engaños y falsas identidades. Cuando el conflicto se resuelve, el resultado es la corrección de fallas morales o de injusticias sociales. Entre los distintos tipos de comedia, se distinguen: *la comedia romántica*, que gira alrededor de problemas entre enamorados o amantes, y *la comedia de costumbres*, que satiriza las costumbres sociales. La comedia suele oponerse a la tragedia, en la cual el protagonista tiene un final desafortunado.

COMIC RELIEF / ALIVIO CÓMICO El *alivio cómico* es una técnica que se usa para interrumpir una parte seria de una obra literaria introduciendo una situación o personaje gracioso.

CONFLICT / CONFLICTO Un *conflicto* es una lucha entre fuerzas opuestas. Los personajes en conflicto forman la base de cuentos, novelas y obras de teatro.

Hay dos tipos de conflicto: *externos* e *internos.* En un *conflicto externo*, el personaje principal lugar contra una fuerza externa.

Un *conflicto interno* atañe a un personaje que entra en conflicto consigo mismo.

CONNOTATION / CONNOTACIÓN La *connotación* de una palabra es el conjunto de ideas que se asocian a ella, además de su significado explícito.

CONSONANCE / CONSONANCIA La *consonancia* es la repetición de los sonidos consonantes finales de sílabas acentuadas con distintos sonidos vocálicos, como en *hat* and *sit*.

COUPLET / PAREADO Un *dístico* o *pareado* es un par de versos rimados, por lo general de la misma extensión y metro.

DENOTATION / DENOTACIÓN La *denotación* de una palabra es su significado en un diccionario, independiente-mente de otras asociaciones que la palabra suscita. Por ejemplo, la denotación de la palabra "lago" es "masa de agua acumulada en medio de un terreno".

DESCRIPTION / DESCRIPCIÓN Una *descripción* es un retrato en palabras de una persona, un lugar o un objeto. La escritura descriptiva utiliza detalles sensoriales, es decir, aquellos que apelan a los sentidos: la vista, el oído, el gusto, el olfato y el tacto. La descripción puede encontrarse en todo tipo de escritos.

DIALECT / DIALECTO El *dialecto* es la forma de un lenguaje hablado por la gente en una región o grupo particular. Puede incluir diferencias en la pronunciación, el vocabulario y la estructura de la oración, con respecto a la forma estandarizada de esa lengua. "Danny Deever", de Rudyard Kipling, es un poema escrito en el dialecto *cockney* del inglés, usado por las clases trabajadoras de Londres.

DIALOGUE / DIÁLOGO Un *diálogo* es una conver-sación entre personajes que puede revelar sus rasgos y hacer progresar la acción de un relato. Ya sea en un género de ficción o de no ficción —en inglés— las comillas repro-ducen las palabras exactas de un personaje, y un nuevo párrafo indica un cambio de personaje. En un guión, es decir, en la versión impresa de una obra de teatro, no se usan comillas, sino que cada parlamento va introducido por el nombre del personaje que debe pronunciarlo.

DICTION / DICCIÓN La *dicción* comprende la elección de palabras que hace el autor, especialmente en relación al vocabulario, al uso de un lenguaje coloquial o jerga y al nivel de formalidad.

DRAMA / DRAMA Un *drama* es una historia escrita para ser representada por actores. El guión de un drama está consituido por *diálogo* —las palabras que dicen los actores— y por *acotaciones*, que son los comentarios acerca de cómo y dónde se sitúa la acción.

La *ambientación* es la época y el lugar donde sucede la acción. Se indica a través de una o varias escenografías, que incluyen el mobiliario y el fondo, o telón de fondo, que sugieren si las escenas son interiores o exteriores. La *tramoya* o *utilería* son los objetos, tales como una espada o una taza de té, que se usan en escena.

Al principio de la mayoría de los dramas, una breve *exposición* le da a la audiencia cierta información de contexto sobre los personajes y la situación. Al igual que en un cuento o una novela, el argumento o trama de una obra dramática se construye a partir de personajes en conflicto.

Los dramas se dividen a grandes unidades llamadas *actos*, que a su vez se dividen en unidades más breves llamadas *escenas*. Un drama de cierta extensión puede incluir muchas escenografías que cambian con las escenas, o pueden indicar un cambio de escena por medio de la iluminación.

ESSAY / ENSAYO Un *ensayo* es una obra breve de no-ficción sobre un tema en particular. Si bien es difícil llegar a una clasificación, suelen diferenciarse cinco tipos de ensayos.

El *ensayo descriptivo* se propone transmitir una impresión acerca de una persona, un lugar o un objeto.

El *ensayo explicativo* describe y resume información sobre un determinado concepto recogida de cierto número de fuentes.

El *ensayo narrativo* narra una historia real.

El *ensayo persuasivo* intenta convencer a los lectores de que hagan algo o que acepten el punto de vista del escritor.

EXPOSITION / EXPOSICIÓN Una *exposición* es un escrito o un discurso que explica un proceso o presenta información. En un cuento o un drama, la exposición es la parte donde se presenta a los personajes, la ambientación y la situación básica.

EXTENDED METAPHOR / METÁFORA EXTENDIDA En una *metáfora extendida*, al igual que en una metáfora habitual, el escritor escribe o habla de algo como si fuera otra cosa. Una metáfora extendida prolonga la comparación a lo largo de varias líneas o de un poema entero.

FANTASY / RELATO FANTÁSTICO Un *relato fantás-tico* es una obra altamente imaginativa que contiene ele-mentos que no se encuentran en la vida real. Ejemplos de relatos fantásticos son los cuentos que incluyen elementos sobrenaturales, tales como los cuentos de hadas, y cuentos que tratan sobre lugares y criaturas imaginarias.

FICTION / FICCIÓN Una obra de *ficción* es un escrito en prosa que cuenta algo sobre personajes y hechos imaginarios. El término se usa por lo general para referirse a novelas y cuentos, pero también se aplica a dramas y poemas narrativos. Algunos escritores se basan solamente en su imaginación para crear sus obras de ficción. Otros basan su ficción en hechos y personas reales, a las que agregan personajes, diálogos y situationes de su propia invención.

FIGURATIVE LANGUAGE / LENGUAJE FIGURADO El *lenguaje figurado* es un escrito o discurso que no se debe interpretar literalmente. A menudo se usa para crear impresiones vívidas, estableciendo comparaciones entre cosas disímiles.

Algunas de las formas más usadas del lenguaje figurado son la *metáfora*, el *símil* y la *personificación*.

FLASHBACK / FLASHBACK Un *flashback* o *escena retrospectiva* es una de las maneras a través de las que los autores presentan materiales, que ocurrieron antes del tiempo presente del relato. Los autores pueden incluir estos materiales, como los recuerdos o sueños de un personaje, o narrar directamente hechos anteriores al momento en que empezó el relato.

FORESHADOWING / PREFIGURACIÓN La *prefiguración* es el uso, en una obra literaria, de claves que sugieren hechos que van a suceder. Esta técnica ayuda a crear suspenso, manteniendo a los lectores interesados preguntándose qué sucederá.

FREE VERSE / VERSO LIBRE El *verso libre* es una forma poética en la que no se sigue un patrón regular o metro o de rima.

GENRE / GÉNERO Un *género* es una categoría o tipo de literatura. La literatura se divide por lo general en tres géneros principales: poesía, prosa y drama. Cada uno de estos géneros principales se divide a su vez en géneros más pequeños. Por ejemplo:

1. **Poesía:** Poesía lírica, Poesía concreta, Poesía dramática, Poesía narrativa y Poesía épica.
2. **Prosa:** Ficción (Novelas y Cuentos) y No-ficción (Biografía, Autobiografía, Cartas, Ensayos, Artículos).
3. **Drama:** Drama serio y Tragedia, Comedia, Melodrama y Farsa.

GOTHIC LITERATURE / LITERATURA GÓTICA La *literatura gótica* es un género que comenzó en Inglaterra a finales del siglo XVIII. Algunas de las características de esta literatura son: ambientaciones en lugares sombríos y remotos, personajes atormentados psicológicamente, trama que incluye violencia o lo supernatural, lenguaje altamente descriptivo e intenso y una atmósfera pesimista, melancólica o fantasmal.

HYPERBOLE / HIPÉRBOLE Una *hipérbole* es una exageración o magnificación deliberada. Las hipérboles se usan a menudo para lograr efectos cómicos.

IMAGERY / IMÁGENES Las *imágenes* son el lenguaje figurado o descriptivo que se usa en la literatura para crear una descripción verbal para los lectores. Estas descripciones verbales, o imágenes, se crean mediante el uso de detalles visuales, auditivos, gustativos, táctiles, olfativos o de movimiento.

INFORMATIONAL GRAPHICS / INFOGRAFÍAS Las *infografías* usan imágenes, símbolos, gráficas y texto para explicar y presentar las partes más complejas de un tema de manera clara y atractiva.

INTERVIEW / ENTREVISTA Una *entrevista* es una conversación entre dos personas estructurada en forma de preguntas y respuestas, en la cual una persona trata de obtener información de la otra persona.

IRONY / IRONÍA *Ironía* es un término general para distintas técnicas literarias que subrayan las diferencias entre apariencia y realidad, o entre expectativas y resultado. En una *ironía verbal*, las palabras se usan para sugerir lo opuesto a lo que se dice. En la *ironía dramática* hay una contradicción entre lo que el personaje piensa y lo que el lector o la audiencia sabe que es verdad. En una *ironía situacional*, ocurre un suceso que contradice directamente las expectativas de los personajes, o del lector o la audiencia.

JUXTAPOSITION / YUXTAPOSICIÓN La *yuxtaposición* es una manera de exponer ideas o detalles uno al lado del otro, lo que ayuda a que los lectores puedan analizar las semejanzas y las diferencias entre dos ideas.

LITERARY NONFICTION / LITERATURA DE NO-FICCIÓN La *literatura de no-ficción* es un texto que emplea muchos de los recursos literarios de la ficción, pero presenta hechos y datos reales. Puede tener una trama, usar detalles sensoriales, incorporar diálogo e, incluso, lenguaje figurado. Las memorias, las autobiografías, los discursos y las conferencias se suelen considerar literatura de no-ficción.

LYRIC POEM / POEMA LÍRICO Un *poema lírico* es una sucesión de versos de mucha musicalidad que expresan los pensamientos, observaciones y sentimientos de un único hablante.

MAGICAL REALISM / REALISMO MÁGICO El *realismo mágico* incorpora elementos de fantasía y mito en una narrativa que es, por lo demás, realista.

METAPHOR / METÁFORA Una *metáfora* es una figura literaria en la que algo se describe como si fuera otra cosa. A diferencia del símil, que compara dos cosas usando el conector *como*, la metáfora establece la comparación entre ellas de modo implícito.

METER / METRO El *metro* de un poema es el patrón rítmico que sigue. Este patrón está determinado por el número y disposición de las sílabas acentuadas en cada verso. Para describir el metro de un poema hay que escandir los versos. Escandir significa marcar las sílabas acentuadas y no acentuadas.

Cada sílaba acentuada se marca con un ('), y cada sílaba no acentuada se marca con un (ˇ). Las sílabas acentuadas y no acentuadas se dividen luego con líneas verticales (|) en grupos llamados *pies*. En la poesía en inglés algunos de los pies más frecuentes son:

1. el *yambo:* un pie con una sílaba no acentuada seguida por una sílaba acentuada, como en la palabra "again"

2. el *troqueo:* un pie con una sílaba acentuada seguida por una sílaba no acentuada, como en la palabra "wonder"

3. el *anapesto:* un pie con dos sílabas no acentuadas seguidas por un acento fuerte, como en la frase "on the beach"

4. el *dáctilo*: un pie con un acento fuerte seguido por dos sílabas no acentuadas, como en la palabra "wonderful"

5. el *espondeo:* un pie con dos acentos fuertes, como en la palabra "spacewalk"

Según el tipo de pie más frecuente en ellos, los versos de un poema se describen como *yámbicos, trocaicos, anapésticos,* etc.

Los versos también se describen según el número de pies que los formen. Por ejemplo:

1. *monómetro:* verso de un solo pie

2. *dímetro:* verso de dos pies

3. *trímetro:* verso de tres pies

4. *tetrámetro:* verso de cuatro pies

5. *pentámetro:* verso de cinco pies

6. *hexámetro:* verso de seis pies

7. *heptámetro:* verso de siete pies

Verso blanco: se dice de la poesía escrita en pentámetros yámbicos sin rima.

Verso libre: se dice de la poesía que no sigue un patrón métrico ni rímico regular.

MODERNISM / MODERNISMO NORTEAMERICANO
El **modernismo norteamericano** es una forma de expresión creativa que se desarrolló a principios del siglo XX en respuesta al rápido crecimiento de la industria, el paso de las sociedades rurales a las urbanas y los horrores de la guerra. La ambigüedad, la desaparición de límites claros entre realidad y fantasía, y los temas de la enajenación del ser humano moderno son algunos de los elementos típicos de este movimiento.

MONOLOGUE / MONÓLOGO Un **monólogo** en una obra de teatro es un parlamento por parte de un personaje que, a diferencia del *soliloquio*, se dirige a otro u otros personajes.

MOOD / ATMÓSFERA La **atmósfera** es la sensación que un pasaje u obra literaria crea en el lector. Por lo general, la atmósfera se crea a través de detalles descriptivos. A menudo puede ser descrita con una sola palabra, tal como *desenfadado, aterrador* o *desesperante.*

NARRATION / NARRACIÓN Una **narración** es un escrito que cuenta una historia. El acto de contar una his-

toria de forma oral también se llama narración. Las novelas y los cuentos son obras narrativas de ficción. Las obras de no-ficción, como las noticias, las biografías y las autobiografías, también son narrativas. Un poema narrativo cuenta una historia en verso.

NARRATIVE / RELATO Se llama **relato** a la historia que se narra en una obra de ficción, obra de de no-ficción, en un poema o en un drama.

NARRRATIVE POEM / POEMA NARRATIVO Un **poema narrativo** es un poema que cuenta una historia.

NARRATOR / NARRADOR Un **narrador** es el hablante o el personaje que cuenta una historia. La elección del narrador por parte del autor determina el *punto de vista* desde el que se va a narrar la historia, lo que determina el tipo y la cantidad de información que se revelará.

Cuando el que cuenta la historia es uno de los personajes, a ese personaje se lo llama *narrador en primera persona.* Este narrador puede ser uno de los personajes principales, un personaje menor, o solo un testigo. Los lectores ven solo lo que este personaje ve, oyen solo lo que este personaje oye, etc. Al ver cómo se desarrollan los sucesos desde la perspectiva de este personaje, el lector comparte sus descubrimientos y experimenta mayor suspenso que el que producen narraciones desde otros puntos de vista.

Cuando la que cuenta la historia es una voz exterior a la historia, hablamos de un *narrador en tercera persona.* Un narrador en tercera persona, *omnisciente* —es decir, que todo lo sabe— puede decirles a los lectores lo que cualquier personaje piensa o siente. Un narrador en tercera persona *limitado* ve el mundo a través de los ojos de un solo personaje y revela solo los pensamientos de ese personaje.

NONFICTION / NO-FICCIÓN La **no-ficción** es un escrito en prosa que presenta y explica ideas o cuenta algo acerca de personas, lugares, ideas o hechos reales. Para ser clasificado como no-ficción un escrito debe ser verdadero.

NOVEL / NOVELA Una **novela** es una obra extensa de ficción. Tiene una trama que explora los personajes en conflicto. Una novela también puede tener una o más tramas secundarias —es decir, historias de menor importancia—, así como tocar varios temas.

ONOMATOPOEIA / ONOMATOPEYA La **onomatopeya** es el uso de palabras que imitan sonidos, tales como *pío-pío, tic-tac* o *susurro.* Los escritores pueden escoger palabras deliberadamente con el fin de producir el efecto sonoro deseado.

OXYMORON / OXÍMORON Un **oxímoron** es una combinación de palabras que se contradicen mutuamente. Por ejemplo, "un silencio ensordecedor", "un ladrón honesto", "la música callada". Este recurso es especialmente efectivo cuando la aparente contradicción revela una verdad más profunda.

PERSONIFICATION / PERSONIFICACIÓN La **personificación** es un tipo de figura retórica en la que se dota a una instancia no humana de rasgos y actitudes humanas: *El musgo se abrazaba al árbol.*

PERSUASION / PERSUASIÓN La **persuasión** es un recurso escrito u oral por el que se intenta convencer al lector de que adopte una opinión o actúe de determinada manera. Un *argumento* es una manera lógica de presentar una creencia, una conclusión o una postura. Un buen argumento se respalda con razones y evidencias.

PLOT / TRAMA o ARGUMENTO La **trama** o **argumento** es la secuencia de los hechos que se suceden en una obra literaria. En la mayoría de las novelas, dramas, cuentos y poemas narrativos, la trama implica tanto a los personajes como al conflicto central. La trama por lo general empieza con una **exposición** que introduce la ambientación, los personajes y la situación básica. A ello le sigue el **suceso desencadenante**, que introduce el conflicto central. Este conflicto aumenta durante el **desarrollo** hasta que alcanza el punto más alto de interés o suspenso, llamado **clímax**. Todos los sucesos que conducen al clímax contribuyen a la **acción dramática creciente**. Al clímax le sigue la **acción dramática decreciente** que conduce al **desenlace,** o **resolución,** en el que se resuelve el conflicto y en el que puede darse a entender cierta idea o percepción más amplia acerca de la situación tratada.

POETIC STRUCTURE / ESTRUCTURA POÉTICA Las **estructuras poéticas** básicas son los versos y las estrofas. Un **verso** es un grupo de palabras ordenadas en un mismo renglón. Un verso puede terminar, o cortarse, de distintas maneras. Versos de distinta extensión pueden crear ritmos imprevistos.
En un **verso no encabalgado** la estructura gramatical y el sentido se completan al final de esa línea.
En un **verso encabalgado** tanto la estructura gramatical como el sentido de un verso continúan en el verso que sigue.

POETRY / POESÍA La **poesía** es uno de los tres géneros literarios más importantes. Los otros dos son la prosa y el drama. La mayoría de los poemas están escritos en un lenguaje altamente conciso, musical y emocionalmente rico. Muchos también hacen uso de imágenes, de figuras retóricas y de recursos sonoros especiales, tales como la rima. Los poemas a menudo se dividen en versos y estrofas, y emplean patrones rítmicos regulares, llamados metros. Los poemas que no siguen un metro regular están escritos en **verso libre**.

POINT OF VIEW / PUNTO DE VISTA El **punto de vista** es la perspectiva desde la cual se narran o describen los hechos. Al usar un punto de vista constante, el escritor controla la cantidad y tipo de información que quiere revelarle al lector. Cuando quien cuenta la historia es uno de los personajes, ese personaje es el **narrador en primera persona** y tiene un **punto de vista limitado**. Cuando quien narra la historia es una voz exterior al relato que sabe y ve todo lo que ocurre, el relato está escrito desde un **punto de vista omnisciente**. El **relato en tercera persona** presenta el mundo desde la perspectiva de un solo personaje y revela solo lo que piensa ese personaje.

PROSE / PROSA La **prosa** es la forma más común del lenguaje escrito. La mayoría de los escritos que no son poesía, ni drama, ni canciones, se consideran prosa. La prosa es uno de los géneros literarios más importantes y puede ser de dos formas: de ficción y de no-ficción.

PROSE POEM / POEMA EN PROSA Un **poema en prosa** es una forma poética que se ve como si fuera prosa, pero que tiene las características propias de la poesía. Los poemas en prosa no tienen los cortes de verso que suelen encontrarse en la poesía, pero tienen otros elementos de la poesía tales como la repetición y el ritmo.

REPETITION / REPETICIÓN La **repetición** es el uso de cualquier elemento del lenguaje —un sonido, una palabra, una frase, una cláusula, o una oración— más de una vez en un mismo pasaje del texto.

Los poetas usan muchos tipos de repeticiones. La **aliteración**, la **asonancia**, la **consonancia**, la **rima** y el **ritmo** son repeticiones de ciertos sonidos o patrones sonoros. Un *estribillo* es un verso o grupo de versos que se repiten. Tanto en prosa como en poesía, la repetición se usa tanto para lograr efectos de musicalidad como para enfatizar algo.

RHETORICAL DEVICES / FIGURAS RETÓRICAS Las **figuras retóricas** son patrones especiales de palabras e ideas que dan énfasis y producen emoción, especialmente en discursos y otras presentaciones orales. El **paralelismo**, por ejemplo, es la repetición de una estructura gramatical con el propósito de crear un ritmo y hacer que las palabras resulten más memorables.

Otras figuras retóricas muy frecuentes son:

la **analogía**: establece una comparación entre dos cosas diferentes

el **lenguaje emocionalmente cargado**: las palabras apelan a las emociones

la **concesión***:* un reconocimiento del argumento del contrario

el **humor***:* uso del lenguaje y detalles que hacen que los personajes y las situaciones resulten graciosos

la **paradoja**: un enunciado que parece contradecirse, pero que en realidad presenta una verdad

la **reafirmación**: expresa la misma idea con distintas palabras

las **preguntas retóricas**: preguntas que no se hacen para contestarse porque las respuestas son obvias. Por ejemplo, *¿Es la libertad un derecho esencial del ser humano?* es una pregunta retórica.

el **tono**: la actitud del autor hacia el tema

RHYME / RIMA La **rima** es la repetición de los sonidos finales de las palabras. Se llama *rima de final de verso* a la rima entre las palabras finales de dos o más versos. La *rima interna* se produce cuando una de las palabras que riman está situada en el interior de un verso. En la *rima perfecta (o consonante)* todas las vocales y las consonantes que siguen a la vocal acentuada son iguales, como en *ball* y *hall*. Se llama *rima falsa* a la que se da entre palabras que suenan de modo parecido pero que en realidad no riman, como *grove* y *love*.

RHYME SCHEME / ESQUEMA DE RIMA Un *esquema de rima* es el patrón de las palabras que riman en un poema. El esquema de rima de un poema se indica con distintas letras del alfabeto para cada tipo de rima. En una estrofa *aabb*, por ejemplo, el verso 1 rima con el verso 2 y el verso 3 rima con el verso 4. Muchos poemas siguen el mismo patrón de rimas, aunque no las mismas rimas, en cada estrofa.

SATIRE / SÁTIRA Una *sátira* es una obra literaria que ridiculiza las tonterías y fallas de ciertos individuos o instituciones, de la sociedad o incluso de la humanidad.

SENSORY LANGUAGE / LENGUAJE SENSORIAL El *lenguaje sensorial* es un escrito o discurso que incluye detalles que apelan a uno o más de los sentidos.

SEQUENCE OF EVENTS / SECUENCIA DE SUCESOS Los autores usan a menudo la *secuencia de sucesos*, es decir, el orden en que suceden los hechos, para estructurar textos de no-ficción que tratan sobre hechos históricos o que explican un cambio que se produjo a lo largo del tiempo. Con frecuencia los escritores presentan los hechos en **orden cronológico**, es decir, en el orden en que se sucedieron.

SETTING / AMBIENTACIÓN La *ambientación* de una obra literaria es la época y el lugar en el que se desarrolla la acción. La época incluye no solo el período histórico —pasado, presente o futuro —, sino también el año específico, la estación, la hora del día. El lugar puede incluir no solo el espacio geográfico —una región, un país, un estado, un pueblo— sino también el entorno social, económico o cultural.

En algunos cuentos, la ambientación sirve solo como un telón de fondo para la acción, un contexto en el que los personajes se mueven y hablan. En otros casos, en cambio, la ambientación es un elemento crucial.

SHORT STORY / CUENTO Un *cuento* es una obra breve de ficción. En la mayoría de los cuentos, un personaje principal se enfrenta a un conflicto que se resuelve a lo largo de la trama. Para escribir un buen cuento se necesita mucho dominio técnico, porque el cuento debe cumplir su cometido en relativamente pocas palabras.

SIMILE / SÍMIL Un *símil* es una figura retórica en la que se usa la palabra *como* para establecer una comparación entre dos cosas aparentemente disímiles. La comparación sorprende al lector ofreciéndole una nueva percepción que se deriva de descubrir una semejanza inesperada.

SOCIAL COMMENTARY / COMENTARIO SOCIAL En las obras de **comentario social** el autor tiene como objetivo resaltar, generalmente de forma crítica, un aspecto de la sociedad. El comentario social suele ser el objetivo de la *sátira*, en la que el autor señala lo absurdo de una práctica, costumbre o institución.

SOLILOQUY / SOLILOQUIO Un *soliloquio* es un largo parlamento en el que un personaje, solo en escena, expresa sus sentimientos.

SONNET / SONETO Un *soneto* es un poema lírico de catorce versos, por lo general escritos en pentámetros yámbicos rimados. El *soneto inglés o shakesperiano* consiste en tres cuartetas (estrofas de cuatro versos) y un pareado (estrofa de dos versos), por lo general con rima *abab cdcd efef gg*. El pareado suele consistir en un comentario sobre las ideas expuestas en los doce versos que lo preceden. El soneto inglés no se suele imprimir con la división interestrófica, pero el lector puede identificar las distintas ideas que se presentan en cada estrofa.

El *soneto italiano o petrarquista* consiste en una octava (una estrofa de ocho versos) y una sextina (una estrofa de seis versos). A menudo, las octavas riman *abbaabba* y las sextinas riman *cdecde*. La octava expone el tema y propone una pregunta. La sextina comenta el tema o responde la pregunta que se planteó en las estrofas anteriores.

SPEAKER / HABLANTE El *hablante* es la voz imaginaria que asume el escritor en un poema. En muchos poemas, el hablante no se identifica con un nombre. Al leer un poema, recuerda que el hablante puede ser una persona, un animal un objeto o una abstracción.

STAGE DIRECTIONS / ACOTACIONES Las *acotaciones* son notas que se incluyen en una obra de teatro para describir cómo debe ser actuada o puesta en escena. Estas instrucciones aparecen en itálicas y no se pronuncian durante la representación. Se usan para describir decorados, la iluminación, los efectos sonoros y el aspecto, la personalidad y los movimientos de los personajes.

STANZA / ESTROFA Una *estrofa* es un grupo de dos o más versos cuya estructura se repite. Las distintas estrofas de un poema suelen seguir un mismo patrón de ritmo y de rima. Las estrofas a menudo reciben su nombre del número de versos que las componen. Por ejemplo, un *dístico* o *pareado* (dos versos), una *cuarteta* (cuatro versos), una *sextina* (seis versos), y una *octavilla* (ocho versos).

STYLE / ESTILO El *estilo* es la manera particular en que escribe un autor. Los elementos que determinan el estilo son: la dicción, el tono; el uso característico de ciertas figuras retóricas, del dialecto, o de los recursos rítmicos; y la sintaxis, es decir, los patrones y estructuras gramaticales que usa con más frecuencia.

SURPRISE ENDING / FINAL SORPRESIVO Un *final sorpresivo* es una conclusión que no responde a las expectativas del lector, pero que de todos modos resulta lógica y verosímil.

SYMBOL / SÍMBOLO Un *símbolo* es algo que representa otra cosa. Además de tener su propio significado y realidad, un símbolo también representa ideas abstractas. Por ejemplo, una bandera es un trozo de tela, pero también representa la idea de un país. Los escritores a veces usan símbolos convencionales como las banderas. Con frecuencia, sin embargo, crean sus propios símbolos, a veces a través del énfasis o la repetición.

SYNTAX / SINTAXIS La *sintaxis* es la estructura de las oraciones.

THEME / TEMA Un *tema* es el mensaje central o la concepción de la vida que revela una obra literaria.

El tema de una obra literaria puede estar implícito o bien puede expresarse directamente. Cuando el tema de una obra está implícito, los lectores hacen inferencias sobre lo que sugiere la obra acerca de la vida o la gente.

Los *temas arquetípicos* son aquellos que aparecen en el folklore y en la literatura de todo el mundo y a lo largo de toda la historia.

TONE / TONO El *tono* de una obra literaria es la actitud del escritor hacia su tema y su audiencia. A menudo puede describirse con un solo adjetivo, tal como *formal* o *informal*, *serio* o *jocoso*, *amargo* o *irónico*.

TRAGEDY / TRAGEDIA Una *tragedia* es una obra literaria, por lo general una obra de teatro, que termina en una catástrofe, un desastre o un gran infortunio para el personaje principal. En el drama de la antigua Grecia, el personaje principal siempre era una persona importante —un rey o un héroe— y la causa de la tragedia era un *error trágico*, una debilidad de su carácter. En el drama moderno, el personaje principal puede ser una persona común, y la causa de la tragedia puede ser algún problema de la sociedad misma. La tragedia no solo despierta miedo y compasión en la audiencia, sino también, en algunos casos, le hace tomar conciencia de la majestuosidad y la nobleza del espíritu humano.

VOICE / VOZ La *voz* es el "sonido" distintivo de un escritor, o la manera en que "habla" en la página. Se relaciona a elementos tales como la elección del vocabulario, la estructura de las oraciones y el tono. Es similar al estilo en que habla un individuo y puede describirse de la misma manera: rápida, lenta, directa, dispersa, jadeante, etc.

La voz se parece al *estilo*, es decir, a la manera típica en que escribe un autor, pero el estilo por lo general se refiere a una cualidad que puede encontrarse a lo largo de toda la obra de un autor, mientras que la voz de un autor puede variar de una obra a otra.

PARTS OF SPEECH

Every English word, depending on its meaning and its use in a sentence, can be identified as one of the eight parts of speech. These are nouns, pronouns, verbs, adjectives, adverbs, prepositions, conjunctions, and interjections. Understanding the parts of speech will help you learn the rules of English grammar and usage.

Nouns A **noun** names a person, place, or thing. A **common noun** names any one of a class of persons, places, or things. A **proper noun** names a specific person, place, or thing.

Common Noun	Proper Noun
writer, country, novel	Charles Dickens, Great Britain, *Hard Times*

Pronouns A **pronoun** is a word that stands for one or more nouns. The word to which a pronoun refers (whose place it takes) is the **antecedent** of the pronoun.

A **personal pronoun** refers to the person speaking (first person); the person spoken to (second person); or the person, place, or thing spoken about (third person).

	Singular	Plural
First Person	I, me, my, mine	we, us, our, ours
Second Person	you, your, yours	you, your, yours
Third Person	he, him, his, she, her, hers, it, its	they, them, their, theirs

A **reflexive pronoun** reflects the action of a verb back on its subject. It indicates that the person or thing performing the action also is receiving the action.

I keep *myself* fit by taking a walk every day.

An **intensive pronoun** adds emphasis to a noun or pronoun.

It took the work of the president *himself* to pass the law.

A **demonstrative** pronoun points out a specific person(s), place(s), or thing(s).

this, that, these, those

A **relative pronoun** begins a subordinate clause and connects it to another idea in the sentence.

that, which, who, whom, whose

An **interrogative pronoun** begins a question.

what, which, who, whom, whose

An **indefinite pronoun** refers to a person, place, or thing that may or may not be specifically named.

all, another, any, both, each, everyone, few, most, none, no one, somebody

Verbs A **verb** expresses action or the existence of a state or condition.

An **action verb** tells what action someone or something is performing.

gather, read, work, jump, imagine, analyze, conclude

A **linking verb** connects the subject with another word that identifies or describes the subject. The most common linking verb is *be*.

appear, be, become, feel, look, remain, seem, smell, sound, stay, taste

A **helping verb,** or **auxiliary verb,** is added to a main verb to make a verb phrase.

be, do, have, should, can, could, may, might, must, will, would

Adjectives An **adjective** modifies a noun or pronoun by describing it or giving it a more specific meaning. An adjective answers the questions:

What kind?	*purple* hat, *happy* face, *loud* sound
Which one?	*this* bowl
How many?	*three* cars
How much?	*enough* food

The articles *the, a,* and *an* are adjectives.

A **proper adjective** is an adjective derived from a proper noun.

French, Shakespearean

Adverbs An **adverb** modifies a verb, an adjective, or another adverb by telling *where, when, how,* or *to what extent*.

will answer *soon, extremely* sad, calls *more* often

Prepositions A **preposition** relates a noun or pronoun that appears with it to another word in the sentence.

Dad made a meal *for* us. We talked *till* dusk. Bo missed school *because of* his illness.

Conjunctions A **conjunction** connects words or groups of words. A **coordinating conjunction** joins words or groups of words of equal rank.

bread *and* cheese, brief *but* powerful

Correlative conjunctions are used in pairs to connect words or groups of words of equal importance.

both Luis *and* Rosa, *neither* you *nor* I

Subordinating conjunctions indicate the connection between two ideas by placing one below the other in rank or importance. A subordinating conjunction introduces a subordinate, or dependent, clause.

We will miss her *if* she leaves. Hank shrieked *when* he slipped on the ice.

Interjections An **interjection** expresses feeling or emotion. It is not related to other words in the sentence.

ah, hey, ouch, well, yippee

PHRASES AND CLAUSES

Phrases A **phrase** is a group of words that does not have both a subject and a verb and that functions as one part of speech. A phrase expresses an idea but cannot stand alone.

Prepositional Phrases A **prepositional phrase** is a group of words that begins with a preposition and ends with a noun or pronoun that is the **object of the preposition.**

before dawn   as a result of the rain

An **adjective phrase** is a prepositional phrase that modifies a noun or pronoun.

Eliza appreciates the beauty **of a well-crafted poem.**

An **adverb phrase** is a prepositional phrase that modifies a verb, an adjective, or an adverb.

She reads Spenser's sonnets **with great pleasure.**

Appositive Phrases An **appositive** is a noun or pronoun placed next to another noun or pronoun to add information about it. An **appositive phrase** consists of an appositive and its modifiers.

Mr. Roth, **my music teacher,** is sick.

Verbal Phrases A **verbal** is a verb form that functions as a different part of speech (not as a verb) in a sentence. **Participles, gerunds,** and **infinitives** are verbals.

A **verbal phrase** includes a verbal and any modifiers or complements it may have. Verbal phrases may function as nouns, as adjectives, or as adverbs.

A **participle** is a verb form that can act as an adjective. Present participles end in *-ing;* past participles of regular verbs end in *-ed.*

A **participial phrase** consists of a participle and its modifiers or complements. The entire phrase acts as an adjective.

Jenna's backpack, **loaded with equipment,** was heavy.
Barking incessantly, the dogs chased the squirrels out of sight.

A **gerund** is a verb form that ends in *-ing* and is used as a noun.

A **gerund phrase** consists of a gerund with any modifiers or complements, all acting together as a noun.

Taking photographs of wildlife is her main hobby. [acts as subject]
We always enjoy **listening to live music.** [acts as object]

An **infinitive** is a verb form, usually preceded by *to,* that can act as a noun, an adjective, or an adverb.

An **infinitive phrase** consists of an infinitive and its modifiers or complements, and sometimes its subject, all acting together as a single part of speech.

She tries **to get out into the wilderness often.** [acts as a noun; direct object of *tries*]
The Tigers are the team **to beat.** [acts as an adjective; describes *team*]
I drove twenty miles **to witness the event.** [acts as an adverb; tells why I drove]

Clauses A **clause** is a group of words with its own subject and verb.

Independent Clauses An independent clause can stand by itself as a complete sentence.

George Orwell wrote with extraordinary insight.

Subordinate Clauses A subordinate clause, also called a dependent clause, cannot stand by itself as a complete sentence. Subordinate clauses always appear connected in some way with one or more independent clauses.

George Orwell, **who wrote with extraordinary insight,** produced many politically relevant works.

An **adjective clause** is a subordinate clause that acts as an adjective. It modifies a noun or a pronoun by telling *what kind* or *which one.* Also called relative clauses, adjective clauses usually begin with a **relative pronoun:** *who, which, that, whom,* or *whose.*

"The Lamb" is the poem **that I memorized for class.**

An **adverb clause** is a subordinate clause that, like an adverb, modifies a verb, an adjective, or an adverb. An adverb clause tells *where, when, in what way, to what extent, under what condition,* or *why.*

The students will read another poetry collection **if their schedule allows.**

When I recited the poem, Mr. Lopez was impressed.

A **noun clause** is a subordinate clause that acts as a noun.

William Blake survived on **whatever he made as an engraver.**

SENTENCE STRUCTURE

Subject and Predicate A **sentence** is a group of words that expresses a complete thought. A sentence has two main parts: a *subject* and a *predicate*.

A **fragment** is a group of words that does not express a complete thought. It lacks an independent clause.

The **subject** tells *whom* or *what* the sentence is about. The **predicate** tells what the subject of the sentence does or is.

A subject or a predicate can consist of a single word or of many words. All the words in the subject make up the **complete subject.** All the words in the predicate make up the **complete predicate.**

Complete Subject	Complete Predicate
Both of those girls	have already read *Macbeth.*

The **simple subject** is the essential noun, pronoun, or group of words acting as a noun that cannot be left out of the complete subject. The **simple predicate** is the essential verb or verb phrase that cannot be left out of the complete predicate.

Both of those girls | **have** already **read** *Macbeth.*
[Simple subject: *Both;* simple predicate: *have read*]

A **compound subject** is two or more subjects that have the same verb and are joined by a conjunction.

Neither the horse nor the driver looked tired.

A **compound predicate** is two or more verbs that have the same subject and are joined by a conjunction.

She **sneezed and coughed** throughout the trip.

Complements A **complement** is a word or word group that completes the meaning of the subject or verb in a sentence. There are four kinds of complements: *direct objects, indirect objects, objective complements,* and *subject complements.*

A **direct object** is a noun, a pronoun, or a group of words acting as a noun that receives the action of a transitive verb.

We watched the **liftoff.**
She drove **Zach** to the launch site.

An **indirect object** is a noun or pronoun that appears with a direct object and names the person or thing to which or for which something is done.

He sold the **family** a mirror. [The direct object is *mirror.*]

An **objective complement** is an adjective or noun that appears with a direct object and describes or renames it.

The decision made her **unhappy.**
[The direct object is *her.*]
Many consider Shakespeare the greatest **playwright.** [The direct object is *Shakespeare.*]

A **subject complement** follows a linking verb and tells something about the subject. There are two kinds: *predicate nominatives* and *predicate adjectives.*

A **predicate nominative** is a noun or pronoun that follows a linking verb and identifies or renames the subject.

"A Modest Proposal" is a **pamphlet.**

A **predicate adjective** is an adjective that follows a linking verb and describes the subject of the sentence.

"A Modest Proposal" is **satirical.**

Classifying Sentences by Structure

Sentences can be classified according to the kind and number of clauses they contain. The four basic sentence structures are *simple, compound, complex,* and *compound-complex.*

A **simple sentence** consists of one independent clause.

Terrence enjoys modern British literature.

A **compound sentence** consists of two or more independent clauses. The clauses are joined by a conjunction or a semicolon.

Terrence enjoys modern British literature, but his brother prefers the classics.

A **complex sentence** consists of one independent clause and one or more subordinate clauses.

Terrence, who reads voraciously, enjoys modern British literature.

A **compound-complex sentence** consists of two or more independent clauses and one or more subordinate clauses.

Terrence, who reads voraciously, enjoys modern British literature, but his brother prefers the classics.

Classifying Sentences by Function

Sentences can be classified according to their function or purpose. The four types are *declarative, interrogative, imperative,* and *exclamatory.*

A **declarative sentence** states an idea and ends with a period.

An **interrogative sentence** asks a question and ends with a question mark.

An **imperative sentence** gives an order or a direction and ends with either a period or an exclamation mark.

An **exclamatory sentence** conveys a strong emotion and ends with an exclamation mark.

PARAGRAPH STRUCTURE

An effective paragraph is organized around one **main idea,** which is often stated in a **topic sentence.** The other sentences support the main idea. To give the paragraph **unity,** make sure the connection between each sentence and the main idea is clear.

Unnecessary Shift in Person

Do not change needlessly from one grammatical person to another. Keep the person consistent in your sentences.

> **Max** went to the bakery, but **you** can't buy mints there. [shift from third person to second person]

> **Max** went to the bakery, but **he** can't buy mints there. [consistent]

Unnecessary Shift in Voice

Do not change needlessly from active voice to passive voice in your use of verbs.

> Elena and I **searched** the trail for evidence, but no clues **were found.** [shift from active voice to passive voice]

> Elena and I **searched** the trail for evidence, but we **found** no clues. [consistent]

AGREEMENT

Subject and Verb Agreement

A singular subject must have a singular verb. A plural subject must have a plural verb.

> **Dr. Boone uses** a telescope to view the night sky.
> The **students use** a telescope to view the night sky.

A verb always agrees with its subject, not its object.

> *Incorrect:* The best part of the show were the jugglers.
> *Correct:* The best part of the show was the jugglers.

A phrase or clause that comes between a subject and verb does not affect subject-verb agreement.

> His **theory,** as well as his claims, **lacks** support.

Two subjects joined by *and* usually take a plural verb.

> The **dog** and the **cat are** healthy.

Two singular subjects joined by *or* or *nor* take a singular verb.

> The **dog** or the **cat is** hiding.

Two plural subjects joined by *or* or *nor* take a plural verb.

> The **dogs** or the **cats are** coming home with us.

When a singular and a plural subject are joined by *or* or *nor,* the verb agrees with the closer subject.

> Either the **dogs** or the **cat is** behind the door.
> Either the **cat** or the **dogs are** behind the door.

Pronoun and Antecedent Agreement

Pronouns must agree with their antecedents in number and gender. Use singular pronouns with singular antecedents and plural pronouns with plural antecedents.

> **Doris Lessing** uses **her** writing to challenge ideas about women's roles.
> **Writers** often use **their** skills to promote social change.

Use a singular pronoun when the antecedent is a singular indefinite pronoun such as *anybody, each, either, everybody, neither, no one, one,* or *someone.*

> Judge **each** of the articles on **its** merits.

Use a plural pronoun when the antecedent is a plural indefinite pronoun such as *both, few, many,* or *several.*

> **Both** of the articles have **their** flaws.

The indefinite pronouns *all, any, more, most, none,* and *some* can be singular or plural depending on the number of the word to which they refer.

> **Most** of the *books* are in **their** proper places.
> **Most** of the *book* has been torn from **its** binding.

Principal Parts of Regular and Irregular Verbs

A verb has four principal parts:

Present	Present Participle	Past	Past Participle
learn	learning	learned	learned
discuss	discussing	discussed	discussed
stand	standing	stood	stood
begin	beginning	began	begun

Regular verbs such as *learn* and *discuss* form the past and past participle by adding *-ed* to the present form. **Irregular verbs** such as *stand* and *begin* form the past and past participle in other ways. If you are in doubt about the principal parts of an irregular verb, check a dictionary.

The Tenses of Verbs

The different tenses of verbs indicate the time an action or condition occurs.

The **present tense** expresses an action that happens regularly or states a current condition or a general truth.

> Tourists **flock** to the site yearly.

Daily exercise **is** good for your heallth.

The **past tense** expresses a completed action or a condition that is no longer true.

> The squirrel **dropped** the nut and **ran** up the tree.
> I **was** very tired last night by 9:00.

The **future tense** indicates an action that will happen in the future or a condition that will be true.

> The Glazers **will visit** us tomorrow.
> They **will be** glad to arrive from their long journey.

The **present perfect tense** expresses an action that happened at an indefinite time in the past or an action that began in the past and continues into the present.

> Someone **has cleaned** the trash from the park.
> The puppy **has been** under the bed all day.

The **past perfect tense** shows an action that was completed before another action in the past.

> Gerard **had revised** his essay before he turned it in.

The **future perfect tense** indicates an action that will have been completed before another action takes place.

> Mimi **will have painted** the kitchen by the time we finish the shutters.

Degrees of Comparison

Adjectives and adverbs take different forms to show the three degrees of comparison: the *positive*, the *comparative*, and the *superlative.*

Positive	Comparative	Superlative
fast	faster	fastest
crafty	craftier	craftiest
abruptly	more abruptly	most abruptly
badly	worse	worst

Using Comparative and Superlative Adjectives and Adverbs

Use comparative adjectives and adverbs to compare two things. Use superlative adjectives and adverbs to compare three or more things.

> This season's weather was **drier** than last year's.
> This season has been one of the **driest** on record.
> Jake practices **more often** than Jamal.
> Of everyone in the band, Jake practices **most often.**

Pronoun Case

The **case** of a pronoun is the form it takes to show its function in a sentence. There are three pronoun cases: *nominative, objective,* and *possessive.*

Nominative	Objective	Possessive
I, you, he, she, it, we, you, they	me, you, him, her, it, us, you, them	my, your, yours, his, her, hers, its, our, ours, their, theirs

Use the **nominative case** when a pronoun functions as a *subject* or as a *predicate nominative.*

> **They** are going to the movies. [subject]
> The biggest movie fan is **she.** [predicate nominative]

Use the **objective case** for a pronoun acting as a *direct object,* an *indirect object,* or the *object of a preposition.*

> The ending of the play surprised **me.** [direct object]
> Mary gave **us** two tickets to the play. [indirect object]
> The audience cheered for **him.** [object of preposition]

Use the **possessive case** to show ownership.

> The red suitcase is **hers.**

Diction The words you choose contribute to the overall effectiveness of your writing. **Diction** refers to word choice and to the clearness and correctness of those words. You can improve one aspect of your diction by choosing carefully between commonly confused words, such as the pairs listed below.

accept, except

Accept is a verb that means "to receive" or "to agree to." *Except* is a preposition that means "other than" or "leaving out."

Please **accept** my offer to buy you lunch this weekend.

He is busy every day **except** the weekends.

affect, effect

Affect is normally a verb meaning "to influence" or "to bring about a change in." *Effect* is usually a noun meaning "result."

The distractions outside **affect** Steven's ability to concentrate.

The teacher's remedies had a positive **effect** on Steven's ability to concentrate.

among, between

Among is usually used with three or more items, and it emphasizes collective relationships or indicates distribution. *Between* is generally used with only two items, but it can be used with more than two if the emphasis is on individual (one-to-one) relationships within the group.

I had to choose a snack **among** the various vegetables.

He handed out the booklets **among** the conference participants.

Our school is **between** a park and an old barn.

The tournament included matches **between** France, Spain, Mexico, and the United States.

amount, number

Amount refers to overall quantity and is mainly used with mass nouns (those that can't be counted). *Number* refers to individual items that can be counted.

The **amount** of attention that great writers have paid to Shakespeare is remarkable.

A **number** of important English writers have been fascinated by the legend of King Arthur.

assure, ensure, insure

Assure means "to convince [someone of something]; to guarantee." *Ensure* means "to make certain [that something happens]." *Insure* means "to arrange for payment in case of loss."

The attorney **assured** us we'd win the case.

The rules **ensure** that no one gets treated unfairly.

Many professional musicians **insure** their valuable instruments.

bad, badly

Use the adjective *bad* before a noun or after linking verbs such as *feel*, *look*, and *seem*. Use *badly* whenever an adverb is required.

The situation may seem **bad**, but it will improve over time.

Though our team played **badly** today, we will focus on practicing for the next match.

beside, besides

Beside means "at the side of" or "close to." *Besides* means "in addition to."

The stapler sits **beside** the pencil sharpener in our classroom.

Besides being very clean, the classroom is also very organized.

can, may

The helping verb *can* generally refers to the ability to do something. The helping verb *may* generally refers to permission to do something.

I **can** run one mile in six minutes.

May we have a race during recess?

complement, compliment

The verb *complement* means "to enhance"; the verb *compliment* means "to praise."

Online exercises **complement** the textbook lessons.

Ms. Lewis **complimented** our team on our excellent debate.

compose, comprise

Compose means "to make up; constitute." *Comprise* means "to include or contain." Remember that the whole comprises its parts or is composed of its parts, and the parts compose the whole.

The assignment **comprises** three different tasks.

The assignment is **composed** of three different tasks.

Three different tasks **compose** the assignment.

different from, different than

Different from is generally preferred over *different than*, but *different than* can be used before a clause. Always use *different from* before a noun or pronoun.

Your point of view is so **different from** mine.

His idea was so **different from** [or **different than**] what we had expected.

farther, further

Use *farther* to refer to distance. Use *further* to mean "to a greater degree or extent" or "additional."

Chiang has traveled **farther** than anybody else in the class.

If I want **further** details about his travels, I can read his blog.

fewer, less

Use *fewer* for things that can be counted. Use *less* for amounts or quantities that cannot be counted. *Fewer* must be followed by a plural noun.

Fewer students drive to school since the weather improved.

There is **less** noise outside in the mornings.

good, well

Use the adjective *good* before a noun or after a linking verb. Use *well* whenever an adverb is required, such as when modifying a verb.

I feel **good** after sleeping for eight hours.

I did **well** on my test, and my soccer team played **well** in that afternoon's game. It was a **good** day!

its, it's

The word *its* with no apostrophe is a possessive pronoun. The word *it's* is a contraction of "it is."

Angelica will try to fix the computer and **its** keyboard.

It's a difficult job, but she can do it.

lay, lie

Lay is a transitive verb meaning "to set or put something down." Its principal parts are *lay, laying, laid, laid*. *Lie* is an intransitive verb meaning "to recline" or "to exist in a certain place." Its principal parts are *lie, lying, lay, lain*.

Please **lay** that box down and help me with the sofa.

When we are done moving, I am going to **lie** down.

My hometown **lies** sixty miles north of here.

like, as

Like is a preposition that usually means "similar to" and precedes a noun or pronoun. The conjunction *as* means "in the way that" and usually precedes a clause.

Like the other students, I was prepared for a quiz.

As I said yesterday, we expect to finish before noon.

Use **such as,** not **like,** before a series of examples.

Foods **such as** apples, nuts, and pretzels make good snacks.

of, have

Do not use *of* in place of *have* after auxiliary verbs such as *would, could, should, may, might,* or *must*. The contraction of *have* is formed by adding *-ve* after these verbs.

I **would have** stayed after school today, but I had to help cook at home.

Mom **must've** called while I was still in the gym.

principal, principle

Principal can be an adjective meaning "main; most important." It can also be a noun meaning "chief officer of a school." *Principle* is a noun meaning "moral rule" or "fundamental truth."

His strange behavior was the **principal** reason for our concern.

Democratic **principles** form the basis of our country's laws.

raise, rise

Raise is a transitive verb that usually takes a direct object. *Rise* is intransitive and never takes a direct object.

Iliana and Josef **raise** the flag every morning.

They **rise** from their seats and volunteer immediately whenever help is needed.

than, then

The conjunction *than* is used to connect the two parts of a comparison. The adverb *then* usually refers to time.

My backpack is heavier **than** hers.

I will finish my homework and **then** meet my friends at the park.

that, which, who

Use the relative pronoun *that* to refer to things or people. Use *which* only for things and *who* only for people.

That introduces a restrictive phrase or clause, that is, one that is essential to the meaning of the sentence. *Which* introduces a nonrestrictive phrase or clause—one that adds information but could be deleted from the sentence—and is preceded by a comma.

Ben ran to the park **that** just reopened.

The park, **which** just reopened, has many attractions.

The man **who** built the park loves to see people smiling.

when, where, why

Do not use *when, where,* or *why* directly after a linking verb, such as *is*. Reword the sentence.

Incorrect: The morning is when he left for the beach.

Correct: He left for the beach in the morning.

who, whom

In formal writing, use *who* only as a subject in clauses and sentences. Use *whom* only as the object of a verb or of a preposition.

Who paid for the tickets?

Whom should I pay for the tickets?

I can't recall to **whom** I gave the money for the tickets.

your, you're

Your is a possessive pronoun expressing ownership. *You're* is the contraction of "you are."

Have you finished writing **your** informative essay?

You're supposed to turn it in tomorrow. If **you're** late, **your** grade will be affected.

GLOSSARY: GRAMMAR HANDBOOK

Capitalization

First Words

Capitalize the first word of a sentence.

Stories about knights and their deeds interest me.

Capitalize the first word of direct speech.

Sharon asked, "**D**o you like stories about knights?"

Capitalize the first word of a quotation that is a complete sentence.

Einstein said, "**A**nyone who has never made a mistake has never tried anything new."

Proper Nouns and Proper Adjectives

Capitalize all proper nouns, including geographical names, historical events and periods, and names of organizations.

Thames **R**iver	**J**ohn **K**eats	the **R**enaissance
United **N**ations	**W**orld **W**ar II	**S**ierra **N**evada

Capitalize all proper adjectives.

Shakespearean play	**B**ritish invaision
American citizen	**L**atin **A**merican literature

Academic Course Names

Capitalize course names only if they are language courses, are followed by a number, or are preceded by a proper noun or adjective.

Spanish	**H**onors **C**hemistry	**H**istory 101
geology	**a**lgebra	**s**ocial **s**tudies

Titles

Capitalize personal titles when followed by the person's name.

Ms. Hughes   **D**r. Perez   **K**ing George

Capitalize titles showing family relationships when they are followed by a specific person's name, unless they are preceded by a possessive noun or pronoun.

Uncle Oscar   Mangan's **s**ister   his **a**unt Tessa

Capitalize the first word and all other key words in the titles of books, stories, songs, and other works of art.

Frankenstein   "**S**hooting an **E**lephant"

Punctuation

End Marks

Use a **period** to end a declarative sentence or an imperative sentence.

We are studying the structure of sonnets.
Read the biography of Mary Shelley.

Use periods with initials and abbreviations.

D. H. Lawrence	Mrs. Browning
Mt. Everest	Maple St.

Use a **question mark** to end an interrogative sentence.

What is Macbeth's fatal flaw?

Use an **exclamation mark** after an exclamatory sentence or a forceful imperative sentence.

That's a beautiful painting!   Let me go now!

Commas

Use a **comma** before a coordinating conjunction to separate two independent clauses in a compound sentence.

The game was very close, but we were victorious.

Use commas to separate three or more words, phrases, or clauses in a series.

William Blake was a writer, artist, and printer.

Use commas to separate coordinate adjectives.

It was a witty, amusing novel.

Use a comma after an introductory word, phrase, or clause.

When the novelist finished his book, he celebrated with his family.

Use commas to set off nonessential expressions.

Old English, of course, requires translation.

Use commas with places and dates.

Coventry, England   September 1, 1939

Semicolons

Use a **semicolon** to join closely related independent clauses that are not already joined by a conjunction.

Tanya likes to write poetry; Heather prefers prose.

Use semicolons to avoid confusion when items in a series contain commas.

They traveled to London, England; Madrid, Spain; and Rome, Italy.

Colons

Use a **colon** before a list of items following an independent clause.

Notable Victorian poets include the following: Tennyson, Arnold, Housman, and Hopkins.

Use a colon to introduce information that summarizes or explains the independent clause before it.

She just wanted to do one thing: rest.
Malcolm loves volunteering: He reads to sick children every Saturday afternoon.

Quotation Marks

Use **quotation marks** to enclose a direct quotation.

"Short stories," Ms. Hildebrand said, "should have rich, well-developed characters."

An **indirect quotation** does not require quotation marks.

Ms. Hildebrand said that short stories should have well-developed characters.

Use quotation marks around the titles of short written works, episodes in a series, songs, and works mentioned as parts of collections.

"The Lagoon"   "Boswell Meets Johnson"

Italics

Italicize the titles of long written works, movies, television and radio shows, lengthy works of music, paintings, and sculptures.

Howards End   *60 Minutes*   *Guernica*

For handwritten material, you can use underlining instead of italics.

<u>The Princess Bride</u>   <u>Mona Lisa</u>

Dashes

Use **dashes** to indicate an abrupt change of thought, a dramatic interrupting idea, or a summary statement.

> I read the entire first act of *Macbeth*—you won't believe what happens next.

> The director—what's her name again?—attended the movie premiere.

Hyphens

Use a **hyphen** with certain numbers, after certain prefixes, with two or more words used as one word, and with a compound modifier that comes before a noun.

> seventy-two
> self-esteem
> president-elect
> five-year contract

Parentheses

Use **parentheses** to set off asides and explanations when the material is not essential or when it consists of one or more sentences. When the sentence in parentheses interrupts the larger sentence, it does not have a capital letter or a period.

> He listened intently (it was too dark to see who was speaking) to try to identify the voices.

When a sentence in parentheses falls between two other complete sentences, it should start with a capital letter and end with a period.

> The quarterback threw three touchdown passes. (We knew he could do it.) Our team won the game by two points.

Apostrophes

Add an **apostrophe** and an *s* to show the possessive case of most singular nouns and of plural nouns that do not end in *-s* or *-es*.

> Blake's poems   the mice's whiskers

Names ending in *s* form their possessives in the same way, except for classical and biblical names, which add only an apostrophe to form the possessive.

> Dickens's   Hercules'

Add an apostrophe to show the possessive case of plural nouns ending in *-s* and *-es*.

> the girls' songs   the Ortizes' car

Use an apostrophe in a contraction to indicate the position of the missing letter or letters.

> She's never read a Coleridge poem she didn't like.

Brackets

Use **brackets** to enclose clarifying information inserted within a quotation.

> Columbus's journal entry from October 21, 1492, begins as follows: "At 10 o'clock, we arrived at a cape of the island [San Salvador], and anchored, the other vessels in company."

Ellipses

Use three ellipsis points, also known as an **ellipsis,** to indicate where you have omitted words from quoted material.

> Wollestonecraft wrote, "The education of women has of late been more attended to than formerly; yet they are still . . . ridiculed or pitied. . . ."

In the example above, the four dots at the end of the sentence are the three ellipsis points plus the period from the original sentence.

Use an ellipsis to indicate a pause or interruption in speech.

> "When he told me the news," said the coach, "I was . . . I was shocked . . . completely shocked."

Spelling

Spelling Rules

Learning the rules of English spelling will help you make **generalizations** about how to spell words.

Word Parts

The three word parts that can combine to form a word are roots, prefixes, and suffixes. Many of these word parts come from the Greek, Latin, and Anglo-Saxon languages.

The **root word** carries a word's basic meaning.

Root and Origin	Meaning	Examples
-leg- (-log-) [Gr.]	to say, speak	*legal, logic*
-pon- (-pos-) [L.]	to put, place	*postpone, deposit*

A **prefix** is one or more syllables added to the beginning of a word that alter the meaning of the root.

Prefix and Origin	Meaning	Example
anti- [Gr.]	against	*antipathy*
inter- [L.]	between	*international*
mis- [A.S.]	wrong	*misplace*

A **suffix** is a letter or group of letters added to the end of a root word that changes the word's meaning or part of speech.

Suffix and Origin	Meaning and Example	Part of Speech
-ful [A.S.]	full of: *scornful*	adjective
-ity [L.]	state of being: *adversity*	noun
-ize (-ise) [Gr.]	to make: *idolize*	verb
-ly [A.S.]	in a manner: *calmly*	adverb

Rules for Adding Suffixes to Root Words

When adding a suffix to a root word ending in *y* preceded by a consonant, change *y* to *i* unless the suffix begins with *i*.

ply + -able = pliable   happy + -ness = happiness
defy + -ing = defying   cry + -ing = crying

For a root word ending in *e*, drop the *e* when adding a suffix beginning with a vowel.

drive + -ing = driving   move + -able = movable
SOME EXCEPTIONS: traceable, seeing, dyeing

For root words ending with a consonant + vowel + consonant in a stressed syllable, double the final consonant when adding a suffix that begins with a vowel.

mud + -y = muddy   submit + -ed = submitted
SOME EXCEPTIONS: mixing, fixed

Rules for Adding Prefixes to Root Words

When a prefix is added to a root word, the spelling of the root remains the same.

un- + certain = uncertain   mis- + spell = misspell

With some prefixes, the spelling of the prefix changes when joined to the root to make the pronunciation easier.

in- + mortal = immortal   ad- + vert = avert

Orthographic Patterns

Certain letter combinations in English make certain sounds. For instance, *ph* sounds like *f*, *eigh* usually makes a long *a* sound, and the *k* before an *n* is often silent.

pharmacy   n**eigh**bor   **k**nowledge

Understanding **orthographic patterns** such as these can help you improve your spelling.

Forming Plurals

The plural form of most nouns is formed by adding -*s* to the singular.

computer**s**   gadget**s**   Washington**s**

For words ending in *s, ss, x, z, sh,* or *ch,* add -*es.*

circus**es**   tax**es**   wish**es**   bench**es**

For words ending in *y* or *o* preceded by a vowel, add -*s.*

key**s**   patio**s**

For words ending in *y* preceded by a consonant, change the *y* to an *i* and add -*es.*

citi**es**   enemi**es**   trophi**es**

For most words ending in *o* preceded by a consonant, add -*es.*

echo**es**   tomato**es**

Some words form the plural in irregular ways.

women   oxen   children   teeth   deer

Foreign Words Used in English

Some words used in English are actually foreign words that have been adopted. Learning to spell these words requires memorization. When in doubt, check a dictionary.

sushi   enchilada   au pair   fiancé
laissez faire   croissant

INDEX OF SKILLS

Analyzing Text

Analyze, 32, 44, 56, 278, 382, 406, 583, 611, 699, 722

  essential question, 32, 44, 56, 78, 96, 110, 180, 188, 208, 220, 228, 242, 278, 288, 296, 315, 332, 340, 382, 426, 438, 457, 465, 476, 569, 583, 598, 611, 630, 640, 722, 742, 754, 782, 798

  media

    essential question, 296, 321, 348, 406

    present and discuss, 88, 321, 348

    review and clarify, 348

    review and synthesize, 88, 321

  prepare to compare, 48

  present and discuss, 78, 96, 110, 208, 220, 228, 242, 315, 332, 340, 426, 438, 457, 465, 476, 630, 640, 742, 754, 782, 798

  review and clarify, 78, 96, 110, 208, 220, 228, 242, 315, 332, 340, 426, 438, 457, 465, 476, 630, 640, 742, 754, 782, 798

  writing to compare, 292, 322, 468, 612

Argument, 225

Argument model, 130, 496

Assess, 551

Author's style

  apostrophe, 632

  author's choices, 467, 784

  character development, 80, 399

  descriptive details, 61

  details, 334

  diction, 98, 210

  Greek Chorus, 701

  information integration, 301

  motifs, 585

  pace, 784

  parallelism, 230, 725

  paraphrase, 617

  poetic form, 222

  poetic language, 440

  poetic structure, 467, 601

  point of view, 112

  quotations, 617

  repetition, 585

  rhetorical devices, 291

  scientific and technical diction, 98

  sentence variety, 478

  sound devices, 440

  syntax, 210

  transitions, 193

  word choice, 342, 428, 553

  word choice and meaning, 756

Characterization, 80

Cite textual evidence, 32, 44, 45, 78, 79, 96, 97, 110, 111, 180, 181, 208, 209, 220, 221, 228, 229, 242, 243, 278, 279, 288, 289, 296, 315, 316, 332, 333, 340, 341, 382, 383, 397, 426, 427, 438, 439, 457, 458, 465, 466, 476, 477, 531, 532, 551, 552, 569, 583, 584, 598, 599, 611, 630, 631, 640, 641, 699, 700, 722, 723, 742, 743, 754, 782, 783, 798, 799

Classify, 699

Close read, 531, 551, 569, 583, 699

  annotate, 32, 44, 78, 96, 110, 119, 180, 208, 220, 228, 242, 251, 278, 288, 355, 382, 396, 476, 485, 509, 598, 630, 640, 649, 722, 742, 754, 782, 798, 807

  close-read guide, 119, 251, 355, 485, 649, 807

  conclude, 32, 44, 78, 96, 110, 119, 180, 208, 220, 228, 242, 251, 278, 288, 315, 332, 339, 355, 382, 396, 426, 438, 457, 465, 476, 485, 509, 598, 611, 630, 640, 649, 722, 742, 754, 782, 798, 807

  question, 32, 44, 78, 96, 110, 119, 180, 208, 220, 228, 242, 251, 278, 288, 315, 332, 339, 355, 382, 396, 426, 438, 457, 465, 476, 485, 509, 598, 611, 630, 640, 649, 722, 742, 754, 782, 798, 807

Close review

  conclude, 56, 88, 188, 296, 321, 348, 406

  question, 56, 188, 296, 321, 348, 406

  synthesize, 88

Compare and contrast, 44, 180, 288, 382, 406, 583, 699

Compare texts, 12, 36, 268, 282, 308, 442, 604

Compare texts to media, 318

Connect, 32, 44, 278, 296, 531, 551, 699

Contrast, 188

Craft and Structure

  author's choices, 221, 333, 439, 466, 743

author's claims, 97

author's purpose, 316

development of ideas, 799

dramatic structure

  aside, 584

  monologue, 584

  plot, 570

  soliloquy, 584

  subplot, 570

drama types

  comedy, 532

  romance, 532

  tragedy, 532

emotional appeals, 289

evidence, 316

  credibility, 229

  relevance, 229

  variety, 229

feature story

  body, 477

  conclusion, 477

  introduction, 477

  title, 477

figurative language

  analogy, 755

  extended metaphor, 333

  hyperbole, 743

  metaphor, 333, 743

  personification, 743

  simile, 333, 743

  theme, 755

Greek play structure

  exodos, 700

  odes, 700

  parados, 700

  prologue, 700

  verse drama, 700

Greek tragedy

  antagonist, 723

  dramatic irony, 723

  hamartia, 723

  protagonist, 723

  tragic hero, 723

literary devices

  irony, 383

  situational irony, 383

  surprise ending, 383

literary nonfiction

  conclusion, 243

  discussion, 243

INDEX OF SKILLS

INDEX OF SKILLS

INDEX OF AUTHORS AND TITLES

The following authors and titles appear in the print and online versions of *my*Perspectives.

ADDITIONAL SELECTIONS: AUTHOR AND TITLE INDEX

The following authors and titles appear in the Interactive Student Edition only.

INDEX OF AUTHORS AND TITLES

Acknowledgments

The following selections appear in Grade 10 of *my*Perspectives. Some selections appear online only.

ABC News - Permissions Dept. Spooky Business: American Economy ©ABC News; Diane Sawyer Sits Down With the Inspirational Malala Yousafzai ©ABC News; 14-Year-Old Teaches Family the 'Power of Half' ©ABC News; Dr. Geoffrey Tabin Helps Blind Ethiopians Gain Sight ©ABC News.

American Folklore. "What We Plant, We Will Eat" by S. E. Schlosser; Used with permission from S.E. Schlosser and American Folklore. Copyright 2015. All rights reserved.

American Foundation for the Blind. "The Empire State Building" by Helen Keller, originally appeared in *New York Times,* January 17, 1932. Courtesy of the American Foundation for the Blind, Helen Keller Archives.

Amnesty International UK. Everybody—we are all born free ©Amnesty International UK.

Anchor Books. "The Sun Parlor" from *The Richer, The Poorer* by Dorothy West, copyright ©1995 by Dorothy West. Used by permission of Doubleday, an imprint of the Knopf Doubleday Publishing Group, a division of Penguin Random House LLC. All rights reserved. Any third party use of this material, outside of this publication, is prohibited. Interested parties must apply directly to Penguin Random House LLC for permission.

Arte Publico Press. "Fences" is reprinted with permission from the publisher of *Communion,* by Pat Mora ©1991 Arte Publico Press—University of Houston.

Atlantic Monthly. "Why Do Some Dreams Enjoy Fear?" ©2013 The Atlantic Media Co., as first published in *The Atlantic Magazine.* All rights reserved. Distributed by Tribune Content Agency, LLC.

BBC News Online. "How Your Eyes Trick Your Mind," from BBC; Used with permission.

BBC Worldwide Americas, Inc. *Franz Kafka and Metamorphosis* ©BBC Worldwide Learning; Socrates ©BBC Worldwide Learning; Episode 1: Rock the Ship ©BBC Worldwide Learning; Blind Teen ©BBC Worldwide Learning; How Your Eyes Trick Your Mind ©BBC Worldwide Learning.

Black Moon Theatre Company. Kafka's *The Metamorphosis* ©Black Moon Theatre Company.

Bowers, Jai. "By Any Other Name" from *Gifts of Passage* by Santha Rama Rau. Copyright ©Santha Rama Rau. Reprinted by permission of the author's estate.

Cambridge University Press - US – Journals. "A Dose of What the Doctor Never Orders," from *The Japanese Family Storehouse* by Ihara Saikaku, translated by G. W. Sargent. Copyright ©1959 Cambridge University Press. Reprinted with the permission of Cambridge University Press.

Carmen Balcells Agencia Literaria. Julio Cortazar, "House Taken Over," *Blow-Up and Other Stories* ©The Estate of Julio Cortazar, 1967.

Curtis Brown, Ltd. (UK). "They are hostile nations" from *Power Politics* by Margaret Atwood. Copyright ©1976 by Margaret Atwood. Used with permission.

Dancing Bear, J. P. "Caliban," Copyright ©J. P. Dancing Bear. Used with permission of the author.

Farrar, Straus and Giroux. "Avarice" from *Talking Dirty to the Gods* by Yusef Komunyakaa. Copyright ©2000 by Yusef Komunyakaa. Reprinted by permission of Farrar, Straus and Giroux, LLC. CAUTION: Users are warned that this work is protected under copyright laws and downloading is strictly prohibited. The right to reproduce or transfer the work via any medium must be secured with Farrar, Straus and Giroux, LLC.

Forgiveness Project. "The Forgiveness Project: Eric Lomax," ©The Forgiveness Project.

Freedom House. "Harsh Laws and Violence Drive Global Decline," Freedom of the Press 2015. By permission of Freedom House.

Frost, Adam. Adapted from "How to tell you're reading a gothic novel—in pictures" by Adam Frost and Zhenia Vasiliev, from *The Guardian,* May 9, 2014.

Getty Images. JFK Inaugural Address ©MediaRecall Holdings/Archive ED/Getty Images.

Gibbons, Reginald. "Money" copyright by Reginald Gibbons. Reprinted by permission of the author.

Goldsmith, Margie. "The Thrill of the Chase" by Margie Goldsmith, from *Hemispheres Magazine,* January 2013. Copyright ©2013 by Margie Goldsmith. Used with permission of the author.

Graywolf Press. Tracy K. Smith, "The Good Life" from *Life on Mars.* Copyright ©2011 by Tracy K. Smith. Reprinted with the permission of The Permissions Company, Inc., on behalf of Graywolf Press, Minneapolis, Minnesota.

Guardian News and Media Limited. "Stone Age man's terrors still stalk modern nightmares," Copyright Guardian News & Media Ltd 2015; "A Dish Best Served Cold," Copyright Guardian News & Media Ltd 2015; "Experience: I first saw my wife 10 years after we married," Copyright Guardian News & Media Ltd 2015.

Hanging Loose Press. "Sonnet With Bird," reprinted from *What I've Stolen, What I've Earned* ©2014 by Sherman Alexie, by permission of Hanging Loose Press.

HarperCollins Publishers. "Harrison Bergeron" from *Welcome to the Monkey House* (audio) by Kurt Vonnegut. Copyright © 1950, 1951, 1953, 1954, 1955, 1956, 1958, 1960, 1961, 1962, 1964, 1966, 1968 by Kurt Vonnegut Jr. (p) & © 2006 HarperCollins Publishers. Used by permission of HarperCollins Publishers.

HarperCollins Publishers Ltd. (UK). "Windigo" from Jacklight by Louise Erdrich. Reprinted by permission of HarperCollins Publishers Ltd ©1984 Louise Erdrich

Houghton Mifflin Harcourt. "They are Hostile Nations" from *Selected Poems I: 1965–1975* by Margaret Atwood. Copyright ©1976 by Margaret Atwood. Reprinted with permission of Houghton Mifflin Harcourt Publishing Company. All rights reserved.

Houghton Mifflin Harcourt Publishing Co. Excerpt from *Blindness* by Jose Saramago, translated from the Portuguese by Giovanni Pontiero. Copyright ©1995 by Jose Saramago and Editorial Caminho, SA. English translation copyright ©1997 by Juan Sager. Reprinted by permission of Houghton Mifflin Harcourt Publishing Company. All rights reserved.

Ivan R. Dee, Publisher. *Oedipus the King.* Copyright ©2000 by Ivan R. Dee, Inc. Translation copyright ©2000 by Nicholas Rudall. All rights reserved.

John Hawkins & Associates, Inc. "Where Is Here?" Copyright ©1992 Ontario Review, Inc. Reprinted by permission of John Hawkins & Associates, Inc.

John Wiley & Sons, Inc. "Encountering the Other—The Challenge for the 21st Century" republished with permission of John Wiley & Sons, "Encountering the Other—The Challenge for the 21st Century" from *New Perspectives Quarterly*, Vol. 22, No. 4 by Ryszard Kapuscinski, 1986; permission conveyed through Copyright Clearance Center, Inc.

Johnston, Ian. *The Metamorphosis,* translated by Ian Johnston. Used with permission of the translator.

LA Theatre Works. *Oedipus the King* ©LA Theatre Works.

Little, Brown and Co. (UK). "Caged Bird" from *And Still I Rise* by Maya Angelou. Copyright ©1983. Used with permission of Little, Brown Book Group Ltd.

Little, Brown and Co. (New York). "The Neglected Senses," From *For the Benefit of Those Who See: Dispatches from the World of the Blind* by Rosemary Mahoney. Copyright ©2014 by Rosemary Mahoney. Reprinted with the permission of Little, Brown and Company. All rights reserved.

Little, Brown Book Group UK. "The Sun Parlor," from *The Richer, The Poorer* by Dorothy Parker. Copyright ©1995. Used with permission of Little, Brown Book Group Ltd.

Lowenstein Associates. "Beware: Do Not Read This Poem," excerpted from *Conjure: Selected Poems* Copyright ©1972 by Ishmael Reed. Permission granted by Lowenstein Associates, Inc.

MacAndrew, Ann. "The Necklace" from *Boule de Suif and Selected Stories* by Guy de Maupassant, translated by Andrew MacAndrew. Reprinted with permission of Ann MacAndew and Guy MacAndrew.

MacAndrew, Charles. "The Necklace" from *Boule de Suif and Selected Stories* by Guy de Maupassant, translated by Andrew MacAndrew. Reprinted with permission of Ann MacAndew and Guy MacAndrew.

Mezey, Robert. "On His Blindness" by Jorge Luis Borges, translated by Robert Mezey, from *Poetry Magazine* (May 1994). Used with permission of Robert Mezey.

Nature Publishing Group. Republished with permission of *Nature,* from "Look and Learn," by Appova Mandavilli, Nature, Vol 441, 18 May 2006; permission conveyed through Copyright Clearance Center, Inc.

New Statesman Limited. "Credo: What I Believe," from *New Statesman,* May 29, 2015 by Neil Gaiman. Used with permission of New Statesman.

Nijland, Kees. "Blind" from *A Longitudinal Section in the Memory* by Fatima Naoot, translated by Cornelis (Kees) Nijland. Used with permission of Kees Nijland.

PARS International Corporation. "How Maurice Sendak's 'Wild Things' moved children's books towards realism," from *The Christian Science Monitor,* May 9, 2012, ©2012 *The Christian Science Monitor.* All rights reserved. Used by permission and protected by the Copyright Laws of the United States. The printing, copying, redistribution, or retransmission of this Content without express written permission is prohibited; "Outsider's Art Is Saluted at Columbia, Then Lost Anew," From *The New York Times,* June 8, 2015, ©2015 *The New York Times.* All rights reserved. Used by permission and protected by the Copyright Laws of the United States. The printing, copying, redistribution, or retransmission of this Content without express written permission is prohibited; "In La Rinconada, Peru, searching for beauty in ugliness," from

The Washington Post, March 2, 2013, ©2013 *Washington Post Company.* All rights reserved. Used by permission and protected by the Copyright Laws of the United States. The printing, copying, redistribution, or retransmission of this Content without express written permission is prohibited; "Ads may spur unhappy kids to embrace materialism," from Reuters, August 21, 2012, ©2012. All rights reserved. Used by permission and protected by the Copyright Laws of the United States. The printing, copying, redistribution, or retransmission of this Content without express written permission is prohibited; "Blind Yet Seeing: The Brain's Subconscious Visual Sense," from *The New York Times,* December 23, 2008, ©2008 *The New York Times.* All rights reserved. Used by permission and protected by the Copyright Laws of the United States. The printing, copying, redistribution, or retransmission of this Content without express written permission is prohibited.

Penguin Books, Ltd. (UK). "Misrule of Law" from *Letters from Burma* by Aung San Suu Kyi, translated by Graeme Wilson (Penguin Books Ltd, 1997). Text copyright © Aung San Suu Kyi 1997. Reproduced by permission of Penguin Books Ltd.

Persea Books, Permissions. "Some Advice to Those Who Will Serve Time in Prison," by Nazim Hikmet, translated by Randy Blasing and Mutlu Konuk, from *Poems of Nazim Hikmet.* Copyright ©1994, 2002 by Randy Blasing and Mutlu Konuk. Reprinted by permission of Persea Books, Inc. (New York). All rights reserved.

Phoebe Larmore Inc. '"They are hostile nations," by Margaret Atwood, included by permission of the Author. Available in the United States in *Selected Poems I,* 1965-1975, Published by Houghton Mifflin, ©1976 by Margaret Atwood; and in Canada, *Selected Poems,* 1966–1984, published by Oxford University Press, ©Margaret Atwood 1990.

Psychology Today. Reprinted with permission from Psychology Today (Copyright ©1988 Sussex Publishers)

Random House, Inc. "House Taken Over," copyright ©1967 by Random House, Inc.; from *End of the Game and Other Stories* by Julio Cortazar. Used by permission of Pantheon Books, an imprint of the Knopf Doubleday Publishing Group, a division of Penguin Random House LLC. All rights reserved. Any third party use of this material, outside of this publication, is prohibited. Interested parties must apply directly to Penguin Random House LLC for permission; Graphic Novel Excerpt from *The Metamorphosis* by Peter Kuper, copyright ©2003 by Peter Kuper. Used by permission of Crown Books, an imprint of the Crown Publishing Group, a division of Penguin Random House LLC. All rights reserved; Excerpts from *The Metamorphosis* by Peter Kuper, copyright ©2003 by Peter Kuper. Used by permission of Crown Books, an imprint of the Crown Publishing Group, a division of Penguin Random House LLC. All rights reserved; "The Orphan Boy and the Elk Dog" from *American Indian Myths and Legends* by Richard Erdoes and Alfonso Ortiz, copyright ©1984 by Richard Erdoes and Alfonso Ortiz. Used by permission of Pantheon Books, an imprint of the Knopf Doubleday Publishing Group, a division of Penguin Random House LLC. All rights reserved. Any third party use of this material, outside of this publication, is prohibited. Interested parties must apply directly to Penguin Random House LLC for permission; "Caged Bird" from *Shaker, Why Don't You Sing?* by Maya Angelou, copyright ©1983 by Maya Angelou. Used by permission of Random House, an imprint and division of Penguin Random House LLC. All rights reserved. Any third party use of this material, outside of this publication, is prohibited. Interested parties must apply directly to Penguin Random House LLC for permission; "Harrison Bergeron," copyright ©1961 by Kurt Vonnegut Jr; from *Welcome to the Monkey House* by Kurt Vonnegut. Used by permission of Dell Publishing, an imprint of Random House, a division of Penguin Random House LLC. All rights reserved. Any third party use of this material, outside of this publication, is prohibited. Interested parties must apply directly to Penguin Random House LLC for permission; "Civil Peace" from *Girls at War: And Other Stories* by Chinua Achebe, copyright ©1972, 1973 by Chinua Achebe. Used by permission of Doubleday, an imprint of the Knopf Doubleday Publishing Group, a division of Penguin Random House LLC. All rights reserved. Any third party use of this material, outside of this publication, is prohibited. Interested parties must apply directly to Penguin Random House LLC for permission; "Civil Peace" from *Girls at War* by Chinua Achebe, copyright © 1972, 1973 by Chinua Achebe. Used by permission of Doubleday, an imprint of the Knopf Doubleday Publishing Group, a division of Penguin Random House LLC. All rights reserved; "The Blind Seer of Ambon" from *Travels* by W.S. Merwin, copyright ©1992 by W.S. Merwin. Used by permission of Alfred A. Knopf, an imprint of the Knopf Doubleday Publishing Group, a division of Penguin Random House LLC. All rights reserved. Any third party use of this material, outside of this publication, is prohibited. Interested parties must apply directly to Penguin Random House LLC for permission.

Robbins, Alexandra. "Revenge of the Geeks," by Alexandra Robins, author of *The Geeks Shall Inherit the Earth: Popularity, Quick Theory, and Why Outsiders Thrive After High School.* "Revenge of the Geeks" from *LA Times,* May 28, 2011.

Simmons, Anne. "King Midas" by Howard Moss, from *Poetry Magazine* (May 1957). Used with permission of the Estate of Howard Moss.

Tutu, Desmond. "Let South Africa Show the World How to Forgive," Copyright ©2000 by Desmond M. Tutu, used with permission. All rights reserved.

Unger, David. "The Censors," ©David Unger, 1982.

United Nations Publications. From "The Universal Declaration of Human Rights" ©United Nations. Reprinted with the permission of the United Nations.

University of California Press. "Elliptical," republished with permission of University of California Press, "Elliptical" from *Sleeping with the Dictionary* by Harryette Mullen, 2002; permission conveyed through Copyright Clearance Center, Inc.

University of Chicago Press. From *Shakespeare & the French Poet* by Yves Bonnefoy. Copyright ©2004 by the University of Chicago. Reprinted with permission of the publisher, University of Chicago Press.

University of Illinois Press. "En El Jardin, de los Espejos Quebrados, Caliban Catches a Glimpse of His Reflection," From *Guide to the Blue Tongue: Poems.* Copyright2002 by Virgil Suárez. Used with permission of the University of Illinois Press.

University of Texas Press, Books. "The Feather Pillow" from *The Decapitated Chicken and Other Stories* by Horacio Quiroga, translated by Margaret Sayers Peden. Copyright ©1976 by the University of Texas Press. By permission of the University of Texas Press.

Vasiliev, Zhenia. Adapted from "How to tell you're reading a gothic novel—in pictures" by Adam Frost and Zhenia Vasiliev, from *The Guardian,* May 9, 2014.

Virginia Polytechnic Institute and State University. "Fleeing to Dismal Swamp, Slaves and Outcasts Found Freedom," by Sandy Hausman, as appeared on NPR, December 28, 2014. ©WVTF; Fleeing To Dismal Swamp, Slaves And Outcasts Found Freedom (audio) ©WVTF.

Visual Capitalist. "The Gold Series," ©Visual Capitalist

W. W. Norton & Co. "Under One Small Star," "Under a Certain Little Star," from *Miracle Fair* by Wislawa Szymborska, translated by Joanna Trzeciak. Copyright ©2012 by Joanna Trzeciak. Used by permission of W.W. Norton & Company, Inc.

WGBH Media Library & Archives. "Understanding Forgiveness," from *This Emotional Life, Understanding Forgiveness* ©2009 WGBH Educational Foundation and Vulcan Productions, Inc.

Wylie Agency. "Windigo" from *Jacklight* by Louise Erdrich. Copyright ©1984 by Louise Erdrich, used by permission of The Wylie Agency LLC.; "Civil Peace" from *Girls at War and Other Stories* by Chinua Achebe. Copyright ©1972, 1973 by Chinua Achebe, used by permission of The Wylie Agency LLC.; "The Blind Seer of Ambon" by W. S. Merwin, collected in *Travels.* Copyright ©1992 by W. S. Merwin, used by permission of The Wylie Agency LLC.

YGS Group. "Heirlooms' value shifts from sentiment to cash" by Rosa Salter Rodriguez. June 15, 2014. ©Associated Press, Reprinted by permission of the YGS Group.

Credits

Photo locators denoted as follows: Top (T), Center (C), Bottom (B), Left (L), Right (R), Background (Bkgd)

vi Larry Lilac/Alamy; **viii** Michael Blann/Stone/Getty Images; **x** Alexey U/Shutterstock; **xii** Abdul Aziz Apu Bangladesh/Ocean/Corbis, **xiv** Glowimages/Getty Images; **2** Larry Lilac/Alamy; **3** (BC) Alexsvirid/Shutterstock, (BCR) Rachel K. Turner/Alamy, (BL) Sfam_photo/Shutterstock, (BR) Zbramwell/Shutterstock, (CT) Arthur Tress copyright 2015; (CTL) Blackwaterimages/E+/Getty Images, (CTR) Bonciutoma/Fotolia, (T) Quavondo/Vetta/Getty Images, (TC) Pixforfun/Getty Images, (TL) Mary Evans Picture Library/ARTHUR RACKHAM, (TR) Hung Chung Chih/Shutterstock; **6** Quavondo/Vetta/Getty Images; **11** (C) Blackwaterimages/E+/Getty Images, (T) Mary Evans Picture Library/ARTHUR RACKHAM; **12** (B) Everett Historical/Shutterstock, (TL) Mary Evans Picture Library/ARTHUR RACKHAM, (TR) Blackwaterimages/E+/Getty Images; **13, 32, 34, 36** (TL), **48** (T) Mary Evans Picture Library/ARTHUR RACKHAM; **18** Tom Tom/Shutterstock; **25** Frozenstarro/Fotolia; **26** Perseo Medusa/Shutterstock; **36** (B) Ulf Andersen/Getty Images, (TR) Blackwaterimages/E+/Getty Images; **37, 44, 46, 48** (B) Blackwaterimages/E+/Getty Images; **50** (B) ZheniaVasiliev, (T) © Adam Frost; **65** (B) Sfam_photo/Shutterstock, (BC) Alexsvirid/Shutterstock, (T) Pixforfun/Getty Images, (TC) Arthur Tress copyright 2015; **68** Francois Durand/Getty Images; **69** Pixforfun/Getty Images; **74** Ken Tannenbaum/Shutterstock; **78** Pixforfun/Getty Images; **80** Pixforfun/Getty Images; **82** Arthur Tress copyright 2015; **83–88** Arthur Tress copyright 2015; **91, 96, 98** Alexsvirid/Shutterstock; **100** Sfam_photo/Shutterstock; **101** (B) Chris Felver/Archive Photos/Getty Images, (C) Everett Historical/Shutterstock, (T) Drew Altizer/Sipa USA/Newscom; **102** Sfam_photo/Shutterstock; **104** SlavaGerj/Shutterstock; **108** Chris Clor/Blend Images/Corbis; **126** Michael Blann/Stone/Getty Images; **127** (BC) Arina P Habich/Shutterstock, (BCR) Sam Steinberg, (BL) Nick Fox/Shutterstock, (BR) Subos/Shutterstock, (C) Tntphototravis/Shutterstock, (CR) V.S.Anandhakrishna/Shutterstock, (T) When They Were Young Benjamin Franklin, Jackson, Peter (1922–2003)/Private Collection/Look and Learn/Bridgeman Art Library, (TL) MarishaSha/Shutterstock, (TR) Aleksey Stemmer/Shutterstock; **130,190** When They Were Young Benjamin Franklin, Jackson, Peter (1922–2003)/Private Collection/Look and Learn/Bridgeman Art Library; **135** (B) BBC Worldwide Learning, (T) MarishaSha/Shutterstock; **136** Lebrecht Music and Arts Photo Library/Alamy; **137** MarishaSha/Shutterstock; **141** Fasphotographic/Shutterstock; **146** Madeleine Forsberg/Shutterstock; **150** VasilyevAlexandr/Shutterstock; **158** Jan Faukner/Shutterstock; **165** Michael ZittelSerr/Shutterstock; **170** Alenavlad/Shutterstock; **180** MarishaSha/Shutterstock; **182** MarishaSha/Shutterstock; **184** MarishaSha/Shutterstock; **187** BBC Worldwide Learning; **197** (BC) Arina P Habich/Shutterstock, (TC) Tntphototravis/Shutterstock; **200** Lebrecht Music and Arts Photo Library/Alamy; **212** Tntphototravis/Shutterstock; **213** (B) © Pat Mora, (C) © Judy Natal 2015 www.judynatal.com, (T) Ulf Andersen/Getty Images; **214** Tntphototravis/Shutterstock; **216** Isaravut/Shutterstock; **218** AlexandrOzerov/Fotolia; **224** David Robbins; **225, 230** Arina P Habich/Shutterstock; **228** Arina P Habich/Shutterstock; **232** S(TR)/AFP/Getty Images; **233** Nick Fox/Shutterstock; **237** Geogphotos/Alamy; **242, 244** Nick Fox/Shutterstock; **258** Alexey U/Shutterstock; **259** (BC) Ub foto/Shutterstock, (BCR) Atlantis Films Limited/Everett Collection, (BL) Andipantz/Vetta/Getty Images, (BR) Art4all/Shutterstock, (T) Hine, Lewis Wickes/Library of Congress, (TC) Fareed Khan/AP Images, (TCL) Bettmann/Corbis, (TCR) Soe Zeya Tun/Reuters, (TL) AP Images, (TR) AC Rider/Shutterstock; **262** Hine, Lewis Wickes/Library of Congress; **267** (B) MediaRecall Holdings/Archive ED/Getty Images, (C) Bettmann/Corbis, (T) AP Images; **268** (B) Fine Art/Corbis, (TL) AP Images, (TR) Bettmann/Corbis; **269** AP Images; **273** BrooklynScribe/Shutterstock; **278, 280, 282** (TL) AP Images; **282** (B), **294** National Archives/Getty Images; **282** (TR), **283, 288, 290, 292, 295, 297** Bettmann/Corbis; **298** Hine, Lewis Wickes/Library of Congress; **305** (BR) Andipantz/Vetta/Getty Images, (C) Ub foto/Shutterstock, (T) Fareed Khan/AP Images, (TR) ABC News; **308** (B) Dpa picture alliance/Alamy,(TL) Fareed Khan/AP Images, (TR) ABC News; **309** Fareed Khan/AP Images; **311** Epaeuropeanpressphoto agency b.v./Alamy; **315,316,318** (TL), **322** (T) Fareed Khan/AP Images; **318** (B) Everett Collection Inc/Alamy; **318** (TR), **319, 321, 322** (B) ABC News; **324,326** Ub foto/Shutterstock; **325** (B) Ozkok/Sipa/Newscom, (T) Ken Charnock/Getty Images; **328** Cunaplus/Shutterstock; **336** Abdel Meza Notimex/Newscom; **337, 340** Andipantz/Vetta/Getty Images; **342** Andipantz/Vetta/Getty Images; **362** Abdul Aziz Apu Bangladesh/Ocean/Corbis; **363** (BC) Arthur Rackman/Mary Evans Picture Library/The Image Works, (BCR) Joy Brown/Shutterstock, (BL) Addison Doty,**363** (BR) LiliGraphie/Shutterstock, (CB) Wiktord/Shutterstock, (CBL) Michael Snell/Alamy Stock Photo/Alamy, (CBR) Sagar Singh Bisht/EyeEm/Getty Images, (CT) Alexskopje/Shutterstock, (CTL) Natasha Owen/Fotolia, (CTR) Ollyy/Shutterstock, (T) Melpomene/Fotolia, (TC) Jan Sochor/Alamy, (TL) Pamela Moore/E+/Getty Images; **366** Melpomene/Fotolia; **371** (B) Michael Snell/Alamy Stock Photo/Alamy, (C) Natasha Owen/Fotolia, **371** (T), **373, 382, 384, 386** Pamela Moore/E+/Getty Images; **372** Culture Club/Hulton Archive/Getty Images; **388** Eamonn McCabe/Hulton Archive/Getty Images; **389** Natasha Owen/Fotolia; **393** Doug McKinlay/Lonely Planet Images/Getty Images; **396, 398, 400** Natasha Owen/Fotolia; **402** Wael Hamdan/Alamy Stock Photo/Alamy; **403** Everett Collection/Newscom; **404** (T) Brendan McDermid/EPA/Newscom, (B) Images of Africa Photobank/Alamy Stock Photo/Alamy; **405** (T) Frank Trapper/Corbis, (B) Michael Snell/Alamy Stock Photo/Alamy; **407** Michael Snell/Alamy Stock Photo/Alamy; **408** Melpomene/Fotolia; **415** (B) Addison Doty, (BL) Arthur Rackman/Mary Evans Picture Library/The Image Works, (C) Wiktord/Shutterstock, (T) Jan Sochor/Alamy, (TL) Alexskopje/Shutterstock; **418** Julia Ewan/The Washington Post/Getty Images; **419, 426, 428** Jan Sochor/Alamy; **423** Heritage Image Partnership Ltd/Alamy; **430** Alexskopje/Shutterstock; **431** (B) Cornelia Spelman, (C) Jason DeCrow/AP Images, (T) Beowulf Sheehan/ZUMA Press/Newscom; **432** Alexskopje/Shutterstock; **434** Daniel Schweinert/Shutterstock; **435** Nina Leen/The Life Picture Collection/Getty Images; **442** (B) Lebrecht Music and Arts Photo Library/Alamy, (TL) Wiktord/Shutterstock, (TR) Arthur Rackman/Mary Evans Picture Library/The Image Works; **443, 457, 458, 460** (TL), **468** (T) Wiktord/Shutterstock; **447** Determined/Fotolia; **451** Lana Langlois/Shutterstock; **460** (B) Oscar White/Corbis; **460** (TR), **461, 465, 466, 468** (B) Arthur Rackman/Mary Evans Picture Library/The Image Works; **470** Margie Goldsmith; **471, 476, 478** Addison Doty; **492** Glowimages/Getty Images; **493** (BCL) Warongdech/Shutterstock, (BCR) Ingram Publishing/Newscom, (BL) sherwood/Shutterstock, (BR) Elena Ray, (C) The Guardian/Alamy, (CBR) Quint & Lox/akg images, (CR) Robert Hoetink/Shutterstock, (CTL) Melinda Sue Gordon/Touchstone Pictures/Everett Collection, (CTR) Infuksc 02/Stockpix/INFphoto/Newscom, (T) 'The Tempest', c.1790 (oil on canvas),Hamilton,William (1751–801)/Royal Pavilion, Libraries & Museums, Brighton & Hove/Bridgeman Art Library, (TC) Prudkov/Shutterstock, (TL) GeorgiosKollidas/Shutterstock, (TR) Robert Walker Macbeth/Hulton Fine Art Collection/Getty Images; **496** 'The Tempest', c.1790 (oil on canvas), Hamilton,William (1751–1801)/Royal Pavilion, Libraries & Museums, Brighton & Hove/Bridgeman Art Library; **501**(BCL), (BL), (CTL), (CTR), (TL) Melinda Sue Gordon/Touchstone Pictures/Everett Collection, (BCR) sherwood/Shutterstock, (BR) Warongdech/Shutterstock, (CL) AF archive/Alamy, (T) GeorgiosKollidas/Shutterstock; **502** (TL) Elizabeth I, Armada Portrait, c.1588 (oil on panel), Gower, George (1540–96) (attr. to)/Woburn Abbey, Bedfordshire, UK/Bridgeman Art Library,(BCL) World History Archive/Alamy, (BCR) Pantheon/Superstock, (BL) The Print Collector/Alamy, (BR) IanDagnall Computing/Alamy, (T) Elizabeth I (1533–1603) (colourlitho), Oliver, Isaac (c.1565–1617) (after)/Private Collection/Ken Welsh/Bridgeman Art Library; **503** (BL) Pantheon/Superstock,(BR) © IanDagnall Computing / Alamy Stock Photo; **504** Mary Evans Picture Library/The Image Works; **505** Travel Pictures/Alamy; **506** Steve Vidler/Superstock; **508** Stocksnapper/Shutterstock; **510, 534, 554, 572, 587** Georgios Kollidas/Shutterstock; **511** Matt Mawson/Corbis; **512, 520, 525, 531, 532, 535, 541, 552, 557, 564–565, 579, 583, 585, 598, 600, 602, 604** (L), **612** (B) Melinda Sue Gordon/Touchstone Pictures/Everett Collection; **569, 571, 596** AF archive/Alamy; **572, 586** Georgios Kollidas/Shutterstock; **597** Victor Schrager; **604** (R), 606 (Bkgd), **612** (B) Warongdech/Shutterstock; **605** © J. P. Dancing Bear; **606, 611, 612**(Bkgd) sherwood/Shutterstock; **608, 611** SasinT/Shutterstock; **614** 'The Tempest', c.1790 (oil on canvas), Hamilton,William (1751–1801)/Royal Pavilion, Libraries & Museums, Brighton & Hove/Bridgeman Art Library; **621** (B) The Guardian/Alamy, (T) Prudkov/Shutterstock; **624** Prudkov/Shutterstock; **625** (B) Polish Press Agency (PAP), (T)

ImehAkpanudosen/Getty Images; **626** Prudkov/Shutterstock; **628** SandratskyDmitriy/Shutterstock; **634** Jennifer Bruce/AFP/Getty Images; **635, 640, 642** The Guardian/Alamy; **656** Bruce Rolff/Shutterstock, **657** (BC) GalynaAndrushko/Shutterstock, (BCL) Neil Hanna/ZUMA Press/Newscom, (BCR) Diana Ong/SuperStock/Getty Images, (BL) Vkara/Fotolia, (BR) Divgradcurl/Shutterstock, (CBR) Stocksnapper/Alamy, (CT) Bphillips/Getty Images, (CTL) Popperfoto/Getty Images, (TC) Everett Collection Historical/Alamy, (TCL) Hercules Milas/Alamy, (TCR) Chanase,Dane (1894–1975)/Private Collection/Photo Christie's Images/Bridgeman Art Library, (TL) Tomgigabite/Shutterstock, (TR) Akg images; **660** Akg images, (Bkgd) Tomgigabite/Shutterstock; **665** (B) Neil Hanna/ZUMA Press/Newscom, (C) Popperfoto/Getty Images, (T) Hercules Milas/Alamy; **666** Cardaf/Shutterstock, (TL) Hercules Milas/Alamy; **668** FedorSelivanov/Shutterstock; **669** Khirman Vladimir/Shutterstock; **670** Imagno/Getty Images; **671** Ingres,JeanAuguste Dominique (1780–1867)/Musee des Beaux Arts, Angers, France/Bridgeman Art Library; **672** Universal Images Group/Getty Images; **673** Ariy/Shutterstock; **674** Popperfoto/Getty Images; **678** akg images/Newscom; **682** Flaxman,John (1755–1826)/York Museums Trust (York Art Gallery),UK/Bridgeman Art Library; **685, 694** Merlyn Severn/Picture Post/Getty Images; **690–691** Neil Hanna/ZUMA Press/Newscom; **699, 701** Popperfoto/Getty Images; **702** Universal Images Group/Getty Images; **703** Neil Hanna/ZUMA Press/Newscom; **709** Eileen Darby/The LIFE Images Collection/Getty Images; **716** John Vickers/University of Bristol Theatre Collection/ArenaPal/The Image Works; **719** Lebrecht Music and Arts Photo Library/Alamy; **722, 724, 726** Neil Hanna/ZUMA Press/Newscom; **728** (L) Tomgigabite/Shutterstock, (R) Akg images; **735** (B) Vkara/Fotolia, (BC) GalynaAndrushko/Shutterstock, (T) Everett Collection Historical/Alamy, (TC) Bphillips/Getty Images; **738** GraphicaArtis/Getty Images; **739, 742,744** Everett Collection Historical/Alamy; **746** Bphillips/Getty Images; **747** (B) Clement/AFP/Getty Images, (C) Don Tormey/Los Angeles Times/Getty Images, (T) AL Youm AL Saabi/Reuters/Reuters; **748** Bphillips/Getty Images; **750** MerkushevVasiliy/Shutterstock; **752** Sophie Bassouls/Sygma/Corbis; **759** GalynaAndrushko/Shutterstock; **764** LenarMusin/Shutterstock; **770** Saraporn/Shutterstock; **777** Nina B/Shutterstock; **782** GalynaAndrushko/Shutterstock; **786** Rosemary Mahoney; **787, 798, 800** Vkara/Fotolia; **793** Wu Hong/EPA/Newscom.

Credits for Images in Interactive Student Edition Only

Unit 1

Colin McPherson/Corbis; Lopris/Shutterstock; Oronoz/Album/SuperStock; Virunja/Shutterstock

Unit 2

© Earl Wilson; © Sarah Cramer; Kevin Day/Shutterstock

Unit 3

Epa european pressphoto agency b.v./Alamy; Oliver Morris/Hulton Archive/Getty Images

Unit 4

Jeff Desjardins; Mark Higgins/Shutterstock; Olivier Le Queinec/Shutterstock; Rose Salter Rodriguez; Russel Belk

Unit 5

Brooks Kraft/Sygma/Corbis; Louis Monier/Gamma-Rapho/Getty Images; The Forgiveness Project/Brian Moody;

Unit 6

Stocksnapper/Alamy; Chanase,Dane (1894–1975)/Private Collection/Photo Christie's Images/Bridgeman Art Library; Hulton Archive/Handout/Getty Images; Hulton Archive/Stringer/Getty Images; Melissa Hogenboom; Sasha/Stringer/Hulton Archive/Getty Images; Shander Herian; Ulf Andersen/Getty Images